THE BROTHERS GRIMM

& THEIR CRITICS

Frontispiece: Jacob and Wilhelm Grimm as professors and members of the Academy of Sciences of Berlin.

The
BROTHERS
GRIMM

❯❯❯❯❯❯❯❯❯❯❯❯❯❯❯❯❯❯❯❯❯❯❯❯❯❯❯❯❯❯❯❯

& THEIR CRITICS

*Folktales and the
Quest for Meaning*

CHRISTA KAMENETSKY

OHIO UNIVERSITY PRESS ⫸ ATHENS

LIBRARY OF CONGRESS CATALOGING-IN-PUBLICATION DATA

Kamenetsky, Christa, 1934–
  The brothers Grimm & their critics : folktales and the quest for meaning /
Christa Kamenetsky.
    p.   cm.
  Includes bibliographical references.
  ISBN 0-8214-1020-2
  1. Grimm, Jacob, 1785–1863. 2. Grimm, Wilhelm, 1786–1859.
3. Philologists—Germany—Biography. 4. Kinder- und Hausmärchen.
5. Fairy tales—Germany—History and criticism. 6. Fairy tales—History
and criticism. I. Title. II. Title: Brothers Grimm and their critics
PD63.K36 1992
410'.92'2—dc20   92-55
[B]   CIP

To the memory of my mother,
Tilly Müller,
and my childhood in Germany

TABLE OF CONTENTS

ILLUSTRATIONS

For additional credits to libraries and collections, please consult the Acknowledgments, and for complete publishing data refer to the Bibliography. A number of the illustrations listed below are from the author's private archives.

FRONTISPIECE. Jacob and Wilhelm Grimm as professors and members of the Academy of Sciences in Berlin. Illustration by Ludwig Emil Grimm (1843), located in the Brüder Grimm Museum. Courtesy of the Brüders Grimm Museum, Kassel.

THESE ILLUSTRATIONS FOLLOW PAGE 52:

1. Title page, *Kinder- und Hausmärchen*, vol. 3, 2d ed. Courtesy of the Osborne Collection of Early Children's Books, Toronto Public Library.

2. Title page, *Kinder- und Hausmärchen*, vol. 3, 2d ed, Courtesy of the Osborne Collection of Early Children's Books, Toronto Public Library.

3. "Little Brother and Little Sister." Illustration by Ludwig Emil Grimm in *Kinder- und Hausmärchen*, vol. 1, 2d ed. Courtesy of the Osborne Collection of Early Children's Books, Toronto Public Library.

4. Cover design, *Kinder- und Hausmärchen*, vol. 3, 2d ed. Courtesy of the Osborne Collection of Early Children's Books, Toronto Public Library.

5. Title page, *German Popular Stories and Fairy Tales as Told by Gammer Grethel*, 3d rev. ed.

6. "Frau Viehmännin." Illustration by Ludwig Emil Grimm in *German Popular Stories and Fairy Tales as Told by Gammer Grethel*, 3d rev. ed. This illustration was originally published in *Kinder- und Hausmärchen*, vol. 1, 2d ed. and was first reprinted in England by Edgar Taylor in 1823.

7. Title page, *Des Knaben Wunderhorn (The Boy's Magic Horn)* by Achim von Arnim and Clemens Brentano.

8. Title page, *Irische Elfenmärchen*, translation of Thomas Crofton Croker's *Fairy Legends and Traditions of the South of Ireland* by Wilhelm and Jacob Grimm.

9. Title Page, *Once Upon a Time*, rpt. ed. Illustration by Ludwig Richter. This illustration and others in this work were first published in Ludwig Bechstein's *Märchenbuch*.

10. "The Blue Light." Illustration by George Cruikshank in *German Popular Stories and Fairy Tales as Told by Gammer Grethel*, 3d rev. ed.

11. "The Man in the Bag." Illustration by George Cruikshank in *German Popular Stories and Fairy Tales as Told by Gammer Grethel*, 3d rev. ed.

12. "The Elfin Grove." Illustration by George Cruikshank in *German Popular Stories and Fairy Tales as Told by Gammer Grethel*, 3d rev. ed.

THESE ILLUSTRATIONS FOLLOW PAGE 116:

13. "The Goose Girl." Illustration by Walter Crane in *Household Stories from the Collection of the Bros. Grimm.*

14. "The Fisherman and His Wife." Illustration by Walter Crane in *Household Stories from the Collection of the Bros. Grimm.*

15. "Cradle Song." Illustration by Ludwig Richter and Marschner's *Alte und Neue Volks-Lieder mit Bildern und Singweisen.*

16. "The Wolf and the Seven Little Kids." Illustration by Ludwig Richter in Schmidt's *Das Märchenbuch für Kinder.*

17. "The Bremen Town Musicians." Illustration by Christa Kamenetsky. The drawing is based on a photograph of a bronze statue located next to the City Hall (Rathaus) in Bremen.

18. "The Frog Prince." Illustration by Arthur Rackham in Grimms' *Es war einmal.*

19. "Hansel and Gretel." Illustration by Ludwig Richter in *Märchenbuch.*

20. "By Railway Through Fairyland." Segment of a poster issued as an advertisement by the Deutsche Bundesbahn, Munich, 1965.

21. Dortchen (Dorothee) Grimm. Drawing by Christa Kamenetsky inspired by a daguerreotype in the Grimms' family album in Ottendorff-Simrock's *Die Grimms und die Simrocks in Briefen.*

22. Illustration by Berta Martin (n.d.). Courtesy of the Brüder Grimm Museum, Kassel.

ACKNOWLEDGMENTS

I thank the following libraries and their staff for having made available to me their holdings of books and other research materials relevant to this project: The Bavarian State Library in Munich, the University Library in Bonn, the Library of Congress in Washington, D.C., the Robarts Library at the University of Toronto, the Toronto Public Library, the Graduate Library at the University of Michigan; the Education Library at Stanford University, the University of Illinois Library at Urbana, and the Central Michigan University Library in Mt. Pleasant, Michigan.

I have deeply appreciated the expert advice and assistance I received from Margaret N. Coughlan at the Children's Literature Center of the Library of Congress, Margaret Crawford Maloney and Dana Tenny at the Osborne Collection of Early Children's Book in Toronto, Erika v. Engelbrechten and J. Garrett at the International Youth Library in Munich, Dieter Hennig at the Brüder Grimm Museum in Kassel, and Evelyn Leasher at the Central Michigan University's Lucile Clarke Memorial Children's Library. Further, I thank Michael Fitzpatrick, Ruth Helwig, and Irena Ionin of C.M.U.'s Interlibrary Loan Division, as well as Dennis Pompilius and David Darst (Graphics Production) for their kind cooperation.

Central Michigan University's Committee on Research and Creative Endeavors deserves thanks for having entrusted me with a research travel grant to Washington, D.C., in October 1987 and with C.M.U.'s Research Professorship Award during the fall semester of 1988. These grants helped me substantially to complete my work on this project that I began in the early eighties. I have appreciated the recommendations and support of Pamela Gray and William Browne (successive Committee Chairpersons), Hans Fetting and Francis Molson (successive Chairpersons of the English Department), John Haeger (Dean of Graduate Studies), Ronald Johnstone (Dean of the College of Arts and Sciences), and Nancy Belck (former Interim Provost).

I warmly thank Alice Breyer, Gisa Prescott, Iris Meltzer Cohen, Marion Mulholland, Dorothea Roth, Annelies Müller, Hannelore Ahlers, Marianne Wannow, and Inge Wehle for having occasionally supplied me with relevant literature, reviews, and illustrations. I am especially grateful to my son, Andrey Kamenetsky, for some valuable research assistance.

INTRODUCTION

THE FOLKTALES OF the *Kinder- und Hausmärchen* (*Children's- and Household Tales*) by the Brothers Grimm have never been the sole property of children, but children have enjoyed them for close to 180 years. Ever since this work of Wilhelm and Jacob Grimm was first published in 1812, parents and educators have wondered about the nature, meaning, and ethics of the tales, trying to decide if they were beneficial for children after all. Anthropologists, linguists, psychologists, folklorists, and literary critics, too, have found intriguing material for study in these tales while trying to answer the same questions from their own points of view. Therefore, it is only logical that the scope of this study should be cross-cultural and interdisciplinary in nature. The vantage point of this work is that of the history of children's literature, from which different issues will be discussed and analyzed. Such multiple perspectives on folktales provide a solid basis for a comparison of cultural, social, and educational trends at a given time and allow for insights into the topic from various academic fields of study.

The age-old issue concerning the suitability of the *Kinder- und Hausmärchen* for children could not be resolved without taking into consideration the Grimms' own stated beliefs on this behalf. The same is true for the issue pertaining to their loyalty to the oral tradition in view of some liberties that Wilhelm Grimm took in editing the folktales, not only in regard to his so-called folktale style but also to the inclusion of some printed sources. Still another issue, the identity of their informants, may be best resolved by a closer analysis of the Grimms' own notes and comments on the subject. Did they indeed claim that all of the storytellers contributing to this volume had been illiterate German peasant folk residing in the country, and is it true that they exclusively traced the tales' "purely German and Nordic origin"? Should critics respect the Grimms' demand for loyalty to tradition, and were the Grimms loyal to it in the first place? Is it possible to distinguish between folktales and literary fairy tales (*Volksmärchen* and *Kunstmärchen*) even if folktales have been edited? In his recent book of original essays on the Grimms' *Kinder- und Hausmärchen*, Heinz Rölleke suggested that these and other issues might be best resolved by taking another look at the international comparative context of the Grimms' work. It is concisely in this context that the present study proceeds.

The aspect that has received little attention so far is the Grimms' own conception of folktales within their quest for *Naturpoesie* (folk poetry). This concept referred not only to folk songs and epic poetry but also to folktales, myths, legends, children's games, chapbooks, and some aspects of medieval literature that the Grimms considered close to the oral folk tradition. What has also escaped many critics is that they pursued their quest from such angles as linguistics, history, and ancient law. Their conception of the folktale, based on international variants, is thus best understood from an interdisciplinary and comparative point of view.

The Grimms' *Kinder- und Hausmärchen* developed within the framework of German Romantic thought, which was both national and international in its orientation. Their prefaces to the work and various essays well reflect their Romantic faith in the soul of nature. In the child, too, they conceived the spirit of nature, along with a certain purity, innocence, and naivete that also characterized *Naturpoesie*. Therefore, it is not only fair but also appropriate to turn our attention first to those ideas that gave rise to their folktale collection. Their scholarly work was a natural outgrowth of these ideas, also with respect to the sources and methods that they employed in their projects. Once we have established the Grimms' own contextual framework on the topic, the stage will be set for discussing the many and often contradictory critical views on the *Kinder- und Hausmärchen*.

The various issues that have been raised in regard to the work should also motivate us to take a closer look at the German text and at the Grimms' own notes on the subject. There exist as many discrepancies in the translations of the Grimms' introductions to the tales as there are confusions regarding their true intent. Many critics have blindly relied on quotes used by others while ignoring not only the Grimms' broader literary, linguistic, and philosophical approaches but also their very detailed annotations, some of which they published separately in later editions of the *Kinder- und Hausmärchen*.

Part I of this work focuses on the background of the Brothers Grimm as well as on the publishing history of their folktale collection. It begins with a biographical sketch of the Brothers Grimm, including their childhood, upbringing, inclinations, and schooling and focuses on their university studies in medieval literature, philology, linguistics, and German law. Their broader academic interests and scholarly contributions are discussed in relation to their sustained interest in various kinds of folklore collections but also in reference to their defense of civil liberties and their quest for democracy. Part I further explores the evolution of the Grimms' folktale collection, beginning with their earliest contributions to folk-song and folktale collections and some stories for the little daughter of Professor Savigny. Some comparisons are drawn between the first published edition of the *Kinder- und Hausmärchen* and later editions, with special attention given to the second edition of the work, whose third volume was dedicated to the Grimms' notes as well as to comparative folktale studies on a worldwide basis. The first English translation entirely omitted the notes. Margaret Hunt's translation included them only late in the nineteenth century but not the original manuscript international folktale analysis that makes up the bulk of the third volume. Many critics continued to ignore the Grimms' notes and studies while carrying on with their own interpretation of the tales. In the light of the Grimms' extensive scholarly apparatus, the question arises why they themselves decided to drop all of the notes in the 1825 edition of the so-called *Kleine Ausgabe* (*Small Edition*). Did they write for children after all, and if so, did the editing still correspond to the Grimms' original objectives?

Part II is dedicated to the theoretical foundation of the collection. It aims at introducing the reader to the Grimms' own philosophy regarding the nature, meaning, and origin of folktales. Beginning with an analysis of Johann Gottfried Herder's influence on the Grimms' concept of *Naturpoesie* and its broad comparative and universal applications, Part II explores the Grimms' quest for naivete in epic poetry and mythology. This analysis forms the core of the subsequent investigation, which also includes an examination of the Grimms' parallel search for naive folk poetry in what they considered "the innocent folktale." The Grimms' epic studies emerge here as a scholarly pursuit that must be considered complementary to their work with folktales, particularly in relation to their analyses of language, plots, themes, characters, and folk motifs. This applies as much to their studies of the *Edda*, the *Nibelungenlied*, and the *Igorlied* as it does to French, Dutch, and Danish versions of the animal epic *Reinhart Fuchs* (*Reynard the Fox*). Their work with epic restorations had a significant bearing upon their interest in the language and theory of folktales, and it also gave direction to their interpretation of Norse and world mythology in relation to their folktale theory. Their concept of an unchanging "epic truth" involving the struggle of light and darkness also influenced their thoughts on folktale ethics.

The Grimms' conception of folktale characters had been illuminated from three angles: the mythical, the humorous (folk-book type), and the universal. Mythical characters, as the Grimms perceived them, emerged in part from the "cosmic struggle," which explained why naive and abused characters such as Dummling (Boots) usually triumphed in the end. The humorous folk-book characters were related to characters in medieval legends and folk books, the so-called *Volksbücher*, in which trickery, thievery, and jolly pranks were paramount. The Grimms recognized as a third type those folktale characters who showed some humane and gentle if not poetic traits. Such gentle characters often had the best educational effect on the minds of children because their humane traits emerged from the vivid images and action of the stories themselves, without preaching. The elements of kindness, love, and fairness cast a mild light over the black-white contrasts of the folktale world, without making them didactic.

One chapter in Part II is dedicated to the Grimms' conception of national as well as universal aspects of *Naturpoesie*. In this context, both the Indo-European theory and Jacob's theory of language dynamics receive close attention, particularly in relation to the concept of folktale variants and the art of "approximation." Wilhelm's theories are examined on a separate plane in view of their tolerance for multiple perspectives.

In two separate chapters, Part II investigates the various sources that the Grimms used for their collection and the methods that they employed in selecting and editing the tales. While examining the role of their oral and written sources, the background of their informants, and the mail contributions that they received for the *Kinder- und Hausmärchen* from children and friends, these chapters also analyze the Grimms' comparative notes, correspondence, and essays on this behalf that give clues to many puzzling questions.

Innovative in folklore research were Wilhelm Grimm's collection and analysis of children's games, nursery rhymes, proverbs, and sayings, especially in relation to his folktale revisions. As such, this aspect of this work also had a significant bearing on what is known as his folktale style. Jacob Grimm's *Circular-Brief*, a folklore questionnaire that he mailed also outside of Germany in more than three hundred copies, represents a more scientific counterpart to Wilhelm's efforts of tracing variants in a broad range of *Naturpoesie*. These approaches receive special attention, as both Grimms utilized the results of their research for their publication of folktales and legends.

Part III of the book is dedicated to the critical reception of the Grimms' folktale collection since the time of its first publication. The methodology is comparative and cross-cultural, including an analysis of critical views voiced over almost two centuries in Germany, Great Britain, Ireland, and the United States. It begins with an analysis of the Grimms' stated intentions, the reception of the *Kinder- und Hausmärchen* during the Romantic movement, and the Grimms' personal response to some parents' requests of changing or eliminating aspects that might be offensive to children. The Romantic reception of these folktales gives clues to some early misconceptions regarding such issues as the "word-by-mouth" recording of tales from illiterate peasants, the Nordic-Germanic interpretation, and the claim of its supposedly nationalistic orientation. A special subchapter is devoted to Wilhelm Grimm's translation of the *Fairy Legends and Traditions of the North of Ireland* and its impact on German-Irish and well as German-Scottish folklore scholarship. Part III traces the reception of the work in Germany and abroad and examines prevailing trends and philosophies that tended to favor the publication of folktales at that time. The ambiguous type of *Ammenmärchen* (nursery tales or simply "fairy tales") often confused the issue, however, even among the

Grimms' best friends and Romantic scholars, while contributing to a slightly diminished publishing of the *Kinder- und Hausmärchen*. Even Sir Walter Scott at the time misunderstood that the Grimms attempted something that had nothing to do with conventional "nursery tales."

Why and to what extent was the Grimms' folktale collection responsible for a tidal wave of folktales being published in Europe during the early nineteenth century? On the basis of some early British reviews and Edgar Taylor's introduction to the first English translation of the work *German Popular Stories*, Part III traces the correlation between a growing interest in folktales and the development of a more imaginative attitude toward children's literature. Simultaneously, it notes the emergence of some myths regarding the Grimms and their collection, some of which have persisted to the present.

Within the framework of didactic trends in nineteenth-century children's literature, Part III further examines various types of responses to the *Kinder- und Hausmärchen* that pursued an objective beyond the tales themselves. It raises the question of why some educators and critics used the Grimms' tales only selectively and with certain adjustments and why others banned them from libraries and schoolrooms. A closer analysis is dedicated to an examination of various didactic responses to the *Kinder- und Hausmärchen* that were employed by religious groups, social organizations, curriculum reformers, patriotic enterprises, and political parties, most of which had nothing more in common than the notion that folktales should serve a particular purpose. Among a great variety of primary sources, school readers and teachers' handbooks have been examined in view of their changing attitudes toward folktales. Around the turn of the century, the so-called *Kunsterziehungsbewegung* (art education movement) once more restored Germany's faith in the aesthetic value of folktales, and at about the same time, both in England and in the United States, a new taste developed for imaginative folk literature and fantasy. Part III further pursues the long struggle of the folktale against didactic and pragmatic trends through the time of political censorship under Hitler, with the intent of identifying some distorted ideological interpretations of the *Kinder- und Hausmärchen* that, in some respects, have also influenced some modern interpretations. This applies in particular to one-sided nationalistic interpretations.

Part III investigates various interdisciplinary approaches to the Grimms' folktale collection. It begins by tracing the theoretical implications of linguistic and anthropological approaches to folktales, as far as the Grimms' folktale collection was concerned. Solar interpretations, ritualistic interpretations, and others are compared and contrasted with approaches that followed the psychoanalytical views of Sigmund Freud, C. G. Jung, and Bruno Bettelheim. The influence of archetypal concepts is further traced in the folktale interpretations of Hedwig von Beit, Max Lüthi, and Hermann Bausinger, among others. Some attention is also given to formalistic and structural approaches that have marked the beginnings of modern folklore research, among them those of Antti Aarne, Stith Thompson, and Vladimir Propp. This part also examines the emergence of some realistic, historical, cultural-sociological, and Marxist approaches, be they in relation to Otto Kahn, Otto Gmelin, or Jack Zipes, as well as feminist approaches and others used by Maria Louise von Franz, Ruth Bottigheimer, and Marie Tatar. Two dominant issues arising from various modern interpretations of the Grimms' folktales are discussed in separate chapters, The Issue of National Character and The Issue of Folktale Ethics. Literary, symbolic, and textual approaches to the Grimms' *Kinder- und Hausmärchen* have received attention throughout the work, mainly in the light of modern German scholarship in this field.

Finally, the work examines different versions of the Grimms' folktales available in translation, both in terms of folktale collections for children and in terms of satirical and journalistic versions. The question is raised to what degree the Grimms' quest for loyalty to tradition should still be observed in modern folktale translations and adaptations for children. Ironic and satirical versions are viewed in historical perspective, beginning with the works of Ludwig Tieck. They also receive attention as critical approaches to the *Kinder- und Hausmärchen* and in part as humorous critical responses to the Grimms and their tales.

One of the major objectives of this work is to examine the Grimms' scholarly approaches to the *Kinder- und Hausmärchen* from the perspective of their own age and philosophy and to clear up some basic misunderstandings regarding the nature and intent of the *Kinder- und Hausmärchen* in light of new evidence based on a close interpretation of the Grimms' essays, original notes, letters to children, published scholarly works, and international correspondence.

The work concludes that the Brothers Grimm did not consider folktales the exclusive property of a single nation. Their broad international and comparative perspective on mythology has shown them to be disciples of Johann Gottfried Herder, whose love of native folklore simultaneously invited a search of *Naturpoesie* around the world. It also brings new evidence that the Grimms neither collected and edited folktales solely for children nor excluded children as contributors and as an audience.

The ideas and methods of Jacob and Wilhelm Grimm's *Kinder- und Hausmärchen* can be best understood within the context of their broader studies during the German Romantic movement. Yet also beyond their own time and ideology, the Grimms' efforts have substantially contributed to the development of scholarship in folklore, comparative literature, and children's literature.

PART I

Background and History

I. Biographical Sketch of the Brothers Grimm

[Childhood and Youth]

ACOB AND WILHELM Grimm were born in Hanau in 1785 and 1786, respectively, as the oldest of five children. Wilhelm, in his autobiography, still remembered his early childhood home, with the garden wall, the red blooming peach tree, and the old church at the town's center. When he and Jacob had walked hand in hand across the market square in the afternoon to take French lessons near the church, they paused at this place and joyfully watched how the golden weather cock turned around at the top of its steeple. In a daily ritual they would visit their two aunts, and twice weekly they visited their retired grandfather in town, who was never at a loss for good advice. Often before supper, they would roam around in the hilly countryside or play marbles and tack in front of their home. Wilhelm vividly recalled how one day their parents took them in a horse carriage to Bergen near Frankfurt, where the duke exercised his colorful troops to safeguard the emperor's election. How their rifles had glistened in the sunshine![1]

Jacob and Wilhelm were five and six years old when the family moved to Steinau, where their father, Philipp Wilhelm Grimm, became the town's *Justizamtmann* (town scribe and legal adviser). The new job promised him not only a stately salary but also a roomy stone house, with big stairways leading up to the front door. It was springtime when Dorothea Grimm accompanied her children on what Wilhelm remembered as a "long journey" to Steinau. Sitting at his mother's feet on a wooden box, he clearly recalled how the carriage rolled along dusty roads, past green meadows and rows of blooming white-thorn bushes. They soon felt at home amidst the winding streets of Steinau, as if they had always lived there.[2]

The family Grimm was well rooted in Hesse. For two generations, they had been associated with the Protestant clergy, and it was here that their grandfather, Friedrich Grimm[3] had preached for close to forty years. Today, the cemetery of Steinau still houses fourteen tomb-stones carrying the name of Grimm, among them that of their great-grandfather, whose name had been Friedrich Grimm also. Accord-ing to one of their aunts, an oil painting in Philipp Wilhelm Grimm's parlor showed that little Jacob bore a remarkable resemblance to his grandfather. Perhaps such talk encouraged Jacob to climb on a chair and to preach, telling everyone that he, too, wanted to become a preacher. Their great-great-grandfather had been Heinrich Grimm, a highway-toll collector in Dörnigheim during the time when Germany was still divided into hundreds of small principalities, each with its own borders, customs, and toll regulations. Heinrich had been the son of Johannes Grimm, known as the postmaster of Hanau.[4]

Education played a significant role in the Grimm family. Jacob and Wilhelm remembered their father as a serious and orderly man who kept his books with meticulous care and was often engaged with his clients. In spite of his busy schedule he always found time for a few kind words, inquiring frequently about their health and schooling. He also saw to it that the children had private lessons at home, which he and their mother would sometimes attend in per-son to check on their progress. Since Jacob and Wilhelm were so close in age, they were instructed together by a tutor, Herr Zinckhahn, who would arrive early every morning in his light-blue coat. In addi-tion to the three R's, he taught them geography, history, and botany. In Jacob's view, Zinckhahn didn't teach them much more than being diligent and paying strict attention to the subject. Consequently, in the afternoons, he and Wilhelm eagerly watched the big clock in their study, waiting impatiently for the time of his departure. Later in the afternoons, they still had to attend private lessons outside of their home in French and Latin. Jacob remembered that later they also had to write Latin. They studied Langens' Latin grammar book, bound in yellow leather, and they were drilled on a great number of rules. Jacob thought that their Latin teacher, who also taught them geography and religion, was rather orderly and pedantic yet neither knowledgeable nor effective. Their father made learning much more interesting. He taught them, for example, to make the Latin words rhyme with German ones, always in sets of two:

mensa — der Tisch
piscis — der Fisch
auris — das Ohr
Aethiops — der Mohr[5]

In addition, Jacob received special lessons in law from his father. As Philipp Wilhelm Grimm had made up his mind that Jacob, his oldest son, would become a lawyer or administrator, he would teach him personally in his study, making sure that he would memorize case studies and their legal implications. In religion, too, they learned more from their family than from their teacher, for aside from their praying together, their aunt would frequently read aloud to them from the Bible and from *Hühners biblische Historie* (*Hühner's Biblical History*).[6]

The two boys shared not only their tutors but also recreational games and hobbies. It is astonishing with what clarity both Wilhelm and Jacob Grimm recalled their childhood games. In their autobiographies each of them dedicated much space to the experiences that had filled the days of their childhood. They were as fascinated by childhood[7] as they were by nature poetry of *Naturpoesie*, be it in relation to folk songs, folktales, legends, or epic poems.

They played the ageless games that children had played before them in small German towns: hide-and-seek, tack, or jumping up and down the stairs in front of their home. Jacob recalled that they traded marbles made of clay, which they kept in elongated grey and brown leather bags that looked like boots. Both he and Wilhelm enjoyed catching butterflies and collecting cock feathers, chestnuts, and acorn shells. Their toys were simple but their imaginations were strong. The double acorns were the officers, and the acorns with crooked stems were the trumpeters and drummer boys, all of them marching off to war. The brothers would pretend to build a country oven simply by pushing a shoe into a firm pile of sand and pulling it out again. Some scraps of paper, a few sticks, and a bit of string were sufficient to fashion windmills or water mills. From wide grass blades or reeds they braided "cat chairs," and from chestnut shells and waxed sewing thread they built toy buggies and wagons. They also knew how to turn chicory sticks into marvelous "hyacinth blossoms," by slitting them at the top, soaking them in water, and then watching them curl up like flower petals.

In May they would catch cockchafers and ladybugs and let them fly away again. June was the best time to pick up green apples that had fallen to the ground and use them as missiles. One simply had to pierce them onto sharp sticks and hurl them through the air. Sometimes they just enjoyed watching the swallows build their nests underneath the roofs.[8] Wilhelm often took long walks by himself through the meadows, where he would give himself up to quiet thoughts. Later in life, he continued to enjoy his long and lonely walks, where nature affected the calm of his soul. To these moments he ascribed a feeling of great happiness and also some of his best and most unexpected ideas.

When winter came, it was time for snowball fights. Sometimes they would also throw snowballs against other people's entrance doors. Above their own door they found a favorite target: a carved head with a funny face, which they called Meierlein, as it resembled Court Secretary Meierlin, a friend of their grandfather's. Of course, their grandfather scolded them for it, and so did their father at one time when they bombarded the Hessian Lion at the *Scheuertor*. He angrily told them to stop that nonsense and show more respect.

On cold and rainy days when they had to stay indoors, they were seldom bored. Jacob liked to climb into the attic and sort out "old things" in boxes and on the floor. It gave him a feeling of calm when he sat there and brought order into chaos—a feeling he recognized in later days when he worked in King Jerome's library. Drawing and sketching was a hobby that they both enjoyed, along with their younger brother Ludwig. Jacob was not as gifted as Wilhelm, but he was fascinated by making drawings on very small pieces of paper—or by creating "wheat fields" with his hair on the fogged-up window pane. One of his favorite drawings was a wheat field through which a man walked holding a stick, with a house in the background that had neatly outlined windows and doors.[9] Wilhelm's favorite indoor pastime was to organize their collection of insects and butterflies and to prepare careful specimen sketches of them in his notebook. Occasionally, he and his brother would also copy some passages from books or poems that they liked especially well. Such occasions were peaceful and serene, giving them both a feeling of deep happiness.

Wilhelm referred to such activities as the early awakening of their "collector spirit" ("*Sammlergeist*"),[10] perhaps realizing that such hobbies foreshadowed their later interest in collecting not only folktales but also folk songs, myths, legends, children's games, proverbs, epic poetry, and thousands upon thousands of words that made up the German dictionary. Their lifelong interest in the lore and language of children reflects the love of their own childhood memories and the warm feelings they had for each other, their friends, and their family. The lore and language of childhood remained a part of their lives, also in their academic and scholarly work. While their active games provided a healthy balance to their rigorous study hours, their quiet and creative pursuits helped them to develop their personal and creative inclinations in a calm and peaceful way. As such, it formed a fruitful basis for their future scholarship, and it also gave them a feeling of identity and inner strength on which they soon came to rely when they were left to fend for themselves in the big city.

Philipp Wilhelm Grimm died when Jacob was barely twelve years old and Wilhelm eleven. Dorothea Grimm and her family were now facing difficult times, for there was no pension forthcoming for widows of town administrators, regardless of the length and loyalty of their service. Being forced to live on small savings, she left the stone house in Steinau and moved with her children to more modest accommodations, determined to make the best of their education. If Jacob and Wilhelm had acquired from their father a spirit of orderliness, diligence, and sense of duty, they learned from their mother a sense of modesty, frugality, sacrifice, and determination. They admired her dedication to her family and were deeply grateful for the feeling of warmth and togetherness that she provided for the entire family, including their three younger brothers, Carl, Ferdinand, and Ludwig, and their sister, Lotte. [11]

In 1798 Dorothea's sister, Henriette Zimmer, invited Jacob and Wilhelm to stay with her at her home in Kassel so that they might attend Lyceum Fredericianum. She was a maid-in-waiting for the marchionesse—a job that she acquired on the basis of family connections, for her father had served the old marquise as a personal attendant during the Seven Years War. Having a secure income and a generosity of heart, she took it upon herself to support Jacob and Wilhelm during their secondary education, but for the boys themselves it was at first painful to be separated from their immediate family. Still, they liked their aunt and well understood that attending the Lyceum was a prerequisite for their future university studies. Occasionally, their mother would send them letters and parcels, reminding Jacob to take his father's place while watching over his younger brother. She told them to study hard, to be polite to Aunt Henriette and their teachers, and to watch their health, but above all to avoid distractions and stay away from bad company. Gently, she let them know that their future careers would very much depend on the success of their studies, since she was unable to support them by herself.

In those years, Jacob indeed tried to assume the role of a protector for his younger brother—a role that he never quite abandoned for the rest of his life. Both boys tried hard to do their best in all subjects. They soon discovered, however, that unfortunately Herr Zinckhahn had not sufficiently prepared them for the rigorous demands of the Lyceum. Among the subjects they studied were geography, history, the natural sciences and physical sciences, anthropology, ethics, logic, philosophy, Latin, French, and Greek. To keep up with the requirements, they had to engage the help of a mentor. In reflecting years later about the value of their education at the Lyceum, Jacob expressed that many of their teachers' demands had been too tedious and a mere waste of time. Their lessons now absorbed as many as eight to ten hours a day, including Saturdays. A ray of sunshine in those years was their mentor, Herr Dietmar Stöhr, who not only taught them creatively but also took an interest in their personal growth and development. [12]

For Wilhelm, school had always been more difficult than for Jacob, and by nature he had been more fragile than his brother, due to the aftereffects of scarlet fever in his childhood. The rigorous demands of the Lyceum and his insufficient preparations increased his stress level and manifested themselves in a series of colds and asthma attacks.

Frequently he felt weak and had breathing problems, and at night he often lay awake, startled by an irregular heartbeat.[13] Jacob was smaller in stature than Wilhelm and also had lived through more childhood diseases than he, including the small pox, yet in Kassel he turned out to be healthier and more robust than his brother. As he had alway been an excellent student, it was easier for him to follow the academic instruction. He, too, had problems, but not so much with his assignments as with the personalities of his teachers. He really liked none of them, with the exception of his German teacher, Professor Richter, who was the school's philologist and principal. Even Richter, he thought, was a bit too old and not demanding enough, but he was at least tactful and kind. Teacher Horbach was a hypochondriac, teacher Robert was clumsy and disorganized, and teacher Caesar was downright discriminatory. Instead of addressing Jacob with the customary polite form of *Sie* (thou or you), Caesar would use the familiar term *er* (he), the third-person singular that was generally reserved for persons of inferior rank. Jacob thought such a manner of address plainly insulting. What gave Caesar the liberty to treat him as if he had come from the country? It was true that Steinau lacked a Lyceum, yet it was not a village and neither were he and his brother the sons of uneducated peasants! Evidently, Caesar did not realize that the boys had a distinguished family background with an emphasis on education that was a rarity in small towns like Steinau.

Many years later, Jacob still was angry about Caesar's discriminatory attitude. It may have been in the Lyceum in Kassel that he first began to feel strongly about the need for justice, fairness, and equal human rights.[14] One day, he and Wilhelm would stand up against a much deeper injustice done to the German people—an injustice committed by the king himself when he abolished the constitution. As mature persons, they were strong enough to forgive personal insults, but they became increasingly sensitive to the plight for freedom and justice that affected the fate of their nation—and the fate of the common man everywhere.

[Studies in Marburg and Abroad]

Jacob and Wilhelm graduated from the Lyceum in 1802 and 1803, respectively. In that order they also entered the University of Marburg to study law within the faculty of philosophy. According to custom, university scholarships in those days were awarded only to the seven upper classes of society. As children of an administrator, Jacob and Wilhelm belonged to the less-privileged middle class and thus could not expect an exemption from tuition. Officially, however, they had no reason to complain, for upon their mother's written requests, exceptions were made in both of their cases, which meant that they received free tuition after all. Having been raised in the spirit of self-reliance, they still believed at that time that poverty promoted character strength and virtue, yet they felt some resentment regarding this incident. When later in life Jacob would take a public stand in favor of abolishing unfair class privileges, he may have done so on the basis of their experience along these lines. His main target was the matter of injustice—which in the case of his teacher Caesar had arisen in the context of prejudice against "country folk"—not the class system as such.[15]

After a year of separation, Jacob and Wilhelm were happily reunited again at Marburg, sharing the same room and desk and attending the same courses within the faculty of philosophy. Together they listened to lectures on medieval literature and ancient law and became close friends with Professor Friedrich Carl von Savigny, a young and highly talented professor who taught courses in old Germanic law. Recognizing their genuine thirst for knowledge, Savigny generously permitted them to browse freely in his private library collection, which was rich in rare medieval manuscripts. Here they discovered for the first time old German and French chronicles and epics. Wilhelm got so carried away by this literature that hour upon hour he would diligently copy some of the texts in his fine handwriting, taking deep delight in reading them again in leisure in the privacy of their room.[16]

Of all professors, they liked Friedrich Carl von Savigny the best, as he truly inspired them to look beyond the letter of the law for traces of a language, customs, and traditions of a bygone age. What Wilhelm especially praised in Savigny's lectures was that they moved freely and in a spirited way from one discipline to another while making meaningful connections among various subjects, including poetry and literature. Sometimes he would recite lines from medieval epics or passages from Goethe's *Wilhelm Meister* to illustrate a point of human interest that had a bearing upon medieval law. His recitations formed a stark contrast with those of other professors, who talked either smoothly and in a well-organized fashion or in a baroque and ornamental style, without, however, touching the minds and hearts of their students. The Grimms owed to Savigny a lifelong debt for having inspired and motivated them to move beyond mere diligence to self-imposed tasks. He awakened their genuine academic interest to the point that they no longer needed tutors or mentors to tell them what to do or how to study.[17]

Jacob had just turned twenty when Professor Savigny invited him as a literary research assistant at the University of Paris. Being delighted to travel and study abroad, Jacob gladly agreed to join him, hoping by this occasion to improve his fluency in French and to explore some of the most famous libraries of Europe. While in France, he avidly corresponded with Wilhelm, expressing his vivid interest in the cultural, social, and political life of the new environment. In his turn, Wilhelm kept his brother up to date on the personal and political life at home but also reminded him to hunt in the libraries for some old French manuscripts of medieval epics, as he needed them for his comparative studies. Being himself fond of medieval French literature, Jacob used his spare time for some research on this behalf and copied by hand some rare manuscripts for his brother.[18]

In 1806 Jacob's trip paid off. His fluency in French and work and study abroad helped him to get a modestly paid job as secretary to the Hessian War Ministry (*Kriegskollegium*). The Ministry direly needed his language skills, for by now administrative affairs in the occupied German territory were conducted in French. Jacob now became the main provider of the Grimm family, for Wilhelm was not permitted to seek employment due to persistent ailments. Since Dorothea Grimm and their sister, Lotte, had moved to Kassel, they now lived together again under one roof. In spite of the modest means that they had available to meet their living expenses, they kept up a cheerful and happy family spirit. Occasionally, Aunt Henriette helped to alleviate some financial problems when Wilhelm's medical bills threatened to absorb all of Jacob's earnings.

It did not bother Jacob to speak French during all of his working hours, for he liked that language and spoke it as if it were his native tongue. Neither did he mind wearing a fancy French uniform and a powdered wig. What did disturb him, however, was that the administration increasingly relied on French laws rather than on German laws, which, in his view, led to all kinds of judicial abuses in the occupied German territory. Wilhelm observed at that time that the French language could be heard everywhere, not just in the city hall but also in the markets and streets of Kassel. While this aspect of the French occupation did not cause him a particular annoyance, he strongly objected, like his brother, to the arbitary rule that manifested itself daily. It touched him deeply when once he observed from his window that foreign soldiers were carrying off German citizens for public execution, wondering if the native residents of Kassel had not been pitifully reduced to mere pawns in a power game.[19] He never lost his admiration for the French people and their culture, yet he loathed the way in which the French occupation forces suppressed all things German. Such thoughts added a further motivation to his plans of retrieving from the Middle Ages the neglected German folk heritage.

It must be understood, however, that his resentment of the foreign rule and the love of their fatherland were not the only driving forces in the scholarly pursuits of the Brothers Grimm. Neither could it be said that the dedication and diligence with which they pursued their work was a compensation for their middle-class status or the loss of the father figure in their lives. As mature and creative persons, they did not consider their work as means to another end of achieving status, prestige, or some narrow nationalistic goals. Thinking about their research enthusiastically and in professional terms also prevented them from looking upon it as a mere obsession. Significant in this connection were Wilhelm's own comments of why it was important to turn to the Middle Ages. In his autobiography, he wrote:

> Only the most limited souls would get the idea of studying the Middle Ages to make it relevant to the present age; yet, it would be equally limited to reject the significance which it has in relation to an understanding and the proper treatment of the present. In this connection it also seems important to me that the Old German literature has directed our attention to the mores, customs, language, and poetry of the people.[20]

In spite of their shared interest in exploring the roots of *Naturpoesie*, Jacob and Wilhelm did not feel or act like identical twins. Since childhood, Jacob had been a more systematic person, capable of long hours of sustained, rigorous, and analytical work.[21] Wilhelm also possessed an admirable stamina for work, yet he relied more on his intuitive powers when approaching a problem. This difference became more pronounced during their university studies, when Jacob began to lean toward comparative linguistics and law while Wilhelm developed a fascination with medieval literature, language, and folklore studies. On the other hand, it would also be exaggerated to consider them as extreme opposites—Jacob a scientist and Wilhelm a poet— for they complemented each other in many ways. Whereas Jacob approached his work more with an eye toward scientific methodology, he was also open to poetry and literature and by no means a demagogue or a pedant.[22] Wilhelm approached his work with the perceptiveness of a poet but did not let his poetic imagination interfere with his scholarly work. Like Jacob, Wilhelm was capable of systematic work in his lectures and studies of comparative literature. It also cannot be overlooked that he spent the greater part of his professional life working together with Jacob on the *German Dictionary*. Both shared a certain amount of intuition, yet both were also disciplined enough to cooperate on scholarly projects.

The Grimms' first great cooperative project was their collection of folk songs and folktales for their friends, Clemens Brentano and Achim von Arnim, which seven years later culminated in their joint publication of folktales, the *Kinder- und Hausmärchen*. This work was innovative at the time, as it committed to print what up until then had still been considered subcultural material. To some earlier related folklore pursuits by Johann Gottfried Herder, Achim von Arnim, and Clemens Brentano, the Brothers Grimm added the method of fieldwork research, the concept of loyalty to tradition, and the idea of attaching comparative notes to the stories. In prefaces and essays they further elaborated on their innovative approach that emerged within the context of European Romantic thought.

[From Libraries to Diplomacy]

Early in 1808, Jacob voluntarily quit his job with the War Ministry in the hope of being accepted to another one at Kassel's city library, a position that he thought would be more suitable to his academic preparation. His qualifications for that position were excellent, as he was fluent in various languages and skilled in the self-taught art of reading medieval manuscripts and deciphering all kinds of peculiar samples of handwriting. Unfortunately, someone else was hired to fill this vacancy, much to the distress of Jacob's mother, who was in ill health at the time and had hoped for some financial support. For several months Jacob was unemployed but did not wish to return to his studies at the university, where Wilhelm had passed his law examination in 1806.

Soon, however, Jacob was recommended for another post that did come much closer to his academic preparations: King Jerome, the brother of Napoleon, offered him a job as royal librarian at the castle in Wilhelmshöhe (Kassel), which at the time was called Napoleonshöhe. Jacob's scholarly articles on the *Meistersinger* and German law and his fluency in the French language had made him a desirable candidate for the position. He very much wished that his mother would have lived long enough to witness the overall improvement of his situation. To the great sorrow of the family Grimm, Dorothea died in May 1808, just weeks prior to this favorable turn of events.[23]

Jacob's new occupation was a quiet one that gave him much time for personal study and contemplation. The Royal Library was not a public lending library but reserved for official use only by the king. Occasionally it served some scholars doing research on ancient and medieval literature or historical topics. On the average, he would not spend more than two hours daily on cataloging new entries, and as the king seldom asked for a book and also rarely called meetings that he had to attend in his richly embroidered uniform, he was able to pursue his scholarly work in leisure, with only a few interruptions. Overall, Jacob found this job especially pleasant, as it permitted him to use all of the Royal Library's resources for his own projects. Among these were stores of Oriental literature and rare documents relating to the Thirty Years War.[24]

After one year had passed, the king was so pleased with Jacob's performance that he gave him an additional job as legal adviser to the City Council. Jacob gladly accepted this position, too, as it did not seem to interfere too much with his research.

There were times, however, when tedious assignments threatened to drown out all creative thought. Such was the case when the king decided to store all of the books and documents upstairs in the castle's attic, as he needed the huge library hall for ceremonial purposes. He ordered about one thousand servants to assist in carrying the books, asking Jacob to see to it that the books were reshelved in a logical order.[25]

During those years when Jacob supported the family, Wilhelm was not idle. Working at home at his desk, he translated Scottish and Danish folktales, edited the *Kinder- und Hausmärchen*, wrote essays and book reviews on medieval literature, and carried on a vast correspondence with contributors to their collection, also on behalf of the German legends. Further, he analyzed and sorted an array of German folklore material that had been sent to him and Jacob from various sources.

When Jacob entered the Hessian diplomatic service in 1813, he was given the title of *Legationssekretär* (Liaison Officer). Again, he came to Paris, where he used every free minute of his spare time in libraries to collect research materials and copy old manuscripts. At that time, he also translated French romances and epics in connection with some comparative literature studies.[26]

In 1815 he accompanied the official Hessian delegate to the Vienna Congress, where he observed firsthand politics in the making. In his letters to Wilhelm he suggested that a pending secession of some states might disturb the unity and balance of the nation. It was at this time that he became more deeply involved with the German question, which undoubtedly motivated him to join a circle of friends concerned with German history and folklore.

Due to Wilhelm's precarious health conditions, his life continued to proceed more calmly. In 1814, however, he managed to get a secretarial post at the Kassel Library, where a year later Jacob joined him as second librarian. These appointments brought them both a modest yet secure income, but especially the joy of being able to work side by side and finding enough time for their scholarly projects. Years later, Jacob commented that not even exile could have disturbed their inner peace, provided it gave them a quiet place such as they had known at the Kassel Library.[27]

This peaceful occupation lasted only a short time, however, for the political turmoil soon affected the library as well. To prevent plundering and destruction, the bulk of the Hessian Archives had been stored in one of the basement rooms in the Wilhelmshöhe Castle, where it stayed until 1824. The packing and crating of books caused much commotion and abruptly terminated the Grimms' quiet pursuits. First, Jacob was placed in charge of shipping a number of valuable manuscripts and books out of the country for safe storage, and then he was sent as a delegate to Paris to retrieve some books that were stolen or lost in the process. Both brothers suffered from the external disorder and disruption. They felt a similar frustration when one day a fire erupted on the floor directly underneath the large library hall. Guards were ordered to wrap the library books in huge pieces of canvas and to dump them from the windows into the library's courtyard. Again, it fell to the Grimms and the other librarian to create order out of chaos.

The Grimms encountered another tedious work situation that arose from an administrative change after the death of the archduke. The new administration demanded of them to prepare a file of itemized purchase orders for every book to be purchased, including those to be acquired at auctions. This process not only slowed down the purchase of books but made it practically impossible for them to make any spontaneous purchases at auction sales. Still more frustrating was the new administration's request that they prepare a handwritten copy of the entire library card catalog—a job that took the Grimms and their fellow librarian more than eighteen months to complete. Jacob called this an absurd assignment, considering it "the most horrid and most boring job" of his entire life.

Much has been said regarding the work ethics and diligence of the Brothers Grimm,[28] but such incidents as these illustrate how conscious they were of the distinction between meaningful work and futile labor. They loved work that could be done with a sense of calm and on the basis of genuine involvement in a scholarly design, yet they loathed mechanical and repetitive work that required little more than tolerance for routine and red tape while underutilizing their academic preparation and innate capacities.

On the basis of their high scholarly achievements, both brothers received honorary doctoral degrees in 1819 from the Faculty of Philosophy at Marburg University. In addition, Jacob was awarded the doctorate of law degree from Berlin University in 1828 and from Breslau University in 1829.[29] Whereas Jacob was mainly recognized for his distinguished work in Germanic law and comparative linguistics (and later in comparative mythology), Wilhelm was honored for his contributions to medieval literature. Together they were cited for their joint work on *Deutsche Sagen* (*German Legends*, 1816) and the two oldest German medieval poems, *Hildebrand and Hadubrand* and *Das Weißenbrunner Gebet* (The Prayer of Weißenbrunn, 1812) as well as their translation and annotation of the *Elder Edda* (1815).[30]

It may come as a surprise to modern readers that the *Kinder- und Hausmärchen*, a work for which the Brothers Grimm are so well known in our time, were not at all mentioned among such honorary citations. Wilhelm did not list the work among his scholarly publications in his official curriculum vitae, most likely because it was not considered of academic significance in those days. Wilhelm himself, whom scholars around the world credit today for having established a dignified place for comparative folktale studies, was too shy to speak up in favor of its academic recognition. A case in point was his personal meeting and conversation with the famous poet Johann Wolfgang von Goethe, during which Goethe politely inquired into the progress of his literary work.

Wilhelm responded by mentioning his work with medieval manuscripts as well as their collection of German legends. When Jacob later asked him if he had mentioned to Goethe their work on the *Kinder- und Hausmärchen*, Wilhelm bashfully admitted that he had not. It turned out that he had also been silent on the topic of *Der armer Heinrich* (*Poor Henry*), an Old German poem, which he and Jacob had edited and which was about to be published. Perhaps he knew that Goethe did not consider German Medieval literature to be on an equal footing with the works of Homer and that, besides, he was less interested in "raw folklore" than in folk themes that appeared within a literary context. Fearing Goethe's indifference to the *Märchen* and not feeling inclined to convert the great poet, Wilhelm preferred to talk about something else. Whatever Wilhelm's reasons may have been, his silence on this account shows his awareness of the fact that the subject of folktales was not yet considered fully emancipated at that time.[31]

The year 1825 marked Wilhelm's marriage to his childhood friend and neighbor, Dortchen Wild (Dorothee Wild, the great-granddaughter of a famous philogist whose work the Grimms very much admired). Until the end of his life, Wilhelm considered this union "God's best blessing." Together they had four children, of which the first one (who died in his infancy) was named Jacob in honor of Wilhelm's brother. Their three other children were named Hermann, Rudolf, and Auguste.[32] As Jacob stayed under the same roof with Wilhelm's family, the lifestyle of the brothers did not essentially change as far as their work was concerned. They maintained separate offices, but the door between them always remained open, which was symbolic of their common goals and efforts. Tranquility was assured by Dortchen's friendly nature, her tactfulness, and her quiet support of their scholarly work. She also was a storyteller in her own right and became one of the living sources of the Grimms' *Kinder- und Hausmärchen*.

[The Grimms' Struggle for Democracy]

In 1929, one year after Hermann Grimm was born (who later became a famous German philologist and a great admirer of Ralph Waldo Emerson),[33] both Jacob and Wilhelm were appointed to the distinguished posts as librarians at the University Library of Göttingen. The library halls, with ceilings as high as those of the castle's ballroom, contained the largest and most distinguished book collection of Hesse. It also was known as the first lending library in Germany, sending upon request books to scholars into every part of the country and even abroad. In 1831 Jacob was also appointed Professor of Law and Linguistics at Göttingen University, thus combining two professions at the same time. He was appointed to this job mainly on the basis of his *Deutsche*

Grammatik (German Grammar, 1819–1839) and *Deutsche Rechtsalter-tümer* (German Legal Antiquities, 1828), as well as various essays and learned treatises. He lectured on Germanic law (including customs, traditions, and Germanic folk wisdom), but he also taught a course on the History of German Literature and another one on International Law. Wilhelm followed him as *Außerordentlicher Professor* (Lecturer of Medieval Literature) in 1831 and in four years was promoted to the rank of *Ordinarius* (full professor), like his brother. Wilhelm had been selected for this assignment on the basis of his *Deutsche Heldensage* (*The German Heroic Legend*, 1829), as well as *Über deutsche Runen* (*About German Runes*, 1821) and *Zur Literatur der Runen* (on the *Literature Regarding Runes*, 1828), but also because he had distinguished himself by a Latin treatise on *The Song of Hildebrand and Hadubrand, De Hildebrando antiquissimi carminis i fragmentum* (1830). He lectured on the medieval poems of *Gudrun* and *Ruodolf* and was especially successful in his lecture on *The Nibelungenlied* (*Song of the Nibelung*). Wilhelm also prepared an innovative comparative lecture on the treatment of the Cyclops theme in literature from Homer to the present.[34]

Their own high academic standards demanded of them a rigorous preparation for lectures, but in spite of this time-consuming work, they still found time between lectures, library work, and meetings with students to continue with their scholarly activities. This was only possible, however, because their classes were relatively small, testing was kept to a minimum, and committee responsibilities were not overbearing. Some transcripts of their lectures that have been preserved to this day show a meaningful connection between their research and teaching.[35]

An inseparable bond developed between Jacob and Wilhelm during their Göttingen years, when they both committed themselves to the cause of democracy and freedom. After King Jerome had been driven away from Kassel and the German residents in a joyous parade had welcomed back the duke and his family, new hope began to dawn for the prospects of freedom, fairness, and democracy. Both Wilhelm and Jacob rejoiced at the turn of events, and in the following months they contributed actively toward the framing of the new Constitution. While putting to work Savigny's philosophy that regarded law not as a dead paragraph in dusty books but as a civil right and "light" belonging to all, they expected the Constitution to grant basic human rights to the native population.[36] All might have gone well if the duke had not died.

On November 1, 1837, the duke's brother, Ernst August of Cumberland, took over the rule and with one stroke he wiped out all of their labor while threatening to quench the newborn spirit of freedom. He simply abolished the Constitution overnight, while instituting his own rule of power. The Brothers Grimm were among the seven dissident professors at the University of Göttingen who publicly protested such arbitrary action. In an open address to students and professors, Jacob defended their democratic rights by citing the famous words of Martin

Luther: "The freedom of Christian man must give us the courage to resist our ruler, if it turns out that he acts contrary to the spirit of God, and if he offends human rights."[37] The punishment for their courageous stand was exile, as all seven dissidents lost their jobs and were forced to move away from Göttingen and Hannover.

The Grimms freely admitted that the Constitution had been based on various compromises and was far from being perfect. They also agreed that some of its framers had been cynics and opportunists while others had been what they called "great levelers" who merely enjoyed pulling down what was up and moving up what was down or, as Jacob put it, "to shave off mountain tops, uproot the proud forests, tear up the good soil, or mow down the flowery meadows."[38] Some had indeed misused the name of democracy to serve their own vanity and profit, being too small-minded to look beyond practical things and personal advantages. He knew all that, and yet in spite of its inherent flaws and some weaknesses among its framers, the Constitution represented the will of the people. Being firmly rooted in representative democracy, it had guaranteed the democratic rights of the citizens that were made sacred by an oath before God. Such an oath could not and should not be dissolved by the sheer power of a king. The Grimms knew that in the face of power and might, courage was needed to affirm the very principle and existence of Truth and that it was immoral to give in to doubts that, according to Jacob, sprang up "like weeds among the cobblestones."[38]

They found the source of such courage and inner strength in their deep faith in democracy and fairness. It was the same faith that they had admired in their former ruler, who had been raised in the spirit of democracy under the British Constitution. Jacob commented that as an inheritor to the throne, and in accordance with an unwritten law based on an ancient custom, the new ruler should have respected his brother's last will instead of destroying it overnight. If every successor to the throne would arbitarily dissolve the constitution, all laws would soon be abandoned and anarchy would prevail.[40]

The Grimms' defense of basic democratic freedoms, including the liberty of speech and the right to participate in self-government, has often been cited as an action arising from the spirit of growing German nationalism.[41] While such an interpretation is not altogether wrong, it bypasses the universal implications of this courageous action that carried the spirit of the American and the French Revolution. Their plight was based on the ideas of Rousseau and Montesquieu, who had advocated the quest for human rights on a universal basis, and they expressed it with a religious sincerity that had already marked Herder's struggle for cultural and political liberation in the late nineteenth century. Like Rousseau, Montesquieu, and Herder, they granted such a quest for freedom to all nations, whether they belonged to Europe, Africa, Asia, or North America.

As humanists and as teachers, the Brothers Grimm affirmed ethical values that had also been shared by the great writers of the ancient classics in whose spirit they were raised. "It is not the arm of justice but sheer power that has forced me to leave the country,"[42] wrote Jacob in an essay on their dismissal from Göttingen University. Their spirit was unbroken, as they had acted in accordance with their conscience, without fearing the consequences of such an action in terms of job security or reputation. Neither had they cared for an applause by their friends. Jacob wrote that what students demanded of those who taught them was an uncorrupted character and an open mind, as well as a serious response to significant questions. They also expected professors to maintain a pure ethical point of view that served no other goal except the spirit of Truth. In the light of such demands, they deserved to receive what they expected, namely nothing less than what was "holiest, simple, and true." The best teachers whom the Grimms themselves remembered with admiration had taught and interpreted the great classics in that spirit. Should their own students demand and receive less from teachers who taught and interpreted democracy and the current state of the nation? The Grimms were convinced that no person serving at a university should allow himself to remain indifferent when the country's Constitution was at stake. As citizens, as Christians, and as teachers, they had the moral obligation to speak for human rights—even if it meant to go against the king himself.

The Brothers Grimm never regretted their stand. In Jacob's written response to the charges brought against him and the other six dissidents at Göttingen University, he wrote:

> Now I have openly exposed to the world my ideas, conclusions, and actions, without considering whether it may be to my benefit or to my disadvantage. If these pages will be discovered by some future generations, let them read in my heart which then will have long stopped beating. Yet as long as I have a living breath in me, I will be glad to have done what I have done; and this I know for sure: whatever part of my work will survive me will not lose but will only gain because of it. . . . Whether any or what kind of fruit shall come of it lies in God's directing hand.[43]

Wilhelm's son, Hermann Grimm, recognized in these words an expression of Jacob's faith and humility but also a prophecy regarding the timeless value of his final commitment.

It was an odd experience for Wilhelm and Jacob Grimm to have been exiled from Göttingen to the place of their youth, the city of Kassel, where the people greeted them with love and respect. Jacob recalled a touching incident shortly upon his arrival in Kassel, when an old grandmother proudly pointed him out to her grandchild with the words: "Shake hands with this gentleman, for he is a refugee!"[44] Having lost their jobs and being without a regular income, they were now facing hard times. The warm welcome with which they were received seemed to alleviate some of their worries, and it helped that they earned some money from publishing occasional articles and reviews, but such subsidies were not sufficient to support the family. Fortunately, their friends and acquaintances helped in various tactful ways, which made it easier for all of them to overcome this crisis.

[Toward an International Scholarship]

The Grimms' scholarly achievements must be viewed within the context of German Romanticism, for it is that movement that explains their impact on national as well as comparative studies.[45] Their concern with the restoration of German and Germanic folk traditions largely corresponded to the awakening Romantic interest of the native language, law, and history, for which the ground had already been prepared by Johann Gottfried Herder. The growing national consciousness in Germany created a climate that favored their search for native roots. Such writers as Clemens Brentano, Achim von Arnim, August Wilhelm Schlegel, Friedrich Schlegel, Ludwig Tieck, Heinrich Wackenroder, and Joseph Görres were similarly involved in retrieving the treasures of the past. In related yet different ways they secretly hoped to strengthen the nation's identity and the quality of German literature as well. Native folklore was to be the "healing power" for the nation, a remedy for its spiritual recovery and creative strength.[46]

At the same time, however, the Brothers Grimm and a number of other German Romantic writers and philosophers also searched beyond their own national borders for the spirit of the past, hoping to retrieve from it the myths, folktales, and legends of other lands. Following in the footsteps of Herder, the early Romantic movement in Germany brought an awakening of studies in comparative literature, comparative philosophy, and comparative mythology.[47] Johann Jacob Bachofen and Joseph Görres, for example, looked toward India as a great source of mythology and poetic inspiration, whereas Friedrich and August Wilhelm Schlegel even talked about developing a new mythology from within the creative mind that would arouse the nation to a new spiritual perception and *inner* unity. Their journal, the *Athenäum*, gave evidence of a universal Romantic quest in folklore and literature that transcended the boundaries of their homeland. Novalis (Friedrich von Hardenberg) dreamed of a united Europe under the banner of Christianity. The Romantic age in Germany was also the age of great translations. Friedrich Schlegel's lectures on world literature in Berlin were partially based on his own translations of works from the ancient Sanskrit *Shakuntala* to the dramas of Sophocles and Shakespeare. The search for *Naturpoesie* was at once national and universal, and it encouraged writers at home and abroad to look for the naive and holistic spirit of the past.[48]

On the surface it appeared as if the Grimms' frequent use of the word *"Deutsche"* (German) in such titles as Jacob's *Deutsche Rechtsalterhümer* (*German Legal Antiquities*), *Deutsche Grammatik* (*German Grammar*), and *Deutsche Mythologie* (*German Mythology*) and in Wilhelm's *Deutsche Sagen* (*German Legends*) and *Deutsche Heldensagen* (*German Heroic Songs*) were symptomatic of an exclusive concern with the German and Germanic folk traditions. A number of nationalistic interpretations of their works strengthened the impression that they had been exclusively concerned with the unity and welfare of the "fatherland." In fact, some critics have taken the frequent use of the word *"deutsch"* in the titles of their works as evidence of their nationalistic inclinations.[49] Yet, such appearances are misleading, especially if we keep in mind that the proper translation of the title *Deutsche Mythologie* should not have been *Teutonic Mythology* but *Germanic and Indo-Germanic Mythology*, for Jacob mainly used the comparative Indo-European approach to language and mythology studies in this work. He consistently drew upon comparisons with Romanic, Italic, Slavonic, Celtic, Baltic, Greek, Armenian, Hittite, and Indic languages and folk beliefs in analyzing examples of German and Nordic myths, folktales, customs, and folk beliefs.[50] The same is true for Jacob's works on grammar, none of which strictly followed a national orientation or a dry analytical method but a historical and comparative approach that had been initiated by the Danish linguist Rask.[51] Even Wilhelm's work with German legends was internationally based, as it embraced legends collected and rooted not only in Germany but also in such neighboring countries as Switzerland, Austria, the Netherlands, France, and Alsace-Lorraine.

The *Kinder- und Hausmärchen* of the Brothers Grimm did not have the word "Deutsche" attached to the title. Only when Edgar Taylor first translated the work in 1826 under the title of *German Popular Stories* did English-speaking readers begin to suspect that nationalistic concerns had been the Grimms' sole motivation for publishing the work. This notion was strengthened by Taylor's preface, which pointed to the *German* sources as the tales that supposedly had been taken directly from the lips of the simple peasant folk. As Taylor did not publish the Grimms' comparative notes and also did not mention their work with comparative literature, law, and philology, English critics for a long time failed to see the broader international significance that the Grimms had attached to them. Not even Margaret Hunt's translation later in the nineteenth century included the unabridged third volume of notes for *Kinder- und Hausmärchen* (2d edition of 1822) that contained, among other things, Wilhelm's very detailed and comparative analysis of folktales by Giambattista Basile.[52]

In their search for linguistic and historical roots of German folktales, the Grimms were preoccupied with Germanic traditions yet never to the point of overlooking possible influences from other cultures or cross-cultural variants. In fact, searching out variants in other cultures was one of the main objectives of their notes, which they attached to every tale with meticulous care.

The Grimms also spent much time and effort encouraging scholars of other nations to search out their own native folktales and legends. Among their correspondents were Sir Walter Scott and his friend Henry Weber in Scotland, Thomas Crofton Croker in Ireland, Edgar Taylor in England, Peter Christian Asbjörnsen and Jörgen Moe in Norway, Bernhard Thiele in Denmark, Josef Dobrovsky in Czechoslovakia, Vuk Stepanovic Karadcik in Serbia, and Aleksandr Afanas'ev in Russia, to mention just a few.[53]

Their various translations and book reviews of foreign publications give further evidence of their genuine interest in the folktales and folk beliefs of other lands. Together they translated not only some Old German and Middle High German epic poems, such as *Rudolf* (or *Ruodolf*) and *The Song of Hildebrand* but also *The Elder Edda* from the Icelandic, along with portions of the Ruthenian epic *The Song of Igor* of the Finnish *Kalevala*, as well as some Old French and Old English manuscripts of epics and romance. In connection with the English epic of *Beowulf*, they closely cooperated with John B. Kemble, who studied under the Grimms in Göttingen and also was a frequent guest in their home. Kemble dedicated to Jacob Grimm his edition of the *Beowulf* epic (1836–39). Jacob's translation of the animal epic *Reinhard Fuchs* (*Reynard the Fox*), for which he translated and analyzed side-by-side Low German, French, Dutch, and Latin poems, represented a truly comparative study.[54]

In 1811, one year prior to the appearance of the *Kinder- und Hausmärchen*, Wilhelm had already translated and published *Altdänische Heldenlieder, Balladen und Märchen* (*Old Danish Heroic Songs, Ballads, and Folktales,* 1811), and in 1813 he brought out *Drei altschottische Lieder, im Original und Übersetzung* (*Three Old Scottish Songs, in the Original and in Translation,* 1813). To all three of these he attached comparative notes along with introductions in praise of the national and universal spirit of folk literature.

The motivation for comparative folktale studies arose in Jacob's case from his scientific interest in the nature of the Indo-European language theory and its application to folklore. He would have liked to see published with international cooperation a vast European folktale collection on which basis he would have carried out further comparative studies related to both language and folk literature. Unlike the German nationalists around the turn of the century and the Nazis in the thirties, Jacob did not use racial determination in his interpretation and application of the Indo-European theory. Instead, he employed a broad comparative approach that was unrelated to an ethnocentric or racial bias.

In Wilhelm's case, comparative studies developed from an almost missionary zeal to encourage writers in other lands to search out their native folk traditions as a tribute to *Naturpoesie*, the simple naive poetry of the common folk everywhere. Essentially, he was more interested in the folktales themselves than in their further use for linguistic studies. While he was shy in personal relations, he was eloquent as well as tactful in his correspondence and managed to promote by his letter a great number of folktale collections in other lands.

The Grimms' efforts in translating, collecting, and comparing folktales, myths, and legends of other countries motivated a number of European writers to follow in their path. To the 1850 edition of the *Kinder- und Hausmärchen* the Grimms attached an annotated bibliography of folktale collections around the world that had come into print since 1812. Already then it encompassed several hundred entries.[55] Even though they did not claim that all of these collections were to be ascribed to an immediate influence of the *Kinder- und Hausmärchen*, they wrote that most of them, by means of letters or preface acknowledgements, had given the Grimms credit for their example. A landmark of cross-cultural understanding was their joint translation of Thomas Crofton Croker's *Fairy Legends and Traditions of the South Ireland* (1826), to which they gave the title *Irische Elfenmärchen*,[56] but even more so Wilhelm's introductory essay dealing with a comparative study of fairy lore in Ireland, England, Wales, and Scotland. Already in his own time, Wilhelm sparked off an interest in comparative folktale studies or "fairy mythologies" that in terms of scope far exceeded the boundaries of Ireland and the British Isles.

Among Jacob's early translations was the *Wuk Stephanowitsch, Kleine serbische Grammatik* (Vuk Stepanovic, Small Serbian Grammar, 1824), which was really a voluminous work encompassing more than a thousand pages. It is of particular importance for two reasons: It established a basis for comparative linguistics, and it helped Jacob to develop a closer relationship with its original author, Vuk Stepanovic Karadcik, who later published *Volksmärchen der Serben* (*Folktales of the Serbians*, 1854), to which were appended several hundred Serbian proverbs. Jacob Grimm wrote the preface to this work, which showed a significant interest in Serbian folk culture. These two publications also revealed that Romantic scholarship in general and Jacob Grimm's in particular combined linguistic studies and folklore studies in an ingenious way.

With a reawakening of the populist movement in Eastern Europe, the nations in the East looked with hope upon Jacob Grimm as they had formerly looked upon Herder, taking his translation of the Serbian works as a sign of encouragement and a movement toward better world understanding. Their admiration for Jacob increased with his appreciative introduction to Anton Dietrich's translation of *Russische Volksmärchen* (*Russian Folktales*, 1832) and his perceptive analysis of the Old Rus' epic *Song of Igor*, which he and Wilhelm had compared favorably with the *Edda* and the *Nibelungenlied*.[57]

The broad scope and sincerity of the Grimms' international scholarship provoked a strong reaction abroad and set the tone for decades to come. As one of the cofounders of the Historical Society of Lower Saxony in Hannover, John Kemble spoke with warmth and enthusiasm about how the Brothers Grimm had presented a breakthrough by the example of their work. Referring to their international contributions to folklore, history, and archaeology, he wrote:

> If we wish that our studies should lead to something more than merely a busy yet useless leisure time activity, then we will all have to work in one spirit and maintain our mutual connections, for in the area of archaeology it would be futile to believe that the research results of one country could suffice. Every country should contribute its appropriate part to the common project. Its beauty and longevity will depend on how carefully each one works on his own collection.[58]

The last sentence also contains the key to the Grimms' thoughts about the relationship between national and cross-cultural folktale collections. They hoped that if each nation would carefully collect its own folk treasures first then the comparative project would have an excellent start.

[Berlin and Beyond]

The Grimms' financial problems were unexpectedly resolved in 1840, when in recognition of their scholarly achievements the king of Prussia himself, Friedrich Wilhelm IV, offered them a generous stipend on the condition that they would move to Berlin and dedicate their efforts to the first German etymological dictionary. Occasionally, they would also be required to lecture at the University of Berlin. The Grimms agreed to these conditions, and soon they moved to larger living quarters in the capital of Prussia, which then was the center of Germany's intellectual life. With them moved Wilhelm's wife, Dortchen, and their three children. The new assignment promised to offer to the Grimms material security and, above all, the intellectual environment of the University of Berlin and released time for their scholarly pursuits.[59]

At the University of Berlin, both Wilhelm and Jacob received a standing applause—not just in recognition of their fame as scholars but in honor of their firm stand on democracy and freedom. By now the courage of the Grimms had become a legend. Personally, the Grimms could do without the fame that surrounded them. They enjoyed their lectures and some social contacts with students and colleagues, but they were happiest with their private quarters at home, where they worked with dedication on a project that would crown all of their previous achievements.

In 1841 Jacob was awarded the Cross of the Honor Legion of France for his scholarly contribution. The notification on this account by the French Foreign Ministry indicated that this recognition was given in the name of peace and cultural cooperation between France and Germany. In his acceptance letter, Jacob wrote that as the origins and ancient roots of their Germany were intimately connected, the future of Europe would depend on their mutual agreement and respect for each other. He was indeed very pleased that in terms of science and literature he had been able to contribute his modest share to the promotion of closer ties between their two countries. In a private letter to his friend Karl Lachmann he later commented that not even a medal from King Ludwig of Bavaria could have given him such a deep pleasure, simply because the Cross of the Honor Legion of France stood for a peaceful international cooperation.[60]

On May 31, 1842, the Prussian court awarded Jacob with the so-called *Orden pour le merité*,[61] which made him an official ambassador of peace. Although Jacob cared little for such public honors and ceremonies and was quite content to work quietly in his study, he did not wish to spoil the fun for his family, who took deep pride in the public recognition of his work.

In 1845 Jacob Grimm was elected president of the newly founded Association of Germanists, and a year later he was chosen to preside over its National Convention in Frankfurt am Main. His keynote address for that occasion marked his new comparative approach to German studies. He emphasized the goal of elevating the study of the German language, history, and law on an interrelated basis and of using the term *Germanistik* (Germanistics) in this connection "in the *broadest possible sense.*" He hoped that henceforth Germanists would be recognized on the same basis as the Romanists, Slavists, and Classicists, who already long ago in Germany had organized their own professional associations. To Jacob Grimm it appeared as an irony that in Germany itself Germanists had to struggle for academic emancipation.[62]

The place and timing of this address offered Jacob a unique occasion to express some strong nationalistic sentiments, yet he did not give in to such a temptation, mainly because he based his ideas on a broader international perspective. Although he expressed enthusiasm at the prospects of seeing the German language as the new determining and uniting factor of the German *Volk*, he was far from appraising Germany's cultural or political leadership position within the European context. To the contrary, he told his audience to use the term "Germanic" with caution. While admitting that it was preferable to use native German words instead of foreign ones whenever they expressed something concisely and well, and that it was indeed a deep pleasure to discover a long-forgotten German word in an old folktale or legend, he warned against the foolishness of a "purist's" approach to language that would radically eliminate all foreign words and phrases.

No language was an island to itself, was Jacob's essential message, for each language among the "family" of languages had influenced the other in an intimate way. The same could be said about culture, regardless if it applied to the German, English, Celtic, Romanic, or Slavic culture. Both linguistically and culturally Germany was as much indebted to France and England, for example, as these countries were to Germany. Languages, cultures, and nationalities should not be clinically separated as if they were products of an exact science, for, as a matter of fact, they were not! Linguistics as well as Germanistics belonged to the *inexact sciences.* To put this definition to a test, he added jokingly that even the most nationalistically inclined *Germanist* who called himself *Dichter* (poet) would have to recognize two foreign influences at once: the ending *ist* in *Germanist* was as non-German as was the word *Dichter* in its entirety, which was derived from the Latin word *dictator.*[63] Jacob's call for an international perspective in the field of Germanistics was eagerly suppressed during times of surging nationalism in Germany around the turn of the century and again during the Nazi period. Yet it has left its mark on modern scholarly orientation in this field, which in modern times has once more taken a broader view of the subject.

The Brothers Grimm found time to continue some of their folktale collections in Berlin, although it was mainly Wilhelm who, since the second edition of the *Kinder- und Hausmärchen*, had been responsible for the new editions and revisions of the tales. Jacob published his two-volume work of *Geschichte der deutschen Sprache* (*History of the German Language*) in 1848, yet his main assignment until the end of his life remained his work on the first German etymological dictionary. Wilhelm assisted him throughout, but Jacob, as a professional linguist, took the leading part. In defining the origins and historical usage of words, the Grimms would resort to literature and folklore studies while frequently quoting German literature of several centuries, from Martin Luther to Johann Wolfgang von Goethe. Also, they would refer to German proverbs, sayings, popular rhymes, medieval jests, old Germanic legal documents, epics, chapbooks, and romance. The work progressed slowly but persistently, word by word and column by column, all in Jacob's and Wilhelm's small, fine penmanship and with many additions and corrections on loose sheets of paper and in the margins. As it gradually took shape, it moved beyond mere words to open up an intricate pattern of German thought, literature, history, law, and culture. The work was unique at the time, as it also made room for colloquial speech and popular literature, which many critics then considered as "subcultural material."[64]

In Berlin the Brothers Grimm were relatively successful in staying aloof from various distractions, yet they did not retreat to an ivory tower to complete their work. There were times when they had to give up the peace and tranquility of their studies for meetings with publishers or visiting scholars, for lectures, for professional conferences, and for literary and political gatherings. Books and papers often piled up so high in their offices that they felt frustrated at what appeared to be an endless project. Even the patient Jacob had moments when he was threatened by visions of getting buried under a blizzard of papers swirling around in his study. The situation got worse when they had to leave their studies for several weeks to follow their professional and political commitments. This was especially true for Jacob, who in 1848 was elected the official delegate to the First National Assembly taking place in Frankfurt's St. Paul Cathedral. Here he presented a significant motion on the floor regarding the guarantee of freedom, not only for all German citizens but also for strangers who came to live on German soil. He made yet another motion that favored the liberty and equality of common man, namely to abolish all privileges of the aristocracy (along with the practice of awarding honorary medals to civilians).[65]

In 1854 the Grimms finally published the first volume of the dictionary under the title *Deutsches Wörterbuch* (German Dictionary), which covered the letters "A–Biermolke." Wilhelm died in 1861 of a lung and heart ailment, before he had been able to complete his entries for the letter "D."

In spite of Jacob's deep sorrow at the loss of his brother, he continued the work with determination, knowing all the while that he would not finish the gigantic task. At the age of seventy-five, one year after Wilhelm's death, he wrote to his publisher that an estimated 20,000 additional pages in his small handwriting would be needed to do justice to the remaining letters of the alphabet—a task he did not think he was destined to complete. In the final weeks of his life, when he was already too weak to work at his desk, he would continue writing while sitting in bed, with a pillow propped behind him. What gave him strength was the growing realization that the project was greater than he and that it was vitally needed for the German language and the German nation. Working in the spirit of true humility, without caring about fame or fortune, Jacob completed two more volumes of the *Wörterbuch* before he died in 1865. His last entry, the word "fruit," may be taken as a symbol of the fruits of his labor that seemed to ripen in their own time.[66]

Some of the greatest German linguists continued the work, among them Rudolf Hildeband, and step-by-step it reached its completion in the early 1970s. In 1985, the year of the Bicentennial celebration of Jacob Grimm's birthday, the Reclam Verlag in West Germany published a paperback edition of the work in sixteen volumes. In view of the many contributors, Jacob Grimm could no longer be considered to be the sole author of the work, although his name still appears on its cover. Properly speaking, he never was the sole author of the book, for Wilhelm certainly deserves credit for having labored on it with him for almost thirty years, even if not with the same linguistic zeal as his brother. Still, there is no doubt among linguists in our time that Jacob was the major driving force behind the project, setting the pace for generations of linguists after him.

Some critics have suggested that if Wilhelm had not been forced to serve Jacob's ambitions regarding the dictionary, he might have accomplished still greater things within the realm of folktale collections.[67] Yet, it must be said in Jacob's defense that Wilhelm accepted the same lifelong fellowship from the king of Prussia as his brother and that officially he never resigned from the job. Also, he did spend the bulk of his time on further revising and enlarging the *Kinder- und Hausmärchen*, for which Jacob gave him the sole responsibility in Göttingen and Berlin. Of course, there is no way of knowing what else Wilhelm might have done if instead of joining hands with Jacob he had dedicated all of his time to folktales and legends. Jacob was not blind to Wilhelm's talents and inclinations and sometimes wondered if he should have talked him into such painstaking work as that required by the *Wörterbuch*. In his eulogy to his brother, Jacob called him *Märchenbruder* (folktale brother),[68] recognizing freely and without envy that it was Wilhelm, with his poetic intuition, who had contributed the most to their folktale collection. He also suggested that without Wilhelm's poetic inclinations, persistence, and loyalty, Jacob might never have accomplished his own scientific work. Wilhelm himself did not consider Jacob his oppressor but rather looked upon him with loving admiration. One may only guess what else he might have accomplished if he had not helped his brother.

On a popular level, the Brothers Grimm are best known around the world today for their folktale collection that appears in many languages and new editions every year. On a scholarly level, Jacob is better known by linguists and comparative philologists than is Wilhelm.[69] In their own time, the Grimms received honorary membership in philological and scientific associations in such German cities as Berlin, Breslau, Brünn, Dresden, Erfurt, Frankfurt, Görlitz, Göttingen, Hamburg, Hannover, Jena, Kassel, Kiel, Königsberg (now in Poland), Laibach (now Ljubljana, Slovenia), Mainz, Marburg, Meiningen, Munich, Münster, Nuremberg, Regensburg, Schwerin, Stettin, Stuttgart, Wiesbaden, and Würzburg. In addition, they received many honorary memberships in professional associations and universities abroad. Among the places mentioned on their membership certificates are Amsterdam, Belgrade, Brussels, Budapest (Pest), Catania, Dublin, Dünkirchen, Florence, Gent, Groningen, Helsinki, Kopenhagen, Leiden, Leuuwarden, St. Petersburg, London, Mitau (Kurland), Mülhausen (Alsace-Lorraine), Paris, Prague, Reykjavik, Stockholm, Tallin (Reval, Estonia), Upsala, Utrecht, Vienna, Zagreb, and Zurich. In the United States too Jacob won high honors as a scholar. New York's American Ethnological Society made him an honorary member in 1845, Boston's American Academy of Arts and Sciences (Class of Moral and Political Sciences, Section of Philology and Archaeology) gave him honorary membership in 1857, and Philadelphia's American Philosophical Society listed him as a member in 1865.[70]

Essentially, however, such honors and others were bestowed upon them mainly because of their contributions to linguistics and philology, not because of their comparative folktale research or their contributions to children's literature. Like the German encyclopedias and universities in their time, the learned societies at home and abroad largely ignored the *Kinder- und Hausmärchen* of the Brothers Grimm.

Free from personal ambitions, vanity, and greed, the Brothers Grimm quietly followed their own quest for knowledge while striving toward higher goals. The spirit of modesty and humility that characterized their work is evident on their tombstones in Berlin. Upon their own request, these bear neither titles nor their honors but merely the dates of their births and deaths, next to the simple inscriptions "Here lies Jacob Grimm" (*Hier liegt Jacob Grimm*) and "Here lies Wilhelm Grimm" (*Hier liegt Wilhelm Grimm*).[71]

To what degree the Grimms' theories and methods have influenced modern folklore research is likely to remain a subject of future debates. Modern beyond doubt were their interdisciplinary and comparative approaches to language, law, literature, and history, which have not yet received the attention they deserve. It may be more relevant to our time that they are remembered not merely for their love of home and country but for their universal quest for *Naturpoesie* and their commitment to democracy and freedom. This legacy has validity beyond their time and meaning beyond the borders of their own nation.

NOTES

1. Wilhelm Grimm, "Selbstbiographie" in *Kleinere Schriften von Wilhelm Grimm*, vol. I (Berlin: Ferdinand Dümmlers Verlagsbuchhandlung, 1881), p. 5.

2. Ibid., pp. 2–3.

3. Wilhelm Grimm named his son, Ferdinand Friedrich, after the boy's maternal grandfather, who had come from Bern, Switzerland, as well as his own grandfather, Friedrich Grimm, whose tombstone was located in Steinau. His firstborn child (who died in infancy) he called Jacob—after his brother, Jacob Grimm.

4. See also Wilhelm Praesent, "Im Hintergrund Steinau: Kleine Beiträge zur Familiengeschichte der Brüder Grimm" in Ludwig Denecke, ed., *Brüder Grimm Gedenken*, vol. I (Marburg: N. G. Elwert Verlag, 1963), pp. 49–67, and Hermann Gerstner, *Die Brüder Grimm. Biographie mit 48 Bildern* (Gerabonn: Hohenloher Verlag, 1971), pp. 9–25.

5. Jacob Grimm, "Selbstbiographie" in *Kleinere Schriften von Jacob Grimm*, 1 (Berlin: Ferdinand Dümmlers Verlagsbuchhandlung, 1864), pp. 2–10. Both Wilhelm's and Jacob's autobiographies are also reprinted in Ingeborg Schnack, *Die Selbstbiographien von Jacob und Wilhelm Grimm* (Kassel: Brüder Grimm Gesellschaft, 1956).

6. Ibid.

7. Ibid.

8. Wilhelm Grimm's fascination with childhood games is evident in his introductory essay: "Kinderwesen und Kindersitten" (The Nature and Customs of Children) in *Kinder- und Hausmärchen*, vol. 2 (Berlin: Reimer, 1819), pp. 359–98, which is framed by an essay on the nature of folktales and another one on children's folk beliefs. Both brothers also contributed children's counting rhymes and songs to Achim von Arnim and Clemens Brentano's *Des Knaben Wunderhorn: Alte deutsche Lieder (Heidelberg: Mohr und Zimmer, 1806–08)*.

9. Jacob Grimm, "Selbstbiographie," pp. 1–5.

10. Wilhelm Grimm, "Selbstbiographie," pp. 11–13.

11. These were Jacob's personal reflections about his parents. See Ulrich Wyss, ed., *Jacob Grimm: Selbstbiographie. Ausgewählte Schriften, Reden und Abhandlungen* (Munich: Deutscher Taschenbuch Verlag, 1984), Part I. Significant in this connection are also Dorothea Grimm's letters which she wrote to Jacob and Wilhelm at the time when they were studying at the Lyceum in Kassel. See: Wilhelm Praesant, *Märchenhaus des deutschen Volkes: Aus der Kinderzeit der Brüder Grimm* (Kassel: Brüder Grimm Gesellschaft, 1957). For a very different view on the subject see Jack Zipes, "Dreams of a Better Bourgeois Life. The Psychosocial Origins of the Grimms' Tales" in James M. MacGlathery, et al. eds., *The Brothers Grimm and Folktale* (Urbana: University of Illinois Press, 1988), pp. 213–15. Zipes' view that the Grimms' compensated for the loss of the father figure in their lives by clinging fervently to the idea of the "fatherland" is not supported by the Grimms' autobiographies, which repeatedly show that they loved both parents equally, but especially admired their mother for having given them spiritual support during difficult times. It may also be argued that there is no rational or scientific basis for the assumption that semi-orphans transfer their loss of a parent to the fatherland or motherland.

12. Of related interest is Murray B. Peppard, *Paths Through the Forest* (New York: Holt, Rinehart and Winston, 1971).

13. In his autobiography, Wilhelm dedicated relatively much space to a description of his various ailments and attempted cures, mainly because his ill health constantly forced him to struggle against the odds. Nevertheless, he retained a sunny disposition throughout his life. See also Hermann Grimm, "Jacob and Wilhelm Grimm" in *Literatur*, Sarah Adams, trans. (Boston: Cupples, Upham & Co. Publ., 1886), pp. 254–85.

14. These comments refer to the Grimms' fight for constitutional rights during the Göttingen years.

15. Jacob Grimm, "Selbstbiographie," p. 5. He wrote: *"Dürftigkeit spornt zu fleisz und arbeit an, bewahrt vor mancher zerstreuung and flöszt einen nicht unedlen stolz ein, den das bewustsein des selbstverdienstes, gegenüber dem, was anderen stand und reichtum gewähren, aufrecht erhält."* (Poverty promotes diligence and work, protects from distraction, and enhances a noble pride that is kept up by the consciousness of having earned something by one's own efforts, instead of having gained it by class and wealth.) Partially, Jacob ascribed the same reasons to the work ethics of the German people, which to him indicated a healthy democratic spirit. (Jacob used lowercase letters for nouns and also had his own rules for spelling such words as *bewustsein* with one "s" and the "sz" for the "ß.")

16. Wilhelm Grimm, "Selbstbiographie," pp. 10–11.

17. *Ibid.* For further references regarding the Marburg years, consult Alfred Höck, "Die Brüder Grimm als Studenten in Marburg," *Brüder Grimm Gedenken*, vol. 1, pp. 67–75, and Ludwig Denecke *Jacob Grimm und sein Bruder Wilhelm* (Stuttgart: Metzler, 1971).

18. Wilhelm Schoof and Ingeborg Schnack, eds., *Briefe der Brüder Grimm an Savigny. Aus dem Savignischen Nachlass* (Berlin: Erich Schmidt Verlag, 1953),

and Hermann Grimm and Gustav Hinrichs, eds., *Briefwechsel zwischen Jacob und Wilhelm Grimm aus der Jugendzeit*, 2d enl. and rev. ed., Wilhelm Schoof, ed. (Weimer: Böhlaus, Nachf; 1963). See also: Theo Schuler, "Jacob Grimm und Savigny: Studien über Gemeinsamkeit und Abstand," *Zeitschrift der Savigny-Stiftung für Rechtsgeschichte* 80 (Weimar, 1963), pp. 197–305.

19. Wilhelm Grimm, "Selbstbiographie," pp. 19–20.

20. Ibid., p. 20. See also Jacob Grimm, "Selbstbiographie," pp. 9–13.

21. Friedrich Panzer, ed., *Kinder- und Hausmärchen der Brüder Grimm. Vollständige Ausgabe in der Urfassung* (Wiesbaden: Emil Vollmer Verlag, n.d.: about 1955). See Panzer's introduction, "Einleitung," pp. 37–41 in which he elaborated on the complementary character qualities of Jacob and Wilhelm.

22. Jacob Grimm, "Über das Pedantische in der deutschen Sprache" in *Kleinere Schriften von Jacob Grimm*, vol. I (1851). In this essay, Jacob characterized pedantry as a shortcoming in linguistic research.

23. Jacob Grimm, "Selbstbiographie." See also note 11.

24. Jacob's responsibilities included, among other things, not only the professional care of rare books and manuscripts but also some research assistance to visiting scholars. This experience accounts for his early acquaintance with Slavic and Oriental literature.

25. Consult note 15.

26. Compare Jacob Grimm's comments on his work in Paris: "Selbstbiographie," p. 13. Also H. Grimm and Hinrichs, *Briefwechsel*. Consult letters between Jacob and Wilhelm for the months following January 1805.

27. Jacob Grimm, "Selbstbiographie," pp. 18–22.

28. Ibid. See also Jacob Grimm, "Über Schule, Universität, Akademie" in *Kleinere Schriften von Jacob Grimm*, vol. I (1819). See also Gerstner, p. 37.

29. Jacob Grimm, "Selbstbiographie."

30. Wilhelm Grimm, "Selbstbiographie." Some critics have commented on the Grimms' Romantic quest for national unity within the context of Napoleon's rule and their growing enthusiasm for Fichte's writings, without mentioning in this connection their translations and contributions to international scholarship. See, for example, Gabriele Seitz, *Die Brüder Grimm: Leben — Werk — Zeit* (Munich: Winkler Verlag, 1984), p. 87.

31. H. Grimm and Hinrichs, *Briefwechsel*.

33. H. Grimm, "Ralph Waldo Emerson" in *Literatur*, pp. 3–45.

34. Only Jacob Grimm mentioned the *Kinder- und Hausmärchen* in his autobiography among his publications, without making reference to Wilhelm. He expressed his regret that the "fairy tales" of Albert Ludwig Grimm, to whom they were not related, neither in blood nor in spirit, had often been confused with this publication. See pp. 20–21.

35. Else Ebel, "Jacob und Wilhelm und ihre Vorlesungstätigkeit in Göttingen 1830–37," in *Brüder Grimm Gedenken*, vol. III (1981), 56–96.

36. The best document on the Grimms' democratic spirit is Jacob's long essay "Über meine Entlassung" (About My Dismissal), which he composed on January 16, 1838. Significantly, he introduced it with a quote from the *Nibelungenlied*: "*War sint de eide komen?*" For related documents and analysis, consult Hans-Bernd Harder and Ekkehard Kaufmann, eds., *Die Brüder Grimm in ihrer amtlichen und politischen Tätigkeit. Vol. 3 of Katalog der Ausstellung* (Kassel: Verlag Weber und Weidemeyer, 1985). See also *Kleinere Schriften von Jacob Grimm*, vol. 1, pp. 25–56.

37. Ibid. Also: "Selbstbiography."

38. Ibid.

39. Ibid.

40. Jacob Grimm, "Über meine Entlassung."

41. See Seitz, pp. 57–59. See also Jack Zipes, "The Enchanted Forest of the

Brothers Grimm: New Modes of Approaching the Grimms' Fairy Tales," *Germanic Review LXII*, 2 (Spring 1987), p. 69. Zipes' quotation marks in the text pertaining to a statement on patriotism are slightly misleading, as the quote does not refer to the Grimms' own statement regarding the fatherland but rather to an undocumented view expressed by Gabriele Seitz, *Die Brüder Grimm*, pp. 57–59 (see Zipes' note 19).

42. Jacob Grimm, "Über meine Entlassung."

43. H. Grimm, "Jacob and Wilhelm Grimm," pp. 275.

44. Jacob Grimm, "Selbstbiographie," p. 1.

45. For a broader perspective on European Romantic thought, consult Ernst Behler, ed., *Die Europäische Romantik* (Frankfurt a. Main: Athenäum, 1972). The national as well as international perspectives of German Romanticism also received attention in René Wellek. *Confrontations: Studies in the Intellectual and Literary Relations between Germany, England, and the United States in the Nineteenth Century* (Princeton: Princeton University Press, 1965).

46. Even in Herder's case, the international perspective prevailed. Christa Kamenetsky, "Herder und der Mythos des Nordens," *Revue de littérature comparée* (Paris) 47, 1, Ja./Mar., 1973.

47. H. G. Schenk, *The Mind of the European Romantics: An Essay in Cultural History* (London: Constable, 1966).

48. Burton Feldman and Robert D. Richardson, eds., *The Rise of Modern Mythology: 1680–1860* (Bloomington: Indiana University Press, 1972). See: "German Romanticism and Myth" and "German Romantic Mythology and India," pp. 302–65.

49. John Ellis underscored Grimms' frequent use of the term "*Volk.*" John Ellis, *One Fairy Story Too Many: The Brothers Grimm and Their Tales*, (Chicago: University of Chicago Press, 1983), pp. 25–26. For an effective counterargument see Donald Ward, "New Misconceptions about Old Folktales: The Brothers Grimm" in McGlathery, et al. eds., pp. 91–101.

50. Jacob Grimm, *Deutsche Mythologie*, 4 vols. (Göttingen: 1835).

51. Jacob Grimm, *Deutsche Grammatik*, 4 vols. (Göttingen: 1819–37).

52. Jacob and Wilhelm Grimm, *Kinder- und Hausmärchen* 2d ed., vol. 3, Part 2 (Berlin: Reimer, 1922). Hunt based her translation on the 1856–57 edition.

53. For anthologized documents regarding the Grimms' professional contacts with scholars in Finland, the Baltic countries, France, Russia, Bohemia, and others, see Dieter Hennig and Bernhard Lauer, eds., *200 Jahre Büder Grimm: Dokumente ihres Lebens und Wirkens,* (Kassel: Verlag Weber und Weidemeyer, 1986), pp. 491–507. See also *Brüder Grimm Gedenken*, vols. 1 and 2, which contain various articles on the Grimms' foreign relations, and Wilhelm Schoof, "Englische und französische Beziehungen der Brüder Grimm," *Wirkendes Wort* 14 (1966), pp. 394–407. For more details on the Grimms' foreign correspondence see: Ruth Michaelis-Jena, *The Brothers Grimm* (New York: Praeger, 1970).

54. Hennig and Lauer, eds., pp. 477–500.

55. *Kinder- und Hausmärchen*, 6th ed. (Göttingen: Dietrich, 1950), Introduction.

56. Thomas Crofton Croker, *Fairy Legends and Traditions of the South of Ireland* (London: Murray, 1926). Trans. by the Brothers Grimm under the title *Irische Elfenmärchen*. See Chapter 8, "The Irish Connection."

57. See, for example, Isidor Levin, "Das russische Grimmbild" in *Brüder Grimm Gedenken*, vol. I (1963), pp. 375–95.

58. Cited in Hans Gummel, "John Kemble," *Nachrichten aus Niedersachsens Urgeschichte* 20 (1951), see pp. 53–54. Gummel's article contradicts Dilkey's assumption that the Grimms never met Kemble personally by giving evidence that young Kemble, then a student of philology, made longer visits at the Grimms' home in Göttingen. It also emphasizes Grimms' comments on Kemble's fluency in German. Marion C. Dilkey and Heinrich Schneider, "John Mitchell Kemble

and the Brothers Grimm," *Journal of English and Germanic Philology* 11 (1941), pp. 461–79.

59. Wilhelm Schoof, *Die Brüder Grimm in Berlin* (Berlin: Haude & Spener, 1964).

60. "Jacob Grimm an Minister Guizot über Frankreich und Deutschland" (Berlin: June 27, 1841) in Hans-Bernd Harder and Ekkehard Kaufmann, eds., *200 Jahre Brüder Grimm: Die Brüder Grimm in ihrer amtlichen und politischen Tätigkeit,* vol. 3, part 1 (Kassel: Verlag Weber & Weidemeyer, 1985), p. 116.

61. Ibid., p. 118.

62. Ibid., p. 121. See also Hennig, ed.

63. Ibid.

64. Will Erich Peuckert, "Wilhelm und Jacob Grimm" in *Die grossen Deutschen: Eine Biographie,* vol. 3 (Berlin: 1961), pp. 124–34 and Peter Ganz, *Jacob Grimm's Conception of German Studies,* an inaugural lecture delivered before the University of Oxford, on 18 May, 1973 (Oxford: Clarendon, 1973).

65. Harder and Kaufmann, eds., pp. 121–23.

66. Peuckert, p. 135.

67. Ibid.

68. Jacob Grimm, "Rede über den Bruder" in *Kleinere Schriften von Jacob Grimm,* vol. 1. See also: Hermann Grimm, ed., *Rede au Wilhelm Grimm and Rede über das Alter,* Oration on Wilhelm Grimm and Lecture about Old Age (Berlin: Druckerei der Königlichen Akademie der Wissenschaften, 1863).

69. Katherine Briggs, "Fairies in Children's Books" in Eloise Speed Norton, ed., *Folk Literature of the British Isles* (London: The Scarecrow Press, Inc., 1978), pp. 11–21.

70. Ludwig Denecke, "Mitgliedschaften der Brüder Grimm bei den Akademien, wissenschaftlichen Gesellschaften, und Vereinen; Ehrendoktorate und andere Auszeichnungen" in *Brüder Grimm Gedenken,* vol. 3 (1981), pp. 471–92.

71. Schoof, *Die Brüder Grimm in Berlin.*

2. The History of the
Kinder- und Hausmärchen

[Collections for Arnim and Brentano (1805–1811)]

RIGINALLY, THE BROTHers Grimm collected folktales as a by-product of a major folk-song collection, which they contributed to *Des Knaben Wunderhorn* (literally: *The Boy's Magic Horn*, published in 1805 by their friends Clemens Brentano and Achim von Arnim.[1] When Brentano planned a second volume of this work, he encouraged the Brothers Grimm to collect folktales too. He thought it might be wise to turn their attention from poetry to prose, including also proverbs, anecdotes, and legends, as these belonged to a relatively neglected aspect in their folklore collection that might turn out to be useful for his creative writing projects. Brentano himself also planned to translate Italian folktales from Basile's *Pentamerone*, hoping to make them available for German children. As it turned out, however, he gave up such plans in favor of writing tales and novels of his own. By 1808, Arnim too turned away from the planned joint publication toward a project of his own: the collection and publication of medieval *Volksbücher* (folk books or chapbooks).[2]

As far as loyalty to tradition was concerned, both Brentano and Arnim had initially expressed a demand similar to that of the Grimms, urging their contributors to the *Wunderhorn* to record the songs concisely and with no additions of their own. Yet they, especially Brentano, hated to be bureaucratically concise in any given method. On his visits to storytellers, Brentano would take only very hasty notes and later usually forget to fill in the rest. He always hoped to supply the details at a later date, but then he usually lacked the time or patience to do so. Jacob was annoyed by Brentano's habits that sometimes caused him to miss out on some valuable tales if his notes were too sketchy, especially in cases when it was not possible for him to return to the same place. Soon Brentano and Arnim also began to neglect the oral tradition while relying largely on printed sources, including Fischart, Rollenhagen, Moscherosch, and Grimmelshausen. Of course, the Grimms too later consulted the same sources, mainly because these were well known to be close to the oral tradition, yet they did so primarily for comparative purposes and not at the expense of the immediate oral folk tradition.[3]

The second difference between the Grimms and their collaborators was the immediate or intended use of the collected folklore material. As students of law, philology, and comparative medieval literature, the Grimms thought of folktales in the same way as folk songs, perceiving in both different yet related aspects of the naive *Naturpoesie* (nature poetry or folk poetry). Arnim and Brentano, on the other hand, valued folklore primarily as a springboard for their own creative imagination, hoping to utilize it for their own tales and novels.[4] The Grimms disagreed with Arnim and Brentano, believing that arbitrary changes in the substance of folktales would make them unfit for collections, especially if such alterations affected the plots, themes, and characters of the stories.

The third difference in their approaches to folklore was that Arnim and Brentano preserved only what they called the best variants, whereas the Grimms preserved as many tale variants as possible, even if sometimes only in the form of fragments. The Grimms believed that these might give some valuable clues to linguistic changes that had occurred over time as well as clues to a comparative study of folk beliefs inside and outside of Germany. Jacob also perceived in variants the evidence of changes in customs and laws that had occurred over time.

Having recorded and collected fifty-three tales for Brentano, Wilhelm and Jacob Grimm mailed them to his Berlin address. The Grimms well knew about Brentano's habit of embellishing and rewriting collected tales to a point that they no longer resembled folklore. They therefore hardly expected to see their tales again in the original form. Nevertheless, out of respect for Brentano as the initiator of the project, they sent him the original versions, yet as a measure of precaution Wilhelm copied all of the tales before sending off the package.

As it turned out, Brentano first misplaced the manuscript and then forgot about it. When the Grimms inquired if he had received it, he admitted that he had but was unable to locate it. In the meantime, he said, he had lost interest in pursuing the matter further, as he was actively engaged in completing his own stories. Brentano's change of mind thus put an abrupt end to their common project. Fortunately, the Grimms' personal relations with Brentano were strong enough to survive this blow so that it did not hurt their friendship.[5]

Determined to turn this loss into a positive venture, Jacob and Wilhelm decided to publish the tales under their own names. They informed Brentano about their plans, asking whether he had objections if they used the copy of the tale manuscript that they had retained. Brentano not only gave them his blessings for this venture but generously mailed them a bundle of his own collected folktales for possible inclusion in this project.

The lost manuscript with the Grimms' original folktales was found a little more than one hundred years later in the Monastery of Oelenberg, along with some original recordings of the tales. Over the years, this so-called Oelenberg Manuscript has provided Grimm scholars with many clues to the editing procedures of the Brothers Grimm, especially in comparison with the first edition of the *Kinder- und Hausmärchen* (1812 and 1815).[6] However, in the light of new insights that scholars have gained into the nature of the original notes, it is legitimate to ask if the Oelenberg Manuscript can be used as a first, solid basis for comparison with the edited tales in the seven published versions during the Grimms' lifetime. Judging by the Oelenberg Manuscript, the original tale that the Grimms sent to Brentano were mere sketches, written in a sort of shorthand style. Neither the notes found among the papers nor tale summaries prepared for Brentano were what we might consider stenographically accurate recordings of the tales. Their sketchy form suggests that the Grimms expected them to be edited, even though with moderation. In some cases the Grimms would take meticulous notes on proverbial expressions or individual speech patterns, but their notes and comparative tale studies indicate that more frequently they prepared some relatively short versions that resembled rough drafts rather than well-composed stories.[7] For that reason, it would be more adequate in textual studies to compare the first printed edition with later editions rather than with the Oelenberg Manuscript, the more so as the Grimms themselves did not believe in an *Urmärchen* (primeval or archetypal tale).

[Folktales for Savigny's Children (1808)]

The oldest tale versions were not those of the Oelenberg Manuscript but those that Jacob sent to Savigny and his children in 1808. Jacob mailed him seven folktales, of which one was intended for him personally and six for his children, Pulettchen (whose real name was Bettine) and Franz. The first tale, "The Fox and Mrs. Fox," he attached to his letter on March 25, 1808, commenting that he now lived up to his promise regarding the *Kindermärchen* (children's tales). Soon Jacob would send Savigny more tales, he wrote, although not those with which Savigny might already be familiar through Perrault's collection. Savigny thanked him sincerely, urging him to send more tales soon: "Don't let this be the last one you've sent."[8]

Such encouraging remarks from his admired professor fell on fertile soil. On April 10, 1808, Jacob mailed to Savigny six more tales: "Child Mary," "The Moon and His Mother," "Rumplestiltskin," "Snow White: Or the Unlucky Child," and "The Stepmother." Of these, five were in Jacob's handwriting, and one had been recorded by Jeannette Hassenpflug, directly from the oral tradition. The first edition of the *Kinder- und Hausmärchen* contained four of these tales and included others that the Grimms collected between 1807 and 1812. These four tales not only are evidence that Jacob himself was the earliest contributor to the collection, but they also are in a category by themselves because he initially did not write them down for publication. He specifically wrote them down for Savigny and his children, especially little Pulettchen, who was then only three years old.

The discovery of these six tales among Savigny's papers contradicts the common stereotype of Jacob as the stiff scientist who cared more for his books than he did for children. The letters reveal that with the six folktales Jacob tried to keep an earlier promise he had made to Pulettchen when he had visited Savigny's family earlier in Frankfurt. He may also have had in mind Pulettchen's birthday on April 11, for Wilhelm added a note at the bottom of Jacob's letter: "Greetings to everybody, but especially to Pulettchen,"[9] thanking her for her previous birthday gift to him and implying that now it was their turn to send a gift to her.

In other letters too, both brothers fondly remembered Pulettchen, sometimes in simple greetings, inquiries about her health and her progress in the French language, or some casual humorous remarks. In December 1807, for example, Wilhelm wrote to Savigny about Brentano's plan of including some of his Danish folktales and "romances" in the *Wunderhorn*. Wilhelm mentioned on that occasion his amazement at certain striking similarities between the Danish tales and the legends of the *Nibelungenlied* and asked—without starting a new paragraph—"How is the child?" Did she still talk in such a pretty and well mannered way about Salzburg and the Bertoldsgarden and the Hartzmann, and did she still remember the young *Kümmelbauer* (Caraway Seed Peasant)?[10] It seems that during an earlier visit Wilhelm had told her a humorous story in which he and Jacob figured each as a *Kümmelbauer*, for in a joking manner he used that term more frequently. Comments such as these reveal that the brothers had talked with Pulettchen and enjoyed telling her stories.

While it is heartwarming to know that Jacob and Wilhelm cared enough for children to communicate with them at their level—an observation that was confirmed by the loving relationship that both brothers had with Wilhelm's children two decades later—it must be observed that the stories were not meant exclusively for Pulettchen. This is particularly evident from the additional variants of the tales that Jacob enclosed in the letter as well as his notes on this behalf addressed to Savigny. Who but a scholar of Old Germanic literature and tradition would have appreciated Jacob's notes on the tales, the enclosed variants, or his comments? They were certainly not meant for Savigny's little daughter. Further, Jacob encouraged Savigny also to collect folktales in case he should happen to come across some interesting versions.

Jacob wrote to Savigny that he considered the tale about the fox his favorite and the most poetic one of all, perhaps because he had heard it so often since his childhood days. For some reason, the conclusion had always been incomplete, just as in the enclosed tale. He had collected and written down the tales somewhat unevenly (as he had heard them), wishing, however, that each one had such an elaborate beginning as the tale of Snow White. Savigny might see for himself how the beginnings were usually the best parts of the tales, perhaps because storytellers seemed to remember them best, whereas the endings were often lost. [11]

These comments reveal two things: first, that Jacob did keep alive his own childhood memories of folktales, and second, that for the sake of loyalty to the folk tradition, he abstained from supplying his own ending to a tale fragment—mainly because he himself remembered the tale only as a fragment.

If the six tales that Jacob included for Pulettchen had been exclusively intended for the child, he might have supplied some missing endings or changed some of the beginnings to make them more pleasing. Yet, in the other cases too, he did not change the tales. Instead, he added a note titled "Another Beginning" to the tale of "Snow White,"[12] which clearly seems to have been intended for Savigny. Jeannette Hassenpflug, who had originally recorded the tale for Jacob, used the familiar opening in which the queen, sitting by the ebony-black windowsill, accidentally stitched her finger. As she observed the drops of red blood coloring the white snow, she made a wish: "Oh, if I just had a child, as white as this snow, as red-cheeked as this red blood, and as black-eyed as this window frame!" The variant, which Jacob included under "Another Beginning," told of a duke and a duchess who first passed by a huge pile of snow during a sleigh ride in winter, then by three pits filled with red blood, and finally by three coal-black ravens. During each incident, the duke himself made a wish for a girl with skin as white as the snow, cheeks as red as blood, and hair as black as that of ravens. Moments later, Snow White passed by the sleigh, as if brought there by magic, whereupon the duke invited her to sit next to him in the sleigh. Being mad with jealousy, the duchess let her glove drop onto the road, ordering Snow White to pick it up, and when Snow White stepped out to do her bidding, the sleigh took off without her.

Jacob did not say which beginning he liked better but merely listed the latter as a variant. Because he also did not ask Savigny to try it out on Pulettchen or her brother Franz, it seems that he followed the very same method of listing variants in the notes to the tales that he used in the *Kinder- und Hausmärchen* in 1812. The same applied to his critical comment that a portion of "Snow White" could also be found in Musäus' story of "Richilde," which would merely indicate that another variant existed in an earlier collection.

Jacob's comments on the ending of "Snow White" were critical. He called that portion "incorrect and too flawed."[13] Hassenpflug's "Snow White" told about some learned doctors who, in the company of the returning king, revived Snow White by suspending her body on four ropes under the ceiling. Jacob insisted that according to "other sources," the dwarfs themselves had brought her back to life by knocking thirty-two times with their little magic hammers against the glass coffin. Jacob added: "But I don't know it for sure." A young child of Pulettchen's age might have wanted a more definite conclusion. If given a choice of two endings, young children will generally insist on knowing: "But which one is true?" Jacob's ambiguity may have caused some frustration to the child, but it would have been welcome to a scholar such as Professor Savigny who, like the Grimms, believed in the coexistence of variants in tradition about which he had lectured in connection with law and the "Old Poetry." If indeed Jacob had meant the story solely for Pulettchen, he might easily have changed the ending, but the fact that he did not change it further confirms that he intended it for both, the more so as he urged Savigny to send him some of his own collections.

The last one of the six tales, "The Stepmother," was actually a short variant of the "Juniper Tree" story that later appeared in a Low German variant in the first edition of the *Kinder- und Hausmärchen*.[14] In this case, Jacob recorded a brief High German variant. In spite of the relative brevity of this variant in comparison with the published version of 1812, the tale is told in a lively and poetic way and contains not only such corresponding motifs as the apples in the box, the magic tree (in this case not a juniper tree but a pear tree), the singing bones, the bird, and the millstone, but also the themes of death and resurrection, suffering and retribution. Above all, the concept of justice appears at the end with great clarity and strength. Whether or not Pulettchen liked or understood this particular tale, we will never know. In 1815, however, Savigny thanked the Grimms for a complimentary copy of the second volume of the *Kinder- und Hausmärchen*, mentioning that the children, as well as his wife and himself, had very much enjoyed the stories and were continuing to enjoy them.

While Pulettchen's role as the sole recipient of the tales must thus be questioned, she still played an important role in motivating Jacob Grimm to send the folktales to Savigny. When, in 1819, Jacob sent to Savigny a copy of the second edition of the *Kinder- und Hausmärchen*, he again remembered Pulettchen. She must be grown up by now, he reflected, and as a young lady, Bettine probably already accompanied her parents on social occasions. While alluding to the passage of time, he added with a touch of humor that still they would never forget how as a small child she had sometimes misbehaved and was made to stand in a corner. Still another decade later when Jacob received the news of Bettine's engagement to a Greek diplomat, he wrote a touching letter to Savigny, reminding him of the events surrounding her birth in Paris. On that day, he had found himself strangely alone at the National Library, yet upon visiting Savigny's home a few hours later, he had been a part of the gentle family happiness that had elated them all.

[The Publishing History (1812–57)]

The first volume of the *Kinder- und Hausmärchen* appeared in 1812 and was published by Reimer in Berlin in an edition of 900 copies. The work consisted of forty-nine tales, to which the Brothers Grimm themselves had contributed twenty-two.[15] Innovative were both the preface on the nature and intent of the collection and the methodology that applied to the recording and editing of the tales. A new feature was the commentary attached to the tales in the form of comparative notes and an indication of sources. From a modern folkloristic point of view, this commentary was not detailed enough, but it was certainly innovative at the time, for no other folktale collector prior to the Grimms had ever taken the trouble to use learned notes for simple folktales. Also, no other folktale collector before them had felt the need to investigate parallel themes and motifs in folktales from various regions and different countries, nor to explore parallel themes, characters, and motifs in myths or legends. Finally, no one before the Grimms had ever looked for parallel expressions in folktales, proverbs, chapbooks, or children's games. What has made the Grimms' approach to folktales so fascinating is its broad interdisciplinary perspective that viewed *Naturpoesie* at one and the same time in national and international terms.

The only writer before the Grimms who had concerned himself with some comparable cross-cultural perspectives was Johann Gottfried Herder, although more in relation to folk songs than to folktales and less from a philological than cultural point of view.[16]

Volume 2 of the *Kinder- und Hausmärchen* followed with additional tales in 1815. It contained a new collection of German folktales as well as a new preface and additional notes, and like the first volume, it was also printed in an edition of 900 copies. According to Wilhelm Grimm, the second volume was originally meant to include a complete translation and interpretation of the Italian folktales of Giambattista Basile's *Pentamerome*. Yet in a letter to Jacob in 1814, at the time when Jacob was on a diplomatic mission to Vienna, Wilhelm mentioned that he had changed his mind, mainly because in the meantime he had accumulated so many German folktales and legends, also from friends and acquaintances, that it was logical to publish these first before going ahead with the Italian tales.

The second edition of the *Kinder- und Hausmärchen* was published in 1819. It consisted of the expanded collection of folktales in two volumes, in which the notes had been omitted. However, the third volume, published in 1822, contained in its first half all of the notes combined for both volumes, and in its second half a content analysis and comparative study of folktale collections around the world.

The publisher in Berlin, Reimer, had foreseen some financial difficulties with the sale of that third volume, because he did not think that the volume of notes and comparative studies would be in as wide popular demand as the folktales themselves. Upon discussing this problem with Reimer, Jacob and Wilhelm agreed to publish the third volume without financial compensation. The honorarium question regarding the first two volumes was solved to the disadvantage of the Grimms, and as a result, a quarrel ensued between the Grimms and their publisher. Reimer had also disappointed them by printing the works on poor-quality paper. Some letters finally settled the issue, with the outcome that Reimer agreed to sell the third volume for only about one half of the price that he charged for the first and second volumes, respectively, while printing only 500 copies. The two folktale volumes were brought out in 1,500 copies each.[17]

Later editions no longer included the third volume of notes or only incorporated portions of it in an altered form, which accounts for the rarity of the work. In subsequent editions, the Grimms again incorporated the notes in an appendix to the tales, but not the synopsis and analysis of international folktales including the comparative historical perspective. The sixth edition of the work of 1850 included an eighty-page introduction concerned with German and international folktale publications, but it was no more than a review article. The seventh edition again included a third volume dedicated to notes (1856) but not in the same form as it had appeared in 1822. Being ambitious to include his reviews of the great bulk of books that had been published in Germany and abroad since 1822, Wilhelm made space for new book reviews by reducing the comparative historical folktale section, including about 100 pages of his analysis of Basile's *Pentamerone* to four and a half pages, rationalizing that a new German translation of the work made his own detailed summary and analysis somewhat redundant. He also deleted, among other items, the table of contents to the international section. As a result of such changes, this portion of the book became more up to date, but it also assumed the cluttered look that characterized the Grimms' international book review sections in the 4th and 5th editions of the *Kinder- und Hausmärchen*. The fact that only 500 copies of the original 1822 volume had been printed, with no reprint editions containing the all-inclusive international part, has made this volume a great rarity.[18]

The Grimms' original comparative folktale studies in the third volume of the *Kinder- und Hausmärchen* (1822) encompassed about two hundred pages, making up about half of the entire volume. In the clearly structured original form they give significant clues to their use of the comparative approach to folktale studies. In a special preface attached to the international part, Wilhelm Grimm commented on the unique as well as universal aspects of folktales in many lands and the strange occurrence of correspondences among them. After a section concerned with general folktale literature and quotations by great writers from ancient to modern times about the significance of folktales, he listed the table of contents, in which he grouped and analyzed folktales from around the world, country by country. The organizational structure alone thus gave the impression that the reader was introduced to a book within a book. In each section of the subsequent discussion, Wilhelm introduced first the history of folktale collections in a given country, and then discussed the most significant ones in greater detail, in most cases giving brief plot summaries of the best-known tales within a collection. He also noted the correspondences of plots, characters, themes, and motifs among the foreign tales and between the foreign and German tales. He noted in his introduction that he had done so, especially in cases in which the tales were from remote areas and from a distant time. Both he and his brother attached significance to such a phenomenon that could not easily be explained. He thought that their task of presenting such a comparative analysis would have been greatly facilitated if they had been able to rely on previous studies in this field, but as nothing of this nature had been written, they had to do the major spade work on their own. This implied, he added, that they had to do substantial background readings of various national folktale collections. Basile's collection, for example, so far had only been mentioned by its title, whereas the Grimms' study was meant to introduce it more closely to the reader by a careful analysis of its contents.

The Grimms' explanation for variants across different cultures merely hinted at some theories, but overall it remained suggestive, tentative, and humble. The main reason why they had taken such pains to indicate folktale variants was, according to Wilhelm, to show possible interconnections but not to claim the discovery of some definite truths.

The international part of the third volume is of great folkloristic and historical value, giving evidence of the existence of folktales in different times and different countries. In taking a comparative perspective on folktale collections from Germany and other nations, while occasionally also considering fables, anecdotes, and legends, the Grimms shared Herder's spirit of fairness and humanity. In evaluating the various collections, for example, they consistently applied the questions: To what degree do they represent genuine folklore, and to what degree are they flavored by a given collector's personal style and fancy. In this connection the Grimms were much harsher in their judgment of the German collectors Johann August Musäus and Albert Ludwig Grimm, and their own brother Ferdinand (writing under the pseudonym of Lothar), for example, than with the French collector Charles Perrault.

Why is it that so many critics are unfamiliar with the Grimms' admiration for folktales beyond their own national borders? In the first place, one may search for an explanation in some German nationalistic interpretations of the *Kinder- und Hausmärchen* around the turn of the nineteenth century that were overly eager to emphasize the "German" and "Nordic Germanic" collection at the expense of all others. The Nazi interpretations added to these some exclusive racial interpretations while considering the Grimms' international interests a mistake that should be ignored. English and American critics have some different excuses: Edgar Taylor's complete omission of the notes, Margaret Hunt's reliance on the 1856 edition containing an altered volume of notes, and finally, the rarity of the original third volume of the *Kinder- und Hausmärchen* with its comparative analysis of folktale collections.[19] It is time to look once again at the way in which the Grimms perceived the homeland of *Naturpoesie* in a world without borders.

Ironically, it was not the extensive three-volume edition of 1819–22 but the shorter 1825 edition of the *Kinder- und Hausmärchen* without notes and international references that became the basis of the Grimms' early fame in Germany and abroad. Yet, the Grimms and their publisher had evidently planned it that way. In a letter to Georg Reimer on August 16, 1823, Wilhelm commented on his plans of bringing out a small German edition of the work which, like Taylor's *German Popular Stories*, would contain a selection of folktales in a single volume. He suggested that Reimer publish it in a pocketbook format, like the *Urania* edition by Brockhaus, and thought it should be sold at Christmas time. Perhaps he might prepare copies of the engravings from the English edition of Cruikshank that were so spirited and pleasant, by transferring them on stone. Wilhelm mentioned that their brother Ludwig would be interested in adding another few engravings to the work, maybe even one that would show children under the Christmas tree. It was mandatory that the price for the book be kept low, so as to enhance its popular appeal. All notes would have to be omitted in this case and along with them everything else that was scholarly.[20]

Around Christmastime 1825, the planned short paperback edition of the *Kinder- und Hausmärchen* indeed appeared in German bookstores—specifically for children. It contained fifty tales and combined, as planned, some illustrations by Cruikshank with those of their brother Ludwig. It was not only small but also inexpensive and made a wonderful gift for young and old. Judging by Jacob's earliest stories for Pulettchen, Wilhelm's correspondence with little Anna von Haxthausen, and the more recently discovered letter by Wilhelm to a little girl named Mili,[21] the Grimms were indeed conscious of children as an audience, even if not exclusively so at all times. In this case, at any rate, they consciously set aside their scholarly studies and ambitions to please children.

The third expanded edition of the *Kinder- und Hausmärchen* appeared in 1837, the fourth in 1840, the fifth in 1843, the sixth in 1850, and the seventh in 1857. In each case, the work was issued in two volumes, including prefaces and notes. The fourth edition and sixth edition deserve special mention, as they included an extensive listing of the Grimms' own book reviews and book notes regarding various folktale editions at home and abroad that had been published in the wake of the *Kinder- und Hausmärchen*. Spanning close to sixty pages in small print, these reviews present additional evidence of the Grimms' broad interest in folktales around the world. Today, the 1857 edition in usually considered the standard edition of the work, as it is the most complete of all, including a total of 211 tales with expanded notes. There was still an eighth edition during the Grimms' lifetime, in 1864, and between 1864 and 1886, the work went through another twenty-one editions.

The small one-volume paperback edition of the 1825, *Kleine Ausgabe (Small Edition),* was a publishing success. The second edition appeared in 1833, and thereafter it was published in new editions about every three years. By 1858, it had been issued in a total of ten editions, and by 1886, in a total of thirty-six. This edition was still reprinted as a facsimile edition by the Insel Verlag in 1911. Today, the 1825 edition has become a rarity, even though in the Grimms' own time it was something like a best seller in comparison with the other editions of the *Kinder- und Hausmärchen*.[22]

On the whole, the Brothers Grimm could not consider the *Kinder- und Hausmärchen* a financial success. Yet, since financial gain had never been one of their major objectives, the sales question did not bother them overly much. To them it was of greater importance that with the tales they had captured the spirit of *Naturpoesie* that otherwise might have been lost or forgotten. By combining their efforts in the areas of language, literature, law, and history, they hoped to capture the poetic meaning that folktales held for their own nation as well as for others.[23]

NOTES

1. L. Achim von Arnim and Clemens Brentano, *Des Knaben Wunderhorn; Alte deutsche Lieder* (Munich: Winkler Verlag, 1964). Complete edition, with a postscript by Willi A. Koch. For a separate edition of the folk songs collected and published by the Brothers Grimm see Charlotte Oberfeld et al., eds., *Brüder Grimm: Volkslieder* (Kassel: Bärenreiter Verlag, 1985–88).

2. Wilhelm Schoof, *Die Entstehungsgeschichte der Grimmschen Märchen* (Hamburg: Hauswedell, 1959), chapters 1–3.

3. Reinhold Steig, *Clemens Brentano und die Brüder Grimm.* (Stuttgart: Cotta, 1914), pp. 164–71. See also: Reinhold Steig, *Achim von Arnim und die Brüder Grimm* (Stuttgart: Cotta, 1940). See also: Wilhelm Schoof, "Neue Beiträge zur Entstehungsgeschichte der Grimmschen Märchen" *Zeitschrift für Volkskunde* 52 (1955), 112–43.

4. Steig, *Clemens Brentano und die Brüder Grimm*, pp. 1–35.

5. Karl Schmidt, *Die Entwicklung der Kinder- und Hausmärchen seit der Urhandschrift; nebst einem kritischen Texte der in die Drucke übergegangenen Stücke.* Series: *Hermaea. Ausgewählte Arbeiten aus dem Deutschen Seminar zu Halle*, eds. Philip Strauch et al. (Halle: Niemeyer, 1933) and R. Danhardt," Grimm-Editionen im Kinderbuchverlag Berlin," in *Die Brüder Grimm: Erbe und Rezeption; Stockholmer Symposium 1984* (Stockholm: Almqvist & Wiksell International, 1985) ed. Astrid Stedje, pp. 51–54.

6. Heinz Rölleke, *Die älteste Märchensammlung der Brüder Grimm: Synopse einer handschriftlichen Deutung*, monograph (Geneva: Fondation Martin Bodmer, 1975).

7. Wilhelm Schoof, *Briefwechsel zwischen Jacob und Wilhelm aus der Jugendzeit* 2d ed. (Weimar: Hermann Böhlaus Nachf., 1963). See Chapter 7, "Jacobs Aufenthalt in Wien."

8. Wilhelm Schoof and Ingeborg Schnack, eds., *Briefe der Brüder Grimm an Savigny: Aus dem Savignyschen Nachlaß* (Berlin: Erich Schmidt Verlag, 1953), p. 41.

9. Ibid., pp. 423–30. For a chronological listing of the correspondence see pp. 503–07.

10. Ibid., pp. 423–30.

11. Ibid. For Jacob Grimm's tale contributions consult appendix.

12. Ibid.

13. In the *Kinder- und Hausmärchen* (1812), the Grimms even listed two endings of "*Rotkäppchen*" ("Little Red-Cap") in the text itself—yet without a didactic commentary. In most cases, however, they would confine such variants to the notes of the tales for comparative purposes.

14. This tale appears to be based on Runge's contributions. See Heinz Rölleke, "Von dem Fischer un syner Fru: Die älteste schriftliche Überlieferung" in "*Wo das Wünschen noch geholfen hat;*" *Gesammelte Aufsätze zu den 'Kinder- und Hausmärchen' der Brüder Grimm*, Heinz Rölleke, ed. (Bonn: Bouvier Verlag Herbert Grundmann, 1985), pp. 161–74. See also: Heinz Rölleke, *Die Märchen der Brüder Grimm.* Series: *Artemis Einführungen*, vol. 18 (Munich: Artemis Verlag, 1987).

15. Jutta Rißmann, "Zum Briefwechsel der Brüder Grimm mit ihrem Verleger Reimer: Zwei neuentdeckte Briefe Wilhelm Grimms" in Ludwig Denecke, ed., *Brüder Grimm Gedenken* vol. 4 (Marburg: Elwert Verlag, 1975), 114–19, and Wilhelm Schoof, "Neue Beiträge zur Entstehungsgeschichte der Grimmschen Märchen" in *Zeitschrift für Volkskunde* 52 (1955), pp. 112–43.

16. See Chapter 3 on "Herder and the Brothers Grimm."

17. Schoof, *Briefwechsel*, pp. 396–420. In January 1815, Jacob too mentioned his plans for a third volume of folktales, although not in relation to Basile's collection.

18. The title is listed as follows: *Kinder- und Hausmärchen* Ges. durch die Brüder Grimm. Dritter Band. Zweite und vermehrte Ausgabe (Berlin, G. Reimer, 1822). One of the rare copies of the third volume (1822 edition) has been preserved in the Osborne Collection in Toronto, Canada, whose director and staff kindly permitted me to use their collection. In the seventh edition of the *Kinder- und Hausmärchen* (1956/57) the Brothers Grimm again reprinted the volume of notes but in a changed form. Bolte and Polivka observed that Wilhelm Grimm had reduced the extensive discussion of Basile's *Pentamerone* in the 1956 re-edition of the volume of notes because Liebrecht's translation had appeared in the meantime, yet they neither commented on the extent nor the significance of this omission, nor did they mention other alterations. Johannes Bolte and Georg Polivka, *Anmerkungen zu den Kinder- und Hausmärchen*, vol. 3 (Hildesheim: Georg Olms Verlag, 1971), p. 461. Heinz Rölleke's three-volume re-edition of the *Kinder- und Hausmärchen* is based on the altered 1956/57 edition (Stuttgart: Philip Reclam, 1980).

19. Margaret Hunt's translation of Grimms' tales is not as complete as it is thought to be, as far as Grimms' comparative international folktale studies in the volume of notes were concerned, as it was based on the altered 1856/57 edition. In addition, Andrew Lang placed his own notes in the appendix prior to Hunt's translated notes of the Grimms, thus introducing a one-sided anthropological interpretation that influenced the reception of the work in England.

20. Hans Gürtler and Albert Leitzman, eds., *Briefe der Brüder Grimm* (Jena: Verlag der Fromannschen Buchhandlung, Walter Biedermann, 1928), pp. 285–86.

21. Heinz Rölleke, "Discovery of Lost Grimm Fairy Tale Not the Sensation it is Claimed to Be," *The German Tribune* 287 (Nov. 1983), p. 11. Reprint from *Frankfurter Allgemeine Zeitung für Deutschland* (17 Oct. 1983).

22. Danhardt, pp. 53–54.

23. Ludwig Denecke observed that Wilhelm had been more concerned than Jacob with questions regarding the origin and variants of folktales, "and by no means just with the German ones" ("*keineswegs nur mit der dt.*"). Ludwig Denecke, "Grimm, Wilhelm Carl" in Enzyklopädie des Märchens: Handwörterbuch zur historischen und vergleichenden Erzählforschung, vol. 5, ed. Ludwig Denecke et al. (Berlin: Walter de Gruyter, 1990), pp. 195–96.

1. (LEFT) Title page, *Kinder- und Hausmärchen* vol. 1 (1819)   2. (RIGHT) Title page, *Kinder- und Hausmärchen*, vol. 3 (1922). Grimms' rare volume of notes also contained their valuable comments on folktale collections around the world, including an extensive discussion of Basile's *Pentamerone*.

3. The humane and gentle spirit of folktales, as the Grimms perceived it. "Little Brother and Little Sister," illustrated by Ludwig Emil Grimm.

GERMAN POPULAR STORIES

AND

FAIRY TALES,

AS

TOLD BY GAMMER GRETHEL

FROM THE COLLECTION OF MM. GRIMM.

Revised Translation

By EDGAR TAYLOR.

WITH ILLUSTRATIONS FROM DESIGNS
By GEORGE CRUIKSHANK AND LUDWIG GRIMM.

LONDON: GEORGE BELL & SONS, YORK STREET,
COVENT GARDEN.
1878.

4. (ABOVE) Cover design of the third volume (*Kinder- und Hausmärchen*, 1822).   5. (RIGHT) Edgar Taylor's preface promoted the myth of the Grimms' exclusive concern with recording oral tales of German and Nordic origin.

6. Frau Viehmännin's folktales were much more lively and versatile than critics generally assumed they were. Illustrated by Ludwig Emil Grimm.

7. The Grimms, too, contributed folk songs to *The Boy's Magic Horn* and began their folktale collection in this process.

Irische Elfenmärchen

übersetzt und eingeleitet von den

Brüdern Grimm

Herausgegeben von Johannes Rutz

Mit vielen Silhouetten von

Maria Lahrs

München 1913 R Piper & Co. Verlag
[1826]

8. The Grimms' translation of Croker's *Fairy Legends* and Wilhelm's comparative essay to this work vitalized folklore research in Ireland, England, and Scotland. Illustration by Maria Lahrs.

Es war einmal

9. "Once Upon a Time" (title of a German folktale anthology of the mid-nineteenth century), illustrated by Ludwig Richter.

10. "The Blue Light," illustrated by George Cruikshank.

11. "The Man in the Bag," illustrated by George Cruikshank.

12. "The Elfin Grove," illustrated by George Cruikshank.

PART II

The Grimms' Theory and Practice of Folktale Collections and History

3. The Nature and Meaning of Folktales

[Herder and The Brothers Grimm]

ORN IN 1744 IN EAST Prussia, Johann Gottfried Herder spent his young years in Riga, which was then under the rule of Catherine I. It was here that he developed not only his warm sympathy for a peaceful coexistence of many nationalities but also his love of native folklore belonging to his German roots. He was a theologian, a philosopher, a literary critic, and a poet in his own right, but he is probably best remembered for his contributions to the concept of the *Volk*, his love of freedom, and his international collection of folk songs.

Herder's ideas had a strong influence upon the German Romantic writers, including the Brothers Grimm. From his essays and folk-song collection they received their inspiration of the *Volk* as a unique and organic entity rooted in the past. Each *Volk* had a "soul," he had taught them. One only had to rediscover it in the old folk songs to regain the inner unity and to be strengthened from the "source." Through his works they learned to value the authentic culture but also the vernacular languages that had been preserved in the traditional songs and tales of the common folk.[1] It was Herder who first called to their attention the neglected treasures of Norse mythology, of the Indian *Shakuntala*, Old Persian poetry, and the poetic spirit of the Bible. His interests in the languages and literatures of the world were all-embracing, ranging from the Icelandic sagas and the supposedly old Celtic *Ossian* to the works of Homer. He taught the Brothers Grimm to judge each work of folk literature on the basis of its own unique cultural merits before comparing it with others on a worldwide scale. No longer were the classics to be considered the ultimate measure of all literature. Although Herder wrote in glowing terms about the *Urpoesie* (primeval or ancient poetry) of Homer's *Iliad* and *Odyssey*, he did not place these works on a pedestal above all others. "Let us follow our own path," he reminded his compatriots. "Let them speak well or ill of our nation, our literature, our language: they are ours, they are ourselves, and let that be enough."[2] Herder longed to restore to the German nation a feeling of cultural unity and self-consciousness. If at times he seemed to pay more attention to the "Nordic roots" of his own nation than to those of others, it was not because he suffered from ethnocentrism or was driven by a quest for power but because he found here the cultural origins of his own *Volk* that for such a long time had been neglected and treated with contempt. Rather than wishing to reserve for Germany a superior status in the world, he merely fought for her recognition in terms of cultural equality. According to his worldview, all nations were equal, as God had created them in their colorful variety to take their place within the one huge painting of humanity.[3]

Nationalism, as Herder understood it, was a cultural rather than a political phenomenon that brought with it the obligation to search for the cultural roots of one's people. Being unrelated to a claim for national superiority or political power, it was closely linked to his concepts of democracy and equality among the nations and not at all to that of a totalitarian super-state.[4] Whatever some late-nineteenth-century writers did with this concept and however much the Nazis distorted it into a prerequisite of Nazism had very little to do with Herder's original ideas.[5] Herder wrote that each nation had to fulfill a dual responsibility: to develop its own creative potential through a collection of *Naturpoesie* and also to participate in the language, folklore, and literature of the world. Not an excessive self-pride or a cultural isolationism were his goals but rather a greater tolerance and appreciation of the unique contributions that each *Volk* could make to humanity at large. His ultimate aim was to lead all nations, big or small, toward a better understanding of self and others.[6]

In the realms of literature and folklore, Herder prepared the ground for the study of comparative literature and comparative folklore. His ideas implied that comparative studies would be substantially enhanced by a preceding examination of one's own literature and folk songs, for according to his belief, a search for native roots would lead to a better understanding of all *Urpoesie* around the world. It was one of his most democratic notions, also in literary terms, that each nation was equal in terms of possessing its own voice within the chorus of humanity.

Herder gave expression to his faith in the humanity of man through his publication of an international folk-song collection of 1778–79. It appeared under the title of *Volkslieder. Stimme der Völker in Liedern (Folk Songs. Voice of the Nations in Songs)*[7] and is still hailed as a milestone in comparative folk literature. As the first international folk-song collection, it recognized the presence of a poetic spirit in the simple language of the common folk, not just in the German nation but also in many other nations. The origin of these songs was anonymous, wrote Herder, but their pulse was alive, speaking vividly in images and strong rhythms. One could still feel in them the heartbeat of the old nations. In these songs, the *Urpoesie* of mankind, one might discover feelings and universal truths that linked nation to nation. Herder's collection included next to old German folk songs a great variety of songs from Greenland, Lapland, Latvia, Greece, Italy, Sicily, Spain, France, Scotland, England, Norway, Iceland, Madagascar, Peru, and the Slavic nations. He believed that each ancient nation's voice was lovely in its own way, yet in harmony with the songs of other nations, they created a symphony that was symbolic of God's creation of mankind.[8] There was unity within the great variety of all *Urpoesie* around the world. As each song bore the innocent trait of its early creation, a voice of spontaneity, and a spirit of naivete born from a closeness to God and nature, it expressed symbolically the unity of all mankind.

To Herder, these were not merely songs but a philosophy of life: reflections of a Golden Age in the past but also hope for a stronger nation in the future. He maintained that the language of the ancient folk songs possessed a visionary quality that far surpassed anything that had been created by poets in modern times. The ancient bard, whom he called the "natural genius" of the *Volk*, had still found a natural synthesis between reason and emotion, which accounted for the inherent vitality of his songs.[9]

Herder compared the "folk genius" of long ago to a tree growing and unfolding its branches, drawing sap from its roots, sending up shoots, then leaves, buds, blossoms, and finally fruit. Such a growth pattern evolved through three stages: childhood, youth, and manhood. The first stage was the most innocent one and also the purest of all. Here human vision had been the strongest and the creative spirit had developed most freely. In the "childhood" of mankind, poetry had been at its best. Later, reason had suppressed some of poet's initial spontaneity, while slackening his excitement. His language had become more abstract, his imagery repetitious, and his expression somewhat tired. Lost was the vision that had grown from his closeness to nature. Being detached from the roots of inspiration, his words no longer possessed the magic touch that had moved the listeners of early times.[10]

Still, Herder was an optimist in the sense that he believed in the recovery of what was lost. Herder thought that if during the stage of "manhood" the bard reached a new synthesis between reason and emotion, then there was hope for a new visionary power and hope for a nation's cultural revival from its source. In this regard, too, he had much in common with the Brothers Grimm, who also encouraged the nations to revitalize their strength by contemplating the inherited folklore of their past.

Through his folk-song collection, Herder expressed his faith in the renewal of the *Volk* and its poetic vigor. He referred to folk poetry by different names, calling it alternately *Urpoesie* (primeval poetry), *Naturpoesie* (nature poetry), or *reine Fabelpoesie* (pure fable poetry). By the word *Fabel* (fable) he meant epic poetry but also folktales and myths based on the inherited folk traditions.[11] Like the Brothers Grimm a few decades later, he felt that *Urpoesie*, having been left untouched by the disintegrating forces of modern civilization, reflected more acutely than anything else the true "soul" of a nation. By collecting folk songs, Herder hoped to retrieve the nation's soul and with it the ancient spirit of purity and naivete.

Herder's focus on the virtues of the past led him to a new appreciation of native history and a rehabilitation of the "savage" lifestyle of the ancestors. Like Jean Jacques Rousseau, he equated the simple peasant life of long ago with a life of purity and honesty while rejecting the term "primitive" when speaking about the past.[12] The Brothers Grimm built substantially on Herder's new concepts of the old Germanic lifestyle and sided strongly with his view that the concept of "savages" was wholly unsuitable to describe the naive spirit and community ethics of their Germanic ancestors.[13] While the Grimms also extended their love of *Naturpoesie* beyond the horizons of their own heritage, they did share with Herder the notion that German poets had neglected their own traditions by meekly imitating the models of others. They could not have agreed more with Herder, who reminded his fellow men that the native heritage had unique merits that should not be overlooked. Why should poets admire only Homer and the great works of classical Greece and Rome if they had within their tradition the genius of the *Edda* and of Shakespeare? Thus Herder wrote:

> In Greece the drama originated as it could not have originated in the North. In Greece it became what it could not have become in the North. Thus it is not and may not be what it used to be in Greece. And if Sophocles portrays, and teaches, and touches, and forms the Greeks, so Shakespeare teaches, and touches, and forms Nordic man. Who can imagine a greater poet of the Nordic world and at that age than Shakespeare?[14]

Norse mythology and Shakespeare were closer to the Germanic spirit than was Homer. In Shakespeare there were *human* drama, vitality, the very spirit of the Germanic North. Jacob and Wilhelm Grimm's fascination with the Nordic Germanic world myths and legends was inspired by Herder's enthusiasm for the Germanic North. In his *Deutsche Mythologie,* Jacob gave due recognition to this influence. [15] In addition, both brothers were motivated by the Indo-European language theory to pursue comparative research within the sphere of related languages and folk literatures. Although their approaches to research differed substantially from Herder's, especially within the context of linguistics and medieval epic studies, they retained the same open-minded attitude toward the myths, songs, and tales of other cultures and traditions.

Patriotism did play an important role in the motivation of Herder and the Brothers Grimm, but in neither case did it become overbearing. The feeling for home and nation was present and strong in both cases, and so was the desire for national unity, but it was well-motivated within the political context of their time. In Herder's time and a few decades later, the unity of the German nation still left much to be desired. Although under the Grimms it no longer represented hundreds of small splintered principalities fighting each other as in earlier days, it was divided into more than thirty states defending their petty regional interests. Also in the cultural sphere, the French occupation under Napoleon had taken its toll, and the German colloquial language was far from being emancipated in the realm of literature. [16] Even though the struggle for German as a literary language was more pronounced in Herder's days than in the Grimms', it was not yet a thing of the past when Jacob and Wilhelm published their *Kinder- und Hausmärchen.* The Grimms, too, had to fight for an acceptance of plain colloquial speech among some of their colleagues, even though the rise of the Romantic movement worked in their favor.

What made the plight of Herder and the Brothers Grimm so similar was not only their discovery of Nordic folk poetry and their belief in its healing power for the life of the nation but also their simultaneous quest for international folklore that lay beyond the sphere of their patriotic interests. Sharing a deep faith in the unity of mankind and an unfailing optimism in a possible resurrection of the naive and wholesome spirit of the past, they expressed a belief in the peaceful coexistence of all men on earth.

There were also differences among them, notably in their academic backgrounds, their conceptions of folktales and education, and their actual approaches to collections. Being a theologian, Herder emphasized to a much greater degree than the Grimms the merits of biblical literature. Even though the Grimms also collected Christian legends, they did not concern themselves in the same intensity as Herder with the spirit of biblical "poetry."

Herder also differed from the Grimms in his views of fairy tales and their uses with children. He strongly disliked fairy tales of the French tradition, both as an art form and as literature for children, considering them too contrived and too nightmarish for the young audience.

The Grimms had some reservations on behalf of the style of French folk-tales too, yet they still approved of the tales of Perrault and commented positively on some of them in their notes to the *Kinder- und Hausmärchen*.

Herder was an admirer of Rousseau but also one of his critics, in the sense that he did not endorse his idea that books should talk down to children or be used primarily for their moral or religious enlightenment. Unlike Rousseau, Herder warmly embraced the value of folklore, recommending to young people the reading of *reine Fabelpoesie* (pure fable poetry), which meant folktales and myths derived from the epic tradition. Among the epic tales he recommended were those based on the *Iliad* and the *Odyssey*, the *Nibelungenlied*, and the Finnish *Kalevala*, referring to these as *Schicksalsfabeln* (fables of fate), a term that he also used for classical myths and the stories of Greek drama. He was fascinated not only with the myths of various nations but also with international folktales, which he collected in various printed sources.[17]

Like Rousseau, Herder recommended the use of Aesop's fables with younger children, referring to these as *Tierfabeln* (animal fables), but he thought that they should be read less for the sake of instruction than for the delight they offered in delineating clear-cut animal characters that behaved—even though in an exaggerated way—like human beings. As Herder recognized the intimate connection among fables, epics, folktales, myths, and legends, he was far from limiting his appreciation of fables to their usefulness in teaching certain lessons.

In connection with a National Institute of German History, he had planned to bring out his own collection of German folktales and legends. Such plans did not materialize, but next to his international folk-song collection, he published a collection of Oriental folktales (predominantly from India) that had a significant influence on the Romantic folktale collections by Clemens Brentano and the Brothers Grimm.[18]

What Herder rejected were embellished and ornate literary fairy tales that, in his view, bore little or no resemblance to the traditional *Märchen*. In particular, he loathed the French fairy tales (contes des fées) and Charles Perrault's *Tales of My Mother Goose* (Contes de ma mère Coyr) that were popular in Germany at his time, suggesting that the latter should have been called the *Tales of Father Goose* because a Mother Goose certainly would have known better than to tell them to her goslings. He thought they were too contrived, too ornate, too cruel, and altogether too spoiled by the extravagant taste of the court to reflect the naive spirit of folklore. While he held up the naive folktale and legend as examples of the simple and spontaneous *Naturpoesie*, he thought that the ogres, giants, and witches in the tales of Perrault caused children to have nightmares that might haunt them until their deathbed. All too often, the tales ended on a note of horror, without giving the child the feeling that evil had been vanquished while justice prevailed.[19]

He warned storytellers and writers not to frighten children by an exaggerated emotional appeal that transformed innocent folktales into horror stories, for young children were sensitive and gullible, believing, in their innocence, that folktales reflected nothing but the truth. Storytellers should try to preserve the traditional themes of justice and redemption and be on their guard not to distort the tales arbitrarily.

> Whoever doubts the holiness of the child's soul should look at children when they are listening to a folktale. "No, that's not the way it goes," they say. "Last time you told me the story differently." They literally *believe* the tale and neither doubt its truth nor its *dream of truth*, even though they well know that you are telling them a fairy tale. And if in this context you offend their sense of logic or morality, if in the course of the tale or its conclusion virtue and vice are not treated accordingly by reward and punishment, the child listens unwillingly and is discontent with the ending. "I don't like the tale; tell me another one." Do we indeed wish to present this holy listener with ghastly images that are neither justified by themselves nor in relation to reality? Do we wish to project into the tales such phantoms of fear and anxiety that may pursue children for the rest of their lives, reappearing as phantoms during moments of weakness or illness, or haunting them in old age and disturbing their final peace?[20]

As far as traditional folktales were concerned, Herder defended them as legitimate reading material for older children, along with myth, legends, and epic tales. While he rejected the embellished fairy tales of the Enlightenment, he warmly embraced traditional folktales, with their epic style and dreamlike imagination, praising them as reflections of the "age of childhood" common to all older nations. "For it is a wondrous thing," he mused, "how our deepest imagination clings to such childhood dreams."[21] It was not important, he felt, that writers of folktales preserved the spirit of naivete that belonged to the genuine folk tradition. Fairy tales told to children left a deeper impression on the human mind than all "dry systems of teaching," he said, yet if told in a distorted and exaggerated way they might create more harm than good. As true folktales were the key for creative thought, embellished tales might unlock some secret fears and superstitions that might haunt children like nightmares. As childhood memories were often linked to stories heard at an early age, such fears might continue to haunt a person at times of illness and old age. Therefore it was doubly important to tell folktales truthfully and imaginatively, with proper respect for their inherent simplicity and power to console.

From the vast treasury of folktales, Herder recommended to older children those tales that had preserved the simple language and wisdom of the past. While it may be considered selective that he advocated a rewriting of such tales for the sake of making their wisdom more relevant to the present, it was not didactic, as he insisted on revisions without embellishments in the interest of preserving the folktale's genuine spirit of naivete, justice, and consolation. He maintained that all older nations had expressed a faith in these qualities through their folktales and folk beliefs. Such great poets as Homer and Shakespeare, too, had known them well. To prove his point, he cited a few lines (in English) from "A Midsummer Night's Dream" that expressed Shakespeare's trust in the power to console: ". . . the nights when no planets strike; no fairy takes, no witch has power to charm; so hallow'd and so gracious is the time."[22] This was the same faith that consoled the child listening to an unembellished folktale, he added.

What saved Herder from being didactic in his approach to fairy tales was his insistence on preserving in folktales the inherent spirit of wisdom and simplicity. In that sense he essentially differed from other writers who willfully imposed on folktales their own conception of conventional morality along with an ornate style. The Brothers Grimm shared Herder's view of the folktale's epic connection, defending it in their time against those who arbitrarily subordinated it to their own fancy or to moral lessons.

The point in which Herder differed from the Brothers Grimm was that he never engaged in the method of fieldwork recordings and also thought little about loyalty to tradition. Although he frequently commented on the oral tradition, expressing his enthusiasm about the songs he had heard around him, he did not think of recording songs or tales by word of mouth but rather relied on printed sources and other collections. Of course, the Grimms also used written sources, although not exclusively. In fact, Wilhelm Grimm translated, like Herder before him, Bishop Thomas Percy's collection of English and Scottish ballads as well as printed sources of Danish ballads and tales. Together with Arnim and Brentano he had also collected and recorded oral songs for *Des Knaben Wunderhorn*, and so had Jacob in connection with his "Circulatory Letter."[23] Yet, overall, it still remains one of the Grimms' most innovative contributions to have discovered the oral tradition as a source for national and international folktale collections.

The Grimms further differed from Herder in their approach to the folk tradition by abstaining from using it as a springboard for their own poetic imagination. Herder rejected embellished tales yet did not consider it inconsistent to compose his own ballads in imitation of folk ballads. In the process of composing, he sometimes did not distinguish clearly between what was traditional and what was his own. The Grimms, on the other hand, strongly disapproved of such a practice for scholarly reasons and consciously tried to maintain a division between editing folk songs and folktales and using them as inspiration for creative writing. Whether they were consistent in their attempt to be loyal to the folk tradition will be subject to a later investigation. There is no question, however, that while Herder established a philosophical basis for folklore collections, the Brothers Grimm developed a methodology for dealing with folklore on a more scholarly level.

[*Naturpoesie:* The Grimms' Search for Naivete]

Like Herder, the Brothers Grimm believed that native folklore reflected the soul of the nation, that it was ancient in nature, and that its origins lay deeply embedded in the epic tradition. To a much greater degree than Herder, the Grimms focused their attention on the oral tradition as well as on a comparative study of myths, legends, and folktales. They were also more intent on emphasizing the difference that they perceived in *Naturpoesie* (nature or folk poetry) and *Kunstpoesie* (art poetry or poetry as an art form). Herder, too, had seen this difference while emphasizing the virtues of the first, yet he had still found it legitimate to create folk ballads of his own. For the Grimms, such a compromise was out of question. In this respect, the Grimms differed in their attitude not only from Herder but also from Goethe and their friends August Wilhelm and Friedrich Schlegel, all of whom had defended the idea of using old folk ballads as an inspiration for new poetry. Being somewhat annoyed with the Grimms' "puristic" stance on this account, the Schlegels let Jacob know that he and his brother grossly exaggerated the virtues of the old epics and tales.

In 1808 Jacob Grimm wrote an essay in which he defined the differences between *Naturpoesie* and *Kunstpoesie*,[24] while emphasizing the relationship of the first to the spirit of history. As such, it represented a powerful organic unity that had arisen with "one voice" from the national epic. Its origin was anonymous, yet it existed with an undeniable strength of vision that could not be matched by modern imitations. Both songs and tales had been remembered by the common folk for ages precisely because the voice of *Naturpoesie* had been so powerful and dynamic and also because it reflected the purity and naivete of a more wholesome age. In his essay "Thoughts about how Legends are Related to Poetry and History" ("Gedanken sich Sagen zur Geschichte und Poesie verhalten"), Jacob wrote: "One may argue and decide whichever way one wishes; the difference between *Naturpoesie* and *Kunstpoesie* is founded in eternity."[25]

Wilhelm Grimm saw the same pronounced differences in folktales and fantasies and consented to deal only with the first. In discussing the great merits of *Naturpoesie* in relation to folktales, he defined more concisely in 1819 what exactly he understood by these qualities.[26]

The first mark of *Naturpoesie* was the natural conditions in which it had been created, he wrote, conditions that made it unconscious of itself, like a flower or a plant. Among the common folk, the old bards had created it spontaneously, without vain self-reflections or stylistic refinements. *Naturpoesie* was as unconscious of itself as had been the bards, and both had been naive in a most positive sense. Naivete was concisely the quality that one now admired in epics, myths, legends, and folktales. *Naturpoesie* spoke with a sense of urgency and directness, yet with ease and spontaneity, without an obvious effort or artificial restraints.

The second quality of *Naturpoesie* was that it told a story in a pure and simple way. It never set out to teach, to preach, or to impress the listener. Its simple style demanded fewer words than modern poetry and writing, yet it was incomparably rich in its vigorous expression. Being rich in itself meant that *Naturpoesie* needed neither morals nor maxims nor adornments, because its language, themes, and images spoke for themselves. Wilhelm compared the old bards to God-like creatures who had been capable of producing children by the mere power of thought or just by "looking at each other intensively,"[27] whereas he compared the modern poets to clumsy amateurs who needed the whole works: embraces, ornate decorations, rational constructions, and stylistic adornments, without coming close to the old poets in terms of quality and effect.

Naturpoesie was always created "from the core"[28] of human experience, thus conveying a feeling of unity and truth. In this act of creation lay its very secret and strength. For that reason, its words possessed a visionary power that would bridge gaps in sentences wherever words had been omitted or had been lost in crumbling manuscripts. Being derived from a mythical power and epic truth, the vision of *Naturpoesie* would always supply the missing parts, even where only small fragments were left. In the old days, the bards had composed their tales intuitively by "reliving" their innermost perception of truth. Sometimes they had changed the traditional wording yet never the core of the tale itself. The intensity and inner unity of the epic songs and tales were so strong that they had never failed the listeners.

As Wilhelm saw it, *Naturpoesie* derived its powerful vision and "eternal quality" from its quest for truth. In that sense, it was not a mere form of entertainment but a significant expression of the humanity of man. A mere play of aesthetics had little to do with this quest. Wilhelm likened *Naturpoesie*'s quest for truth to the powerful current of a mighty river. In comparison, modern poems and fantasies were nothing but meandering brooks or shallow streams.[29]

Wilhelm Grimm perceived the greatest quality of *Naturpoesie* in its childlike innocence and simplicity, its naivete. It was wiser than a man who had spent a lifetime studying the rules of composition, he wrote, even though it looked so humble and unassuming. Its wisdom really was that of a pastor's small child speaking from the quiet faith of a pure heart. How much more convincing and touching was such a child's talk than the learned speech of a clever theologian giving a pompous sermon during Sunday's mass! Childlike naivete and wisdom made *Naturpoesie* credible, as it touched upon an eternal truth.[30]

Herder, too, had seen such qualities in the *Urpoesie* of the ancient nations, but Wilhelm Grimm attached them more consciously to the folktale tradition and the world of the child. Wilhelm also insisted that folktales should be read with the mind of an innocent child, not with the mind of a superstitious or prejudiced adult. Still, both he and his brother ascribed an even stronger reflection of these virtues to epic poetry and myths from which folktales supposedly had been derived. Folktales were like dew drops or diamonds sparkling in the grass,[31] Wilhelm wrote in the preface of the first edition of the *Kinder- und Hausmär-chen*, splinters of larger "jewels," the myths and epics that had been forgotten with the past. As such, they were innocent reminders of another age in which mythical images had still occupied the minds and hearts of the simple folk. As reflections of an older, purer age, they deserved to be gathered like the last sheaves of wheat that had been left in the field long after the harvest.

In contrast to the legend, Wilhelm defined the folktale as a folk narrative that was not bound to a geographical location or a definite time in history. Whereas the legend was either tied to historical circumstances or an identifiable place, the folktale was free from both. The opening formula: "Once upon a time, there was . . ." implied that the folktale stood aloof from the world in a sheltered, undisturbed place, somewhere beyond time and place.[32] Mainly because it had neither historical nor geographical ties and was free from local color, it could be found wherever there was a sheltered, quiet, and "secret" place, away from the turmoil of civilization: "It know neither name nor place, nor a definite home, and it is something that belongs to the entire fatherland." ("*Darum kennt es weder Namen und Orte noch eine bestimmte Heimath, und es ist etwas dem ganzen Vaterlande Gemeinsames.*")[33] In referring to the fatherland, Wilhelm meant that the folktale was not bound to a specific German region but that it represented a unifying force with a universal appeal.

Did Wilhelm suggest that German folktales belonged to the German fatherland alone? To answer this question, one first has to examine his statement against the background of the historical context. Before Napoleon's conquest, Germany had still been divided into more than 300 principalities, each marked by its own local history, folk traditions, and regional dialects, and even after the unification, there were still more than thirty distinct principalities. If Wilhelm considered the folktale as something that belonged to the entire nation, he ascribed to it a force capable of overcoming such given regional differences. That he did not mean to imply chauvinism may well be perceived from his vital interest in the folktales of other nations. Very much like Herder, both he and Jacob believed in the universal appeal of *Naturpoesie* that transcended the boundaries of a single nation.

If the folktale's place was so secret, where, then, should one look for it? The Grimms generally agreed that "quiet places" seemed to be conducive to its growth and development. It was logical to turn away from the turmoil and noise of the cities and search for folktales in the countryside among shepherds and peasants where indeed traditions had been well preserved. Wilhelm gave us a hint that remote areas were indeed their secret hiding place, but he also indicated that it was neither confined to the peasantry of the German fatherland alone, and not even to simple folk in the meadows of Denmark or the fjords of Norway. In his notes to some early collected tales, he wrote:

> It is the poetry of the simple, naive life that we may find among the negroes in Africa or even among the Greeks. Folktales are the harvest of forgotten places, cherished by the common folk and preserved by them. They possess the same purity as we see it reflected in the souls and eyes of children; they are simple, yet always fresh in their appeal.[34]

He spoke of the folktale's animated nature that reflected the mythical view of the Golden Age of mankind: a language of concrete symbols in which all creatures, big or small, spoke with a human voice. The characteristics that he ascribed to folktales and the simple folk were by no means not restricted to the fatherland alone but were shared by all ancient nations, although more likely in remote areas than in highly populated places. The key phrase is "the simple, naive life," a life that was not confined to one nation or the countryside but was ever-present in the souls and eyes of children. The condition of "purity" that Wilhelm ascribes here to "forgotten places" may well be one that has been preserved wherever the love of traditional storytelling is still alive.

In a letter to his friends asking them to contribute to their collection of folktales, Jacob Grimm wrote in 1815:

> On the high mountains and in the small villages, where there are neither paths nor roads, and where the false Enlightenment has had no access and was unable to do its work, there still lies hidden in darkness a treasure: the customs of our forefathers, their sagas and their faith. We, the Undersigned, have experienced this truth quite often, yet we also know how difficult it is to lift the treasure. Needed for this task is not only a certain innocent naivete, but also an education enabling us to grasp this naivete in the virtue that is unconscious of itself. Needed especially are a strict loyalty to tradition and a mild friendliness . . .[35]

Neither the "high mountains" nor the "small villages" would have to be taken too literally in this context, although both locations fit the previous description of remote areas and forgotten places. Significant above all is Jacob's emphasis on discovering a "certain innocent naivete," a state of mind that he considered a prerequisite for the storyteller as well as the folktale collector. In other words, in order to recognize the tale grown in the quiet conditions of a pure and childlike soul, a folktale collector would have to be naive in spirit. This implied that the task involved was not merely a rational or mechnical one but required a certain innocence and "mild friendliness" to make a person receptive to such tales. We may interpret this not merely as an "open mind" but a warm feeling for the common folk and their tradition. Secondly, however, it also required an education enabling the collector to "grasp the naivete that was unconscious of itself." This meant that he had to learn how to distinguish between what was genuine and what was not. It was not a simple thing after all, Jacob seemed to say, to understand the unity of *Naturpoesie* in its vision of the epic truth. Even though genuine folktales reflected the truth as simply as an innocent child, one might confuse it with the lesson of moralistic or artificially constructed tales meant to enlighten or to entertain the audience. The idea of "loyalty to tradition" in this context referred to the collector's obligation to record the tales in the same naive spirit as he had heard them, without the addition of morals or embellishments.

The idea that an education was needed to comprehend the naive mind that was unconscious of itself is an intriguing one, for it is commonly believed that simple things can easily be grasped by a simple mind. Upon second thought, however, one may remember the Socratic wisdom that it is not simple at all to be simple again. In fact, it may turn out to be the most difficult task facing us all. The type of naivete that Jacob Grimm expected of a folktale collector certainly was not identical with that experienced unconsciously by the traditional storyteller, for it had to be conscious enough to grasp and record the naive tale. Schiller had spoken in similar terms about naive poetry as the reflection of a first nature that in modern times could be re-created only as a second nature.[36] The first nature was unconscious of itself in its visionary state of naivete, whereas the second nature represented a modern poet's conscious attempt to be simple and visionary again after having received his education in naive poetry. While he could not dare to hope that his own poetry would reflect the same powerful naivete of epic poetry that was "created from the core" of a visionary mind, it might come close to it through his conscious effort to create from the depth of inspiration. To achieve that state of mind, a poet would have to become simple again, forgetting all modern rules and embellishments.

From this perspective, to say that the Brothers Grimm looked for folktales "among the peasants" is truly an understatement. Aside from the fact that according to their own notes they did not restrict themselves to the peasant class by any means, their philosophical definitions of quiet and sheltered places and particularly of naivete, suggest a condition of the mind rather than a mere topographical place, a naive state of mind that had remained untouched by the spirit of the "false Enlightenment." Jacob's definition of the folktale collector further suggests that the type of education needed for this task had little to do with formal schooling but required a deeper understanding of *Natur-poesie* and a full grasp of naivete.

[The Epic Connection]

Both Wilhelm and Jacob Grimm were fascinated by epic literature. They already developed their taste for medieval manuscripts as young students of Professor Karl von Savigny, who permitted them to visit his home and browse freely in his extensive library. In looking for materials related to ancient Germanic law, they would come across old manuscripts stacked away in the shelves, and especially Wilhelm made it his hobby to copy with painstaking effort some long poems in his neat handwriting. Occasionally, Savigny permitted them to take home a book so as to give the brothers a chance to finish reading some of these works at their leisure. When as a young man Jacob Grimm followed Savigny for a year to France on a research excursion, Wilhelm begged him in a letter not to forget to look for old and quaint manuscripts and to bring back some copies of medieval materials to which he might have access in the libraries of Paris.[37]

This interest in old manuscripts and epic literature, which persisted throughout their lives, also had significant bearing on the Grimms' work with myths and folktales, for all of these belonged in the realm of *Natur-poesie*. Among their scholarly contributions were numerous studies related to medieval epics and romances that concerned folk beliefs, themes, motifs, and character traits that found an echo in the oral folk tradition. Vice versa, in many folktales they perceived a strange echo of epic literature upon which they commented frequently in their notes to the *Kinder- und Hausmärchen*, be it in relation to peculiar archaic expressions, proverbs, or related folk motifs.

Toward the beginning of the 1830s, when Wilhelm had already become a professor of medieval literature at the University of Göttingen, his main field of specialization concerned medieval epics whereas Jacob moved toward linguistics and Germanic law. But from that perspective, too, Jacob remained in contact with epic literature, especially in regard to the *Nibelungenlied* and the *Elder Edda*, both of which he edited with Wilhelm. These provided the most substantial sources for his work with comparative mythology, which culminated in the *Deutsche Mythologie (Teutonic Mythology)*, published in 1835.

Jacob and Wilhelm Grimm translated the *Elder Edda* (with a commentary) on the basis of the Icelandic manuscript, at about the same time when they both worked on the *Nibelungenlied*. Since in both cases they encountered a rival publication by Heinrich von der Hagen, they did not proceed with their work beyond the first volume.[38] Still, their research connected with these epic restorations was substantial, and it helped Wilhelm considerably to prepare for his lectures on the *Nibelungenlied*. Jacob used his findings for some later Göttingen lectures on comparative mythology related to European variants on the Norse god Thor.[39] Most significantly, however, it helped him in preparing the ground for three volumes of the *Teutonic Mythology*, which established his fame in philological circles in both Europe and the United States.

Jacob and Wilhelm recognized in the Nordic epics what they had long known from the oral folktale tradition. There were surprising correspondences not only between characters of dwarfs and elves, dwights and fairies but also between motifs related to magic rings, fierce dragons, sleeping beauties, and the "water of life." Even though their comparative research of other folk traditions also revealed similar folk motifs, Jacob reasoned that the correspondences were strongest among those cultures that shared some language roots and ancient folk beliefs. In his first volume of the *Teutonic Mythology* he gave the following reasons for the affinity between German and Old Nordic folk motifs:

1. An undisputed and very close affinity of speech between German and Nordic languages and an identity of form in their oldest poetry.

2. The joint possession of many terms relating to religious worship among all Teutonic languages.

3. The identity of mythic notions and nomenclature (*muspilli* in Old High German, *mudspelli* in Old Saxon, and *muspell* in the Eddic poems, for example, all pointed to the same "land of fire" in the creation story of the world).

4. The reflection of mythic elements in the names of plants and constellations.

5. The gradual transformation of gods into devils.

6. The evident deposit from god-myths in various folktales, games, rhymes, curses, names of days and months, and idiomatic phrases.

7. The undeniable intermixture of the old religious doctrines with the Germanic system of law.[40]

In the last point, Jacob Grimm was an expert, for he had studied Germanic law under Savigny for several years before becoming Professor of Germanic Law at the University of Göttingen. Especially in regard to points 6 and 7 Jacob hints at the intimate interrelationship among epic literature, ancient folk religion, and folktales, a topic that he and Wilhelm explored their entire lives from various angles. Even their final work, the *Deutsches Wörterbuch*,[41] is full of cross-references linking language to myths, epics, folk beliefs, and children's games. Yet neither Jacob nor Wilhelm Grimm confined their research to interdisciplinary studies of this sort but included into the scope of their interests also the epics of other cultures. Significantly, Jacob wrote in his *Teutonic Mythology* that an unraveling of such complex relations made it indispensable not to overlook the mythologies of neighboring nations, especially of the Celts, Slavs, Lithuanians, and Finns. By themselves such contacts were most fruitful, he wrote, but a study of those myths might also reveal more clearly the course of development that the myths and languages had taken over time and what relationship they had to each other.

We learn more about Wilhelm's involvement in epic studies from his autobiography.[42] Here he referred to his doctoral degree in philosophy from the University of Marburg in 1819 and his lectures on the *Nibelungenlied* and the *Gudrunlied (Song of Gudrun)* in Göttingen a decade later. He also listed his memberships in various literary and philological associations that show the wide range of his scholarly acceptance within the field of his expertise: the Netherlandic Literature Society, the Scandinavian Literature Society, the Language Association in Berlin, the German Association in Leipzig, the Historical Association of Westfalia, and the Royal Academy of Sciences in Kopenhagen. He was too shy to enumerate the various publications he had co-authored with his older brother, yet among his own scholarly productions he mentioned the *Aldänische Heldenlieder, Balladen und Märchen (Old Danish Heroic Songs, Ballads, and Folktales*, 1811), two volumes of *Deutsche Sagen (German Legends*, 1816), and his essay "Über deutsche Runen" ("About German Runes," 1828). Among the epic fragments that he edited mainly on the basis of medieval manuscripts were *Grâve Ruodolf (Count Rudolph*, 1828), fragments of the poem of *Assundin* (1830), and *De Hildebrando antiquissimi carminis teutonici fragmentum (The Song of Hildebrand;* a Teutonic fragment, 1830), as well as *Der arme Heinrich (Poor Henry*, 1838). He also published numerous book reviews related to medieval epics. The reviews addressed the songs of the Troubadors, Spanish romances, and the *Igorlied (Tale of Igor)*. The *Igorlied*, to which Wilhelm referred as an "epic in the Old Slavic tongue," had been translated into German by Joseph Müller in 1802. In a lengthy review in the *Göttingische Gelehrte Anzeigen* of 1820, Wilhelm praised it highly as a national epic that should be compared to the *Nibelungenlied,* the *Edda,* and the works of Homer. Jacob, too, commented on the *Tale of Igor* in positive terms, perceiving in it, a close relationship to Slavic folktales. He felt that the *Naturpoesie* of this epic was so powerful and unique that it stood above that of *Ossian*[43] It is worth noting that in these reviews and others both Brothers Grimm shared Herder's broadminded attitude toward other cultures and traditions.

Jacob Grimm's attitude toward epics was slightly more nationalistic in regard to the animal epic of *Reinhart Fuchs (Reynard the Fox)*, which fascinated them over many years. While in Brussels in 1823, he prepared a handwritten copy on the basis of two manuscripts that he discovered.

In the same year, he published an essay about Reinhard Fuchs in Berlin, in which he explained what he conceived to be a definite connection between the animal epic and German animal folktales.[44] While giving an extensive review of European variants of animal fables belonging to this cycle of tales, he tried to establish the dominant themes and character traits. Next to a comparative approach to motifs, he used a linguistic-historical analysis in tracing some recurrent names and themes in Germany, the Netherlands, and Northern France.[45] Like Wilhelm, who wrote on a related topic from the angle of German animal folktales, he concluded that these tales possessed "the fragrance of the German forest" and were distinctly homegrown in relation to the German folk tradition.

Wilhelm observed that animal epics had developed from an uninterrupted human interaction with animals and consequently reflected a familiarity with their unique and secret life. This close association had led to an elevation of some animal traits into the human sphere and to a projection of some human traits into animal behavior. The nature of the animals had not changed over time. The plot of the tales was clearly delineated, and the actions evolved from the natural attributes of the animals that were somehow fixed in the human imagination: the lion or bear, being the strongest, was always shown to be the ruler; the wolf was consistently depicted as gruesome and wild; the deer appeared as the fastest, the fox as the slyest, the donkey as the most patient, and the hare the most fearful creature.[46]

It appears peculiar that among the many accomplishments that Wilhelm listed in his autobiography he did not mention the *Kinder- und Hausmärchen*. Jacob, too, did not make too much of the fame that both he and his brother earned on account of that work. On the other hand, it was Jacob who emphasized in an oration on Wilhelm that it was Wilhelm who truly deserved to be called the "fairy tale brother."[47] Jacob knew better than anybody else that their work with folktales had been inseparably linked with studies of the epic tradition and that both had been equally worthy of their attention.

[Folktales and Norse Mythology]

Following Herder's theory that the old speech had been rich in its poetry, spontaneity, and closeness to nature, Jacob and Wilhelm Grimm both agreed that folktales contained remnants of this folk speech. Long before Jacob systematically traced the origins of such remnants in his *Deutsche Mythologie (Teutonic Mythology,* 1935), Wilhelm detected them in the language of myths and folktales. In elaborating on some of the mythic origins of German folktales, Wilhelm referred mostly to Norse mythology, as he adhered to his brother's theory regarding their common Indo-European roots. Yet he would also write about folktales and myths in universal terms as the common language of humanity and "the living breath of poetry" ("*der lebendige Odem der Poesie*").[48]

To Wilhelm, folktales were the essence of "the old poetry" created by the people. The folktale language was the language of poetry. By animating the inanimate world and by speaking in symbols, it encompassed the spirit of humanity, giving evidence of ancient man's poetic vision that modern poetry no longer possessed. In such symbols he perceived the mythical qualities of the folktale language that young and old could understand equally well. In referring to the folktale's powerful capacity to animate the inanimate world, he wrote in his 1812 introduction to the *Kinder- und Hausmärchen*:

> Like myths, they reflect an animated nature of a golden age: nature is humanized, alive. Sun, moon, and stars have dresses and give gifts; there are dwarfs working in the mountains, digging for metal; mermaids inhabit the waters; animals, stones, and plants can talk and are capable of human compassion . . . the very blood talks. . . . This innocent and intimate relationship between the largest and the smallest creatures creates a beauty beyond comparison.[49]

According to Wilhelm, the theme of the eternal struggle of the elements was particularly strong in German folktales and the related Nordic Germanic myths. It involved the battle between the powers of light and the powers of darkness, which found an echo in the battle between the good and the evil forces within the folktale world.[50] As darkness fought light in myths and epics, so evil, fear, and destruction struggled to overcome goodness, hope, and love. One might rediscover such mythical and symbolic battles in the folktale character of the Prince of Night, for example, who was doomed to die if the first ray of the morning sun would touch his face. There lay embedded the ancient struggle of such a solar myth. In Norse mythology, the Black Elves (Alfs) were the ones who were doomed if touched by the rays of the sun. In the folktale of "The Goose Girl," Berhta with the shiny golden hair represented the image of the bright sun, and so did Snow White, who was beautiful and radiant even in death. When the Norse god Odin would ride across the lands on his swift eight-legged horse, Sleipnir, the ancient folk knew that he would battle the evil forces while returning victoriously to Asgard. The *Edda* spoke of the sons of Day (Dassynir, Megir) and the daughter of the Night (in *Sigurdrifa's Song*), but it also knew Surtur, the "Black One," who consistently fought against the mild and radiant Aesir. Such characters undoubtedly influenced the portrayal of evil and darkness in folktales, wrote Wilhelm. The folktale theme of punishment, too, had mythological origins in the battle theme. The idea of killing someone in a snake pit, for example, was derived from the *Edda* but also from the Norse image of "Hel." Wherever folktales showed snakes or dragons guarding a golden treasure, one might search for the related image of Fafnir, the dragon, in Norse mythology and the *Song of the Nibelung (Nibelungenlied).*[51]

To Wilhelm, the fair images of innocence and purity, too, were an integral part of such battle myths, for they were the foil to the threat of destruction. Balder, the radiant Nordic sun god, and Siegfried of the *Song of the Nibelung* were primeval images of innocence, of which traces could be rediscovered in the folktale world. Both were threatened with death yet continued to live as bright images in myth and legend. Related images and symbols could also be found in Homer's *Odyssey* and in the Greek legend of Perseus.[52] Besides, there were many other ancient cultures that depicted in their myths and folktales how a radiant hero would defeat the powers of evil. In most cases, evil would finally be defeated, and the monsters and fear would be destroyed or banned forever, just as the fair Sigurd had slain Fafnir, and the fair Perseus had overpowered the Hydra. After victorious battles, once again there would emerge a period of calm, harmony, and peace, and people would regain their unity with God and nature.[53] Such examples, drawn from the Greek epics and hero tales, did not contradict the Indo-European theory of the Brothers Grimm, as both Greece and Persia were related to the same "family" of languages. Rather the examples show clearly that the Grimms interpreted such a relationship in much broader terms than some fanatic antiquarians at a later time who limited their comparisons strictly to the "Nordic countries" of Europe.

Wilhelm cited many other parallel motifs in German folktales and Norse mythology. The theme of becoming invisible, for example, had predecessors in the Nibelung's cap of invisibility and the magic helmet of the Aegir. Many of the magic objects in folktales also could be traced back to the Norse myths, be they in form of magic wands, hats, scarves, or tables. The theme of "getting stuck" in the folktale of "The Golden Goose" was an echo of the myth about the Giant Thijazi, who with Loki sticking to his back, took off in the form of a bird. The tale of "The Water of Life" could be found in the myth of Mimir's Well containing the magic dew of the World Ash. The magic water in the folktale restored health and youth to people, whereas it possessed the power of wisdom in the old myth. For a sip of that water, Odin had even sacrificed one eye.[54]

Within the context of his broader comparative analysis of mythical themes throughout the Germanic (Teutonic) world, Jacob Grimm also mentioned a number of German folktale motifs that could be traced back to Norse mythology. Consistent with the main thesis, he drew his examples mainly from Norse mythology yet not to the exclusion of other Indo-European myths and legends. In comparing motifs of wise women, apples, dwarfs, spindles, local haunts, sacred rocks, birthmarks, tests, magic spells, and miraculous number schemes of three, seven, nine, and twelve he generally traced their occurrences in folktales to the older myths.[55] The vast scope of his cited examples are bound to overwhelm the general reader, although they never fail to impress the specialist. To the older collections and epic sources he referred in a sort of "shorthand" style that had little in common with Wilhelm's poetic discourses. One might be tempted to compare it to that used by Sir James Frazer in the *The Golden Bough*.[56]

What distinguishes Jacob's approach from others is the close attention he gives to clues arising from a comparison of older names and words, from proverbs, and from colloquial expressions. In this connection, two of his examples are of particular interest, as they refer to the better known folktales of the *Kinder- und Hausmärchen*, "Mother Hulda" ("Frau Holle"), and "Thornrosa" ("Dornröschen"). The name "Frau Holle" was derived from Holda, who was a kind, benign, merciful goddess or lady, a word derived from the German *hold* (the Latin *propitius*) and the Gothic *hulps*.

Jacob further elaborated on the etymology of the word *Holle:*

> Root: hilpan halp hulpun (to bend, bow), ON, hoor; the Gothic form of it would be *Hulpa*. For the opposite notion of a malignant diabolic being, Ulphilas employs both the fem. unholpo and the masc. *unholpa*; one more confirmation of the double sex running through these divinities.[57]

In his usual stenographic style, Jacob commented on the modern German term of *unhold*, which, like the Old Nordic feminine word *unholde*, referred to a dark, malignant, yet mighty being. These words again had a certain bearing on the German folktale character of *Frau Holle*, also called *Hulda, Holle*, or *Frau Holl*. She, too, was a superior being, although she was considered a benevolent, kind, and helpful creature who never became angry with people except when she noticed a disorder in household affairs. She was well known in Hesse, Thuringia, and Voigtland, the Rhön mountains in northern Franconia, the Westerwald, Lower Saxony, Swabia, Bavaria, and even Switzerland. In North Saxony and Friesland, however, she was not known by that name.[58]

In considering snowflakes as the specific old Germanic folk belief associated with "Frau Holle," also in proverbial expressions and old sayings, Jacob related the old folk belief that whenever she made her feather bed, snowflakes would begin to swirl in the sky, covering the earth with a soft, white blanket. In this role, she resembled Donar (Thor), the Norse god of thunder, who was known to have stirred up the rain. Viewed as a weather goddess, she even bore certain similarities to Zeus, the Greek god of lightning. According to another Germanic folk belief, Frau Holle haunted the lakes, fountains, and wells and also rode on her chariot across the skies between Christmas and the Twelfth Night, bringing fertility to the land. In that role she resembled the Norse fertility god, Freyr.[59]

In the folktales of *Kinder- und Hausmärchen* (tale number 24), Frau Holle appeared as a rather ugly old woman resembling a witch with her long teeth, which meant that the mythical image of a kind and benevolent goddess of fertility had been transformed into an ugly and dreadful one. On the other hand she still appeared as a spinning woman who rewarded industrious girls while punishing the lazy ones. In Jacob's view, such an appearance confirmed her association with the early gods of agriculture and domestic order, a motherly deity whom one might encounter in the Egyptian goddess Isis or in the Norse goddess Hulle, who had presided over cattle grazing and milking. According to old Germanic customs, the special care of flax and spinning was left to the housewives, while the men were expected to take up the sword. [60]

Jacob used a similar methodology in his analysis of the folktale "Dornröschen" (Thornrosa or Sleeping Beauty), by first searching out the etymology of the word *Feen* (fairies) and then relating to the variant spellings the folktale variants of different cultures. In this case, too, he did not restrict his comparison to the Nordic Germanic sphere but moved freely among customs and languages of other nations, especially Italy and France, while including in his discussion the printed sources of earlier collections, namely *Pentamerone* and Perrault's *La belle au bois dormante*, which he treated as "fixed forms of variants."[61] The thirteen fairies (*dreizehn Feen*) in the German "Dornröschen" tale had been preceded by Basile's three fairies (*tre fate*), of which the first (like fate itself) had bestowed blessings and the last one curses. Pervonto had built a bower for them, and they had lived in a rocky hole, dowered the children who descended, and appeared at the birth of children. In Perrault's *La belle au bois dormante* seven fairies appeared who asked to be godmothers to a child. After seats of honor had been prepared for them at the table, six took their places, but the seventh discovered to her dismay that none had been reserved for her. The six fairies who had been well treated endowed the child with blessings and good things, but the seventh one in her anger murmured an evil spell, just like the thirteenth *Fee* in the German "Dornröschen."

Jacob Grimm compared further variants on this theme with some Arthurian legends and a German tale about the children of Limburg, concluding that in these, as well as in numerous other related tales, only three fairies had been mentioned, which suggested that there existed a close connection with the motif of "three women" in Norse and Greek mythology. The three Norns of the Germanic myth had spun the threat of life at Mimir's well, whereas in Greek mythology, the three Fates — Lachesis, Clotho, and Athropos (the three *Parcae* in Roman mythology) — had been associated with spinning. [62] The spindle motif was especially related to Clotho, whose name meant "to spin" or "to twine." The activity of weaving was an indication that a motherly divinity had been involved, very much like in the case of Frau Holle. In many cases, the three fairies also had been associated with wells and springs as they bestowed boons on babies and children. Numerous other examples from Latvia and Lithuania and even from Swiss nursery rhymes affirmed the intimate relationship of folktales with old myths in various cultures.[63]

Unlike his brother Wilhelm, who was most fascinated by the rich imagery of folktales, Jacob felt that myths deserved more attention, as they had a greater aura of respectability and also some nobler elements than folktales. This difference in attitude may explain why after publication of the first edition of the *Kinder- und Hausmärchen* he left most of the revisions of the folktales to Wilhelm. By following a more exacting scientific approach informed by linguistics, Jacob enjoyed playing the detective in tracking down the etymology of key words as much as he enjoyed tracing variants in mythical themes. Like Wilhelm, however, Jacob retained an international perspective in his research while choosing his examples freely from other myths and folk beliefs, be they Greek, Lithuanian, or Egyptian, wherever the etymology of a given word or the mythical relationship of a theme justified it. Only in strictly etymological terms did he focus more intensively on the related Nordic Germanic cultures than on others. To some degree his comparisons were limited by the scope of his Indo-European myth and language theory, but they still reflected Herder's legacy regarding his warm interest in other cultures and traditions and were far removed from the Nazis' ethnocentric and racial myth interpretation a century later.

NOTES

1. Alexander Gillies, "Herder's Preparation of Romantic Theory," *Modern Language Review* 39 (1940), pp. 257–61; Reinhold Steig, "Wilhelm Grimm und Herder," *Vierteljahresschrift für Literature* 3 (1890), pp. 573–78; August Coss, "Wurzeln der Romantik bei Herder" *Modern Language Quarterly* 2 (1941), pp. 611–18; Oscar Walzel, *German Romanticism* (New York: Putnam's Sons, 1965), pp. 3–73.

2. Johann Gottfried Herder, "Über die neuere deutsche Litteratur (sic)," in *Herders Sämmtliche Werke* 6, 2, Bernhard Suphan, ed. (Berlin: Weidmannsche Buchhandlung, 1894), p. 161. Subsequent references to this edition will be made to Herder, *Werke*. In the same essay Herder asked, "Where are our Chaucers, Spensers, Shakespeares?" expressing his hope that a renewed national consciousness might lead to a more vigorous German national literature.

3. "No one can contribute to all of mankind who does not make out of himself what he can and should," said Herder. "Everyone must first cultivate the spirit of humanity in his own soil, where it grows as a tree or blossoms as a flower." Herder, *Werke* 17, 153. Yet, he insisted that beyond one's own culture one should always seek that of others, for all mankind could look back to *one* origin and *one* original language. Richard Benz, "Johann Gottfried Herder," in *Die Grossen Deutschen: Eine Biographie*, Hermann Hempel, Theodor Heuss, Bruno Reifenberg, eds., (Berlin: Deutsche Buch-Gemeinschaft, 1965), p. 220. On behalf of Herder's quest for cultural diversity rather than uniformity, consult Isaiah Berlin, *Vico and Herder: Two Studies in the History of Ideas* (New York: Vintage, 1976), p. 176.

4. Hans Kohn, *Prelude to Nation-States: The French-German Experience 1781–1815* (Princeton: Princeton University Press, 1964), p. 388. In the Third Reich, Herder's cultural nationalism was distorted into racism. Dahmen's book, for example, presented Herder as if he had paved the way for Nazism. See Hans Dahmen, *Die nationale Idee von Herder bis Hitler* (Cologne: Hermann Schaffstein Verlag, 1934).

5. Ibid. See also Christa Kamenetsky, "Herder und der Mythos des Nordens," *Revue de littérature comparée* 47 (1973) 23–41. Christa Kamenetsky, "Herder and the Romantic Folklore Revival," in *Journal of Popular Culture* (1973) 54–68.

6. It is for this reason that Herder is called the father of comparative literature. See René Wellek, "The Name and Nature of Comparative Literature," in Stephen Nichols et al., eds. *Comparatists at Work: Studies in Comparative Literature* (New York: Waltham, Massachusetts: Blaisdell Publishing Company, 1968), p. 18. Kamenetsky, "Herder und der Mythos des Nordens," 23–41.

7. Johann Gottfried Herder, *Volkslieder: Stimme der Völker in Liedern* 2 vols. (Leipzig: Weygandsche Buchhandlung, 1778–1779, 1787). See also Herder, *Werke* 5, introduction. This introduction was awarded a prize from the Bavarian Academy in Munich in 1778. Originally, Herder used the singular form of the noun *Stimme* (*Voice*) in the title, so as to indicate the unity and universality of *Urpoesie* that was shared by many nations of the world. Later editions used the plural form of *Stimmen* (*Voices*).

8. Herder, *Werke* 5, Part 1, introduction., p. iv. See also introduction to Part 2 of the same volume, where he talks about the necessity of capturing the unique mood of every song arising from a people's emotions and passions. Herder's introductions to *Volkslieder* became a landmark in terms of expressing a deep respect for the differences among all nationalities as well as their universal human aspects marking them as "children of God" within the "brotherhood of mankind." For a commentary on these introductions consult Konrad Nussbacher, "Einleitung," in *Johann Gottfried Herder: Von der Urpoesie der Völker* (Stuttgart: Reclam Verlag, 1975), pp. 4–13. This Reclam edition contains Herder's essays on Shakespeare, Ossian, the folk songs, and the "Book of Hiob."

9. Herder, *Werke* 9, pp. 541–45.

10. Ibid. Herder expanded Winckelmann's concept of *Naturpoesie*, which originally had applied only to Greek epics, by including in it also myths, legends, folk songs, and folktales.

11. Herder, "Über die Fabel" and "Märchen und Romane," in Herder, *Werke* 23, pp. 225–39. Of particular significance is his reference to the concept of *Schicksalsfabel* (fable of fate).

12. Herder, *Werke, 5*, p. 168.

13. Hermann Gerstner, *Die Brüder Grimm. Biographie mit 48 Bildern* (Gerabonn-Crailsheim: Hohenloher Druck- und Verlagshaus, 1970), Chapter 4. See also Gabriele Seitz, *Die Brüder Grimm: Leben-Werk-Zeit* (Munich: Winkler Verlag, 1984), Chapter 3.

14. Herder, "Shakespear," [sic] in Herder, *Werke* 5, p. 210.

15. Jacob Grimm, *Teutonic Mythology* 1 (New York: Dover, 1968), Introduction. Jacob published this work under the original title of *Deutsche Mythologie* (Göttingen: 1835), dedicating the third volume to his brother Wilhelm. He also used the term "*Deutsche*" in the title of his earlier work on grammar, *Deutsche Grammatik* (Göttingen: 1819), implying in both cases a comparative approach to Germanic myths and languages in the broadest sense, while using many comparative notes on other cultures and traditions.

16. Herder, "Gallicomanie," in Herder, *Werke* 17, p. 161. Also Kohn, p. 165.

17. Herder, "Über die Fabel," Herder, *Werke* 23, pp. 225–39. See also: Johann Gottfried Herder, "Adrastea: Über die Fabel," in *Sämmtliche Werke* Vol. 15 (Berlin: Düntzer Verlag), p. 235. Herder discussed at lengths myths and legends under the

name of *kosmogonische Märchen* (cosmic or epic tales) and praised them highly, yet he referred in derogatory terms to the *Feenmärchen* (fairy tales of the French tradition).

18. Herder, "Märchen und Romane," *Sämmtliche Werke*, pp. 239–45. See also notes. Herder hoped to bring out *"eine reine Sammlung von Kindermärchen"* (a pure or undiluted collection of folktales for children) as a "Christmas gift for the young people in future generations." See also: Johann Gottfried Herder, "Adrastea: Über die Fabel," in *Sämmtliche Werke* 24 vols. in 15, Heinrich Düntzer and Wollheim da Fonseca, eds. (Berlin: Hempel, 1869–1879), p. 235. With respect to a general academy for the promotion of German studies, he defined his goals in *Idee zum ersten patriotischen Institut für den Allgemeingeist Deutschlands* (Plan for the First Patriotic Institute for the Community Spirit of Germany). Robert Clark, *Herder: His Life and Thought* (Berkeley: University of California Press, 1969), p. 353.

19. Herder, "Über Märchen und Romane," p. 246–59.

20. Ibid.

21. Ibid., p. 260. Herder considered Shakespeare a "natural genius," like Homer, and very much admired his use of folklore.

22. See Robert Clark, "Herder, Percy and the Song of Songs," *Publication of the Modern Language Association* 61 (Sept. 1964), pp. 428–41.

23. Joseph Prestel, "Volksmärchen," in *Handbuch zur Jugendliteratur*, ed. Joseph Prestel (Freiburg i. Brsg.: Herder Verlag, 1933), pp. 35–46.

24. Wilhelm Grimm, "Natur- und Kunstpoesie," in *Kleinere Schriften by Wilhelm Grimm* vol. 1 (Berlin: Ferdinand Dümmlers Verlagsbuchhandlung, 1881), pp. 154–264. This section refers to various essays by Wilhelm concerned with aspects of epic literature and folk literature. Also: "Achim von Arnim und Jacob Grimm, über Natur- und Kunstpoesie," in *Romantische Wissenschaft*. Series: *Deutsche Literatur, Reihe Romantik,* vol. 13, ed. Paul Kluckhorn (Darmstadt: Wissenschaftlicher Buchverlag, 1966), pp. 185–88.

25. Jacob Grimm, "Gedanken wie sich Sagen zur Poesie und Geschichte verhalten (1808)," in *Kleinere Schriften von Jacob Grimm* 1 (Berlin: Ferdinand Dümmlers Verlagsbuchhandlung, 1889), and "Gedanken über Mythos, Epos, und Geschichte (1813/14)," Ibid., 4.

26. See also Wilhelm Grimm, "Vorrede" *Kinder- und Hausmärchen* (Berlin: Reimer, 1919).

27. Wilhelm Grimm, "Vorrede" in *Kinder- und Hausmärchen* (Berlin: Reimer, 1812).

28. Ibid.

29. Ibid.

30. Ibid.

31. Ibid. The expression: "splintered diamonds strewn about in the grass" refers to the old myths and epics that have been partially lost and forgotten yet that are still fresh and "sparkling" with vitality.

32. Ibid.

33. Ibid.

34. In the 1930s, the National Socialists conveniently omitted Wilhelm Grimm's universal references to the Negroes of Africa, considering such comments "an error on the part of the Grimms."

35. Jacob Grimm, *Circular wegen Aufsammlung der Volkspoesie* (Vienna: 1815). Facsimile edition (with Jacob's handwritten notes on counting the returns of the questionnaire) Ludwig Denecke, ed., postscript by Kurt Ranke (Kassel: Bärenreiter Verlag, 1968). A similar appeal of 1811, titled "Aufforderung an die gesammten Freunde altdeutscher Poesie und Geschichte erlassen" ("Appeal to All Friends of Old German Poetry and History") was not mailed. For a discussion of Grimms' concept of *Naturpoesie* and early folklore collection efforts also consult Reinhold

Steig, *Clemens Brentano und die Brüder Grimm* (Stuttgart: Cotta, 1914), pp. 164–71. See also: *Kleinere Schriften von Jacob Grimm* vol. 7 (Berlin: Ferdinand Dümmlers Verlagsbuchhandlung, 1889).

36. Friedrich von Schiller, *Über naive und sentimentalische Dichtung* (first published as an essay in 1795) (Stuttgart: Reclam, 1966). To some degree, Schiller was inspired by Heinrich Winckelmann's conception of the naive poetry of the Greeks. In his own interpretations of naive and sentimental art, Schiller emphasized the distinction between ancient and sentimental art, Schiller emphasized the distinction between ancient and modern literature that found an echo in the writing of Herder as well as the Brothers Grimm. Schiller already identified here the search for naivete with the search for epic "truth." See also Jacob Grimm, "Rede auf Schiller," *Kleinere Schriften von Jacob Grimm* vol. 1.

37. Manfred Lemmer, *Die Brüder Grimm* (Leipzig: Bibliographisches Institut, 1967), pp. 6–20.

38. For a commentary on Grimms' work on the *Nibelungenlied* and other epic literature, consult Dieter Hennig und Bernhard Lauer, eds., *200 Jahre Brüder Grimm; Dokumente ihres Lebens und Wirkens* (Kassel: Verlag Weber & Weidemeyer, 1985), pp. 411–22.

39. Jacob Grimm, "Uber die Namen des Donners. Eine akademische Abhandlung vorgelesen am 12. Mai 1953" (About the Name of Thunder: A Scholarly Lecture Delivered on May 12, 1853) (Berlin: 1853). This lecture was comparative throughout and not confined to the sphere of Norse mythology. See also Jacob Grimm, *Kleinere Schriften von Jacob Grimm* vol. 2.

40. Jacob Grimm, *Teutonic Mythology* vol. 1, trans. from the 4th ed. with notes and appendix in a separate volume (New York: Dover, 1966), pp. 9–11. The points listed represent the author's summary of points made by Jacob Grimm on these pages.

41. Jacob and Wilhelm Grimm, *Deutsches Wörterbuch* (Berlin: Weidmannsche Buchhandlung and the Wissenschaftliche Akademie, Berlin: 1852–1863). The work was continued after the Brothers Grimm and published in this century under the title *Das Deutsche Wörterbuch von Jacob und Wilhelm Grimm* 33 vols. (Leipzig: Verlag Hirzel, 1960–1971). See also: Hennig and Lauer, eds., pp. 352–53.

42. Wilhelm Grimm, "Selbstbiographie" in Wilhelm Grimm, *Kleinere Schriften von Wilhelm Grimm*, Vol. 1 (Berlin: Ferdinand Dümmlers Verlagsbuchhandlung, 1881), pp. 11–28.

43. "Arbeiten zur Mittellateinischen Philologie und zur Tiersage," cited in Hennig and Lauer, eds., pp. 477–84.

44. Jacob Grimm, *Reinhart Fuchs* (Berlin: Reimer, 1834). Reprint Kassel: Brüder Grimm Gesellschaft, 1962. The original work encompassed 600 pages and represented the result of twenty-five years of research of both brothers, even though Jacob is listed here as the sole editor of the animal epic. See Hennig and Lauer, p. 481.

45. Hennig and Lauer, eds., Ibid. Also: *Kleinere Schriften von Jacob Grimm*, vol. 1.

46. Wilhelm Grimm, "Vorrede," *Kinder- und Hausmärchen*, vol. 1 (Berlin: Reimer, 1919).

47. Jacob Grimm, *Rede auf Wilhelm Grimm und Rede über das Alter*, Hermann Grimm, ed. (Berlin: Druckerei der Königlichen Akademie der Wissenschaften, 1863).

48. Wilhelm Grimm, "Vorrede," *Kinder- und Hausmärchen* (Berlin: Reimer, 1812).

49. Ibid.

50. Wilhelm Grimm, "Über die Märchen," *Kinder- und Hausmärchen* (1819), pp. xxi–liv. The myth interpretation of the folktales was reprinted in the sixth edition of 1850. See also Johannes Bolte und Georg Polivka, *Anmerkungen zu den*

Kinder-u. Hausmärchen der Brüder Grimm, Vol. 5 (Leipzig: Dieterichsche Verlagsbuchhandlung, 1932).

51. Wilhelm Grimm, "Über die Märchen."

52. Ibid.

53. Ibid.

54. Ibid.

55. Jacob Grimm, *Teutonic Mythology* vol. I, pp. 265–77. Jacob's comparisons of dominant themes in Norse myths, myths of other countries, and German folktales is not limited to the examples of "Mother Hulda" and "Sleeping Beauty" but can be found throughout his work, sometimes in the form of brief reference notes. Thus, he concluded his discussion of the three Norse deities Vili, Ve, and Odin, for example, by referring to the Scythian story of the three brothers, Leipoxais, Arpoxais, and Kolaxais, in which a golden plough, yoke, and sword had fallen from heaven, which only the youngest one was able to seize. "The same thing occurs in many *Märchen*." See p. 395. Interesting in this connection is also his observation that sometimes in the *Märchen* sons were born with a star on their forehead, which he interpreted as an indication that they were descendents of older heroes or deities. See p. 391. For a modern comparative study of motifs in myths, legends, and folktales, see Katalin Horn, "Helfer," in *Enzyklopädie des Märchens. Handwörterbuch zur historischen und vergleichenden Erzählforschung,* Kurt Ranke, et al., eds. (Berlin: Walter De Gruyter, 1987), pp. 772–88.

56. Sir James George Frazer, *The New Golden Bough.* Theodor H. Gaster, ed. (New York: The New American Library, 1959), ed. Theodor H. Gaster. This work is based on Sir James George Frazer, *The Golden Bough* 12 vols. (London: Collier Macmillan, Ltd., 1890). Frazer made frequent references to Jacob Grimm's *Deutsche Mythologie (Teutonic Mythology),* yet he did not employ his comparative philological method but rather pursued the course of anthropology.

57. Jacob Grimm, *Teutonic Mythology* vol. 1, p. 266. See also p. 271.

58. Ibid., p. 277.

59. Ibid.

60. Ibid., p. 270.

61. Ibid., p. 411.

62. Ibid., p. 412.

63. Ibid., p. 423.

4. FOLKTALE CHARACTERS

[Mythical and Epic Dimensions]

YTHICAL AND EPIC ORIGINS DETERmined not only the deeper meaning of folktales but also the nature and dimensions of their characters, according to the Brothers Grimm. Folktale characters appeared in many forms, some human, some superhuman, some in the shape of birds, fish, animals, plants, trees, or even stars and stones. Creatures of land, sea, air, and the very firmament above were animated and alive, spoke with a human voice, and had a human soul.[1] They laughed, wept, and took an active part in human thoughts and endeavors, assumed various human shapes, and ultimately returned to their original forms. A clear line of division between the animate and inanimate world did not exist among the folktale characters of long ago, for in one way or another they all shared in God's creation.[2]

Many folktale characters themselves embodied the mythical powers of good and evil. Whereas in myths and epics there had been gods and goddesses, in folktales often these were in human shapes while the magic power of the gods was transferred to heroes or to magic objects. In that sense, magic objects in folktales were mythical too, for they aided the hero in his struggle or protected him in times of danger. Wizards, witches, magic wands, magic potions, and magic spells all had their mythical counterparts in various cultures, and so did the very power capable of transformation used to perform great feats or to escape a foe. As the theme of metamorphosis was deeply rooted in world mythology, explained Wilhelm, so also the smaller magic objects like golden apples, the water of life, or the speaking well represented echoes of myths and epics. One might only recall the *Edda*'s reference to Idun's magic apples, the water of Mimir's well, or the speaking falcon in the myth of Thjalfi to recognize their echoes in folktales.[3]

In his discussions of folktale heroes, Wilhelm Grimm drew upon many comparisons with heroes of German and Germanic myths and epics, especially while identifying forces of good and evil. Among others, he referred to Sigurd and Siegfried, who were kind, courageous, fearless, and strong, while seeking a symbolic power of evil and treachery in Loki and Hagen. Yet, he also sought out for his comparison some heroes of Greek mythology and epic, be they the glorious Odysseus, Perseus, or the infamous Ajax. In facing the human struggle against the forces of evil, he said, folktale heroes everywhere affirmed a folk belief in the universal need for justice.[4]

Like the world of myth and epic, the folktale world was governed by such universal laws of justice. If a protagonist was unable in this life to assert himself by good deeds and strong actions because perhaps he was treacherously slain, justice would follow after his death. Of course, there were some humorous tales to which this rule did not apply, but in most folktales sooner or later justice would reign. If humans did not carry out justice, some spirits might appear in the shape of animals, fish, or birds to set things right. In the folktale "The Juniper Tree," for example, the spirit of the dead mother appeared in the shape of a white bird to avenge the murder of the little boy. Corresponding to the mythical theme of resurrection, a dead soul might rise again from the waters of the river to seek its love or its due revenge. In that sense, the speaking head of the dead horse Fallada in "The Goose Girl" might remind one of Mimir's head in Norse mythology, just as talking ravens in the folktale "The Seven Ravens" might evoke the mythical image of Hugin and Munin (Thought and Memory), the wise birds of Wotan.

In folktales, as in myths and epics, the old God or Eternal Justice most often would come to the aid of those who were innocent. From the mistletoe to the dwarfs working with metals underground, numerous examples show how the folktale world sided with the one who was at a natural disadvantage. This aspect was an integral part of the universal folk belief in justice.[5]

Folktale characters also shared with characters of myths and epics certain exaggerated features that, at least to some degree, set them apart from reality. Often, they were very tall or very small, very clever or very dumb, very fast or very slow, very powerful or very weak. Whatever happened in folktales was not told on a human scale but rather in super-dimensional or diminutive terms. With respect to human emotions and ethics, too, there were no in-between situations. A person was either very sad or very happy, very wicked or very good. Such an exaggeration, both in physical and spiritual terms, added a powerful emotional appeal to folktale characters and plots, because it enhanced with clarity the necessity and probability of any given situation while adding suspense to the folktale's action.

Wilhelm urged modern storytellers and editors of folktales to respect their element of exaggeration, as it represented a significant heritage of epic literature and the inherited folk tradition. An attempt to reduce a folktale character or action to human size by cutting it down or softening some traits meant to deprive the folktale character of its mythical dimensions. In some cases such a reduction might even deprive the story of its emotional appeal and its innate sense of humor.

Another mythical quality of the folktale character was its reflection of naivete and purity, both of which were an integral part of *Naturpoesie* that was also evident in myths and epics. Characters possessing such radiant qualities remained untouched by the turmoil of event, they were immune to temptations and even to a head-on attack by the dark forces of evil. According to Wilhelm Grimm, it was the folktale character of Boots who best represented these qualities. As such, Boots certainly was not a modern invention but had numerous predecessors in myths, epics, folk books, and legends.

In trying to determine the most predominant characters in the common folktale, Wilhelm Grimm called attention to the following types: Boots (Dummling; Dümmling), The Giant and Tom Thumb (der Riese and der Däumling, Daumesdick, or dwarf), the Fool (der Narr, der Lalenbürger, or Schildbürger), the Braggart or Liar (der Aufschneider or Lügner), the Thief (der Dieb), and the Practical Joker or Brother Jolly (Bruder Lustig). [6] He pointed out in his analysis that especially Boots, the Giant, and Tom Thumb bore a strong relationship to characters known in mythology and some older literary sources, whereas the Fool, the Braggart, the Liar, the Thief, and the Practical Joker were more closely related to characters in the German *Volksbücher* (folk books) and other legends dating back to the Middle Ages, including Baron von Münchhausen and Merry Tyll (Till Eulenspiegel).

Boots was the "*Dummling*" or "*Dümmling*" in German folktales, a sort of male Cinderella. His name derived from the word *dumm*, which may mean naive or dumb but not necessarily stupid in the ordinary sense, for he was wise in his own way and usually also successful at the end. He was the abused fellow who was forced to sleep in the ashes or under the stairwell, to scrub the floors, and to do the meanest jobs. Yet even though he was kicked around, despised, ridiculed, and rejected, he never turned angry nor plotted revenge. Suffering silently, he remained kind, loving, patient, and sincere. The evil nature of others simply left his soul untouched.

In focusing on the quality of naivete that marked the character of Boots, Wilhelm compared him to the legendary British Perceval (Parzival), who was also called the *tumbe klare*, suggesting that even though both characters appeared to be dumb, dull, and a bit slow-witted to everyone around, they had in common a certain inner clarity and purity that set them apart from others and also above fate. Unrelated to worldly cleverness, their wisdom consisted of a pure heart and a clear moral vision. Both saw and judged the world only with the heart. Free from greed and vanity, they were unaware of their goodness and also free of calculation involving their own advantages.[7]

Wilhelm compared Boots to the naive character of Rennewart in an old French legend who, in spite of having to render the meanest services in the kitchen, never lost the innocence of his heart. Wilhelm also compared him in his innocence and kindness to the radiant Norse sun god, Balder, who was mortally wounded by the mistletoe yet, according to the *Edda*, had risen after death. There were also parallel traits in the characters of Sigurd and Siegfried, both of whom were remembered in folk tradition as innocent heroes who died at treacherous hands.

For centuries, Boots had always been a favorite folktale character among children and grown-ups, mainly because he was always good-willed, good-humored, and kind. When people and events turned against him, his inner strength and joyous disposition helped him to overcome all adversaries and fate itself. Somehow he always managed to come out on top, for usually a good spirit protected and saved him in a miraculous way. Even if he died in a folktale, his innocence and purity remained triumphant, for he would live on forever in the hearts of listeners.

Why was it Boots and not Ashputtel or Cinderella whom Wilhelm Grimm singled out as a predominant folktale type? Judging by the known variants in the oral and printed variants of related tales in the European folktale tradition, this character type was predominantly male, not female. Still, at his time, Boots was more dominant in folktales than Ashputtel, as far as this type of naive character was concerned. Undoubtedly, this conclusion was based on his definition of the type.

In Wilhelm's view, the "core" of the Boots tale did not involve a change of fortune or status (from rags to riches) but rather the character's retention of purity and naivete. He emphasized in this connection some dominant ethical dimensions derived from the theme of justice. Boots did not passively wait for his good fortune, he wrote, and neither was the happy ending merely a result of good luck. He was successful not because he was lucky, said Wilhelm, but because he deserved it. In such a reversal of fortune the folktale firmly expressed the folk belief in God's reign of justice—that justice would prevail whenever an innocent person was wronged or slain. Such endings ultimately gave proof of man's optimism in the eternal victory of good over evil. By no means was such a character as Boots to be understood as a weak person. By showing him as a naive and altruistic person who accepted poverty and hardships with humility and kindliness, the folktale marked his inner strength.

The same inner strength that marked the character of Boots was also present in Ashputtel. Wilhelm Grimm's analysis shows that good looks, however, were irrelevant to her character, unless the "fair face" and graceful appearance became true mirrors of a beautiful soul. Naive folktale characters became "beautiful" only when they mastered their fate without suffering damage in the purity of their souls. To qualify for the Boots type, it was also not sufficient if a character suffered abuse and ridicule or had to sleep in the ashes. Prerequisites were an inner radiance, a kind and joyous disposition, and a purity of heart. By such prerequisites, Disney's Cinderella would not fit under this type, as she was too pretty and not radiant enough from within. What she altogether lacked was naivete.

The big, clumsy Giant was another significant folktale type. Yet he did not come alone: usually a small fellow outsmarted him at the end. Wilhelm Grimm recognized this folktale character also in variants in Norse mythology and in folktales around the world. His physical prowess, ill matched by his slow wit, made him a rather ridiculous figure, especially when he was outwitted by a little fellow like Tom Thumb called *Däumling*, who was named after the *Daumen* or thumb. Däumling means "little thumb." Folktales involving the Giant as a type usually were humorous in nature, as they underscored his bigness by contrasting him with the physical and mental oppposite, be it a small and clever dwarf, a featherweight Jolly Taylor, a dwarf, or a witty Däumling. As foils, both the Giant and the Däumling were well-liked character types in many countries, for young and old everywhere enjoyed how the little guy teased the big fellow. It was especially humorous when the Giant first bragged about doing some impossible things and then was frightened out of his wits by the littlest creature. In some cases, the little guy, too, was a braggart when he tried to overcome some physical disadvantages in this manner, but unlike the Giant, he was usually successful in resolving difficult problems, simply by putting to work his mind.[8]

Wilhelm referred to a broad range of variants in folktales, myths, and legends as he discussed such stock characters of the Giant and Tom Thumb. In doing so, he was free from all domestic considerations that later so much bewildered educators as they contemplated the ethics of folktale characters and their possible influence on children. Of course, he knew that it was neither well-mannered nor decent of the Däumling to brag, to lie, to cheat, and to steal, but he felt that young and old gladly forgave him his tall tales and misdeeds, because he used them by law of compensation as a means of self-defense. Instead of being angry with him, they laughed at how he tricked his enemy. Besides, he pleased the audience by the ways in which he cleverly managed to live up to some of his most incredible promises. In the interest of folk humor and folk justice, people had come to embrace gladly in folktale characters what in real life they looked upon with contempt, said Wilhelm. This type of humor had been accepted since the Middle Ages, and it still appealed at the present.

[Characters from Folk Books and Legends]

The Brothers Grimm thought that folk books *Volksbücher* or chapbooks) were one of the greatest sources of folktale characters, next to medieval manuscripts and epics. One of the most predominant character types that emerged from the folk books was the Fool. He was the silly character, known in German legends also as the *Lalenbürger* (later called *Schildbürger*). Variants of this type could be found in the legendary Till Eulenspiegel (Merry Tyll), with his fool's cap, as well as in the Seven Swabians. In the German tradition, the female counterpart of the male Fool was dumb little Catherlieschen, who appeared in various folktales. In India, the male fool was known as Paramarta, in Finland as the giant Kullervo (in the epic of *Kalevala*), and in Ireland as Darly Duly.⁹ All of these characters pretended to be innocent while doing the most outrageous and absurd things. They carried out all orders literally yet in the wrong way, either because they didn't know better or because they truly enjoyed playing tricks on people. They appeared to be obedient to the letter of the law, and in spite of it, or because of it, they usually affected the very opposite. The humor arising from the related stories was derived from the stark contrast between what they hoped to achieve and what they actually did achieve. The endings of such fool's tales often held in store a surprise for the listeners: a completely unexpected turn of events that evoked cascades of laughter.

The Fool usually set out to do impossible things from the beginning to the end of the given story. He might climb to the sky on a thin blade of grass and slide down again on a rope made of hay. Wilhelm Grimm referred in this context to the tales numbered 112, 138, and 159 in the *Kinder- und Hausmärchen*, all of which focused on the Fool as the main character. He made reference to the legendary character of Baron von Münchhausen, but in comparative terms also fools in several foreign collections, such as Norway or the Slavic countries. In Serbia the Fool appeared as King Beardless and in Ireland as Daniel O'Rourke. Still, Wilhelm felt that the Fool in some medieval tales of the tenth century emerged more convincingly than in all of these combined. As a genre, the fool's tale was unsurpassed in its humor, and as a character type, the Fool added life and laughter to folklore on the broadest scale.¹⁰

Another folktale character that could be traced back to the tradition of the *Volksbücher* was the Braggart or the Habitual Liar. He lied throughout the entire tale while maintaining the appearance of credibility. Granted, there were also some purely nonsensical tales in which eagles swam, fish flew, and hares skated on ice, yet in contrast with such stories or tales from the "Schlaraffenland," where the laziest man was king, the best liar's tales always retained some element of probability.

Many of the liar's tales depicted characters and used a language that were truly creative. By defying all laws of reason and logic, they had a liberating effect upon the listener's imagination. Wilhelm wrote that in such tales, "the human imagination satisfies the longing to use with full liberty that knife that cuts all restraints."[11] These comments show that Wilhelm Grimm was far ahead of the European didactic age in which educators tried to find a moral purpose in every story they heard or read. Instead of looking for a moral or purpose in folktales, he recognized the need for imaginative stories and emotional freedom. He knew from his studies of medieval literature, as well as from his own love of the oral tradition, that braggarts, liars, and fools had a legitimate place in storytelling. Their humor was needed to bring vigor and warmth to the heart. Remarkable were his insights into the need for nonsense—the upside-down world of tomfoolery in the storytelling tradition—that was not always considered legitimate literature for children in the nineteenth century.

Wilhelm felt that compared with epic literature and some medieval legends and poems, many folktales of the oral tradition gave merely a weak reflection of the humor contained in the printed sources. The *Modus florum* of Ebert's transmission (Vol. 13, 20), for example, or the tales of Merry Tyll (Till Eulenspiegel) and of Baron von Münchhausen were unsurpassed in their vitality and humorous appeal. Some medieval literary tales, such as the old folk-book story of the king who promised his daughter to the one who would tell the biggest lies, were told so vigorously that the best living storyteller would have a hard time competing with them.

He felt it especially remarkable to what degree the medieval German *Volksbücher* had retained traces of the old folk speech that transmitted the humor of the Middle Ages in such a lively, direct, and colloquial way. Compared with the language of the *Volksbücher*, the language of folktales was sometimes a bit pale and repetitious. These observations on the language of the old folk books and their sources for folktale variants give significant insight into the reasons why both Wilhelm and Jacob considered some medieval literary sources worthy of inclusion in their folktale collection.

The Thief was another folktale character who had been well-known in the medieval folk-book tradition. In the *Kinder- und Hausmärchen* this character found its best expression in the tale "The Master Thief." Wilhelm compared this character with the trickster in North American Indian tales, finding him compatible in terms of his cleverness. Folktales depicting the Thief as the main character were meant for enjoyment, not for teaching vices or virtues. The character of the Thief was as timeless and poetic in folktales as he had been in myths and epic poetry. In whatever folk tradition he might appear, he was always in a humorous context.

Finally, there was the character of the Practical Joker, who in German folktales was best known as Brother Jolly (*Bruder Lustig*). He not only fooled people of all ranks and classes but even played jokes on Holy Peter and the Devil himself. Yet instead of receiving his due punishment at the end of the tale, he sometimes reaped the highest reward. In one case, he even managed to gain admittance into Heaven — not because he repented or was forgiven but because he used another clever trick.

Such a seemingly antimoralistic outcome in a folktale, explained Wilhelm, could also be found in certain blasphemous folk comedies. The outcome was always to be understood within a humorous context and not otherwise. Tales of this type were simply not meant to convey a useful lesson. He admitted that a type like Brother Jolly certainly taught us nothing except resourcefulness, cleverness, a bit of cheer. Yet wasn't that enough for a good story? Granted, all that Brother Jolly cared about was having a good time. Yet even if he seldom, if ever, worried about the difference between justice or injustice, good or evil, he was never malicious or ill-natured himself.

Why was Bruder Lustig so well-liked by young and old? He was popular because his tricks were humorous but without malice and because he himself was basically good-hearted. Above all, however, they liked him on account of his freedom of action. Without bothering about possible consequences, he took liberties that no one else did take, disregarding all taboos, rules, or obstacles, jumping over hurdles, and doing exactly what was strictly forbidden. In that sense he resembled Shakespeare's Falstaff, said Wilhelm, who, as a Fool, was as well-liked in Germany and elsewhere as was the German folktale character. Whether Brother Jolly appeared in the company of God or Holy Peter or as the Bear-Skinner (Bärenhäuter), he consistently took advantage of them all and usually escaped punishment and death. Even when he was finally caught, he remained undefeated in his spirit.

Laughter and wit were always on Brother Jolly's side. He possessed neither the innocence of a Perceval nor the purity and inner radiance of Boots, but the audience warmed up to him because of his cheerfulness, self-confidence, defiance, and cleverness. Above all, however, they liked him because of his undefeated optimism and spirit of liberation. All of these qualities, claimed Wilhelm, represented an integral, lovable part of the native tradition and should never be changed.

Wilhelm Grimm accepted the full range of human characters that had been popular in the oral and printed tradition. As he embraced the folktale characters' purity, innocence, and generosity of heart, so he also accepted their nonsense, tomfoolery, thievery, trickery, and practical jokes. Such characters as tricksters, braggarts, liars, fools, and thieves were, of course, no ideal models for character training, yet together with the *Dummling* and the other good-hearted creatures, they expressed the full, vigorous spirit of the folk heritage, both at home and abroad. This was the spirit of *Naturpoesie* that taught children to appreciate life and nature without preaching.

The Grimms thought that cosmetic modifications or added moralities most certainly would detract from the vitality of the characters' poetic substance.[12] They would also undermine the traditional folk humor that belonged to their substance. With all their exaggerated traits, both good and evil, these characters should be accepted just as they were and had been known for ages. He knew, of course, that some persons would raise objections. The Giant, believing in might above right, was often too rude and too crude; Tom Thumb showed off, lied, stole, and used sly tricks; and the Fool, the Braggart, the Liar, the Thief, and Brother Jolly were constantly engaged in outrageous, irreverent, and unlawful things. Yet essentially folktale characters yielded no more than what was already present in nature and life itself and also no more than what could be found in myths and epics. To soften such character traits even mildly meant to go against nature and against life as well, but especially against the folk tradition. It was a different matter, insisted Wilhelm, if one modified some crude expressions contained in the folk books and other medieval sources, for these were unrelated to the major characters or a given tale's substance. In referring to crude expressions Wilhelm had in mind the bawdy and crafty language used in some medieval sources, such as the works of Hans Sachs and Johann Fischart, which in an undiluted form might still shock some readers in our time.

Within the context of their medieval literary studies, both Jacob and Wilhelm Grimm concerned themselves intensively also with animal characters, especially with those related to the verse poem of *Reynard the Fox*. They looked for parallel characters in the oral folk tradition, be they in regard to the slyness of the fox, the viciousness of the wolf, or the gentleness of the dove. When, in cooperation with his brother, Jacob published in 1834 his six-hundred-page edition of *Reinhart Fuchs (Reynard the Fox)*, he observed in his preface that the character types among the animals were modeled upon human types. Yet, they differed from human characters in that they admitted neither change nor development: a fox always remained sly, just as a wolf remained vicious and a dove gentle. The same was true for the animal characters in folktales, where, very much like in fables, some exaggerated human traits remained fixed to them throughout the ages and also throughout proverbs and stock expressions. In an essay "The Nature and Origin of Animal Tales,"[13] Wilhelm emphasized the creatures' unchanging characters, noting that nothing else was said about their sins or virtues that fell outside of these stereotypes. In their actions, the animals usually followed their natural instincts. In spite of many variants and developments throughout history, their characters had essentially remained the same.

Both Brothers Grimm agreed that such characters should not be changed in the editing process either, as they were deeply rooted in epics, myths, and medieval folk literature. They searched in these animal epics, like in folktales, for some traces of *Naturpoesie*. In Wilhelm's essay "On the Mythological Significance of the Wolf,[14] which he published in the *Zeitschrift für deutsches Alterthum* in 1865, he called attention to the unchanging symbolic nature of animal characters that took on an almost fablelike rigidity. He also noted parallel traits based on tradition in fables, folktales, myths, and epics but especially with the animal characters in the fables of Aesop and Babrius.

In an essay that Jacob wrote in 1812 for Friedrich Schlegel's *Deutsches Museum*,[15] he presented his findings of a detailed comparative study of *Reynard the Fox* in various cultures, including France and the Netherlands. In discussing the language and motifs of this epic, he acknowledged its rootedness in various cultures and traditions. Among others, he referred to the Latin version of *Echasis captivi* (1043–1046), the Flemish *Isengrimus* by the poet Nivardus (about 1150), the Old French epic *Roman de renart* (between 1174 and 1250), and the Dutch version of *Van den Vos Renarde* (thirteenth century), comparing them to folktale variants that existed within a widespread naturally grown structure that resembled that of "branches and buds." His German sources, to which he also alluded with this organic simile, were the Middle High German *Reinhart Fuchs* by the poet Heinrich den Glichezare (1182), the Low German *Reynke de Vos* (1498), and some folk-book versions of the Middle Ages.

When Jacob responded to the animal epic in terms of expressing a feeling for home and country by writing: "It appears to me that I still sense in this epic the Germanic fragrance of the forest in the essential qualities and structure of these tales. . . ."[16] He did not think it was possible to tell which of the various epics had preceded the other, as far as the origin of the folktale characters was concerned. Rather, it satisfied his scholarly and personal interest to discover as many European variants of the tale as possible.

In France Jacob had prepared handwritten copies of the Old French *Roman de renard,* of which he attached to his essay a sample of his own vivid translation. In reflecting about the animal characters in this epic, he expressed his surprise at their correspondence with those of a Hessian folktale and also with respect to certain motifs that he had not seen in either the Low German, Flemish, or Dutch versions of the tale. Upon presenting to his readers the need for a more systematic exploration of animal-tale variants in the folk tradition, he appealed for their cooperation to collect for him stories in poetry, song, or prose, in a complete form or in fragments, about such creatures as the fox, the wolf, the bear, the dog, the cock, the sparrow, and the cat. He urged them to search for these in "remotely situated mountain and forest villages, where nature itself has granted something like a refuge even for the old customs and traditions."[17] This appeal was similar to another one, designed on a much broader scale, that Jacob sent out as a *Circular-*

Brief three years later, also with respect to his request for accuracy in the recording of such tales.

It is evident from both Wilhelm's and Jacob's discussion of animal characters that they considered them an integral part of the *Kinder- und Hausmärchen*.

[Humane and Poetic Character Traits]

The Grimms' various essays on folktale characters and types show that they were looking with particular interest for German and Germanic sources in order to obtain the native flavor of traditional folk characters in relation to their naivete and purity, a vigorous folk humor, or the symbolic language of *Naturpoesie*. In this connection, they used both oral and literary sources in complementary terms. In their editing and translation work with medieval literary sources, they were often informed by their oral folktale collections, and in their work with folktales, they were enriched by a close reading of medieval manuscripts and epics. The poetic and symbolic nature of myth and epics was common to both.

The Grimms were delighted whenever they came across a homey flavor in folktales, be it in the image of a native character, in a motif, or in a colloquial expression, one that, as Jacob put it, still carried the "fragrance of the native forest." On the other hand, their search for *Naturpoesie* in folktales was as universal as folk poetry itself, and they never lost sight of international and comparative perspectives. It is this broad-minded attitude that added a humanistic touch to their scholarship, also within the realm of folktales.

The humane aspects of folktales were derived from their rootedness in the reality of the past. They emanated a warm and intimate feeling for the Middle Ages, the countryside, the small towns and villages, and the simple life within them. Viewed from this perspective, folktale characters, too, could be partially considered a reflection of the Middle Ages, for they concerned themselves intimately with the life of the simple folk in forests and valleys as well as of kings, queens, princes, and princesses residing in hilltop castles and landed estates. As Wilhelm saw it, the main heroes and heroines of folktales were mainly descendants of simple peasants, shepherds, charcoal burners, fishermen, shoemakers, blacksmiths, and various other craftspeople, most of whom were engaged in a quiet and steady occupation.

As the folktale dwelt on exaggerated types rather than on unique individuals, it was self-evident that the historical reality of such characters had some definite limitations, but the setting, the structure of society, and the common-folk environment in villages and towns were reflections of reality. This was especially true in regard to the ways in which it mirrored poverty and hardships encountered by many characters at the beginning of the tales. To a large degree, such adverse conditions reflected the life of the common man as it had been throughout the centuries and as it still is to some extent today. Poverty in folktales, like cruelty and war, brought about suffering, tears, and unhappiness. Such conditions reflected the reality of life, and they belonged to the folktale world as they belonged to life because they always had been an integral part of the true experiences of mankind. Reading about such harsh life conditions would make us more humane, as it would induce us to take part in the life of others who were less fortunate than us.

In contrast to epic heroes who often were descendants of gods or kings or both, folktale heroes were mostly simple fellows and young girls of humble origin. They were unspoiled, innocent, and content with the bare necessities for survival. Yet poverty never made them greedy but rather fostered their altruism. They were used to getting along on a crust of bread, asked little or nothing for themselves, and were ready to share what little they had with others. Their ancestry was unknown, they inherited nothing, and they struggled for survival from day to day. Sometimes they were poor young orphans or semi-orphans forced to wander into the wide world to earn their daily bread. The little girl in "The Twelve Months" had to walk into the snowy woods with bare feet, clad only in a paper dress, to search for strawberries in the middle of the winter. The Star Child parted with her shirt and shared her last crust of bread to help a poor stranger; Hansel and Gretel were neither bitter nor angry when their parents deserted them in the dark forest, but understood their plight and prayed for God's help. [18]

Reminders of life's harsh reality were ever-present in folktales, said Wilhelm Grimm. This was so because they represented a truth with which the storytellers themselves had been well familiar. Having customarily come from the peasant class or the lower classes of society, they had experienced first-hand what it meant to be poor, thus projecting their own problems into the stories. Simple folk had always known such hardships, and in the past had not objected to rediscovering them again in the folktale world, because hardships made the stories more credible. Within the context of human hardships, even the character of the stepmother was realistic too, said Wilhelm Grimm. On and off, one could still hear and read reports in the newspapers about child abuse and child desertion that made one shiver. In such cases, it was usually extreme poverty, not an evil nature, that drove some parents to abandon their children — unfortunately even at the present time. In that sense, the stepmother represented some realistic traits derived from adverse conditions of the life of common folk rather than the portrayal of a monster.

But folktales also showed the bright side of life in terms of miracles, rich rewards, and happy endings that transformed all sadness into happiness: a dwarf would help the freezing little girl in the paper dress; a good child would be blessed by a rain of golden coins or a radiant new shirt embroidered with stars; and Hansel and Gretel would return to their father's house with boxes full of money to last them a lifetime. Such transformations of fate were not merely wishful thinking but rather a reflection of common-folk optimism based on their faith in eternal justice. Regardless of how cruel the human condition might be, they believed that justice would come to set things right.

Moreover, a struggle against the harsh reality would set the stage for the folktale character's courageous actions. Thus it was not the background of action but rather a needed challenge that brought out the best in the protagonists. It gave rise to hope, strength, and determination but especially to the power of love, which was capable of overcoming all powers of evil. In that sense, folktales did not present poverty and hardships as permanent conditions, for they were meant to be overcome. In struggling against the odds, folktale characters were blessed with hopeful actions but not crushed by the spirit of resignation. Sometimes they were assisted by helpers and miracles, but mostly they fended for themselves.

Folktale characters often had very little education, yet they were close to nature and possessed a fine intuition, a good common sense, and a remarkable wit. Some were more serious in nature whereas others were more humorous, but they all struggled against the odds and in the end usually overcame all obstacles—even if it meant to outwit the Devil himself. The folktale's portrayal of such a successful struggle showed, said Wilhelm, that the storytellers had a deep faith in the resourcefulness, wit, and ingenuity of the common folk.

Would some traditional folktale characters frighten children listening to the tales? Wilhelm did not think so. He emphasized that the reflection of adverse conditions of life would lead children to a strong feeling of empathy for those who were lonely, frightened, and abused and thus would humanize children in the best sense of the word. Such an effect could also be expected from listening to folktales involving evil stepmothers. In this connection, he referred to a legend of *Stiefmütterchen* (Little Stepmother),[19] which is the German name for the pansy. The legend esssentially called attention to the plight of poor children by relating the story that the yellow and purple flower petals were the chairs for the mother's real children, while the small green leaves supporting the flower petals were the seats of the deprived children who had no chairs. What did this legend mean? Wilhelm thought that it reminded children of the lot of unfortunate creatures. Some children had no mother and were so poor that they didn't even have a chair to sit upon. The young listeners would realize by themselves, he thought, that these poor children did not deserve such a fate, and upon experiencing such a realization, they would extend to the children a feeling of warm sympathy in their prayers.

Wilhelm's views on reality undoubtedly reflected the Romantic vision of the child. With his own kindness he projected nothing but kindness

into others, always believing that good would prevail.[20] It is important to realize his own innocent and naive perspective on the world
that was far removed from the perspective of gore and evil of which
some critics are still accusing him in our time. His detached mythical
view of the subject seemed to tame the dark and threatening forces
in folktales, for he considered them merely an antithesis to the powers
of love, goodness, empathy, and justice. Who but Wilhelm Grimm
would have thought that the characters of a dragon or an evil stepmother were needed to arouse the listener's love and empathy for the
suppressed? In this context, the unpleasant and potentially fearful aspects
of folktale characters were not merely reflections of folk reality; they
served to develop the child's sensitivity and love for others. The symbolic and literary interpretations of Max Lüthi, the aesthetic views of
Hermann Bausinger, and the psychological views of Bruno Bettelheim[21]
are not so very far removed from such thoughts, although they are based
on different premises and also follow different lines of argumentation.

Wilhelm not only addressed with his discussion questions of ethics
and folklore in general but he also anticipated the needs of the child.
Children exposed to such harsh characters and events would not at
all feel depressed and dejected, he wrote, but liberated and free, for
in the folktale hero's struggle against evil they would rediscover in their
own soul a spark of warmth and affection for those who suffered or
were lost or abandoned. These were the gentle and liberating forces
of folktales that had a positive effect upon the child's soul. Folktales
had a strange yet fascinating way of blending history with the present
conditions of simple life, he observed, and, even more so, of transform-
ing the world of reality by the power of the soul.

To the child, the folktale world was really a gentle world, he said,
for if it seemed that "might was right" and that evil powers gained the
upper hand, one should wait for the power of love and magic to take
their effect. Folktales also had frail and gentle characters, those who
merely smiled and transformed the world. These were the ones who
won the greatest battles. The folktale's most touching moments were
the ones that appealed to the heart. It was the greatest miracle of all
when the innocent laughter of a frail little princess banished an evil
spell or when a simple truth spoken by a small child destroyed a mighty
castle of falsehood and pretense. A single tear, wept in sympathy for
a suffering creature or human being, transformed a fearful monster
into a loving prince. Such was the power of love that it changed the
world. In this gentle, humanizing touch lay embedded the true magic
of the folktale. Such thoughts, he said, were no idle dreams of an
idealist. Feelings were as much a reality as the world outside, and
the feelings that a child experienced in listening to a story were a
powerful reality indeed.

A most humane aspect of the folktale was its power to console. In
the folktale world no harsh reality would ever be present without its

counterpart: hope, brotherly love, pity, empathy, or simple sharing. When, after a long and lonesome walk through the dark forest, Hansel comforted Gretel and both sent their prayers to God, all fear was wiped away and the listeners glowed in a feeling of warmth and affection. There was also faith in God, who would help those asking for his support, provided their hearts were innocent and pure. It was this faith that dominated the impression that a child would gain from a folktale, not the image of the harsh and cruel life conditions affecting the common man. As the protagonists struggled toward freedom, their love and resourcefulness would dominate in the end and push back the harsh reality with its powers of evil. In the focus of attention was the struggle itself, led on by hope. In that sense, folktales had much to offer to make the world more gentle and more humane.[22]

Sometimes folktale characters would only partially succeed in gaining such a freedom. In such a case, a character might discover to his dismay that he had retained the wing of a swan instead of an arm or that he had lost an eye along with his tears. Such elements were not arbitrary inventions of individual storytellers, claimed Wilhelm, but expressed symbolically traditional images revealing the loss of inner purity or the loss of a truth. Their origin could be traced back to myths and epics, where human symbols abounded within a sphere of vivid images of this kind. Such folktale symbols were as true to life as were the images of reality contained in others. No effort was needed through sermons or long explanations to convey their meaning to the child, because they spoke a language of true human experience that appealed directly to the heart.

The most significant thing that folktales had to offer, said Wilhelm, was that they taught us about ourselves, our inner resources, altruism, kindness, empathy, and genuine strength. This, too, was a reality, as it focused on the hidden powers of all humane aspects in this world that lay embedded in our souls. The folktale helped us to rediscover it and put it to work. There was poetic justice in the tale in which the *Dummling* gained at the end all of the fortunes, for he had suffered from abuse and ridicule. Yet it was more than that, said Wilhelm, namely "a lesson in poetry itself," for it spoke of the power of purity, goodness, truth, innocence, compassion, and love. Wherever such powers were evident, there was sunshine, there was *Naturpoesie.*

Finally, Wilhelm warned readers not to make folktale characters the object of a lesson or a moralistic example. Folktales never preached. Lessons derived from folktales were lessons in poetry, not in morality.[23] Even though this poetry had not been the folktale's original purpose and the folktale was not told because of it, poetry was its natural attribute and the secret of its universal appeal. It developed from the folktale "as a fruit grows from a healthy blossom—without any additions" by a storyteller. The vivid images and symbols of this poetry needed no explanation, as the listening child would instantly recognize in them his own experiences, his compassion for others, or his own true self and his soul. Such a discovery gave the reader a feeling of elation while making him rejoice in his own better self and, above all, in his newly won relationship with others. In reading folktales, he would cast off the bondages of selfishness and falsehood and commit himself to the spirit of light, truth, and freedom.

NOTES

1. Jacob and Wilhelm Grimm, *Kinder- und Hausmärchen* (Berlin: Reimer, 1812). Preface.

2. The Grimms shared such Romantic thoughts with other German Romantic writers. These ideas were especially close to the philosophy of Friedrich W. J. Schelling. See Burton Feldmann and Robert D. Richardson, eds., *The Rise of Modern Mythology: 1680–1860* (Bloomington, Indiana: Indiana University Press, 1972), pp. 302–05.

3. Wilhelm Grimm, "Über das Wesen der Märchen," in *Kinder- und Hausmärchen*, 2d ed. (Berlin: Reimer, 1819), Introduction, pp. xxi–liv. The analysis of Wilhelm's ideas in relation to folktales is based on the unabridged text of his essay in the 1819 edition.

4. Wilhelm Grimm, "Über das Wesen der Märchen," in Gustav Hinrichs, ed. *Kleinere Schriften von Wilhelm Grimm* Vol. I (Berlin: Ferdinand Dümmlers Verlagsbuchhandlung, 1881), pp. 344–48; 350–51. For the reader's convenience, page references are given to the shorter version of this essay that is more readily available in Hinrich's edition.

5. Ibid., pp. 332. (See Wilhelm's notes on this account.)

6. Ibid., pp. 355–587.

7. Ibid.

8. Ibid., p. 335.

9. These detailed comparisons appear only in the original 1819 edition of the *Kinder- und Hausmärchen* but not in Hinrich's abridged versions of the introductory essays in *Kleinere Schriften*.

10. For a comprehensive discussion of German *Volksbücher* and their relevance to an understanding of the Grimms' concept of *Naturpoesie*, see Max Lüthi, "Europäische Volksliteratur" in Albert Schaefer, ed., *Weltliteratur und Volksliteratur* (Munich, Beck, 1972), pp. 55–80.

11. Wilhelm Girmm, "Über das Wesen der Märchen."

12. In the preface to the same edition Wilhelm wrote his famous words about an education in *Naturpoesie* (nature or folk poetry), which frequently have been mistranslated or misinterpreted as a didactic message: "*Wir wollten indes durch unsere Sammlung nicht bloss der Geschichte der Poesie einen Dienst erweisen, es war zugleich Absicht dass die Poesie selbst, die darin lebendig ist, wirke: erfreue, wen sie erfreuen kann, und darum auch, dass es ein eigentliches Erziehungsbuch daraus werde.*" ("We wish to offer with our collection not only a service to the history of poetry but simultaneously the intention to make effective the poetry itself that is alive within it: to delight those who are capable of enjoying it. It is for this reason that it (the *Kinder- und Hausmärchen*) should become a true book of education."

13. Wilhelm Grimm, "Über das Wesen und den Ursprung der Tierfabeln" and "Tierfabeln bei den Meistersingern," in Hinrichs, ed. *Kleinere Schriften von Wilhelm*

Grimm vol. 4 (1887), and Wilhelm Grimm, "Die mythische Bedeutung des Wolfes," Ibid. This essay was first published in Grimms' journal *Altdeutsche Wälder* (1813–1816). See also Jacob Grimm, *Reinhart Fuchs* (Berlin: Reimer, 1834).

14. See Dieter Hennig and Berhard Lauer, eds. *Die Brüder Grimm. Dokumente ihres Lebens und Wirkens* (Kassel: Verlag Weber & Weidemeyer, 1986), especially pp. 475–84 in reference to various works by the Brothers Grimm pertaining to "Reinhart Fuchs" (also called Reineke Fuchs or Reynke de Vos in fables) and related animal fables. The sources listed and discussed in this work were prepared on the basis of exhibits in the Museum Fridericianum in Kassel, as well as in Berlin and Hanau, between 1985 and 1986.

15. Jacob Grimm, "Über das Wesen der Tierfabel," *Aus den Kleineren Schriften von Jacob Grimm; Die Schriften der Brüder Grimm in einer Auswahl für das deutsche Volk* (Berlin: Meijer & Jessen, 1911), pp. 343–63.

16. Ibid.

17. Jacob Grimm, "Reinhart Fuchs" *Kleinere Schriften von Jacob Grimm* vol. 4 (Berlin: Dümmler, 1869), pp. 53–63.

18. Hennig and Lauer, eds., p. 333.

19. Ibid., pp. 334–35.

20. Hermann Grimm, "Jacob und Wilhelm Grimm," in *Literatur* trans. Sarah Adams (Boston: Cupples, Upham & Company, Publ., 1886), pp. 254–85.

21. The ideas of these critics and others are discussed in Chapter 10.

22. Hennig and Lauer, eds., p. 335.

23. Ibid., pp. 336–37.

5. THE ORIGIN OF MYTHS AND FOLKTALES

[Indo-European and Comparative Theories]

HE BROTHERS GRIMM BELIEVED that folktales were old, even though younger than myths and epics, and that their language gave evidence of the naive and poetic spirit of ancient man. Like Herder, they perceived a definite advantage in older languages and dialects, because in their vivid and concrete expressions they adhered more closely to the folk reality, the "core" of tradition. The Grimms' approaches differed, yet their conclusions were similar. Wilhelm examined the old languages in relation to myths, folktales, and epic literature, whereas Jacob analyzed them in relation to medieval laws and customs and also within the broader framework of his historical and comparative approach to grammar. Both praised the strong rhythm, natural imagery, simplicity, directness, and symbolic force of the old languages.

In principle, the Brothers Grimm subscribed to the Indo-European language theory that had been developed by the Danish linguist Rasmus Christian Rask. In his Anglo-Saxon and Icelandic grammars, Rask had produced some new insights into interrelationships of Indo-European languages that strongly influenced both brothers. This theory derived its name from the Indo-European family of languages that was assumed to have originated in the area between India and Europe, and it embraced the following major language groups: Anatolian, Baltic, Celtic, Germanic, Greek, Indo-Iranian, Italic, Slavic or Slavonic, Thraco-Illyrian, Thraco-Phrygian, and Tokharonian (West China).[1] Rask and Jacob Grimm assumed that these languages were most closely related within their many subgroups, sharing a common vocabulary and grammar. Jacob perceived such relationships especially in personal nouns denoting kinship (mother, father, etc.) but also in numerals and body parts as well as in myths, heroic legends, and folktales.

Jacob Grimm was the first scholar who applied the Indo-European languages theory to a comparative study of folklore. He explained variants of myths and folktales in different cultures on the basis of common language roots, concluding that similarities in major themes and characters were more likely to occur wherever the languages were closely related. In his preface to *Deutsche Mythologie* (Teutonic Mythology),[2] he pronounced as his main goal the study of certain affinities between the folklore of Germany and the North European countries, mainly since the proximity in speech patterns and folk beliefs in these countries warranted such an approach, for over time it had produced close variants in myths and folktales.

Jacob was also a pioneer in terms of relating myth and folktale variants to medieval laws, customs, rituals, and folk beliefs, believing that language provided clues to deeper meanings that lay embedded in tradition. In comparing, for example, some striking correspondences among the Old High German *muspilli*, Old Saxon *mudspelli* and the Eddic *muspell*,[3] he concluded that in spite of minor variations, the respective cultures had shared a conception of fate and heroic action. Following linguistic clues, he traced parallel and divergent themes in myths, folktales, and legends while drawing upon a comparison of Gothic, Frankish, and Norse family names as well as on names of plants and constellations.

Jacob's historical and comparative approach to grammar demanded a documentation based on linguistic evidence, which he was able to supply on the basis of his knowledge of such languages as Burgundian, Gothic, Vandalic, Old Norse, Danish, Faeroese, Icelandic, Norwegian, Swedish, Dutch, English and Flemish. It was logical to turn to the documents in these languages for comparative studies. Because he was fluent in Danish, Swedish, English, Norwegian, and Icelandic, he had easy access to oral and printed sources belonging to his closest "relatives" within the Indo-Germanic language family. His studies of German folktales and Norse mythology were also greatly enhanced by his intimate acquaintance with numerous German dialects, including Frisian and several variations of Low German.[4]

From a professional linguistic point of view he felt that both the language and the heritage of his ancestors had been greatly underrated in their importance. Here was an untapped treasure of research materials that promised to give answers to questions of etymology and cultural development that, in his view, had worldwide implications. Yet by no means did he confine himself exclusively to the sphere of the Germanic North but frequently sought out parallels in the languages and folk traditions of other cultures within the Indo-European sphere. Such cross-cultural approaches were particularly evident in Jacob Grimm's comparative mythology, *Deutsche Mythologie* (Teutonic Mythology), a multivolume work dedicated to a study of variants in myths, folktales, rituals, and folk beliefs of related cultures and language groups. In drawing upon a wide range of parallels in Slavic, Greek, Egyptian, and Hindu mythology, he often cited sources that he translated himself. His fascination with the epic of *The Song of Igor*, for example, arose from his earlier efforts of related translations, and the same was true for his analysis of French, Spanish, and Celtic songs and tales and those of the *Kalevala*. His broad comparative approach strongly influenced Thomas Keightley in Ireland and later Sir James Frazer in England to pursue comparative folklore studied on a world-wide scale.[5]

Acknowledging certain mutual influences of the Nordic and Christian religion, Jacob contended that some Nordic gods and elves had been transformed into Christian saints, angels, or devils while such Christian saints as Mother Mary could still be traced in the German folktale character of Mother Hulda (Berhta). Occasionally, he discovered remnants of the old faith in colloquial speech and even in nursery rhymes and folk songs. In this connection, he usually expressed his anger at the Christian missionaries who had suppressed the early religion, thus destroying many valuable documents pertaining to language, customs, and what they had considered a "barbaric heathen faith." In his view, the Nordic faith had not been barbaric at all but deserved to be measured by its unique inherited values. Why should Germans turn to Greece and Rome if they had their own epic and mythological heritage? The dignity that he granted to other nations in searching out their folk heritage he also granted to his own.[6]

Some critics have perceived a sign of patriotism or nationalism in such observations as well as in Jacob's studies of Nordic Germanic languages and folk traditions. Jacob Grimm differed substantially in this regard from the Nazis, whose "Aryan theory" narrowed the broad comparative perspective to Nordic Germanic and racial concepts tainted by a "*Volkish*" ideology. Unlike the Nazis a century later, he interpreted the word "Nordic" in linguistic terms that included value-free comparisons with other languages, cultures, and folk traditions. Racial and ethnic concepts were alien to his way of thinking. Like Rask, he understood the Indo-European theory in linguistic terms.[7]

Neither was Jacob dogmatic in his approach to the Indo-European language theory. He also considered other theories and approaches to the study of folk traditions. He even humbly accepted the limitations of his own scientific method. In a speech at a Germanistics Conference in the 1840s, he referred to the linguistic-historical method itself as an "inexact science"[8] while making no claims for having found the ultimate truth. He stated, for example, that each dialect, like each folktale variant, expressed only an approximation of the truth and should be respected in its own right. He thought that it was often difficult, if not impossible, to decide which dialects or folktale variants were the best, for there were no standards of value judgments in absolute terms. Scholars had not yet invented scientific instruments by which to measure language and folklore objectively, he observed, and therefore tolerance toward various forms of folk traditions, be it in language or *Naturpoesie*, would be the wisest policy.

As exacting as Jacob was in his demand for linguistic documentation, he kept an open mind also for ideas and theories that differed from his own, always showing a readiness to debate them in a truly democratic spirit. When Theodore Benfey challenged his Indo-European theory by insisting that all myths had originated in India, Jacob did not defy him but rather granted him a share of the "truth" by personally recommending him for membership in the Berlin Academy of Sciences, a gesture that spoke for his generosity and professional fairness.[9]

Wilhelm, too, was open-minded in regard to theories about the nature and origin of folktales and languages, perhaps even more so than Jacob, as he felt less restricted than his brother by the need for linguistic evidence. Like Jacob, he pointed out certain limitations of the Indo-European theory in regard to broader comparative studies. He thought it made sense to explain the mutual influences of folktales in countries that shared common borders but not where the countries or cultures in question were far remote from each other in time and space. Where cultures shared neither historical roots nor geographical proximity, the language theory, in Wilhelm's view, simply did not apply. In the preface to the 1819 edition of the *Kinder- und Hausmärchen*, Wilhelm bluntly stated that actually no one could prove where a given folktale had originated. Who could tell whether it had come from Hesse and then moved to Serbia or if it had come from Serbia and then moved to Hesse? Similar ambiguities existed in regard to tales shared by unconnected German religions and landscapes. Who could tell with certainty from what religions a tale or dialect had originally come and what direction an influence had taken? In such cases, he even questioned the concept of "influence" itself.

[Universal Folktale Origins]

Wilhelm was more inclined to explain folktale origins and variants in universal terms. In pondering the question of what elements in folktales were significant enough to account for variants, he pointed to the so-called stable elements that made up the substance of the tales,[10] namely the basic plots, themes, and characters. Changes occurring with respect to language often were so drastic that they led to basic differences rather than to variants. He also called such stable elements *"die Sache"* (the thing or substance), which he considered universal. This applied, for example, to basic challenges and problem solutions in folktales—themes that recurred in all folktales around the world. While the wording, names, subthemes, minor plot elements, and individual motifs usually differed drastically from one culture to the next, the folktale substance was stable. In this connection, language was the least reliable element in determining a variant, with the exception of certain proverbial or formulaic expressions that occurred in many parallel forms in different cultures.

Such insights into the nature of variants led Wilhelm to ponder the question of how variants in countries far remote from each other and outside of the Indo-European sphere of influence might have been created. He came to the conclusion that in cases where linguistic, geographical, and historical theories didn't apply, one had to look for another phenomenon that he called simply "mysterious." He suggested that such variants, folktales, and myths had created themselves independently from each other (*unabhängig voneinander*). Rather than speculating how exactly such spontaneous creations of variants might have occurred, he preferred to conclude cautiously that the origins of folktale variants were shrouded in the mist of history and that the exact route influence was "like something unexplorable and mysterious that remained hidden in darkness" (*"Es bleibt wie etwas Unerforschliches und Geheimnisreiches in der Dunkelheit zurück"*).[11] His use of the word "*Unerforschliches*" (unexplorable)—not "*Unerforschtes*" (unexplored)—implies that he thought it impossible to find a rational answer for this riddle. He suggested that under the circumstances it might be wise just to "speculate" rather than to insist on a definite answer. In the meantime, one should enjoy the very existence of variants as proof of the universal aspects of folklore that existed everywhere around the world. He added that he had listed numerous variants in the notes to the *Kinder- und Hausmärchen* because they might bring readers a little closer to the truth.

While refusing to commit himself to a single theory of folktale origins, Wilhelm did affirm his belief in the oral transmission of folktales throughout history. He considered the existence of variants in itself proof of oral transmission because it represented a sure sign of man's shared experience with a primeval poetry (*Urpoesie*). Variants showed that similar human conditions had existed everywhere. The folktale language, too, was universal in terms of expressing early man's natural experiences and poetic thought. Its closeness to nature and spirit of naivete were proof of what Herder had called the "one humanity of man."

Wilhelm's universal theory regarding the origin and dissemination of folktale variants resembles that of the anthropologist Andrew Lang around the turn of the century, although it had little to do with "savage customs and traditions" as he understood it. Unlike Lang, who defended his theory fanatically against others proposed by Max Müller and his followers,[12] Wilhelm had no problems with reconciling opposing points of view. If he had lived long enough to witness the battle that ensured between the defenders of the *polygenesis* theory or the *monogenesis* theory, he might have been the perfect mediator, finding some positive aspects in each. Such an inclination toward compromise solutions was already evident in Wilhelm's 1822 preface to the third volume of the *Kinder- und Hausmärchen*, where he cited side by side a great number of diverse opinions on folktales, from Plato to Goethe.[13] Neither the pattern in which he organized these quotations nor the framework of his essay gave a hint at the viewpoint that he personally favored. By listing them chronologically, he left it entirely to the readers to form their own opinion on the subject.

The open-minded attitude that both Jacob and Wilhelm showed in regard to the origin and nature of folktales contradicts the widely held belief that the Grimms had pursued one-sidedly the Indo-European theory. Jacob's declaration that linguistics was far from an objective science further shows his humility as a scholar.

[The Art and Age of Storytelling]

Unlike many other European linguists of his time, Jacob rejected an authoritarian, corrective attitude toward language and grammar, advocating instead a comparative historical study of language growth and development. He characterized such an approach as *"Gewaltlosigkeit"*[14] (lack of force or coercion) as it was not prescriptive but descriptive in nature.

He did base his historical and descriptive analysis of language on the theories of Rask, yet he went beyond Rask's approach by applying them not only to grammar but also to folklore, the *Naturpoesie* of the ancient nations. In myths, legends, epics, folktales, songs, proverbs, sayings, rhymes, riddles, folk songs, ancient laws, customs, and superstitions he noted that laws governing their mutations corresponded to those that he had observed in relation to language. In that sense, he perceived in the folklore collection more than mere remnants of the past, namely evidence of an evolution of language and concepts shared by ancient cultures. Their languages, tales, and folk beliefs alike reflected the animated worldview of the simple, naive life everywhere, the *Naturpoesie* of the nations.

Wilhelm basically shared his brother's linguistic theories, yet while focusing less on the close relationship between the evolution of language and that of folk literature, he concentrated his efforts more on recurring motifs and themes in folk literature in various cultures, including not only folktales, myths, and legends but also the living tradition of children's games and customs, their songs and sayings.

The most innovative aspect of Jacob's language theory was that it emphasized the significance of a time prior to the age of language formation, which he called the "realm beyond words." In that age, long before the age of storytelling, he perceived the "core" of human experience, the "historical reality" or "folk reality." In his view, that age contained the spiritual truth of tradition on the basis of which folktales were later formed. As such, it harbored the most stable and permanent element of tradition, the very soil and substance that later gave rise to stories through words and music. This source of tradition contained the substance of myths and folktales from which storytellers at a later time absorbed the essential truth of the tales, as if it were a "wellspring" of words.

Jacob Grimm's belief in a "core" of tradition or a "realm beyond words" implied that there was no single "primeval tale" or *Urmärchen* out there somewhere which storytellers merely imitated or copied. Rather, it suggested that several good traditional storytellers might come up with similar "true" stories, none of which was identical with the others. According to Jacob's theory, the exact wording of a particular myth or folktale was of secondary importance in comparison with its traditional substance. Only a given storyteller's proximity (*Annäherung*) to the core of the tale would determine if the story was loyal to tradition or not. The language of a given tale itself was subject to change, as was language itself. Both would evolve in natural variations not only over time but also from one storyteller to another.

The Grimms defined the core or substance of tradition as the basic plots, themes, and characters of folktales and myths. These they considered the relatively stable elements in folktales that experienced only minor variations. With respect to language, the only stable elements were certain recurring archaic patterns that one might find in proverbial expressions, beginning or closing formulas, and traditional rhymes or chants within the folk narratives. As the rest was subject to change, one should look primarily to the stable elements for clues to the approximate age and authenticity of a given tale.

By insisting that all storytelling was an *approximation of the truth*[15] but not the truth itself, Jacob affirmed that the original story idea was intangible because it lay hidden in the "mist of history," the folk reality, or the "core." He did grant that some gifted storytellers might succeed in "forming a tight ring around the core," as he put it, thus coming very close to the original story idea, yet more likely several storytellers might come up with similar versions, all of which were based on approximations. In this way, variants were born, and several variants combined together might come closer to the truth of the tale than one alone. Like each dialect in a given language, each variant contained a part of the truth, but individually none was ever capable of touching the absolute core of a tale.

Since according to Jacob's theory, the core or truth of folktales lay hidden in the story, in the mist of historical reality, much depended upon a storyteller's intuitive power of vision to approach it as closely as possible. No single storyteller could possibly be in possession of the entire truth regarding a given story. Inevitably, some storytellers were more gifted than other in grasping the core, yet none would ever grasp it entirely.[17]

Jacob Grimm went one step further by insisting that the "folk reality" of a given tale determined language itself. Therefore, he insisted that as soon as storytellers had grasped the essential core of a tale, they should cling to it as to a holy truth, without altering the basic plots, themes, or characters. He granted them a certain liberty in altering individual expressions by choosing their own words, as long as they did not embellish the tale with personal fantasies that distracted from the tale's substance and deviated from its core.

Jacob Grimm's theory was refreshingly original yet also controversial at the time, especially with respect to the idea that popular traditions preceded the formation of language, which implied that the historical reality, too, had preceded the word and story. Linguists at his time defended the notion that words had preceded reality and history, and not the other way around. Thinking that Jacob did not attach the primary importance to language that it deserved, they attacked his theory. Jacob defied his colleagues by maintaining that in regard to the history of language and the concept of storytelling, they had overemphasized the importance of words, syntax, and the aesthetic rules.[18]

It appears paradoxical that a researcher who spent more than thirty years of his life deciphering the etymology of words and who was so insistent on praising the virtues of the older language ultimately attached only secondary importance to words themselves. Jacob defended his theory by stating that language was important to the degree that it did express the life and thought of the people who had created it, be it in relation to early history, religion, or folklore. Language gave significant clues for studying a given culture and its folklore within the context of history—yet it was no more than a tool or a means to another end. In that sense, he placed history, the folk reality, and also the story idea above language itself. "It is more important to interpret the word from the legend," he wrote "than to interpret the legend from the word." He openly rejected a "clinging to words" in a pedantic way, for fear such a practice would lead to an inevitable separation of words from the core or substance of traditional tales.

Three stages of language development could be seen throughout history, observed Jacob.[19] All of these had supposedly emerged after the nonverbal age characterizing the core of folk reality. The first stage was that of the *Ursprache* (primeval or original language.) Language at that time had been immensely alive, as people had been in close contact with nature and the folk reality. Being content with naming things in their immediate environment, they had communicated primarily by means of nouns, concrete nouns that expressed immediate sense impressions gained from contact with nature. For that reason, the older nouns in many languages still appealed to the senses, with their clear references to sight, sound, smell, touch, and taste. At that time, language captured the right words directly from sense experience in naming things, and there was nothing abstract about them.

The evolution of man's lifestyle and the hierarchy in real life had also shaped a certain evolution in the hierarchy among the words, claimed Jacob. Speaking directly from his immediate life experience and perception of reality in naming animals, trees, plants, earth, stones, metals, water, air, and light, the nouns, in turn, revealed his attitude about them and their relative importance at a given stage of civilization. He wrote that in the first stage of language development the male noun had been predominant, mainly because the male had played a predominant role in primitive society. Correspondingly, female and neuter nouns then appeared less frequently because females and children had then played a less significant role in real life.

Jacob did not think that the first stage of language development was especially poetic or sophisticated. It was close to nature, sensual, rhythmic, melodious, and far from being monotonous or simplistic, but its main reliance on nouns for naming things allowed only for a very simple system of grammar. Among the melodious sounds, vowels had been predominant, which corresponded to the role of music in older societies. If older languages in general were more melodious than the modern languages, this was because early speech had consisted of song. In principle, Jacob admired the language at the first stage of development yet thought that it was altogether too functional to give rise to creative stories.

The Grimms placed the beginnings of folk poetry into the second stage, with the discovery of the active verb. Wilhelm, too, perceived in the verb the key element for the creation of *Naturpoesie*. In this point they differed from Herder, who had characterized the first stage of language development as the most poetic age, or the age of *Urpoesie* primeval poetry). The Grimms thought that language at the second stage was still very close to nature, reflecting the naive world view of natural man by vivid, concrete, and melodious expression, yet in addition, it had acquired a greater coherence of thought, a richer vocabulary, and a more complex grammatical structure.

Man's greatest discovery in the second stage of language development was the verb, as it allowed him a greater subtlety of expression. Language was no longer a simple tool of naming things but it became capable of revealing inner relationships and deeper reflections, touching upon feelings, emotions, and the creative imagination. With the simultaneous birth of imagination and poetic thought arose a deep joy in storytelling. He called it the age of *Naturpoesie* (nature poetry), the stage that gave life to folk poetry. It was only now that epics, myths, folktales, and legends were born, of which so many had survived to the present day. The age of *Naturpoesie* was the age of storytelling in its most vital form.

Then came the third stage, which Jacob called the age of reason and abstraction. As language grew more complex, it also lost its vitality and became removed from nature and the immediate sense experience. As storytellers became more sophisticated, they got entangled in a maze of words and embellishments that obstructed their vision. On the surface this stage appeared to represent progress in language development because it showed a growing capacity for more eloquent and refined expressions. Yet paradoxically, what it gained in terms of articulation it lost in terms of proximity to the core of tradition. Neither newly coined words nor greater clarity or logic could make up for its loss of visionary quality and vitality.

What were the symptoms of language decay? Jacob perceived these as the loss of active verbs and the increase of abstract nouns. Abstractions, circumscriptions, elaborations, and explanations were all signs of a weakening creative power of language and also signs of a decline in the quality of traditional storytelling.[20] The more self-conscious storytellers had become and the more they strove for effect, the more they lost touch with the spirit of naivete and the power to convince. Partially, their language became abstract, pale, monotonous, and tired because it imitated others or fashionable trends rather than turning to the core of tradition and the primary source of inspiration. Sometimes it captured an audience momentarily, yet lacking vision and credibility it was soon forgotten. Gone was the great age of poetic perception and with it the storyteller's power to convince. Only very few tellers of tales preserved the visionary power of the second age of means of maintaining contact with the core.

[Language Dynamics and Loyalty to Tradition]

Jacob's theory of language dynamics holds the key to an understanding of what he meant by a balance between loyalty to tradition and the art of paraphrasing. Language dynamics meant that language had a dynamics of its own. Drawing its initial inspiration from the core of reality, tradition and history, it developed an energy from within itself that contributed substantially to the perpetuation of a folk tradition.

In his essay "Die Geschichte der deutschen Sprache" ("The History of the German Language")[21] he developed the *Pendeltheorie* (pendulum theory) that substantiated the concept of a dynamic interaction of language and reality. He maintained that at the very moment when traditional storytellers re-created traditional tales by communicating them orally, they gave them a new force of life. He called the creative process at work in traditional storyteller's language the process of *Eigendynamik* (self-dynamics). Over time, the *Eigendynamik* of a given tale interacted with the core of the tale, thus creating what he called "language dynamics" within a dialectical process. This interaction or dialectical process was mainly responsible for the development of tale variants. None of the tale variants were identical with the core of the tale, but each one in its own way represented an approximation of the truth.

The pendulum theory implied that the life and perpetuation of folktales depended as much on the core of the folk tradition as they did on the creative words of an inspired storyteller. If storytellers drew their tales in proximity to the wellspring of tradition, their tales were by no means fixed but fluid and flexible. Being inspired by the core, they might tell the tales in variations, although never arbitrarily, as they were bound by tradition. Yet this process was not one-sided, because the language of storytellers interacted with the core.

Jacob believed in the need for a storyteller's creativity, which he called a "spirited retelling" of the tales. Such an interaction was needed to keep the folktale alive. While strongly objecting to the traditional storytellers' license to embellish the tales or to change them at will, he insisted that they "recreate" the tales "from within." The *Eigendynamik* of language would produce variants in the course of time.

What, then, were the attributes that the Grimms ascribed to the best traditional storytellers? Jacob felt that ideally they would reach for the core of the folktale in an intuitive yet concentrated way, drawing as closely as possible to its truth within the folk reality. At the same time, however, they would try to use a language that was traditional without being imitative and sterile. While drawing upon the wellspring of words to express the folktales in a truthful yet lively and spirited way, they would give life and dynamics to an old story. Good storytellers were close to nature and tradition and were gifted by the power of intuition and a spontaneous expression while possessing a certain simplicity of mind and a power of vision. Sharing the naivete of the ancient bards, they were unconscious of themselves as artists. They needed a strong intuition to get as closely as possible to the core of tales, but they also needed a creative mind to activate the dynamics of language. The *Pendeldynamik* would keep the stories alive in the oral tradition. The so-called *Urmärchen* (primeval or archetypal tale) was a modern "myth" that did not exist, for the core of the tale could only be reached by approximation.

Wilhelm shared his brother's theory in an infinitely rich core of tradition within the folk experience that gave rise to multiple variants, all of which might come close to the truth of a given tale. In commenting on the numerous variants that he and his brother had listed in their notes to the *Kinder- und Hausmärchen*, Wilhelm explained that they had selected for the collection those variants that, in their judgment, represented the best. Yet they had some other equally good variants in the notes for the following reasons: "To us, such variants appeared to be more peculiar than to those who regarded them only as certain changes or distortions of a supposed primeval image. Yet such variants might perhaps be, on the contrary, some attempts (by storytellers) to get close to something that exists only in terms of an inexhaustible idea."[22]

Why did some folktales survive in the oral tradition whereas other were forgotten? To Jacob Grimm, the key to the survival of a traditional story lay in the storyteller's art of choosing the middle path between the core or substance of tradition and a creative retelling of the tales. In his view, the best folk stories were told as if the storytellers had just invented them. The words should follow the spirit of the "folk reality" or core of the tale, not the other way around. Rote memory, imitation and a dull recital not only were the sure signs of a "tiredness" of language but also signalled the death of traditional storytelling and the folktale itself. While Jacob objected to artificial embellishments, he also opposed a pedantic approach to storytelling that missed out on the self-dynamics of language. Only in the dialectical process of historical consciousness and creative thought could the folktale have survived throughout the centuries.

As the Grimms perceived it, good storytellers never repeated themselves, and their language was not "fixed" or static but alive with the spirit of creativity. They did not believe in the fixed wording of an *Urmärchen* that would prescribe the exact wording for all tales that followed its example. They also rejected the idea of rote memory and a mechanical recital. Believing that traditional storytelling was a *continuous process* subject to an evolutionary process like language itself, they supported the art of paraphrasing as a key to keeping the stories alive.

The implications of this definition are that it renders irrelevant many critical discussions regarding the issue of the Grimms' loyalty to tradition, for the Grimms did not believe in a fixed *Urmärchen* but in storytelling as a dynamic, continuous, and changing process. The question is not whether the Grimms insisted on loyalty to tradition but how they defined such a loyalty within the context of language dynamics. It is evident that they had in mind neither a slavish imitation nor pedantry in terms of the exact vocabulary and syntax of a given story. Rather than advocating the search for the perfect truth or the mythical *Urmärchen*, they urged storytellers to cling as tightly as possible to the core or substance of a tale and then to activate their own creativity, the *Eigendynamik* of language, in bringing it back to life. While no single storyteller could ever hope to render the perfect truth of a given tale, the best folktales were "reborn" in a dialectical process involving tradition as well as the perceptive and creative individual.

NOTES

1. Rask's works on the Icelandic and Nordic languages were first published in Copenhagen in 1811 and 1818. On Rask's influence on Jacob Grimm, consult Ulrich Wyss, *Die wilde Philologie; Jacob Grimm und der Historismus* (Munich: F. C. H. Beck'sche Verlagsbuchhandlung, 1979), pp. 130–35. See also Peter Ganz, *Jacob Grimm's Conception of German Studies. An inaugural lecture delivered before the University of Oxford*, 1973 (Oxford: Clarendon Press, 1973).

2. Jacob Grimm, *Deutsche Mythologie.* See Jacob Grimm, *Teutonic Mythology* 1 (New York: Dover, 1966). Preface by Jacob Grimm.

3. Ibid., vol. 4, p. 1540. In a further comparative study Jacob relates this word to the Nordic World Ash, Yggdrasil.

4. Jacob Grimm, "Die Poesie im Recht," *in Kleinere Schriften von Jacob Grimm* vo. 4. Reprint Hildesheim: Georg Olms Verlagsbuchhandlung, 1965, p. 153.

5. The broad international scope of Jacob's language theories is especially evident in the preface and outline of: Jacob Grimm, *Geschichte der deutschen Sprache* 1, 4th ed. (Leipzig: Verlag von S. Hirzel, 1880). See the chapter on "Zeitalter und Sprachen," pp. 1–11. For a discussion of Jacob's influence on the comparative studies of Frazer and Keightley, refer to chapter 10 of this work.

6. *Teutonic Mythology* 1, Preface.

7. For discussion of the Nazis' *"Volkish"* cultural policy and its distorted view of German Romanticism (including the works of the Brothers Grimm), consult Christa Kamenetsky, *Children's Literature in Hitler's Germany. The Cultural Policy of National Socialism* Athens, Ohio: Ohio University Press, 1984), Chapters 1 and 5.

8. Jacob Grimm, "Reden und Aufsätze," in *Kleinere Schriften von Jacob Grimm* 4 (Berlin: Dümmlers Verlagsbuchhandlung, 1889).

9. Wyss, pp. 136–55.

10. "Introduction," *Kinder- und Hausmärchen* (Berlin: Reimer, 1812).

11. Wilhelm Grimm, *Kinder- und Hausmärchen*, Vol. 3 (Berlin: Reimer, 1822), Preface. Bolte and Polivka omit this reference, yet they do refer to Wilhelm's notes in the 1856/57 edition of the *Kinder- und Hausmärchen*, pp. 405–14, in which he commented on the recurrence of basic themes and characters in folktales around the world. Johannes Bolte and Georg Polivka. *Anmerkungen zu den Kinder- und Hausmärchen der Brüder Grimm* 5 (Leipzig: Dieterich'sche Verlagsbuchhandlung, 1932), pp. 239–45.

12. Richard Dorson. "The Decline of Solar Mythology," in *Myth: A Symposium*, Thomas A. Sebeok, ed. (Bloomington, Indiana: Indiana University Press, 1965. For a closer analysis of the nineteenth-century controversy among the theorists, see also Chapter 10 in this work.

13. Wilhelm Grimm, *Kinder- und Hausmärchen* 3 (1921).

14. Wyss, pp. 240–47.

15. Ibid.

16. Ibid., Chapter 12.

17. Ibid., p. 155.

18. Robert A. Fowkes, "The Linguistic Modernity of Jacob Grimm" *Linguistics* 8 (1964), pp. 54–61. Also "A-Zypressenzweig," *Der Spiegel* 15 (1961), pp. 65–74, and Leo Stern, *Der geistige und politische Standort von Jacob Grimm in der deutschen Geschichte.* Monograph (Berlin: Akademie Verlag, 1963).

19. See Wyss, pp. 160–72.

20. Jacob Grimm, "Über den Ursprung der Sprache. Gelesen in der Akademie der Wissenschaften am 9. Januar 1851" in *Kleinere Schriften von Jacob Grimm* 1 (Hildesheim: Olms Verlag, 1965), pp. 255–98.

21. Ibid., p. 277. In this context, Jacob also commented on the interrelationship of all languages in the world: *"Diese sprache, dieses denken steht aber nicht abgesondert da für einzelne menschen, sondern alle sprachen sind eine in die geschichte eingegangene gemeinschaft und knüpfen die welt aneinander.* ("Such words and thoughts, however, do not just exist in isolation for individual human beings. Rather, all languages form a historical community and knit together the world.") [Author's note: Jacob used lower case letters throughout the essay.]

22. Ibid. This statement confirms the Grimms' faith in the coexistence of variants in languages and folktales of the world. It also implies a rejection of the static model of one original tale or an *Urmärchen*. The concept of variants as it is discussed here, encourages a loyal yet spontaneous folktale recital.

6. The Sources of the Collection

[The Background of the Informants]

OME RECENT STUDIES have thrown new light on the informants of the Grimms' folktale collection. It used to be a common misconception among critics that the Grimms made actual trips into the countryside to collect folktales from the common peasants so as to capture the living folk tradition. While such an assumption was not altogether wrong,[1] it represented by no means the true conditions under which they gathered the tales nor did it reflect the true identity of their informants. Research has shown that the Grimms did collect some of their stories from simple folk in rural areas and in some cases indeed made an effort to visit them in more remote places, but as a rule they did not. They gathered only a few tales directly from shepherds and peasants, but others they received indirectly from friends or acquaintances who gathered the tales for them, either orally or in a written form. Besides, they also received many tales from informants residing in small towns or cities, of which some had an impressive educational background.

Much of the information that is now generally available about the Grimms' sources is based on the documentary evidence supplied from their archives by Hermann Grimm, Wilhelm Grimm's son. On the basis of such primary sources Wilhelm Schoof identified, among others, the following major informants: Catherine Wild and her daughters; "Old Marie" of the Wild household; the families Engelhard and Hassenpflug; the family von Haxthausen; Ludovica Jordis, the sister of Brentano; Friedrich Krause, a retired night watchman; Friederike Mannel, the daughter of a minister; and a certain candidate named Ferdinand Siebert.[2]

The myth that the Grimms' informants had mainly been illiterate German peasant folk from the rural areas of Hesse has now been largely dispelled. The most striking evidence regarding the higher educational background of some of the informants is that they themselves were contributors to the collection. To the first edition of the *Kinder- und Hausmärchen*, Jacob himself contributed seventeen folktales and Wilhelm nine. Both Brothers Grimm certainly did not represent the illiterate peasant folk but the educated middle class. By their contributions they gave living proof of their own theory that an education might enhance the taste for *Naturpoesie* rather than interfere with its growth. It is true that in Wilhelm's 1812 introduction to this work, he emphasized that the folktales had been best preserved in "quiet places" away from the "false enlightenment." In this context he did not refer to a particular class in sociological terms but rather to a state of mind that favored the preservation of *Naturpoesie*. It is evident from their correspondence and various essays that they found some of the best storytellers in their own middle class who possessed the same qualities that they themselves had acquired, namely a strong positive feeling for traditional lore that was simple, childlike, and naive. In their view, an education of the best kind enhanced such a feeling and did not destroy it like the enlightenment. Their own studies of medieval literature and ancient law, especially under Savigny, had promoted their quest for *Naturpoesie*.

Recent studies have shown that more of the Grimms' informants belonged to the educated middle class residing in small towns and cities than critics had formerly assumed.[3] The Wild family, for example, were educated neighbors of the Grimms in Kassel, and the Grimms had to step only outside of their front door to obtain some of their best stories. Herr Wild, a native of Switzerland, owned the Sonnenapotheke (Sun Pharmacy), and he and his wife, along with their four daughters Dortchen (Dorothee, who later became Wilhelm's wife), Gretchen (Margarete), Lisette (Elizabeth), and Mie, contributed substantially to the folktale collection.

Hermann Grimm could not have been mistaken about the tales told by Dortchen and her sisters, as he remembered at least some of them as a part of his own childhood experience. Dortchen was his mother and her sisters were his aunts. Even though they had originally told their tales to Wilhelm and Jacob Grimm, with whom they used to play together when they were young, he still remembered their tales as a definite part in the many tales told in the Grimm household. In the Grimm archives he was also able to identify with relative ease some letters and story contributions signed "Jeannette" and "Male," whom he remembered personally as the sisters Johanna and Amalie Hassenpflug, the family's friends who were known for their contributions to the *Kinder- und Hausmärchen*. With admirable skill and patience, Hermann Grimm joined together the puzzle pieces as he tried to identify the various contributors to the collection.[4] In one case, however, he was mistaken.

According to more-recent findings of Heinz Rölleke, Hermann Grimm accredited too many tales to "Old Marie," the Wild's housekeeper. Rölleke discovered some flaws in his background and source identification and consequently also in that of Wilhelm Schoof, whose standard work on the history of the collection substantially relied on Hermann Grimm's findings. The main question that he raised pertained to the identity of Marie. Was she indeed the "Old Marie," the housekeeper of the Wilds, who used to live upstairs in the pharmacy building next door to the Grimms in Kassel? Rölleke noticed some discrepancies in the titles and also in the number of stories that had supposedly come from "Old Marie," pointing out that while Hermann Grimm had ascribed only seven stories to her, Johannes Bolte listed the number of her contributions as ten. Wilhelm Schoof first mentioned six in 1930 and then thirteen in 1959. Rölleke found it peculiar that none of the mentioned critics had taken notice of such a discrepancy.[5]

By carefully examining the Grimms' notes to all tales attributed to the Wild's housekeeper, Rölleke found that the Grimms themselves had not always used the term "Old" along with the name of "Marie." Since the Grimms had customarily mentioned the first name of a person only in cases where that person was of the same age or younger than they, he deduced that whenever they referred only to "Marie," they must have meant a younger person than the housekeeper. His choice fell upon the young Marie Hassenpflug, a well-known contributor to the *Kinder- und Hausmärchen* who belonged to the educated middle class. These findings substantially changed some general assumptions about the background of the informants.

Rölleke further supported his findings by referring the reader to the place names that the Grimms had attached to the respective tales. In an earlier recording, Wilhelm had clearly identified the place for "Old Marie" as "Kassel." Jacob, on the other hand, however, who recorded the later tales accredited to "Marie," identified it as "Hesse" or "Area around Main"—the very place names that both Grimms had consistently used in relation to contributions by the Hassenpflug family.

Rölleke obtained still another clue from the respective dates attached to the tales. In one case, he identified one tale from Marie Hassenpflug and another one for "Marie" that came rather close to the dates on which Jacob had recorded stories from the Hassenpflugs. In another instance—a Sunday afternoon—the dates were even identical. Deducing that the Grimms could not possibly have recorded folktales on the same

Sunday from both persons, even less so as it was unlikely that the "Old Marie" would have crossed the social barrier by joining Marie Hassen-pflug's Sunday afternoon circle of friends to read and recite poetry, Rölleke concluded that the name "Marie" must have applied to Marie Hassenpflug. As far as the Grimms were concerned, it was well-known that they used to join such gatherings at her place. Consequently, there was no question that they actually recorded the tales from the young Marie.

In this debate concerning the identity of tales by the "Old Marie" and tales by the young Marie, the age of the informants actually carried less weight than their respective social and educational background. Rölleke worked on the assumption that the humble housekeeper would have not crossed the social and educational barrier to join the literary circle at the Hassenpflugs. He suggested that some critics had consciously perpetuated the myth of the "old German storyteller" because it fitted the popular image of an uneducated peasant woman. By trying to make another Frau Viehmännin of "Old Marie," they had added an undue nationalistic emphasis to the *Kinder- und Hausmärchen*.

On the skeptical side it might be said that the nature of their "literary discussions" may have made a difference, for it did not focus on elegant French poetry but on *Naturpoesie*, the humble folklore of the common folk. Yet there is indeed no evidence to suggest the "Old Marie" ever set foot in the Hassenpflug's house.

The origins of this issue go back to an earlier debate regarding the identity of Frau Viehmännin. Specifically, it concerned a basic misunderstanding regarding the supposedly simple and idyllic origin of a peasant woman. As she contributed about one-third of the tales contained in the first edition of the *Kinder- und Hausmärchen*, she was supposedly one of the Grimms' most important informants, but when it turned out that she was neither a peasant woman nor the wife of a farmer but the poor widow of a tailor living in the rural area of Zwehrn, critics began to reconsider the common notion that the bulk of the Grimms' tales had originated among illiterate peasants. Modern research has revealed that she would come to Kassel twice a week to sell some agricultural products, mainly vegetables and potatoes, also to the Grimms. This alone did not make her a peasant. Neither did she come from a family of peasants, for her father was an innkeeper in the area. Research has also shown that instead of making excursions to the village of Zwehrn to record tales from Frau Viehmännin directly in the countryside, the Grimms used to record her stories at their own apartment, where she would come to sell her produce, usually prodding her on with a cup of hot coffee.[6] Possibly because Ludwig Grimm's engraving of Frau Viehmännin (whom Edgar Taylor called "Gammer Grethel" in his first English translation of the *Kinder- und Hausmärchen* in 1823) became so popular, earlier critics mistakenly associated her image with that of the simple Mother Goose, the legendary storyteller of

13. "The Goose Girl," illustrated by Walter Crane.

14. "The Fisherman and His Wife," illustrated by Walter Crane.

15. "Cradle Song." Next to folktales, myths, and legends, children's games and lullabies, too, belonged to Wilhelm Grimm's folklore collections. Illustration by Ludwig Richter.

16. (ABOVE) "The Bremen Town Musicians,"
illustrated by Christa Kamenetsky. 17. (RIGHT)
"The Wolf and the Seven Little Kids," illustrated by
Ludwig Richter.

18. "The Frog Prince," illustrated by Arthur Rackham.

19. "Hansel and Gretel," illustrated by Ludwig Richter.

20. "By Railway Through Fairyland." Map of folktales and local legends in Germany.

21. Dorothea Grimm (Wild), Wilhelm's wife, in her sixties.

22. "In the Beginning was the Word." Frontispiece to Jacob and Wilhelm Grimms' *Deutsches Wörterbuch*.

23. The Marktgasse in Kassel, where the Grimms lived in an upstairs apartment (house on the left) between 1805 and 1819.

Charles Perrault's fairy tales and the supposed creator of John Newbery's nursery rhymes.

It must be noted, however, that Wilhelm Grimm was not at fault in spreading the myth of a simple woman in an idyllic rural setting when he called her a "Bäuerin von Zwehrn" (a peasant woman of Zwehrn). To the contrary, he was the one who explained in a footnote that Frau Viehmännin was the widow of a tailor with a meager income who took care of her daughter and six grandchildren and that she died in poverty under adverse circumstances brought on by war. Did the Grimms purposely mislead their readers when they referred to her as a Bäuerin (peasant woman)? John Ellis definitely thought so.[7] He also accused the Grimms of various other forms of conscious deceit pertaining to an identification of sources and their editing process. Ellis's problem was that he took Wilhelm's words too literally and without the context of Romantic thought that attached a special significance to the concept of the peasant.

The Grimms never insisted that most of their informants were illiterate folk belonging to the peasant class. This notion was first introduced by Taylor's preface to the *German Popular Stories*.[8] Like other Romantic writers at that time, the Bothers Grimm understood the concept of the *Bäuerin* in symbolic terms, not in a literal or sociological sense reminiscent of class and occupation. In German Romanticism, the peasant became a symbol of the ancestor who had lived in closeness to God and nature, marked by a simplicity and naivete of spirit that had become very rare in modern life.[9] Such a pure and naive state of mind, thought the Brothers Grimm, was as rare as a violet blooming under thorny bushes in springtime. They considered it a treasure beyond comparison—the very precondition for traditional storytelling—as it favored an intuitive power of vision needed to make contact with the "core" of tradition. Just as Herder had associated the "folk soul" of the people with the simple peasant folk, so the Grimms associated it with the peasant, the shepherd, or the mountaineer—with people who had been left untouched by the chaos and distraction of modern times. They felt that it had been best preserved in more isolated regions of the world, among shepherds and peasant folk, as well as among all those who had retained a certain innocence in their hearts and souls. What they admired in Frau Viehmännin was that she possessed the calm and naive soul needed to grasp the poetic spirit of the native folk tradition. Along such lines, not only Frau Viehmännin fulfilled their expectations but also little Anna von Haxthausen, Gretchen and Dortchen Wild, and various other contributors, who had little to do with the peasantry but had a great perception for the oral tradition.

[The Issue of Ethnic Origin]

The question of the informants' ethnic identity has intrigued many critics in recent times, undoubtedly due to the growing sociological influence on folktales studies. When Rölleke suggested that some critics had tried to build up the myth of the "Old Marie" and enhance the nationalistic interpretation of the *Kinder- und Hausmärchen*, he had already been informed about her French Huguenot descent yet insisted that many critics still considered her the archetype of the female German storyteller, as her foreign background belonged to the generation of her grandfather (or great-grandfather). As such, it was further removed from the present than that of young Marie Hassenpflug's father, who was of direct French Huguenot descent.[10]

Unlike many American critics, Rölleke did not attach too much importance to the question of the informants' ethnic identity. Even though he did point out that Frau Viehmännin's father, too, had been of French Huguenot origin and that Frau Viehmännin and the Hassenpflugs in their childhood indeed may have spoken French at the dinner table and read the French tales of Charles Perrault, he did not think that such deductions were enough evidence to prove that their oral tale contributions to the Grimms' *Kinder- und Hausmärchen* were based on Perrault's influence. Judging by the tales and the Grimms' comments on German variants, he maintained that except for those tales that the Grimms had already identified as tainted by the French tradition, they were based on the German tradition. If Perrault had been the sole influence, Rölleke reasoned, then the Hassenpflugs would have used Perrault's ending in the tale of "Thornrosa" ("Sleeping Beauty" or "Dornröschen") or Perrault's beginning and ending in the tale of "Little Red Riding Hood," for they were not given to invent such matters on their own. As they were known for their loyalty to tradition, one might well see that their tale contributions were based on the German oral tradition. Their style showed that they did not add their own fantasies or adornments to the tales but rather relied on existing German variants.[11]

The very fact that the Hassenpflug's concerned themselves on Sunday afternoons with Old German poetry and native folklore supports Rölleke's findings on this behalf. This close-knit circle of friends met regularly but rather informally at the Hassenpflug's home. It was a private social meeting of women, called *Kränzchen*, to which also belonged the Grimms' sister Lotte. If after enjoying coffee, hot chocolate, and cake served at a cozy *Kränzchen*-table they would recite some Old German poetry, it was not the equivalent of formally reciting Hugo or Voltaire at a French literary "salon." Their active and persistent contributions to the Grimms' folktale collections indicate that it is more likely they recited epic poetry or literature of the *Volksbücher* (folk books) that contained various types of *Naturpoesie*, adding to these well-known folk songs and the folktales they knew.[12]

Of course it is possible that Madame Hassenpflug passed on to her children the French folktales from her childhood, but such a possibility would not make irrelevant that variants of the same folktales have existed side by side in the German and French oral tradition to this day. The Grimms themselves attested to the existence of oral variants in their notes and did not venture to say which influenced which. The fact remains that regardless of their Huguenot relations, the Hassenpflug girls enjoyed their involvement in old German *Naturpoesie*. It would have been interesting to find out if they shared Jacob and Wilhelm Grimm's interest in comparative and cross-cultural discussions as well.

The Huguenot ancestry of Frau Viehmännin has probably caused the greatest confusion among critics. Modern research has shown that her maiden name was Pierson, identifying her as the daughter of a well-to-do innkeeper at the "Knallhütte" whose grandfather was the first mayor of the French Huguenot settlement in Schöneberg near Hofgeismar. Walter Scherf speculated that he may not have been of French Huguenot origin after all but of Dutch descent.[13] Whatever the case may be, the genealogical findings dispelled the myth of her purely bred Hessian peasant origin. Critics deduced that she was not the German storyteller whom the Grimms had made her out to be and that in all likelihood she had not even spoken German but French at the dinner table, reciting French and not German tales for the Grimms. In his work *One Fairy Story Too Many: The Brothers Grimm and Their Tales* John Ellis drove the ethnic question to the verge of the absurd, accusing the Grimms of conscious deceit.[14]

In a rebuttal, Donald Ward pointed out that Frau Viehmännin might well have possessed a firm knowledge of the oral German folk tradition, not only because her mother was German but also because she may have heard the tales at her father's inn and certainly was familiar with others told in the area where she was born and raised. Walter Scherf, too, argued that the Huguenot origin applied only to the second and third generation of some of the Grimms' informants, not to the informants themselves. In the case of Frau Viehmännin and the von Haxthausen girls, only one parent (the father) had been of Huguenot origin, and in the case of "Old Marie" only the grandmother. Most likely, these children and grandchildren of Huguenots who were all born and raised in Hesse had absorbed the oral tradition from the German environment as well as from the other side of the family, which in all cases had been German.[15] Finally one may raise the question of why children of immigrants would be less capable of developing a firm grasp of a country's language and tradition into which they were born, the more so if one of their parents was a native of Germany. The fact that they may have spoken French at the dinner table would not render them incapable of being firmly rooted in the native German tradition. There is no linguistic proof that persons exposed to bilingual conversations at home are, as a rule, less well versed in the language and folk tradition of their home environment than those who have no immigrants in their immediate ancestry.

The bilingualism in the von Haxthausen family, too, has been vastly overplayed in this connection. It was in Bökendorf, in the midst of the von Haxthausen family circle, that Wilhelm felt the warmest bond with the German folk tradition. When in 1815 Wilhelm sent Ludowina von Haxthausen a copy of the newly published second volume of the *Kinder- und Hausmärchen* in appreciation of her contributions to the volume, she responded with warm enthusiasm, not just to the folktales themselves but particularly to the language in which they were written. Thanking him for this gift, she wrote:

> Still greater was my joy in receiving the new book of folktales. It is to all of us a reminder of eternal youth, of the enlivening spirit of uniqueness that grows from the root and spreads into all of the most tender branches. It is impossible not to notice with some sadness that in the language that we hear daily, this originality of expression, this perceptiveness and relationship to nature has faded away. It seems that long ago people were much closer to the spirit of wonder than they are today. When I read these tales, I recalled some of the things that I had lost since my childhood.[16]

In the vivid language of the folktales she recognized the language that she had known as a child: a language that in its closeness to nature had still emitted a sense of wonder that she thought was largely lost in everyday modern speech. This statement gives evidence not only of the language she remembers best from her childhood but also of her capacity to appreciate it in its great simplicity. Not with one word did she refer to the French language, by comparison or otherwise. Rather, she seemed to identify with the Grimms' attempt to preserve the language and spirit of the collected tales. She herself had been an active contributor to the *Kinder- und Hausmärchen*—while respecting their advice in recording the tales in loyalty to tradition. There is no evidence that her bilingual background would have interfered with such an endeavor.

The Grimms made no mention of Frau Viehmännin's or the von Haxthausens' ethnic background. Rather, they emphasized that their stories were of "truly Hessian stock." What mattered in this connection was not German ethnicity but the living oral tradition that they gleaned from Hesse. That the Grimms dropped the reference to "purely Hessian tales" in the second edition to the work by no means proves that they admitted the Huguenot origin of some of the tales.[17] It is more likely that in the meantime they had become acquainted with additional variants from other regions of Germany that they partially integrated in the text and partially in the notes of the *Kinder- und Hausmärchen*.

What Ellis overlooked in this context is that the Grimms never referred to ethnic or racial concepts when speaking about the German origin of their tales. Also there is no proof in the Grimms' own writings nor in their correspondence that they ever considered a given storyteller's ethnic background. Actually, only three of about twenty stories contributed by Frau Viehmännin bear some resemblance to the tales of Perrault, and these may well have circulated both in the French and German oral tradition.

It was Edgar Taylor, the first English translator of the collection, who used the term "German" in the English title of *German Popular Stories,* claiming that these tales were of "purely German" origin. The Grimms had made a case for "mainly Hessian stories" in the first edition of the *Kinder- und Hausmärchen* yet even then modified their claim by citing variants from numerous other cultures in the tales. A closer reading of the Grimms' prefaces and notes reveals that they considered the question of locating German national tales. Even if in their immediate fieldwork they confined themselves to the surrounding regions of Hesse and the Main area, they went far beyond those boundaries in collecting recording from friends and acquaintances, namely not only all German regions but also Austria, Switzerland, and the Netherlands, for example.[18] Especially their comparative folktale studies in volume three of the second edition of the *Kinder- und Hausmärchen* showed a genuine interest also in worldwide folktale collections, including all that had been published in France. Such studies speak for the Grimms' wider comparative and scholarly concern that had little to do with narrow ethnocentric thinking related to the French Huguenot question.

For the Grimms it was sufficient to know that variants existed—without necessarily wishing to speculate about which one had influenced which. As they did not believe in an *Urmärchen* but rather in the need for a parallel existence of several oral variants of a given tale, they were more concerned with the folktales themselves than with their given age. Neither did the question regarding the ethnic origin of an informant play a role in their way of thinking. In some cases, they thought that both the German and the French variants could be traced back to a common Nordic Germanic ancestry, for the common roots of French and German epics in mythology were certainly older than any single folktale variant. In the context of such broad comparative discussions, especially in their notes to the tales, the Grimms gave more attention to folktale variants and the dissemination of folktales within the Indo-European context than to the question of ethnic origin.

In regard to folktale variants in printed sources, the Grimms generously pointed to the common Italian collections that seemed to contain the oldest tales in the European tradition. They found that especially the works of Giambattista Basile's *Il Pentamerone* (*Le Cunto de li Cunti,* 1674) and Gianfrancesco Straparola's *The Delightful Nights* (*Le piacevoli Notti,* 2 vols., 1550–1553) were a common resource for

German and French tales and collections. Beyond the Italian origin, the Grimms traced several stories back to still older branches of the Indo-European family of languages, be it the Middle East or India. They even cited variants in Jewish and Persian collections. In still other cases, they admitted that there were some "unexplainable" connections that pointed to a shared origin and early experience of mankind. Judging by their notes, the Grimms often merely confirmed that variants existed "side by side" without speculating much further. [19]

More so than modern critics may expect, the Grimms considered the common roots of the French and German languages and folk traditions in folklore within the context of the Indo-European theory. Significantly, they included the legends of Charlemagne among the *Deutsche Sagen* (German Legends), not because they felt driven by German imperialistic thoughts but because the legends dated back to a time when Germany and France had been one country under the Franks. Still to this day the Roland statue dominates the marketplace in Bremen as a reminder of the time when both countries shared a common heritage. As far as Perrault's folktales were concerned, the Grimms let no patriotic sentiments interfere with their judgment. They praised them for their natural flow of speech and proximity to the folk tradition, giving them a higher rating than the tales the French *Cabinet des fées* or the German tales of Albert Ludwig Grimm and Musäus.

By no means did the Grimms hate the French people or loathe French culture. Even though they themselves were of "purely Hessian stock," they spoke and read French in their early childhood days, as did other children of the better-educated middle class and aristocracy in their time. Even Savigny's little daughter, Pulettchen, learned to speak French fluently at the age of three. The Grimms knew the tales of Charles Perrault still before they entered the first grade, and they were quite at home with the French language throughout their lives. Speaking and reading French certainly did not diminish their love of the native German language and dialects. [20]

Undoubtedly the limitation on German freedom under the French occupation induced the Grimms to contemplate more than before the roots of their own heritage in linguistic, historical, and literary terms, but not to the degree that they cut off their interest in the French cultural heritage. In spite of their growing national sentiments, they continued to speak French, travel to France, and promote French-German cultural relations.

If they had indeed thought in racial, ethnocentric, or strictly political terms, they would have avoided contacts with those informants and friends who were of French Huguenot origin while mingling only with persons of "purely German" origin. However, the Grimms selected their storytellers not on the basis of ethnicity or political party but on the basis of their familiarity with the German folk tradition. They themselves were the judges on this behalf, as native Hessians and as students of linguistics, law, and medieval literature. With such a background, they certainly knew better than anyone else in their time how to distinguish a "home-grown" story from an "imported" one.

[The Child as Informant]

Among the contributors to the Grimms' folktale collection was Anna von Haxthausen. She was the youngest of eight daughters of Hermann von Haxthausen and his wife, who lived with his family on an estate in Bökendorf. Born in 1801, Anna was only ten years old when Wilhelm met her during a visit there in July 1811. During a walk together, he asked her to tell him a story, and later he admitted that he was quite impressed by her lively and spirited performance. She had the honor of being the first one to present Wilhelm with a folktale at Bökendorf. Many more tales were to follow in the years to come.[21]

Whenever Wilhelm and Jacob visited the von Haxthausens at their estate in the countryside, they would walk and hike together or sit in the living room and sing old German folk songs. Known as the "Böken-dorf Folktale Group," they enchanted each other with tales and legends of the past. The family was of aristocratic origin and well-to-do but by no means given to the frills of court life. They thought especially of Wilhelm Grimm as a most welcome guest, because he participated actively in their oral recitals and also was a most attentive listener. At the von Haxthausens' place the Grimms also met the von Haxthausen's cousins, Annette von Droste Hülshoff and her sister Jeannette, who, according to some sources, felt a strong sympathy for Wilhelm.[22]

Actually, it was her older sister, Ludowine von Haxthausen, who became known as a major contributor to the Grimms' folktale collections. In all, she wrote nine letters to Wilhelm Grimm, always including her own stories that she collected from the common folk in the village, but sometimes she also included stories collected and written down by Anna, by her older sister Ferdinandine, and by her mother. It appears that the entire family was engaged in cooperating with the Brothers Grimm.

Following the Grimms' directives, they tried to record the stories exactly as they had heard them and also took notes when listening to tales on their excursions to the surrounding rural areas. Ludowine recalled in a letter to Wilhelm that Anna was by far the best folktale collector of the family, in spite of her young age. When they would go together to the villages on their folktale expeditions, Anna was not just a little "tagalong" but an active participant. Ludowine wrote to Wilhelm: "Anna is truly a lucky child. She catches the best stories under our noses, before we even get around to them."[23] She thought that Anna was much more successful than they in getting people to tell her stories.

Probably this had something to do with her friendly and trusting face, for wherever she turned, she got some stories.

Anna was an unusual child. With an astonishing dedication and diligence, she wrote down the stories for Wilhelm as she had heard them, sometimes covering three and four pages with her small penmanship. Most of the tales she reconstructed at home on the basis of her notes, never forgetting to include dialogues and lively turns of speech. Because she was ten, her spelling and syntax left something to be desired, but she seemed to have a good ear for the oral tradition. How much she enjoyed collecting and writing up is evident from a letter of November 3, 1814, in which her older sister Ferdinandine wrote to Wilhelm: "Anna is busy collecting folktales, and we think that during the winter season, which offers an excellent opportunity for such an activity, we will still discover quite a bit more."[24] On some occasions, her older brother August would collect some stories, too, and dictate them to Anna.

It is assumed that several of Anna's tales made it into the *Kinder- und Hausmärchen*, although they were not necessarily under her name, as the Grimms often identified the stories submitted by her and her sisters only by the words: "from Bökendorf" or "von Haxthausen." In critical discussions of the topic, Ludowine received most of the credit, but Anna has well been recognized as the second most important tale collector of the von Haxthausen family. Among the correspondence that the Grimms (especially Wilhelm) carried on with Haxthausen girls, only three letters were found by Anna herself addressed to Wilhelm (none of which mentioned the folktales), yet thirty-three from Wilhelm to Anna alone. Schoof thinks that this uneven distribution of letters is because as a child, Anna used to enclose her stories in Ludowina's letters, thus indirectly extending her greetings, and also because she relied on the fact that her sisters would mention her frequently in their letters to Wilhelm.

Several of Anna's stories ended up in the Grimms' big file of "unpublishable tales." They have a swift and lively style yet are marked by numerous errors in spelling and syntax. Still, Anna's stories have a certain charm. The writing errors (not counting the many words that she crossed out) give evidence of her independent work, and they also show her family's respect for Wilhelm's demand that folktales be written down in loyalty to tradition—including all corrections. Anna's parents or her older and well-educated sisters might normally have corrected them, for in some letters even the older sisters admitted that occasionally they had copied their letters to enhance their legibility, but then they would no longer have been Anna's own contributions as an informant, it is also possible, of course, that Wilhelm had reminded the older von Haxthausens beforehand not to "spoil" Anna's stories by forcing her to make formal corrections. With the few words that she herself crossed out, the stories transmit a touch of childhood.

Among the rejected tales that Professor Rölleke and his students identified in the Grimms' archives as Anna's tales were "The Prince Who Feared Nothing" ("Königssohn, der sich nicht fürchtet"), "The Stone as a Back Pack" ("Der Stein als Aufhocker"), and "The Bells Underground" ("Die unterirdischen Glocken").[25] They bore her signature and showed flaws in grammar and spelling. The Grimms may have kept them as a lovable souvenir, but they may also have valued them as variants of the tales they published.[26]

One additional tale, "How Six Men Got on in the World," was found a few years ago among the papers of the Arnswaldt Estate that belonged to Anna, who had become Frau von Arnswaldt when she married August von Arnswaldt. Jutta Rißmann suspected that it somehow belonged to the tale collection of the Brothers Grimm. It was written anonymously, in a clumsy handwriting on both sides of lined paper, and with a number of spelling errors. Because two small flowers had been drawn with ink into the margins, she deduced that the writer must have been female, and because of some dialectical forms, such as "*Fleiße*" instead of "*Flasche*" (bottle), she concluded that the tale and its writer most likely came from Westphalia. Westphalia was also the region of Bökendorf, where the von Haxthausens had their estate, yet she ruled out categorically the possibility that the writer had been one of the Haxthausens. Too many spelling errors pointed to an unskilled writer, she reasoned, whereas the von Haxthausen sisters had been too well educated to write such a piece. She thought it possible, however, that the writer of the story had turned to the von Haxthausen girls to have it corrected by them, which might also explain why the tale fell into Anna's hands.[27]

Rißmann did not think about the possibility that Anna herself wrote the story as a child and kept it for sentimental reasons, since she forgot to send it off to Wilhelm, or that it was the rough draft of a tale that Ludowine sent for her to Wilhelm. She assumed that it could not have originated in the family von Haxthausen or Arnswaldt as they were highly educated people. Also, the paper had no water marks. What escaped her attention is that Anna might have written the letter as a child. There are some striking correspondences of orthographical and syntactical errors in this manuscript compared with those of Anna's tales that were cited by Rölleke and his students. For example, *ch* is used instead of the *g* in the verb *frachte* (*fragte*, or asked) in the Arnswaldt version, and it also occurs in the noun *Jacht* (*Jagd*, or hunt) in Rölleke's anthologized tale by Anna; the *ß* is used instead of the *s* in *dieß* (instead of *dies*) in both, or there is a general confusion about the use of the *ß* in its right place, such as in *Schlos* (*Schloß*, or castle) in the Arnswaldt version and *Princeßin* (*Prinzessin*, or princess) in the identified tale by Anna in Rölleke's work. Most striking is the similar childlike error with the added *h* in *einmahl* and *ein mahl* (*einmal*, or once) in the respective tale openings. The Arnswaldt version begins: "*Es war ein mahl ein Mann der hatte eine sehr schöne Tochter.* . . .

(There was once a man who had a very beautiful daughter. . . .) Anna's tale of the "Prince Who Feared Nothing" begins "*Es war einmahl ein Prinz, der ging so gerne auf auf [sic] die Jacht. . . .*" (There was once a prince who very much liked to go hunting. . . .) Both tale openings are based on traditional tale formulas, which might make the similarity coincidental, but there are also numerous fused sentences and sentence fragments that correspond to the style of the child Anna.

The ruled inexpensive paper would not be proof that a poorer person than the von Haxthausens had written the story, for one might assume that even in a well-to-do aristocratic family, children were asked to write their rough drafts on less expensive ruled paper rather than on expensive paper with water marks. More importantly, the scribbled ink flowers, too, point to a little girl rather than to a woman.

The tale itself is a variant of Frau Viehmännin's version from Hesse, which the Grimms published in the second edition of the *Kinder- und Hausmärchen* in 1819. In their notes to the tale the Grimms mention another variant from the region of Paderborn that was almost identical to the Hessian version, with the exception that it included a fellow who had to cork up his ears, for if he would remove the corks, he could hear the dead folks singing under the earth. The Grimms still mentioned in their notes a third variant of the Schwalm area that had the same motifs yet was incomplete.[28]

The unidentified folktale recording from the Arnswaldt files was incomplete, and it did include the motif of the fellow with the corked up ears. When he opened his ears, said the tale, he could hear "*was die Todten unter der Erde anfangen*" (what the dead are doing under the earth). Rißmann was convinced that this version was an early recording based entirely on the oral tradition.

Did Wilhelm favor little Anna's tales over other variants because he loved children? There is no evidence that he preferred her contributions to those submitted by other informants. To the contrary, the fact that several of Anna's tales were never printed shows that he evaluated them first of all in regard to their loyalty to the "core" of tradition. Regardless of his warm sentiments for the child, he judged them in the same objective way that he judged other contributions. In the margins of one of Anna's tales he wrote: "It's overwhelming and invented." Similar remarks also appeared in Wilhelm's handwriting on other rejected tales, and they were not meant as a compliment. Even Wilhelm's son, Hermann, had his own experience with rejected tales, and so had a boy named Willi, who loved to tell stories to the Grimms, but whose tales were not always coherent and therefore were not printed.[29]

Whatever some handwriting experts may find out in the future, one or more tales from Anna among the big pile of unprinted tales related to the *Kinder- und Hausmärchen* would not make much difference to our understanding of the work itself. Yet the case of Anna as a whole makes it seem important to emphasize more than it has been in the past that a child contributed actively to the Grimms' folktale collection and that starting at the age of ten, Anna faithfully recorded from the oral tradition, without assistance from her parents or siblings in the technical aspects of writing. The rediscovered Arnswaldt tale also gives more evidence that the Grimms encouraged their informants to stay close to the oral tradition. When we think of children as potential writers, we usually focus on creativity, not on their potential talent in fieldwork recordings of popular tales. Anna's example may be encouraging for our children as well. Her serious and dedicated involvement in writing down stories for the Brothers Grimm became a lifetime hobby that she also pursued in later years. As a young child of ten, she may not have been the best "recorder" of tales, but she certainly turned out to be one of the most enthusiastic contributors to the Grimms' folktale collection.

[The Language and Games of Children]

Among the oral sources that the Grimms explored was the language of children. This included the language of folk songs, prayers, proverbs, sayings, and nursery rhymes as well as children's games and superstitions, all of which were rich in folktale motifs and archaic and idiomatic expressions. On a selective basis, the Grimms integrated some aspects of the traditional language of children into the text of the *Kinder- und Hausmärchen*, either to restore some missing portions to the tales or to add life and credibility to their folktale style. They maintained that the language of childhood had been an integral part of the storytelling tradition and that it still belonged to the oral tale in the present.

Both Brothers Grimm were keen listeners. On their daily walks to town and during visits with friends and strangers, they noted their speaking habits, such as dialectical or colloquial expressions, archaic words and phrases, proverbs, and traditional sayings. They also lent an open ear to children, whose songs and sayings they had already recorded for the third volume of *The Boy's Wonderhorn*. By watching children at play, Wilhelm observed a close relationship with the language of folktales. In counting rhymes, songs, and children's games, he also noted parallels in medieval manuscripts and chapbooks. These had in common the concrete and lively nature imagery of *Naturpoesie* and the spirit of naivete that he and his brother hoped to recapture in folktales. He also observed that the language of children and folktales had retained some archaic elements that had largely been lost in modern abstractions.

Jacob shared Wilhelm's interest in the lore and language of children and integrated various observations into his linguistic studies, mostly in relation to language change and development. Wilhelm was less inclined to follow an analytical approach and rather noted in descriptive terms some parallels in folktales and epics. Each time he came across some corresponding archaic expressions, he was delighted as if he had rediscovered a precious treasure of the long-forgotten past. He collected children's expressions and rhymes in a similar way as he collected folktales, writing them down as he heard them and adding to his notes parallel expressions used in medieval manuscripts. Occasionally, he would also relate them to native folk beliefs and common superstitions. By loosely arranging his selected examples, he would comment on their relationship to each other in a somewhat impressionistic way. Far from being dry in his approach, he always retained a lively tone that seemed to express a sense of wonder. Evidently he was delighted at the discovery that the child's way of thinking and speaking so much resembled that of the finest *Naturpoesie.*

To the preface of the second edition of the *Kinder- und Hausmärchen* in 1819 he attached an essay titled "Kindersprache und Kinderglaube" ("The Language and Faith of Children").[30] The placement of this essay is significant, as it indicates its internal relationship with the folktale collection. Due to its length and lack of a clear structure, critics have largely ignored this essay or brushed it aside as unrelated to the *Märchen.* Yet there is an inner connection that links the folktales to the language of children as well as to the poetic language of medieval literature. The way in which Wilhelm hinted at this connection reveals that he perceived a direct link between some games, rhymes, and expressions used by children from past to present and their reflection in traditional folktales. The essay also gives some clues to Wilhelm's folktale style, as it explores the sound patterns and imagery that are so prevalent in the language of children.

Wilhelm observed that young children preferred to use diminutives, perhaps because grown-ups customarily spoke to them this way. While the Swiss word "*Dädi*" (daddy) might be explained in terms of its relationship to such older words as "*Atte*" and "*Tatte*," this was hardly the case with "*Nännä*" (*Mutter*, or mother) or "*Dodoah*" (*Großmutter*, or grandmother). On the basis of etymology it would also be difficult to explain the word "*Ditti*" (*Kind*, or child) that was still used in Hesse near the River Main (*Maingegend*), or such terms as "*Appeli*" (*Närrchen*, or little fool) and other terms used as nicknames for small children that belonged solely to the Swiss German dialect. In Germany, parents might still call their young ones "*Täubchen*" (little dove) or "*Hühnchen*" (little chicken). In some areas, the term "*Neshäkchen*" (little nest clinger, or literally: little nest hook) was still in use for the youngest child, which in the Low German dialect was "*Neest-kiken*" (chick-in-the-nest or little nest bird).

Why, then, were such diminutives used with children? Wilhelm found a simple explanation: Most adults enjoyed using the vivid and concrete language of diminutes as much as their own children, as it helped them to communicate with them in an affectionate way. Such sound words used in baby talk with young childen as *"Mu-kuh"* (mooh-cow), for example, or *"Piephuhn"* (beep-chicken), *"Kikeriki-Hahn"* (cockedoodle-doo-cock), *"Blä-Lamm"* (baah-lamb), *"Wauhund"* or *"Wauwau"* (bow-wow dog or bow-wow), *"Misekatz"* (pussy-cat), or *"Hottpferd"* (hotti horse), were not derived etymologically from another root but merely imitated the natural sounds of creatures. Children liked such words as they were vivid and concrete.

Still more dynamic were the imaginative and humorous aspects of the language that adults often used with children. If a grown-up offered a child some drinking water, he might call it *"Gänsewein"* (goose wine), a name that evoked the humorous image of wine served to geese — a most distinguished drink indeed! To avoid the usual preaching at bedtime, parents sometimes told their children that it was time for them to get ready for "marching into the cradle" (*"in die Wiege marschieren"*). In Low German, the euphemism for bed would be *"Eija"* (*"in die Eija marschieren"*), a word based on a mere rhyming word in the children's song "Eija, popaija, what moves in the straw?" ("Eija, popaia, was raschelt im Stroh"). Another common expression used at bedtime related to the folktale of Frau Holle (Mother Hulda). Jokingly, a parent might say that the child should "take a walk in the feather-bed road" (*"in der Federallee spazierengehen*). In Pomerania, a naughty child was called "a little weed" *"een Krüdken,"* or *Kräutchen* in High German). When a child misbehaved, a parent might say, tongue-in-cheek, that he'd soon give him the "Lenten bread" (*Lendenbrood*, or *Lentenbrot* in High German) or that he might get him with a bundle of sticks (*Ruthe* or *Rute*). Children knew that at Christmas time Ruprecht would come, the dark companion of St. Nicholas, who would bring the *Rute* for naughty children but gifts and candies for the good ones. Adults might also use the teasing expression "The little mouse will bite you" (". . . *dat di dat Mäuseken beit"*).

Some traditional prayers, too, touched upon tradition as well as the childlike imagination. Wilhelm singled out one that combined Christian elements with folk beliefs of pre-Christian times while sending the child to sleep. While the first verse alludes to children's faith in the protective love of the guardian angel, the second verse directs their attention to the tree in Heaven, an image that suggests the Nordic World Ash, Yggdrasil:

In Heaven stands a tree
On which I hang my dream
On which I hang my sins.
In God's name go to sleep.

(Im Himmel steht ein Baum
Dran häng ich meinen Traum.
Dran häng ich meine Sünden.
In Gottes Namen schlafe ein.)[31]

Childlike is the image of the tree on which one may hang up one's dream along with one's sins, as if both were concrete objects, like clothes that one might hang in a closet at bedtime. As nightmares and sins have been put away into their proper place, neither one can now disturb his peace. The child can manage his fears and sleep in God's name. Like in the language of myths and folktales, concrete nouns and verbs take the place of abstractions. The closing of the prayer is what Wilhelm called "consoling and comforting" in regard to the ending of folktales.

Several more of Wilhelm's examples point to the rich imagery of the child's language as well as to its self-dynamics. In referring to the inter-relationship of the language of children and common folk beliefs, he explained that childlike expressions sometimes had a tendency to create a new story. The common expression "*Hasenbrot*" (hare bread or rabbit bread), for example, which was often used colloquially in relation to fresh bread made from new grain, gave rise to the myth of the hare who used to bake his bread along the roadside. Sometimes natural phenomena were the source of imaginative expressions that had a special appeal to children while stimulating the storytelling process. When the fog was hovering over the mountains, grown-ups would say "the hare is cooking in his kitchen," or "the fox takes a bath." Such traditional expressions, based on the understanding that children had an imaginative view of nature and reality, made children believe that the hare was indeed cooking something in his kitchen and that the fox was truly taking a bath. In talking with children, adults often catered to this language, as they enjoyed its imaginative quality and its closeness to nature. But in doing so, they also stimulated children's interest in stories.

He further observed that some children's games were based on such concrete and vivid expressions that language and action had become inseparable. This was the case with such customary expressions as "snowballing," for example, "making angels" in the snow, building a snowman, or playing top and the whip. One game in which two children hit each other's fingers on the table top by using only their forefingers, characteristically was called *Paw* (paw) in Switzerland and *Tatze* or *Datze* (claw) in Germany. Such words vividly evoked the very nature of the game and hardly needed a footnote or instructions to be understood by young and old alike. Different regions of the country had different names for such games, as they were often derived from dialectical ex-pressions, but they were based on the same instant communication in terms of their childlike imagery. Making flat stones "jump" on the surface of the water, for example, was a game called by such names as "Throw-ing a Frog," "Letting the Virgin Dance," "Freeing a Peasant," or "Cutting

Bread." In each case, such expressions represented vivid folk speech that was flavored by the visual resemblance of a certain movement.

The language used in conversations with children often assumed a dynamics of its own while leading the child on toward creative storytelling. This was also true for such casual expressions as: "My little finger has told me," which adults would sometimes use if they wished to hide from children whoever had told them about a certain incident. Interpreting such expressions literally, young children might think that the little finger had really betrayed the secret. Sometimes adults would speak to them figuratively on purpose, just to tease them a little. If childen pressured them too much for a gift, for example, they might say: "Sure, sure, I'll bring you a 'Wait-a-while!'" Being pressured for storytelling, they sometimes also teased them with a never-ending story: "There was once a little man who wished to pick some nuts. 'Would you like me to tell you a story?' he asked the children. 'Yes, please!' they responded eagerly. 'All right, then,' said the little man. 'There was once a little man who wished to pick some nuts. Would you like me to tell you a story?' . . ." Parents enjoyed using the child's language at the sight of sparks flying away from a burning piece of paper. It was customary to say:

> The paper is the church
> The fire's in the steeple
> The sexton locks the door
> And out jump the people![32]

Nature herself might remind grown-ups of traditional stories simply because some natural objects reminded them of children. Thus, two apples growing together on a branch were called "*Kindsappel*" (child's apple), an expression based on the common perception that children, like friends, often loved each other. Many Nordic sagas as well as some medieval poems vividly illustrated the mutual affection of young children. To children as well as to the common folk, nature was animated and alive. In fluffy little clouds they usually saw little lambs (*Lämmerchen*); in a red evening sky they recognized "God feeding his herd of sheep." A certain cloud formation might be a spider web or an umbrella. Upon seeing some blinking stars, one would say: "Now God shuts the door to Heaven," an expression that was meant to incite little children to go to bed quickly. Stars were "the golden nails on the heavenly gate," the moon was "the lock of the door to Heaven," and the snowflakes were "feathers."

Wilhelm related in this context some examples from the folktale collection that illustrated the poetic origin of some expressions. Everyone knew, of course, that when it snowed on earth it was because Mother Hulda (Frau Holle) or the Golden Marie shook the feather beds. In reference to snow, children might also say that the miller and the baker were fighting each other. The image of flour for snow related to an old folk belief in which people during a heavy snowstorm would throw flour out of the window to "feed" the "greedy wind." An old children's rhyme still reminded of this custom:

> Calm down, dear Wind
> Bring this to your child!
>
> (Lege dich, lieber Wind
> Bring dies deinem Kind!)[33]

Such an animated view of nature reminds one of Hansel's response to the witch's question of who had nibbled on her roof:

> The Wind, the Wind,
> The Heavenly Child . . .
>
> Der Wind, der Wind,
> das himmlische Kind . . .[34]

In folktales and children's verse, the world was animated and alive. The language of children revealed the old folk belief that gave life and speech to the sun, the moon, the stars, and the trees. Flowers, rocks, stones, and birds were alive and spoke with human voices, and even the wind blew with human anger and whispered a secret warning. As in the world of myths and folktales, children spoke to the elements and natural objects, and these, in turn, responded with human speech. In Wilhelm's essay "The Nature of Folktales," he commented on the folktale's animated worldview: "Already the *animation of all of nature* could be considered as a continuing tradition from pagan times. We are no strangers to such a worldview, as we know that it belonged to heathenism everywhere. . . ."[35] These words echo the philosophy of the German Romantic poets, but we also recognize in them the child's imaginative view of reality. Wilhelm Grimm recognized in both the naivete of a bygone age that was still alive in *Naturpoesie* and the language of children.

What was it that characterized children and childhood? Wilhelm pondered this question in relation to the image of children in medieval literature, where children had been portrayed as pure and naive creatures that were touching in their natural state of innocence, purity, loyalty, and honesty. By citing relevant passages from the *Elder Edda*, the Nordic sagas, from Wernher, Fischart, Freidank, and Walter von der Vogelweide, he painted an image of children as graceful creatures who were often so absorbed in play that they forgot the reality. Young children generally lived in the present, took pleasure in bright and glistening things, and sometimes cried for instantaneous satisfaction. More so than adults, they were easily guided by their imagination. Already some medieval poems had shown how very young children would press their little hands against their eyes to make themselves "invisible." Rather than scolding them for such an illusion, grown-ups would smile at such an innocence and enjoy it, as much as they enjoyed the child's contentment as he played with such simple objects as stones, eggs, balls or apples.

Literature and art throughout the ages had shown children at play in such a simple and imaginative way, be it in ancient Egypt or in ancient Greece. The same innocent spirit of childhood was also reflected in folktales and legends, in which children were close to nature, pure, honest, and absorbed in play. In folktales, epics, and the Bible, as well, the innocence of childhood also appeared in relation to medieval and ancient concepts of law and justice. In older societies, be it in the Germanic North or in ancient Egypt, a person accused of crime was often tested in his innocence. The Nordic sagas told of a little boy who had killed his little sister in a game. Testing the boy's innocence, the judge took into one hand a nice red apple and in the other a gold piece (*Rhenish Gulden*). Then stretching both hands toward the boy, he asked him to choose one or the other. Because the boy chose the apple, he was declared innocent. In a related Bible story, the Pharaoh had played with a little boy (young Moses). Suddenly the boy took advantage of him by plucking hard at his beard and kicking his crown into the dust. The angered Pharaoh wanted to punish the boy severely, but his advisers persuaded him to put the boy's innocence to a test. In this case, the judge placed red-hot coals on one platter and gold coins on another, letting him choose between them. Guided by the archangel Gabriel, Moses reached for the coals—and was freed.[36]

Walther von der Vogelweide had already observed that the rod would not chasten the child, observed Wilhelm, which meant that he had perceived the child's true character in its innocence and purity. Wilhelm supported the ancient wisdom of such stories while considering them "documents" of certain universal qualities that had characterized children everywhere and at all times. For each example cited, he listed many more variants in the folk tradition to prove his point.

Literature and customs of many ancient nations had depicted a certain reverence and respect for the child because of such qualities. One form of respect had been to bestow gifts upon them as a symbolic gesture of expressing one's blessings or good wishes. At the present time it was still a custom for godparents to bring a gift to their godchildren on the day of baptism, just as it had been a custom among the ancient Germanic people to bring gifts to children on teething day (the day when a child grew his first tooth) or on name's day, when children received their surnames. In this connection Wilhelm related a tale of the baby Hrorwardshad from the *Elder Edda* (2, 33), who uttered his first words when his mother gave him the name of Helge. He had cried out loud demanding, "I want a gift!" In another Nordic myth, Freija had received her residence of Alfheim as a "tooth gift" from the gods. According to an old custom, parents would be expected to bring a gift for their children upon returning from a trip. Often, they would ask beforehand, "What shall I bring you?" Whereas boys usually received toys (wooden horses, flutes, pictures), girls would receive dresses or jewelry. Such customs were still reflected in such folktales as "Ashputtel"("Aschenputtel") and "The Singing, Soaring Lark" ("Löweneckerchen").[37]

Children's games reflected the same universal joy and imagination of childhood as the language of children, observed Wilhelm, and the same spirit of naivete and simplicity. Often they involved simple sticks, stones, chips, tops, broomstick "riding horses," or a small paper windmill fastened upon a wooden rod. Most of such games are still customary at present day, whether children played them alone or in small groups, in the streets, on playgrounds. Konrad von Würzburg had mentioned a game with stones in his well-researched book *Die Jugend des Paris* (*The Youth of Paris*), and a certain Berthold had observed the game in his work *Reise durch Rußland* (*Travels in Russia*). Niebuhr had found it among the ancient people of Arabia, and there was also an illustration of it on a Grecian urn.

Especially traditional games of younger children showed an animated worldview—translated into action. As children assumed different roles, they *were* the wolf or the sheep, as the rules demanded it. In the following dialogue Wilhelm especially noted the verbal challenges that added dynamics to the game:

> *Shepherd:* Sheep, sheep, come here.
> *Sheep:*   We aren't allowed to come.
> *Shepherd:* Why not?
> *Sheep:*   There is a big wolf at the front door.
> *Shepherd:* What is he doing there?
> *Sheep:*   He sharpens his knife.
> *Shepherd:* What does he want to do with it?
> *Sheep:*   He wants to cut our throats.[38]

In vain the shepherd came running to protect the sheep, for the vicious wolf stopped chasing them only after he had caught one with his teeth. The rule of the game was that the sheep that had been caught would now become the big bad wolf, and the game would then start over again from the beginning. Forgetting momentarily the real world around them, children *became* a part of nature and a part of the natural law, but they also exercised the ancient rules of justice.

The game touches upon some fable elements but more so upon some familiar themes in such folktales as "Little Red Cap" and "The Wolf and the Seven Kids." The sharpening of the knife reminds one of a scene in "Fitcher's Bird" or "Bluebeard." Wilhelm did ask if the wolf might create a phobia in the young child. He knew then what Bettelheim revealed in our time that children have the world of light and darkness within themselves, even without playing wolf and sheep or without reading folktales. The role reversal at the end of the game seems to have been part of the ancient system of justice.

Among the other action games that caught Wilhelm's imagination were Cat and Mouse, Pulling Someone Down from the Mountain, Ring-a-Wreath, and the Pea Game, all of which involved a similar reversal of roles. Several of these also focused on verbal battles derived from such seasonal rituals as the battle of King Summer and King Winter on the first day of spring. Games such as these reflected folk festivals and folk beliefs of long ago—a subject that Jacob pursued on an extended scale in *Deutsche Mythologie* (*Teutonic Mythology*).

Many children's games also related to seasonal festivals that had been celebrated throughout the ages. On St. Nicholas Day on December 6, Mardi Gras (called Fastnacht), Epiphany (day of the Three Wise Kings), Spring Day (battle of King Summer and King Winter), May Day (dance around the maypole), and St. John's Day (the ancient summer solstice), for example, children would dress up and recite traditional songs and verses. Wilhelm's comments on each of these traditional festivals may be considered an extension of a number of related songs and verses that he and Jacob had already included in *The Boy's Wonderhorn*. Some of the verses also recurred in folktales, and Wilhelm recognized them as such.

Among children's superstitions and folk beliefs, he cited the familiar "Lady-Bug" song ("*Marienkäferchen*"),[39] along with songs about storks, wells, and Mother Hulda, all of which were endowed with the power of fulfilling the wish for a new baby. Wilhelm also related children's prophecies involving good-luck omens and bad-luck omens, such as drawing the shorter straw or holding a buttercup up to a child's chin. Well-known in the Grimms' time was the prophetic game of plucking the petals of a small wild daisy, the "star flower" (*Sternblume*), also called "little goose flower" (*Gänseblümchen*): "He loves me, he loves me not. He loves me." Wilhelm Grimm recorded it as follows:

Du liebst mich	You love me
Von Herzen	With your heart
Mit Schmerzen	With sorrow
Wenig	A little
Gar nicht.	Not at all.[40]

He observed that such wishing games, too, occurred in folktales, myths, and legends, perhaps as remnants of an old faith in the power of words and magic. There was a certain word magic in the "Fisherman's Game," for example, that bore a faint resemblance to the word game in "Rumpelstiltskin." The "fisherman" was assigned to "catch" different kinds of "fish" by touching the other children. The child who was caught quickly had to name a fish, such as salmon, herring, or sprout, to become free again. If he failed to remember a name or did not react fast enough, he had to be "fisherman" in turn. Evidently, in children's games and folktales, the belief in the magic power of a name or word was still alive.

Rather modern were Wilhelm's views of verbal nonsense in children's games. Wilhelm realized that it could not possibly be explained by ancient laws, rituals, or magic. The only meaning he tried to detect was its humor and capacity to stimulate children to an agile and quick response. This applied to the "Beer Game," for example, in which children hid behind trees and upon a clue quickly changed places like in "Musical Chairs," as well as to the "Snail Game," the "Ring Game," the "Bran Game" and the "Bell Game," all of which dealt with something hidden, covered up, or secretly handed around while children quickly had to guess its hiding place or secret location. Such games and others seemed to aim at nothing but action and fun. This was especially true for the "Pea Game," which involved a verbal "tug-o-war" yet culminated in nothing but blowing, puffing, huffing—and laughter. There were no skills involved, no folk beliefs, rituals, or ancient themes of justice— and certainly no lessons and no morals!

> *Pea Master:* Give me a pea.
> *Children:*   I don't have any.
> *Pea Master:* Go to the Miller and get yourself one.
> *Children:*   He won't give me any.
> *Pea Master:* Then search for one.
> *Children:*   I can't find any.
> *Pea Master:* Then I'll blow on you.
> *Children:*   Then I'll defend myself. [41]

At the end, the children would take a deep breath and blow into each other's faces. The child who would blow the longest (without bursting into fits of laughter) would be "it" and become the new Pea Master. Perhaps this category showed best of all how much Wilhelm appreciated the pure delight of childhood games free from a didactic purpose. As such, his appreciative comments on such games are to be read, like a commentary on his 1812 preface in which he praised folktales as an education in *Naturpoesie*.

Wilhelm traced international variants in childhood games just as he traced international variants in folktales. Among others, he mentioned such Scottish and Welsh variants as "Blind Man's Buff" and "The Fox Goes About," games that were also mentioned in German medieval literature and folktales. He even cited English language variants in the text of his essay to show how close English children's games were to German ones. In loyalty to his theory of universal folktale origins, he made no attempt to find out in what country the game might have originated. As a possible source for some games he mentioned German medieval literature—but also the works of Shakespeare.

The Grimms' much-discussed folktale of the "Frog King" or "Frog Prince" ("*Froschkönig*") received attention in the context of Wilhelm's comparative study of children's ball games. Wilhelm perceived a universal motif in the opening scene where the princess played with her golden ball and accidentally dropped it into the well. Rather than contemplating the psychology of the young girl, her authoritative father, and her potential lover, as modern critics have done in many variations, he commented extensively on variants of ball games around the world, be it in folktales, folk songs, or medieval epics. He even discussed "stick golf" (croquet) in Scotland, and he simply concluded that throughout the ages and everywhere, boys and girls had always enjoyed playing ball, especially in springtime.[42]

With great ease and genuine delight, Wilhelm thus explored the traditional world of children, observing that the meaning of childhood games, like the meaning of folktales, lay deeply embedded in age-old mores, customs, and festivals that had been preserved but also in real life, involving childhood games and the children's traditional language. He thought that the language of children—with its strong rhythm, vivid imagery, affinity with nature, and reflection of magic, laws, and rituals—derived its dynamics from the oral tradition. As children sang their songs, told their tales, and played their games, they had added a new vitality that had kept it alive on playgrounds as well as in folktales. Just as in folktales, he also recognized in children's games a source of rich archaic expressions, including metaphors, symbols, and magic chants, as well as half-forgotten ancient laws and customs, a sense of humor, and a sense of justice. All of those showed that games were part of *Naturpoesie* that deserved to be preserved like folktales and medieval epics. Above all, children's games were universal and testified to a shared human experience around the world.

Jacob Grimm agreed with Wilhelm's conclusions, although he observed the phenomenon of shared human experience from another perspective. Instead of looking primarily at the language and games of children and noting some remnants of ancient laws, he turned his primary attention to ancient Germanic laws, as Savigny had taught him, noting in these some remarkable shards of *Naturpoesie*. In his essay "Law and Poetry" ("Das Recht and Poesie") he wrote: "Whatever emerges from one source is akin to itself and shows some mutual relations. Consequently, folk poetry will sustain the law and law will sustain folk poetry."[43]

[Printed Sources]

It should not come as a revelation that the Grimms also relied on printed sources, for not only have several modern critics examined this issue but the Grimms themselves did comment on these substantially in various essays as well in their notes to the *Kinder- und Hausmärchen*. Of the eighty-six folktales in the first edition of the *Kinder- und Hausmärchen*, only twelve came from literary sources, which means that the overwhelming number of collected tales was based on the oral tradition. While modern scholars generally agree that the *Kinder- und Hausmärchen* was innovative for its predominant use of oral sources, they express a wide range of opinions regarding the questions of under what circumstances and to what extent the Brothers Grimm used printed sources. Even though the Grimms listed some references to sources in their first and subsequent editions of the work and dedicated more than two hundred pages of combined notes in the third volume in 1822, not all of their notes have been widely available, and the ones that have been acceptable did not entirely satisfy the more exacting demands of modern scholars. While some critics ignored the bulk of their notes, others translated them incorrectly or interpreted them without the context of the Grimms' theories of language dynamics and folktale variants.

The Grimms listed a number of printed sources of folktales for three distinct reasons: to indicate variants in earlier publications, to establish the authenticity of a tale they had collected by word-of-mouth, and to give credit to sources from which they had paraphrased certain tale variants or other information.

In regard to the listing of variants, the Grimms essentially used the same method that they followed in annotating oral sources, namely to indicate a given tale's existence in various forms either in the German or foreign folktale collections. While rejecting the idea of an archetypal tale (*Urmärchen*), they searched for the truth among those variants of a given tale that, in their view, came relatively close to the core of tradition. They also searched for variants and traditional expressions in folk songs, proverbs, and children's games, as well as in earlier printed sources that closely reflected the oral folk tradition. In comparing their collected oral versions with corresponding earlier printed versions, they would write: "Like in the *Pentamerone*" or "Similar to a tale in Straparola" or "Already listed by Hans Sachs, but better" or "Appears in a slightly different form in the *Rollwagenbüchlein*." Sometimes the Grimms would elaborate on the similarities and differences among the variants. Whenever they wrote "*Wie in . . .*" (Like in . . .), such as "Like in Perrault,"[44] it meant that they indicated variants in different collections, regardless of whether these were tales based on folktales or other sources. Some critics all too quickly concluded that such notes were meant to acknowledge their direct use of a printed source, namely the collections of Perrault, Straparola, and Basile, etc. Although there were exceptions to the rule, such notes were not meant as acknowledgements of entire tales or tale portions quoted or paraphrased from another collection but rather as the Grimms' learned references to existing national or international variants.

Having served in one of the richest private library collections in their time in Göttingen, with access to the libraries of King Jerome, the Royal Library Collection, and valuable books lent to them by their friends, the Grimms took an obvious pleasure in establishing some interconnections between the oral tale and earlier collections, not for the sake of satisfying a collector's drive but to verify the older existence of a tale motif, theme, or character. In that sense they were much more than antiquarians satisfied with the accumulation of a wealth of stories. Rather, they made it their lifelong occupation to study the intimate interconnections of the oral and printed folk tradition, also in relation to their etymological dictionary.[45]

In the second type of notes, the Grimms pointed to an earlier printed source to prove a given tale's age in the German folk tradition. They worked on the assumption that if an oral tale showed some definite similarities with an earlier printed source that itself was closely based on the oral tradition, they would be able to show its established tradition on German soil. For that purpose, they searched out such printed sources that in terms of language and substance were relatively close to the oral folk tradition and therefore genuine and considered as landmarks of tradition. They might cite in this connection some German chapbooks, German medieval manuscripts, and sixteenth- and seventeenth-century writers known for their "rootedness" in dialects and the German folk tradition. Simultaneously, however, they never neglected to search out international variants as well, be it in regard to folktale collections from England, Scotland, Ireland, Wales, the Slavic countries, the Middle East, or Africa.

Already toward the end of the nineteenth century, German critics with nationalistic inclinations showed little interest in such broad international references, and modern folklorists have largely ignored them, as they have long used different ways of establishing the age and authenticity of a folktale.[46]

The third type of notes unmistakably did show the Grimms' effort to give credit to direct quotations or paraphrases from published sources. This type has been the most problematic one for many critics, as it seemed to prove beyond doubt from specific printed sources that the Grimms had "borrowed" some of their tales. In the seventh edition of 1857, for example, the Grimms supposedly based 49 out of a total of 211 tales on literary sources. Does this mean that they had become disloyal to their own principles of searching out the oral tradition? This is not the case if we consider that they primarily selected from the printed sources those that in substance were based on the oral tradition. They were consistent in terms of rejecting for this purpose printed tales based on fantasy or fiction. Among such acknowledged sources were the medieval chapbooks or folk books (*Volksbücher*), for example, which Joseph Görres at the time collected and published as a significant part of *Naturpoesie*. Dating back to the fifteenth and sixteenth centuries, they were written in a simple, sometimes crafty language, entailing such well-known popular legends as "The Haimond's Children," "Emperor Octavian," "The History of Doctor Faustus," "The Horned Siegfried," and "Melusine." The legends of Barbarossa and Duke Ernst were also available in chapbook form, and so were the tales of "Genovefa," "Griseldis," and "Helena," in which legendary material was combined with romance. Besides, there was the jolly trickster tale of "The Merry Tyll" and the Numskull story of "The Seven Swabians," based on earlier *Lalebuch* (*Fool's Book*).[47] While the Grimms used the bulk of chapbook sources for the *German Legends*, some of them also made it into the *Kinder- und Hausmärchen*, to the extent that they still lived in the oral tradition as well.

The *Rollwagenbüchlein* (*Little Rolling Wagon Book*), which was published by the scribe and book-store manager Georg Wickram in Colmar in 1555, inspired the Grimms with its folkloristic inclinations. So did Jakob Frey's *Gartengesellschaft* (*Garden Society*), partially based on works by Bebel Poggio and J. A. Muling in Strassburgh, which was known for its proximity to the oral folk tradition. Seventeen tales in that collection alone were based on oral sources, among which were also some of Wickram's tales. Among the Grimms' printed sources was further Martin Montanus's *Der Wegkürzer* (*The Path Shortener*), published in 1557. Like his work of 1560, *Das Ander Theyl der Gartengesellschaft* (*The Other Part of the Garden Society*), it was largely based on the oral tradition, especially as far as jokes and anecdotes were concerned, even though it also borrowed from the popular works by Wickram, Pauli, Poggio, and others. In the *Wegkürzer* we find the Grimms' tale "The Valiant Tailor," which evidently had been preserved since that time in the German oral tradition.[48]

Frequently, the Grimms referred their readers to Johann Fischart's books, many of which preserved the oral folklore of the sixteenth and earlier centuries. Some called him a plagiarist, for more than thirty of the eighty-six tales contained in his *Schildwacht* (*Sentinel*) of 1560 were taken from older printed tales, including the *Rastbüchlein* (*Little Book of Rest*) of 1558, yet it is estimated that twenty-seven tales were directly based on the oral tradition. The Brothers Grimm considered Fischart's works invaluable source books for the German oral tradition, not only for anecdotes, jests, plays, and folktales (tale number 33, "The Best Friend and the Worst Friend" may also be found in Fischart) but also for folk songs, proverbs, and children's games of Elsace-Lorraine. The latter inspired especially Wilhelm in his own collection of children's games. In his essays on the lore and language of children Wilhelm Grimm made frequent references also on Fischart's observations of the poetic expression of some sayings and songs used by children.[49]

The works of Hans Sachs were another valuable source of folklore for the Brothers Grimm. He was a writer of satires and vigorously defended the Reformation. Between 1494 and 1576 he produced close to 200 plays, integrating into these not only colloquial speech and dialects but also themes of antiquity, medieval legends, fables, and folktales. Goethe rediscovered Hans Sachs's great art of using in his work the common folk theme and language, particularly authentic folk jest and folk humor. Four of the Grimms' folktales may be traced back to Hans Sachs (even though not entirely), "The Unequal Daughters of Eve" (number 180), "The Seven Swabians," (number 119), "The Devil's Animals and God's" (number 148), and "The Rejuvenated Little Man" (number 147). Wilhelm Grimm himself gave credit to Hans Sachs to the earlier form of the "liar's tale," of which some also appeared in the *Kinder- und Hausmärchen*. He accredited him for having used popular braggart's tales, a type of folktale that Wilhelm discussed in detail in his analysis of predominant folktale characters. Hans Sachs also mentioned in his work the never-never land of "*Schlaraffenland*" (known by Fischart as *Gargantua*) that in the *Kinder- und Hausmärchen* appeared under the title of "*Schlauraffenland*"[50] In all cases it is the wonderful upside-down land of milk and honey, where candies grow on trees and roasted ducks fly through the air, where fences are made of sausages and houses of gingerbread, and where diligence gets punished while laziness rules.

It would be exaggerated, however, to believe that the Brothers Grimm relied exclusively on such printed sources, even if they mentioned them in their notes. In most cases, they were familiar with at least portions of the printed tales from the oral tradition. In the case of oral-tale fragments, however, they relied on printed versions to supplement the missing parts, for in consistency with their own principles they did not wish to rely solely on their memory or mere intuition. Some tales had indeed been well-known for a long time, from both the oral and the printed versions. Already in 1595, Georg Rollenhagen had referred to such "wunderschöne Hausmärchen" (wonderful household tales as "Aschenpössel" ("Ashputtel") and "Iron Henry" ("Der eiserne Heinrich," who later evolved into a character in the "Frog King"), tales that reappeared in the Grimms' collection.[51]

The list of published "folk sources" to which the Grimms referred in their notes seems to be endless and overwhelming. Among these were also the seventeenth-century works of Michael Moscherosch, Johannes Prätorius, and Philip Harsdörffer, as well as the collections of J. R. Wyss and the theologian Nachtigall, who published under the pseudonym of Otmar. The Grimms utilized a number of legends and chronicles from these sources for the *Deutsche Sagen* (*German Legends*), which appeared in 1816. They told these legends in chronological order, in keeping with the historical events to which they were related, beginning with the Germanic tribes and moving on to the Goths, Langobards, and Franks. They arranged the regional legends thematically, for such folktale creatures as dwarfs, giants, witches, devils, and monsters appeared everywhere, with little relevance to historical periods or geographical areas. To the extent that they recognized in some of these legends parallel themes or motifs in folktales, they would cite them in their notes to the *Kinder- und Hausmärchen*.

Such a misunderstanding is particularly evident with respect to the Grimms' supposed "borrowing" from the collection of Charles Perrault. Perrault's *Contes de ma mère l'oye* (*Tales of My Mother Goose*) appeared in 1697, more than a century prior to the *Kinder- und Hausmärchen*, sharing with that work such tales as "Little Red Riding Hood," "Sleeping Beauty," "Cinderella," "Toads and Diamonds," "Hop O' My Thumb," and "Puss in Boots." Some critics simplified the issue by assuming that because the Grimms had published their tales later than Perrault, because they had known his tales since their childhood days, and because some of their informants had some French Huguenot blood, they must have taken the stories directly from that source.

What did the Grimms themselves have to say about Perrault? First of all, they well knew that he had not given his readers an unpolluted folk tradition. "It appears," wrote Wilhelm in his introduction to the 1812 edition of the *Kinder- und Hausmärchen*, "as if in some cases Perrault first invented stories before they were disseminated among the people. It is said that [his] Tom Thumb was aimed at becoming an imitation of Homer, for the purpose of making it clear to children what a hard lot Odysseus had with Polyphemos."[52] Nevertheless, Wilhelm expressed respect for his style, considering his use of vivid dialogues and colloquial expressions far superior to that of Madame d'Aulnoy.

> Perrault has perceived the folktales in an undiluted form and, aside from some minor elements, has nothing added to them. The style is simple and natural, and to the degree that the smooth and polished literary language permitted it at his time, he also captured the childlike tone. He preserved some good colloquial expressions, such as: she comes *"tant que la terre put la porter,"* or: she went *"de douze mille lieues de la,"* or: *je vais manger ma viande:* "I want to eat," and quite certainly Bluebeard's question and answer are derived from the oral tradition: *"Anne, ma soeur Anne, ne vois tu rien venir?"* —*"Je ne vois rien, que le soleil, qui pondroie, et l'herbe, qui verdoie."* It is without doubt due to such advantages that the book has survived to the present time.[53]

At first glance it appears quite self-evident that the Grimms should have based the story of "Bluebeard" ("Blaubart"), for example, directly on Charles Perrault's "La barbe bleue." However, their corresponding notes show that in spite of their close knowledge of Perrault, they relied on the variant that was alive in Germany at the time. How little they were concerned to claim it as a "German" tale, however, is evident from their reference to the journal *Schwedische Fliegende Blätter* (Swedish Flying Leaves) in 1810, where it had first appeared in print, "yet as a mere translation." In this version, Sister Anne had climbed on the tower to look out for the rescuers, which was not the case in the German variant that they had heard. The Grimms wrote, "As we heard it, this part is altogether missing. Instead, another aspect occurs, namely that the frightened woman hides the bloody key in the hay—a variant that truly corresponds to the German folk belief that hay draws out the blood. They also referred to *Des Knaben Wunderhorn* (Vol. 1, p. 274) and to Herder's *Volkslieder* (part 3, p. 79), as well as to Gräter's edition of *Folk Songs from Breslau*, which essentially contained the same tale, yet in some variations—and without the blue beard. Further, certain motifs of this tale were to be found in such tales of the *Kinder- und Hausmärchen* as tales number 43 and 76. In a comparative gesture, they introduced the reader to related stories in the Old Scottish Song of Cospatrik, the tale of King Pork in Straparola, and the frame story of the *Arabian Nights*, in which the sultan used to kill his wives after the wedding night. The *Gesta Romanorum* (late thirteenth-century England) contained a story in which a mother, who had killed four of her own children, unsuccessfully tried to wipe off the blood from her hand, which then motivated her to wear one glove.[54]

Whenever the Grimms were conscious that one of their own collected tales strongly resembled a tale by Perrault, they tested its rootedness in the German oral tradition also in other regions of Germany, in earlier printed German collections, or in medieval chapbooks, manuscripts, or epics. Where they could establish the existence of such a variant, they would retain the respective tale, yet where this was not the case, they would drop it. Such was the case, for example, with "Puss in Boots," which Wilhelm Grimm already in 1815 had referred to as "the only exception" to the rule, as far as his selection process was concerned. At that time, he once more emphasized that he did not believe in an archetypal tale or *Urmärchen* that served as a model for all subsequent tales in tradition. Most of the Italian, French, and Oriental collections were not read by the common folk in the country, as they lacked foreign-language skills and anyhow read very little. No variant was either right or wrong, but each one, in accordance with its own oral tradition, had its legitimate existence. It was only natural that, over time, smaller elements in the tale had taken on different colors. Instead of projecting a perfect "primeval image" of one given tale into a certain region or country, one should get accustomed to the idea that each tale variant represented an attempt of the people to get closer to a tale that existed as an inexhaustible idea in manyfold ways (". . . *da es im Gegentheil vielleicht nur Versuche sind, einem im Geist blos vorhandenen, unerschöpflichen Wesen sich zu nähern*")[55]

The case of "Little Red Riding Hood" was less clear-cut than that of "Puss in Boots." Wilhelm left open the question of influence, indicating that it might give readers something to wonder about that the tale appeared nowhere else except in Perrault. This comment shows his awareness of the possible influence of Perrault on the oral folk tradition in Germany, but it hinted at no definite conclusions. In most cases they found enough evidence of variants among the oral and printed German sources.

It belongs to Edgar Taylor's myth (and later to that of the German nationalists and the Nazis) to believe that the Grimms searched exclusively for folktale variants in the myths and sagas of the Nordic Germanic tradition. In some German tales (as well as in Perrault's) the Grimms noted primarily a strong Italian influence, particularly in regard to the famous folktale collections of Francisco Straparola and Giambattista Basile.

Without necessarily deciding the question of which tale had influenced which, they frequently referred to these sources in their notes to the *Kinder- und Hausmärchen*. Overall, however, the Grimms were more given to believe that the Italian tales had influenced the German tales rather than the other way around. In 1822 Wilhelm commented that there was an intimate interconnection among Italian, French, and German folktales, and that in all likelihood, the Italians had come first.[56] Such an admission hardly sounds like the ethnocentric view of a nationalist wishing to prove under all circumstances that the folktales were German. Rather, it reaffirms the Grimms' open-minded international approach to folktale collections.

The Grimms admired the tales of Basile so much that they planned on publishing an entire volume of them in their own translation. In 1813, while Jacob resided in Vienna, Wilhelm reminded his brother of such plans, yet mentioned simultaneously that in the meantime he had accumulated so many German folktales that they might as well postpone the Italian project. As it turned out, the second volume of the *Kinder- und Hausmärchen* in 1815 indeed included only German tales, but Wilhelm realized the plan in a slightly different context in the 1819 second edition of this work. He dedicated a substantial portion of the third volume to Straparola's *Nights* and Basile's *Pentamerone*, within a broadly conceived analysis of world folklore collections spanning from Europe to Asia, Africa to North America.

Wilhelm Grimm analyzed Straparola's *Nights* before he discussed Basile's *Pentamerone* because it was published earlier and also because it was better-known in Germany than Basile's. The earliest German translation had been made by a certain Caravaggio in Vienna in 1791, and another shorter edition had come out in Berlin in 1817, translated by Friedrich Wilhelm Valentin Schmidt, under the title of *Märchen-Saal (Folktale Ballroom)*. Wilhelm, however, relied on his own translation in neither one of these translations but rather on the more complete Venetian edition of 1573, as well as a French translation, believing that in this way he would get closer to the original version of the work. To facilitate a comparison of variants for his readers, however, he referred in his notes to page numbers in Schmidt and tale numbers in the *Kinder- und Hausmärchen*. His tale summaries represent a sort of shorthand style and essentially aim at the major theme of the tale, its core or essence.

> *Master Carpacifico.* Is cheated and cheats in turn. Schmidt, p. 133. Related to the German tale of "The Little Peasant," No. 61.[57]

Occasionally, he added a value judgment regarding the better variant of the two:

> *The Three Brothers.* Schmidt, p. 262. More complete and better in Pentamerone's "The Five Sons," No. 47, and in the German tale of "The Four Brothers," No. 129. *Kinder- und Hausmärchen,* 3rd ed.[58]

Wilhelm was fascinated by Basile's collection, partially because it was written in the vivid Neapolitan dialect and partially because he was convinced that Basile had added nothing to the tales in terms of his own inventions or literary adornments.

In his international folktale analysis of 1822, Wilhelm introduced Giambattista Basile by his assumed name of Giam Alesiv Abbatutis, who had lived at the beginning of the sixteenth century, spending his youth on the island of Crete, where he met with some Venetians. Later, he followed his sister, a famous singer, to Mantua and entered the service of a duke, whose favors permitted him to travel widely through Italy. He published the *Pentamerone* in 1737 in Naples, a work that was reedited six or seven times until 1788. Wilhelm mentioned that he had access to a relatively unknown 1749 edition, owned by his friend Clemens Brentano.

Brentano originally inspired him to read the tales of Basile, for he had made some plans of publishing a popular translation for German children. When he had abandoned this project—as he abandoned the German folktale collection—to pursue his own writing of fantasies, he opened the way for Wilhelm to continue the job.

Wilhelm found a noticeable difference in the styles of Straparola and Basile on the one hand and the traditional German storytelling style on the other. The tone of the German style was generally calm, childlike, simple, and naive, he wrote, whereas the Italian style, being geared toward an audience of adults, was spiced with wit, irony, and quick turns of speech based on proverbial and idiomatic expressions. He found that such a style was difficult to render in German translation, the more so as it included a number of gross and erotic expressions that might be deemed offensive if translated too literally. Nevertheless, he praised especially in Basile a thorough and immediate knowledge of the dialect and an extraordinary skill in perceiving and rendering the tales in a complete, lively, and convincing way. He thought that Basile had found the right tone of the tales as he rendered them in a homey Neapolitan dialect. By contrast, Straparola had used a smooth narrative style that conformed too much to the literary taste of his time. Wilhelm concluded:

Consequently, one can consider Basile's collection with its rich contents as the very basis by which to evaluate all others. Even though in reality this collection may not have been the basis of all European tales—for, to the contrary, it was not even known outside of the country [Italy] and had not even been translated into French—it has the advantage of demonstrating a great inter-connection among the (European) tales. With respect to their essential elements, two-thirds of the tales correspond to German tales that are still alive in modern times.[59]

Wilhelm's statement confirms his theory regarding the mysterious interconnection of folktales in various nations. Without being obsessed by wishing to prove the German influence abroad or the Italian influence in Germany, he merely praised as a great advantage the existence of folktale variants within the European tradition. He felt that the strong correspondence between Basile's tales and those of the German folk tradition proved that Basile had substantially relied on the oral tradition, for if he had largely used printed sources, their appeal would certainly be less universal. He felt that, more so than Perrault, Straparola, and others, Basile had also abstained from imposing his own fantasies upon the folktales. His tales were as true to the folk tradition as they were to the Neapolitan dialect.

In the third volume of the *Kinder- und Hausmärchen* of 1822, Wilhelm dedicated almost 200 pages, or about half of that volume, to a discussion of foreign folktale collections. In this context, he discussed at length the *Gesta Ramanorum,* which had already inspired Shake-speare, as well as folktale collections of England, Scotland, Ireland, and Denmark. Among the French tales, he gave detailed attention to Perrault, Madame d'Aulnoy, and such imitators of the *Cabinet des fées* as Countess Mural, Countess d'Anneuil, M. de Presschac, Count Hamil-ton, M. de Monarif, Mademoiselle de la Force, and the *Nouveau contes de les fées* by Madame de Beaumont. Then followed an analysis of folktale collections of Hungary and Greece.

In regard to the Slavic tales (Slawische Märchen), Wilhelm analyzed various collections and collectors under the broader titles of such coun-tries as Serbia, Russia, Bohemia, and Poland, and in regard to Oriental tales, he gave attention to some tale collections in Persia, as well as the *Arabian Nights*, the *Bidpai* Fables, and tale collections from India, the Kalmucks, China, Japan, and many other countries.

German tale collections were also included under the heading of Ger-many, right after Denmark. The space given to these was relatively modest in comparison with that dedicated to foreign cultures, but it gave a good survey of whatever had been published more recently in terms of German fairy tale collections. The listing of names and titles of works followed no particular sequence and also mixed the genres of *Kunstmärchen* and *Volksmärchen*, but in the discussion itself, Wilhelm pointed out differences in the methods and styles of the individual collections. Among others, he mentioned Johann Karl Musäus, Benedicte C. Naubert, Albert Ludwig Grimm, Countess Fouqué, E. T. A. Hoffman, Ernst Moritz Arndt, Caroline Stahl, J. A. C. Löhr, Lothar (their brother Ferdinand), and Franz Ziske.

In most cases, Wilhelm introduced the individual subdivisions by a history of folktale collections in the respective countries and then gave brief plot summaries with commentaries for individual tales within the collections. With meticulous care, he also attached notes to the tales to indicate parallel themes or motifs in collections of other countries.

What Wilhelm Grimm compiled in this volume in 1822 served as an outline for a worldwide folktale analysis by the famous scholars Johannes Bolte and Georg Polivka that filled one out of five big volumes, encompassing close to 400 pages. They added and enlarged the Grimms' notes, using for that purpose also the later editions of the *Kinder- und Hausmärchen*, but in their basic design, tracing the Grimms' sources and background knowledge of international collections, they followed the very schemes that Wilhelm Grimm had developed in this work.

NOTES

1. In spite of such corrective views, it must be noted that the Grimms did engage in fieldwork recordings, but more so prior to 1808, when they were still collecting folk songs and folktales for Brentano.

2. Wilhelm Schoof, *Zur Entstehungsgeschichte der Grimmschen Märchen* (Hamburg: Hauswedell, 1959), Chapter 1.

3. Heinz Rölleke, ed., *"Wo das Wünschen noch geholfen hat"*; *Gesammelte Aufsätze zu den "Kinder- und Hausmärchen" der Brüder Grimm* (Bonn: Bouvier Verlag, Herbert Grundmann, 1985), pp. 161–74.

4. Hermann Grimm, "Jacob and Wilhelm Grimm" in *Literatur*, Sarah Adams, trans. (Boston: Cupples, Upham & Company, 1886), pp. 254–85.

5. Rölleke, ed., pp. 163–65.

6. Ibid.

7. John Ellis, *One Fairy Story Too Many: The Brothers Grimm and Their Tales* (Chicago: University of Chicago Press, 1983).

8. *German Popular Stories* (London: Murray, 1823), Preface. Taylor wrote: "The collection from which the following tales are mainly taken is one of great extent, obtained for the most part by M. M. Grimm from the mouths of German peasants." Also, Taylor called them "national tales" while referring to their "highest northern antiquity."

9. Schoof, pp. 10–35.

10. Rölleke, ed., pp. 165–67. See also: Heinz Rölleke, *Die Märchen der Brüder Grimm: Eine Einführung*. Series: *Artemis Einführungen* (Munich: Artemis Verlag, 1987).

11. Rölleke, ed., *"Wo das Wünschen noch geholfen hat."*

12. This is also true for the Grimms' visits at the Haxthausens' place.

13. Walter Scherf, "Jacob and Wilhelm Grimm: A Few Small Corrections to a Commonly Held Image" in *The Brothers Grimm and Folktale*, James MacGlathery, et al., eds. (Urbana: The University of Illinois Press, 1988), 178–92.

14. Ellis, p. 103. His verdict is "fraud and forgery," with the emphasis that the Grimms' case was supposedly far more serious than that of James Macpherson.

15. See Donald Ward, "New Misconceptions about Old Folktales: The Brothers Grimm" in McGlathery, ed. et al., pp. 92–93. Among other things, Ward pointed out that Frau Viehmännin's paternal great-grandfather had emigrated to Hesse from Holland 128 years before the Grimms began to collect stories from her and that her mother had come from a long line of Hessian innkeepers.

16. Schoof, p. 99. Altogether, Ludowine wrote nine letters to Wilhelm. See the chapter "Der Bökendorfer Märchenkreis" and Reinhold Steig, "Zur Entstehungsgeschichte der Märchen und Sagen" *Archiv für das Studium der neueren Sprachen* 107 (1901), pp. 378–87.

17. The Grimms did not confess to having made a mistake.

18. For more details, consult Chapter 7.

19. All of these relate to *Kinder- und Hausmärchen* 3 (Berlin: Reimer, 1922).

20. See Chapter 1.

21. Wilhelm Schoof and Ingeborg Schnack, eds., *Briefe der Brüder Grimm an Savigny. Aus dem Savignyschen Nachlaß* (Kassel: Brüder Grimm Gesellschaft, 1956), Appendix, p. 423.

22. Karl Schulte-Kemminghausen, "Dokumente zu Besuchen des westälischen Freundeskreises der Brüder Grimm in Kassel," in *Brüder Grimm Gedenken* 1, Ludwig Denecke, ed. (Marburg: Elwert Verlag, 1963), pp. 125–46. Also: Karl Schulte-Kemminghausen, *Westfälische Märchen und Sagen aus dem Nachlaß der Brüder Grimm* 2d ed. (Münster: Beiträge des Droste-Kreises, 1957).

23. Schoof, *Entstehungsgeschichte,* p. 136.

24. Ibid.

25. Heinz Rölleke, ed., *Märchen aus dem Nachlaß der Brüder Grimm.* Series: *Literaturwissenschaft* 2d ed. (Wuppertal: Gesamthochschule, 1979). See tales number 8, 35, and 36. Bouvier, 1972), no. 8; 35; 36. See also appendix with notes to these tales.

26. For related tales from the Grimms' archives see: Heinz Rölleke, "Texte die beinahe 'Grimms Märchen' geworden wären" *Zeitschrift für Deutsche Philologie* 102, 4 (1983), pp. 481–500.

27. Jutta Rißmann, "Eine bisher unbekannte Fassung des Grimmschen Märchen KHM 71," *Brüder Grimm Gedenken* 4 (1978).

28. See also Johannes Bolte and Georg Polivka, "Sechse kommen durch die Welt" in *Anmerkungen zu den Kinder- u. Hausmärchen der Brüder Grimm* 1 (Leipzig: Dieterich'sche Verlagsbuchhandlung, 1913), pp. 73–87. This volume is dedicated to Grimms' notes to the folktales.

29. Rölleke, ed. *Märchen aus dem Nachlaß.* The title of Willi's tale is "Der gläserne Berg" ("The Glass Mountain"), tale number 7.

30. The following analysis is based on the unabridged essay "Kinderwesen und Kindersitten," which Wilhelm wrote as an introduction to the second edition of the *Kinder- und Hausmärchen* (Berlin: Reimer, 1819).

31. Ibid.

32. Ibid.

33. Ibid.

34. See the relevant notes to the tale of "Hänsel und Gretel" in *Kinder- und Hausmärchen* (1812).

35. Wilhelm Grimm, "Über das Wesen der Märchen" in *Kinder- und Hausmärchen* 2d ed. (Berlin: Reimer, 1819), pp. xxi–liv.

36. Like Herder, Wilhelm Grimm considered biblical tales, too, as *Naturpoesie.*

37. The interrelationship of language, customs, folk beliefs, and myths was Jacob's main objective in the *Deutsche Mythologie.* It is of interest to note that Wilhelm already began such comparative studies in 1812—about twenty years before Jacob brought out his work on comparative mythology. The same is true

for Wilhelm's comparative studies of Danish, Irish, Scottish, and Welsh folk motifs, all of which became an integral part of Jacob's *Deutsche Mythologie*.

38. Modern variants of this game can still be observed among young children. Grimms' shared interest in children's song and games significantly influenced the Germanist Karl Simrock, whose publication of traditional German children's rhymes had certain parallels with the works of John Newbery. See Karl Simrock. *Das deutsche Kinderbuch. Altherkömmliche Reime, Lieder, Erzählungen, Rätsel und Scherze für Kinder (The German Children's Book. Traditional Rhymes, Songs, Games, Riddles, and Jokes for Children)* (Frankfurt am Main: Brönner, 1848). On behalf of modern German variants of related songs and games see: Hanna Wolf, ed. *Mudder, Mudder, de Melk kokt öber! Kinderspiele und Geschichten aus der Raabestraße im alten Geestemünde (Mother, Mother, the Milk Boils Over! Children's Games and Stories from the Raabe Street in the Old Geestemünde)* (Bremerhaven-Langen: Selbstverlag Hanna Wolf. Druckhaus Lehe-Nord, 1986).

39. The "Lady-Bug" song already received attention in *Des Knaben Wunderhorn* where it was listed as a children's song in two variants, one of which was based on Otmar's collection (Bremen) and the other on an oral contribution. See: L. Achim von Arnim und Clemens Brentano, eds., *Des Knaben Wunderhorn: Alte deutsche Lieder* (Munich: Winkler Verlag, 1957), p. 159. References to "Marienwürmchen" and "Marienkäferchen" also occur in Jacob Grimm's *Deutsche Mythologie*. See index, Vol. 4 in *Teutonic Mythology* (New York: Dover, 1966).

40. This popular game finds a modern echo in the "Tale of Three Little Pigs": "And I huff, and I puff, and I blow your house in . . ."

41. Possibly the greatest contrast may be perceived between Grimms' Romantic perception of childlike innocence and the modern Freudian interpretation of the golden ball as a sex symbol.

42. Jacob Grimm, "Von der Poesie im Recht" in *Kleinere Schriften von Jacob Grimm 6.* Eduard Ippel, ed. (Berlin: Dümmler, 1871). This essay was first published in 1815.

43. This aspect shows that they rediscovered in printed versions what they heard in the oral tradition. Rölleke also called attention to the opposite process, namely that the Grimms rediscovered in the oral tradition what they had read in books.

44. Jacob and Wilhelm Grimm, *Deutsches Wörterbuch* (Leipzig: Weidmannsche Buchhandlung, 1854–1862) (first ed.: a–Allverein). Volume 1 was completed by 1854. The second volume appeared in 1860, and the third in 1862. The project was completed only a little more than one hundred years later (early in the 1960s) with the help of numerous scholarly contributions by German linguists. Even though the final volumes no longer follow Jacob Grimm's initial design, the work as a whole is still unique, with its broad comparative references, proverbial expressions, customs, folkways, and literary documents.

45. Kurt Ranke, "Alterbestimmung der Märchen" in *Enzyklopädie des Märchens; Handwörterbuch zur historischen und vergleichenden Erzählforschung 1,* Kurt Ranke, et al., eds. (Berlin: Walter de Gruyter, 1979). Modern theories show that folktales are much younger than the Grimms thought they were. Some critics have also pointed to their colloquial speech patterns as a modern trend rather than an archaic one. See Dietz-Rüdiger Moser, "Altersbestimmung des Märchens" in *Enzyklopädie des Märchens 1,* pp. 7–19.

46. See Kurt Ranke, Manfred Grätz, and Elfriede Moser-Rath's contributions to the essay, "Deutschland" in *Enzyklopädie des Märchens 3,* pp. 475–525. See also: Heinrich Hamann. *Die literarischen Vorlagen der Kinder- und Hausmärchen* (Series: *Palaestra. Untersuchungen und Texte aus der deutschen und englischen Philologie,* Number 57) (Berlin: Mayer & Müller, 1906).

47. Hamann, pp. 15–29.

48. Ibid.

49. Ranke, pp. 475–81. See also W. Eckehart Spengler, "Fischart" in *Enzyklopädie des Märchens* 4 (1984), pp. 1,222–28.

50. *Kinder- und Hausmärchen* 3 (1822) Notes. See also the long book review article in the 1850 edition which precedes the *Märchen*.

51. *Kinder- und Hausmärchen* (1812), Introduction.

52. *Kinder- und Hausmärchen* 3 (1819) part 1, Notes.

53. Ibid., 3 (1822) Part II. All of these are discussed in the cross-cultural analysis.

54. Ibid., 3 (1822) Part II. Vorrede by Wilhelm Grimm, p. 4.

55. Ibid., "Italien"; "Frankreich."

56. Ibid., "Die Nächte des Straparola," p. 273.

57. Ibid., "Pentamaron des Basile," pp. 277–78.

58. Ibid. *"Man kann demnach diese Sammlung von Märchen bei ihrem reichen Inhalt als Grundlage der übrigen betrachten und diese danach messen; denn ob sie es gleich in der That nicht war, im Gegentheil außer dem Lande nicht bekannt, nicht einmal in das französische übersetzt wurde, so hat es doch bei dem Zusammenhang der Überlieferung das Ansehen davon. Zwei Drittel finden sich den Grundzügen nach im Deutschen und noch zu jetziger Zeit lebendig."*

59. The volume of notes published by the Grimms in 1856 encompassed more page numbers because it integrated the long international book review article from the preface of the 1850 edition. However, as it omitted the table of contents in the international part and considerably reduced the comparative section on Basile and other historical collections, it lost the appearance as a book within a book dedicated to cross-cultural folktale studies.

7. THE METHODS OF THE COLLECTION

[Recording and Annotating Oral Sources]

IN OUR TIME, THE ORAL BASIS of the *Kinder- und Hausmärchen* still largely remains its landmark, even though it is known that the collection is based on printed sources as well. The Brothers Grimm were the first ones to introduce the fieldwork-research method. Some earlier folktale collectors had also relied on the oral tradition but only to a limited extent. While embellishing the tales with personal fantasies, they showed little or no awareness of the need to indicate oral or printed sources.

The idea of collecting stories from the oral tradition originated with Achim von Arnim, but Arnim did not carry it through as a method. Shortly after the publication of the first volume of *Des Knaben Wunderhorn* in 1805, he issued an appeal to his friends, encouraging them to continue the collection of folk songs from the oral tradition and to expand the search to legends and folktales as well. The Grimms took this project seriously. They also developed the method of collecting and editing tales in loyalty to tradition. Yet they understood the concept of loyalty in Romantic terms—not in modern terms—and they also did not rely exclusively on the oral tradition or on their own collection.[1]

We may well perceive the broad scope of their initial collection and their early demand for loyalty to tradition from a letter that Wilhelm wrote to their friend Paul Wiegand in 1809. While asking him for various folktale contributions, Wilhelm also inquired if he might not send him some notes from court hearings pertaining to folklore about criminals, such as songs he might have heard about robbers and thieves, some verses, or superstitious tales. He reminded him to record these very carefully, without making editorial changes.[2] It was not that he did not trust Wiegand, but both Wilhelm and Jacob already had experience in editing medieval manuscripts and found it more reliable to undertake the editing of folklore by themselves.

In comparison with their friends, the Grimms were more exacting in recording tales from the oral tradition, and even if they merely summarized an oral tale, they would exert all of their efforts in reconstructing its oral style in loyalty to its spirit. Arnim and Brentano, for example, did not take the spirit of tradition too seriously. They, too, had insisted on loyalty in the recording of tales, yet all too frequently they felt tempted to use folktales as springboards for their own creative writing. Brentano customarily took very sketchy notes, a habit that he shared with the Grimms, who only occasionally would record phrases verbatim to catch on to certain idiomatic expressions. The difference was that the Grimms would later reconstruct the tales on the basis of their notes and other reliable documents, whereas their friends would be too hard-pressed with other tasks to find time for such painstaking efforts. Especially Brentano didn't take the editing job too seriously. If he could not make out his own scribbled notes, he either relied entirely on his memory in reconstructing them or simply dropped them from his memory. In the case of the fairy tale woman of Marburg, for example, he lost six tales because his notes were illegible or incoherent. Finally, he merely gave up the project, leaving it to the Brothers Grimm to retrace his steps to the hospital.[3]

The first person that comes to mind in regard to the Grimms' recording of oral sources is the famous Frau Viehmännin of the village of Zwehrn. Ever since Wilhelm Grimm praised the oral contributions of Frau Viehmännin to the second edition of the *Kinder- und Hausmärchen*, critics have come to believe that to the Grimms she represented the ideal storyteller of all times. The pleasant engraving that Ludwig Grimm made of her[4] did much to enhance her image as the archetype of storytellers. Yet was she indeed the Grimms' ideal of a storyteller—and if so, was she the type of storyteller that the critics make her out to be? All too often, she has been praised for her fabulous memory, as if she had told the stories by rote. If she indeed told her tales in this manner, the question arises how such a storytelling technique could possibly be reconciled with the Grimms' theory of language dynamics.

By examining Wilhelm Grimm's appraisal of Frau Viehmännin more closely, some misunderstandings surface that throw a new light on her genius. According to Wilhelm, she qualified as an ideal storyteller for several other reasons. First, in spite of her harsh life experience, she retained a calm and naive spirit that permitted her to get close to the core of folk tradition. Coming from the village of Zwehrn, a rural area where, in Wilhelm's words, the "unpolluted imagination" still thrived "under hedges" without having been driving away by the "false Enlightenment," she was blessed with a naivete that had characterized the ancient bards.[5]

Wilhelm wrote that she told her stories "with reflection and self-assurance and in an unusually lively way" (*bedächtig, sicher, und ungemein lebendig*). In using such words, he expressed his admiration for her sure grasp for the core of tradition, her genuine involvement in the tales, and her vigor in reciting them. The expression "unusually lively" ("*ungemein lebendig*"), however, has little to do with a mechanical recital but rather indicates that her stories were enlivened by paraphrase and vivid expressions. In his essay on the vices of pedantry, Jacob characterized the word "lively" ("*lebendig*") as an expression of a desirable improvised oral tale recital while contrasting it with the words "tired" ("*müde*") and "lame" ("*lahm*"), which, in his view, signaled the death of storytelling. Frau Viehmännin's storytelling was lively, but it also was calm and unaffected—but never "tired" or "lame" from repetition.

By emphasizing a certain calmness and steadiness in her expression (*Ruhe und Festigkeit im Ausdruck*), Wilhelm further hinted at a certain serenity: "There was something steady, understanding, and pleasant in her expression, and her eyes were bright and penetrating." These words were similar to those that he used to describe the calm and serene spirit of epic poetry: "the color of green, spread evenly throughout nature in manyfold variations, a green that satisfies and calms, without making one tired." In both cases, he did not identify calmness with sameness but rather a gentle variety that lay embedded in natural speech as well as in nature itself.

If it is unlikely that Frau Viehmännin recited her tales with an accuracy based on a photographic memory, it is also unlikely that the Grimms recorded them word by word. By misunderstanding Frau Viehmännin's manner of recital, critics often also misunderstood the Grimms' method of recording the tales. Of course, Wilhelm himself emphasized that, first, she would tell her tales in a free and lively way (*ganz frei und lebendig*) and then upon request more slowly. In this process, she would also repeat some portions of the tale, which made it possible for them to take notes. He added: "In repeating a tale, she never changes anything in regard to the substance, and as soon as she notices a mistake, she corrects it right away herself in the middle of her speech." ("*Sie ändert niemals bei einer Wiederholung etwas in der Sache ab und ändert ein Versehen, sobald sie es bemerkt, mitten in der Rede gleich selber.*")[6] Contrary to what many critics have said, this does not mean, however, that she corrected the wording of the tale or that she recited the tales verbatim. Wilhelm wrote *Sache* (substance), not *Wort* or *Wörter* (word or words). His expression "*sich an die Sache*

halten" means "to stick to the subject" or "to hold the main line of
a story," but it does not mean to cling pedantically to each word of
the tale. Essentially, then, he emphasized that she clung to the core
of tradition, the very substance of the tale, and would not change plots,
themes, or characters.

If she indeed occasionally interrupted her tale "*mitten in der Rede*"
(in the middle of her speech or tale) to correct herself, it did not mean
that she stopped in the middle of a sentence, for then Wilhelm would
have written "*mitten im Satz*" (in the middle of a sentence). Therefore,
Wilhelm's comment that she corrected herself "*mitten in der Rede*" refers
more likely to the correction of a paragraph idea pertaining to the
substance of plot, theme, or character. It is as absurd as it is unsubstan-
tiated to claim, as many critics have done, that she literally stopped
talking in the middle of a sentence to correct a word or phrase. Had
she indeed repeated every word of the tale like a parrot, it is unlikely
that the Grimms would have praised her as a storyteller who told her
tales in a lively and spirited way. The very wording of such an appraisal
corresponds to Jacob's appraisal of language dynamics that supposedly
kept storytelling from becoming weak and tired by mere imitation.

In referring to the method of their recordings, Wilhelm further wrote:
"In this way, we were able to capture some things word by word." (*Auf
diese Weise ist uns manches wortwörtlich beigekommen.*)[7] Again, we
have to watch the wording, Wilhelm wrote: "some things" ("*manches*"),
but he did not say: "all things" ("*alles*"), or "every word" ("*jedes Wort*").
The expression "some things" refers to some portions of the given tale,
not to an individual word or exactly the same syntax. It is likely that
they asked her to repeat some stock phrases, opening and closing formulas, archaic expressions, or certain folk rhymes and riddles that were
a part of the traditional tale rather than the exact wording of her stories,
for the Grimms did not usually record tales verbatim, unless it pertained to such traditional aspects of speech. The *Oelenberg Manuscript*
has revealed the sketchy nature of their original tales, and so have their
recordings of variants in the Grimms' notes.

If Frau Viehmännin had told her tales in a mechanical way that
allowed her to repeat them word by word, it is unlikely that Wilhelm
would have praised her performance. Judging by the Grimms' concept
of language "self dynamics" and "approximation," they were generally
quite satisfied with storytellers who came close to the core of tradition
in terms of the tale's substance. They didn't seem to mind so much
if the wording was flawed, for with their own feeling for folk speech
they could easily improve the style of a given tale. Among the tales
they rejected, they usually perceived the major problem in their lack
of spiritual loyalty to tradition. If the spirit was flawed, they would
not consider it for publication.

Of significance in this connection is a tale among the rejects by a
person named Willi. Wilhelm wrote that Willi had first told it to him

personally yet in such a mixed up and incomplete way that Wilhelm ended up writing it down once more in a coherent way. He added, however, that the tale, thus summarized more concisely, represented more truly Willi's words than his own.[8] He had merely put together more coherently whatever he had been able to record in fits and spurts through numerous questions. Finally, however, he decided to reject the tale, nevertheless. Since Wilhelm had already spent so much time and effort on Willi's tale, one may wonder why he would not shape it up a little more to make it fit for inclusion in the *Kinder- und Hausmärchen*. His own words indicate, however, that he did not consider it a part of the editing process when he first helped Willi along a little to get the story on paper, for up to that point he still regarded it as Willi's story.

It seems that Wilhelm Grimm was consistent in regard to his own concept of "loyalty" to tradition, as far as the core of the tale was concerned. Viewed from that perspective, the tale simply did not hold, and therefore he would not tamper with it. He wrote into the margin of the story: "Invented? Good is the diamond horseshoe."[9] It is self-evident that he did not consider the diamond horseshoe motif substantial enough to make up for the tale's missing substance.

The length of the Grimms' initial recordings varied, depending on the informant. In most cases, they used brief tale summaries that captured the core of the story (plot, theme, character), giving only minute attention to certain tale formulas, proverbial and idiomatic expressions, and archaic turns of speech. Sometimes both Brothers Grimm were also curious about a certain manner of expression belonging to a particular storyteller, but in such matters, the exact wording initially did not matter. If they judged a tale as "made up" in the first place, they would lay it aside without editing it at all.

Following the initial recording stage, Wilhelm would make a clear distinction between acceptable and unacceptable tales, mainly on the basis of their loyalty to the substance or core of the folk tradition, not on the basis of the exact wording. If a tale appeared to them to be made up, they rejected it regardless of the wording or style of the storyteller. This is why among the tales that they accepted were even some from little Anna, whose contributions were often flawed by awkward expressions, and why they rejected some her others that were more elegant in style. Since there were quite a number of well-told tales among those they rejected, it is evident that the style of a given storyteller had little to do with a tale's acceptability, unless some expressions served as clues that marked it as genuine folklore.

Wilhelm was generally consistent in his approach to the oral tradition, as he searched for substance rather than the exact wording of a given folktale, although he was highly perceptive to traditional patterns of speech in folktales, such as formulaic openings, chants, rhymes, and songs. For Jacob the exact wording of a recorded tale was mainly important in connection with his comparative study of languages, dialects, and speech patterns but not at the expense of spontaneity and language dynamics. Occasionally, his interests in storytelling and grammatical research overlapped, but overall, he, too, thought less about the exact wording of a given tale than critics generally assume.

The Grimms' attitude was more meticulous in regard to printed sources, even though they related many of the folktale plots in the form of brief summaries within their notes. They showed particular care in indicating concise references to individual variants in national and foreign folktale collections, often not only including the collector's name and the title of the work but also the complete publishing data and inclusive page numbers. Further, they gave detailed attention to proverbs, quaint expressions, or relevant passages from their foreign correspondence to note some striking similarities or variations in individual tales from other regions and other lands. They would also indicate tale fragments pertaining to different openings or closings of stories to give proof of the existence of variants. On the basis of such notes, scholars have been able to trace a wealth of information regarding international folk literature, customs, laws, comparative philology, and comparative linguistics. Modern scholars who are accustomed to expect one or another form of documented publications could hardly hope to improve on the accuracy in the Grimms' notes.

The identification of oral sources was a different matter. The Grimms' methods of identifying oral sources has posed problems for modern scholars because the Grimms often failed to indicate the exact places where they recorded a tale from the oral tradition or the circumstances under which some of their informants had recorded it for them. This omission has led to confusion regarding the way in which they obtained their tales from oral sources. Often they only referred in rather general terms to such areas as Hesse, Paderborn, the environment of Main, or Bökendorf, without indicating the exact location where they had recorded a given tale. In some cases, they did not even give the person's last name.[10] This is why until recently many critics relied on the myth that the Grimms collected all folktales personally and directly from oral sources while traveling to farms and villages to listen to old women's tales in spinning chambers. Even after Heinz Rölleke dispelled that myth with his findings, many still tended to believe that the few tales that they did record orally were recorded directly by word-of-mouth.[11]

Now we know that such a word-of-mouth approach applied to some of their recordings but by no means to all. Yet the Grimms also received indirect oral sources, and not all were "tales by mail" based on fantasies or printed sources. In case of the shepherd of Höxter, Wilhelm made a personal visit to the Brunsberg, a mountain near Höxter. where he collected some tales directly from a shepherd. The same applies to the case of Friedrich Krause, a retired soldier, whom he gave used clothes in exchange for some stories. Yet in cases where they obtained stories from visitors coming to their apartment in the city, it is less clear if they received the stories directly or indirectly.[12]

The most obscure cases for scholars are those that pertain to hand-written tale contributions that the Grimms received by mail, for among them were oral recordings based on their own memory of tales, direct recordings of oral tales gleaned from a trip into the country or from an interview with a family member or another friend, or tales that someone else had recorded for them. Readers were left to guess which method such informants had used when the Grimms did not write more into the margins than "*mündlich*" ("oral"). In the case of Frau Lehmann's, for example, the wife of a doctor in Frankfurt, critics have assumed that she told (or wrote) the story "Eisenhans" ("Iron Hans") at her home, at the time when the Grimms attended the National Convention in Frankfurt in the 1840s. The Grimms themselves did not indicate whether they recorded the story directly from Frau Lehmann while visiting or just took a few notes during their visit and reconstructed the rest at home. The Grimms' source identification as "*mündlich*" might also be interpreted in such a way that Frau Lehmann had obtained the story from another person in a storytelling session or while going shopping. There might still be another possibility that Frau Lehmann first told the story to the Grimms when they visited her and that she later mailed to them her own version.[13]

Another ambiguous case refers to the von Haxthausen sisters, who would frequently tour the countryside for the Grimms to record folktales for their collection. When the Grimms later published some of their tales (most of which they received by mail), they did not always indi-cate which sister had recorded them or where. They merely attached the note: "oral—from Bökendorf." Neither did the notes identify the origin of various tales they received on the basis of a folklore ques-tionnaire that Jacob mailed to friends and acquaintances in 1815. Conse-quently, critics had to glean such information from correspondence and manuscript notes. Therefore, it is no wonder that critics have felt frustra-tions in dealing with this issue.

The roundabout way in which the Grimms sometimes obtained their "oral sources" is well-illustrated by the example of the Marburg fairy tale woman in the Elisabeth Hospital in Höxter, from whom Brentano originally collected six stories. As usual, he had relied too much on his memory as he had listened to her tales, and later he felt unable to reconstruct them on the basis of his sketchy notes. Since he was con-vinced of the genuine merits of the tales, he asked the Brothers Grimm to retrace his steps. Jacob thereupon assigned to Wilhelm the task of visiting the old woman to record the tales once more. Yet, as Wilhelm after several attempts was still unsuccessful in securing her coopera-tion, he used the "detour" approach to obtain the stories.

An acquaintance of the Grimms had a sister-in-law who knew the wife of the hospital director. The hospital director influenced his sister to speak with her friend, a nurse in the hospital, who, in turn, knew the old woman's grown children. He hoped that the children might be more successful than Wilhelm in getting the old woman to tell her stories. Surprisingly, this scheme worked—not without amusement to Wilhelm. The old woman indeed told her stories to her grown children, the children wrote down the stories and gave them to the nurse, the nurse forwarded them to the sister of the hospital director, and the director forwarded them to the Grimms.

The Grimms still considered this approach as a legitimate oral source, but it had little to do with the generalized conception of a word-of-mouth recording of folktales as Edgar Taylor still presented it in his introduction to the *German Popular Stories*. Again, we must observe that if the exact wording had been of supreme importance, the Grimms would have rejected such an approach. Neither could it be said that the Grimms' attempted to mislead the public on the nature of their oral sources. In the above mentioned case, for example, it was Wilhelm Grimm himself who, with a touch of humor, related the odd method of recording the oral tales.[14]

Where, then, lies the truth regarding the Grimms' methods of collecting and recording the tales? A recent discovery of a letter that was supposedly written by one of Jacob Grimm's students, who had interviewed him in his study to establish the exact method of his tale recordings, turned out to be a hoax. In all likelihood, such an interview never took place, for not only does it contradict the Grimms' own notes on the subject but it is also well-known that they were relatively tight-lipped about their methods. Evidently, the writer of this essay wished to perpetuate the myth that the Grimms recorded every tale "exactly as he had heard them."[15]

In view of all that has been said about the shortcomings of the Grimms' exact method of recording and clear identification of informants, should one conclude that their procedures were inconcise and inconsistent? It is true that modern folklore research in our time insists on more exacting standards while paying closer attention to circumstantial information than did the Grimms. Such a judgment would bypass the Grimms' own definition of loyalty to tradition and impose standards that were alien to their Romantic concept of folktale collections. It is evident from the concise and elaborate procedure with which they recorded printed sources and folktale variants that the purpose of their notes differed widely from that of modern folklore scholarship. It partially served to remind the reader, as Wilhelm put it, that there was something mysterious about the strange correspondences among some tales around the world. Inspiring readers with a sense of wonder is hardly the goal of modern folklore, but certainly that was a part of Wilhelm Grimm's romantic scholarship. For Jacob, it was sufficient to know that variants existed and that they were genuine. He was definitely more interested in a comparative linguistic and folkloristic study based on the variants themselves than in the background of the informants or the methods in which they obtained the tales.

[Jacob Grimm's Folklore Questionnaire]

In 1811 Clemens Brentano suggested to Jacob Grimm the idea of bringing out an anthology under the title of *The Old German Collector (Altdeutscher Sammler)*. Two weeks later, the Grimms sent him a plan for such an anthology, suggesting that they invite their friends and acquaintances to contribute to it. In the draft of a letter entitled *"Aufruf an alle Freunde der deutschen Poesie und Geschichte"* ("Appeal to All Friends of German Poetry and History") they sketched a more detailed outline of what they expected them to contribute and how. They asked for idiomatic expressions and proverbs of the common folk, legends, customs, and traditions, among other things, all of which were to be written down *"buchstabengetreu"* ("with minute accuracy"). They also suggested that they record the tales in exact dialectical forms, concluding that in this way they hoped to receive contributions from every region of Germany.[16]

In the same year, Jacob wrote to Joseph Görres that some time ago he had suggested a detailed plan to Clemens Brentano regarding a German anthology of folklore that would contain oral narratives representing all major areas of Germany. "Yet, nothing came of it," he concluded in a tone of resignation. Some critics who read this letter among the published correspondence of the Brothers Grimm came to the conclusion that indeed all such plans of a systematic collection of folklore had come to nothing. They were right, as far as the planned anthology and the initial sketch of the plan were concerned, yet not on behalf of the questionnaire that was still to come four years later.

In 1815, Jacob Grimm once more wrote a letter in the form of an appeal to collect more systematically various aspects of *Naturpoesie*. In Vienna, he published a "round-letter," titled *Circular wegen Auffassung der Volkspoesie (Round-Letter on Behalf of Collecting Folk Poetry)*,[17] to which he later referred for short as the *Circular-Brief*. To this letter, he attached an invitation to his friends and acquaintances not only in all regions of Germany but this time also in the neighboring countries of Austria, Switzerland, Denmark, the Netherlands, and Belgium to contribute to the collection their personal recordings of folktales, legends, proverbs, rhymes, and popular sayings. The *Circular-Brief* was more like an invitation for a folkloristic cooperation, or what we would call a folklore questionnaire in our time. It mainly served the purpose of gathering information on a large scale on various aspects of oral and printed folklore, indicating various categories that would come into consideration, as well as concise methodological instruction.

The *Circular-Brief* represents a pioneering attempt to conduct systematic folklore research. In a letter to Wilhelm, Jacob wrote on January 18, 1815, that the questionnaire had been printed and was ready to be mailed to at least one hundred different places. His handwritten annotations on his master copy indicates that he mailed it to a much larger number of persons. He sent out 50 copies in February of that year, a total of 122 by October, and 360 by April 1816. Compared with the folklore questionnaire mailed out by Wilhelm Mannhardt in 150,000 copies (1868) these are relatively modest figures, yet by mailing out the forms and keeping track of the returns, Jacob initiated one of the first folklore questionnaires in European history. At the time it was an entirely new method that paved the way for systematic investigations of various kinds in the second half of the nineteenth century.[18] For the Grimms' own projects, the questionnaire returns were undoubtedly of great significance. Even though the bulk of them stayed in their offices and were never analyzed and evaluated as a project, they made their way into their various notes to the Grimms' subsequent publications of folktales, legends, and comparative mythology. It is likely that Jacob also used contributions in the areas of dialects and idiomatic expressions for his comparative grammar.

The idea of the large-scale questionnaire, the *Circular-Brief*, was born in Vienna, where a small group gathered on a weekly basis between 1813 and 1824. They would regularly meet at a reserved table in a cozy beer house called Zum Strobelkopf, located behind St. Stephan's Cathedral. Clemens Brentano had introduced the Grimms here to Friedrich Schlegel, Adam Müller, Joseph von Eichendorff, the painter Philip Veit, Friedrich Klinkerström, Clemens Maria Hofbaus, Georg Passy, and Heinrich Eckstein. Passy was a librarian and Eckstein a bookstore manager, and both later became known as contributors to the *Kinder- und Hausmärchen*. Calling themselves "A Society for the Collection of Folk Poetry," they would discuss medieval German literature, *Naturpoesie*, and the need for a collection of folklore that would supplement and perhaps even excel *The Boy's Wunderhorn*. In a letter to Professor Tydemann in Leyden, Jacob wrote in May 1815 that the newly formed society had been expanded to include members from all regions of Germany, with the main purpose of preserving the German oral tradition in the very dialects in which they had been transmitted for centuries.[19]

The questionnaire was the visible outcome of this effort. In a brief introduction, Jacob explained his request for cooperation, expressing his hope that such a collection of folklore would save from oblivion those remnants of the German past that were still "alive" in the oral tradition. Specifically, he asked for folk songs and rhymes related to seasonal celebrations sung in spinning chambers or by laborers in the fields. These should be recorded very carefully and, if possible, with the traditional melodies. In a way, the request for folk-song contributions was a parallel to an earlier call for cooperation by Arnim and

Brentano in relation to *The Boy's Wunderhorn*, yet new in the *Circular-Brief* was Jacob's call for folk narratives, such as legends, simple nursery tales, and children's tales (*Kindermärchen*) about giants, dwarfs, monsters, enchanted princes and princesses, spells, devils, treasures, and charms, as well as for well-known local legends related to such topographical and regional features as mountains, rivers, lakes, swamps, castle ruins, towers, rocks, and historical markers. He asked that special attention also be given to traditional animal fables with such stock characters as the fox, the wolf, the cock, the dog, the cat, the frog, the mouse, the raven, and the sparrow.

Innovative also was his request for contributions regarding jolly trickster tales, anecdotes, jests, old puppet plays (with Hanswurst and the Devil as traditional characters), folk festivals, customs, rituals, and children's games. We may assume that some returns from this portion of the questionnaire served Wilhelm as a basis for his essay on children's language and children's games, which he attached to the second edition of the *Kinder- und Hausmärchen* in 1819. Jacob further asked here for recordings connected with celebrating the birth of a child (on which Wilhelm also elaborated in that essay), but also with weddings, old codes of justice and laws, superstitions related to ghosts, spooks, witches, good and bad omens, apparitions, dreams, proverbs, sayings, idiomatic expressions, and traditional parables. The interdisciplinary interests of the Brothers Grimm is particularly evident in a category that involves aspects of language, law, and old folk beliefs. He also listed the possibility of tales related to unusual interest payments, taxes, land-winning activities, and corrections of border lines, all of which might have a legal dispute as a basis.

With respect to the methodology that the contributors were expected to observe, Jacob stated that the legends should be recorded in natural speech patterns, just as they were told. It was of primary importance that all entries be recorded truthfully, without addition or embellishments, and directly from the mouth of the people. Even tale fragments might be included, as well as variants, repetitions, and corrections made by a storyteller within the same tale. Even if a tale was already well-known, it should be recorded, as it might contain a valuable clue with respect to variants.

They further advised their friends that the best places for them to obtain such unadulterated folklore would be in more remote areas away from the cities, especially in villages among older persons, women and children, and shepherds, but also among fishermen and miners—in short, wherever the memory of the oral folk tradition was still alive.

In a postscript, he urged their friends to visit archives and monasteries in their home regions to search out old manuscripts, for in these they might discover an amazing treasure of folklore resources. Whenever they came across some items that might fit the collection, they should forward it to the Brothers Grimm along with all of the relevant information.

This blueprint for folklore collectors might have pleased modern folklorists so much more than the few hints about "loyalty to tradition" that the Brothers Grimm gave in their various introductions to the *Kinder- und Hausmärchen*. It is evident from the Grimms' writings, however, that they themselves never expected to print the contributions exactly as they had received them. They tried to ensure an accurate recording of folklore by their friends, mainly so as to avoid some stylistic embellishments of the tales that would spoil their authenticity. They reserved the final editing job entirely for themselves. For slightly different reasons they instructed the recipients of the questionnaire to record all corrections made by storytellers, for they themselves wished to make their own selections among the variants told and recorded.

One may wonder why the Grimms instructed their friends to visit the villagers and people in more remote areas of the country while they themselves were often quite content with collecting folktales in the city. It seems that in this regard, too, they wished to play it safe, for in the city many tales had already been tainted with literary embellishments. It required a trained ear and a good knowledge of tradition to detect which was a genuine folktale and which tale was made up. [20]

[The Editing Process]

The Brothers Grimm took pride in the fact that their collection of folktales preserved what they called "loyalty to tradition." They stated in their introduction to the first edition of the *Kinder- und Hausmärchen* that in this respect it resembled no other collection they knew.

By mistaking the Grimms' insistence on "loyalty" for a pedantic word-by-word recording of the tales, as well as for a publication that followed their notes in minute detail, the earliest English critics perpetuated the myth that the word-of-mouth recording was the landmark of the *Kinder- und Hausmärchen*. When in more recent times it became widely known, also in the United States, that the Grimms had changed the wording and syntax of the tales from one edition to the next, critics began to support the opposite idea, maintaining that the Grimms had "doctored" the tales by imposing upon them their own words and values. [21] Consequently, some of them concluded that their so-called *Volksmärchen* (folk tales) were undistinguishable from *Kunstmärchen* (literary fairy tales) and that their proclamations of "loyalty to tradition" were no less of a hoax than Macpherson's claims regarding *Ossian*. A few among them even applied to the *Kinder- und Hausmärchen* the term of "fakelore."

The question arises whether the Grimms indeed were inconsistent with their own principles regarding the editing process or whether they made promises that they did not keep. Some critics developed more suspicions on this behalf upon discovering that the Grimms had also used published sources and, in some cases, had even combined tale fragments from different regions of the country. They accused them of the same faults in editing the work that the Grimms themselves had condemned in regard to the collections by Musäus and Brentano.

What critics failed to recognize from the beginning was, first of all, that the Grimms' concept of loyalty to tradition referred to the substance of the tales (*die Sache*) rather than to their exact wording and syntax. Secondly, they ignored in this context the Grimms' substantial notes regarding additional variants on which they had relied in subsequent editions. Concluding prematurely that the Grimms had changed the "original" tales of the *Oelenberg Manuscript* arbitrarily throughout the seven editions, they further perpetuated the myth that there had been such a thing as an *Urmärchen* in the Grimms' collection, an idea that the Grimms rejected. They failed to grasp that they constantly worked with *variants* and that changes found in different editions had to do with new variants that they had obtained in the meantime, not only with language changes that occurred within the editing process.[22]

In his preface to the second edition of the *Kinder- und Hausmärchen* (third volume), Wilhelm Grimm commented on their placement of variants in the notes. He apologized to the readers for their unusual method of including such elaborate notes to the tales—perhaps many more than they might wish to read—yet he hoped that such notes would make the reader aware of the existence of a great number of folktale variants around the world. Perhaps they would also help the reader to get closer to the "truth" of the tales. What he meant was that all of the variants combined might reflect more concisely the core of the traditional tale than the single variants that they had selected for the text of the collection.

It is informative to take a closer look at how the Grimms treated the numerous variants that crossed their desks. Already at the beginning of this century, the opening of the Grimm Archives revealed that the Grimms had laid aside many more contributions than they actually published. Among these were variants and stories that they considered too fragmentary or too incoherent to be useful or others that were too embellished or altogether "fabricated" to be credible as genuine folklore. They also rejected tales that had already appeared in other collections published more recently, unless they were convinced that they had come across a more authentic version than the one that was published. They further laid aside tales that lacked the structure of folktales but rather resembled jests, riddles, or anecdotes.[23]

How did the Grimms determine which variants were acceptable and which ones were not? In some cases, they undoubtedly relied on their personal knowledge of the oral tradition, but in others they used their professional expertise in medieval literature, law, and linguistics in determining the authenticity of a given tale. Their penciled notes in the margins of the tales that they had received by mail clearly indicate that they read them in view of their credibility and authenticity and that they did not hesitate to reject those that did not meet their standards. Such rejects in the Grimms' files speak of their principled selection in regard to the oral tradition. They also reveal consistency in the application of the standards they set forth in their prefaces to the *Kinder- und Hausmärchen* and in the *Circular-Brief*.

Given their extensive firsthand experience with the oral tradition as well as their professional work with folk-song collections and the restoration of medieval manuscripts, they developed a good ear for what was genuine and what was not. They also possessed the traditional storyteller's intuition of getting close to the core of traditional stories. Occasionally, they relied on certain language clues, such as proverbial expressions and sayings, to determine if a tale was genuine or not, but because they later inserted such elements into the tales they had already collected, they must have realized that this method was not too reliable. Overall, in selecting the best variant, they relied less on the exact wording of a given tale than on its substance (*Sache*). Wherever such a decision was difficult to make, they would reserve some equally credible variants for their notes and sometimes use these in the next edition.

This does not mean that Wilhelm Grimm had begun to fantasize in cases in which a comparison of two or several editions of the *Kinder- und Hausmärchen* revealed different opening passages, for example. He may have replaced an opening by a variant, either from the published notes to the tales or from his archival collection of tale contributions.

Jacob once commented that for the task of collecting folktales, a person needed not only a certain love of tradition but also an education enabling him to grasp this naivete. By "education" he did not mean interviewing skills or recording skills but a sensitivity to the naive spirit of folktales that addressed the perceptive listener in an unpremeditated, spontaneous, lively, and convincing way.[24] Editing folktales required the same sensitivity and perception. In addition, it demanded their knowledge of etymology and medieval epics that helped them in the restoration process. With some instructions, many persons might learn to record tales from the oral tradition, but not everyone was to be trusted with the editing job. In the case of the folktale collection, it also demanded their knowledge of etymology, comparative mythology, and medieval epics.

Both Brothers Grimm also brought to this task the gift of traditional storytellers. They had experience in retelling epic tales for the common reader, thus rendering in a simple prose form what had been known before only in medieval poetry. An example of this is Wilhelm's *Der Arme Heinrich* (*Poor Henry*) and Jacob's *Das Waltharilied* (*The Song of Walthari*). They considered the editing job in relation to folktales on a similar plane. In a way, it was a "translation" too, as it demanded loyalty to the original yet also a lively and credible way of rendering them for the common reader. In his introduction to the 1819 edition of the *Kinder- und Hausmärchen*, Wilhelm wrote:

> In regard to the way in which we collected the tales, it must be noted that first of all we were concerned with loyalty and truth, for we did not add anything on our own account, but did not beautify (idealize) the circumstances or traits of the tale. Rather, we have related the contents just as we had received them; it is self evident that the expression [exact wording] and the individual details stem from us, yet we have tried to preserve every unique element that we have observed, so that also in this respect we have left to the collection the variations that occur in nature. [25]

Wilhelm once commented that ideally he would have preferred to render all of the folktales in the *Kinder- und Hausmärchen* in the original dialects. He somewhat regretted that for the sake of better communication, he had to translate most of them into High German. He expressed similar sentiments in regard to Norwegian and Swedish folktales, saying he would have liked very much to travel more extensively to Norway and Sweden so as to get a closer feeling for the original dialects in which the tales had been told. "But then I would have to know all of the dialects," he reflected, "for it appears to me very essential that even mistakes be honored and rendered faithfully, so as to preserve the unique idiomatic expression of the individual storyteller." [26]

Beginning with the second edition of the work, Wilhelm mainly was responsible for editing the language of the collected tales. He relied not only on his poetic intuition as a storyteller but also on his experience with epics and medieval manuscripts. First, he would try to grasp the core of the story, yet then he would largely use his own words while trying to preserve some archaic expressions with which he was also familiar from children's songs, games, and folk beliefs as well as from proverbs and sayings that had survived in current colloquial speech. As long as he had captured the substance of the tale, it was safe for him to work into it some folk proverbs and sayings, for such an endeavor would not disturb the "core" of tradition.

With tact and a feeling for the appropriate place and timing, he handled each tale individually. In some cases, he skillfully introduced idiomatic expressions into the flow of the narrative, whereas in others, he would modernize some obscure archaic or dialectical expressions by paraphrasing them in a vivid "folk speech" that was more easily understood at the present time. He proceeded with the certainty of an artist, yet also with caution, so as to preserve the substance of the tales.

To what extent Wilhelm succeeded in doing so has been the subject of a continuing debate. While some critics have accused him of censoring the tales by omitting bawdy or licentious expressions others have accused him of not censoring enough. The most hotly debated issue concerns Wilhelm Grimm's "folktale style," which, according to some critics, has imposed his own wording and his own values upon the tales.

Did the Grimms take too many liberties in editing the tales? The emphasis which this work has placed on their use of variants in different editions and their rejection of an archetypal tale or *Urmärchen* may induce some critics to recall their hasty conclusions on this behalf. Jacob's theory of language dynamics may also provide additional food for thought, for it encouraged not only the storyteller but also the editor to paraphrase folktales without altering its core. A case in point is Wilhelm's preface to the second edition of the *Kinder- und Hausmärchen* (1819), where he wrote: "In this new edition we have carefully eliminated every expression that is not suitable for the young age." (*Dabei haben wir jeden für das Kindesalter nicht passenden Ausdruck in dieser neuen Auflage sorgfältig gelöscht.*) Did this mean that Jacob and Wilhelm had caved in to pressures from their publisher and friends by eliminating all cruel elements from the tales? Several critics have suggested that the Grimms exercised a certain self-censorship while becoming disloyal to their own professed beliefs in "loyalty to tradition."

A careful reading of Wilhelm's qualifying definitions of language change is needed to avoid hasty conclusions. What Wilhelm had in mind was a careful elimination of bawdy and erotic talk customary in medieval jests and folk books but not an embellishment or alteration of traditional plots, themes, and characters. Nor did he timidly try to shield children from certain harsh and cruel aspects of reality reflected in traditional tales. He neither softened the endings nor did he eliminate characters that parents might find "objectionable" on account of their evil actions. He also did not swing into the opposite extreme by setting up characters as models of good behavior. On the contrary, he tried to preserve what he called the purity (*die Reinheit*) of traditional tales. Wilhelm defined purity as the straightforward truth: "We search for purity in the truth of a tale that does not hide things that are wrong or injust." ("*Wir suchen die Reinheit in der Wahrheit einer geraden, nichts Unrechtes im Rückhalt bergenden Erzählung.*") This meant that he still considered it his primary goal to preserve the truth of the traditional tales' themes and characters. In this context, it is important to remember that making certain changes in the language of the folktales was a practice that did not contradict the Grimms' principle of "loyalty" to tradition, as long as such changes were not arbitrary and did not affect the tales' substance.

Another issue that has been widely debated refers to Grimms' editing practice of occasionally combining tale fragments. Some critics have found it detrimental to the authenticity of the collected tales, stating that it seriously undermined Grimms' credibility as folktale editors. After 1819, Wilhelm was mainly responsible for the revisions. It is then that we notice some greater liberties of style, also in regard to the combination of tale fragments. Wilhelm's own comments, however, show that he would insert tale fragments into another tale only if the main folktale essentially convinced him of its substance. He proceeded in the "restoration" of the folktale like an archaeologist who fits together the shards of a broken urn, following the logic of its internal structure yet carefully avoiding any imposition of his personal fantasy.[27] Essentially he would not change characters, basic themes, or plots but confined himself to supplying minor portions of the tale, such as subthemes, closing formulas, or individual motifs with which he knew that they belonged. In cases in which he employed such a method, he did so only if he could verify or knew from firsthand experience that the given story existed in the oral folk tradition as an organic whole. In his preface to the 1822 volume of notes, he explained this method as follows:

> The notes to the folktales first of all mention the area from where we have collected them from the oral tradition and indicate precisely those cases where we have inserted some portions from other tales or where two have been joined together. An actual fusion of tales has not taken place, and whatever was inserted can easily be taken away again.[28]

There was nothing arbitrary about the way in which he combined tale fragments. In some cases he was familiar with the tales from his own fieldwork experience and in others from recurring themes and characters in myths, chapbooks, medieval epics, or variants in older German and foreign folktale collections.

The Grimms believed that editing folktales required a vision that enabled a person to get close to the core of the folktale and the spirit of the folk tradition. It also required an intimate knowledge of speech patterns used by the common folk and children, such as proverbial and idiomatic expressions, sayings, rhymes, riddles, and the language in children's songs and children's games. For recording purposes it was essential to grasp the substance of traditional plots, characters, and themes, yet for editing purposes, one would also have to possess an intimate feeling for language. This was especially important in cases in which a storyteller or informer changed the syntax and wording of a tale, overlooked a rhyme or a riddle that belonged to the tale tradition, or simply forgot a particular ending. The Grimms observed that storytellers, like children, usually remembered the openings best and most often would forget the endings.[29]

In spite of their principled approach to the editing task, the Grimms sometimes encountered circumstances beyond their control. This referred specifically to the interference of their publisher, Georg Reimer, in Berlin, who was responsible for all editions of the Kinder- und Hausmärchen until 1832. He definitely had his own views on what was loyal tradition and what was not, and sometimes he took it on his own to change the wording of folktales before he sent them on to the printer. Ironically, one of the Grimms' supposedly most authentic tales, "The Fisherman and his Wife," underwent a strange transformation for which they were not responsible. Knowing that the Grimms had received the tale in the Low German dialect from Otto Philipp Runge, who had already published a version of it in Arnim's journal, Reimer assumed the authority to edit the folktale by himself. Since he was familiar with the story as well as with the dialect, he claimed that he knew the wording of the tale better than Runge and the Grimms combined and merely proceeded to change it. Heinz Rölleke reconstructed the complex editing process regarding this tale, demonstrating concisely on the basis of a comparative chart that the tale was much further removed from the oral tradition than it is generally assumed to be.[30] These findings are valuable in terms of giving insight into the complex editing and publishing process regarding the tales. They do not suggest, however, that the Grimms had lost control over their tales, for Rölleke did not question the Grimms' loyalty to the "substance" of the tale.

In view of Jacob Grimm's *Pendeltheorie*, the seemingly endless debate among critics regarding the Grimms' "loyalty" to the oral folk tradition should be laid to rest, for it also applied to their conception of editing folktales. The Grimms considered it only natural that the wording of folktales should undergo some mutations, both in a traditional storytelling setting and in the editing process. While trying to get close to the substance of the tales, they also tried to recapture the colorful variety of folk speech, either by recording it, if it was present in an oral version, or by inserting it, if it happened to be absent. They believed that an editor, like a good traditional storyteller, should move back and forth between the core of tradition and an inspired and lively rendition. An occasional insertion of archaic or idiomatic expressions did not spoil the tale's authenticity but rather enhanced its value in relation to the folk tradition.

[The Grimms' Folktale Style]

Jacob's concept of language dynamics had definite implications for the Grimms' folktale style. His pendulum theory applied to the storyteller's closeness to the core of tradition but also to a lively and animated way in retelling of the tales, which suggested paraphrasing rather than a mechanical repetition. Essentially, he applied the same basic principle to the editing process from which evolved the "folktale style."

A clear line divided Wilhelm's folktale style from a merely personal literary style, even though at times the dividing line may have appeared blurred. Max Lüthi felt that Wilhelm's folktale style, also known as the *Märchenstil*, was free from subjective meanings and moralities and flowed naturally from the oral tradition while helping to preserve it.[31] With great sensitivity, Wilhelm had grasped the right words at the right time, keeping the stories traditional yet also alive. Wilhelm Steig and Hermann Grimm paid similar compliments to his style, particularly to Wilhelm's skill in dividing up the plots into successive phases that became best known as the style's two-dimensional or linear quality.

They did not think that such structural changes altered the substance of the tales but rather enhanced the credibility of their characters and actions. Such alterations also added vividness and conciseness to the folk narrative while offering a better psychological motivation for the characters' actions. Overall, his careful composition had introduced some desirable logical transitions that emphasized a sense of poetic symmetry and a dramatic climax. Essentially, Wilhelm's folktale style took away nothing from the stories themselves, and neither did it detract anything from their substance. Possibly the positive effect of Wilhelm's folktale style was that it made the tales more comprehensible to children than the original texts.

In appraising Wilhelm's folktale style, critics have usually called attention to its sense of rhythm and smooth flow of dialogues. They have also noted the correct syntax and logic and a consistent use of the past tense instead of the present tense or mixed tenses that once dominated the style of earlier tale collections. Further, they have generally thought that his use of folk proverbs, sayings, and idiomatic expressions enhanced the traditional style rather than detracted from it. In the sixth enlarged edition of 1850, Wilhelm Grimm himself commented on that aspect of his folktale style:

> I have been constantly trying to integrate into the tales proverbs and quaint expressions of the common people. I always listen for these, ready to record them. Here is an example that may also serve as an explanation. If the farmer wants to express his satisfaction, he says: "I have to praise this more than the green clover." In doing so, he chooses the image of the fresh green field of clover. [32]

Wilhelm commented that the same vivid and concrete expressions could be observed in medieval epic literature and that they were still alive in colloquial speech and dialects. One could hear them in everyday conversations in the country as well as in the town's marketplaces, on street corners, and among children, especially in their games, songs, and sayings. This striking link between the past and the present showed that the common folk then and now had preserved the same poetic way of speaking, along with a sense of *Naturpoesie*.

Most critics have given Wilhelm credit for his "good ear" for the oral tradition and also for his attempt to preserve at least some tales in the original dialects. Few have found fault with his translation of most of the collected tales into High German, as it promoted a better understanding and a wider popular appeal. Jacob, too, supported Wilhelm in this effort, and he subscribed to this practice. Together they also decided on changing some of the original tale titles. "Foundling" they made into "Foundling Bird," "The Wolf" became "The Wolf and the Seven Kids," and "The Princess and the Enchanted Frog" became

"The Frog King." They translated such dialectical forms as "*stak*" ("stuck") into the modernized "*steckte*," "*rotbäckig*" ("red-cheeked") into "*rot*" (red), and "*verbrennt*" ("burnt") into "*verbrannt*." In the second edition, they saw to it that some foreign words such as "*Prinz*" and "*Prinzessin*" were Germanized and replaced by the words "*Königssohn*" and "*Königstochter*."[33] However, in consistency with Jacob's belief that the German language should respect foreign words that still held meaning for the people, they did not become "purists" along these lines and practiced moderation.

The Grimms' folktale style is a significant reason of why the *Kinder- und Hausmärchen* are still with us today—and *alive*. It differs vastly from the *Kunstmärchenstil* (style of the literary fairy tale) that dominated in France as well as in Germany during that time. Sometimes, critics use the term "*Buchmärchenstil*" (book folktale style) as a synonym for Wilhelm's folktale style, not realizing perhaps that Wilhelm was very much concerned with banning everything "bookish" from it while associating it with living oral speech patterns. By no means did he wish to cast the folktale into a permanently fixed printed form but rather hoped to keep it "alive" in the oral tradition. His various stylistic revisions clearly demonstrate his belief in an open-minded attitude toward variants as well as in a certain fluidity of expression. *Buchmärchenstil* suggests a static form of expression that is unrelated to language dynamics. Besides, it lends itself to a confusion with the *Kunstmärchenstil*, which the Grimms rejected for the folktale, as it permitted the intrusion of stylistic embellishments and personal fantasies.[34] Jacob thought that if a storyteller or editor moved beyond a certain level of poetic expression toward personal self-expression and artistry, it meant the sure end of a traditional tale. Ginschel observed that both Brothers Grimm consciously avoided such pitfalls while giving back to the "folk" what belonged to it.

For some time, critics have begun to realize that not just Wilhelm Grimm alone but Jacob, too, deserved credit for the folktale style. The idea that Jacob's style was essentially different from Wilhelm's may be traced back to a casual remark by Achim von Arnim, in a letter that he addressed to Wilhelm. Having received a copy of the second edition of the *Kinder- und Hausmärchen*, he thanked him sincerely while letting him know that he had enjoyed the style of this volume much more than that of the first volume. In a jovial tone he added that this was probably because Wilhelm had escaped his brother's watchful eye in assuming the major role in the editing job. Arnim advised Wilhelm to be cautious not to let his brother know. Arnim appeared to take sides with Wilhelm against Jacob, seeming to poke fun at the older brother's strict attitude regarding the exact wording of the tales.[35]

Yet were Arnim's words to be taken literally? Did he really mean what he wrote? The light tone of his letter suggests a joke at Jacob's expense. The irony of the matter is that Arnim knew better than anyone else that Jacob was perhaps a little overprotective of his younger brother, yet by no means pedantic. Still on December 31, 1812, a week after the

Grimms had published the first volume of the *Kinder- und Haus-märchen*, Jacob had written Arnim a letter stating his true attitude regarding the need for change and variation in folktales. Such mutations, as he called them, were "the consequence of the human element. . . ." ("*Dies ist die folge alles menschlichen.*")[36] He clearly told Arnim that he took kindly to changes that had occurred in the wording of tales as they were passed on in the oral tradition.

If occasionally Jacob reminded his brother not to get carried away by his enthusiasm and imagination, as Panzer suggested,[37] he certainly never accused him of having embellished the folktales with his own fantasies or of having changed their essential substance. The differences in the brothers' approaches to the editing process were not as great as some critics made them out to be. Overall, Jacob indeed was more scientific and exacting in his approach as a linguist, but he had also read, studied, translated, and even taught a university course in literature and, above all, deeply appreciated Wilhelm's poetic perception in the editing process. Their differences were more pronounced in regard to editing medieval epics and manuscripts than in relation to folktales. In that connection, Jacob tolerated no paraphrased material but insisted on minute accuracy and a literal translation in rendering the older texts.

Jacob was a linguist and a scientist in his own right, but he was also a man of letters and occasionally also gave lectures on literature, not just on law and linguistics. He was perceptive in his approach to historical grammar and definitely not pedantic. In fact, his friends and colleagues usually thought that he was not pedantic enough. In his "On the Pedantic Elements in the German Language,"[38] he accused grammarians of having sinned by their pedantry against the German language. One of the greatest mistakes a linguist could make, he said, would be to insist too dogmatically on rules while ignoring the exceptions, and to be closed-minded to language change and development. He especially attacked the ridiculous practice of retranslating adopted French words into quaint German compound words, so as to satisfy the demands of the "purists." Like George Orwell in our century, who spoke so vehemently in favor of "simplicity," Jacob also advocated the use of colloquial short forms rather than the more "correct" yet cumbersome expressions. Thus, he preferred the word "*Rechenlehrer*" ("math teacher") to the grammatically more correct word of "*Rechnenlehrer*" (with an *n* inserted to show its derivation from the verb "*rechnen*," or "doing math"), for the first word corresponded to simple colloquial speech and was less artificial.

In regard to translations, he used the same principle of simplicity, clearly rejecting an "accurate" but "dead" word-by-word approach to another language. Jacob said that a translator should never proceed in a strictly literal way. Rather than using minute accuracy in striving toward perfection, he should aim at an "approximation" of words derived from a perception of the work as a whole. Taking too many liberties so as to deviate from the substance of the tale was just as bad as "cling-ing" to every single word and phrase in retelling it. A good translator should avoid both extremes. Jacob felt that German translators in par-ticular were often driven by pedantry and ended up with cumbersome translations that took up about twice as many words as the original without doing justice to its spirit. The ideal translator should balance both form and thought. Such a philosophy of translation applies to Grimms' editing job of folktales as well. An editor taking too many liberties in revising the tale might threaten its traditional substance, yet an editor following the pedantic approach might kill the spirit of the tale just as well.

Today, critical views lean toward giving Jacob a good deal more credit for the folktale style than was the case some decades ago. Hermann Hamann and K. Schmidt in separate studies came to the conclusion that there were no essential differences between Wilhelm's and Jacob's styles, as both had paid more attention to the poetic spirit of folktales than to their exact wording and syntax.[39] More recently, Schulte-Kemminghausen reexamined Jacob's folktale style in these terms, as did Gunhild Ginschel. In a step-by-step analysis of Jacob's stylistic revi-sions of "The Foundling Bird"—a tale that Wilhelm Schoof had mis-takenly ascribed to Wilhelm—Ginschel proved that Jacob had used the same basic principles as his brother. By examining more closely Jacob's translation of Basile's folktale "Le serpe" ("The Snake"), she demonstrated that he had skillfully replaced the more wordy style of Basile by the simple and concrete folktale style of the *Kinder- und Hausmärchen*. Instead of following a pedantic word-by-word translation of Basile's passage "As soon as the sun with his golden broom had swept aside the dust of night from the dew-covered meadows. . . ." Or instead of saying in a word-by-word translation from Basile "As soon as night had been exiled from land because of having given some advantages to thieves, he packaged his bundle, scattering the shadows of dawn. . . ." he merely wrote, "Early in the morning at daybreak. . . ." Such a transla-tion caught the essence of the matter without getting entangled in wordy statements. Nothing was lost in Jacob's paraphrase, except some quaint expressions belonging the Neapolitan dialect that would have sounded bombastic in a literal translation.[40]

He also avoided the ironic tone and licentious dialogues hinting at sex and impotence that belonged to some everyday expressions of the Neapolitan dialect yet sounded crude and offensive in translation. Fur-ther, he cut some elaborate descriptions of such Catholic practices as fasting and church processions that did not belong to the basic plots or themes, thus making the stories more readable and more univer-sally acceptable. Even if he deleted some specific derogatory comments by Basile (as a storyteller) regarding the stupidity of the peasant Cola Matteo, he saw to it that the stupidity emerged from the peasant's action itself rather than from the storyteller's interpolations. He certainly would not whitewash the peasant's character and left his basic stupidity unchanged as a dominant trait. Jacob never tampered with the substance of the tales.

Ginschel observed that Jacob's translation made the tale more credible, also from a psychological perspective, as he added logic and dramatic tension to some scenes. She considered his most successful stylistic device one of "epic sequence." Whereas Basile's version would show how a dove broke a windowpane rather swiftly and without an effort, Jacob introduced a sequence of phases to the action, thus adding credibility to the dove's escape. Wilhelm, too, used the same device rather effectively in the *Kinder- und Hausmärchen*. Lüthi called it the "linear quality" of the Grimms' folktale style, which, by creating a step-by-step progression of the story, made it much easier for younger children to follow the story line.

Regarding the descriptive quality of Jacob's folktale style, she observed that Jacob used colorful adjectives instead of plain nouns and added a strong sense of rhythm to the word order. He also used such adverbial phrases as *"ast bei ast"* ("branch by branch")[41] so vividly that the narrative turned out to be much more lively than the original text. Like Wilhelm, he, too, introduced into the folktale texts some proverbs, sayings, and idiomatic expressions, corrected some faulty grammatical constructions, and used the past tense throughout. She thought that overall, however, the differences in the style of the two brothers were minor.

Yet there were some more obvious differences in style, and the Grimms both knew it. In his eulogy on his brother, Jacob alluded to Wilhelm's folktale style, saying that whenever he opened the *Kinder- und Hausmärchen*, he seemed to perceive his voice. There was indeed something special in Wilhelm's voice or tone of writing. Perhaps it emanated from his kind, gentle, and poetic personality and his love of children. It is also evident it some dedications that he wrote for children, as well as in a letter addressed "Dear Mili,"[42] to which Maurice Sendak added his own imaginative illustrations. While this story is not a folktale at all but only a letter that makes use of some folktale themes, it unmistakenly reflects Wilhelm's way of writing. It is another question whether he would have liked to see it published in his lifetime. Given his honest approach in judging the core of tradition, most likely he would have considered it unacceptable as a *Märchen*.

Like Hans Christian Andersen, Wilhelm used to make up his own stories when he wrote to children. He would write such letters with love and imagination solely for the individual child, without even considering the idea of publishing them. Among the many papers of the Grimm archives is a letter addressed to Malchen (Amalie von Zuydtwyck) in 1817.[43] It is not a folktale either and also was not meant for the eyes of others, but it is a loving reminder of the way he spoke to children.

Thanking her for a note and some drawings, he wrote that he hoped he might visit her soon. It had already become quite cold outside. As soon as frost had arrived, the flowers could hardly manage to keep themselves upright, and they had begun to stoop forward. The leaves, too, didn't feel like sitting a minute longer on the branches and were beginning to fall off, one by one. Truly, it was no longer fun to sit up there, and he himself certainly didn't want to be in their place! And how the wind was blowing! She probably couldn't imagine how violently it blew! Did the wind think one should take off one's hat to salute him? Not long ago, the wind had tried to blow off his own hat by force, but he had held onto it very tightly. . . . Wilhelm concluded the letter saying that if Amalie would come to visit him, he would get her something pretty—perhaps a little white mouse, just such a one as he had seen not long ago. She might then get a little black mouse, just to keep it company, so that they might play together as miller and chimney sweep.

Wilhelm's letter has the simplicity and warmth that marks his folktale style. It also has the same animated view of nature as it freely moves back and forth between the world of reality and the world of the childlike imagination. The frost emerges here like an authoritarian person taking pleasure in intimidating his subjects and trying out the limits of his power. He makes the flowers "stoop down" before him and shakes the leaves from the branches—yet doesn't manage to take away Wilhelm's hat. It's almost as if he were telling little Malchen a parable of the seven Göttingen professors who didn't bow to the king. It's as comforting and consoling as the ending of a folktale to know that Wilhelm held on to his hat!

Wilhelm's letter to Malchen, like his story for Mili, shows him as a storyteller in his own right, without regard for the core of the folk tradition. Yet, the tone and the worldview reflected in these letters is similar to the one we perceive in his preface to the *Kinder- und Hausmärchen* (1812), where he spoke about animals, stones, and plants that talked and were capable of human compassion; about the sun, the moon, and the stars that wore dresses and were alive; about the innocent and intimate relationship between the largest and the smallest creatures of this world. . . . When Wilhelm wrote this way, he did not merely convey a given style. His very words breathed the spirit of *Naturpoesie* but also the spirit of the Romantic poet. They reflected the animated world of myths and folktales but also that of Schelling's transcendental philosophy. For Wilhelm the world was filled with the innocence and purity of nature and childhood. If in his folktale style we detect the same warmth and sensitivity that we sense in his letters to children, it is because his own soul was alive with *Naturpoesie*. He fully realized that in this regard, Jacob was no match for him.

The German people recognized in the language of the *Kinder- und Hausmärchen* the simple and naive language of *Naturpoesie* that they already knew from folk songs, legends, and the language and games of children. It was archaic enough to be true to tradition and colloquial enough not to be obscure, yet it was never antiquated but alive. By combining traditional speech patterns with informal colloquial speech, Wilhelm breathed new life into the language of folktales from which emerged a dynamic of its own. Its poetry appealed to children as well as to adults, thus making German folktales once more what they used to be: stories for all ages.

NOTES

1. Reinhold Steig, *Achim von Arnim und Jacob und Wilhelm Grimm* (Stuttgart: Cotta, 1940).

2. Wilhelm Schoof, *Die Entstehungsgeschichte der Grimmschen Märchen* (Hamburg: Hauswedell, 1959), Chapter 1.

3. Ibid.

4. This engraving first appeared with the 1819 edition of the work.

5. Jacob and Wilhelm Grimm, *Kinder- und Hausmärchen* 2d ed., Vol. 1 (Berlin: Reimer, 1819), Preface.

6. Ibid.

7. Ibid.

8. Heinz Rölleke, ed., *Märchen aus dem Nachlaß der Brüder Grimm* 2d ed., Series: *Schriftenreihe Literaturwissenschaft* (Bonn: Bouvier, 1972). Tale number 7.

9. Ibid.

10. John Ellis, *One Fairy Story Too Many: The Brothers Grimm and Their Tales* (Chicago: University of Chicago Press, 1983).

11. Heinz Rölleke, ed., '*Wo das Wünschen noch geholfen hat'; Gesammelte Aufsätze zu den 'Kinder- und Hausmärchen' der Brüder Grimm* (Bonn: Bouvier Verlag Herbert Grundmann, 1985), pp. 161–74.

12. Schoof, Chapter 3.

13. Ibid., Chapter 5.

14. Heinrich Hamann, *Die literarischen Vorlagen der Kinder- und Hausmärchen.* Series: *Palaestra. Untersuchungen und Texte aus der deutschen und englischen Philologie*, number 57 (Berlin: Mayer & Müller, 1906).

15. Rölleke, ed., '*Wo das Wünschen noch geholfen hat'*, pp. 167–74.

16. Rölleke reprinted the earlier appeal of 1811, titled "*Aufforderung an die gesammten Freunde deutscher Poesie und Geschichte erlassen,*" in Heinz Rölleke, *Die Märchen der Brüder Grimm: Eine Einführung.* Series: Artemis Einführungen (Munich: Artemis Verlag, 1987), pp. 63–69. This appeal, however, unlike the folklore questionnaire of 1815, remained only a plan.

17. Jacob Grimm, *Circular wegen Aufsammlung der Volkspoesie* (Vienna, 1815). Facsimile edition by Ludwig von Denecke, with a preface by Kurt Ranke (Kassel: Bärenreiter Verlag, 1965). The Grimms referred to this questionnaire for short as the *Circular-Brief.*

18. See also Ludwig Denecke, "Grimm, Jacob Ludwig Carl" *Enzyklopädie des Märchens; Handwörterbuch zur historischen und vergleichenden Erzählforschung* 5, Kurt Ranke, et al. eds. (Berlin: Walter de Gruyter, 1989), pp. 171–86.

19. Kurt Ranke, "Introduction" to *Circular-Brief.* Further, it must be noted that the questionnaire was not confined to German-speaking countries. Jacob Grimm also gave a copy of it to B. Kopitar in Vienna who on May 12, 1815, sent it on to Vuk Karadcik in Serbia—a fact to which some scholars ascribe the beginning of systematic Serbian folk song and folktale collections. Miljan Mojašević, "Jacob

Grimm und die Jugoslawen; Skizze und Stoff zu einter Studie" in *Brüder Grimm Gedenken* 1, Ludwig Denecke, ed. (Marburg: Elwert Verlag, 1963), pp. 341–44. Mojašević compared the warm and appreciative comments of both Brothers Grimm on Serbiann folk songs to those uttered earlier by Herder and Goethe, ascribing to them also the same liberal, cosmopolitan, and humanitarian worldview that had characterized the beginnings of comparative literature. See pp. 345–46.

20. Jacob also issued a direct appeal for contributions to their collection through review articles that he published. See Chapter 4, ref. "Reinhart Fuchs."

21. See Chapter 10, reference notes to Jack Zipes and Alan Dundes.

22. Schoof, Chapter 5. See also: Christa Kamenetsky, "Wilhelm and Jacob Grimm (1785–1863 and 1786–1859)" Jane Bingham, ed. *Writers for Children: Critical Studies of Major Authors Since the Seventeenth Century* (New York: Charles Scribner's Sons, 1987), 379–83.

23. Their annotations betray that they were consistent with their stated principles of selection.

24. Jacob wrote in his "Appeal to all Friends of German Poetry and History": "Needed for this task is not only a certain innocent naivete but also an education enabling us to grasp this naivete in the virtue that is unconscious of itself." Cited in Reinhold Steig, *Clemens Brentano und die Brüder Grimm* (Stuttgart: Cotta, 1914), pp. 164–71. See also Christa Kamenetsky, "The Brothers Grimm: Folktale Style and Romantic Theories," *Elementary English* (March 1974), p. 383.

25. *Kinder- und Hausmärchen* 3 (1822) Part 2, Preface.

26. Ina Maria Greverius, "Wege zu Wilhelm Grimms 'Altdänischen Heldenliedern' " in *Brüder Grimm Gedenken* 1, Ludwig Denecke, ed. (Marburg: Elwert Verlag, 1963), pp. 74–84.

27. *Kinder- und Hausmärchen* 1 (1819), Introduction.

28. Ibid.

29. *Kinder- und Hausmärchen* 3 (1819) Part I, Notes.

30. Heinz Rölleke, "Von dem Fischer un syner Fru. Die älteste schriftliche Überlieferung," in *'Wo das Wünschen noch geholfen hat'* Heinz Rölleke, ed., pp. 161–74.

31. Max Lüthi, *The European Folktale: Form and Nature* (New York: Institute for the Study of Human Issues, 1986), Chapters 1, 4 and 5. Also Max Lüthi, *Märchen* 2d rev. ed. Series: *Realienbücher für Germanisten* (Stuttgart: Metzlersche Verlagsbuchhandlung, 1964). Relevant are also several chapters in Lüthi's *The Fairytale as Art Form and Portrait of Man*. Jan Erickson, trans. (Bloomington: Indiana University Press, 1970).

32. The German proverb is: "Jemanden über den grünen Klee loben." For related studies of the Grimms' use of proverbial expressions, see Wolfgang Mieder, "Ever Eager to Incorporate Folk Proverbs: Wilhelm Grimm's Proverbial Additions in the Fairy Tales" in James McGlathery et al., eds., *The Brothers Grimm and Folktale* (University of Illinois Press, 1988) pp. 112–33.

33. Gunhild Ginschel, "Der Märchenstil Jacob Grimms," *Deutsches Jahrbuch für Volkskunde* 9 (1963), pp. 131–68.

34. Lüthi, *The Fairy Tale*, Chapter 2.

35. Steig, p. 156.

36. Ibid.

37. Friedrich Panzer, *Kinder- und Hausmärchen*. Vollständige Ausgabe in der Urfassung (Wiesbaden: Emil Vollmer Verlag, n.d., about 1955), Introduction.

38. Jacob Grimm, "Über das Pedantische in der deutschen Sprache" in *Kleinere Schriften von Jacob Grimm* I (Berlin: Dümmler, 1864).

39. Hamann, pp. 109–22. See also Kurt Schmidt, *Die Entwicklung der Grimmschen Kinder- und Hausmärchen seit der Urhandschrift*. Series: *Ausgewählte*

Arbeiten aus dem Deutschen Seminar zu Halle, Philip Strauch et al., eds. (Halle: Niemeyer, 1932, pp. 7–32.)

40. Ginschel, pp. 131–78.

41. This expression related to Jacob's translation of the French "Renard" ("Reynard the Fox") into German.

42. This work is a fantasy, not a folktale, although it does contain a similar theme as Grimms' collected tale "St. Joseph in the Woods" (a Christian legend in the *Kinder- und Hausmärchen*).

43. Wilhelm's letter to Malchen, dated November 8, 1817, is reprinted in Schoof, p. 180. Malchen (Amalie von Zuydtwyck) was the little daughter of one of the eight von Haxthausen sisters, Ferdinandine von Zuydtwyck. For a related correspondence see also Wilhelm Schoof and Jörn Göres, eds., *Unbekannte Briefe der Brüder Grimm. Unter Ausnutzung des Grimmschen Nachlasses* (Bonn: Athenäum, 1960).

PART III

Critical Appraisal of the *Kinder- und Hausmärchen*

8. *MÄRCHENKRITIK* IN THE CONTEXT OF EUROPEAN ROMANTICISM

[Folklore and the Middle Ages]

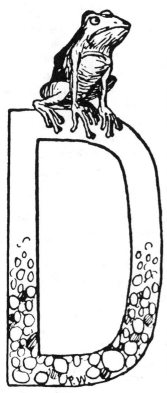

URING THE ROMANTIC MOVEMENT, the critical reception of the *Kinder- und Hausmärchen* in Germany and abroad coincided with a new appreciation of nature, myths, and the medieval past. Being inspired by Rousseau, Johann Gottfried Herder had prepared the ground for this trend by urging all nations to search out their native folklore and traditions. In folk songs, folktales, myths, and legends, one believed to see remnants of a Golden Age in which people had still lived in harmony with God and nature. It was this quest for native *Naturpoesie* (folk or nature poetry) that motivated Clemens Brentano and Achim von Arnim to publish a German folk-song collection, titled *Des Knaben Wunderhorn* (*The Boy's Wunderhorn*) in 1805. Brentano then too urged his friends, among whom were poets, painters, scholars, and writers, to make a further search for legends and tales among the common folk. His call also reached the Brothers Grimm, who contributed more than their due share to his collection.[1]

Only a few decades earlier, the German philosopher Immanuel Kant still had regarded the Middle Ages as an aberration of the human mind, yet since Herder's days the trend had swung in the opposite direction. In Germany as well as in the British Isles, the growing preconcern with native "roots" drew particular attention to the Nordic and Celtic traditions rather than to those of classical Greece and Rome. The storm clouds of Macpherson's *Ossian* seemed to correspond more closely to the mood of Herder and Goethe at that time, who even learned Celtic to grasp the full meaning of what they believed to be a genuine epic. Inspired by Herder's essays, one also began to feel closer to "the wild genius" of Shakespeare, discovering in his writings the spirit of the "Nordic" homeland. A book review editor of the *Edinburgh Review* noted in 1827: "Of all literatures, accordingly, the German has the best as well as the most translations; men like Goethe, Wieland, Schlegel, Tieck have not disdained this task. Of Shakespeare three entire versions are admitted to be good, and we know not how many partial or considered as bad."[2] August Wilhelm Schlegel's Shakespeare translation at that time expressed the same love of *Naturpoesie* as did Brentano's and Arnim's folk-song collection. A similar spirit moved Sir Walter Scott to search for folk ballads in the border countries of Southern Scotland[3] and Wilhelm Grimm to translate Sir Walter Scott's ballads along with others from Denmark.

When, in 1806, Heinrich von der Hagen published a new edition of the *Nibelungenlied* (*Song of the Nibelung*), August Wilhelm Schlegel and Ludwig Tieck hailed it as evidence of national poetry, as proof of *Naturpoesie* belonging to the "folk soul" of the nation. Jacob Grimm enthusiastically compared it to the epics of Homer. Following a similar motivation, both Jacob and Wilhelm Grimm had prepared a translation of the *Elder Edda* and the *Nibelungenlied*, although they abandoned the latter project after the first volume upon discovering that Hagen's edition had reached the market before they had time to finish their work.[4]

It is often overlooked that the Romantics needed courage and perseverance to publish *Naturpoesie*, as they were swimming against the tide of a literary establishment. All too fresh in their memories were the harsh words that King Frederick the Great had spoken against the *Nibelungenlied*, calling the great Austrian epic "nothing but plunder—not worth a shot of gun powder."[5] A number of critics still continued to feel that way as they attacked the Romantics from the rigid standpoints of the neoclassical tradition. Even as they gradually began to appreciate medieval epics, they still considered folklore as subliterary material not worthy of the printer's ink. The transition toward a new conception of literature and language was not a smooth one that merely happened without a struggle. It turned out to be a particularly rough road for the Brothers Grimm, who came to defend not only epic literature but also the simple folktale as a living tradition of the vernacular. The general Romantic quest for *Naturpoesie* favored their folktale publication,[6] yet they still had to defend their endeavors against different conceptions of folktales held by a number of their colleagues, not just by a critical opposition.

Only gradually did an awakening interest in epic poetry make room for the legitimate use of the German vernacular and dialects in literary publications. In the preceding decades many German poets had still preferred to write in French, Latin, Italian, or Greek, although Hamann and Herder had already paved the way for a new appreciation of the old languages in their epic vitality. As the Romantics rediscovered the native folk spirit of the past in the language of the simple peasant and of the child, they also began to see a link between the language of medieval poetry and the traditional folk song, in all of which they recognized the vivid, concrete, and spontaneous expression of another, more wholesome age. The Brothers Grimm went one step further by searching for that naive spirit also in the prose of traditional legends and folktales, which up until that time had not been taken too seriously. Knowing that their friends were still preoccupied with the collection of poetry rather than with prose, Jacob wrote prophetically in 1807: "In our time a great love of folk songs has developed, and it will also draw attention to the legends and folktales that still circulate among the peasants and that have been preserved for us in forgotten places."[7]

The revived interest in the Middle Ages gradually drew the Romantic poets' attention from the *Minnelieder* (medieval love songs) and the old folk songs to the more zesty and humorous works of Hans Sachs and the German folk-book tradition. In 1807 Joseph Görres published *Die teutschen Volkbücher* (*The German Folk Books*),[8] which became a literary as well as a popular success. The *Volksbücher* (also called chapbooks) included such popular medieval legends as "Dr. Faustus," "The Horned Siegfried," and "Beautiful Magelone," as well as humorous anecdotes, proverbs, and swanks. Their language was often crude and not meant for children, yet it closely resembled the spoken speech of earlier days, and as such, it appealed to the Romantics so much more than the tired prose of more-pretentious literary works. What formerly had been treated with contempt now arose as a new wellspring for the poetic imagination. The folk books were not just literature by the people and for the people, but they were living evidence of the "folk soul" of the past. To many Romantic writers they promised an inspiration of their own work in regard to both theme and style, a true revival from the source of folkdom.

The Brothers Grimm were fascinated by the folk books, for poetic as well as for scholarly reasons. In the language of these medieval tales they discovered traces of the old folkways, quaint expressions and dialects that resembled those of the vernacular language and the oral folk tradition of their own time. Many themes and character traits, too, seemed to correspond with those that occurred in the folktales that they recorded from storytellers. Thus, the folk books also provided them with valuable resource material for a comparative study of folktale variants, of which they later made use in their notes to the *Kinder- und Hausmärchen*.

To the German Romantics, tradition was not a rigid or dead subject that had been transmitted mechanically from one generation to the next. Rather, it was alive and demanded to be kept alive by a creative mind open to the ancient folk imagination. It was in this spirit that Wilhelm published the *Altdänische Heldenlieder, Balladen und Märchen* (*Old Danish Hero Songs, Ballads, and Folktales*) in 1811. Believing in the vigor of the old languages, he selected among the folk ballads only the oldest ones, and among these only those that appeared to have been preserved most loyally since the thirteenth century. In translating the ballads and tales, he made his primary concern to bring alive again what had almost been forgotten. Even though he took some liberties in the word choice, he managed to recreate the essential imagery, mood, and rhythm in a masterly fashion. Especially because he avoided clinging pedantically to every single word, he came very close to the original feeling and spirit of the songs, so that even today scholars compliment him on the art of his translation. Wilhelm's skill in translation and his feeling for language were talents that seemed to predetermine his later success with what has come to be known as his folktale style. He wrote in his introduction to this work: "The poetry of these folktales touch upon everyone's heart and soul. In these tales there is a sense of magic that can also be found here (in Germany) and conveyed to children: in secret forests, in subterranean caverns, and in the depth of the sea."[9] Wilhelm expressed similar thoughts about the poetic effect of folktales in his introduction to the first edition of the *Kinder- und Hausmärchen*.

Jacob and Wilhelm Grimm published the *Kinder- und Hausmärchen* in 1812. Their previous collection activities and the general Romantic interest in *Naturpoesie* were encouraging factors in this endeavor. Still, it needed courage on their part to concern themselves with stories that in their time were still somewhat contemptuously called "nursery tales." Their friends had primarily focused attention on folk songs, ballads, and epics, while considering folktales as subliterary material that belonged nowhere except in the nursery. The *Volksbücher*, too, had contained some tales, but generally these seemed to belong to a greater degree to grown-ups, not to children. The Grimms titled their collection of folktales *Kinder- und Hausmärchen* (*Children's and Household Stories*), so as to indicate that these tales were not merely of interest to children but to the entire household, be it parents, grandparents, or servants. To play it safe, Wilhelm added a long preface to the first edition of the work, explaining and justifying their endeavor. In this preface as well as in later ones and related essays, he and Jacob contemplated the age and nature of the tales and their relation to myths and medieval epics of older times, as well as their universal human significance.[10]

[*Volksmärchen* versus *Kunstmärchen*]

The hallmark of the *Kinder- und Hausmärchen* was its supposed loyalty to tradition. "In this sense," wrote Wilhelm in his preface to the 1812 edition, "there exists in Germany not a single collection."[11] The method with which the Grimms collected the tales differed from that of their predecessors. Herder, for example, had still composed ballads in imitation of the folk ballads, in a similar way as Scott, who followed his trail; Brentano, too, had felt no qualms about inventing his own "fairy tales" while mingling folktale motifs with his own story elements. Like Heinrich Wackenroder and Novalis (Friedrich von Hardenberg), he concerned himself to a greater degree with the *Kunstmärchen*, or literary fairy tale, as an art form. In and by themselves, *Kunstmärchen* were a highly respected form of imaginative writing,[12] yet they had little bearing on the search for genuine folk traditions. The Grimms were concerned with the *Volksmärchen*, or folktale, not with the literary fairy tale. Both genres were related and in some cases overlapped, yet as scholars of linguistics and medieval literature, the Grimms were embarking on a comparative study of *Naturpoesie*[13] in which only the folktale could be considered suitable for research. Substantial changes in folktales would have presented a serious obstacle to their goal. Even though Jacob and Wilhelm at times differed in their views regarding the question to what extent a collector was permitted to change a ballad, song, or tale without becoming disloyal to tradition, they both agreed on one essential point, namely that *Naturpoesie* should be preserved in loyalty to the style and substance of medieval epics.

Well known among the "fairy tale" collections prior to the *Kinder- und Hausmärchen* had been the tales of *Pentamerone* by Giambattista Basile (originally called *La cunto di la cunti* or *The Tale of Tales,* 1634–36), the *Contes de ma mère l'Oye* (*Tales of My Mother Goose,* 1697) by Charles Perrault, the *Contes des fées* (*Fairy Tales,* 1697–98) by Madame d'Aulnoy, and the collection by Musäus, titled *Volksmährchen der Deutschen* [*sic*] (*Folktales of the Germans,* 5 vols., 1782–87). All of these and others were commonly called "*Märchen*" or "*Mährchen*,"[14] (a term derived from the word *Mare* or *Märe*), meaning tales, news, tidings, or "fairy tales," which made it difficult for the Grimms to defend their own tales as "different." What distinguished the Grimms' folktale collection from the other collections may be partially explained by the general distinction between the *Volksmärchen* (folktales) and *Kunstmärchen* (literary fairy tale or fantasies), for it was only the first that belonged to the inherited oral folk tradition. In their essays and correspondence, the Grimms used the terms *Volksmärchen* and *Kindermärchen* (children's tales) synonymously, while setting them off against the *Kunstmärchen* or *Wundermärchen* (tales of wonder) as something that had to be treated with a similar reverence as medieval manuscripts.

How sensitive the Grimms were to a confusion of folktales with literary fairy tales or tales of wonder we may gather from Jacob Grimm's letter addressed to Sir Walter Scott in 1815. Jacob had initially inquired about a possible exchange of medieval manuscripts with Scott. In the course of his correspondence he mentioned his own and Wilhelm's work on *Tristem*, his research on Nordic languages and dialects, as well as their recent publication of the *Kinder- und Hausmärchen*, to which he referred here simply as *Kindermärchen*. In return, Scott had sent to the Grimms some of the requested materials, replying, among other things, that he had not seen the Berlin edition of this work yet and that he should like to possess it. He remembered having read with delight the *Volksmärchen* of Musäus, recognizing in these the story of "The Mountain Spirit of Rammelsberg" and other tales in which he perceived similarities with Scottish tales, in fact the very ". . . outline of the stories of our nurseries and schools." Scott continued, "I have also a curious and miscellaneous collection of books in German containing the *Gehörnte Siegfried* and other romantic tales,"[15] Even though Jacob's return letter indicates that he was happy about Scott's kind response, it also showed that he was unwilling to accept Scott's basic misunderstanding regarding the true nature of the *Kinder- und Hausmärchen*. After thanking him for the manuscripts, he tried to convey to him that their *Kindermärchen* were not exactly what he perceived them to be:

> The tales of Musäus are generally touching, yet this quality may be ascribed to their unexplainable substance, not to their manneristic style that, while not without spirit, is but modern and often French in its satirical aspects. Therefore, it has been one of my most pronounced efforts to be as different as possible in style from Musäus. What I have gained or lost in this process you may be better able to judge for yourself after you have seen the book.[16]

Jacob evidently felt embarrassed that Scott had not understood the scholarly or poetic reasons behind their collection. Perhaps Jacob expected too much of Scott at that time, for after all, Scott had not seen the work and consequently also did not know Wilhelm's elaborate defense of the uniqueness of their collection. It turned out that later Scott became one of the Grimm's most ardent supporters in the British Isles.

The aspect to which the Grimms objected most in Musäus's collection was his stylistic embellishment of folktales. By imposing upon traditional tales his own fantasy and a satiric style, Musäus came close to the mannerism of Charles Perrault and Madame d'Aulnoy, thus removing himself substantially from the tone and language of the old storytellers. The Grimms, on the other hand, used every means of research available to them in medieval studies and linguistics to come as close as possible to the original folktale language. The style that especially Wilhelm Grimm created in rewriting the collected tales is generally known and revered today as the "folktale style." It is self-evident that Wilhelm, too, changed the language to some degree in this process, but he never did so arbitrarily. The issue of his loyalty to tradition still needs closer attention in a later chapter.

It was not only Scott who at first did not quite grasp the Grimms' original intentions. Clemens Brentano, for example, who initially had motivated them to collect folk songs as well as folktales, also did not quite understand the significance of the folktales' epic connection, or else he did not care enough about the subject to continue his endeavor. It had been a generous gesture on Brentano's part that he handed over his own collected folktales to the Brothers Grimm in 1811, yet by misplacing the Grimms' final manuscript during the same year, he almost destroyed their project.[17] It was fortunate that in anticipation of Brentano's unpredictable attitudes Wilhelm had prepared a copy of more than thirty folktales which they had mailed to his Berlin address, a precaution that saved these tales for inclusion in the *Kinder- und Hausmärchen*. Wilhelm had also indicated to Jacob at that time that he was afraid Clemens might change the tales too much before submitting them to the printer.[18] The entire incident shows that Brentano did not share the Grimms' fascination with the historical and poetic value of folktales but rather preferred to use them as a springboard for his own imagination.

For different reasons also the Grimms' friends August Wilhelm and Friedrich Schlegel did not quite understand the value of their endeavors on behalf of the folktale collection. Whereas Brentano had moved toward writing *Kunstmärchen*, the Schlegels swayed in the opposite direction of medieval scholarship. Being actively involved in editing their literary journal, *Das Athenaeum*, and in writing scholarly essays on mythology, philosophy, and *Naturpoesie*, they failed to understand how intelligent men like the Brothers Grimm should have wasted so much time on children's stories. Thus Friedrich Schlegel wrote somewhat cynically in 1815:

> As far as *Ammenmärchen* (nursery tales) are concerned, we do not wish to underestimate their value too much, but we believe that excellent qualities are just as rare in this genre of literature as in all other ones. Every good nurse shall entertain children, or at least calm them down and put them to sleep. If she manages to accomplish this through her stories, we can't expect more of her. Yet to clean out the entire attic stuffed with well-intended nonsense while insisting that every piece of junk be honored in the name of an age-old legend, this is indeed asking too much of an educated person.[19]

Personally, Friedrich Schlegel enjoyed folktales, and the Brothers Grimm knew it, but he thought it below his dignity to take them all too seriously. In this case, too, the misunderstanding was based on a superficial association of the Grimms' *Kindermärchen* with other collections known at that time. There was Ludwig Tieck's *Ritter Blaubart* (*Knight Bluebeard*) of 1797, for example, which bore the ironic subtitle *Ein Ammenmärchen* (*A Nurse's Tale*), although in its psychological complexity it was no children's tale at all but rather a refined *Kunst-märchen* with literary merits in its own right. Johann Gustav Büsching's publication of *Volks-Sagen, Märchen und Legenden* (*Folk Sagas, Folktales, and Legends*) which he published only three months prior to the *Kinder- und Hausmärchen*,[20] may further have added to the confusion of terms. This work contained some local legends collected orally but also tales gleaned from the works of Musäus and others who had no connection with Grimm. Possibly the greatest confusion arose on account of a rival publication of folktales by Albert Ludwig Grimm, which had appeared in 1808 under the title of *Kindermährchen* (sic.) (*Children's Tales*). Wilhelm Grimm noted explicitly in his introduction to the 1812 edition of the *Kinder- und Hausmärchen* that their collection had absolutely nothing in common with that of a certain Mr. A. L. Grimm who accidentally shared their name.[21] In his turn, A. L. Grimm emphatically disassociated himself from the Brothers Grimm by criticizing the "all-inclusive" nature of their tales that exposed children prematurely to cruel characters and events.[22]

[*Märchen* at Home and Abroad]

In spite of such misunderstandings and confusions, however, the critical reception of the *Kinder- und Hausmärchen* was overwhelmingly positive, and so was the popular response shortly after its publication. How much support the Grimms received from their friends and colleagues in the Romantic age may well be perceived by the returns of his folklore questionnaire, the *Circular wegen Auffassung der Volkspoesie* (*Round-Letter on Behalf of Collecting Folk Poetry*)[23] that Jacob mailed to his friends and acquaintances in 1815. Over a period of a little more than a year, he counted 360 responses from all regions of Germany, as well as from Bohemia, Austria, and the Netherlands. In accordance with his instructions, these friends not only sent him folktales but also nursery rhymes, children's songs, children's games, ballads, legends, proverbs, folk superstitions, and even some "quaint" colloquial expressions that seemed to belong to an older age. All of these they recorded in loyalty to those versions that they had heard in their own environment. In his instructions, Jacob had reminded his friends that they should look out for variants in the songs and tales they heard, because these would undoubtedly provide valuable insights into the living folk tradition. From the questionnaire returns, the Grimms then collected a number of variants, on the basis of which they undertook comparative folktale studies. The Grimms later incorporated some of these responses in their notes, which they published in the third volume of the second edition of the *Kinder- und Hausmärchen* in 1819[24] It is regrettable that they did not make a concise analysis of the questionnaire returns, as it might have provided folklorists today with more evidence regarding the exact origins of some variants and the circumstances under which they had been recorded. Alone the data pertaining to the informants would have made invaluable research material for a modern scientific analysis. One copy of the questionnaire itself, however, was found among the Grimm papers. Jacob had scribbled into its margins the numbers of the returns and the respective dates when he had received them. Still, it was the first large-scale research of its kind, and it fully served the purpose that the Grimms had in mind.

In itself the questionnaire provides valuable evidence not only of Jacob's inquiring mind and systematic approach to folklore research but also of the wide support that he received from his acquaintances and friends who shared his love of *Naturpoesie*. As Brentano had inspired the Grimms to set out in search of the oral tradition, so the Grimms, in turn, inspired others to do the same. The *Kinder- und Hausmärchen* provided the living example of the results of such a search, yet the questionnaire provided clear-cut instructions for the methods to be used in fieldwork collections. As such, it was equally encouraging for others to collect folktales on their own.

From the perspective of children's literature, the *Kinder- und Hausmärchen* was an instant success in Germany and abroad. Especially because the language of the tale followed so closely the oral tradition of the common folk, the work appealed to children as well as to adults. Here was storytelling at its very best: the colloquial language flowed smoothly, rhythmically, and with ease while plots and themes spoke of human endeavors, be they within the context of adventure, reality, or the realm of the imagination. Both the language and the themes spoke directly to the heart and soul of the people.

The warm popular response to the *Kinder- und Hausmärchen* is well reflected in its publishing history. Even though the editions were not large and the sales were relatively modest, every edition had an increasing number of tales, with the exception of the *Kleine Ausgabe* (*Short Edition*) of 1825 that was especially designed for children. In all, seven editions were published between 1812 and 1857, and already in the 1820s numerous translations of the work spoke for its success. A sure sign of the work's influence were the many collections that were directly or indirectly inspired by the *Kinder- und Hausmärchen*. In his introduction to the third volume of the work in 1822, Wilhelm Grimm humbly observed: "The loyal perception of tradition, the natural expression, and, if it does not sound presumptuous, the richness and variety of the work have evoked a continuous interest in and recognition of the work at home and abroad."[25]

Wilhelm Grimm himself carefully took stock of the influence that their collection had exercised at home and abroad. An annotated bibliography that he attached to the sixth edition of the *Kinder- und Hausmärchen* (1850) encompassed numerous translations of their work in European countries. Among these were also Edgar Taylor's first English translation, the *German Popular Stories* (1823), which Wilhelm praised on account of its completeness and accuracy. His comments on this translation also betray his acquaintance with Cohen's complimentary review of their work in the English *Quarterly Review*. He further mentioned another English translation by Richard Doyle and John Edward Taylor, entitled *Fairy Ring: A New Collection of Popular Tales* (London, 1846), illustrated by Otto Spekter in 1847. He further listed with a note of satisfaction a Dutch translation by Hegermann and Lindencrone (1820), several Danish translations by Lindencrone, Öhlenschläger, and Molbeck (1835–1842), a Swedish translation by Reutendahl (1832), and some French translations (1834–1838), of which the first had been a single story, "The Juniper Tree," which appeared in the *Journal de débats* in Paris.[26]

To the sixth edition of the *Kinder- und Hausmärchen* Wilhelm also added a still longer supplementary list of folktale publications in Germany and abroad. Among the German-language works, he mentioned in his introduction collections from Austria, Bohemia, Prussia, Saxony, and Westphalia, and among individual works, he singled out the collections of W. Bechstein and W. Panzer. He also listed Hans Christian Andersen's *Eventyr fortalis for børn* (*Fairy Tales*), which had been published in Copenhagen in 1840.[27] Through Jessen's German translation he was familiar with this work, but since he also knew Danish, he may have read the original version as well. It is peculiar that he did include this work, as it is only partially based on the Danish folk tradition and generally would be classified as a volume of literary fairy tales rather than folktales. Yet, since Wilhelm included no other *Kunstmärchen* except for these, we may deduce that he considered Andersen's tales much closer to the folk tradition than the rest.[28]

Wilhelm's review of folktale publications also concerned collections of Scotland, Norway, and Sweden, although it was by no means restricted to the sphere of the Nordic Germanic traditions. It encompassed folktale collections of Ireland, Brittany, Finland, Livland, Kurland, Estland, Walachia, Hungary, Poland, Russia, the "Slavonic peoples," and Greece. Even the tales of the North American Indians won his attention with one of the longest reviews of the entire essay. Particular mention must be made of Wilhelm's appraisal regarding Thomas Crofton Croker's *Fairy Legends of the South of Ireland* (London, 1823), which had been the first work in the British Isles to follow the Romantic folklore revival and specifically the model of the Grimms' *Kinder- und Hausmärchen*. Having read the Grimms' tales as a young lad, Croker wandered across the countryside of Southern Ireland for three years, collecting songs and tales from the Irish peasants, shepherds, and miners.[29] Wilhelm was so thoroughly charmed by the spirit of these old Celtic traditions that he translated the work during the same year it appeared, publishing it under the title of *Irische Elfenmärchen*.

Croker, in his turn, translated Wilhelm's long introduction "Über die Elfen" ("About the Fairies") into English. He attached it to the second edition of his work, along with a "Dedicatory Letter" to the Brothers Grimm.[30]

The warm enthusiasm with which Wilhelm embraced the folktale collections of many lands unmistakenly bears the stamp of Herder's international orientation. His extensive comments (spanning more than seventy pages) testify to his genuine interest in other folk cultures and traditions, not just his own. Like Herder, he first of all perceived in the folktale collection of each culture the unique spirit and language of its own folk heritage, and then some universal elements reflecting the spirit of humanity shared by all.[31] This world-open attitude on the part of both Brothers Grimm has not yet received the attention it deserves. Partially because of mistranslations or misinterpretations and partially because of political distortions, a number of critics during the last century and ours did portray the Grimms one-sidedly as German nationalists with little or no concern for other cultures and traditions.

The positive critical responses to the Grimms' *Kinder- und Hausmärchen* came from two quarters: namely from those concerned with a revival of the medieval past and from those who believed in the merits of imaginative literature for children. Many critics during the early and mid-nineteenth century, in both Germany and the British Isles, still considered folk literature and children's literature on separate planes and were not ready for the Grimms' revolutionary idea that both were essentially related. Consequently, those who supported the cultivation of folklore used a different set of arguments than those who supported folklore as literature for children. The Grimms themselves were quite aware of the fact that their work had a two-fold appeal. On the one hand, it had attracted scholars who, by following their example, had made folktales the basis of philological and comparative studies while on the other hand, it had caught the attention of those who wished to free children from the narrow confines of a moralistic and didactic approach to education. Jacob Grimm consciously referred to this duality in the reception of their *Kindermärchen* in his preface to Anton Dietrich's *Russische Volksmärchen* (*Russian Folktales*) in 1831.[32] Folktales had recently become a two-fold center of interest, he observed, namely for students of medieval literature as well as for children. One had also begun to discover an important link between the language and ethics of folktales and those of medieval poetry. He reminded medieval scholars that they should not neglect to consult both folktales and epics mutually, for only an understanding of both could help in establishing their deeper meaning. He left no doubt that this meaning lay embedded in their mythical symbols, their childlike naivete, and their very language.[33]

[The Grimms' Response to the Fearful]

The great appeal that folktales had for children proved that children needed food for the imagination, Jacob wrote. Folktales were so much richer in substance and language than those rationally constructed tales written especially for them. To be honest, hadn't children long grown weary of barren tales that had nothing to offer to them except, as Jacob put it, "the thin suds of an empty morality"? By contrast, folktales were endowed with a poetic spirit that provided children with a much more nutritious diet. At last, children could be happy that one had returned to them what rightfully belonged to their domain, namely "the full taste of the still undiminished source of the old fantasy" ("*den unversiegten Quell der alten Fantasie*").[34] Jacob implied that the native tradition in every land poured forth a never-ending stream of songs and tales that were sparkling and alive with the old folk imagination. As the spiritual history of the nation's past, and as the very essence of poetry, they appealed to all ages and needed neither embellishments nor added moralities to make them especially suitable for children.[35] In reflecting the humanity of man, the language of folktales was easily understood by all: It was naive yet vivid and concrete, and as it mirrored the childhood of mankind, so it appealed to the heart of the child.

Among Jacob Grimm's correspondences with Reimer, his publisher, exists an often-quoted letter stating explicitly that their folktale collection was not at all intended for children but that he was glad it appealed to them.[36] Does this letter represent a contradiction to his assertion that folktales belonged to children? Did he perhaps change his mind, as some critics suggested, or, what may be worse, did he live with the contradictions without bothering to resolve them in his mind? Was he ambiguous in regard to the question whether or not folktales were suitable for children, or did he have a definite theory of their value for young readers?

If we consider the Grimms' theory of the folktales' epic context,[37] this question may be resolved. What appears to be a dilemma in reality is nothing but a respect for the dual appeal of the vivid epic language that was an integral part of the folktale world. To the Grimms there was no clear-cut "either-or" solution to this question, for they thought that folktales were rich enough in themselves to appeal to adults and children alike. As they did not recognize a sharp line of division between folktales and epics, they considered both simultaneously as resource material for medieval and linguistic studies and as food for the child's imagination. They saw no reason why children should be artificially separated from the "old fantasy" that had existed in the childhood of mankind. Folktales were as much the domain of children as they were the domain of scholars.[38]

The dual nature and appeal of folktales, as the Grimms perceived it, was not evident to those among their contemporaries who were used to considering simple "nursery tales" and epic literature in two entirely different compartments. Achim von Arnim, for example, strongly advised them to change some tales in the *Kinder- und Hausmärchen* so as to make them more digestible for children. Unlike Friedrich Schlegel, who did not wish to spend much time thinking about the nature of folktales at all, Arnim did value the folktales' poetic appeal to children but thought they should be adapted to their taste and age. Why should some selections not be altered or omitted, so as to render the work as a whole more suitable for young readers? He never quite understood why at that time the Grimms insisted that children should read the folktales as they read the Bible, without adornments, abridgements, or alterations regarding their epic substance.

On January 28, 1813, Jacob responded in a letter to Arnim that he did not think that folktales were meant for children alone. Children were as imaginatively receptive to folktales as were older folks, he observed, and he saw no reason why the tales should be tailored for them in a special way.

> I believe that, in God's name, all children should read the entire folktale collection and be left to themselves in this process. What is the difference if there are some incomprehensible elements in the language and narrative of the folktales, such as in the Low German tales? One can always skip those things and even be glad if something is left for the future. Anyhow, you won't ever be able to give a book to children that is perfectly comprehensible to them, for there will always be some aspects of composition or syntax that, while clear to us, will be unclear to them. Yet, it's always pleasant to guess a little, which usually brings out some new aspects . . . My old principle, that I have already defended earlier, has always been that one shall write to please oneself rather than to give in to external pressures. Therefore, this book of folktales has not been written for children at all, but it makes me very glad that they do like it. I would not have worked on it with such a pleasure if I had not believed that with respect to poetry, mythology, and history it would have appeared just as important to the more serious and older adults as it has to me.[39]

Jacob stated that parents and educators expected too much of children too early, and altogether the wrong things from literature. Literature should not be used to teach children or to preach to them. The true "lessons" of literature emerged from a certain wisdom in the stories themselves that ignited and illuminated what the child already knew and possessed. Neither parents, nor teachers, nor books could bring wisdom to children from the "outside" "as if it were a bundle of firewood." Children had to be ready for a given tale to respond to it in a meaningful way. Jacob's remarks on reading readiness have a rather modern ring, but even more so his comments on the need for a non-didactic approach to folktales.

In his introduction to the second edition of the *Kinder- und Hausmärchen* (1819) Wilhelm Grimm, too, reacted to the criticism voiced by Arnim and others. It appears from his comments that a number of concerned parents and educators, too, had voiced the question of whether the tales were indeed suitable reading material for children. Were not some of the stories too harsh and cruel for young and sensitive minds? Wilhelm argued that in depicting good and evil forces in the world, folktales reflected the natural balance of life and an age-old human experience. Why should children be protected from what was natural? By using an analogy of nature, he explained that as the sunlight was unthinkable without the shadow, and as day would be incomplete without night, so evil in folktales was the foil for all that was good. For every sadness there was joy, for every fear there was consolation. Together, good and evil made up the substance of life and were true symbols of humanity. It would be a mistake to shield children from what they had a right to know and from what they wanted to know.

He still used another analogy in which he compared children to young plants in need of sunlight and the fresh air outdoors:

> Rain and dew fall on everything that exists on earth, as a blessing to all. Whoever does not dare to place his plants outside under the weather, fearing that they might be too sensitive and suffer damage, certainly will not demand that the rain and the dew should stay away because of it. Yet everything can grow under natural conditions, and this is what we shall keep in mind. By the way, we do not know of a healthy and strong book created by the people to which such objections would not apply to an ever greater degree. The Bible would have to be ranked at the top of such a list.[40]

Wilhelm's very choice of words betrays his Romantic belief that children should be raised naturally, without the artificial constraints that overprotective parents placed on them. In this case being "outside under the weather" meant to expose children to folktales without fear that they might catch a cold or suffer emotional damage. We recognize in such parables some educational theories of John Locke,[41] but more so those of Jean Jacques Rousseau, who permitted Emile to roam around freely under all weather conditions in the natural environment of the countryside, without having to fit himself into a tight schedule and, more importantly, without having to listen to moralistic lectures.[42] The contrast that Wilhelm Grimm creates here between the stuffy indoors and the fresh outdoors indicates his acceptance of the new Romantic trends in education. Romantic also is his association of the concepts

of organic growth, health, and nature. He perceived the same reflection of vigor, purity, and wholeness in nature as in children and the
age-old folktale. Confirming his Romantic faith in the innocence, health,
and wisdom of both, he referred to the old proverb that the truth lay
in the eye of the beholder. Those who wished to see evil certainly would
find it, he wrote, yet to the pure everything was pure. Wilhelm wrote,
"Children point without fear toward the stars, yet others who are steeped
in folk superstitions are afraid they might offend an angel by doing
so."[43] These "others" were exactly those who objected to unabridged
folktales for children: parents and educators to whom he responded
in this introduction. To grasp the deeper meaning of folktales, he advised
them, one should read them with the naive mind of the child, not with
the fears and phobias of an adult. While admitting that in this edition
he had excised from the text of the tales some crude and offensive expressions, he insisted that in principle he would not consent to change the
epic substance of the tales to the extent that they would alter the traditional concepts of good and evil.

[The English Quest for Nordic Roots]

In the British Isles, the earliest critics of the *Kinder- und Hausmärchen*
at first did not bother too much about children as a potential audience
of the tales but rather saw the tales' greatest significance as a valuable
resource for medieval scholarship. Mr. Francis Cohen, who in 1819
first called attention to the merits of this work in the *Quarterly Review*,
devoted nearly the entire length of his essay to the "northern antiquities"
that the Brothers Grimm had discovered in these quaint old tales.
Although Cohen's book review was indexed under the title of "Antiquities of Nursery Literature," the reviewer seemed to ignore the fact
that the book was also intended for children. Being primarily impressed
by the new potential that the Grimms' comparative approach offered
to a study of other cultures and traditions, and especially his own,
he wrote:

> Under the title of *Kinder- und Hausmärchen* they [the Brothers
> Grimm] have published a collection of German popular stories,
> singular in its kind, both for extent and variety, and from which
> we have acquired much information. In this collection we
> recognize a host of English and French and Italian stories of the
> same genre and species and extent in printed books, but the
> greatest part of the German popular nursery stories are stated
> by the editors to be traditionary [*sic*], some local, others widely
> known; and MM. Grimm say that they are confident that all
> those which they have so gathered from the oral tradition, with
> the exception indeed of Puss in Boots, are pure German and not
> borrowed from the stranger.[44]

What impressed him most was that the Grimms had taken considerable pains to show the relationship between folktales and Norse mythology, which the Grimms had emphasized in various essays and introductions. While ignoring the Grimms' argument, however, that precisely because of this epic relationship, folktales were suitable for children, he insisted that the tales were mainly material for interested scholars and only for "children of larger growth." Nevertheless, he commented enthusiastically on the Grimms' own analysis, indicating that the tales held many old folk beliefs that had almost been forgotten:

> *Thornrosa*, who is set a sleeping in consequence of the wounds inflicted by her spindle, is *Brynhilda* cast into slumber by the *Sleep Thorn* of Odin. The manner in which Loke hangs to the giant-eagle is better understood after a perusal of the story of *The Golden Goose*, to which the lads and lasses who touch it, adhere inseparably. In the stories of the *Wicked Goldsmith*, the *Speaking Fish*, and the *Eating of the Bird's Heart*, who does not recognize the fable of Sigurd?[45]

Over several pages at length, he then continued to draw upon other parallels in "Teutonic" folk traditions that the famous Dr. John Leyden had already observed in relation to German and Scottish ballads and folktales. There was the tale of "Frog-Lover," for example, which in every part of Germany, and also in the Grimms' collection, was known under the name of "King of the Frogs." In citing a similar passage in each, he called the readers' attention to the fact that "the rhythmical address of the aquatic lover, who is, of course, an enchanted prince, corresponds in the two languages":[46]

> "The Frog Lover"
> Open the door, my hinny, my heart,
> Open the door mine ain wee thing.
> And mind the words that you and I spak
> Down in the Meadow at the well spring.

> "Der Froschkönig" ("King of the Frogs")
> Königstochter, Jüngste,
> Mach mir auf.
> Weisst du nicht was gestern
> Du zu mir gesagt
> Bei dem kühlen Brunnenwasser?
> Königstochter, Jüngste,
> mach mir auf.[47]

> (Princess, youngest,
> Open the door.
> Don't you remember what you told me yesterday
> At the cool well water?
> Princess, youngest,
> Open the door.)[48]

He concluded that such similarities spoke of the common "Teutonic stock" of all folktales in the Nordic countries, which proved that also English folktales were older than epics and romances.

The reviewer ascribed such similarities in folktales to the common origin of all popular fictions in the Nordic countries. Especially in England and in the Scottish Lowlands one might discover "offsets and grafts from the Teutonic stock,"[49] so much more as possibly most of the English folktales were of Nordic origin. As far as the age of folktales was concerned, he speculated that they were older than the epics and romances. In that sense, he disagreed with Dr. Leyden (and also with the Brothers Grimm), who had ascribed an older age to the epic tradition. At this point it is also essential to note that the Grimms had not made a claim to the purely German nor to the purely Nordic origin of German, English, or Scottish folktales. Ironically, it was Cohen, not the Grimms, who confined his comparisons to examples in folktales belonging to the northern or Teutonic sphere of influence. The Grimms themselves had also included in their study of variants the broader context of world mythology and epics. A case in point was the reviewer's limited analysis of comparable sound patterns in three tales: the voice of a bird in the Grimms' "The Juniper Tree" ("Der Machandelbaum"), the mewing of a cat in a Scottish tale, and the song of a troll in a Danish story.[50] Regardless of the basic themes underlying all three tales, he focused only on similar-sounding folk rhymes. This method of comparing variants differed substantially from that used by Wilhelm Grimm in his notes to the same tale of "The Juniper Tree." First, he singled out a basic motif, the bones collected and buried by the little girl, and then the main theme of the tale: death and resurrection. From here he would draw upon parallel bone motifs in relation to the death and recollection theme in the Egyptian myth of "Osiris," the Norse myth of "Thor and his Goat," and a comparable scene in the English *Perceval* (on which Jacob had written a long essay).[51] In all three of these examples in the discussion, he never left out of sight the great epic themes in folktales, thus never permitting the sound to take over the sense or meaning of their epic substance. This does not mean that Wilhelm was insensitive to comparable sound patterns. While referring in his notes to Dr. Leyden's study of this folktale, for example, he compared the "Kyvitt! Kyvitt!" of "The Juniper Tree" verse to the Scottish verse "Pew, wew, pew, wew (Pipi, wiwi), my minny me slew,"[52] yet in this case, too, the selection called attention to comparable themes, not just to similar sounds. It appears, then, that the reviewer learned only a part of the Grimms' comparative method without grasping its essential epic and thematic approach.

If at times the reviewer ventured beyond the realm of the Nordic sphere into other regions of the world, he did so in an exaggerated and arbitrary manner that bordered on the ridiculous. Thus, he interpreted the occurrence of frog motifs in German and Scottish folktales to their common origin in crocodiles that might be traced to the Calmuck Tartars. Yet even more of a pseudo-scientific "Giantology" was apparent in his suggestions that Tom Thumb might trace his noble ancestry to Anglo-Saxon kings, that Tom Hickathrift was related to the hammer-throwing Thor, the Norse god of thunder, and that Jack's famous beanstalk was a descendent of Yggdrasil, the mythical Nordic World Ash. What he omitted was the needed epic and linguistic documentation based on a close comparative study of language and major themes. Such exaggerations were bound to introduce some misunderstandings regarding the Grimms' methodology of comparative folktale studies. Ironically, Cohen reaped nothing but praise for his review of the book, but the review itself contributed to some of the first myths about the Grimms regarding the nature, method, and meaning of the *Kinder- und Hausmärchen*.

[The Plea for Imagination: Taylor and Scott]

Edgar Taylor, a lawyer and former student of medieval and comparative literature, was so fascinated with the essay on the Grimms' collection in the *Quarterly Review* that he invited Francis Cohen to translate the work together with him into English. Under the title of *German Popular Stories*, the Grimms' folktales entered the English-speaking world in 1823. The volume consisted only of a selection of tales and a few additional ones from other sources, but it was well-written and achieved popular success, partially because Taylor had consciously used a simple folk style in which the purely English elements were predominant. In this effort he sacrificed some accuracy in the translation, but the work read well and helped to disseminate the German traditions in England. Taylor had also omitted the notes accompanying the German edition and rather apologetically wrote to the Grimms: "I am afraid you will still think I am sacrificing too much to the public taste, but in truth, I began the work less as antiquarian Man [than] as one who meant to amuse."[53]

Judging by the Grimms' earlier negative reaction to Arnim's proposal of adjusting the tales to children's needs, one might have expected a similar response to Taylor's translation, but the opposite was the case. As a matter of fact, Wilhelm found the translation "accurate" precisely because Taylor had remained loyal to the epic spirit and substance of the tales, which had also been his own objective throughout. In this context, it did not matter to them that he had taken a few liberties in the translation. The Grimms thanked Taylor for the copy of the work that he had sent them, congratulating him on a job well done.[54] Soon thereafter, Wilhelm began to warm up to the idea of bringing out a shorter German edition of the *Kinder- und Hausmärchen*, also without the scholarly notes. To his publisher, Reimer, he wrote in 1824:

In London a translation of the *Kindermärchen* has appeared under the title of *German Popular Stories*. . . . It has found such a popular response that already now, after only three quarters of a year has passed since its publication, they are preparing a second edition of the work. Now I, too, wish we could bring out a *small German edition* [kleine deutsche Ausgabe] which, like the English edition, would contain only a selection of stories in a *single volume.*[55]

Not only the Grimms themselves but also their friend Professor George Benecke of Göttingen commented enthusiastically about Taylor's translation in a letter addressed to Wilhelm Grimm on March 1, 1826, in which he wrote: "These tales please me even more in translation than in the German edition. They sound more childlike, more naive, and more spirited." In this connection he still complimented Wilhelm on his own folktale style by adding that the editor of the *Fairy Legends* and especially Mr. Steward might learn much from him.[56] It was implied that Taylor had come much closer to Wilhelm's folktale style than either Thomas Crofton Croker or William Grant Stewart. Such judgments on the part of both the Brothers Grimm and Benecke are important ones to observe, especially in view of our analysis of the Grimms' concept of loyalty to tradition and the nature of Wilhelm's folktale style.

Such a short edition that Wilhelm had mentioned was indeed published at Christmastime in 1825, subtitled *Kleine Ausgabe* (Small Edition), and its publishing success in Germany may well be ascribed to Taylor's inspiration. In this small volume Wilhelm not only made the tale selections for younger children but he also included seven illustrations of his brother, Ludwig Grimm, inspired by the copper engravings of George Cruikshank, that had first appeared in the English translation. Even though some of his language modifications are more evident in this edition than in the previous ones, Wilhelm did not follow Arnim's proposal of altering the tales substantially so as to please young children.[57]

Viewed from the perspective of the history of children's literature, Taylor's preface to the *German Popular Stories* represents a milestone in the direction of imaginative folk literature for children. Like Jacob and Wilhelm Grimm, he clearly perceived that children needed food for the imagination, not just lessons in manners and morals. He wrote that he had compiled this work because his young friends to whom he had told the tales had induced him to it by their "eager relish."[58] This indicates that he had actually told the stories to children before he published them in translation. Such an experience in storytelling may have helped him in developing a prose that resembled the oral style, but it must also have made him more aware of children's needs for the "old fantasy," as Jacob Grimm used to call it.

Taylor's interest in the child as a potential reading audience of folktales is particularly evident in the objections he raised against the severe restrictions that adults placed on children's reading choices at his time:

> Much might be urged against that too rigid and philosophic (we may rather say unphilosophic) exclusion of works of fancy and fiction from the libraries of children, which is advocated by some. Our imagination is surely as susceptible to improvement by exercise as our judgment or our memory; and so long as such fictions only are presented to the young mind as do not interfere with the important department of moral education, there can surely be no objection to their pleasurable employment of a faculty in which so much of our happiness in every period of life consists. [59]

His plea for imagination in children's literature sounds like an apology, and yet, against the background of didactic tales at his time, an explanation on his part was needed to overcome prevailing didactic trends. Sir Walter Scott made a similar point in a letter addressed to Taylor on January 16, 1823, which Taylor attached to a later edition of the *German Popular Stories:*

> There is also a sort of wild fairy interest in them, which makes me think them fully better adapted to awaken the imagination and soften the heart of childhood than the good-boy stories which have been in later years composed for them. In the latter case, their minds are as if they were put into the stocks, like their feet at the dancing-school, and the moral always consists in good moral conduct being crowned with temporal success. Truth is, I would not give one tear shed over Little Red Riding Hood, for all the benefit to be derived from a hundred histories of Jemmy Goodchild. . . . In a word, I think the selfish tendencies will be soon enough acquired in this arithmetical age; and that, to make a higher class of character, our wild fictions—like our own wild music—will have more effect in awakening the fancy and elevating the disposition than the cooler and more elaborate compositions of modern authors and composers. [60]

Scott claimed that contrary to what most parents believed, not only the folktales were unsuitable for children but also dozens of stories that had been especially written for them. The tales of Marie Edgeworth represented an exception to the rule, but the rest of what was called "children's literature" missed out on life and literature altogether by being too obsessed with the element of rational instruction.

Judging by the support that the *German Popular Stories* received from the Grimms themselves, their friend Benecke, and Scott, Taylor indeed deserves credit for his translation. On the other hand, he, too, contributed some myths to the Grimms' supposed intent of the work and their method of collecting the tales, which have persisted up to the present. In the first place, since he omitted the Grimms' notes, his words in the preface were taken at their face value. Potentially they might have been corrected when Margaret Hunt brought out another complete translation with the notes later in the nineteenth century,[61] but these still did not place the notes within the context of the Grimms' epic theories, and the original works were difficult to obtain. First, Taylor repeated Cohen's mistaken notion that all of the tales were of "the highest Northern antiquity," including the tale "Tom Thumb," even though he admitted that there existed variants of this tale in the Russian, Celtic, and Scandinavian folk tradition. Secondly, he introduced the mistaken notion that the Grimms' tales were based solely on the oral tradition, and thirdly, that most of them were derived from peasants: "The collection from which the following Tales are mainly taken is one of great extent, obtained for the most part by M.M. Grimm from the mouths of German peasants."[62]

Even though at the beginning of his preface Taylor acknowledged that the Grimms had "so admirably edited" the tales, his expression "by word of mouth" was the phrase that many critics after his time mistook for the Grimms' sole method of recording the tales. They simply assumed that the Grimms had committed them to print "exactly as they heard them." When twentieth-century researchers established as a fact that the Grimms had recorded the tales not only from peasants but also from townsfolk and educated persons, that they had changed the style and also individual motifs in the tales (although never the epic tale substance) from one edition to the next, and that, finally, they had also included tales from "printed sources" (folk books, chronicles, etc.), they assumed that the Grimms had not lived up to their promises. It has been particularly disconcerting to modern critics to discover that some of the Grimms' informants had been of French Huguenot descent, which seemed to contradict their claim that these were German popular stories. Yet, did the Grimms make such a claim? It was Taylor who changed the title of the *Kinder- und Hausmärchen* into *German Popular Stories*, and it was he (together with Cohen) who claimed that these stories were of purely German and Nordic descent. It remains to be examined in a later chapter to what degree both Cohen and Taylor misrepresented the Grimms' methods and intent. Although initially such misunderstandings were barely noticed, they snowballed at a later age when more distortions were added to them. In our time, they even culminated in a character assassination of the Grimms in Ellis's book *One Fairy Story Too Many, The Brothers Grimm and Their Tales.*[63]

How such myths took their course may well be observed in an 1824 review of the Grimms' *German Popular Stories* in the *Emperial Magazine.* While focusing solely on their "purely German and Nordic origin," the reviewer altogether ignored the Grimms' comparative view of international variants within the context of myth and epic. In taking over some notions of Cohen and Taylor, he further embellished these with his own fantasies. Simultaneously, he also ignored the folk tales' appeal to the childlike imagination. Instead, he merely referred to them as "quaint nursery stories" that really were not suitable for children of a younger age, as it was their main purpose to show "the antiquity of many of our nursery tales, and their evident Saxon and Germanic origin."[64] Evidently, he had mistaken a portion of Taylor's interpretation for the Grimms' own views on that subject, without consulting the original source.

Later in the century, Taylor's plea for imaginative children's stories fortunately dominated over the didactic voices raised against folktales. At least they motivated John Ruskin to call to his readers' attention that children needed folktales as they needed food for the imagination. In the best spirit of Taylor and Scott, he urged them to use folktales with children while doing away with the tiresome new tales whose sole purpose it was to teach a moral lesson. "Lost in the new tales is a simplicity of their conception of love and beauty, as they emphasize too much deliberate wisdom," he wrote. Children should not be told explicitly in stories how to choose between right or wrong but rather should be allowed the freedom of making their own judgments by following the course of the story plot. Being given such a freedom of interpretation, they would undoubtedly develop what he called a self command. "Children so trained," he explained, "have no need of moral fairy tales. The effect of the endeavor to make stories moral upon the literary merit of the work itself is as harmful as the motive of the effort is false, for every fairy tale worth recording at all is the remnant of a tradition possessing true historical value."[65]

Ruskin's words once more focused attention on the need for fairy tales without a purpose, tales that were to be enjoyed for their own imaginative contents and also for their traditional value. Yet he did not speak the last word on the subject. Didactic writers preceding him did a thorough job in spreading their gospel against "fairy tales" in general and the Grimms' collection in particular. Their arguments against the reading of folktales may be worth a closer examination, especially in view of the question of how and to what extent they resemble or differ from those that, for one reason or another, are still voiced in the twentieth century.

[The Irish Connection]

The Grimms' relationship with Thomas Crofton Croker is of significance for our understanding of the *Kinder- und Hausmärchen* for several reasons. One of these relates to the influence of this work on fieldwork collections as well as comparative folktale studies in

Ireland. Another reason is that it reveals the Grimms' attitude toward the concept of loyalty to tradition, perhaps even more clearly than do Wilhelm's various prefaces to the work. In itself, the story of mutual respect and translations attests to the Grimms' persistent efforts toward a better understanding of folk cultures other than their own.

In 1815 Jacob and Wilhelm Grimm received a gift from a friend who had just purchased it during a trip to London: a newly published work by an anonymous author, entitled *Fairy Legends and Traditions of the South of Ireland*. As the Grimms recognized his style from an earlier publication, *Researches of the South of Ireland*, they assumed that the author was Thomas Crofton Croker of Cork, Ireland. An inquiry placed with the London publisher of the work soon proved that they were correct. In less than a year the Grimms translated the work and published it under the title of *Irische Elfenmärchen* (*Irish Fairy Tales*), to which Wilhelm added a sixty-two page essay "Über die Elfen" ("About the Fairies"). What caught their interest in this work was Croker's claim that he had loyally collected these tales from the mouths of the Irish peasants, hoping to capture the flavor of the Irish language, customs, folk beliefs, and ways of thinking. [66]

As a boy, Thomas Crofton Croker had read the Grimms' *Kinder- und Hausmärchen*, and the idea of fieldwork research so much inspired him that at the age of fourteen he set out with an older friend to wander for two years across Southern Ireland, collecting and recording the tales of the common folk. To these tales he later added tales from Scotland and Wales, as well as from England.

An accident happened shortly before the manuscript went to the printer, which had some serious implications: Croker lost the manuscript. After an unsuccessful search, he tried to reconstruct the tales, turning in this process to the help of some of his friends who had formerly supplied him with tales for the work. Croker then published the work anonymously, hoping in this way to acknowledge the help of others. Unfortunately, one of his friends later took advantage of this humble gesture by claiming the copyright of these stories and discrediting their authenticity.

The Grimms' translation of the work revealed their deep respect for folktales and legends of Ireland and promoted a broader interest in Celtic tradition. The long comparative essay that Wilhelm attached to the translation, titled "Über die Elfen," was the first of its kind by attempting a systematic comparison of fairy lore and folk beliefs in Ireland, Scotland, England, and Wales. Wilhelm's system of numbering the titles and subtitles of his essay gives the appearance of an encyclopedic essay, which in fact it is, judging by its objective to classify the fairy lore of the British Isles. Such a format lent an air of scientific objectivity to the essay, setting the stage for numerous other comparative works of fairy lore later in the century and in our time, such as Katherine Briggs's *Dictionary of the Fairies*. Wilhelm drew upon examples and comparisons contained in Croker's *Fairy Legends*, but he broadened the scope of comparison by relating examples from Danish, Swedish, Norwegian, Icelandic, German, and Serbian folklore.

Far from being dry and schematic, however, the essay remained lively and poetic throughout. Characteristic of Wilhelm's style is his fine perception of the old *Naturpoesie*, enhanced by the descriptive quality of the text. The poetic tone of his narrative reminds one of his famous introductions to the *Kinder- und Hausmärchen*.

> The Elves, which in their true share are but a few inches high, have an airy, almost transparent body so delicate in their form, that a dew drop, when they dance on it, trembles indeed but never breaks. Both sexes are of extraordinary beauty and mortal beings cannot be compared with them. They do not live alone or in pairs but always in large societies. They are invisible to us, particularly in the day-time . . .[67]

As it was his main objective to describe and analyze yet not to embellish and entertain his audience, his style had little to do with fantasy writing, even though its tone and use of imagery contributed substantially to the poetic nature of its subject.

Systematic and modern in his approach was that he analyzed the topic first of all from a typological perspective, considering separately the fairies, the cluricauns, the banshee, the phooka, along with dwarfs, mermaids, brownies, witches, and other creatures. Within each category he proceeded like an anthropologist, giving close attention to their respective habitat, dress, food, age, social life, magic powers, and interactions with humans. Thus, he informed the reader about the various group gatherings of the elves, for example, their fondness of secrecy, dancing, singing, playing ball—and occasionally, of throwing small pebbles at humans. He explained their light side in terms of their helpfulness, kindness, and cooperation and their dark and evil side in terms of their mean tricks, obnoxious behavior, and vengeful actions.

While trying to maintain a clear distinction among various fairy creatures along national and cultural lines, Wilhelm also pointed out cross-cultural correspondences and striking similarities. Further, he would draw upon comparisons with fairy superstitions reflected in folk songs, ballads, legends, epic literature, customs, laws, and folk beliefs in such countries as Denmark, Norway, Sweden, Germany, Iceland, France, and Serbia. Among these, he gave special attention to stories about elves and dwarfs from the *Elder Edda* and the *Younger Edda*, discussing in conclusion how even the well-meaning "light elves" of Norse mythology over time had assumed darker and meaner features because of the impact of Christianity. Like Jacob in the *Deutsche Mythologie*, Wilhelm blamed it largely on missionaries and priests that the folk belief in fairy lore around the world was gradually vanishing.

In an attempt to destroy "evil pagan superstitions," they had blackened the pagan folk beliefs in the minds of the people while absorbing others into church customs and rituals. Over the centuries, angels had assumed some features of the fairies. This could be observed in designs of the eighth century, which still showed them as men in long white robes, whereas paintings of the twelfth century already depicted them like fairies: as women or fragile young children with long, flowing hair.[68]

When, in 1826, the Grimms sent to Croker a copy of the newly published translation, titled *Irische Elfenmärchen*, he was delighted about it and even more so about Wilhelm's essay. In the preface to the second edition of *Fairy Legends* (1828), he wrote that normally an author had little reason to plume himself if his work appeared in French or German, as the exchange of ideas among European nations had become a common thing. This case was different, he said, as the work had been translated by no lesser persons than the eminent Brothers Grimm, whose friendship and valuable correspondence it had also procured him. He called their translation "faithful and spirited," announcing that they had prefixed to it a most learned and valuable introduction respecting fairy superstition in general. With pride he quoted Wilhelm Grimm: "Whoever has a relish for innocent and simple poetry will feel attracted by these tales. They possess a peculiar flavour, which is not without its charm."[69] They came from a country, wrote Wilhelm, with whom Germany had only had few relations, and those few had not even been pleasant ones, but whose people could trace back their history to ancient roots and still spoke their own language. Perhaps more so than elsewhere, the language of the Irish folktales and legends bore traces of this ancient past, and so did Irish folk beliefs and superstitions.

Croker dedicated the second edition of *Fairy Legends* to Wilhelm Grimm with the words: "To Dr. Wilhelm Grimm, Secretary of the Prince's Library, Member of the Royal Scientific Society of Göttingen etc., etc., etc., At Cassel in Hesse." The greatest compliment that Croker paid Wilhelm was that, in his turn, he had translated his essay "About the Fairies" from German into English, attaching it to the same edition as an introduction. He stated that he had given this essay without note or comment of his own, because he perfectly agreed with him in every point regarding a scientific analysis of fairy lore.

Croker commented favorably about Wilhelm's scientific method of supplying comparative notes to the tales. He fully appreciated what he called "a clear and firm view of the subject" rather than "a poetic amplification." It might be argued that Croker's own style in the *The Fairy Legends* did reflect some "poetic amplification,"[70] yet his comments show that he was quite conscious of the dangers of taking too many liberties in rendering folktales by turning them into fantasies.

At first, Croker reaped due applause for his contributions to Irish folktales, also in England and Scotland. *Frazer's Magazine* introduced him as "The King of All Fairies," who had appointed himself "the historiographer to King Oberon and all his Cluricauns." In an illustration it introduced the "Fairy King," mentioning that this famous author, who was only the size of a leprechaun, standing only four and a half feet high, had won many national and international honors.[71] An article in the *Quarterly Review* of 1825 praised Croker for having captured in his tales "the very smoke flavor of the turf in simple pleasant huts."[72] The German translation of his work still further enhanced his fame. It was through this translation that Sir Walter Scott first became acquainted with the book in Abbotsford. Like Thomas Moore and Henry Crabbe, Scott had admired Croker's earlier publications, among them his collection of early Irish folk poetry, the "keens" of Ireland (traditional funeral songs), as well as his *Researches of the South of Ireland*, which included travel descriptions along with legends and local superstitions. Being especially impressed with the *Fairy Legends*, he wrote to him in a letter: "You are our—I speak of the Celtic Nation—great authority now on Fairy Superstitions and have made Fairy Land your Kingdom. . . . I have been reading the German translation of your tales," he added as an explanation, "and the Grimms' very elaborate introduction."[73]

Scott sensed in many Irish fairy tales some tales of his own country. Both hinted at the Gaelic-Celtic connection in folklore, which he had long pursued in language and history. "The extreme similarities of your fictions to ours is striking," he wrote to Croker. "The Cluricaune (which is the admirable subject for a pantomime) is not known here. The beautiful superstition of the Banshee seems in a great measure peculiar to Ireland, . . . but I think I could match all of your other tales with something similar."[74] He related to him a number of additional tales of the Highlanders that, in his view, resembled those of the Irish.

Croker's reputation began to suffer severely after Thomas Keightley published in 1828 a comparative folklore study, titled *Fairy Mythology*, in which he confessed that he and his friends had merely played a joke on him by telling him their own fantasies instead of geniune Irish folktales. Gleefully, he pointed to "The Soul Cages," a tale which he claimed as his invention, even though he admitted that two persons whom he met occasionally were, for unknown reasons, quite familiar with the story. Taking advantage of the first anonymous edition of Croker's *Fairy Legends*, Keightley then replenished those tales that he claimed to have contributed to the work, without giving credit to Croker for having first recorded them prior to losing the manuscript. Without betraying that his "assistance" to the work had in reality consisted only of reconstructing four tales, he vainly claimed to have supplied him with "the bulk" of them.[75]

It is unlikely that Croker would have printed "The Soul Cages" if he had not heard and recorded it himself previously. The fact that Keightley reprinted the tale himself in his *Fairy Mythology* further attests to the fact that he considered it a genuine folktale after all. That his academic honesty left something to be desired is also evident in that he failed to acknowledge in his work Wilhelm Grimm's essay "About the Fairies," whose method he adopted throughout in his comparative study of fairy lore. He did mention the Brothers Grimm in his notes, but only in very general terms and without reference to this essay.

In the second edition of *Fairy Legends* Croker did take a stand on Keightley's accusation, affirming the loyalty of his approach to the folk tradition: "Deeply as I lament that such delusions should exist," he wrote, "these facts will sufficiently prove that I have not (as has been insinuated) conjured up forgotten tales, or attempted to perpetuate the creed which has disappeared."[76]

The Grimms were convinced that Croker had generally caught the tone of the genuine Celtic fairy tales and, more significantly, that his tales did justice to the Irish oral tradition. Wilhelm Grimm warmly reviewed the work in *Göttingische Gelehrte Anzeigen* in 1826, in which he especially praised the choice of language in which Croker had rendered the tales.

> The anonymous author has captured the traditions of the place with an obvious loyalty, and he has spent an unusual care in rendering them. . . . The Irishmen themselves will have a special pleasure in recognizing in these tales scenes reflecting their own character, proverbial expressions, native jokes and analogues, and untranslateable idioms; but foreigners, too, have a feeling for these things and value them.[77]

Wilhelm considered Croker's tales loyal to the "spirit of tradition." These words are of significance in relation to his own proclamation of loyalty in the 1812 preface to the *Kinder- und Hausmärchen*, as he in neither case said anything about a requirement regarding a "word-by-word" accuracy. Instead, he commented favorably on Croker's skillful use of proverbs, "and other little things of this kind that add a lively touch to his presentation—all of which cannot be learned through books."[78] In the rhythm of proverbial speech patterns, he felt the very breath of the folk tradition or, as he put it, "the very smoke flavor of the turf in simple peasant huts." He liked Croker's use of the natural colloquial style. He fully realized that Croker had "translated" these tales from the original Gaelic, just as he and Jacob had translated many of the contributions to the *Kinder- und Hausmärchen* from various German dialects. Jacob was more exacting in his critique of the *Fairy Legends*, as far as the concept of loyalty to tradition was concerned. He had the advantage over Wilhelm of knowing Gaelic as well as English and thus used the judgment of a linguist in criticizing some of the liberties Croker had taken in rendering the tales:

> The content of this collection is genuine, and in a skillful way the tales are interwoven with strange, daring, but lively turns of speech, with images and proverbs of the common folk, all of

which contribute to its realism. It is regrettable, however, that the narrative leans a little to the taste of the time, still more so than one might wish for, especially when he makes use of irony. This easily creates the impression that the fairy tale elements are only the products of an excited imagination — an impression that is detrimental to the deeper significance of the work.[79]

Overall, however, Jacob's evaluation of *The Fairy Legends* was positive, for otherwise he would not have cooperated with Wilhelm in translating the work into German. Given his knowledge of Celtic and Gaelic folklore and his acquaintance with the Gaelic language, it is not likely that he would have become the victim of another *Ossian* delusion. In his *Deutsche Mythologie*, in which he used a similar comparative method that Wilhelm had introduced in his essay "About the Fairies," he made substantial use of Croker's work, also in connection with comparisons based on a linguistic analysis. It must be noted, however, that Jacob, too, failed to give credit to Wilhelm for his pioneer work in comparative fairy-lore studies, although he recognized the contributions of Croker and Keightley in corresponding footnotes. In his chapter "Wights and Elves," he stated:

> Celtic tradition, which runs particularly rich on this subject, I draw from the following works: *Fairy Legends and Traditions of the South of Ireland*, by Crofton Croker, Lond. 1825; 2nd ed., parts 1,2,2, Lond. 1828. The *Fairy Mythology*, by Th. Keightley, vols. 1,2, Lond. 1828.[80]

Jacob did not mention the controversy, yet his critical comments on Croker's style betray that Keightley's derogatory comments had not escaped him. This is further evident from the fact that neither he nor Keightley included in their translated work *Über die Elfen* the most controversial story, "The Soul Cages," thus giving Keightley the benefit of the doubt.

A British reviewer caught up with the controversy and spared no words to express his contempt for Keightley. Praising Croker's efforts in capturing the genuine flavor of the Irish folktale, he wrote: "It's like the peat taste of whiskey which touches the Irish origin of liquor, and it is liked and appreciated for its peculiar flavor." Yet, chiding Keightley, he added "And since he has had so much intercourse with the 'good people,' we would have him consider how severely they punish those witless mortals who approach them with presumption and selfishness. Even the legend of the peasant has its moral."[81]

It is possible that the high esteem that especially Wilhelm Grimm and Sir Walter Scott had for Croker did influence the reviewer's opinion at that time, yet also Croker's other folkloristic and historical contributions attest to his loyalty to the spirit of tradition. The poet Harry Crabbe praised him highly for rendering "the sense of the original keens" with great skill and loyalty. Croker's biographical work on Joseph Holt, General of the Irish Rebels, also received high praise regarding its respect for historical details. There is no question that Croker added his own flavor to the tales, but he did not embellish the tales as some of the fairy-tale writers of the *Cabinet des fées* had done before him.

The Grimms' tolerance of the occasional intrusion of Croker's personal style illustrates well that they were not dogmatic about the concept of loyalty, as long as it reflected the spirit of the native folk tradition. Overall, they ranked his loyalty to the folk tradition much higher than that of Musäus, Albert Ludwig Grimm, and other German folktale collectors at the time.

Additional unpublished translations of nine Irish fairy legends by Wilhelm Grimm were discovered among the Grimms' manuscripts in the Hessian State Archives of Marburg in 1985 that attest to Wilhelm's fondness for the Irish folk tradition. With support from the European Folktale Society (Europäische Märchengesellschaft), Werner Moritz and Charlotte Oberfeld edited and published these under the title of *Irische Land- und Seenmärchen* (*Irish Folktales of Land and Sea*) in 1986, giving reference to Thomas Crofton Croker as the original collector of the tales and Wilhelm Grimm as the translator.[82] This work provides new testimony to Wilhelm's sustained interest in Irish folklore within the context of international folktale collections.

NOTES

1. Heinz Rölleke, *Die Märchen der Brüder Grimm*. Series: *Artemis Einführungen*, vol. 18 (Munich: Artemis Verlag, 1985), pp. 70–85. See also T. F. Crane, "The External History of the Kinder- und Hausmärchen of the Brothers Grimm," *Modern Philology* 14, 10, 1917, pp. 577–611. Rölleke substantially revised the critical perception of the role of the Grimms' informants while also calling attention to the need for investigating the folktales from a comparative rather than a strictly national perspective.

2. Herder established his name as a humanist not only through his writings on the philosophy of the history of mankind and his international folk song collection *Stimme der Völker in Liedern: Volkslieder* (1778–79) but also by his essays on Homer, Ossian, and Shakespeare. He defined his concept of *Naturpoesie* in his essay "Auszug aus einem Briefwechsel über Ossian und die Lieder alter Völker" ("Excerpt from a Correspondence about Ossian and Songs of the Old Nations"). Herder's approach to *Naturpoesie* differed from that of the Brothers Grimm not only because he included in the poetry of "poetic geniuses" but also in that he used such poetry as an inspiration to write his own "folk ballads." Johann Gottfried Herder, *Sämmtliche Werke 5* (Berlin: Weidmannsche Verlagsbuchhandlung, 1894), Bernard Suphan, ed.

3. "The State of German Literature," *Edinburgh Review* 24 (June–Oct., 1927), p. 304.

4. Sir Walter Scott, *Minstrelsy of the Scottish Border Countries: Consisting of Historical and Romantic Ballads Collected in the Southern Countries of Scotland* (Edinburgh: Ballantyne, 1802–03). See Preface of the 1830 edition.

5. Hans Kohn, *Prelude to Nation-States: The French-German Experience, 1781–1815* (Princeton, N.J.: Princeton University Press, 1964), p. 127.

6. Richard Benz, *Die deutsche Romantik: Geschichte einer geistlichen Bewegung* (Stuttgart: Klett, 1956), pp. 239–45. Also H. G. Schenk, *The Mind of the European Romantics: An Essay on Cultural History* (London: Constable, 1966), with a preface by Isaiah Berlin. See in particular Chapter 5, "Forebodings and Nostalgia for the Past," pp. 32–46.

7. Jacob Grimm, "*Alte und neue Sagen und Wahrsagungen,*" in *Zeitung für Einsiedler (Trosteinsamkeit)*, 1804, cited by Kohn, p. 178.

8. Joseph Görres, *Die teutschen Volksbücher* (Heidelberg: Mohr und Zimmer, 1807). Goethe, too, had concerned himself with the *Volksbücher*. Next to the tale of Melusine (which he reworked into a *Kunstmärchen*), he used the folk book story of Dr. Johannes Faustus as a model for his *Urfaust* und *Faust*. The Brothers Grimm recognized certain "stock characters" of folktales in the folk book characters of the Schildbürger and others, which convinced them of the close connection between these words and German folktales.

9. Wilhelm Grimm, *Altdänische Heldenlieder, Balladen und Märchen* (Heidelberg: Mohr und Zimmer, 1811). See also Maria Greverius, "*Wege zu Wilhelm Grimm's 'Altdänischen Heldenliedern,'* " in *Brüder Grimm Gedenken 1*, Ludwig Denecke, ed. (Marburg: Elvert Verlag, 1963), pp. 469–88. Unlike Herder and Scott, Wilhelm Grimm did not compose his own "folk ballads."

10. Jacob and Wilhelm Grimm, *Kinder- und Hausmärchen* (Berlin: Reimer, 1812).

11. Ibid., Introduction, p. iv.

12. Marianne Thalmann, *The Romantic Fairy Tale: Seeds of Surrealism* (Ann Arbor: University of Michigan Press, 1970), pp. 4–24. Thalmann predominantly discusses the *Kunstmärchen*. For a thorough discussion of the *Volksmärchen* see Stith Thompson, *The Folktale* (Bloomington: Indiana University Press, 1963); Max Lüthi, *Once Upon a Time: On the Nature of Fairy Tales* (Bloomington: Indiana University Press, 1970); and Max Lüthi, *Volksmärchen und Volkssage: Zwei Grundformen erzählender Dichtung* (Bern: Franke Verlag, 1961).

13. At first, the major motivation for a correspondence between Jacob Grimm and Sir Walter Scott was an exchange of medieval manuscripts on which both of them had been working independently, yet Jacob also expressed his hope that he would motivate Scott to aid him in an international folktale collection project. Walter Schoof and Jörn Göres, eds., *Unbekannte Briefe der Brüder Grimm. Unter Ausnutzung des Grimmschen Nachlasses* (Bonn: Althenäum, 1960). Of particular relevance is Jacob Grimm's letter to Sir Walter Scott on June 9, 1814.

14. Joseph Prestel, *Handbuch zur Jugendliteratur. Geschichte der deutschen Jugendschriften* (Freiburg, Brsg.: Herder Verlag, 1933). Consult the chapter on folk literature for youth.

15. H. J. G. Grierson, David Cook and W. M. Parker, eds., *The Letters of Sir Walter Scott 1811–1814* vol. 3 (London: Constable & Company, 1933) (Centenary edition), pp. 285–89.

16. Ibid.

17. Joseph Lefftz, ed., *Märchen der Brüder Grimm: Urfassung im der Original-handschrift der Abtei Oelenberg im Elsass*. Series: *Wissenschaftliche Reihe der Lothring. Wissenschaftl. Gesellschaft*. Series C, vol. 1 (Straßbourg: Wissenschaftliche Gesellschaft zu Straßburg, 1927). Already in 1924 Franz Schulz published the manuscript of the tales with the Bibliophile-Society in Frankfurt am Main. See Friedrich Panzer, ed., *Die Kinder- und Hausmärchen der Brüder Grimm. Vollständige Ausgabe in der Urfassung* (Wiesbaden: Emil Vollmer Verlag, n.d., about 1955), p. 42n. The rediscovered manuscript is usually referred to as the *Oelenberg-Handschrift*. See also Hermann Gerstner, *Die Brüder Grimm: Biographie mit 48 Bildern* (Gerabonn: Hohenloher Verlag, 1971), pp. 85–98; and Gabriele Seitz,

Die Brüder Grimm: Leben, Werk, Zeit (Munich: Winkler Verlag, 1984), pp. 90–122.

18. Gerstner, p. 108.

19. Prestel, p. 258.

20. Johann Gustav Büsching, ed., *Volks-Sagen, Märchen und Legenden* (Leipzig: Carl Heinrich Reclam, 1812).

21. Wilhelm Grimm, *Kinder- und Hausmärchen* (Berlin: Reimer, 1812), Introduction.

22. Albert Ludwig Grimm, *Kindermärchen* (Heidelberg: Mohr and Zimmer, 1809) and Peter Leberecht (Ludwig Tieck's pseudonym), *Ritter Blaubart: Ein Ammenmärchen (in vier Akten)* (Leipzig: Karl August Nicolai, 1797). See also Ludwick Tieck, *Werke* 4 vols., Marianne Thalmann, ed. (Munich: Winkler Verlag, 1964).

23. Jacob Grimm, *Circular wegen Aufsammlung der Volkspoesie*, Ludwig Denecke, ed., with an introduction by Kurt Ranke (Kassel: Bärenreiter Verlag, 1965). Jacob actually did send out this questionnaire of 360 copies. See Chapter 7.

24. Jacob and Wilhelm Grimm, *Kinder- und Hausmärchen*, 2d ed., Vol. 3 (Berlin: Reimer, 1822). Vol. 1 contained Wilhelm's essay about the nature of folktales.

25. *Kinder- und Hausmärchen*, 7th ed., 3 vols. (Göttingen: Diederichs, 1856/57). Like the third, fourth, fifth, and sixth editions, this work was subtitled *Grosse Ausgabe* (Large Edition). Grimms' notes to the folktales were published separately in its first volume of 1856, and the two expanded folktale volumes followed in 1857. The seventh edition has become popularly known as the *Grosse Ausgabe*, even though its two folktale volumes alone had less pages than the sixth edition.

26. Johannes Bolte and Georg Polivka, *Anmerkungen zu den Kinder- und Hausmärchen der Brüder Grimm* (Leipzig: Diederich'sche Verlagsbuchhandlung 1913–1918). Vol. 5 contains an analysis of the Grimms' international influences on folktale collections around the world.

27. *Kinder- und Hausmärchen* 6th ed. (Göttingen: Verlag der Dieterich'schen Buchhandlung, 1850), Introduction, pp. i–lxxvi.

28. Gerstner, pp. 168–85. In his autobiography Andersen himself comments on this meeting with Jacob Grimm in Berlin and Copenhagen. See Hans Christian Andersen. *Das Märchen meines Lebens: Briefe und Tagebücher*, trans. from the Danish with an afterword by Erling Nielsen (Munich: Winkler Verlag, 1967), pp. 349–53.

29. See also Christa Kamenetsky, "The Irish Fairy Legends and the Brothers Grimm," *Proceedings of the Ninth Annual Children's Literature Association in Gainesville, Florida, 1981* (Ann Arbor, Mi.: Malloy Lith. and the Children's Literature Association, 1983), pp. 77–87.

30. *Irische Elfenmärchen*, trans. Wilhelm and Jacob Grimm (Leipzig: Friedrich Fleischer, 1826). Walzel, pp. 3–73.

31. Christa Kamenetsky, "Herder und der Mythos des Nordens," *Revue de littérature comparée* 47, 1 (Jan.–Mar. 1973), pp. 23–41.

32. Jacob Grimm, "Vorwort" (Introduction) in *Russische Volksmärchen in den Urschriften gesammelt und ins Deutsche übersetzt,* trans. and ed. Anton Dietrich (Jena: Diederichs, 1931).

33. Jacob Grimm, ibid.

34. Ibid.

35. Walter Schoof, *Die Entstehungsgeschichte der Kinder- und Hausmärchen* (Hamburg: Hauswedell, 1959), pp. 10–15.

36. Prestel, p. 235.

37. Bolte and Polivka, Vol. 5, pp. 533–49.

38. Panzer, Introduction, p. 37. See also Ulrike Bastian, *Die Kinder- und Hausmärchen der Brüder Grimm in der literaturpädagogischen Diskussion des 19. und 20. Jahrhunderts* (Frankfurt am Main: M. Haag und Herchen, 1986).

39. Reinhold, Steig, *Achim von Arnim und Jacob und Wilhelm Grimm* (Stuttgart: Cotta Verlag), p. 269.

40. *Kinder- und Hausmärchen*, 2d ed. (Berlin: Reimer, 1819). Introduction.

41. John Locke, "Dialogues Concerning Education" (London, 1745) in John Locke, *The Educational Writing of John Locke*, James L. Axtell, ed. (Cambridge: Harvard University Press, 1970), pp. 270–74. See also Samuel F. Pickering, Jr., *John Locke and Children's Books in Eighteenth Century England* (Knoxville: University of Tennessee Press, 1981). Also Bettina Hürlimann, *Three Centuries of Children's Books in Europe* (Cleveland: World Publishing Company, 1968), Chapters 3 and 4.

42. Jean Jacques Rousseau, *Emile*, trans. B. Foxley (London: J. M. Dent & Sons, 1911). For Rousseau's influence on the history of children's literature, consult John Rowe Townsend, *Written for Children: An Outline of English Language Children's Literature*, 2d ed. (Boston: The Horn Book and Lippincott Company, 1975), Part 3.

43. *Kinder- und Hausmärchen*, 2d ed. (1819), Introduction.

44. "Fairy Tales of the Lilliputian Cabinet, Containing Twenty-Five Choice Pieces of Fancy and Fiction, collected by Benjamin Tabart" *Quarterly Review* 21 (1819), pp. 91–114. The review was anonymous, but Taylor made reference to Mr. Francis Cohen as its author, who was also the (unnamed) co-translator of the *German Popular Tales* in 1823. See also Ruth Michaelis Jena and Ludwig Denecke, "Edgar and John Edward Taylor, die ersten englischen Übersetzer der Kinder- und Hausmärchen" in *Brüder Grimm Gedenken*, vol. 2, pp. 190–95.

45. Ibid. The reviewer took this quote out of context from Wilhelm Grimm's folktale analysis of the 1819 edition of the *Kinder- und Hausmärchen* (see introduction). Both Brothers Grimm followed the Indo-Germanic myth theory of Rask, but simultaneously they also made room for other theories. A subsequent review article on the *Kinder- und Hausmärchen* in the *Emperial Magazine* 5 (1824) followed the simplistic interpretation of the Grimms' ideas in the *Quarterly Review*, without reexamining the Grimms' own views on the subject on the basis of original research.

46. *Quarterly Review.*

47. Ibid.

48. Ibid.

49. Ibid.

50. Compare Wilhelm's notes on "The Juniper Tree" in *Kinder- und Hausmärchen*, 2d ed., Vol. 2.

51. Ibid.

52. Ibid.

53. Otto Hartwig, "Zur ersten englischen Übersetzung der Kinder- und Hausmärchen der Brüder Grimm," *Zentralblatt für Bibliothekswesen* (Jan.–Fb. 1898), pp. 6–7.

54. Ibid.

55. Wilhelm Grimm's letter to Georg Reimer, dated August 16, 1823. Hans Gürtler and Albert Leitzmann, eds. *Briefe der Brüder Grimm* (Jena: Verlag der Fromannschen Buchhandlung, 1823), p. 127.

56. Wilhelm Grimm's letter to Professor Georg Benecke, dated March 1, 1826. Hartwig, pp. 20–28. Wilhelm's references to William Grant Stewart show his familiarity with Stewart's work *The Popular Superstitions and Festive Amusements of the Highlanders of Scotland* (Edinburgh, 1823) that discussed the powers and traits of fairies, ghosts, witches, and brownies. See also Richard Dorson. *The British Folklorists: A History* (Chicago: University of Chicago Press, 1968), pp. 156–57. It is possible that Stewart's work in some ways inspired Wilhelm to compose his comparative essay "About the Fairies" that he attached to the German translation of Croker's work. In turn, Wilhelm's almost anthropological survey of leprechauns

and related fairy spirits may have inspired Katherine Briggs and other folklorists in this century to compile dictionaries of the fairies.

57. *Kinder- und Hausmärchen. Kleine Ausgabe* (Berlin: Reimer, 1825). This short edition was the most popular one with children and exceeded all other editions in terms of sales. Still in his introduction to the 1850 edition of the *Kinder- und Hausmärchen* Wilhelm commented favorably about the illustrations by George Cruikshank, as well as those of Richard Doyle and Otto Specter in later English editions of the work (1846 and 1847), mentioning that Specter's illustrations were attached to individual tales published separately in London.

58. Edgar Taylor, "Introduction" in *German Popular Stories*, trans. Edgar Taylor (London: Murray, 1823).

59. John Ruskin, "Preface," in *Grimm's Household Tales* 3d ed., Margaret Hunt, trans. and ed. (London: George Bell & Sons, 1910).

60. Letter of Sir Walter Scott to John Taylor, Abbotsford, January 16, 1823. Taylor attached this letter to *German Popular Tales* 2d ed., 1826.

61. Ruskin.

62. Taylor, "Introduction."

63. John M. Ellis, *One Fairy Story Too Many. The Brothers Grimm and Their Tales* (Chicago: University of Chicago Press, 1983). The author of this work prematurely draws his conclusions without having investigated Grimms' own notes on the subject (for example, Vol. 3 of the 1819 edition or the Grimms' volume of notes published in 1856) and without comprehending Grimms' concept of "loyalty" to tradition within the context of their research on epic literature. He uncritically disseminates some misinformation initiated by Taylor and other early critics regarding the supposed "purely Nordic," "purely German" peasant origin of the Grimms' folktales. He is also mistaken in his notion that Jacob Grimm's *Circular-Brief*, the first European folk questionnaire, supposedly remained only a plan that was never carried out (see note 23).

64. "Popular Tales and Romances of Northern Nations" *Emperial Magazine* VI (1824): 192–96.

65. Ruskin.

(London: Murray, 1925). Croker first published this work anonymously. See also Wilhelm Grimm, "Über die Elfen" ("About the Fairies") in *Irische Elfenmärchen*. This more than sixty-page essay that already contained the comparative framework of Jacob Grimm's *Deutsche Mythologie*. For a related analysis see Kamenetsky, "The Irish Fairy Legends and the Brothers Grimm."

67. Thomas Crofton Croker, "Preface," *Fairy Legends*, 2d ed. (London: Murray, 1828).

68. Wilhelm Grimm, "About the Fairies," Ibid. Wilhelm commented in general terms about the *Edda* as a vital source of Norse mythology, meaning the *Elder Edda* (about 800 A.D.) as well as the *Younger Edda* or *Snorri Edda* (about 1250 A.D.).

69. Croker, "Preface," *Fairy Legends*, 2d ed.

70. Ibid.

71. Thomas Wright, "The National Fairy Mythology of England," *Frazer's Magazine* (July 1834), pp. 51–67.

72. "Fairy Legends and Traditions of the South of Ireland" (review) *Quarterly Review* (June/Oct. 1825), pp. 197–210.

73. "Sir Walter Scott and Mr. Crofton Croker," *Gentlemen's Magazine* (October 1854), pp. 453–56.

74. Ibid.

75. See John Hennig, "The Brothers Grimm and T. C. Croker" *Modern Language Review* 41 (1946), pp. 44–54.

76. Croker, "Introduction," *Fairy Legends*, 2d ed.

77. Wilhelm Grimm (untitled review of *Fairy Legends of the South of Ireland*) *Göttingische Gelehrte Anzeigen* (Ja. 12, 1826), in *Kleinere Schriften von Wilhelm Grimm* vol. 2 (Berlin: Dümmler, 1881).

78. Hennig, pp. 52–53.

79. Bolte and Polivka, vol. 1, pp. 551–52.

80. Jacob Grimm, *Teutonic Mythology* vol. 1 (New York: Dover, 1975).

81. Wright, p. 51.

82. *Irische Land- und Seenmärchen*, collected by Thomas Crofton Croker, trans. Wilhelm Grimm, eds. Werner Moritz and Charlotte Oberfeld, in cooperation with Siegfried Heyer (Marburg: N. G. Elwert Verlag, 1986).

9. DIDACTIC APPROACHES TO FOLKTALES AND FAIRY TALES

[Philosophical Objections to Fairy Tales]

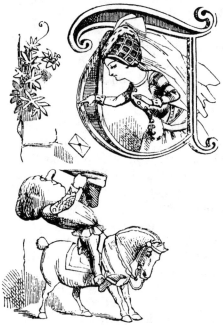

HROUGHOUT HISTORY DI-dactic views of children's books have been voiced from different quarters. Within the context of their own ideas or prevailing patterns of thought, some philosophers, educators, religious groups, social reformers, and authors of children's books have at various times raised their objections to folktales, be it in the name of reason, religion, secular morality, or social norms. Attitudes have ranged from the extreme position of banning folktales, entertaining fiction, and fantasy for children to a seemingly more moderate position of selecting and revising folktales, so as to adjust them to specific goals, such as the promotion of certain moral values, patriotism, or a political ideology. In the latter case, they sometimes ignored or remolded folktales for their own purposes.

On the surface, it may appear that a selective approach to folktales would be preferable as it keeps folktales on children's bookshelves and inside the schoolrooms, which seems to imply tolerance toward the folk tradition. Such an impression, however, is misleading for two reasons. First, a selective approach usually involved a careful screening process in the course of which many folktales were discarded merely because they did not fit a certain goal or purpose. Secondly, the initial censorship process was usually followed by an editing job, in the course of which folktales were retailored to specific needs. In some cases, such a rewriting of folktales resembled propaganda rather than folklore or children's literature. Whenever some interest groups used folktales mainly as a means of instruction, however noble their didactic intentions may have been, they ran the danger of distorting the original folk tradition. Rewriting folktales "with a purpose" has led to various abuses of folk literature, including moral preaching, abstinence campaigns, and political propaganda.

With the elevation of reason during the seventeenth and eighteenth centuries, some philosophies emerged that systematically opposed the pursuit of folktales in the name of educational objectives. In Germany, Immanuel Kant rejected works of fiction and folklore for young people, believing that they obstructed their comprehension of truth and reality, as well as their development of logic and reason. He may have inherited some of his distrust of folktales from Plato, who already in the Golden Age of Greece had warned against the corruptive influence of drama and fiction.[1]

During the late seventeenth century, John Locke raised strong objections to the use of folktales with children. In *Some Thoughts Concerning Education* (1693) he introduced the idea of combining instruction with amusement, suggesting that young children be given pleasant books to read that would be suited to their reading capacity.[2] By pleasant, however, he did not mean folktales but rather illustrated books that were specifically written for children to capture their attention for the purpose of instruction. While these books emphasized motivational aspects, such as illustrations, toys, and even games for children, their primary purpose was to teach useful and practical lessons. Locke specifically warned parents and educators not to tell children tales about sprites and goblins, as these would only fill their heads with "useless trumpery." Even though he abstained from the old-fashioned method of preaching by example, he still believed that reading was meant to lay the foundations of morality. He thought that folktales were ill suited to give desirable examples and that by dwelling on vice and folly they would only confuse the minds of children. To young people he recommended instead the fables of Aesop, with their clear-cut moralities, the animal epic *Reynard the Fox*, and Bishop Comenius' *Orbis Sensualium Pictus* (*The World in Pictures*), but not much beyond those texts and some innovative school books.[3]

Another philosopher who laid the foundations of the rational moralists in England was Jean Jacques Rousseau. His works were of special importance to the English "Rousseauists," as they provided new concepts of nature and experience that influenced the conception of childhood. In 1762 Rousseau published a book under the title of *Emile*.[4] Even though it concerned a young boy named Emile and his tutor, it was not a boy's book at all, in the modern sense of the word, but rather a long treatise on child-rearing and education.[5] Rousseau believed, as had Locke, that children should be raised in the fresh outdoors and with a certain amount of freedom. He emphasized the development of their natural instincts, which, in his view, had nothing to do with savage instincts. In fact, he denounced the term "savage" itself, considering both the child and the primitive man as human beings that were blessed by the spirit of simplicity and naivete. This naivete, he thought, contained the core of morality. Unlike Locke, he did not think it sufficient to form children's habits through practice and routine. For a more lasting effect he recommended that educators let children suffer the consequences of their own deeds.

Having faith in the innate goodness of nature and children, Rousseau believed that children raised in nature would bring upon this earth a new dawn of innocence and unspoiled morality. Given some time and freedom, they would come to their senses and see by themselves that it was best to act in accordance with reason and necessity. In his view, the child was not a "blank slate," as Locke had put it, on which one inscribed some moral laws. On the contrary, moral laws existed already within the child, and they would emerge by themselves within the natural environment. Of course, he did feel that occasionally a tutor was needed to guide children in such a way that they would come to their own conclusions, even if only by the pressure of necessity, yet he did not doubt that such conclusions would be morally sound.

Rousseau agreed with Locke that folktales were unsuitable reading material for children, mainly because they were rooted in dark superstitions that interfered with the tutor's task of cultivating their insight and understanding. He also rejected the reading of fiction, fantasy, myths, and legends, arguing that they would confuse children's perception of truth and reality. As far as Emile was concerned, his tutor recommended to him the fables of Aesop and La Fontaine. In general, Rousseau found it more advantageous for children to experience "the Book of Nature" by stimulating curiosity and motivation than to spend much time in dusty libraries. Consequently, he thought it wise not to bother Emile with books at all (except with fables) until the age of fourteen and then to give him only one book: Daniel Defoe's *Robinson Crusoe*.[6]

It was John Newbery who first rediscovered for England the value of the oral folk tradition. By publishing traditional nursery rhymes along with lullabies, tongue twisters, folk rhymes, and riddles, he did for the British what Clemens Brentano and Achim von Arnim had done for the Germans. Newbery, too, raised to a new esteem the inherited folk tradition, and like Herder, he perceived a link between Shakespeare's sonnets and the "natural poetry" of the people.[7] On the other hand, Newbery's work was still strongly didactic. To the nursery rhymes he added orals or "maxims" to remind children of the wisdom of their parents and the folly of their disobedience. Being inspired by John Locke, he tried to link reading with pleasure, but never left out the principle of instruction. To children who would buy his books, he would sell a little pincushion for two pence extra so that they might mark their bad deeds with black pins on one side and their good deeds with red ones on the other. Such extra-literary tokens were meant to help them in keeping track of their vices and virtues.

In consistency with Locke's philosophy of education, John Newbery did not include a single fairy tale among his publications. His *Little Pretty Pocket Book* in 1744, a book with pictures, rhymes, and games that was intended "for the Instruction and Amusement of Little Master Tommy and Pretty Miss Polly," did include a letter from Jack the Giant Killer (that was also mentioned in the advertisement of the book). Yet, this letter had very little to do with the folktale by that title, for it explicitly served the purpose of making a good boy of Master Tommy and a good little girl of Miss Polly.[8]

The ideas of John Locke and Jean Jacques Rousseau fell on fertile soil in England. As children's book writers began to appeal to the child's power of motivation and experience, their stories became more lively and interesting. Before their time, many writers had preached only rules of morality and proper behavior, sometimes without bothering about dialogues and plot development at all. The tales of the English Rousseauists were modern in the sense that at the end, they often showed children who gratefully acknowledged that they had learned by experience, but they were sometimes predictable and didactic, too. They also contributed to some restrictive critical views of folklore and imaginative fiction. Like Locke and Rousseau, the Rousseauists denounced imaginative fiction as they denounced folktales.

In an unadulterated form folktales were popular and widely available in chapbook form, but the Rousseauists considered them too crude to be used with children. In an overly refined form they were available in English translation from the French *Contes des fées*, yet these, too, did not find their approval, because they thought that their language was too pretentious and their plots too involved with such adult matters as love and intrigue. Neither did they look favorably on Perraults' *Contes de ma mère l'oye* (*Tales of My Mother Goose*) that had been available in English translation since the beginning of the seventeenth century.[9]

The most refreshing thing about the English Rousseauists was that they depicted children in a more realistic setting, while introducing story plots and dialogues that revealed some spontaneous actions. They also had a positive conception of childhood and believed as much in the benefits of reason and experience as they did in the wholesome effects of the natural environment. Still, they did not trust folktales and excluded them from their publications, considering them uncouth and uncontrolled, a "literature in the raw," that interfered with lessons to be learned from nature. Whereas Herder had applied Rousseau's concepts of nature and freedom to the idea of reviving the "natural poetry" of *Naturpoesie* of the common man, the Rousseauists did not perceive this connection and measured folklore together with fiction by their own didactic standards. They used the same rigid criticism in regard to other works of imaginative literature, such as fantasy and fiction, unless these were tempered by moral lessons or an abundance of "useful" information.

An innovative aspect of he Rousseauists' stories was that they dared to show how children sometimes erred from the path of virtue. In *The History of Sandford and Merton* (1783),[10] for example, Thomas Day presented two boys who occasionally failed to conform to their tutor's expectations and even used foul language. Ultimately, however, they would always correct themselves, confessing at the end that they had made a mistake. Far from being natural or convincing, such conversions all too obviously tried to manipulate young minds in the right way of thinking and acting.

Day would also include fablelike stories within his stories to drive home a lesson. In one scene, young Harry would read aloud to Tommy and their tutor a story about two dogs. One of the dogs, which had been raised in the country by a farmer and left to fend for itself in the open air, turned out to be rough, ragged, and meager in appearance but tough and courageous in action. The other dog, which had been raised in the luxury of a rich landowner's home in the city, where it was stuffed with "pot-liquor and broken victuals," grew to be sleek and comely but also unwieldy and cowardly. One day, when its rich master was attacked by a wolf, the dog simply ran away with its tail between his legs instead of coming to his assistance. The main point of the story was the reversal that took place in the characters of the dogs once they had switched their masters and seats of residence. A "magic" transformation took place in the character of each dog, just after a little time had passed: the courageous dog became unwieldy and cowardly, and the cowardly dog became tough and courageous. At the end of the tale within the tale, the landowner let the farmer know that finally he understood how a life of indolence and repose led to nothing but a contemptible character, whereas proper discipline and constant exercise achieved the very opposite. In explaining the story, the tutor would point out to the boys how such fables applied to the natural yet disciplined upbringing of children. In their turn, the boys would praise the tutor for having taught them such a valuable lesson.

In his preface, Day had stated that he hoped the reader would not mistake this book for a treatise on education, but he never left the reader in doubt as to which character was right and which one was wrong. Neither the dialogues nor the fables could hide his didactic purpose.

Like Locke and Rousseau, Day thought that children would fare much better without fairy tales. Aside from his own didactic tales within his books, he recommended to them traditional and modern fables, Defoe's *Robinson Crusoe*, selected passages from Henry Brooke's *Fool of Quality*, and stories from Plutarch and Xenophon. [11] He felt that it was more important to develop in the child a sense of reason than a sense of the imagination. The only magic that he admitted into his stories showed a character's transformation as the result of a changed environment involving self-discipline and self-reliance.

Maria Edgeworth's tales won a wider audience with children than Day's, also in the United States, possibly because she was the more gifted writer of the two and managed to create some more credible characters. Still, her stories, too, were written with a "purpose." In "The Purpose Jar," a story that first appeared in *The Parent's Assistant* (1796), [12] little Rosamond at first showed signs of childlike behavior by choosing for her birthday a lovely purple jar instead of a new pair of shoes. However, as soon as she put water into the jar and the purple color turned into an evil-smelling liquid, she began to understand how foolishly she had acted. She fully realized the extent of her when the soles of her old shoes came off, which kept her from joining a family excursion. [13] This scene parallels an incident in Rousseau's novel, where Emile purposely broke a windowpane of his own bedroom, only to realize by and by that he had made a mistake—especially since the pane was not replaced and the chilly autumn winds began to blow through the cracks. Like Emile, Rosamond promised at the end to act more wisely in the future.

The lesson that Rosamond learned in the story reveals Maria Edgeworth's utilitarian mode of thinking that admitted no "idle dreaming"—be it about purple jars or other "nonsense." She strongly disapproved of fairy tales. In the preface to *The Parent's Assistant*, she chided Dr. Johnson for having been lenient in regard to tales about giants, fairies, castles, and enchantments. She was convinced that such tales were nothing but "sweetmeats" that spoiled the child's appetite. Instead of filling children's minds with fantastic visions of fairy lore, she expected that literature should teach them some useful lessons. In her view, folktales were neither reasonable nor useful enough to suit the educational goals that she hoped to reach through her own stories for children.

[Religious and Moralistic Approaches (England)]

During the early nineteenth century in England, religious groups gained a strong influence on children's literature, mainly through Mrs. Sarah Trimmer, the founder of a well-organized Sunday School movement. As the editor of *The Guardian of Education* [14] and the author of various children's books and stories, she advocated the gentle use of moral and religious principles that would form their mind and enlighten their understanding. In her journal she consistently gave bad reviews of "fairy tales," never failing to condemn their use with children. In principle, she opposed folktales and other "superstitious tales," as they invited children to dangerous flights of fancy. Along such lines she also renounced fiction and fantasy writings, unless they combined entertainment with moral instruction. As a loyal follower of John Locke, she thought that imaginative tales of any kind, whether frightful or pleasant, interfered with the child's perception of reality and contained the core of corruption. Within the framework of her religious task, she would not tolerate books that were written for the amusement of children without a good dose of added moral instruction. [15] She wrote some books for younger children that were meant to familiarize them with the catechism of the Church of England, the New Testament, and Scripture history. Her writing was innovative in the sense that she introduced characters and analogies from nature that involved vivid dialogues. Well received was her *Fabulous Histories*, [16] a work pertaining to the history of a family of robins that also involved some incidents with children who took care of them. Yet instead of appealing to the child's imagination, she insisted on the development of reason and an impeccable moral conduct — even among the families of birds. As an author, she herself abstained from preaching, but she often let her birds and other creatures do that job for her.

Mrs. Trimmer's thorough dislike of "fairy tales" was based on her reading of the French *Contes des fées* and Perrault's collection of fairy tales. She argued that they only filled the heads of children with confused notions of wonderful and supernatural events brought about by the agency of supernatural beings, causing them nightmares and inviting them to sick flights of fancy. While admitting that as a child she had read such tales as "Little Red Riding Hood" and "Blue Beard," she wrote that she would not wish to disturb the tender minds of her grandchildren by "exciting, unreasonable, and groundless fears." Referring to "fairy tales" in general, she wrote: "Neither do the generality of tales of this kind supply any moral instruction level to infantile capacity." [17]

The British moralists especially attacked the French *Contes des fées*, and among these the tales of Madame d'Aulnoy, whose idyllic love stories and lavish descriptions of the court of the fairies had been intended for an older audience. They found these tales even less edifying than those of Perrault, as they included literary conceits and intricate plots involving romance and political intrigues. They also objected to the lavish descriptions of dresses, gardens with fountains and marble statues, and tapestry designs that even related such minute details as hunting scenes woven with red silk and golden threads. Considering them lacking in moral intent, British moralists also thought that they would seduce children by their indulgence in a life of luxury and leisure. Also, they wondered why children should ever be exposed to such nonsense as carriages drawn by lions, leopards, or dragons, dogs hatching from nutshells, or diamonds falling from a princess's hair.[18] Such scenes had no relationship to truth and reality and therefore should be banned.

Some of Mme. D'Aulnoy's tales have become classics, especially "The White Cat," "The Blue Bird," and "The Yellow Dwarf." Even though today some critics still raise objections to their ornate style, they give due credit to the author for having taken her plots from the folk tradition.[19] This argument would have meant little to the British moralists in the early nineteenth century. Unlike Herder, who rejected some tales on the basis of their conceited style yet recommended genuine folk stories (myth, legends, and folktales) to older children, the British moralists rejected all "fairy tales" on the basis that they lacked a clear-cut moral emphasis and distracted children from the more essential things in life.

Anticipating some moral objections to fairy tales by the critics, even in France some writers "adjusted" their tales in such a way as to combine amusement with instruction. Interesting in this connection are the tales of Madame de Beaumont, which were translated in 1761 under the title *The Young Misses' Magazine*.[20] By alternating the folktales with dialogues, she tried to gear them to the understanding of girls between the ages of ten and twelve. Throughout the tales themselves, she combined the "agreeable" with the "useful," thus making sure that the amusing aspect of "fairy tales" always found its practical counterpart or application. Yet these tales, too, were rejected by Mrs. Trimmer.

Some of the earliest fairy tale writers in England were eager to imitate the abaresque style of the *Contes des fées*, still adding in a manneristic way some allegorical themes based on classical mythology. The results were fairy tales "with a purpose" that tried to combine amusement with instruction while using a language that was too sophisticated for young children to understand. When Henry Brooke published in 1750 *A New Collection of Fairy Tales*, he used the subtitle *Containing many Useful Lessons, Moral Sentiments, Surprising Incidents, and Amusing Adventures*.[21] Imitating the elaborate style of Madame d'Aulnoy's *Contes des fées* (without reaching her level of inventiveness), he spiced up the text with allegories and classical allusions, even using such French names as Bleuette, Mignonette, and Papillon and pseudo-mythological references Daphne, Iris, and "Silvia," most likely in an attempt to raise fairy tales to the level of elegant literature. At the same time, he tried to please the moralists by choosing for some of his characters such names as Prince Constant or Princess Luminiscence, which would hint at their particular virtues. Describing the noble company at the court of the fairies, he wrote: "Valour and Activity were the Distinctions among the Men and Grace and Beauty of the Women were their Titles and Dowries."[22] Yet instead of letting such qualities emerge through the story plots, he merely listed the desirable "Qualities of the Mind" in a catalogue form. In a chapter entitled "Palace of Ideas," for example, he tried to impress his readers with "the beauty of morality," while constantly interrupting the flow of the narrative by stating his own views on the nature of virtue.

> The Fairy of the Flower inhabited a Palace and kept her Court in the midst of Fountains and Gardens. Trianon and Marly are best indifferent Copies of her delicious Abode. In the Choice and in the furnishing of a Place we generally unfold our own private Character. . . . Many young Princes and Princesses (for she was very fond of young People) she either educated them up from their Infancy or had them brought to her at the Age of Thirteen and Sixteen, and she commonly endowed them with whatever Gift they desired. There was the Court of the Fairy composed of and adorned with, all the Delights of the Heart and Mind; In those Points very different from that of other Fairies who have not always known the Pleasure of obliging; the only Thing in my Opinion that can make Authority supportable.[23]

Page upon page Brooke gave himself up to abstract contemplations of vices and virtues at the fairy court, as if he had fallen in love with his own pretentious diction. With his many asides, he often lost the thread of the stories and most certainly would have lost the attention of young children.

One might assume that since the English moralists based their bias against fairy tales mainly on the French *Contes des fées* and their translations and imitations in England, they rejected them because of their fanciful style and allegorical themes. Yet, they also rejected the better writers, such as Charles Perrault, without considering their styles or their proximity to the folk tradition. One may indeed wonder why they would reject Perrault's *Contes de ma mere l'oye* (*Tales of My Mother Goose*) along with the rest, especially since he not only had written in a relatively simple style with swiftly moving plots but had also added the subtitle to his work *Avec des moralités* (*With Morals*).[24] The answer lies in the ironic tone of his tales and also of his morals. Especially his morals lacked the high seriousness that educators would have required. Perrault had originally aimed the tales, tongue-in-cheek, at an older audience at the court but not at younger children. Feeling that irony had no place in the serious business of moral education, the critics felt that these tales, too, were too trivial and not Christian enough to deserve attention. Overall, they cared as little about style per se as they did about children's reading interests. Being mainly concerned to improve the hearts and minds of children, they felt that folk and fairy tales did not pass the acid test of high morality.

Edgar Taylor's translation of the Grimms' fairy tales was a refreshing event against the backdrop of so much artificiality and morality. His style was simple and direct, following the English colloquial style in all its vivid simplicity. On the other hand, Taylor, too, was not quite free from didactic intentions. Even though in his preface to *German*

Popular Stories he had made a strong appeal for the free use of the imagination, already the second edition of his work contained a revised translation with various changes in the titles as well as the text.[25] Some of these appear to have been made not so much for the sake of amusing children than for appeasing the British moralists. While admitting in a footnote that he had freely combined some of the Grimms' tales, he did not tell the reader why he had done so. He mentioned only that he had made "variations which diverse considerations dictated."

What these "diverse considerations" may have been is easy to guess from his new version of "Hansel and Grethel." In a footnote to this tale, Taylor confessed that he had taken the liberty to create a composite version of three tales: "Hansel and Grethel," "Little Brother and Sister," and "Roland."[26] What he did not say was that in this way he avoided the evil stepmother motif along with such cruelties as shoving the old witch into the oven. Taylor's new story presented Grethel as an adopted child whom the woodsman, Hansel's father, had found in the bough of a tree where her own mother had deserted her. This way, the woodsman's wife, who was Hansel's real mother, became a stepmother to Grethel, which seemed to prove that stepmothers as well as real mothers were capable of evil thoughts and child desertion. Further, by changing the old witch into a fairy who finally just vanishes into the woods, Taylor managed to bypass the scenes when the witch locks up Hansel in a cage and when Grethel reverses her fate by killing the witch. In conclusion, he let Hansel marry Grethel, his adopted sister, while letting them both stay on for the rest of their lives at the king's palace. Such changes were not minor ones, as they substantially affected the plot, themes, and characters of the story.

Taylor also pruned the ending of "The Frog Prince" by deleting the dramatic scene in which the princess threw the frog against the wall. Taylor's princess suffered no temper tantrum, and neither did she seem to be overly eager to watch with her own eyes the transformation of frog-to-prince in the middle of her bedroom. Instead, she just placed the frog onto her pillow and then left the room discreetly, three nights in a row, only to discover on the third morning that it had been transformed into a charming prince.[27] In "The Blue Light" he softened the fate of the old woman by letting the soldier make a wish that brought her to the bottom of the well instead of to the gallows.[28] In "Ashputtel" he said nothing about the fate of the stepmother and stepsisters at the end of the tale except that they were frightened and turned pale with anger as the prince took Ashputtel on his horse and rode away with her.[29] Thus Taylor left the reader guessing what happened to the stepmother. It is possible that through such editorial changes Taylor tried to protect children from harsh and cruel scenes, but the pattern of the various changes he made shows that he also bowed to the expectations of the moralistic critics.

Generally, the moralistic critics of fairy tales in England did not seem to make a distinction along national lines in their evaluation of the merits of a given work. Following a utilitarian bent, they rather suspected fairy tales as a genre as they suspected fiction. Even after the publication of *German Popular Stories*, which caused a watershed of folktale publications in England,[30] those critics who had been skeptical to begin with continued to be skeptical, on the assumption that all "fairy tales" offered amusement but little or no moral instruction.

In an attempt to please children yet also to appease the moralistic critics, publishers promoted still another type of fairy story that left some of the traditional plot elements intact yet modified the themes and inserted elements that alleviated cruelties or "unreasonable" aspects of the stories. Among these was Benjamin Tabart's *Popular Fairy Tales; or a Lilliputian Library*,[31] a work that cautiously presented children with some pruned and refined fairy tales, in which even Jack the Giant Killer was given a proper excuse to kill the Giant, as this monster had supposedly first robbed Jack's father.

By mid-century, a new quest for folktales emerged against the background of an overemphasis on instructional books that had invaded the shores of "both Englands." Under the pseudonym of Felix Summerly, Sir Henry Cole published his *Home Treasury* series in 1843 and successive years.[32] As this series no longer alluded in its subtitle to moral sentiments but rather professed "To Cultivate the Affections, Fancy, Imagination and Taste of Children," it seemed to usher in a new era in children's literature that included stories written merely for the child's enjoyment. This impression was strengthened by Cole's preface to the work, in which he defied the common notion that the worst literature was good enough for children. He rejected what he called "the deplorable Peter Parleyism" in children's literature with its overemphasis on utilitarian values. Instead, he called for fairy tales. Within his series, he published such well-known French tales as "The Sleeping Beauty," "Little Red Riding Hood," "Cinderella," and "Beauty and the Beast" and English tales such as "Jack and the Giant Killer," "Jack and the Beanstalk," and "Dick Wittington," as well as several volumes of fables and nursery rhymes. Historians of children's literature have generally hailed the publication of this series as a refreshing new trend that introduced genuine folktales to children, tales that seemed to have survived unpruned only in the chapbook tradition.[33]

Like Taylor, however, Cole was not entirely immune to didactic trends. A closer look at some tales that he included in *Traditional Faery Tales* reveals that he still followed the example of Locke by setting up examples of virtues and vices. Thus he transformed Little Red Riding Hood into an exemplary child—at least in the first half of the story—while introducing Jack the Giant Killer as a bad little boy, a lazy good-for-nothing who didn't even wish to help his mother. He told the reader that Red Riding Hood was helpful, obedient, and diligent and that she had learned from her grandmother how to spin, bake bread, make butter, and even sing "so that she might join in the musick in the Church."[34] At length, he commented on what a kind, good-natured, charitable, courageous, grateful, honest, and pious girl she was, a child who "never told a lie" and "constantly prayed for God's blessing and providence." Instead of showing some of these qualities through the story's action, he merely pointed them out in an abstract way, quite in line with the old didactic style that always tried to underscore some exemplary traits along with some vices. Yet at the end of the tale, when in loyalty to Perrault's version he let the wolf eat up Little Red Riding Hood, he seemed to have second thoughts. In small print, he added:

> This is the traditional ending of the tale—but it is a grievous one, which most children dislike. And as I have heard a version related in which poetical justice is done to the wolf, I insert it for those who prefer it.

The second ending related how some faggot makers happened to pass by the house just in time to kill the wolf and to release Little Red Riding Hood. They played a similar role here as the hunter in the Grimms' version of the tale, thus adding a bit of consolation. Unlike the Grimms, however, Cole listed the second ending not because he was interested in variants for their own sake but because he wished to please children.

Cole's portrayal of Jack appears like a foil to Little Red Riding Hood. While Red Riding Hood embodied all female virtues, Jack was the very image of what the author called "the vice of idleness." He climbed on the biggest trees, lay on the high branches overhanging some steep precipices, always screaming with delight. "He spent all his time in fun and frolic, but he never did anything useful."[35] Toward the end of the tale, Jack's attitude changed radically—at least that is what the fairy reported who suddenly appeared out of nowhere: "If you had remained as idle and lazy as you once were," she told Jack, "I should not have exerted my power to help you recover your property and care for your old mother in old age. I trust you will make good use of it as your father once did, and now farewell."[36] How and why he changed she did not say, but she made it clear that now he morally deserved his reward. Cole also made sure that legally Jack deserved his reward. As in the version of *The Holiday House*, Jack never stole gold from the giant, for supposedly he took only a treasure that had originally belonged to his father. However, in accordance with the English folk tradition, Cole did permit Jack to cut off the Giant's head, which shows that in this case he was not overly protective. Cole's editing affected the characters of the tales, and definitely the style, for long asides about virtuous and lazy children do not belong to the oral tradition. However, to a greater degree than other writers of "fairy tales" before him, he respected the basic plots of the traditional stories and only occasionally would soften the ending by adding an alternate version for the child's pleasure.

Supposedly Cole's entire series of books for children was inspired by the Brothers Grimm, but it did not include a single tale by the Grimms themselves. As a folktale collector, he did have some short-comings, for he did not worry too much about loyalty to tradition, as far as folktale characters were concerned. On the other hand, it must be said to his credit that, aside from his dry commentaries on vices and virtues that belonged to the old didactic school, he contributed to a revival of the British interest in folktales and he also cared enough about children to take into consideration at least some of their interests.

Some writers of fairy tales, too, thought it safer not just to tell a good story for the sake of amusement and entertainment but to include some "useful lessons" as well. Sometimes they would even go so far as to use fairy tales merely as a pretext for the purpose of teaching morals. In the *The Holiday House*, Master No-Book is first drawn to the kingdom of Fairy Do-Nothing.[37] The young reader is instructed by the very choice of names that children who don't read (or who don't like school) are likely to end up as lazy kids or loafers. In that sense, Fairy Do-Nothing was the embodiment of a vice. When Master No-Book finally came to the rescue of Fairy Teach-All, the reader is again told what to think, namely that a life full of fun and frolic leads to nothing, whereas a life dedicated to learning is the right choice, or the only choice. Under the pretext of providing children with fairy tales, such lessons within the tales severely curtailed the free range of their imagination while reminding them of their sense of duty. In this context, magic itself became a vehicle of instruction and the fairies were nothing but old-fashioned teachers in disguise.

Other authors in the early nineteenth century went so far as to use the word "fairy" in the title of their books while offering to the child nothing but useful lessons or bland instruction. Under the disguise of such a title as *Fairy Fairstar's Cabinet of Gems*, A. Park published several series of *New and Original Toy Books* in 1854,[38] with colored illustrations. Yet, where were the fairies? The books were supposedly dedicated to the "Instruction and Amusement" of children, yet evidently they used the name of fairyland only as a bait to convey some instructions along with moral lessons. The series included several alphabet books, such as *Alphabetical London Cries*, *The Alphabet of Trades*, and *The Illuminated Scriptural Alphabet*. These were not even storybooks but rather toy books that in verse form conveyed some useful information. The only amusement they offered was the color provided by the illustrations that covered every page of these short books. Being inspired by the philosophy of John Locke, the editor also included didactic stories that were meant to show the pitfalls of vices, illustrated, of course, and in color. Such titles as "The Mishaps of Unlucky Benny," "The Sorrows of Poor Toby," and "The Selfish Boy" left no doubt that vices led to great unhappiness and sorrows. Among the thirty-seven titles of the series, only two slim volumes included fairy tales, namely *History of Cinderella* and *Life and Adventures of Jack, the Giant-Killer*.[39]

George Cruikshank's "fairy stories" that first appeared in 1853,[40] represented a step backward in comparison with Cole's *Traditional Faery Tales*. Not finding it sufficient to use a descriptive style and elements of personal fantasy, he felt it necessary to impose upon the tales his moral visions of a society that was free from alcohol abuse, thus using them as a sort of utopian land of "ABSTINENCE." When the king prepared for Cinderella's wedding and in a generous mood ordered that all fountains in the courtyard and in the streets should be "running with wine," the kingdom was on the brink of ruin—had it not been for the good advice of a fairy. A female dwarf appeared just in time to save the kingdom. She introduced herself as Cinderella's godmother (an invention by Cruikshank) and pleaded with the king to reconsider the ill side effects that drinking would have on the royal wedding party. There would be ill health, she warned, along with misery and crimes, all leading to quarrels, brutal fights, and even death. When the king ventured to ask if Providence had not intended the wine for human consumption, he replied that if the *Almighty* had indeed thought it necessary for man to take stimulating drinks, he would certainly have supplied it to him "free from *all intoxicating qualities*."[41] Besides, he should just take a look at lovely Cinderella. Had she ever taken a drop of alcohol in her life? She certainly had not and never would in the future! And how did the good king respond to such wisdom? Becoming converted by the dwarf's argument, he immediately collected together all the wine, beer, and spirits in his kingdom, piled them on top of a mountain near the castle, and started a big bonfire on the wedding day.

Charles Dickens was enraged when he read Cruikshank's tales, calling them "frauds on the fairies." In response to his "Cinderella" tale and others, he complained that he had lately observed "the intrusion of a Whole Hog of unwieldy dimensions into the fairy flower garden."[42] He was referring specifically to George Cruikshank, who had "edited" ogres and hop-o'-my-thumbs in order to propagate "Total Abstinence, Prohibition of the Sale of spirituous liquors, Free Trade, and Popular Education" while substantially altering the text of the fairy stories. Being in a satirical mood, Dickens suggested how, following such a logic, one might imagine a "Total Abstinence Edition" of *Robinson Crusoe* by leaving out all of the rum, a "Peace Edition" by leaving out all of the gunpowder, or a "Vegetarian Edition" by leaving out the goat's flesh. This way, Robinson Crusoe would be edited out of his island in a hundred years, he prophesied, and the island itself would be swallowed up in an editorial ocean.[43]

Gradually a new trend asserted itself that ultimately led to the Golden Age in children's literature during the latter part of the nineteenth century. Several writers and publishers no longer felt it necessary to add morals to folktales and fantasies, thus freeing themselves from didactic restraints. Being inspired by Jacob Grimms' studies in comparative mythology, some folktale collectors also began to add a broader cross-cultural perspective to their folktale collections. Among such "liberated" folktale publications were Anthony Montalba's *Fairy Tales of All Nations* and C. B. Burkhardt's *Fairy Tales and Legends of Many Nations* (1849), and Sir George Dasent's *Popular Tales from the Norse* (1859), based on the collections of Asbjörnsen and Moe.[44] These works also came much closer to the Grimms' simple, straightforward folktale style while showing a remarkable freedom from abstract talk about virtues and vices.

Charles Kingsley came perhaps closest to Herder and the Brothers Grimm in terms of recognizing the cross-cultural epic connection of folktales, myths, and hero tales. In his preface to *The Heroes: or Greek Fairy Tales for My Children* (1856) he wrote:

> For nations begin at first by being children like you, though they are made up of grown men. They are children at first like you — men and women with children's hearts; frank, and affectionate, and full of trust, and teachable, and loving to see and learn all the wonders round them; and greedy also, too often, and passionate and silly, as children are. . . . Now, while they were young and simple they loved fairy tales, as you do now. All nations do so when they are young: our old forefathers did, and called their stories "Sagas." I will read you some of them some day — some of the Eddas, and the Voluspa, and Beowulf, and the noble old Romances.[45]

Unlike the Grimms, however, Kingsley did not bother to define the various genres of folktales, myths, legends, and sagas but referred to all of these as "fairy tales." Nevertheless, his writings helped to promote a new understanding of folktales as an integral part of the inherited broader folk tradition, especially in relation to the epic. Kingsley's fantasies, on the other hand, had only a vague connection with folklore and reflected to a large degree his own imagination. In his self-conscious style he all too often got side-tracked by topics that ranged from arguments on political economy to crinolines and educational theories, thus leaving the reader to wonder whether he truly did or did not believe in fairies. Harvey Darton judged that in spite of his fine imagination and pure simplicity of soul, Kingsley simply could not write without a moral purpose.[46]

Here and there, didactic "fairy tales" were still alive in the last two decades of the nineteenth century. In 1882 there appeared in London a book titled *Old Fashioned Fairy Tales*, collected and edited by Juliana Horatia Ewing.[47] In her preface, Mrs. Ewing claimed that the use of fairy tales with children no longer needed an excuse, as they were the "most valuable literature for the young." Such claims, however, did not keep her from praising the "positive uses" of fairy tales in education, thus reaffirming the old-fashioned theory that tales of amusement should be combined with elements of instruction. Mrs. Ewing's book was written in a simple and vivid style and preserved some traditional folktale themes, but the tales were mostly her own. In calling them "handmaidens of Faith, Hope, and, perhaps most of all, of Charity," she betrayed the didactic intent of the London Society for the Promotion of Christian Knowledge, under whose auspices she had published them. As such, they had a didactic tendency and followed the trend of the pruned fairy tales with a purpose.

Folktale publications in England truly emerged in their own right with Andrew Lang's *Fairy Book Series* of folktale collections that included not only English but also European and Oriental tales. It began with the *Blue Fairy Book* in 1889 and ended with the *Lilac Fairy Book* in 1911.[48] Even though this series was still based on published sources rather than on fieldwork research, it primarily served the pleasure of the child rather than some specific didactic goals. The broad international scope of these volumes, of which each one represented a different color, introduced children to folktales around the world, helping them realize that a rich folk imagination was the common property of older nationalities everywhere.

From a modern folkloristic perspective, it is generally considered a shortcoming that Lang did not bother to indicate his sources other than by country and that he also did not separate folktales from fantasies. In his lengthy preface to Margaret Hunt's translation of the *Kinder- und Hausmärchen*, he had shown a lively interest in the authenticity of folktales by pointing out their relationship with "savage customs and traditions." By the time he published his *Colour Fairy Books*, however, he had already written another preface to *Perrault's Popular Tales*, which indicated a new appreciation of the fruitful interconnection between the traditional folktale and the accomplished literary fairy tale. Because he finally did not view them on two separate planes, he felt no scruples in listing in the *Blue Fairy Book* some tales of the Brothers Grimm side by side with others by Hans Christian Andersen.[49]

Between 1890 and 1894, Jacob Jacobs published *English Fairy Tales*, *More English Fairy Tales*, *Celtic Fairy Tales*, *More Celtic Fairy Tales*, and *Indian Fairy Tales*, expressing his desire to surpass the Brothers Grimm in publishing folktales that appealed to both children and adults. Jacobs differed in his approach from Lang by including folktales only and, further, by carefully listing the sources of each.[50] He shared with Lang an admiration for international tales and rejected moral or "useful" lessons that were not an integral part of the inherited folk tradition.

[Pragmatic and Realistic Approaches (U.S.A.)]

While philologists in the United States praised the Brothers Grimm (especially Jacob) in the nineteenth century on the basis of their philological contributions, they largely ignored the folktale collection. In spite of the fact that in the wake of the *Kinder- und Hausmärchen* a watershed of folktale collections was published by the mid-nineteenth century, both in England and the United States, these did not yet necessarily win the approval of educators in either country.

As in England, for a long time a didactic trend prevailed in this country that emphasized the need to combine amusement with instruction. "If you do not grow wiser, in some way, by what you read," stated a youth magazine for the benefit of its young readers in 1858, "that is, if you are only amused and not instructed by what you read, you are throwing away the greater part of the time spent reading."[51] Another writer for children advocated, in the name of the Savior, "TOTAL ABSTINENCE . . . from the reading of works of fiction."[52] A recommended book list issued by the Michigan Superintendent of Public Instruction in 1859 for school libraries contained primarily works of a moralistic and informative character, including the didactic works of Hannah More and such titles as *I'll be a Lady*, and *I'll be a Gentleman*. Next to "moral lesson" books, biographies, geographies, and histories, there were also the travel books by Peter Parley and John Abbott. The only true tales of adventure listed were Defoe's *Robinson Crusoe* and Heinrich Wyss's *Swiss Family Robinson*. Under the category of folklore were, next to Aesop's fables, only Dwight's *Mythology* and Bulfinch's *Age of Chivalry*.[53] The list did not contain a single work of folktales. It is of interest to note that other books of supposedly "corruptive influence" on young minds, such as Edward Lear's *The Book of Nonsense* and Mark Twain's *Tom Sawyer*, were also not included on the Michigan Superintendent's recommended book list until the last decade of the nineteenth century, that is, about twenty years after their original publication date. The same conservative pattern may be observed in public library catalogues at the time. The Bay City Public Library catalogue of 1878 still did not yet list Jacob and Wilhelm Grimm's *Tales of the Household*, although it referred to a variety of new acquisitions in the realm of fantasy for children, namely the works of Hans Christian Andersen and Lewis Carroll.[54] The list of the township and district libraries of Michigan included the Grimms' tales only in 1886—which was more than half a century after its first American translation.[55]

Following the pragmatic trend, parents and educators preferred that their children read informational and didactic books while shunning folktales, fantasies, and tales of adventure, which they considered not only a distraction from what was useful and practical but also a source of moral corruption. Still toward the end of the nineteenth century, an editor warned young readers:

> Reading has become a downright vice—a vulgar, detrimental habit, like damdrinking; an excuse for idleness . . . a softening, a demoralizing, relaxing practice, which, if persisted in, will end by enfeebling the minds of men and women. . . . Books which neither confer information which is worth having, nor lift the spiritual part of us up to loftier regions, have no merit.[56]

Children's books were still calculated to improve manners and morals of young ladies and young gentlemen, serving the end of promoting virtue along with propriety and piety. Parents and educators generally tolerated Aesop's fables because they taught virtues that coincided with common sense, yet many of them felt inclined to group folktales with entertaining fiction, condemning both as useless plunder. Even though the first American edition of the Grimms' folktales in 1826 had been a popular success, many adults were still far from considering folktales as a "suitable" literature for young people. Especially in the Midwest, the philosophy of reading was dominated by principles of instruction and propriety far beyond the mid-nineteenth century. Partially, this was so because of certain religious influences, including the Sunday School movement, yet partially also because of pragmatic considerations. In the Midwest there prevailed the spirit of pragmatism, which promoted an anticultural attitude, a "distaste for study deeply inimical to education."[57] Henry Philip Tappan, one of Michigan's greatest educational philosophers, noted in 1851 that such an attitude was related to the political condition in the Midwest at the time, in which a high education and a high order of talent did not generally form a guarantee of success. Such an attitude could also be detected in other parts of the country. On the one hand, the Puritan obsession with sins, saints, and early death still lingered on in literature, promoted by the Sunday School movement and the American Tract Society, and on the other hand, the spirit of pragmatism invaded children's literature as it did the public life with its emphasis on what was useful and practical. As neither one of these trends favored the use of traditional and imaginative literature for children, children were often deprived of both, even though such books were already in print.[58]

Pragmatic and cautious attitudes toward reading matters for children could also be found in other states. Folktales that were printed individually or in anthologies for recreational reading often underwent some transformation in the name of morality, regardless of if they were related to the French collection of Charles Perrault or the German collection of the Brothers Grimm. Sometimes a folktale that survived the keen eye of an American educator was rewritten to suit the spiritual and educational values of the time. An example of such a revision was an 1863 "shape book" edition of *Red Riding Hood* by Lydia Very, a Massachusetts schoolteacher. The revision affected the plot, the theme, and the main characters of the tale. Fitting the conventional concept of morality, Red Riding Hood emerged here as an "exemplary child":

> For she was good and loving
> And beautiful as good,
> With daily acts of kindness
> Little Red Riding Hood.[59]

Not only did she visit her ill grandmother but she would go to her once a week, bringing her wild berries and honey, which she herself had gathered in the woods. Instead of bringing her grandmother custard and a pot of butter as in Perrault's version of the tale, or cake and wine as in the Grimms' version, she brought her faggots and butter. The illustration shows her bent over forward, with a huge bundle of firewood on her back, obviously trying to underline her virtue of going to such pains of trying to be helpful. In the context of so many virtues, the wine obviously did not fit into Mrs. Very's tale. Perhaps she feared that it would have evoked the anger of the prohibitionists.

A major change occurred in the ending of the story. The author thought it wise to let the grandmother leave the room on an errand, just moments before the wolf arrived, thus denying him the opportunity to swallow her up. Furthermore, just when the wolf was ready to eat little Red Riding Hood, some faggot makers entered the room and shot the wolf dead. Unlike in Perrault's version, where both lost their lives, the new American version let them both stay alive. On the other hand, the author took great pains to emphasize the lessons that children were to derive from the story. The last illustration in the book depicted a white marble cross on a graveyard. In the accompanying text, the author reminded her readers that with "fear and trembling," Red Riding Hood contemplated how close she had come to death, confessing to her grandmother that fright had taught her a lesson. In the Grimms' tale Red Riding Hood and her grandmother were far from having morbid thoughts of death and dying. Instead of preaching, grandmother enjoyed the cake and the wine, and together with the hunter, they celebrated their survival.[60]

Toward the end of the nineteenth century, some American critics still argued against the use of the Grimms' folktales with children. Speaking mainly from a realistic and social point of view, an educator wrote in a North American journal in 1885, the centenary year of Jacob Grimm's birthday: "The folktales [by the Brothers Grimm] mirror all too loyally the entire medieval worldview and culture with all its stark prejudice, its crudeness and barbarities as they are so characteristic for those dark times."[61] He objected to the gruesome descriptions of

torture and death, citing numerous examples of death by decapita-
tion, hanging, or burning alive: "An evil brother is sown into a gunny-
sack and drowned at sea, a queen is suffocated in her bath tub, a
witch's daughter is thrown to the wild beasts, and an evil stepmother
has to dance in red-hot iron shoes until she falls down dead."[62] Such
descriptions neither taught children basic ethics nor contributed to
their sense of social reality. Why should American children read about
outdated savage customs, according to which a king gave away his
daughters in marriage as if they were cattle for sale? No lessons could
be derived from tales that unduly emphasized the differences between
rich and poor, gentiles and Jews, as they taught intolerance against
the underprivileged and members of another race. He added: "But
the main mistake of these tales is that they are altogether lacking
a moral foundation."[63]

Unlike in Germany, reading textbooks in the United States made very
little use of folktales in the nineteenth century. This was partially because
schools, too, considered folktales on the same level as fiction and both
as unworthy literature for the young as they were less concerned with
instruction than with amusement. Reading, however, was primarily
meant to serve the first goal and not the second. An essay "On Reading,"
published in the *Fourth Reader* of Parker's *National Series of Selections
for Reading*, stated explicitly:

> Reading can be considered as a mere amusement only by the most
> vulgar or the most frivolous part of mankind. Every one, whom
> natural good sense and a liberal education have qualified to form
> a judgment upon the subject, will acknowledge that it is capable
> of being applied to an endless variety of useful purposes. This
> is, indeed, sufficiently evident, without any studied proof, from
> the nature of the thing.[64]

Reading folktales was not even a subject of discussion. Whereas in
Germany, school readers included folktales in a selective way to enhance
the spirit of nationalism, readers in the United States preferred a different type of literature to achieve a similar goal. At first, they would
include legends about Abe Lincoln, George Washington, or Paul Revere
in order to strengthen children's faith in the spirit of the nation. The
McGuffey Readers added to these the patriotic poems of Walt Whit-
man, speeches by American senators and congressmen, and essays by
Daniel Webster.[65] American legends and folktales only occasionally
made their way into school textbooks, with the exception of "Sleepy
Hollow." As European folktales did not play a vital role in the American
search for national identity, they were rarely included in school textbooks at that time. Only around the turn of the century, when American
educators awakened to a new interest in the imaginative qualities of
folk literature, did the school readers begin to include American tall

tales and American regional tales, along with European folktales and others from around the world.

The growing number of American editions of *German Popular Stories* gave evidence of the work's increasing popularity in the United States. Between 1876 and 1910 the number of new editions alone ranged from seven to fourteen every five years, and in 1902 alone a total of forty-five editions were available in American bookstores. That number rose dramatically to a total of ninety various available editions by 1928.[66]

Writing about her experiences as a children's librarian at the New York City Library in 1914, Sarah Comstock recalled in an essay in the children's journal *St. Nicholas* that in New York alone, thirty-six different branches of the New York Public Library held regular story hours in those years, a trend that found an echo also in Chicago, Cleveland, Pittsburgh, and St. Louis. She had been working with children whose homes were barren of books and whose families were so busy that there was no room for stories. She took special pleasure in reading aloud to them the Norwegian "Troll" stories of Asbjörnsen and Moe, and also those of Hans Christian Andersen and the Brothers Grimm:

> Many children are too ignorant to know how to use and enjoy books when they come. The librarians say, "We must invite them, urge them, then show them the treasures we have here, and tempt them to seek those treasures for themselves." Such volumes as Grimm's and Andersen's tales, Hawthorne's "Grandfather's Chair," Seton's "Rolf" often stood unopened on the shelves. The children knew how to read—the schools had taught them—but many of them did not know how to enjoy reading.[67]

Miss Comstock observed that "the heads and hearts of children were just as hungry as their stomach," for dainty, creepy, or heroic fairy tales or for tales of fun, pranks, travel, biography, or history. They had also come to love the numerous folktales and legends from around the world that she had introduced to them. Significantly, among the works mentioned was not a single didactic tale. She also recalled a multilingual storytelling program that the New York Public Library had initiated so as to give children of immigrants the experience once a week of listening to their native tales in their native tongue, be it Chinese, Italian, Bohemian, or German. In this context she again mentioned the prominent place that the Grimms' folktales had taken up, next to the jolly tales of Wilhelm Busch.

The concept of enjoying literature for its own sake had already begun taking root in the first Golden Age of children's literature during the 1870s, but in only a few decades it was also embraced by educators with Frank L. Baum's *Wizard of Oz*, a book that soon outnumbered

all folktale editions combined. Still, objections to the Grimms' folktales are still voiced in our time, partially from the quarters of feminist
criticism and partially from those concerned with interracial books
for children.[68]

[Early Social and Nationalistic
Approaches (Germany)]

In the second part of the nineteenth century, some German school
textbook reformers strongly opposed the Grimms' folktales on the basis
that they lacked social values. The arguments used were rather similar
to those used by opponents to folktales in England and the United
States, especially with respect to the concepts of cruelty and elements
of social justice. In addition, the reformers raised some objections to the
folktales' "black-white" portrayals of human characters. Thus, W. Prahn
reminded teachers and librarians in the children's literature journal *Die
Jugendschriften-Warte* that by portraying beauty as synonymous with
goodness and ugliness with evil, folktales were counterproductive to the
schools' efforts of teaching children a clear concept of reality.[69]

With the rise of the Workers' movement in the 1880s the issue of
social justice in folktales gained special attention, the more so as at
that time its leaders had a considerable influence on the school curriculum. They contended that the values of the Grimms' folktales were
incompatible with the values prevalent in an industrial society, and that
folktale dreams of magic wands and silver castles served only to spread
discontent among workers' children while alienating them from their
own realistic conditions within the working world. They maintained
that a socialist education could not afford to tolerate idle fantasies,
myths, and "fairy tales." In their estimate, the Grimms' *Kinder- und
Hausmärchen* contributed nothing to the child's character education
and therefore was irrelevant to the German school curriculum. Children's
literature, they demanded, should teach children that dreams of a better
life could only be fulfilled through hard labor and self-reliance, but
not through the magic of a fairy. The only literature they considered
worthy of promotion was one that gave children a sense of social reality
within a realistic setting.[70]

Under the rule of Emperor Wilhelm II, a new interest arose in the
Grimms' folktales and others, primarily for the sake of promoting social
and patriotic values. Ironically, the *Kinder- und Hausmärchen*, which
had formerly been condemned for its supposed lack of social values,
was now promoted because of them. Wilhelm II made a conscious
effort to revive national folklore and history in the German schools,
hoping that such an emphasis would enhance the spirit of patriotism
in the name of Christianity while building a bulwark against socialism
and communism, which he despised.

To implement his reforms, he engaged the educational theorists Georg Herbart and Tuiscon Ziller. Within the context of the so-called "*Volkserziehungsprogramm*" (folk-education program), they now began to reevaluate folktales as "positive forces" in childhood education for the sake of perpetuating the existing order of the state. On the surface, both Christian ideals and conventional morality were to be derived from an intensive study of Geman folklore, literature, and history, yet the primary goal was the order of the state. While paying lip service to the folktales' simplicity of style, imaginative quality, and concern with nature and society, Ziller advised teachers to screen them primarily for their usefulness within the context of German folk education.[71]

In preparing discussion guides for teachers, he gave a step-by-step advice of how such goals were to be accomplished. He told teachers first to emphasize such themes and characters that seemed to document Christian values and conventional morality and then those that appeared to document the native German and Germanic folk tradition. He also showed them how to extract from the Grimms' work some portions of the tales that were ill-suited to revive patriotic sentiments. Tales or passages that did not fit the concept of *Volkserziehung* were supposed to be ignored or eliminated. Discussions of the Grimms' tales "Star Child" and "Ashputtel," for example, were to focus first on the need for trust in God and such Christian virtues as patience, forgiveness, and the love of one's neighbors. Teachers were told to teach children such maxims as "Trust in God!" and "God takes care of everyone!"[72] Yet instead of dwelling extensively on religious themes, they were to move on from here to talk about the life of the individual within the German folk community. In that sense religion served only as a pretext to discuss patriotic and national values. The inherent value of the Grimms' folktale collection as a whole and the international orientation of the Grimms' notes and prefaces received no attention at all.

Ziller also ignored in this context some serious objections to folktales that had been voiced by religious groups earlier in the century in regard to some "pagan elements" in the tales that supposedly manifested themselves in their cruelties and concept of justice. Deploring the themes of hatred and revenge in the *Kinder- und Hausmärchen* and finding them detrimental to their efforts of teaching children the Christian concept of love and forgiveness, religious groups had condemned the work as a "heathen book." It is ironic that Ziller and other educators should now recommend the Grimms' folktales because of their Christian spirit. The values had changed, yet the didactic emphasis was still present, and both the opponents and the defendants of the *Kinder- und Hausmärchen* used similar selective approaches to the tales to support their arguments on either side of the fence.

Ziller raised the Grimms' *Kinder- und Hausmärchen* to a level of prime importance within the curriculum, calling it a "household book" of the German people. In this effort, however, he did not care to defend the folktales for their own sake but rather for their usefulness in German folk education. This is particularly evident in his interpretation of "The Bremen Town Musicians." Evidently, it was his main concern to teach respect for property, which is not a theme that is an integral part of the tale itself. He pointed out didactically that the donkey, the dog, the cat, and the cock had shunned decent work, and instead of looking for a new job, they had behaved like mean thieves when they broke into a home in the forest. He failed to point out that each one of these characters was of retirement age and had received from their masters nothing but abuse. He also did not mention that the "home in the forest" had been taken over by robbers and was not the property of a respectable neighbor. Such a willful distortion of the folktale's original meaning made Ziller's interpretation more like a moralistic tract than a meaningful discussion guide.[73]

In the second half of the nineteenth century there also appeared in print some moralistic additions to folktales, emphasizing the value of family based on solid moral foundations. To make sure that children would derive some moral lessons from the tales, regardless of whether they were related to them or not, some editors would go so far as to print morals at the end of each tale. Such additions included: "Oh, how glad I am that I have good parents!" or "A good child obeys instantly!" or "Whoever does evil things will be punished!"[74] were also meant to appease some parents who still held some reservations against folktales. Wilhelm and Jacob Grimm would have recoiled from the use of such morals or maxims, considering them contradictory to the poetic nature and epic substance of folktales. Not only were such additions alien to the folktale style, but they also deprived children of their own imaginative interpretations of folktales.

In 1895 Dr. Ernst Siecke spoke in Berlin "On the Significance of Grimms' Folktales for Our Nation." His lecture was sponsored by the local chapter of the Pan-Germanic League, which pursued the strengthening of German national consciousness and the unity of all German regions. The league began its formation in 1890 and was formally organized in 1894. As in several other groups of the Germanic movement that preceded it, the members of the league aimed at promoting German *Kultur* at home and abroad, with the ultimate goal of "fostering a racial and cultural kinship of all sections of the German people."[75]

Rather than assessing the literary value of the Grimms' *Kinder- und Hausmärchen*, Siecke hoped to underscore its national significance, from the perspective of both the past and the future. The league, he added, whose ideological objective it was "to form the cement that will spiritually keep together the separate members of our folk community," recognized the value that the work had for the nation as a whole. The Grimms' folktales actually represented only a fraction of the many tales that were still alive among the German people, yet more than all other collected tales they represented the very essence of "Germandom." It was a great credit to the Brothers Grimm that they had rediscovered whatever was childlike, naive, and natural in German folklore, thus adding dignity to the German and Germanic past. He reminded his readers of the earlier "misguided" emphasis of Frederick the Great, who had promoted only a taste for French architecture and the French language, preferring the poetry of Virgil to that of Homer and despising the *Song of the Nibelung* along with everything that was German.

In his discussion of the Grimms' folktales, Siecke underscored the German and Hessian origin of the tales, as if the Grimms had made such a universal claim without hinting at variants in other cultures. Granted, he said, some tales had come to Germany from the Orient, and a few other foreign traits, too, had become intermingled with the German ones, but this had little significance and in no way diminished the German character of these German tales. When commenting on the great number of folktale collections that had been published in the wake of the *Kinder- und Hausmärchen*, he used Wilhelm Grimm's own words: "How lonely our collection used to be when it was first published, and what a rich crop has sprung up since that time . . ."[76] Yet whereas Wilhelm Grimm had referred in almost sixty long pages to international folktale collections as well, Siecke listed only publications of German regional folktales next to German collections in Austria, Swabia, and Alsace-Lorraine. Not with one word did he hint at the great impact that the work had on folktale collections around the world.

Dr. Siecke perceived it as his main task to prove two particular points: First, he claimed that the Grimms' folktales were the remnants of an old faith shared by the German forefathers. None of the Grimms' folktales should ever be changed, he insisted, as they were like holy ancestral shrines dating back thousands of years. The remaining foundations of this shrine should serve all future German children and children's children not as a memory of heathen days and worship but as a reminder of their faith in the future of the German *Volk*. Secondly, Dr. Siecke insisted that these German forefathers had been identical not just with the Germanic tribes but also with the Indo-Germanic tribes. In this context, he blurred the distinction between Germanic and Indo-Germanic while using these terms interchangeably. While dedicating the bulk of his thirty-five-page essay to astral-mythological and solar interpretation of folktales applied to such characters Snow White, Thousand-Furs, and Sleeping Beauty, with numerous references to the *Edda*, he made no attempt to draw upon folktale comparisons outside of the Nordic Germanic sphere, not even to those that had been mentioned in abundance in the Grimms' own notes. In conclusion he wrote: "I repeat: In these tales we possess a treasure of common beliefs and worldviews that will not only sustain and strengthen our folk consciousness but that will also help us overbridge the many differences that separate us from each other."[77]

Heinrich Wolgast had emphasized the need for a liberation from didacticism of every kind, including freedom from a moralistic, socialist, or chauvinist bias in children's books. Deploring the general abuse of children's literature for extraliterary purposes, he had successfully advocated aesthetic, literary, and artistic approaches to children's books that would preserve a world-open perspective. His major work of 1896, *Das Elend in unserer Jugendliteratur* (*The Deplorable State of our Youth Literature*),[78] found a warm response among many educators who also supported him in his endeavor of founding the first professional children's literature journal, *Die Jugendschriften-Warte*, and the first professional children's literature movement, the *Jugendschriftenbewegung* (Youth Book movement). Wolgast belonged to the earlier *Kunsterziehungsbewegung* (Art Education movement), founded in Hamburg a few years earlier, and had initially supported the idea that art and folklore were to be used to cure German civilization from the superficialities of a fragmented modern lifestyle. Under the leadership of Alfred Lichtwark and Ferdinand Avenarius, art education was also meant to counteract cosmopolitanism while establishing a link between art, morality, and nationalism.[79] When turning to children's literature, however, Wolgast felt that more was needed than a national emphasis that all too often turned into chauvinism. Thus he demanded that children's books be works of literature and art — not functional books serving the purpose of one or another interest group. As quality was his main concern, he tried to bring to children the very best that the world had to offer. Among other books, he published German folk songs and nursery rhymes under the title of *Schöne Kinderreime* (*Beautiful Children's Rhymes*), along with the tales of the Brothers Grimm, the tales by Wilhelm Hauff, and the *Nibelungenlied* (*Song of the Nibelung*), and also a number of international classics. In regard to children's book illustrations, too, he promoted the highest standards. Judging by the long-range impact of their efforts, Wolgast and his movement were successful — at least during the first two decades of the twentieth century and again after World War II.[80]

In 1897 the German Youth movement began in Steglitz, and two years later the *Wandervogel* movement, revising at campfires the old German folk songs, folktales, myths, and legends. Both called attention to links with the German and Germanic past while building their hope for a national future. The folklore revival of the German Youth movement in some respects resembled its counterpart during the German Romantic movement, with the difference that it combined storytelling with such activities as marching, hiking, camping, and solstice celebrations in the Old Germanic style.[81] In 1921 there came the Prussian School Reform, emphasizing the need for a renewal of German folklore in the public schools, and in the successive years the German minister of the interior issued a decree that stressed the central role of German folktales, legends, sagas, and history in the curriculum.[82]

In the wake of such developments, Severin Rüttgers fought for the systematic implementation of German folklore in the curriculum. As early as 1914 he had advocated in *Deutsche Dichtung in der Volksschule* (*German Literature in the Elementary School*) the "spiritual renaissance" of the German people, demanding of the schools a conscious return to German "roots" through an emphasis on the native folk heritage. In various publications he laid out plans on how German educators might overcome what he called an "obsession" with critical, artistic, and purely literary perspectives on children's literature. Defying Wolgast's notion that aesthetics should play a role in the selection of children's books, he elaborated on the "communical function" of language and the need to revive it through national folklore. He believed that language, literature, and education expressed the "natural functions of the community" and were to be cultivated as such. Therefore it was less important that children learned to distinguish "good" literature from *Schundliteratur* (trash) than to feel the pulse of their "homegrown" literature and folklore. As German folktales and Germanic myths and legends were the spiritual basis of German community life, he said, they should play a central role in the school curriculum. He also issued several series of books for children that contributed to the German and Germanic folklore emphasis, including *Blaue Bändchen* (*Little Blue Volumes*) and *Quellen* (*Sources*). The term "German blood and fate"— an expression echoed in many publications during Hitler's regime — originally came from Severin Rüttgers.[83]

Overall, however, children's book publications during the Weimar Republic were still characterized by a variety of trends rather than by a one-sided nationalistic emphasis. Even Rüttgers himself still published next to *Nordische Heldensagen* (*Nordic Hero Tales*) a book of Christian legends, and side by side with numerous German folktale collections there still appeared in print a number of books that were banned or no longer recommended after the Nazis came to power. Among these were such children's classics as Jonathan Swift's *Gulliver's Travels*, Harriet Beecher Stowe's *Uncle Tom's Cabin*, Mark Twain's *Tom Sawyer*, and Charles Dickens' *Oliver Twist*, as well as such young adult books as Scharrelmann's *Piddl Hundertmark* (*Piddl One-Hundred-Marks*), dealing with contemporary problems, or Remarque's *Im Westen nichts Neues* (*All Quiet on the Western Front*), focusing on the horrors of war.[84]

[Political-Ideological Approaches: The Nazi Era]

Shortly after the Nazis seized power in 1933, they called for a conscious cultivation of German folklore on all levels of education, claiming that they wished to continue the legacy of Johann Gottfried

Herder and the Brothers Grimm. By means of nationwide curricular reforms and a series of folklore publications for young and old, they implemented a new folklore policy that became binding for all public schools and the Hitler Youth Organization. For teachers and youth leaders they organized conferences and workshops that were meant to help them to implement National Socialist guidelines for a new and uniform interpretation of the national folk heritage. In spite of various political quarrels, party and state organizations agreed not only on the official banning of "folk-alien" literature in schools, libraries, and bookstores around the country but also on a simultaneous promotion of "heroic literature," which included a systematic promotion of folktales, myths, and legends of German and Nordic Germanic origin.[85]

The Nazis' renewed interest in German national folktales was partially founded in a search for national "roots," but more so in a quest for national unity. In their view, national folk traditions were to be exploited not just for "romantic" reasons of glorifying the past but for the sake of ideological goals aimed at building the National Socialist future. This implied that folktales were to be used selectively for the purpose of disseminating the National Socialist *Weltanschauung*.[86]

The selective folklore policy under the Nazi regime essentially deprived German children of international folktale editions as well as of Christian tales and legends. At the same time, it promoted a folktale interpretation with a Nordic Germanic and racial orientation. Publishers were instructed to add new prefaces to older folklore publications and to issue folktale discussion guides for teachers and youth leaders that would emphasize the spirit of the National Socialist *Weltanschauung*.

With its centralized control, the cultural policy of the Third Reich led to a highly selective approach to folktales in general and to the Grimms' *Kinder- und Hausmärchen* in particular. While the Nazis promoted German folktales on an unprecedented scale, they ignored folktales of other lands as well as tales by the Brothers Grimm that did not seem to fit their educational plans. They also distorted some traditional folk values that did not seem to fit the ideological scheme. In the name of the "Nordic past," the "unity of the German folk community," and desired "role models" for German children and youth, editors at that time took substantial liberties in reshaping the Grimms' folktales in accordance with ideological goals.

Nazi critics of the Grimms' folktale collection claimed a straight line of continuity from German Romanticism to the Third Reich, pretending that the Brothers Grimm had already prophesied the coming of German "folk community." In doing so, they used a highly selective approach to the *Kinder- und Hausmärchen*, both in discussion guides and new editions of the work. New prefaces would praise folkish contribution of the Grimms, emphasizing repeatedly their Nordic and German emphasis and research interest, as if these had been as racial and exclusive in nature as the Nazi ideology.[87] They presented the Brothers

Grimm themselves in such a way that they appeared like fanatic Germanists and nationalists with an ethnocentric point of view. Saying little or nothing about their international folktale research, their translations of foreign works, their concern with democratic principles, or their Christian faith, the Nazis made the Brothers Grimm appear like forerunners of the Nazi regime. Some newer folktale editions deleted not only all notes and prefaces but also the Grimms' Christian legends and biblical references within the tales, be it in relation to Mother Mary, St. Peter, the Archangel, or the Devil. Ernst Dobers and Kurt Higelke's guidebook for elementary schoolteachers suggested that new editions rearrange the Grimms' folktales with new ideological headings, such as: "The Strongest One Always Wins" or "Might is Always Right," so as to demonstrate more clearly the folktales' linkage with the Nazis "master race" concept.[88]

According to the new interpretation guidelines, the Grimms' "German" folktale characters had demonstrated their racial superiority in every respect. Following their "racial instincts," they fought for their goals with determination and success and usually chose a marriage partner from the common people, so as to "upgrade" their racial strength. Joseph Prestel considered German folktales as *community tales* in the best sense of the word, as they supposedly provided young readers with excellent role models of "folkish virtues." Thus he wrote: "In vivid images folktales mirror the ethical world. . . . Yet [today], they become a direct visual reflection of such folkish virtues as loyalty, steadfastness, endurance, fearless courage in male protagonists, and a sense of sacrifice, humble devotion, and pity in female protagonists."[89] By "folkish virtues" he did not mean traditional virtues of courage, sacrifice, and devotion as they had been understood for centuries. "Folkish" implied that they were tainted with ideological intent, mainly in relation to the *Volk* as a whole. As such, folktale characters were to serve as models for German children and youth within the new German "folk community" of the Third Reich. Their heroic fighting spirit and devotion to the Führer were meant to indicate that no sacrifice was too great if it served the glory of the Third Reich and its leader, the Führer.

In looking for German and Nordic character types and archetypes in native folktales, myths, and legends, the Nazis tried to create the impression that they were continuing to do what the Grimms had done themselves a long time ago. In that manner they hoped to establish a certain legitimacy to their ideological goals. Occasionally, they also simulated the voice of C. G. Jung by invoking what they said were "archetypes" that spoke with "one voice" for the nation, so as to lead the German *Volk* to its glorious destiny. Such allusions, too, were meant to establish the legitimacy of the Nazi regime and its pursuit of ideological goals. Yet whereas Jung had spoken about archetypes in terms of *liberating* the individual in his inner quest for self-knowledge, the Nazis spoke only from the individual's *bondage* in relation to *Volk* and Führer.

Jung had considered the individual human being unique unto himself, capable of discovering through archetypes his own creative potential.[90] The Nazis, by contrast, urged the individual only to become a "folk personality" in which the self would be subordinated to the German Reich. "*Du bist nichts! Dein Volk ist alles!*" ("You are nothing! Your *Volk* is everything!") proclaimed the Nazi posters. Children were told to identify with folktale heroes not as individuals but as potential members of the larger unit: the German folk community. Nothing could have been farther remote from an inner quest for self-knowledge. Jung had conceived of archetypes as involuntary a priori ideas that could not be ascertained except by their effect.[91] The Nazis consciously constructed archetypes in an effort to subordinate the individual to the German folk community, to the "will" of the Führer. In designing their "pseudo-archetypes" on the basis of traditional folktales and myths, they cared very little about traditional values and rather distorted them in the process. Contrary to C. G. Jung, they had a deep contempt for whatever human beings might have in common on a worldwide scale, for it was not the Nazis' aim to study either folklore or human psychology but to manipulate people for their own political ends. In such a context, the Grimms' folktale collection, too, was to the Nazis mainly a political tool and a means of ideological indoctrination.

One may wonder what happened in this context to all those character types in the Grimms' folktales that did not fit the new ideology. The answer was simple: They were omitted from discussions and new folktale anthologies. In that sense, the censors proceeded on a similar selective basis as had those of the old didactic school. Such a censorship applied, for example, to "stupid peasants" or naive simpletons in folktales whom some extremists considered "unworthy" of consideration within the new racial peasant policy that tried to project the image of racial strength and superiority. Dobers and Higelke considered a character like Dummling or Boots too slow-witted, too sluggish, and altogether too unheroic to serve as a role model for German children and therefore suggested that stories about him be ignored in new anthologies.[92] They also thought him much too pacifistic to be a descendant of the heroic peasant warrior of the Nordic Germanic past. We may perceive how far remote such criteria were from Wilhelm Grimm's if we recall how fond he was of Dummling as the archetype of a naive peasant character who symbolized the radiance of purity and genuine kindness. Purity and kindness were the very qualities that, in Wilhelm's view, had added the "humane touch" to folktales.[93] From the Nazis' point of view, such qualities had no relevance to the new man of the future. Significant in this context was the folktale hero's "fighting attitude." In an essay "The Folktale Story Hour as a Preparation for History Lessons," Dietrich Klagges claimed that the basic theme of all folktales was fight:

> But it is not fight per se, not fight by all means, but the ethical
> fight that has to be fought against evil and destructive forces,
> against evil in every form. It is the fight which serves the sur-
> vival and resurrection of an organized, healthy, and therefore
> ethical order of life.[94]

He clearly identified this "ethical order of life" with the order of the
German folk community under the leadership of Adolf Hitler. By no
means did such an ideological view of folktales overtax the understanding of a seven-year-old. To prove his point, he cited a conversation with
a four-year-old girl. "Father," she had asked him after listening to a
folktale by the Brothers Grimm, "who is the most courageous person
in the world?" "Well," the father had replied, "I don't really know, but
perhaps you know the answer." "It's you and Adolf Hitler!" the little
girl had responded. According to Klagges, this answer proved that the
Grimms' folktales were ideally suited even for the youngest children
to teach the social virtues of the Third Reich.

To achieve a maximum effect with the new folktale interpretation,
Klagges suggested the following methods:

1. Select suitable folktales and legends.
2. Choose new subtitles and headings for folktales.
3. Emphasize the fighting attitude of the heroes.
4. Summarize frequently the protagonists' folkish virtues.[95]

The last point implied that editors were asked to interrupt the folktale
narrative periodically for the sake of getting across an ideological point
of view.

Essentially, didactic writers of previous centuries had used a similar
method in talking down to children. The substance of the message had
changed but the didactic method of preaching was still the same. As
in earlier days, folktales were not appreciated for their own sake but
mainly for teaching some lessons on virtues and vices—in this case,
for teaching the ideology of the Third Reich.

In 1936 a prominent article in *Zeitschrift für deutsche Bildung* (*Journal
for German Education*) proposed two approaches to the Grimms'
Kinder- und Hausmärchen. The first was to show how the folktale symbolized the *German* way of life and thought. The second approach
was to indicate step-by-step how folktales gave proof of older German
myths rooted in the Nordic Germanic past. Both approaches were meant
to lead children to the recognition that German myths and folktales
were steeped in symbols of life and war. On the one hand, there were
numerous symbols of trees, water, swans, frogs, the moon, the spindle,
and the sun, all of which represented life (as well as nature, instinct,
and German "blood consciousness"), and on the other hand there were
symbols of war, represented by giants, dragons, wolves, and Midgard-

Snake. The world of Germanic man was a world of fight, of honor, of self-sacrifice, said author Ulrich Haacke, that should serve as a model to young people:

> The worldview of Germanic man is tragic one, but at the same time, it represents a *positive* attitude toward life. The deciding factor is that the individual faces his fate; that he shows his determination, his readiness to act; that he will not start wavering under the influence of external events but, on the contrary, that his character will be steeled and strengthened in proportion to the burden of his fate, and that in spite of his natural love of life he will rise above his individual self.[96]

Rising above one's self meant only one thing during the Third Reich: to sacrifice one's own will to the will of the Führer and, if necessary, to sacrifice one's life as well.

In 1938 the *Workshop for German Folklore* (*Arbeitsgemeinschaft für Deutsche Volkskunde*) brought out an annotated bibliography that was published by the National Socialist Party (*Zentralverlag der N.S.D.A.P.*). It was meant as a guide for educators as well as for leaders of the Hitler Youth. Among other books, the Grimms' *Kinder- und Hausmärchen* received major attention. In glowing terms, the reviewers reappraised the work as "a gift to the German folk" and a "house book" (*Hausbuch*) for the nation.[97] Such words strongly evoke the praise that Goethe uttered in response to *The Boy's Magic Horn*.[98] Goethe, too, had expressed the wish that it might become a true *Hausbuch* for every household in the nation—without, however, wishing to utilize it for the sake of political propaganda. Rather, such words came closer to Siecke's Pan-Germanic call for a "household book" that would unify the German nation. The *Workshop* praised the Grimms for having initiated a scientific perspective on Germanic traditions that until then had hardly been recognized, in the sense that they had supposedly discovered the thoroughly *German* and Nordic Germanic character of the folktales. As a common heritage of the German *Volk*, the work had great meaning today for the entire nation, as it might "weld together" the entire folk community.

In discussing Bolte and Polivka's scholarly study of the Grimms' *Kinder- und Hausmärchen*, a classic work had emphasized the Grimms' international perspective on folktale research at the beginning of the century, the *Workshop* pointed out that modern folklore, as "a young National Socialist science," might profit greatly from its bibliographical selections that pertained to folktales in "Greater Germany." It mentioned selectively folktales from "German regions and landscapes," such as Pomerania, Posen, Silesia, Hesse, Rhineland, Lower Saxony, the Harz Mountains, Mecklenburg, Westphalia, Lower Austria, etc., but not a single international folktale collection listed in this work. In a one-sided effort to raise the German consciousness at home and abroad, it also ignored Bolte and Polivka's substantial references to the Grimms' international variants and foreign correspondence and their translations, thus giving the impression that they had been concerned only with German and Nordic Germanic perspectives. This impression was further strengthened by the *Workshop*'s appraisal of Matthes Ziegler's *The Woman in Folktales (Die Frau im Märchen)*,[99] a work with a strong racial emphasis that had been issued within the series of *German Ancestral Heritage (Deutsches Ahnenerbe)*. Ziegler gave what the *Workshop* called "a comprehensive picture of women as they appeared in folktales, and . . . a total view of the Nordic image of women in folklore." According to Ziegler, the folktale was a characteristic narrative of the Nordic race — a view that, according to the *Workshop*, was identical with that of the Brothers Grimm. Without bothering to explain in what sense the Grimms had advocated a "racial" point of view, the *Workshop* praised Ziegler's interpretation as if it were a perfect match of the Grimms' philosophy of life.

The *Workshop* gave high praise to Maria Führer's interpretation that had viewed the *Kinder- und Hausmärchen* of the Brothers Grimm exclusively from a "Nordic Germanic" and racial perspective.[100] Far from being skeptical toward her extremely selective and distorted view, the *Workshop* commended her on an "objective" interpretation of German folktales, adding that with its emphasis on the "myths of our people and our race," it stood out favorably against some rather subjective and arbitrary interpretations. By grouping the Grimms' folktales under such new subheadings as "Worlds and Halls of Asgard," "Nordic Germanic Gods and Goddesses," "The World Ash Yggdrasil," and "The Water of Life," she had paid homage to a beautiful and familiar Nordic worldview that was to be especially recommended to educators and youth leaders.

Some aspects of the Nazis' folklore interpretation may be traced back to Pan-Germanic and racial thought around the turn of the century, but now they emerged on a large scale as the only policy promoted by a totalitarian regime. As such, it was more than a "didactic trend" enhancing the value system of a particular interest group, bourgeois, religious, or otherwise. The new "folkish" didacticism was aimed at promoting the ideals of blind followership within the folk community of the future. Both party and state censorship offices used a vast bureaucratic machinery to control children's literature through curricular and library reforms and various decrees on "cultural guidance." By promoting the Grimms' folktales on a selective basis and in a distorted way, they tried to enhance a narrow racial and ethnocentric ideology that was intended to indoctrinate children and youth in the "fighting spirit" of the future.[101]

In their selective approach to folktales, the Nazis emphasized a new paganism that was but an extension of their folkish propaganda. While denying the Grimms' broader international perspective on folktale research, they also denied the Grimms' essential concern with a vast spectrum of human qualities, including kindness, gentility, altruism, and empathy for others.

NOTES

1. Joseph Prestel, "Das Märchen" in *Handbuch der Jugendliteratur. Geschichte der deutschen Jugendschriften* (Freiburg i. Brsg.: Herder Verlag, 1933), pp. 185–93. For a general discussion of didactic trends prior to the Grimms' time, see also Ulrike Bastian, *Die Kinder- und Hausmärchen in der literaturpädagogischen Betrachtung* (Frankfurt am Main: M. Haag und Herchen, 1986).

2. John Locke, *Some Thoughts Concerning Education* (London: 1745) Repr. ed. (Cambridge: The University Press, 1880), and Samuel Pickering, *John Locke and Children's Books in 18th Century England* (Knoxville: University of Tennessee Press, 1981), pp. 40–70.

3. Harvey Darton, *Children's Books in England*, 3d ed. rev., Brian Alderson, ed. (Cambridge: Cambridge University Press, 1982, p. 111. See also John Rowe Townsend, *Written for Children. An Outline of English Language Children's Literature* (Boston: The Horn Book Inc. and Lippincott, 1974), pp. 27–36.

4. Jean Jacques Rousseau, *Emile*, B. Foxley, trans. (London: J. M. Dent & Sons, 1911).

5. See also Patricia Demers and Gordon Moyles, eds., *From Instruction to Delight. An Anthology of Children's Literature to 1850* (Toronto: Oxford University Press, 1982), pp. 120–22.

6. Rousseau, pp. 147–48. Rousseau thought that *Robinson Crusoe* showed boys how to preserve life and how to procure a certain amount of comfort. Stripped of all irrelevant matters, Robinson learned by doing, not by reading books. He expected boys to take the world as it was, not as it appeared to be, hoping that necessity would motivate them to work toward some practical ends. He judged work in general mainly by its contribution to personal usefulness, safety, self-preservation, and comfort.

7. John Newbery, *Mother Goose's Melody; Sonnets for the Cradle; Instruction with Delight* (London: about 1765. The exact publication date is unknown. The second edition, by Francis Power, was issued in 1791.) The work contained fifty nursery rhymes and twenty pages of songs from Shakespeare. Townsend, p. 133.

8. Darton, pp. 85–106.

9. Townsend, pp. 39–41.

10. Maria Edgeworth, *The Parent's Assistant* Part II, Vol. I (London: Stockdale, of Piccadilly, 1796). Richard Lovell Edgeworth, Maria Edgeworth's father, had a similar concept for fairy tales.

11. Darton, p. 148.

12. Darton, p. 140.

13. Ibid. For an early critical review of Maria Edgeworth's books from a didactic perspective consult *The Juvenile Review or Moral and Critical Observations in Children's Books; Intended as a Guide to Parents and Teachers in Their Choice of Books of Instruction and Amusement*. Part I (London: Printed for N. Hailes Juvenile Library, London Museum, Piccadilly, 1817), repr. in two parts (Toronto: Toronto Public Library and the Friends of the Osborne and Lillian Smith Collections, 1982), p. 16.

14. *The Guardian of Education* (1802–1806). The editor stated the intent of the journal as follows: "To Assist in the Choice of Books for instruction and amusement of Children and Youth, as far as Principles of Religion and good morals

are concerned." Some book reviews of this journal were reprinted in Nicholas Tucker, ed., *Suitable for Children? Controversies in Children's Literature* (Berkeley: University of California Press, 1976), pp. 37–41.

15. See Humphrey Carpenter and Mari Prichard, eds., *The Oxford Companion to Children's Literature* (New York: Oxford University Press, 1985), p. 231.

16. Sarah Trimmer, *Fabulous Histories. Designed for the Instruction of Children, respecting Treatment of Animals* (London: T. Longman, 1786). The work later became known under the title of *History of Two Robins*. Pickering, pp. 19–29.

17. Darton, p. 127.

18. Marie Catherine Comtesse d'Aulnoy, *The Tales of the Fairies in Three Parts, Compleat (sic)*. (Extracted from the second edition in English of *The Diverting Works of the Countess d'Anois*, London, 1715). rprt. ed. (New York: Garland Publishing, Inc., 1977). See Preface by Michael Patrick Hearn, pp. v–xi. Countess d'Aulnoy's *Contes des fées* was first published in Paris in 1697. According to Hearn, no copies of the first English trans by T. Cockerill (London, 1699) have survived. D'Aulnoy's name also appears under such spellings as d'Anois, d'Aulnoi, and Dunois, and her works were published under such titles as *The History of the Tales of the Fairies* (London, 1716), *The Court of Queen Mab* (London, 1752), and *Mother Bunch's Fairy Tales* (London, 1773).

19. Iona and Peter Opie, *The Classic Fairy Tales* (New York: Oxford University Press, 1974), pp. 14–15.

20. Darton, pp. 89–91.

21. Henry Brooke, *A New Collection of Fairy Tales; Containing many Useful Lessons, Moral Sentiments, Surprising Incidents, and Amusing Adventures* 2 vols. (London: Printed for R. Dodsley in Pall Mall, Holborn C. Hitch in Pater-Noster Row, W. Bowyer in Whitechapel, and S. Fryer and G. Woodfall at Charing-Cross, 1750). A rare copy of this edition is a part of the Lucile Clarke Memorial Children's Library, at the Clarke Historical Library, Central Michigan University, Mt. Pleasant, Michigan. No review of the work has appeared so far.

22. Ibid., Vol. 1, Part 2, p. 47.

23. Ibid., Vol. 1, Part 4, p. 206.

24. Charles Perrault, *Contes de ma mère l'oye. Histoires due temps passé avec des moralités* (Paris: Claude Barbin, 1896). The first edition of this work appeared anonymously, yet it contained a dedication signed by P. Darmoncour, who was the son of Charles Perrault. Some critics believe that Pierre was the author, as an earlier manuscript of the work, too, was signed "P. P." See Carpenter and Prichard, p. 402. Other critics have suggested that Perrault used a pseudonym.

25. M. M. Grimm (sic.), *German Popular Stories and Fairy Tales as Told by Gammer Grethel*, Edgar Taylor, rev. trans. (London: George Bell & Sons, 1874). Ill. by George Cruikshank and Ludwig Grimm. This work was based on the second revised translation of 1829.

26. Ibid., "Hansel and Grethel," p. 266.

27. Ibid., "The Frog Prince," p. 214.

28. Ibid., "The Blue Light," p. 195.

29. Ibid., "Ashputtel," p. 51.

30. Katherine M. Briggs, "The Influence of the Brothers Grimm in England" in *Brüder Grimm Gedenken*, Ludwig Denecke, ed., Vol. 1 (Marburg; Elwert Verlag, 1963), pp. 511–25. Briggs referred to Thomas Crofton Croker and S. O. Addy as the earliest exponent of the Grimm methods, but also gave credit to E. S. Hartland and Andrew Lang for having examined the Grimms' theory of folktale origin and dispersion. In her view, the moralizing stories of Countess d'Aulnoy and the later authors of what came to be popularly known as the "*Cabinet des fées*" had substantially weakened the English folktale tradition earlier in the century. See p. 514.

31. Benjamin Tabart, *Fairy Tales of the Lilliputian Cabinet; Containing twenty-four Choice Pieces of Fancy and Fiction* (London: Tabart & Company, 1818). See also *Quarterly Review* 21 (1919), 91–114. The article contained a rather negative review of Tabart's work yet high praise of the *Kinder- und Hausmärchen* by the Brothers Grimm.

32. Series: *Home Treasury of Books, Toys, etc. purposed to cultivate the Affection, Fancy, Imagination, and Taste of Children*, Felix Summerly, ed. (London: Joseph Cundall, 1843–1847). Later works in this series were published in London by Chapman and Hill.

33. Series: *Classics in Children's Literature: The Garland Collection*, Justin Schiller, ed. (New York: Garland, 1975), Vol. I. See Margaret Crawford Maloney, Introduction.

34. Ibid., Vol. 1, "Red Riding Hood."

35. Ibid., "Jack the Giant-Killer."

36. Ibid.

37. Gillian Avery, "Fairy Tales with a Purpose," in *Nineteenth Century Children: Heroes and Heroines in English Children's Stories 1780–1900*, Gillian Avery, ed. (London: Hodder and Stoughton, Limited, 1965), pp. 41–48. On *The Holiday House*, consult Carpenter and Prichard, p. 256.

38. Richard Green Parker, *Fairy Fairstar's Cabinet of Gems* in Series: *New and Original Toy Books* (Boston: A. Park, 1854).

39. A list of complete titles in the series is given on the back page of the cover.

40. George Cruikshank, "Cinderella," in the series: *The Fairy Library*, George Cruikshank, ed. (London: Bell and Daldy, 1870). Reprinted by Tucker, p. 43. Cruikshank's "Cinderella" first appeared in 1853. His versions of "Jack and the Beanstalk" and "Puss in Boots," were also first published individually before they came out in *The Fairy Library*. See also: Darton, pp. 98–99.

41. Cruikshank, p. 44.

42. Charles Dickens, "Frauds on the Fairies," *Household Word* 184 (October 1859). Tucker, ed., p. 53.

43. Ibid., pp. 54–55.

44. Townsend, pp. 90–100.

45. See Charles Kingsley, *The Heroes; or Greek Fairy Tales for My Children* 2d ed. (New York: E. P. Dutton, 1885). Preface by Charles Kingsley, p. 9. This work was first published in 1856.

46. Darton, p. 254.

47. Juliana Horatia Ewing, *Old-Fashioned Fairy Tales* (New York: Society for Promoting Christian Knowledge; Pott & Young, 1848). Preface, pp. vi–vii.

48. Andrew Lang. *The Blue Fairy Book* (London: Longmans, Green, 1889). Among Lang's series titled *Colour Fairy Books* (London: Longman's Green, 1884–1910) were such titles as *The Red Fairy Book* (1890), *The Yellow Fairy Book* (1894), *The Pink Fairy Book* (1892), *The Violet Fairy Book* (1901), and *The Lilac Fairy Book* (1910). An anthologized version of this international folktale and fairy tale series is available under the title: *The Andrew Lang Fairy Tale Book* (New York: Signet New American Library, 1981).

49. Richard M. Dorson, *The British Folklorists. A History* (Chicago: University of Chicago Press, 1968), pp. 208–10; 218.

50. Ibid., pp. 269–70.

51. "On Reading; Editorial," *Sergent's School Monthly* (January 1858), p. 3.

52. Anna Fergurson, *The Young Lady* (Lowell, Mass.: N. L. Dayton, 1848), p. 71.

53. John M. Gregory, *School Funds and School Laws of Michigan; with Notes and Forms, to which are added Elements of School Architecture, with Lists of Text Books and Library Books* (Lansing, Mi.: Office of the Superintendent, 1859), p. 425.

54. *Catalogue of the Public Library Bay City* (Bay City, Mi.: Bay City Public Library, 1878).

55. Superintendent of Public Instruction, *Forty-eighth Annual Report; with accompanying documents for the year 1887* (Lansing, Mi.: Office of the Superintendent, 1888). See also W. L. Smith, *Education in Michigan* (Lansing, Mi.: Office of the Superintendent, 1881), p. 57.

56. "The Vice of Reading," *Littell's Living Age*, 8, No. 2582 (Oct. 3, 1874) and "Bad Literature," *Isabella County Enterprise*, Mt. Pleasant, Mi., May 21, 1879. Youth Column, 3.

57. Edwin McClellan, "The Educational Ideas of Philip Tappan," *Michigan History* (Mar. 1954), pp. 69–78.

58. Christa Kamenetsky, "In Quest of Virtue; Popular Trends Reflected in Children's Literature in Nineteenth Century Michigan," *Keystone Folklore Quarterly* (Summer 1965), pp. 63–85.

59. Lydia Very, *Red Riding Hood* (Boston, Ma.: L. Prang & Company, 1863), reprint, Washington, D.C.: Library of Congress, 1985.

60. For a discussion of a great variety of Red Riding Hood tales throughout history, including their origin, analysis, and parodies, consult Hans Ritz, *Die Geschichte von Rotkäppchen: Ursprünge, Analysen und Parodien eines Märchens* (Emstal: Muri Verlag, 1981), and Jack Zipes, *The Trials and Tribulations of Little Red Riding Hood. Versions of the Tale in Sociocultural Context* (South Hadley: Bergin and Garvey Publ. Inc., 1983).

61. See Prestel, *Handbuch*, pp. 166–67. Prestel refers to *Amerikanische Erziehungsblätter* (1885). Much more favorable was an earlier review of Grimms' tales in the *North American Review* (1861), p. 283, which referred to "*German Popular Tales and Household Stories* 2 vols., collected by the Brothers Grimm and newly translated with illustrations by Edward H. Wehnert." See Wayland D. Hand, "Die Märchen der Brüder Grimm in den Vereinigten Staaten" in *Brüder Grimm Gedenken*, Vol. 1, Ludwig Denecke, ed. (Marburg: Elwert, 1963), p. 542 and note 31. For a longer quote from this article (in German translation) see Prestel, pp. 187–88.

62. Ibid.

63. Ibid.

64. "On Reading," *Fourth Reader* of *National Series of Selections for Reading* (New York: A. S. Barnes & Company, 1856), pp. 40–43.

65. Regarding the theme of patriotism in the *McGuffey Readers*, see Henry Steele Commager, *The American Mind. An Interpretation of American Thought and Character Since the 1880s* (New Haven: Yale University Press, 1950), pp. 38–40.

66. Hand, p. 532.

67. Sarah Comstock, "The Story Corner." *St. Nicholas* 41, 4 (February 1914), pp. 308–13.

68. Hand, pp. 530–31.

69. Prestel, pp. 165–68.

70. Ibid.

71. Tuiscon Ziller, "Die Bremer Stadtmusikanten; ethisch—psychologische Zergliederung" *Ethisches Lesebuch* (Leipzig: Dürr'sche Buchhandlung, 1897), pp. 182–84. See also Bastian, pp. 64–65.

72. Karl-Heinrich Hiemesch, *Der Gesinnungsunterricht* (Leipzig, Dürr, 1925), p. 14.

73. Ziller, p. 184; Bastian, p. 64.

74. Hiemesch, p. 14.

75. Ernst Siecke, *Über die Bedeutung der Grimmschen Märchen für unser Volksthum*. Rede, gehalten in der Ortsgruppe Berlin des Alldeutschen Verbandes am 15. März 1895. (Series: *Sammlung gemeinverständlicher wissenschaftlicher Vorträge*) (Hamburg: Königliche Hofverlagshandlung, 1896), pp. 2–3.

76. Ibid., p. 10.

77. Ibid., p. 35. For a discussion of the cultural-political context of the Pan-Germanic League, consult Georg Mosse, *The Crisis of German Ideology. Intellectual Origins of the Third Reich* (New York: Grosset and Dunlap, 1964), pp. 224–26 and Christa Kamenetsky, *Children's Literature in Hitler's Germany. The Cultural Policy of National Socialism* (Athens, Ohio: Ohio University Press, 1984), p. 18.

78. Heinrich Wolgast, *Das Elend in unserer Jugendliteratur; Beiträge zur künstlerischen Erziehung unserer Jugend*, repr. ed. (Hamburg: Selbstverlag, 1950), pp. 12–14. Wolgast became the chief editor of the first professional German children's literature journal, *Die Jugendschriften-Warte*, which aimed at promoting high artistic and aesthetic qualities in children's literature publications. He strongly opposed didactic trends in children's literature.

79. Horst Kunze, ed., *Schatzbehalter alter Kinderbücher. Vom Besten aus der älteren deutschen Kinderliteratur* (Hanau/Main: Verlag Werner Dausien, 1965), pp. 92–94.

80. Wilhelm Fronemann, *Das Erbe Wolgasts* (Langensalza: Beltz Verlag, 1927).

81. The name Wandervogel is the singular form of Wandervögel (migrating birds) and is easily associated with the concepts of hiking and enjoying the outdoors. See also Werner Klose, *Lebensformen deutscher Jugend. Vom Wandervogel zur Popgeneration* (Munich: Günter Olzog Verlag, 1970), and Walther Z. Lacqueur, *Young Germany: A History of the German Youth Movement* (New York: Basic Books, 1962).

82. *Preussische Richtlinien zur Erstellung von Lehrplänen für die Grundschule, March 1921. Erlaß des Innenministers von 1923* (Prussian Guidelines for the Development of Elementary School Curricula, March 1921. Decree of the Reich Minister of the Interior, 1923). Both the Prussian Education Minister's guidelines and the decree emphasized a renewed emphasis on German and Germanic folklore in the curriculum. Cited in Reichsministerium des Innern, eds., *Die Reichsschulkonferenz 1920. Ihre Vorgeschichte und Vorbereitung und ihre Verhandlungen. Amtlicher Bericht* (Leipzig: Dürr'sche Buchhandlung, 1921), p. 698.

83. Severin Rüttgers, *Deutsche Dichtung in der Volksschule* (Leipzig: Dürr'sche Buchhandlung, 1914) and *Erweckung des Volkes durch seine Dichtung* (Leipzig: Dürr'sche Buchhandlung, 1919). The Nazis reprinted the second work by Rüttgers in 1933.

84. Irene Graebsch (Dyrenfurth), *Geschichte des deutschen Jugendbuches* (Leipzig: A. Harrassowitz, 1942), pp. 191–210.

85. Kamenetsky. *Children's Literature in Hitler's Germany*, pp. 236–44.

86. Ibid., pp. 74–84.

87. Christa Kamenetsky, "Folktale and Ideology in the Third Reich" *Journal of American Folklore* 90, 356 (April/June, 1977), pp. 169–78 and "Folklore as a Political Tool in Nazi Germany," *Journal of American Folklore* 85, 337 (July/Sept., 1972), pp. 221–38.

88. Ernst Dobers and Kurt Higelke, eds., *Rassenpolitische Unterrichtsgestaltung der Volksschulfächer* (Leipzig: Klinckhardt, 1940).

89. Prestel, pp. 165–69.

90. C. G. Jung, "On the Relation of Analytical Psychology to Poetry" in *The Portable Jung*, Joseph Campbell, ed., F. C. Hall, trans., (New York: Viking Press, 183), pp. 301–22. Jung distinguishes here between the collective unconscious and the personal unconscious. The Nazis, however, referred only to "collective consciousness" (*Kollektivbewusstsein*). The Nazis employed similar-sounding words and concepts in an effort to strengthen their propaganda efforts. In that sense, they attached ideological meanings to such familiar Romantic terms as "*Volk*," '*Gemeinschaft*," "*romantisch*," and "*Weltanschauung*." Christa Kamenetsky, "Political Distortion of Philosophical Concepts: A Case History—Nazism and the Romantic Movement," *Metaphilosophy* 3, 3 (July, 1973), 198–218.

91. Ibid.

92. Dobers and Higelke, eds. pp. 43–44.

93. Wilhelm Grimm, "Über das Wesen der Märchen" ("About Fairy Tales"). Preface to *Kinder- und Hausmärchen* (Berlin: Reimer, 1919). Reprinted in *Kleinere Schriften von Wilhelm Grimm*, Vol. 1 (Berlin: Dümmler, 1881), Gustav Hinrichs, ed. By comparing the German folktale character *Dummling* with the British Perceval and the French legendary character Rennevart, Wilhelm emphasized the need for viewing folktales on an international basis within the context of the European epic tradition.

94. Dietrich Klagges, "Die Märchenstunde als Vorstufe des Geschichtsunterrichts," *Jugendschriften-Warte* (July/August 1940), pp. 49–51.

95. Ibid., p. 50.

96. Ulrich Haacke, "Germanisch-deutsche Weltanschauung in Märchen und Mythen im Deutschunterricht," *Zeitschrift für deutsche Bildung* 12, 12 (December 1936), pp. 608–12. See also Friedrich Panzer, "Sage und Märchen in ihrer Bedeutung für das Leben der Nation," *Dichtung und Volkstum* 2 (1935), pp. 203–45.

97. *Arbeitsgemeinschaft für deutsche Volkskunde* (Berlin: Zentralverlag der N.S.D.A.P., 1938), p. 3.

98. L. Achim von Arnim and Clemens Brentano, eds., *Des Knaben Wunderhorn: Alte deutsche Lieder* (Munich: Winkler Verlag, 1974), reprint of the complete edition of 1806–1808. In a postscript Willi A. Koch cites Johann Wolfgang von Goethe, p. 897.

99. Matthes Ziegler, *Die Frau im Märchen* (Leipzig: Köhler and Amelang, 1937). See also Ziegler's *Volkskunde auf rassischer Grundlange: Voraussetzungen und Aufgaben*. Series: *Deutsche Volkskunde für Schulungs- und Erziehungsarbeit der N.S.D.A.P.* (Munich: Hoheneichen Verlag, 1939).

100. Maria Führer, *Nordgermanische Götterüberlieferungund deutsches Volkstum. 80 Märchen der Gebrüder Grimm vom Mythus her beleuchtet* (Munich: Neuer Filser Verlag, 1938). This work, which had a pronounced racial bias, was issued and promoted by the Bavarian State Office for Folklore. The National Socialist Teachers Association which in 1933 had taken over the editorship of the *Jugend-Schriftenwarte*, the leading professional children's literature journal, also sanctioned her work. See Maria Führer, "Nordgermanische Götterüberlieferung und deutsche Volksmärchen," *Jugendschriften-Warte* 44, 7 (July 1939), pp. 98–114.

101. Kamenetsky, *Children's Literature in Hitler's Germany*. On the Nazis' folklore interpretation, consult chapters 4, 5, and 6.

10. Interdisciplinary Approaches to the Grimms' Folktales

[Linguistics and Solar Mythology]

I N THE LATE NINETEENTH CEN- tury, Oxford linguist and Sanskrit scholar Max Müller developed a theory that iden- tified the origins of myths and folktales as India. Even though he did not invent the Indo-European myth theory, he was the first one to apply it systematically to com- parative mythology studies while postulat- ing a "mythopoeic" age in which people had spoken a vivid and concrete language. This language, he said, could still be recog- nized in the rich metaphors of myths and folktales. Originally, words had carried many meanings (polyonymy), and con- versely, many ideas had been attached to a single word (homonymy). This meant that the metaphorical language operated in two ways. The same verb root, such as "shine," for example, might be understood as the name of the sun or a bright thought or idea, whereas different words might be used to express the same thing: various types of cloud formations were called "mountains," "cows with heavy udders," "fingers," or "grazing sheep." Such words, which formed the basis of myths and folktales, Müller called "appellatives."[1]

At the basis of Müller's theory was the ancient conception of the sun. In the mythopoeic age, man had created his first conception of the gods by using the sun as the basic concept. Ultimately, all myths and folktales, too, were derived from this concept, yet over time, their original connection with the sun was forgotten and variants developed because of misunderstandings. In this process of "forgetting," which he also called "the disease of language," people created new stories that no longer had a basis in solar mythology. Just as rumors begin with one idea and end with another as the result of a series of misunderstandings, so the disease of language was responsible for a number of myths and folktales that no longer had a reasonable explanation. As an example of a certain creative power of storytelling that lay embedded in such verbal confusions, Müller cited the yarn of a barnacle that was hatched from shellfish. He traced the word "barnacle" to *Hiberniculae*, a word used for Irish birds, which he found in a twelfth-century poem. In the course of time, this word first had been shortened to *Berniculae*, then to *Bernacula*, and finally was confused with "barnacles." Just as in this case a confusion of words and their original meanings had led to the yarn that barnacle geese hatched from shellfish, so other oddities in myths and folktales, too, might easily be explained on the basis of a disease of language.[2] Why, for instance would there be such an oddity that ascribed the wealth of Dick Wittington to a cat? Müller explained that the tale might have arisen from a misunderstanding of the French word *achat*, meaning trade, for it was trade to which Dick Wittington owed his wealth, not really his cat.

Müller also used the idea of a disease of language to explain certain cruelties and strange occurrences in folk stories that could hardly be explained in rational terms. How was it possible, for example, that such a highly civilized people as the Greeks would perpetuate the cruel myth of Cronus, who swallowed his own newborn children? Not less cruel was the myth of Cronus's son, Zeus, who forced him to disgorge his brothers and sisters, only to deprive him of his power. Did such myths indicate ancient savagery or perhaps even cannibalism? In pointing to the theory of forgetfulness, Müller explained that the expression of "swallowing one's pride" had been understood figuratively in the mythopoeic age—just as poets still understood it today. Yet, someone in ancient history used this expression literally, thus creating the story of how Cronus swallowed his children. Another explanation related to the ancient idea that night swallowed day or that darkness swallowed the sun. Again, people might have misunderstood the original meaning of the term, which merely meant that the sun was setting and it was getting dark. Conversely, the myth of Zeus forcing Cronus to disgorge his brothers and sisters again probably had meant nothing more than that the sun was rising again. Müller cited numerous passages from ancient Sanskrit literature to prove that the ancient Sanskrit language had been rich in such metaphors.[3] Instead of saying "Good morning!" they might refer to the glorious god of the sun who climbed into his carriage to begin his course through the skies. . . . No wonder, he said, that myths and folktales were derived from such expressions.

In a systematic and conscientious way, Müller employed linguistic evidence to trace the origins of myths and folktales by means of tracing the origins of names, individual words, or metaphorical expressions. His approach was scientific and based on a vast knowledge of many languages, including Sanskrit. Some of his students, however, paid only lip service to his methodology while basing their arguments on vague speculations, without bothering to support their theories by linguistic evidence. Using Müller's premise that the sun had been at the center of early mythologies, George William Cox in his *Mythology of the Aryan Nations*,[4] for example, generalized about gods and heroes of various nations, explaining their spearheads as "rays of the sun" and their descent into the underworlds as "the darkness of night." Folklorist Richard Dorson gave Cox credit for having prepared the ground for later comparative type and motif indexes, yet accused him of interpreting the "borrowing" practices among nations all too literally while abandoning the more solid footing of linguistic evidence. There was no end to Cox's solar explanations, for he applied them not only to myths and heroes but also to legends and folktales. In every hero who set out on a journey he perceived the rising sun, in his conquest of a monster he saw the glorious sun at noon, and in his death he contemplated the setting sun in the evening or the beginning of night. The hero's resurrection simply meant the beginning of a new day or another "good morning," and his fame after death was a sure sign of spring after a long winter. As Cox transformed all traditional heroes into symbols of the sun, he made them suffer the very same fate, regardless of if it was Odysseus, Beowulf, Sigurd, William Tell, or even Hamlet, while essentially denying the differences of their literary and cultural contexts.[5]

Cox's interpretations became especially conspicuous when he applied them to folktales. Little Red Riding Hood with her red cap became the rising sun. The wolf swallowed her up just as night had swallowed day. Symbols of darkness were night. Cinderella, the Frog Prince, Hansel and Gretel, and even Puss in Boots were children of dawn. Heroes wearing "gowns of humiliation" (as did Thousandfurs and Ashputtel) were the toiling and unrequited sun, yet Cinderella rising from the ashes or the Frog Prince's transformation into a prince again meant the rising sun. Even common sense told observers that such interpretations were far-fetched, for to turn all folktale heroes into solar heroes meant to view them as one and the same. With all of his trust in solar mythology, even Max Müller felt uneasy when he began to realize the extremities of such theories, as these were no longer founded on linguistic evidence; the more so as his followers applied his own findings indiscriminately even to myths and folktales outside of the Indo-European language family.

It may indeed be true, as Dorson observed, that today, "Müller's sun has set,"[6] for serious critics no longer subscribe to his solar mythology. On the other hand it must be noted that some of Müller's linguistic and comparative methods have survived to the present. This applies to folktale studies involving riddles, proverbs, and colloquial speech patterns, as well as to others concerned with the etymology of certain words and concepts. Solar myths aside, Müller followed the Grimms' own comparative and linguistic methods that are still respected in our time. Wilhelm Grimm, for example, even used such examples as the "disease of language" (without calling it such) in referring to Basile's possible confusion of words in regard to an earlier tale by Straparola. Straparola had related a folktale about a *pipata* (doll), which Basile had made into tale about a *papara* goose.[7] Especially in his essays on the language and games of children, Wilhelm paid considerable attention to the impact of traditional expressions, rhymes, and phrases on the storytelling process. Even more relevant to modern-day folktale studies is Jacob Grimm's comparative study of myths based on a combination of linguistic approaches and a study of ancient laws, customs, and folk beliefs.[8] Modern scholarship has shown that just as myths have survived in names of places and persons, so metaphors and similes have survived in proverbs, traditional riddles, and folktales. This is true for studies by Carl W. von Sydow, Reidar Th. Christiansen, and more recently by Wolfgang Mieder, all of which, without making reference to solar mythology, have used various types of comparative linguistic approaches that resembled those employed by Max Müller.[9]

[Anthropology: Savage Customs and Rituals]

As an anthropologist, Andrew Lang challenged Max Müller's theories, contending that fieldwork research, not linguistic evidence, could explain the diffusion of folktales around the world. In his introduction to Margaret Hunt's translation of the Grimms' *Household Tales*,[10] he pondered the question of why some people living far apart from each other in time and space had in common so many myths and folktales. Why did a German folktale resemble one that came from Russia, the Celtic Highlands, or even New Zealand? Lang accused Müller of having locked himself up in dusty offices over dusty books while bypassing the living evidence in primitive societies.[11] He also thought that he should have looked outside of the Indo-Germanic influence sphere, for not all myths could be explained as having come from that part of the world, and besides, some folktales were not even based on myths at all but showed some infusion of modern elements. He also dismissed the theory of conscious borrowing from one people to another, for peasants, as the main carriers of folk culture, had generally read very little, travelled even less, and were thus the last likely group to absorb foreign tales.

Lang did agree with Max Müller and Sir George Cox that there might be some truth to the theory of "slow transmission." Just as in the distant past primitive tradesmen had carried amber and jade halfway across the world, so folktales, too, had been scattered abroad. But then again, "nursery tales" were probably "the last things that nations borrowed from each other." At any rate, he felt it was a futile task to trace the diffusion of any given tale. On the other hand, one might try to trace some older folktale elements in various primitive customs around the world in an effort to detect some correspondences, for primitive men everywhere shared certain forms of a "savage imagination" or an "early fancy."[12]

Lang proposed a comparative approach to folktales on a worldwide basis that would focus on the older elements of customs, rituals, and folk beliefs. Folktales were a hunting ground for such "survivals," provided one would first separate out skillfully the older folktale elements from the modern ones. Under no circumstances should modern aspects of folktales be treated as if they were derived from mythical times.

As a case in point, Lang referred to the Grimms' tale of "The Wolf and the Kids,"[13] explaining how this tale combined both older and newer folktale motifs. Here the wolf deceived seven little kids, eating them all—except the youngest, who hid in the clock-case. The tale was based on two old and universal themes, many parallels of which existed in folklore around the world. The first involved that of a weak creature's victory over a stronger creature by means of outsmarting it, and the second was that of a big creature swallowing and disgorging a weak creature. For the first theme, there were many parallels in tales of the Bushmen in Africa and also in those of Uncle Remus, and for the second one, there were parallels in the Greek myth of Cronus swallowing his children or in the legend of Gargantua from Brittany. The Zulus, the North American Indians, and the natives of British Guinea, too, could supply numerous stories with such themes. The very existence of such age-old universal themes proved, said Lang, that primitive peoples everywhere tended to come up with similar tales without an outside influence, as they shared what he called a "savage imagination." On the other hand, the clock-case motif was an infusion of a theme belonging to the modern era. It was odd indeed that Mr. Cox had failed to recognize it as such by making the clock-case motif the major part of his thesis. It was one thing to interpret the wolf as the symbol of night and day, as he had threatened to swallow up seven days of the week (seven kids in the Grimms' folktale), but it was another to build his major thesis on the seventh little kid hiding in the clock-case. Lang called Cox's suggestion absurd that the seventh day of the week (the seventh kid) would hide in a clock-case, a piece of furniture that was certainly unknown in mythical times. Cox had simply followed the wrong track by getting entangled in a modern motif while overlooking the major ancient and universal themes of the story.

The so-called Märchen or Household Stories of the Brothers Grimm occupied a middle place between the tales of savages and the myths of early civilizations, according to Lang. While he admitted that over time some modern elements had been so imposed on the original or older tales, he still insisted that the older tales, if properly "cleansed" from the intrusion of modern elements, were remnants of genuine myths that gave the most valuable clues to customs, rituals, and folk beliefs of ancient tribes. He suggested that in analyzing folktales, one might do well to ignore some modern infusions while focusing on universal themes that all uncivilized peoples had in common.[14]

In this context, Lang made no allowance for certain differences between folktales arising from primitive tribes and those related to epic literature. Müller had been deeply inspired by the beauty of Sanskrit poetry and the Homeric epics and perceived the greatest source of myths and folktales in the wellspring of images, metaphors, and poetic symbols of epics. Lang, on the other hand, primarily searched for traces of savage customs and rituals among primitive tribes, believing that these were older and thus much more reliable sources of folktales than epics.

With this ritual-based theory of polygenesis (many origins), Lang challenged Müller's idea of monogenesis (one origin).[15] As an anthropologist, he advocated fieldwork research based on the living context of customs and rituals. Where Müller had found ideas about savages extremely untrustworthy in regard to myth interpretations, Lang felt they were the only reliable aspects, as they still reflected ancient taboos, good luck and bad luck omens, or even the practice of cannibalism. In savage ideas he also discovered ideas of kinship with animals, metamorphoses, and certain cruelties, all of which had appeared natural to primitives yet strange and wondrous in folktales. Such early religious beliefs and rituals as animal or stone worship, taboos in regard to certain types of foods or clothing, or marriage and funeral customs had survived from ancient times in peasant tales, be it among those of the Zulus, the Australians, or the Germans. In various travel descriptions, the Greek and Roman writers Herodotus, Aristotle, Strabo, Pliny, Plutarch, and Ptolemy, as well as early explorers, missionaries, merchants, and even evangelists of the Christian church had given evidence of the ancient existence of extraordinary savage customs, rituals, and myths everywhere. Lang agreed that it would be hard to establish what the illiterate savage really had been thinking, yet he felt that it was fairly easy to find out what he had *done*.[16]

Two major factors regulated savage life: social customs (such as marriages and festivals) and savage belief in magic. Savages believed that the medicine man or sorcerer could transform himself and others into animal shapes and enter the abodes of the dead. They also believed that they could move inanimate objects by incantations, act as intermediaries in a personal intercourse between gods and men, and influence the migration of the spirit from humans into animals. They were also convinced that it was possible that women might bear animal children and that spirits might inflict or cure diseases. In savage societies sorcerers had political and priestly powers that had shaped the beliefs, rituals, and *stories* of primitive man. Such a spiritual worldview could still be observed among the American Indians today. To them, all animate and inanimate objects were endowed with a magic power, differing from human beings only in terms of their bodily form. Myths and folktales still reflected this animated view of nature. In summary, Lang pointed out the following chief relationships among rituals, folk beliefs, and predominant themes in the Grimms' folktale collection:

1. *Kinship with Animals*: A girl marries a frog or a tick, or a man weds a girl whose brothers are ravens; a queen is accused of bearing puppies or cats; a man marries a frog.

2. *Metamorphosis*: A hero is transformed into a dragon (worm), a roebuck, or a bird (or a girl becomes a bird).

3. *Inanimate Objects Obey Incantations and Speak*: A hero uses incantations with success; some drops of spittle begin to speak.

4. *Animals Help Favored Men and Women*: A heroine is helped by a bull or sheep; a hero is helped by various beasts.

5. *Cannibals are a Constant Danger*: Hero and heroine are captured by cannibals; hero or heroine flees from home to avoid being eaten.

6. *Belief in Possible Descents into Hades, a Place Guarded by Strange Beasts and Where Living Man Must Not Eat*: Psyche descends to the underworld.

7. *Savage Custom*: Husband and wife are forbidden to see each other or to name each other's names: Husband or wife disappear when seen, or when the name is named (these acts being prohibited by savage custom).

8. *Savage Custom*: The youngest son in the polygamous family is the heir: Youngest son or daughter succeeds where the elders fail and is betrayed by jealousy of the elders.

9. *Savage Idea (A)*: Human strength, or soul, resides in this or that part of the body, and the strength of one man may be acquired by another who secures this part: The giant who has no heart in his body; the man whose life or force depends on a lock of hair and is lost when the hair is lost.

   Savage Idea (B): Souls of dead enter animal forms: A dead boy becomes a bird.[17]

Lang concluded that the folktales contained in the Grimms' *Kinder-und Hausmärchen* were rich in terms of examples illustrating such correspondences between folktale themes and older beliefs and rituals. Whatever appeared cruel or unnatural in these tales was merely a sort of "survival of past savagery" shared by all civilizations.

As fascinating as Lang's theories were to his followers at the time, they did little to improve the status of folktales with educators, perhaps because the theories emphasized the word "savage" too much at the expense of all that the Brothers Grimm themselves had considered poetic. As Lang made no allowance for the epic connection, nor for a symbolic view in relation to mythology, some parents began to question whether such "savage" tales belonged on their children's bookshelves.

On the other hand, Lang's theory was enlightening in the sense that it increased public awareness of recurrent universal and cross-cultural folktale themes. By promoting the idea that similar folktale themes and motifs might have sprung up simultaneously in different parts of the world and without traceable influences, he emphasized some universal human needs and concerns that all ancient nations had in common. Wilhelm Grimm, too, had touched upon the idea of a common source of all folktales around the world when he wrote in the preface to the third volume of the *Kinder- und Hausmärchen*: "This common element [in folktales] resembles a well whose depth one does not know, yet from which everyone draws water in accordance with his need."[18] Yet as a Romantic writer, Wilhelm was far from thinking of primitive tribes in terms of "savages." In correspondence with Romantic philosophy he referred to the Golden Age of mankind, not to the "savage age" as did the anthropologist Andrew Lang. In many respects, he also considered the Golden Age superior to the present age. What he did share with Lang was the belief that all older nations had a rich treasure store of myths, folktales, festivals, customs, and folk beliefs that spoke of man's closeness to God and nature. Using a more eclectic approach than Lang, he had no difficulties in reconciling this theory with others that followed a linguistic line of interpretation.

Bronislaw Malinowski, a cultural anthropologist studying indigenous people in New Guinea and Africa, thought that primitive tribes were far from considering myths and folktales as mere "stories." More explicitly than Andrew Lang he emphasized their belief of the "reality" behind myth and folktales as an expression of primitive rites. He contended that once they entered the storytelling tradition, they reinforced traditional rituals and customs of primitive communities. For that reason, folktales and myths were much more than mere entertainment, as they served the definite function of holding together the primitive tribes.[19]

Folktales and myths were similar in many tribes and countries around the world, he said, simply because rituals among primitive tribes were similar. Music, dancing, painting, dramatic performances, and storytelling all had arisen from the tribal ritual, and all had been sacred before they had become secular. Consequently, myths and folktales, too, had a sacred origin. Since primitive man had considered rituals as "real" and "true," he had respected folktales and myths on the same level as truths anchored in religion. Far from representing symbolic expressions or figurative language meant to entertain the audience, myths and folktales expressed the rituals directly. They themselves embodied sacred actions that had perpetuated the community life, and as such, they had nothing to do with an individual's fantasy. For this reason, it was also wrong to ask what a traditional story meant or what it symbolized. According to Malinowski, the best way to approach an underlying meaning of a folktale or myth was to try to detect, whenever possible, what rituals had preceded a given tale or had given rise to it. [20]

As an example, Malinowski cited the story "Trobiand." In this tale people lost their power to rejuvenate themselves by taking off their skins because a young girl had failed to recognize her rejuvenated grandmother. Being offended by the girl's ignorance, the grandmother had put the old skin on again, which had led to the loss of eternal youth for the entire people. This tale was not to be interpreted in a philosophical, symbolic, educational, or psychological way—or in any speculative way, said Malinowski, for its "deeper meaning" lay in the annual ritual of springtime that was practiced by these folks. As in hundreds of other cases, the tale only fulfilled the indispensable function of reminding people of the ritual, as well as of reinforcing the ritual. Ultimately rituals themselves were to be considered as communal functions that enhanced the old folk beliefs while safeguarding and enforcing tribal morality. They also vouched for the perpetuation of the community by promoting its efficiency and enforcing its rules.

Since not all folktales are related to myths and their functions, and since not even all myths can possibly be related to primitive rituals, Malinowski's theory might be of limited use to educators or literary critics. Nevertheless, it did have a considerable effect on folklore scholarship. Paul Saintyves, for example, explained Perrault's tales of "Bluebeard," "Sleeping Beauty," "Little Red Riding Hood," "Cinderella," and "The Fairies" on the basis of seasonal rites of initiation. Like Malinowski, he warned readers not to interpret these tales in symbolic or moralistic terms. In the case of "The Fairies," one might well be tempted to do so when frogs jumped from the mouth of the evil girl while jewels fell from the mouth of the good girl, as such marvels appeared to be the direct consequence of their respective behavior toward the fairy. Yet, to read the story in such terms meant to bypass its original function related to an annual ritual in France. On New Year's Eve, the women of the household prepared food and drink, setting these in dishes next to a lighted candle near an open window so that the good fairies would partake of them and bless the household in return. Such a ritual had to be observed punctiliously in order to ensure prosperity and a successful marriage. A failure to do so would inevitably invite the rage of the fairies. According to Saintyves, most folktales were based on rituals of one kind or another and should be interpreted only in terms of ancient folkways and traditions, many of which were still practiced in remote communities. [21]

Sir James Frazer, too, used the ritualistic interpretation of folklore in *The New Golden Bough*. Throughout his voluminous work he tried to demonstrate the origin of myths and folktales in ancient rituals, laws, customs, traditions, and folk beliefs. By citing an overwhelming number of examples of ancient rituals and festivals, he demonstrated again and again how we had come to forget the "real" origin of folktales and myths. He even showed how in some cases we had forgotten the origin of rituals as well. Thus he showed the connection between the tale of Balder and the lighting of bonfires and straw puppets at Christmastime, by pointing to their common origin in the ancient solstice celebration.[22] Myths and folktales still gave clues to the origin of rituals, whose sacred purpose had served a function within the community. As there had been rituals to celebrate the birth of a god and springtime, so there had been rituals to celebrate his death and the coming of winter. Both still found their reflections in myths and folktales related to the battle of King Summer and King Winter. Tales of magic and transformation, too, were no mere "tales," according to Frazer, but reflections of ancient rituals that had been reenacted periodically by primitive communities to alleviate hunger and fear of death or to reensure the blessings of fruitfulness and a safe harvest. Some tales were even reminders of an ancient initiation rite, in accordance with which the old king had to die to make room for the new king.[23]

In his bibliographical sources, Frazer relied on a vast array of literary sources and older folklore studies, among which he frequently mentioned Jacob Grimm's *Teutonic Mythology*. Frazer matched Jacob Grimm in a sheer endless exploration of parallel examples from myths and rituals around the world. The scope of his comparative studies was even broader than Jacob Grimm's, including also some African, Asian, and North American myths and folktales, but in overemphasizing the materialistic side of rituals and festivals as a basis of folklore origins, he bypassed the linguistic evidence that Grimm had provided with meticulous care. Occasionally, he also leaned more toward the speculative than the theoretical side. Jacob Grimm had relied to a much greater extent on folk narratives than did Frazer while also paying close attention to the significance of etymological changes of names, words, and phrases, which to him gave clues to folktale variants over time. On the whole, it seems that Frazer was more interested in the rituals and related folk beliefs than in the tales themselves.

In his work *The Hero*,[24] Lord Raglan tried to trace a certain pattern of action in international hero tales. In this venture, he followed the example of Otto Rank's *The Myth of the Birth of a Hero*,[25] which had been written under the influence of C. G. Jung. Rank, a student of Jung, had added to his comparative essay on the hero pattern several chapters on the psychological interpretation of myths, whereas Raglan clung to Malinowski and the ritual origin theory. Neither Raglan nor Rank concerned himself with the link between the epic hero and the folktale hero, but their theories, nevertheless, have sometimes been applied to folktale research. In a cross-cultural study, Rank detected more than thirty recurrent elements characterizing the structure of traditional hero tales. Raglan reduced the pattern to ten. Both relied predominantly on the myth of Oedipus as the "stable element" in comparing the unusual conception and birth of the hero, his exposure to the wilderness, his early youth among strangers far away from home, his conquest of a wild beast, his rise to power and prestige, and finally, his death and burial in a "high place."

The Brothers Grimm had also viewed hero tales within a traditional epic context but were more concerned with tracing their individual characteristics within a cultural and literary context. As the chapter on Folktale Characters has pointed out, they did make allowance for epic characteristics of certain folktale characters but by no means for all, mainly because they recognized various origins of the tales, including farcical tales and jests from the Middle Ages that had little or no bearing on epic character traits.[26]

[Formalistic and Structural Approaches]

Since the late nineteenth century, the Finns were leading in developing a method of classifying folktales according to a scheme that attempted to bring order into chaos. Under the leadership of Kaarle Krohn, they used a geographic method to identify folktales collected orally and a historical method to identify printed sources. Combined, the geographic historical method tried to trace the origin and dissemination of entire tales as well as of individual motifs. Their research results were published in a series of monographs that were usually dedicated to a single folk narrative (folktale, myth, or legend) in terms of a vast cross-cultural perspective. Scholars undertaking such a study would focus on a single folktale, such as "The Two Brothers," and study all of its variants in numerous printed and unprinted versions available to them. They would closely identify each variant with respect to its themes, subthemes, individual motifs, formulaic expressions, etc., making sure that in each case the time and place of each variant would be closely identified and recorded. The bulky indexes of these monographs listing by number, country, and collection the numerous variants of individual themes and motifs resemble scientific works on mathematics, chemistry, or medicine while dwarfing the relatively short analytical essays preceding them.[27]

Antti Aarne, a student of Kaarle Krohn, also approached folktales from an international perspective, but as he worked on his thesis with 26,000 folktales in the Folklore Archives of Finland, he soon recognized the difficulty of proceeding rationally and in a comparative manner without a more definite system of cataloguing the tales. Krohn had developed a system for Finnish folktales, but Aarne expanded it by using also the resources of the Grimms' *Kinder- und Hausmärchen* and those of the Danish folktale collection by Sven Grundtvig. His aim was to make available for cross-cultural study a gigantic register of folktale types, motifs, and themes. In this project he also cooperated with, among others, Johannes Bolte, Axel Olrik, and Carl Wilhelm von Sydow.[28] In 1910 he published *Das Verzeichnis der Märchentypen* (*Index of Folktale Types*, generally identified as *FFC 3*) in Helsingfors.

Aarne divided folktales into three major groups: (1) Animal Tales (2) Ordinary Folktales, and (3) Farce and Jokes. Under the second category, he would group, among others, magic tales, tales of enchantment, and tales of superstitions, with further subdivisions dedicated to legendary tales, novella-type folktales, and tales of stupid giants and devils. Tales of superstition, for example, would have separate entries of supernatural objects, tasks, enemies, marriage partners, knowledge, and skills. Under Farce and Jokes, he would list numskull tales, jokes about parsons, liars' tales and stories about married couples, a woman or girl, a man or boy, a clever man, or lucky accidents. In addition, there were formula tales, cumulative tales, catch tales, and many others. In ordering the entries of major folktale collections, including the Grimms' tales, he numbered each by type and subtype, with specific references to the respective folktale collection in which it could be located. These number references to Aarne's catalogue are still commonly used by scholars today in reference to international folktale types.[29]

Aarne's system has been applied to national folklore archives in Norway, Romania, Hungary, Iceland, Spain, and numerous other countries, and it has aided researchers in various ways by its systematic approach. Still, the different national catalogues show much variation in their catalogues and systems, which sometimes adds to confusion rather than to a greater clarification.[30]

Similar catalogues were also prepared by J. G. von Hahn, G. L. Gomme, L. Sainenu, L. Katona, and Sven Grundtvig, yet they were based on different conceptions that have been found less suitable for international comparative studies than Aarne's. Gomme's catalogue system, for example, was based on 77 folktale collections from around the world yet included only a total of 3,000 tales.[31] Neither did the later efforts of Reinhold Köhler, E. Cosquin, Carl W. von Sydow, or André Jolles match the efficiency of Aarne's system. Jan de Vries tried an independent catalogue system for folktales of Southeast Asia.

In 1928 Antti Aarne and Stith Thompson cooperated on the voluminous index titled *The Types of Folktale*,[32] a classification that broadened the international scope of Aarne's original catalogue. Between 1931 and 1936 Thompson published numerous volumes of a gigantic *Motif Index of Folk Literature*[33] that became an indispensable international reference tool for folktale research. This last work may be considered a fair match to Aarne's catalogue. A valuable aid to researchers has also been Thompson's work *The Folktale* (1946),[34] which, even though on a smaller scale, gives a systematic survey of folktale theories, international organizations of folktale study, methods of collecting folktales, and bibliographical surveys of principal folktale collections. Most significant is his chapter on "Classifying Folk Narratives," which provides insight into the various systems and definitions used in the study of the folktale.

The most exhaustive study of German and international folktales with a clear focus on the *Kinder- und Hausmärchen* was published by Johannes Bolte and Georg Polivka between 1913 and 1918 in five volumes, under the title of *Anmerkungen zu den Kinder- und Hausmärchen*.[35] The work largely utilized the archival materials made available by Wilhelm Grimm's son, Hermann Grimm, but more so the notes that the Grimms had attached to their various editions. In addition, the authors also paraphrased and expanded numerous essays by the Brothers Grimm on the history of German folktale collections, the theories of folktale origin, and various approaches to folktale interpretations. Friedrich Ranke called this work a "crowning achievement"[36] while recognizing that hardly a single study of the Grimms' *Kinder- und Hausmärchen* dared to ignore this exhaustive authoritative study. Volumes 4 and 5 of *Anmerkungen* gave a remarkable historical folktale survey of many nations and ages, be it in relation to ancient Egypt, Babylon, Assyria, Israel, Greece, Rome, England, Ireland, Scotland, Denmark, Norway, or the Slavic nations, to name just a few. New folktale collections, too, were listed from five continents, preceded by historical surveys and review articles. E. Kutzer wrote an essay on Indian folktales, B. Heller discussed Hebraic and Arabic tales as well as the Grimms' Italian tales of the sixteenth and seventeenth centuries, with some excerpts of Basile's *Pentamerone*. Bolte and Polivka introduced the vast bibliographical survey itself by various chapters on the characteristics of folktales and testimonies regarding the history of folktales. All of these, says Ranke, had been written mainly by "Bolte's master pen."[37]

Yet even this work had its shortcomings, largely because Bolte often left quotes from the Brothers Grimm unidentified, which made it difficult to distinguish the Grimms' own analysis from Bolte's commentaries and additions. Occasionally some unmistaken longer quotes by the Grimms were clearly set off from the text, yet in many instances this was not the case. In one of his prefaces, Bolte explained that since the material bulk of their study had been so overwhelming, he had taken the liberty of inserting some materials here and there while omitting others, without trying to disentangle the material by adding some cumbersome notes.[38] Yet in 1922 (*Kinder- und Hausmärchen*, Volume 3) the Grimms had already done the essential spade work for comparative folktale studies by analyzing folktales from more than thirty countries.[38]

While Bolte and Polivka systematically explored the Grimms' commentary and essays and expanded these on a large scale, they might have done a better service to future researchers by identifying more clearly their own additions and elaborations. As it is, Bolte's international comparative studies look as if they were mainly the result of Bolte and Polivka's scholarly efforts. Evidently, Friedrich Ranke thought so, for he wrote in praise of Bolte: "If we compare the stately five volumes [of Bolte-Polivka] with the thin little volume [the Grimms' shorter edition of 1825] . . . we feel a rising gratitude for the two learned men and their assistants whose dedication, diligence, and unselfish objectivity have created a work that for generations to come will always offer materials for new investigations."[39] Yet here Ranke compared the wrong things, for the 1825 edition of the Grimms' *Kinder- und Hausmärchen* was a shortened children's book edition *without* notes, which had little or no bearing on Bolte and Polivka's work. It would have been more fair to the Grimms to make reference to the spade work on international folktale studies that they did in the above mentioned edition of 1922.[40]

Undoubtedly, great recognition is due to Bolte and Polivka, but the prime credit must be given to the Brothers Grimm for their exhaustive international and comparative studies of folktales. Whereas many of their footnotes followed a sort of shorthand style by suggesting various oral and literary variants for the selected tales, they wrote their essays on international folktale research with clarity and insight while laying out a broad framework for future studies.

Lutz Mackensen and Johannes Bolte together edited the *Handwörterbuch des deutschen Märchens* (*Handbook of the German Folktale*) in several volumes between 1930 and 1933.[41] The first volume, covering letters A–E was issued in several sections between 1930 and 1933, with the second volume (I–Fr) following between 1934 and 1945. With a kaleidoscopic view of the folktale and the various theories and studies surrounding it, the individual entries, in the form of documented essays, were prepared by numerous scholars in the field, covering such topics as the age of folktales, the origin of folktale motifs, organizational principles used in classifying folktales, and variants and dialogues in folktales. There were even essays on such themes as thievery in folktales and French and Arabic influences on German folktales. The more recent publication of *Enzyklopädie des Märchens* (*Encyclopedia of the Folktale*),[42] edited by Kurt Ranke, is based largely on the same conception as Mackensen's *Handbuch* and in part uses the same topical entries. Significantly, it was prepared by the same publisher: Walter de Gruyter, in Berlin and New York. On the whole, however, it has consistently updated the individual entries and added so many new ones that it has certainly made a mark of its own. The *Enzyklopädie* has also brought in modern theories, methodologies, and research results, including a vast array of bibliographical entries following each entry. So far, five volumes have appeared in print (A–Gr). In its objective presentation of the many topics and issues related to the folktale and folk narratives in general, the work is an invaluable tool for researchers in the field.

The structural approach to folktales by Vladimir Propp contributed much to folktale studies in general, although it had little bearing upon a specific interpretation of the Grimms' *Kinder- und Hausmärchen*. For his pioneering study, *Morphology of the Folktale* (1928; first English translation 1958),[43] Propp used one hundred Russian folktales, examining the individual structural components as parts related to the whole. In this context, he focused primarily on the plots of the tales, examining their structures as one might examine specific building blocks. He singled out thirty-one distinct functions of folktales in accordance with the peculiar patterns formed by their sequence of actions. He documented such patterns by various examples, claiming that they were highly predictable. In this context, he did not emphasize so much the characters as bearers of the actions as he did the actions themselves and the ways in which they proceeded and led toward a resolution of problems.

Propp suggested that in approaching a folktale, researchers follow a structural sequence and understand the chain of functions, such as the initial situation, special needs, problems, reactions of the hero, means or magic used in fighting battle or achieving victory, methods of betrayal, maneuvers of deceit, the role of helpers, errors, misconceptions, difficult tasks, solutions of problems, or the ways in which punishment was meted out, obstacles were removed, and final salvation was achieved.[44]

Today folklorists emphasize to a much greater degree than the Grimms themselves the method of fieldwork recordings. The use of phonograph records, tape recorders, and concise transcripts have considerably enhanced the accuracy of the word-of-mouth recording technique. While giving credit to the Brothers Grimm for having called attention to the need for oral recordings, they tend to look down upon their recording methods as inaccurate, incomplete, and inconsistent.[45] Some folklorists still continue to concern themselves with theories regarding the origin and dissemination of folktales, but many have brushed aside such questions in favor of accumulating and analyzing data pertaining to folk life and folk culture.

A new type of "scientism" has taken hold among folklorists, not only in regard to the minute accuracy with which they record and transcribe the collected tales but also with respect to the methods they use to take representative samples in the study of distribution patterns and relevant population data. Circumstantial data, too, have come to be valued for establishing every detail of what is called *Erzählgemeinschaft* (tale community).[46] The Grimms used to be casual about recording the exact circumstances under which they collected their tales, mentioning only occasionally some details about their informants. They mentioned, for example, that Frau Viehmännin used to sit down to drink a cup of black coffee when she delivered fresh garden produce at their home, and they also commented on

her status as a tailor's widow struck by poverty, but they did not investigate from whom and under what circumstances she had acquired her
stories. Thus, researchers were left to speculate as to whom one should
consider the greatest storytelling influence: her Huguenot father, her
German mother, the country travellers at her father's inn, or the village
community of Zwehrn in which she had been raised. Modern folklorists
try to avoid such guesswork by establishing more exact data regarding
the *Erzählgemeinschaft*, including its psychosocial environment and even
the individual storyteller's habits.

Modern folktale research has vastly expanded its scope from an initial
preoccupation with peasant lore to present-day urban lore, including
the lore of ethnic groups and occupational groups. Motif and type indexes
and their various supplements, arranged like libraries in accordance with
the Dewey Decimal System, have turned out to be a major tool
of classifying folklore. To this vast data system have been added a great
number of archival resources, many of which are concerned not just
with an accumulation of historical data but also with references to contemporary attitudes and events. In the late fifties folkloristic-sociological
studies emerged with a new call for social relevance and objectivity,
which developed into a so-called "value-free" research that was meant
to raise folklore to a historical science. In addition, there have been
studies of religious folklore and new analytical studies of regional and
local culture. [47]

[Psychoanalysis and Archetypes]

Both Sigmund Freud and his student C. G. Jung realized that myths
and folktales speak in symbols corresponding to the unconscious
elements in our lives. While Freud drew upon certain analogies in
dreams, fears, phobias, and repressions, as well as in the hope for wish
fulfillment, Jung spoke in much broader cultural terms about the "collective unconscious." Both perceived in myths and folktales certain symbols that corresponded to elements of the unconscious, but Jung also
saw in them the quest for an inner renewal through archetypes. What
he expected from a participation in the unconscious forces was an elevation above an experience that was singular and unique toward one that
had been shared throughout the ages by mankind. In archetypes he
searched for a universal human element that would confirm a higher
state of selfhood.

In their various references to myths and folktales, Freud and Jung
were rather eclectic. As long as myths and folktales corresponded to
certain symbols of the unconscious, neither Freud nor Jung did seem
to mind if they drew their examples from tales specifically mentioned
in the Grimms' *Kinder- und Hausmärchen* or from other folktale col-

lections. Yet, because they both were familiar with the Grimms' tales, they mentioned them more frequently than others. Overall, Freud referred to "fairy tales" not so much in relation to their specific cultural context as to their symbolic relationship to the individual and the conflict of the id, ego, and superego. He used them at random, mainly to illustrate the meaning of dreams, fears, phobias, or desires in general human terms. In the same eclectic way he also used other aspects of folklore, such as Jewish anecdotes or traditional jests.[48]

In dealing with the development of a neurosis, for example, he referred to a dream that a patient had experienced at the age of four. It involved seven white wolves sitting in a walnut tree and staring at him. Upon waking up with a big scream, the patient had associated his fear with an illustration from "Little Red Riding Hood" that his older sister had used to frighten him. Yet, he also associated it with another folktale, "The Wolf Puts his Tail through the Window," which involved several wolves climbing on each other's backs. Following the vagueness and complexity of the dream, Freud then related the seven wolves of the dream to a tale emphasizing the number seven, namely the Grimm's "The Wolf and the Seven Little Kids." In this story the wolf, upon having dipped one paw into white flour, pretended to be the mother goat and tricked the kids into opening the door. He devoured six of them, sparing only the youngest, who had hidden away in the big grandfather clock. Freud explained that the wolves in both stories, like the wolves in the dream, symbolized the boy's fear of his father. He diagnosed this fear as "castration anxiety."[49]

Essentially, then, Freud was more concerned with interpreting the dream than with discovering the meaning of the folktales themselves, for ultimately, he cared more about the diagnosis of a given psychological ailment and its possible cure than about a folkloristic analysis. Even though he did pose the question of whether perhaps both "Little Red Riding Hood" and "The Wolf and the Seven Little Kids" contained the hidden meaning of a child's fear of the father figure, he did not elaborate on certain definite symbolic interpretations of folktales. Only occasionally did he hint at the possibility that a close study of recurring folktale elements in a person's dreams might give us clues to an interpretation of folktales themselves, without, however, following through with such observations.

C. G. Jung, as well as his student Otto Rank, were much more thorough in studying myths and folktales from a comparative cultural perspective, so as to establish an underlying archetypal pattern, especially in the hero tales. In the few essays that Jung dedicated to folktales, he often relied on the Grimms' collection, but not exclusively so and never with the purpose of understanding the Grimms' own approach to myths and folktales. Neither did he or Rank study recurrent themes entirely for the sake of establishing cultural variants.

Jung conceived of archetypes as involuntary a priori ideas that liberated the individual in his inner quest for self-knowledge. Considering the human being as unique, he hoped that archetypes would lead him toward self-identification as well as toward his unique creative development. Significant in this connection was a lecture that he gave in Zurich in 1922.[50] In discussing the relationship between psychology and literature, he distinguished between the collective unconscious and the personal unconscious, emphasizing above all man's freedom in regard to his creative potential. Jung considered Freud's approach to art and literature as "reductive," mainly because it was directed at the treatment of neurosis. Such an approach was "stripping the work of art of the golden gleam of artistic creation," as he put it. He called it essentially a medical "corrosive" method used in analyzing the fantasies of hysteria and other morbid psychic phenomena, such as infantile sexual traits or even criminal inclinations that had been repressed into the unconscious background of the psyche. Jung felt that Freud had done well in recognizing that the unconscious background does not remain inactive but may cause psychic and behavioral disturbances, which, in turn, may also cause dream images and fantasies to be projected onto the real world—or into art and literature. Yet such projections were not real symbols or archetypes, said Jung, but only signs or symptoms of a state of mind, symptoms of the subliminal processes. True symbols differed essentially from these, as they expressed broader concepts for which as yet no words existed. In Plato's "Allegory of the Cave" there had been a true symbol of the whole problem of the theory of knowledge. To Freud, said Jung, Plato's symbol would have meant nothing more than the uterus or Plato's personal infantile sexuality.[51]

While trying to do away with purely clinical, biological, and medical terms, Jung still believed in analytical psychology as applied to art. In his approach to art, literature, and folklore, he made a considerable allowance for the unconscious factor, yet rather than addressing in this connection merely the question of the libido, he drew upon archetypal experiences and patterns that addressed human needs in much broader terms. According to Jung, the ancient storytellers had drawn unconsciously upon archetypes and symbols that were larger than their personal biological needs or frustrations.[52]

Marie Louise von Franz, a great admirer and student of C. G. Jung, believed that nowhere else except in folktales did the human collective unconscious manifest itself so clearly. She respected individual folktales within their own given structure and uniqueness, yet in various clusters of them she perceived a psychological meaning that related to the human soul. In some folktales she also saw the reflection of different phases of the spirit of man. Von Franz defined folktales as the spontaneous and naive product of the soul of mankind, which had a power to regulate society.[53]

Von Franz differed from Jung in her view of archetypes in the sense that she thought that they stood not for the entire collective unconscious but just for a part of it. Only if one combined a number of archetypes that were reflected in folktales could one symbolically arrive at the concept of a complex individual. She saw it as the function of folktales to guide the individual instinctively toward his true self. As such, folktales were ideally suited first to help readers to identify with the various problem situations and then to show them how to overcome these problems through the folktale theme of redemption.

Bruno Bettelheim followed in the footsteps of Freud as well as Jung by interpreting folktales mainly to help the human being toward his full self-realization. In using the term "fairy tales," he made no clear distinction between folktale and literary fairy tale but used both interchangeably in an attempt to explain to parents and patients alike that they were significant instruments in helping children learn about life, human nature, and themselves. Alternately, he drew upon examples from fairy tales by Hans Christian Andersen ("The Ugly Duckling," "The Little Match Girl"), folktales from England and Russia ("Goldilocks and the Three Bears"), from Romania ("The Enchanted Pig"), from Italy ("Basile's *Pentamerone*), from France (Perrault's fairy tales), and from Germany (the Grimm's "Snow White"), as well as from the Greek myth of Oedipus and the Riddle of the Sphinx. In this eclectic approach to "fairy tales" Bettelheim referred alternately to folktales by the Brothers Grimm and by Charles Perrault without explaining whose version he was using, and he also did not care to make a distinction between traditional folktales on the one hand and literary fairy tales on the other. His emphasis throughout was on the psychological meanings that "fairy tales" held for children and the insights they might give them into what he called the "driving forces" of human life.[54]

A closer look at Bettelheim's interpretation of the Grimms' "The Frog Prince," for example, shows that he interpreted the tale in broader terms within the so-called "animal groom cycle." He viewed the deeper meaning of "The Frog King" (identical with the Grimms' "The Frog Prince") in strictly psychological terms, suggesting that the story depicted a speeded-up process of maturation in a child. In the ball he perceived an underdeveloped narcissistic psyche containing all unrealized potential. When the young princess dropped the ball into the well, it meant that she had lost her naivete, yet for some time thereafter she continued to hold onto the "pleasure principle" by going about life as usual. She finally matured—yet not without the constant prodding of the king, her father, who symbolically represented the superego, reminding her of her promises and duties.[55]

Bettelheim interpreted the climax of the story as the girl's awakening to sex, which was at first overshadowed by disgust, anger, and anxiety. When she finally threw the frog against the wall, it meant, he said, that she asserted herself by becoming her own agent and thus turned hatred into love—a theme in which he perceived certain parallels to "Beauty and the Beast" and "Cupid and Psyche." Just as Beauty's love had restored the Beast to human form and Psyche's love had led to a happy reunion with Cupid, so love was triumphant at the end of this tale. In contrast to Max Lüthi, however, Bettelheim emphasized love not so much as a spiritual force as a matter of self-assertion and maturity. In that sense, his interpretation retained the biological flavor of Freud's psychoanalysis, especially when he commented at the end that one should not expect first erotic encounters to be pleasant, because they were fraught with anxiety.[56]

Jungian was Bettelheim's suggestion that historically fairy tales had anticipated our knowledge of embryology in various forms. Following Jung's interpretation of the story of Moses—Jung had seen in the basket of reeds floating on the river a symbol of the child swimming in the amniotic fluid of the mother's womb—Bettelheim traced the archetypal meaning of the story to the experience of the unborn child. The frog emerging from the water thus represented not only the animal bridegroom but also the child in fetal development, and the story as a whole supposedly demonstrated the stages of child development from oedipal attachment toward maturity and freedom.[57] Fairy tales, according to Bettelheim, anticipate our knowledge of embryology in various forms but also such development crises as the question of how to overcome oedipal difficulties or how to master oral anxieties (Hansel's symbolic oral craving for the gingerbread). Fairy tales also express symbolically sibling rivalries, maternal or paternal jealousies, and decisions between the pleasure principle and the reality principle ("Little Red Riding Hood").

More so than either Freud or Jung, Bettelheim focused on the uses of fairy tales, both in children's normal reading experiences and in therapeutic situations. It is one of his most important contributions that he encouraged parents to read fairy tales to their children without worrying that they might cause phobias or unhealthy daydreams. He tried to convince parents that fairy tales help children outgrow their fears and phobias and, more importantly, that they help them to expand their fantasies and come to terms with their anxieties. Fairy tales thus were the best aid for children in learning to cope with themselves and the daily realities of life. To such realities of life belonged the forces of good and evil. Bettelheim felt that fairy tales represented these forces symbolically as a struggle that children experienced daily within themselves. Even if children would never hear about monsters and witches through fairy tales, he contended, they would simply invent them, for they were part and parcel of their inner selves. Yet in living through the world of fairy tales, they learned to accept fear and danger as an integral part of life. Folktales showed them how to gain courage, perseverance, and empathy as they identified with the hero or heroine who overcame the various challenges of evil. In that sense, he called folktales "the great comforters" that gave children inner strength through the power of identification and imagination.[58] He promised that children would return from fairy tales to the real world refreshed and strengthened. Fairy tales essentially helped children work out their unconscious problems. By submerging themselves in the world of make-believe they were really getting in touch with their inner selves, thus starting a healthy road toward maturity.

[Symbolic and Literary Interpretations]

A leading work in terms of symbolic interpretations of folktales is Hedwig von Beit's two-volume *Symbolik des Märchens*.[59] Even though Von Beit was strongly influenced by Jungian psychology, she also used philosophical and literary approaches in searching out the symbolic meanings of folktale themes on a cross-cultural basis. Her method differed from that of Jung in that she used a close textual analysis of folktales, particularly in relation to the *Kinder- und Hausmärchen*. Like Jung, she recognized in folktales symbols representing the conscious and unconscious forces of the world in general human terms, but she also perceived separate archetypes for male and female characters. She thought that difficult human problems, tragic events, and the powers of magic, mystery, and creativity that inhabited the world of folktales were far too complex to be dealt with from a single gender perspective.

In battles of heroes and demons Hedwig von Beit recognized the general human struggle for insight and inner freedom. Whenever a folktale protagonist faced a seemingly insurmountable obstacle, such as a deep, dark forest, an endless ocean, or a huge mountain, she thought that he moved away from the known world toward the unknown world of the "beyond," a realm that might be represented by the underworld of the dead, the paradise, or the land of the sun, the moon, or the stars. In other themes she saw several archetypes: the archetype of Mother Nature, who gave life and threatened to destroy it; the archetype of the Primeval Father, who revealed his spirit through the inanimate and materialistic world; and the archetype of the Son (also called the Shadow), who either threatened his parents or brought them good fortune, happiness, and power. Further, there was the Magic Virgin, endowed with demonic powers, who, like her mother, appeared in several forms: as a wild animal, a witch, or a beguiling beauty.[60]

At the center of all folktale action Hedwig von Beit perceived the most treasured jewel: the human personality, which she called "the symbol of the highest spiritual being." By searching out the various folktale symbols and their magic functions in folktales, she tried to get to a deeper understanding of the human personality. Unlike Jung, however, she did not use folktales mainly as a means to another end but made the tales and their symbols the center of her discussion. In this analysis she was strongly influenced by Carl Gustav Carus's concept of the existence of the unconscious, as well as by related ideas expressed by Arthur Schopenhauer. Even though neither one of these philosophers had concerned themselves specifically with folktales, she felt that she was indebted to them for her own conception of folktale symbols. [61]

Von Beit was especially grateful to Carus for the idea that the subconscious was the foundation of our conscious life and that the life of the soul might be compared to a swiftly moving river that reflected the sunlight only in one little spot. It was this spot of light that, according to Carus, represented our consciousness. Occasionally, wrote von Beit, a few more blotches of light would illuminate our understanding of what went on in the world of the unconscious. The symbolic language of myths and folktales represented many spots of light that gave clues to the life of the soul. She considered it her task to decipher them and to connect them meaningfully to the entire symbolic language of folktales and myths so as to gain a better understanding of the human soul—a task to which she devoted a lifetime.

Rudolf Steiner's symbolic approach to folktales was related to the theory of anthroposophy. On that basis, he explained the belief in the evolution of the "Pure Spirit," which supposedly accounted for metamorphosis in myth and folktale. Whenever changes took place from the material world toward the world of spiritual existence—Steiner would interpret these as a development toward a growing spiritual consciousness. According to the anthroposophical interpretation, all folktales known in the Middle Ages moved the human being toward his higher spiritual goal. [62]

In trying to explain the principle of anthroposophy on the basis of the Grimms' tales of magic, for example, Steiner would generally select tales that seemed to project some symbolic meaning and thus would lend themselves to such an interpretation. At the same time, he would ignore others that did not deal with magic at all, such as the numskull stories or jests, which could hardly be interpreted in this manner. Yet because a clear-cut yardstick for selection was evidently missing, he also made some odd choices among tales that seemed to defy such an interpretation or made it appear ridiculous. One of these was the Grimms' tale of "The Bremen Town Musicians," in which he insisted that the spirit reigned supreme throughout the tale. The donkey represented the lowest instinct, the physical body; the dog, the ether or aerial body; the cat, the astral body or the stars; and the cock, the ego. The light that the cock saw in the robbers' house symbolized spiritual enlightenment. In this case Steiner completely ignored the humor of the tale and its inherent theme of self-reliance that emerges from an initial state of abuse and slavery. [63]

A master of the symbolic folktale interpretation is Max Lüthi. In the various books and essays in which he concerned himself with the

European folktale he followed in some essential points the symbolic interpretation of Hedwig von Beit. While he also employed some other theoretical approaches, the symbolic view took the upper hand in his view of folktales. Lüthi contrasted folktales with literary fairy tales, or *Buchmärchen*, as the Grimms had contrasted *Naturpoesie* with *Kunstpoesie*, stating that ideally the folktale should not have been written down but preserved in the oral tradition, because writing would cast it into a rigid form, whereas the oral tradition was characterized by change. In this regard he agreed with the Brothers Grimm, who believed that in spite of great loyalty to tradition even the best storytellers had to improvise a little to keep the tale alive in the oral tradition. [64]

In pondering the meaning of folktales, Lüthi did not exclude the possibility that it might represent wishful thinking on the one hand and fears and phobias on the other, yet overall, he leaned more toward a symbolic view that reflected the "inner reality of human experience." He felt that with their strong emphasis on actions, folktales undeniably did represent an element of reality, yet that they were far more significant as reflections of the *inner life* and *inner reality* of human experience than as manifestations of realistic events, be it in terms of history or social life. [65]

Lüthi considered the folktale as an art form that spoke symbolically in terms of polarity and contrast. While it reflected what actually was and had been, it also showed what appeared to be. In other words, illusions, enchantments, and transformations were just as important in folktales as were themes reflecting the social or historical reality.

The style of the folktale was a language of contrasts. Every aspect of the folktale had its foil: for white there was black, for beauty there was ugliness, for kindness there was evil. Hard objects, especially glass and metal, belonged to the characteristic style of folktales, as they expressed this contrast with greatest clarity. Yet the folktale also dwelt on the contrast between good and evil, teaching implicitly that for every spell there was a disenchantment and that for every curse there was a redemption. Thus it revealed that the suffering brought about by injury and destruction was redeemed by the comfort arising from its secret of healing, be it through a kind and innocent soul or the magic water of life. [66]

In such "foils" or "contrasts" Lüthi perceived still more than a mere "style" in a conventional sense, but rather an aesthetic principle. This principle was not to be confused with an element of morality. The folktale did not teach or preach, even though images and actions taught lessons implicitly. However, such implicit lessons had nothing to do with schoolroom morality. Sometimes it was merely good luck that decided the fate of a hero, whereas at other times it was his kindness toward animals or toward those in need that brought him a reward. Implicitly, the folktale did not just demand that one should be good and kind but revealed the wisdom that good deeds demanded true commitment and sacrifice and that there were no easy solutions in life.

Why did folktales so often follow a pattern of three? Usually twice things went wrong, but the third time they turned out to be successful. What did it mean if the two older brothers or two older sisters were unsuccessful in their endeavors because they were selfish or greedy or lacked respect for a certain unwritten law or taboo, whereas the third or youngest were successful because of the opposite qualities? It meant that good common sense asserted itself. The folktale did not preach against vices, but through patterns of action like these, the folktale informed the listener that egotistical, materialistic, and disrespectful characters got what they deserved.[67]

Following the literary bent, Lüthi called attention to the significance of the Romantic "search motif" in folktales. Young heroes and heroines often set out to wander across vast spaces of the earth, searching for something that seemed to lie beyond human reach, be it the top of a glass mountain or the end of the world. Another Romantic motif was the "escape motif" often found in a fleeing couple that changed shapes in an attempt to escape their pursuers. Humans might take on the shape of animals, stones, or mountains, or they might use magic powers, even turning a simple comb into an entire forest or a drop of water into the sea. While human beings changed into inanimate objects, inanimate objects took on human form. Often small creatures inhabited a small world of their own. One might enter a house or palace in which there was no living creatures, yet inside a table was laid for many.[68] Referring to the "living spirit" that animated all creatures and things alike, Lüthi echoed the Romantic philosophy of Friedrich W. J. Schelling and Friedrich Schlegel, but also that of Wilhelm Grimm who saw the world animated and alive with the spirit of God and nature. Schelling through that myths expressed a primeval knowledge of man's unity with God and nature that had manifested itself in unbroken moments throughout history, and Friedrich Schlegel wrote in his "Rede über die Mythologie" ("Lecture About Mythology"):

> Mythology is a work of art by nature. In its very fabric it reveals the highest things. All aspects are related to each other and everything is metamorphosis, is shaped and reshaped within its unique process, and this shaping and reshaping of myth is its inner life, its very method, if I may say so.[69]

The Romantics believed that there was more to the world than the eye could behold and that both folktale and myth revealed its secret.

By calling the folktale a symbolic expression of man's "inner reality," Max Lüthi also related the reversal of roles, the theme of unsuccessful imitation, and the age-old theme of death and resurrection. Rather than perceiving these in ritualistic terms, he saw them in strictly human terms expressing the inner conflicts of man. Like Marie Louise von Franz, Hedwig von Beit, and Rudolf Steiner, he perceived an intimate connection in the symbolic language of myths and folktales, whose secret lay embedded in its universal human significance.

[Feminist Views and Counter-Arguments]

Our age has seen a gender revolution, a new consciousness regarding the human rights of women. Feminist critics have closely scrutinized chauvinistic attitudes that have led to a discrimination against women, whether at home or in job situations. In this context, they have taken a closer look at the roots of such attitudes in history as well as in myths, legends, nursery rhymes, and folktales. The Grimms' *Kinder- und Hausmärchen* have been singled out with special intensity, perhaps because they reflect what feminist critics have considered outdated values regarding the supposed virtues of the female sex. They have also given attention to female suffering at the hands of those who happened to be in a dominant social position within the folktale world.

Among the feminist critics concerned with folktales, we may distinguish between two major approaches. The first one, represented by Marie Louise von Franz, focuses primarily on women as archetypes or gender specific symbols with both positive and negative connotations. The second one, represented by Ruth Bottigheimer and others, shows women as passive victims. By far the most popular one has been the second (and more recent) approach, as it has called to the reader's attention certain injustices done to women by a supposedly stereotypical assignment of roles, but it has also resulted in some effective counter-arguments by Maria Tartar and Sigrid Früh. Besides, there is still a third approach that has taken stock of the representation of female characters in the Grimms' folktales in quantitative terms.

In *Problems of the Feminine in Fairytales*, Marie Louise von Franz viewed folktales from the perspective of a psychiatrist and from the feminine point of view. In folktales as well as in myths and legends, she perceived both positive and negative attitudes about women in a clear and undiluted way. Greek mythology provided her with the primeval "dual image of motherhood" through Demeter, the goddess of fertility, childbirth, and grain who also became the goddess of sorrow and revenge. With all of her blessings and all of her threats of doom and destruction, she was what von Franz called "the vital impulse of nature."[70] From this image of duality within the mythical goddess were derived the two types of women in folktales and legends: the good fairies with all their blessings on the one side and the evil witches with their ominous spells on the other. Whereas the kind spirit also existed in folktales in the form of the deceased mother who was like a secret blessing and guardian to her orphaned child, so the evil spirit existed in form of the plotting and jealous stepmother. The good mother in folktales died or was already dead before the story opened, yet she was ever-present as a consoling power in various forms, be it in "Ashput-tel" or in "The Juniper Tree." If she was such a wonderful source of comfort, why did the good mother die in folktales? Von Franz felt that both in reality and in the world of the folktale, the presence of a good mother often prevented the child's individuation. Her death, even though an obvious loss, implied that the child was now forced to begin the process of individuation, although never without problems and obsta-cles, one of which often came up in form of the stepmother.

From her perspective as a psychiatrist, von Franz observed that as soon as a girl got the first hunch of her own self, she was immediately attacked by an outsider, which in the folktale world corresponded to an attack by the stepmother. Yet, even within her own self, the girl would experience a voice from within that tended to pull her back. She called this voice an attack by the inner stepmother. In other words, she felt that both in folktales and in real life, there was the necessary struggle toward selfhood that involved the "two mothers" in every female. To give in to the inner stepmother meant to fall back upon the old collective pattern of femininity by repression. The good mother and the stepmother in folktales helped or hindered a female character in the process of growth, but the struggle of both was needed to make progress toward individuation. The conflict arising in this process was always a painful one that required a truly heroic and superhuman effort, yet life without conflict was a life of inertia, and a life of inertia, said von Franz, was for men no life at all but only the old collective role of femininity. The new self demanded a breaking of the magic spell.

By no means did von Franz view femininity in purely heroic terms. Some of her definitions of female archetypes were, in fact, rather unflat-tering to the female sex. As a psychiatrist she had come to know women in their most critical hours, receiving insight into their special or what she called "typically feminist" ways of dealing with life, its joys, and its problems. One of these she defined as the domineering trait that arose from injured pride. Hurt pride had been at the source of Artemis's demand that Agamemnon sacrifice his daughter before he sailed to Troy. It was also at the source of the evil spell the thirteenth fairy cast over the newborn child in "Sleeping Beauty," for the fairy had been left out at the banquet invitation. Von Franz explained that in neurotic behavior the feeling of being left out manifested itself in females by irregular eating habits, stomach disorders, and an outbreak of wrath (anger or revenge). As she drew upon parallels in myth, folktales, and real-life situations, she said that especially folktales were full of female characters who had turned sour because of injured pride or vanity, which, in her view, was a reflection of neurotic female behavior. The failure to get over hurt feelings opened the door to "animus attacks," during which the person was possessed by a bad mood or a lamenting reproachfulness. In such a mood, women tended to blame others for their own shortings or engage in erratic behavior. Such behavior, however, was actually nothing but a disguised appeal for love that arose from an insufficient self-esteem, yet by giving rise to a domineering and vengeful attitude it had the wrong effect and chased away the very thing it wanted.[71]

Another negative motif—in folktales and in real life—was that of women's peculiar ways of reacting to the principles and laws of justice. In her view, women did not deal with justice objectively and openly but sometimes "with nastiness, more like nature, as it were." This aspect of the female character represented the dark side of nature and the Mother Goddess, which in folktales again might appear in the form of a stepmother or an evil witch.

In *Grimms' Bad Girls and Bold Boys; The Moral and Social Vision of the Tales*, Ruth Bottigheimer made a case of women as helpless victims. She pointed out that whereas male protagonists were usually active and aggressive and finally gained reward for their actions, regardless of their ethical merits, female protagonists were often punished by being sent into the dark forest, an old crumbling tower, or the desolate wilderness. In deep isolation, they often spent years as mute victims, communicating with no one in the outside world. Pressing forward, the male folktale protagonists usually got away with devious behavior, such as lying, cheating, and stealing (as did Bruder Lustig), yet the female protagonists were caught in their dishonesty and literally "ended up in nail-studded barrels." She felt that, with few exceptions, the Grimms' folktales portrayed women as mute and passive victims dominated by circumstance, a perverted one-sided system of justice, or a powerful male figure (king, prince, or father).[72]

In the "femaleness of isolation and isolation of femaleness" Bottigheimer perceived a certain buried social message of a patriarchal conservative interest. Spinning tales, she said, reflected the conventional morality of hard work rewarded, whereas towers, trees, and forests gave us a glimpse not only of women's social isolation but also of the subservient position they had experienced for ages.[73]

Partially, Bottigheimer blamed such a gender stereotyping on older social attitudes, but she also blamed the Brothers Grimm themselves for having superimposed upon the tales a certain conventional morality based on a patriarchal and conservative social interest.

In developing her argument of how the Grimms' folktales depicted women as passive victims, Bottigheimer paid special attention to the kinds of punishment meted out in the tales to boys and girls respectively. She concluded that in the overwhelming majority of cases women were the ones to be condemned, not men. Men frequently got away with their crimes, yet women suffered harsh punishments, often through loss of speech. By focusing on the frequency of certain verbs used in the Grimms' 1957 edition of such selected tales as "Ashputtel," "The Frog King," "Jorinda and Joringel," "King Thrushbeard," and the so-called "Christian Tales" (some legends), she tried to prove by means of charts that the Grimms employed direct speech with figures of authority, predominantly with male protagonists and some vicious females, such as witches and stepmothers, while reserving indirect speech for the "good girls." After counting the number of times in which females and males employed the verbs *sagen* (to say), *sprechen* (to speak), *rufen* (to call), *fragen* (to ask), and *antworten* (to answer), she concluded that the active role of speaking and asking was decidedly left to males, whereas the passive role of saying and answering was left to subordinated females.[74]

While such observations appear stunning at first sight, they invite the question of whether the Grimms themselves considered *sagen* and *antworten* weaker expressions than *sprechen* and *fragen*. Even if the reader would buy Bottigheimer's thesis that they did make such preferences on the basis of an unconscious bias, it must be observed that both in formal and colloquial German the verbs *sprechen* and *sagen* are mostly used interchangeably and that their respective active or passive connotations depend entirely on the context in which they occur and the gestures or the tone that accompany them. Context, gesture, and tone would also determine whether *rufen*, *fragen*, or *antworten* are to be understood as clues to a dominant or a submissive character or attitude. A question may be posed in a shy and rather timid way or it may be stated in a demanding and forceful way, and an answer, too, may be weak and dutiful (like that of a demure little schoolgirl) or it may be powerful and even prophetic (like that of a sibyl or prophetess). Without such a context, the use of a verb alone could not well be taken as evidence of a character trait.

Valuable is Bottigheimer's gestalt approach to folktale motifs, in which she grouped together "motif clusters" from various tales under some given chapter topics, for it adds a more comprehensive scheme to the discussion than one that singles out individual motifs.[75] It also enhances the reader's interest in such selected topics as "Deaths and Executions," "Towers, Forests, and Trees," or "Spinning and Discontent" because it uses the motifs as supportive evidence. Bottigheimer wrote that in this way she hoped to avoid coloring her interpretation by a particular school of thought, be it anthropological, psychological, Christian, nationalist, Marxist, or feminist. The weakness of this approach lies in the absence of a clear rationale for the selection of the individual motifs that make up such "motif clusters." As such, some do seem to follow a feminist bias. One might suggest that among the more than 200 tales in Grimms' complete edition of the *Kinder- und Hausmärchen* it would not be difficult to group together some other "motif clusters" that would prove the very opposite of each view presented. Let it suffice to say that in the Grimms' tales there are a number of aggressive young females who do not obey their authoritarian fathers, who do not stay at home to spin and clean house, who do not sit back passively to wait for a suitor, and who do not lose their speech.

Wilhelm Grimm's own point of view received little attention in Bottigheimer's analysis. Regarding the case of women as victims, it may be observed that Wilhelm singled out as a "stock character" of the tales the suffering male, not the suffering female, namely the naive Dummling who slept under the stairwell and had to do all of the dirty work.[76] He recognized the character and theme of Cinderella in a comparative background study, pointing out that she had been better known in older German folk literature as a servant boy named Eschengrudel or Eschengründel (Geile von Kaisersberg). Thereafter, the character had been female, as reference to Aschenpoßel by Rollenhagen (known as a younger sister of three abusive brothers) or Askenpösel, Askenpüster, and Askenböel by Adelung. In Dutch folklore she was popular as the girl Aschenpöselken and Sudelsödelken, and in both German and Dutch the verb *pöseln* was used to indicate her tedious job of selecting the good peas and the bad peas from the ashes into which the stepmothers had dumped them, just as the Polish name of Kopciuszek was related to the word *Kopec*, meaning soot or smoke. Grimm discussed in great detail also some parallel motifs in Perrault's *Cendrillon*, Madame d'Aulnoy's *Finette Cendron*, and Basile's *Cennerentola* (*Pentamerone I, 6*),[77] thus showing his awareness of the Cinderella theme in European folktales. Nevertheless, in analyzing predominant folktale characters in the *Kinder- und Hausmärchen*, he singled out not Ashenputtel but Dummling, "the boy of the ashes." A close reading of the Grimms' tales will confirm that females were by no means the only creatures who suffered from abuse and repression. It will also reveal a number of aggressive female characters who disobey their fathers and are not cowed into submission.

Nevertheless, Bottigheimer's observations have done much to alert modern readers to certain sociopsychological values within the tales that are relevant to our growing consciousness of the gender gap and the need for women's rights. Even though some of her observations may be challenged, they follow an original design and provide excellent material for discussion.

Maria Tatar in *The Hard Fact about Grimms' Fairy Tales* also underscored the traditional sex-role assignment for female characters in folktales. She agreed with Bottigheimer that the Grimms supposedly had reworked the tales in such a way as to emphasize the harsh and cruel treatment of women within the work ethics of the nineteenth century.[78] Still, she voiced some reservations regarding the role of women as victims. To the contrary, she found that there were a great number of female villains in the Grimms' tales that played an active role as agents of evil, such as nags, witches, and stepmothers, and that their victims were by no means just girls or women. It was true that the suffering of females was a bit more extensive in the Grimms' folktales than the suffering males, but on the whole, both male and female characters had an even share of it.[79]

Refreshing in Tatar's discussion is the revisionist view of the male protagonist. Although she did not question the dominant characters of kings and fathers, she felt that their portrayal was well balanced by dominant queens and stepmothers respectively. Instead of calling attention to the suppressed female, she focused on the maltreatment of the naive village boy, the underdog, and the fool, who instead of slaying dragons or giants would delouse them or befriend them. Block-heads, numskulls, or simpletons in the Grimms' tales exorcised demons, withstood horrors, and always triumphed at the end. They also knew how to turn their shortcomings into assets. Some of them had certain tall-tale characteristics that produced a comic effect in folktales. Tatar cited certain parallel characters in literature, such as Wolfram von Eschenbach's Parzival, Goethe's Wilhelm Meister, and Thomas Mann's Hans Castorp (*The Magic Mountain*).[80]

In focusing on the weak male character in the Grimms' folktales who is often hesitant to act, sometimes stupid, and overall so unlike the heroic superhero for whom one might search in folktales, Tatar's views came close to Wilhelm Grimms' own observations regarding Dummling or Boots. However, she emphasized to a greater degree the harsh realities of everyday life rather than the purity and kindness of his naive character. What she did not mention, however, was the quality of kindness and the spirit of forgiveness that, in Wilhelm Grimm's view, distinguished Dummling from other characters. To Wilhelm he was more than a mere numskull or stupid fool but the very embodiment of naivete and purity, which the Romantics valued so highly, be it in the peasant, the "savage," or the child. One might say that Wilhelm was less concerned about the particular sex of a child than about the quality of naivete as such—a quality that he saw reflected in the pure eyes of children. Sometimes Dummling's innocence evoked laughter and thus had humorous effect, but more often, it evoked empathy—the very response that Wilhelm characterized as the "humanizing effect" of folktales.[81]

Tatar combined various approaches in her interpretation of gender in the Grimms' *Kinder- und Hausmärchen*. As far as the folktale's reflection of internal conflicts was concerned, she leaned toward Bettelheim's theory that fairy tales translated psychic realities into concrete images, characters, and events, but in regard to folktale symbols, her comprehensive approach reflected the enlightened views of Max Lüthi. On the other hand, by warning readers not to be carried away by abstract symbols but to respect in the folktales the mental life and culture of the time, she showed herself as a follower of Robert Darnton. Especially her interpretation of violence and cruelty revealed her belief that folktales were a mirror of the hard facts of life. The catalogue of horrors that she listed in her first chapter on "Sex and Violence" has a certain sensational appeal. It is a question whether she did justice to the Grimms by listing the various cruelties out of context (very much in the fashion of nineteenth-century didactic critics), for in this way she obscured their relationship to ethics. Regardless of whether one agrees with the pagan system of justice and the cruelties that it entailed, one cannot well deny that it had meaning within a context of crime and punishment. Cruelty is as integral a part of mythology and epic as it is of the folktale world— but rarely without this context. Who would call Hesiod cruel for having passed on to future generations the myth of Cronus, who swallowed his children? Or who would call Homer cruel for having permitted Odysseus to blind Polyphemus? That the Grimms added to the initial cruelties by exaggerating them is difficult to prove, as they used different variants of the tales for different editions. The same is true for their portrayal of women or females in general. What Bottigheimer or Tatar may have considered the Grimms' own phobias or values may well have been loyal recordings of additional folktale version that they collected for a later edition.

Sigrid Früh in *Die Frau im Märchen* (*The Woman in Folktales*) took the opposite view of Bottigheimer by emphasizing that the Grimms' folktale characters were far from demure and passive. Ashputtel, for example, was as active, adventuresome, and cleverly scheming as had been the French Cinderella. By escaping three times shortly before midnight, she had made herself more desirable to the prince by playing hard to get, and also by finally making the prince kneel down before her. Significantly, she further brought him to the point that he accepted her in her own ash-stained dress, which meant he accepted her in her own identity. According to Früh, this scene represented a symbolic gesture of the prince's *subordination* to the will of Ashputtel.[82]

Früh consciously tried to contradict the common notion that Ashputtel merely sat back passively to wait for her prince. In doing so, she challenged the reader to reread the story carefully and think about it creatively and in modern terms. The question arises whether, in doing so, she did not violate the spirit of the folktale. In the German tradition, Acshenputtel (often translated as Ashputtel) is commonly known for her naivete, purity, kindness, unselfishness—qualities that seem to defy the notions of self-interest and clever scheming. The French Cinderella places more emphasis on vanity, yet she, too, could not be called a schemer—a role that would be better suited for her older sisters (or, according to an older German version by Rollenhagen, for her two older brothers). As refreshing as it may be to take a new look at an old tale, it is advisable to stay within the boundaries of the traditional folktale character traits—unless one wishes to rework it into a satire or travesty.

Heinz Rölleke took a quantitative approach to the study of female characters in the Grimms' *Kinder- und Hausmärchen*. First, he pointed out some general misconceptions regarding the number of tales concerned with female protagonists. Critics had often used the 1857 edition of the work to count how many of the 211 tales were actually concerned with female characters. In doing so, they had come up with the number 30, which had led them to the conclusion that only about one-seventh of the tales were concerned with women. Rölleke pointed out that such mathematics was wrong, as only about 60 folktales in this edition could be considered *Märchen* (defined as magic tales, or *Voll- und Zaubermärchen*) that had a childlike appeal. The rest of the folktales should not be counted, as they resembled legends, jests, animal tales, or cumulative tales and did not fit this definition. On the other hand, the first shorter edition of the *Kinder- und Hausmärchen* of 1825 (which included 50 *Märchen* that all had a childlike appeal) contained 30 tales that dealt with female heroines, which meant 60 percent. Among these tales were such well-known titles as "The Frog Prince," "Child Mary," "Snow White," "Sleeping Beauty," "Mother Holle," "Little Red Cap," "Star Child," "Goose Girl," "Brother and Sister," "Hansel and Gretel," and "The Fisherman and his Wife." Rölleke observed that many of these tales had become so much associated with the female protagonist that even in cases where the story talked in neutral terms about a child, as in "Star Child," most readers automatically associated the child with a girl rather than with a boy.[83]

Rölleke felt that 60 percent was an extraordinary high percentage of tales with female protagonists. As a reason for this preference he did not cite the Grimms' personal interest in women but rather the predominant role of female storytellers in their time. Earlier, German storytellers had been predominantly male, he said, which explained why the character of Dummling, for example, had been much better known than the character of Ashputtel. In his view, the change in gender emphasis in the folktales was a direct result of the rising importance of female storytellers, for it was natural that females would subsequently project their own views of work, suffering, and success into the tales. He suspected that the main reason for the relatively large number of female protagonists in the Grimms' *Kinder- und Hausmärchen* was that women had played a predominant role among the Grimms' informants.[84] While Rölleke agreed that Wilhelm Grimm, who married only in his thirties, had a certain fondness for idyllic womanhood—which may have had a certain influence on the *Biedermeier* idyll in the folktales—he did not think that Wilhelm's personal views had been decisive. Admittedly, there were some exceptions. In a rather domestic scene in "Snow White and Rose Red," for example, Wilhelm had depicted the two girls as perhaps too kind, docile, obedient, clean, and amiable in the *Biedermeier* fashion, yet on the whole, the tales reflected the taste of the informants, most of whom had been women: the Hassenpflugs, the Haxthausens, the Droste-Hülshoffs, Old Marie, and Frau Viehmännin. By examining six tales told by Frau Viehmännin, for example, he found that all of them dealt with girls. In contrast, the tales told by Wachtmeister Krause had no female heroines at all! As a woman, Frau Viehmännin had suffered herself, and it was only natural that she related many of her own life experiences to the tales she told, especially those involving suffering due to poverty, hardships, and labor. Why should Wilhelm Grimm have superimposed his own values on her tales or those of others?

With respect to the Grimm's editorial changes, Rölleke had a different opinion from those expressed by Bottigheimer and Tatar respectively, for he concluded that the Grimms let the stories speak for themselves without meddling with their essential qualities.[85] By contrast, Bottigheimer and Tatar thought that the changes had been substantial enough to color the value judgments about women in the tales—or at least the prevalent views regarding the role of women in their time.

[Social-Historical Perspectives]

August Nitschke in *Soziale Ordnung im Spiegel der Märchen* (*Social Order in the Mirror of Folktales*)[86] suggested that the tale of "Rapunzel" might have its roots in primitive "puberty huts," in which young girls used to be locked away to spend their formative years in safe isolation. In seeking out folktale interpretations that were related to medieval customs and rituals, he essentially followed the lead of Lang, Malinowski, and Frazer, even though his interest gradually moved away from primitive tribes toward social life in Europe. When Lutz Röhrich suggested in *Märchen und Wirklichkeit* (*Folktale and Reality*)[87] that in folktales local color and cultural milieu were derived from real situations and real persons, he, too, followed a historical interpretation that seemed to affirm the "reality" of social customs, mores, and traditions. The basis of such an interpretation was neither symbolic nor literary but mainly realistic, with a view toward the social environment and social forces. In more recent years it has also included bourgeois middle-class values toward work, leisure, education, and sex roles. Folktales, viewed from the historical and social perspective, betray stages of culturalization and socialization. They can be dated, and as manifestations of representative value systems they have even been used to document certain prevailing attitudes and trends.

Yet, Röhrich and others did not necessarily follow the anthropological interpretation of folktales in tracing the folktale's reflection of history and "reality." Von Sydow was one of the first critics who rejected the anthropological interpretation on the basis that it confused the spiritual heritage of the Australian aborigines with the cultural heritage of European countries. Even if the historical evidence of European folktales might lead back as far as 6,000 years, it provided very different insights into history than an equally old tale from a "savage tribe." He thus insisted that a distinction be made between the study of folktales from primitive tribes and from what he called "high civilization."[88]

In a comparative study of the "Rumpelstiltskin" tale, Otto Kahn took Röhrich's lead by emphasizing the "reality" behind the tale. Refusing to see Rumpelstiltskin merely as a dwarf or "little man" endowed with the magic of myth and folktale, he suggested that he was a representative of a conquered and enslaved people, perhaps one of the original inhabitants of a given region that was occupied by more powerful tribes. Folktales and legends often took the perspective of the loser, said Kahn. Calling attention to the need for reading the folktale texts closely, he referred to various references of "wild folks" living in valleys, remote forests, or mountain caves that hinted at a tribe living in the "underground." Far from being creatures of myth or fantasy derived from the imagination, the "little people" were real folk who had lived within real and known history, often revealing the tragic fate of entire peoples. Hidden away among valleys and mountains, they had suffered yet survived, be it as slaves or resistance fighters, moving about secretly only at night and trying to be as "invisible" as possible. Perhaps they had served as hired workers or slaves to the ruling peasant class yet then had fought—even though unsuccessfully—for regaining their status on their own land.[89]

Kahn gave two "realistic" explanations of why Rumpelstiltskin showed an interest in the miller's beautiful daughter. First, the "little people," like all suppressed peoples, were inclined to be kind and helpful to those in need, as they had suffered serious hardships themselves. Secondly, they tried to upgrade their race by intermarrying with the dominant group so as to regain their lost status. The fact that "little people" in folktales were often known "helpers" or "doers of good deed" rather than as wicked creatures supported the idea that they had been real people who were glad to help others in need, simply because they themselves had known trouble.

Following a cultural-historical interpretation, Kahn also made a case for giants as people who had really lived in history. In that case, they had been enemies or foreign invaders from faraway lands. Giants in the Grimms' folktales were just as real as were girls and women with their spinning wheels, he maintained. Until about one hundred years ago, spinning had been a major household chore and the usual customary evening activity of girls and women everywhere in the villages. Generally, such an activity had some positive connotations, as it had made every household self-sufficient in the textile and garment industry. In Greek, Roman, and Norse mythology, spinning women had even been elevated to goddesses spinning the thread of life, and the graves of aristocratic women had been enriched with spinning wheels and spindles to enable them to continue their activity in life beyond death.[90]

In the particular context of "Rumpelstiltskin," however, Kahn noticed that the king's demand for his daughter's labor was much too high to begin with to make spinning a pleasure. Not only did he raise his demands from day to day but he also deprived her of her sleep, locked her up in a room by herself, and finally threatened her by death if she would not manage to fulfill the assigned task. Such labor demands, wrote Kahn, suggested ancient slavery conditions or the conditions of serfdom. From here he moved on to a contemplation of medieval and ancient labor laws, customs and laws regulating slave labor, the role of parents in determining the choice of a girl's bridegroom, and the daughter's attitude toward such pressures and demands. While he did not overlook a certain cleverness in the girl's attitudes and actions by means of which she asserted herself against the king's order, he felt that the overall moral of the tale still pointed to an inevitable reality of history: the king, her master, was victorious in the end.

Viewed from such cultural-historical perspectives, folktales represented a mirror of reality, said Kahn. Far from reflecting the fate of individuals within the context of magic and folk imagination, they reflected the reality of long ago — in this case, the fate of an entire suppressed people who had once owned the land on which they now slaved and the fate of women within the power structure of the medieval as well as ancient society.

Otto Gmelin in *Böses kommt aus Kinderbüchern* (*Evil Originates in Children's Books*) considered folktales unrelated to free fantasy but rather as historically and economically founded instructions for children and adults.[91] They mirrored not only certain historical conditions but also family situations and family values. Because of their predominant work ethics, he called them didactic instructions for work that had become necessary due to certain historical and economic conditions.

Like a number of other critics in the seventies, Gmelin felt that folktales arose, like dreams, from suppressed unconscious desires. Dieter Richter and Johannes Merkel drew certain parallels between dream fantasies as viewed by psychoanalysis and "fantasies of the people" or the *Volk*, yet they noted a substantial difference between the two. Whereas dreams were the products of individuals, fantasies of the people expressed through folktales were dreams of a group of people who had shared a certain historical and economic situation within society. Consequently, an interpretation of folktales inevitably would yield some insights into the reality of a particular people's social structure, their historical experiences, and their values.

Some critics of the antiauthoritarian movement in West Germany argued during the sixties that folktales were too deeply rooted in the values of a feudal authoritarian society to be suitable educational material for children. Either the king or the father figure had ruled with an almost unlimited power, imposing his patriarchal will. While male protagonists in folktales played the dominant role, female protagonists assumed mostly subordinate roles and lived a life of lowly existence on the brink of poverty. Such was the case with the Grimms' "The Goose Girl," for example, in which the servant girl would perform menial tasks, or with "Aschenputtel," the German Cinderella.[92]

They could move up the social ladder (as did the abused girl in "Frau Holle," for example) but only if they were extremely diligent and useful. In this case, the girls had to pass a test by shaking the feather beds and cleaning house. Snow White, too, had to prove her worth by keeping house for seven dwarfs. If a female protagonist exceptionally assumed the role of a clever girl posing riddles, she was usually outwitted at the end by a male protagonist who turned out to be smarter and stronger than she.

The more recent folktale interpretations of Jack Zipes, too, fall under the cultural-historical approach, as they emphasize that folktales reflect the "real life" background and social order or the bourgeois entanglements of modern society. Working on the premise that social, cultural, and political forces shape the individual and his fate, Zipes believes that German folktales are the product of German nationalism and an overconcern with such bourgeois virtues as industriousness and the spirit of the bourgeois entrepreneur. Zipes claimed that the Grimms had "reworked and revised" the collected folktales, mainly in order to convey their notion of family, ethical behavior, and homeland. In the Grimms' tales the male heroes tended to be adventurous, cunning, opportunistic, and reasonable, taking calculated risks and expecting these to pay off, whereas the female protagonists reflected to a greater extent the values of industriousness, order, and thrift.[93] The way in which the two sisters in "Snow White and Rose Red" were described as inseparable and supportive of each other moreover reflected the Grimm Brothers' own relationship to each other. Comparing the *Kinder- und Hausmärchen* version with a summarized tale in Wilhelm's notes, Zipes judged that Wilhelm had taken great liberties in reshaping a literary variant that reflected not only his favored idyllic setting but also an idealized sibling relationship corresponding to the one that he experienced with his brother. Zipes even went so far as to say that the Grimms had redesigned the bulk of the "magic fairy tales" as literary products, so as "to put an end to magic."[94]

Zipes viewed the Grimms' *Kinder- und Hausmärchen* on a similar level as literary fairy tales, projecting into both the formative influences of a bourgeois age. He contended that as members of the middle class, the Grimms had been obsessed with bourgeois norms and values of their age, such as diligence, order, and thrift. In compensation for a lack of aristocratic background and the privileges that went along with it, they had striven for a distinction and prestige in terms of education, or *Bildung*. Both their quest for *Bildung* and their valor to succeed had been obvious in their struggle for an academic career and their lifelong striving for scholarship.[95]

Evidently, Zipes's socialist theory did not make an allowance for the word *Bildung* in altruistic terms as it had been understood by Goethe, the Romantics, and even Thomas Mann. Goethe had spoken about *Bildung* in connection with an idealistic demand for education that also meant the formation of "inner man," implying the formation of self-discipline and civic responsibility. The term *Bildungsbürger* is a compound noun coined by Zipes that is neither used in present-day Germany nor was known as such in the time of Goethe or the Brothers Grimm. In *The Buddenbrooks*, Thomas Mann connected only the concepts of *Bildung* and *Bürgertum* (without coining a new compound noun) while emphasizing the cultural leadership and civic responsibility of the Hanseatic citizen of the upper middle class. Yet Mann also showed in his novel the decline of the *Bürger* as a result of the driving power of his materialistic ambitions and his growing lust for money, power, and prestige. Thus, when he contrasted the truly educated and responsible *Weltbürger* (citizen of the world) with the thrifty yet small-minded and provincial *Spießbürger* (petit bourgeois), he created an awareness of the decline of idealistic values in reverse proportion to the rise of materialism.[96] Zipes did not make such a distinction. Rather, he gave the impression that all German *Bürger*, the Grimms included, had been of the *Spießbürger* type who molded their own lives, and the folktales as well, in accordance with a narrow set of such social virtues as orderliness, cleanliness, and obedience to authority.

In addition to Marxist theories, Zipes also used some psychological speculations to support his views. In discussing the attitudes of the Grimms themselves, for example, he suggested that it was the loss of the father figure in their lives that motivated them to "substitute" the love of the fatherland and all things German.[97] In this connection he referred selectively to some biographical data and excerpts from letters. Curiously, he ignored in this context both Wilhelm's and Jacob's closeness to their mother and sister (a point raised in passing more recently by Rölleke). More importantly, however, he also ignored their international orientation, including their contributions to comparative linguistics, comparative philology, and international folklore research.

Unlike the Romantics and the Grimms themselves, Zipes believed that social forces within the environment shape man's desires and destinies and, further, that all persons live in accordance with the values in which they are raised. Consequently, he concluded that in editing the folktales the Grimms had not only changed the wording of the tales but had also imposed upon conflicts and resolutions the Protestant ethics and the code of the bourgeois enlightenment by which they themselves had been raised. Supposedly this was evident in many tales within the *Kinder- und Hausmärchen*, he claimed, which not only reflected the bourgeois values of diligence, perseverance, and honesty but also that of patriarchal domination, which meant autonomy and power. Often, the folktales concluded in such a way that it seemed perfectly right to accumulate personal wealth and power for private benefit, even if this happened by devious means. These were bourgeois values asserting a master/slave relationship within the context of an accepted male dominance within society. The folktale's function of male socialization within such an hierarchical pattern could well be observed in the Grimms' tale of "The Table, the Ass, and the Stick." The tale demonstrated that as long as masters (or fathers) were benevolent and used power justly, they could do as they pleased within an authoritarian context.[98] In a number of other folktales in the Grimms' collection, Zipes observed a similar hierarchical pattern of the rising nineteenth-century German bourgeois society that took its departure from feudal society, without possessing the skills and qualities needed to compete for a high place in the hierarchy based on property, wealth, and power. Even in such tales where the downtrodden protagonists revolted by over-throwing their oppressors, neither the social relations nor the work ethos underwent a drastic change. This was evident in "How Six Travelled through the World," "The Bremen Town Musicians," "Clever Gretel," and "The Blue Light," which mirrored the values of the German bourgeois society that had been capable of making a revolution but ended up in making compromises at the expense of the peasantry.[99] It was no wonder, wrote Zipes, that many critics of the West German antiauthoritarian movement in the late sixties had questioned the use of the Grimms' folktales with children.

[The Issue of National Character]

Louis L. Snyder contended in *Roots of German Nationalism* that the primary goal of the Brothers Grimm had been to transmit through their folktale collection a fanatic love of the Fatherland.[100] Allegedly he followed in this respect the historical views of Hans Kohn and the folkloristic interpretation of Richard Dorson, yet his documentation reveals that he relied directly and selectively on quotes from such older German nationalistic interpretations as T. Matthias's *Der deutsche Gedanke bei Jacob Grimm* (*The German Idea in the Works of Jacob Grimm*) of 1915 and Carl Franke's *Die Brüder Grimm: Ihr Leben und Werk* (*The Brothers Grimm: Their Life and Works*) of 1898.[101] When Franke wrote, "They [the Brothers Grimm] have en-abled us to understand that we, the German people, bear the power and conditions in ourselves to take up and carry on the civilization of old times, that we are a folk of a high historical mission,"[102] he essentially echoed the view of the Pan-Germanic League regarding the "world mission" of the German people. Yet the Grimms were not so conceited as to consider it their "mission" to impose German folktales or the German way of thinking upon other nations. To the contrary, they spent a lifetime encouraging other nations to search out their identity by exploring their own native folk heritage. Did Snyder know that the Nazis, too, presented the Grimms as if they had been the forerunners of Pan-Germanic thought?

By interpreting certain statements out of context, Snyder presented some ideas as if they had been identical with the true intent of the Brothers Grimm. Occasionally, he would also quote the Grimms themselves out of context to prove their obsession with the Fatherland. In referring to Jacob's research assignment in Paris, for example, he only pointed out that Jacob had searched in French libraries for medieval German manuscripts while ignoring that Jacob had been involved in translations of old Spanish romances and studied medieval French literature at that time. He also used a quote from Jacob's letter, which he had written while in Paris, to prove that he had even been dreaming about the Fatherland. [103] What he ignored in this context was that the quote came from a personal letter that the twenty-year-old Jacob, who was away from home for the first time, had written to his mother. What was more natural under those circumstances than that he should have dreamed about home? Such a "documentation" could hardly be used to prove Jacob's narrow ethnocentrism. [104]

Regardless of the fact that such historians as Leopold von Ranke and Rudolf Stadelmann had sharply rejected the idea of the Grimms' "overweening national pride," [105] Snyder also brushed aside all arguments to the contrary pertaining to the Grimms' "preferred knowledge of national literature to all foreign lore." He simply bypassed all evidence linking the Grimms' research to cross-cultural and comparative studies in literature, folklore, and philology, without even mentioning their foreign correspondence, numerous translations, and prefaces to foreign folktale collections.

A point that has often been raised in regard to the Grimms' alleged nationalism is that they were discontent with the Napoleonic rule and the French occupation of Germany at the time. While this statement is logical under the given historical circumstances, it takes into consideration only the political situation. However, it ignores their cultural point of view that aimed at building bridges of human understanding. The Grimms were always fond of the French people, their language, literature, and folktales (at least as far as those of Perrault were concerned). In recognition of their contribution to the cultural ties between the two nations, they were even honored with a French medal. [106]

Some critics have also used an oversimplified approach to German Romanticism while accusing the Grimms bluntly of fanatic nationalism. While ignoring the complexity of this movement and its early international orientation, they have tended to dwell on the later Romantic fascination with nationalism and the Hegelian concept of the state, making no allowance for the wide differentiation of views prevailing at an earlier time. Historian Robert M. Berdahl observed quite poignantly that a portrayal of German Romanticism frequently overemphasized an exclusive concern with nationalism, thus treating the movement as if it had been a homogenous unit. [107]

Is it true that the Grimms also rejected the Western concept of democracy while clinging to the Hegelian concept of the state? Were they indeed ardent admirers of militarism who "bowed to the voice of authority"? In response to such generalizations, one might point to the theory of the Grimms' friend and colleague Friedrich Dahlmann that defended a "divine order" based on ethical principles of justice that he considered superior to the worldly state. More significantly, however, one should point to the Grimms themselves, who justified the existence of the state primarily in terms of its function as a moral agency of the individual. A state, in their view, was bound by the principles of ethics and certainly was not above the law. Probably the best proof that they believed in a state of justice and democracy is their own courageous stand on behalf of the constitutional rights that had guaranteed the freedom of the individual. They firmly believed that no ruler was justified to amend or abolish such rights without the express consent of the people. In their quest for human rights and democracy, the Grimms sacrificed their jobs as professors along with their personal safety.[108]

Folklorist Richard Dorson pointed out that there were certain similarities between the Grimms' nationalistic view of folktales and the view that had dominated the ideological interpretation of the Third Reich. Yet even though he perceived a continuity of thought from the Grimms to the Nazi period, as far as nationalism was concerned, he did alert his readers to the Nazis' distortion of the Grimms' folktales that differed substantially from the Grimms' own perspective on the subject.[109]

Not all critics made such a distinction, however. In pointing to the national character of the German people, some perceived nationalism as a constant factor throughout German history. In claiming that the Nazis had used the Grimms' "unexpurgated fairy tales," Snyder gave the impression that they had to change nothing in their attempt to use these tales to indoctrinate youth with a glorification of war and power, reckless courage, theft, brigandage, and militarism. Consequently, the Grimms' folktales appear in this interpretation as if they had been perfect blueprints for authoritarianism, "primitive sadistic and even masochistic social attitudes," and other atrocities committed under Hitler's regime. As a matter of warning he wrote: "The effects of such tales upon German youth might well be imagined,"[110] thus hinting at the official warnings against the Grimms' fairy tales, issued by the allied occupation forces after World War II.

Arguments such as these are based on the assumption that there is such a thing as a static national character. Snyder, for example, agreed with Hans Kohn that modern developments in West Germany had shown a movement toward democracy within the NATO alliance and that change was possible. He insisted that the Grimms' folktales, nevertheless, reflected the German people's true national character. This observation was not meant as a compliment, for he pointed out that Germany's most stable and influential aspects throughout its history had been some persistent negative traits. His specific targets were such traits as authoritarianism (usually in relation to the father image of a king or hero), the idea of the family as a cohesive unit ruled by a male (husband, brother, or father), a pronounced class consciousness (distinct roles assigned to the peasantry, the aristocracy, the military, professional merchants, artisans, old people, or children), and an antagonism, or even an open hostility, toward the outsider (particularly the Jew). Yet there were also such traits as respect for order and discipline, subservience to the leader, an overemphasis on valor, an acceptance of cruelty and violence, and a supposedly very primitive concept of "justice."[111]

To prove his point, Snyder singled out selected folktales by number and then analyzed specific recurring character traits, attitudes, and actions. He made no mention of other tales that might prove the opposite, nor did he make reference to other possible approaches that viewed folktales from psychological, symbolic, literary, or ethnological points of view. Neither did he mention the Grimms' own notes regarding international variants of the tales. When discussing the Grimms' tale "The Girl without Hands," for example, he pointed out the girl's blind obedience to authority and the cruelty of her treatment, as both of these traits embodied a typically German theme. Yet he ignored the Grimms' comparative notes on the tale that had pointed to earlier variants by Basile and Straparola.[112] Did he keep silent on this account because such evidence would have implied that the Italians, too, possessed these negative character traits?

Both the issue of national character and the question of the Grimms' nationalistic values in the *Kinder- und Hausmärchen* are the subject of an ongoing debate. The more recent "discovery" pertaining to the Huguenot origin of some of the Grimms' informants did not essentially undermine the argumentation of the critics in question. Ellis solved this dilemma by contending that the Grimms had purposely passed off as German what was not German at all, which meant that they had imposed their own values upon the tales. Zipes essentially took the same perspective on the issue by claiming that the Grimms had reconstituted the folktales in accordance with their own needs and ethics, partially as a compensation for the loss of father and homeland. Snyder decided that such findings were irrelevant to the issue in question, as the children or grandchildren of Huguenot immigrants were less capable of transmitting their native folk tradition than Germans who had lived in a given place for many generations, which meant that in his view the Grimms' folktales were predominantly German in character.

The other question that has had a certain bearing on the issue of the Grimms' nationalism pertains to the accuracy of the Grimms' recordings of the tales. If they had invented some of the tales or changed them drastically, as some critics have claimed, one may wonder how they could still be considered German traditional tales. Snyder brushed aside this argument by affirming that the Grimms had printed the tales "with fanatical accuracy,"[113] which to him implied that they consciously preserved in the tales what he considered the German national character. Jack Zipes used the opposite argument by insisting that the Grimms had imposed upon the tales their own sociocultural values and that they were German because of these values. Curiously, even though both critics used arguments on opposite sides, they tried to prove the same point, namely that the Grimms' tales were essentially representative of the German national character.

We may leave it up to the reader to decide to what degree the Grimms' folktales reflected the kinds of values that the Grimms themselves recognized in their analysis of folktale characters, for example. Their high interest in international variants and their broad-minded attitude toward a great variety of different interpretations regarding folktale origins made it unlikely that they imposed upon the folktales a narrow social perspective flavored by a "bourgeois" environment and "patriotic" inclinations. In this regard and elsewhere it might be more appropriate to respect their own concept of folktales as *Naturpoesie*, both in poetic and international terms.

[The Issue of Folktale Ethics]

In the aftermath of World War II, the British and American occupation forces raised the question of whether it would be wholesome for German children to continue reading the folktales of the Brothers Grimm. German students and professors of folklore and literature responded comprehensively to the issue of folktale ethics by pointing out literary, symbolic, and psychological perspectives that had only intangible relations to real-life events. It is interesting to observe that they distanced themselves from realistic, social, and cultural-historical interpretations of folktales in responding to the issue involved.

Will Erich Peuckert, in his work *Wiedergeburt: Gespräche in Hörsälen und unterwegs*[114] (*Rebirth: Conversation in Lecture Halls and on the Road*), contemplated the fate of the Grimm's *Kinder- und Hausmärchen* after World War II. The question of folktale ethics had become an acute one, as the occupation forces not only had made a definite connection between the Grimms' tales and the horrors of the Nazi concentration camps but also had prohibited the sale and circulation of the Grimms' tales. Was such a censorship fair to the Grimms and the inherent meaning of the *Märchen*? Were the tales to be taken literally or rather symbolically? Did not "good" outweigh "evil" in these tales by siding with justice?

These and many more questions were at the center of attention at an international folktale workshop sponsored by the Hessian universities and colleges at Marburg in the summer of 1947. Discussions of the participating students, professors, and teachers focused on the ethics of the Grimms' *Kinder- und Hausmärchen*, which had been seriously challenged by the occupation forces. The workshop was called to investigate the issue of folktale ethics and its relevance to historical events.

In summarizing the essential points raised at the workshop, Peuckert once more defined the nature of the folktale, in the sense as it was generally accepted by those present. He then contrasted the folktale with the legend, just as the Grimms had done, ascribing to the folktale more of an evocative, imaginative appeal, yet less realism in terms of historical flavor and local color and overall less credibility. He made it clear that such a distinction held true only for the European folktale, as in India folktales were considered true stories. Legends often dwelt on creatures and incidents close to home: the brook behind grandfather's barn, a nearby lake or forest, an inhabited well, or a spirit in a particular haunted house. The neighborhood was alive with spirits that came and went by day or night. The folktale world, by contrast, usually kept a certain distance from home. It was on his travels away from home that the hero met witches, giants, talking beasts, and sorcerers, or that somewhere in the deep, dark forest, in the shelter of a cave, or in the underworld he met with his challenge. Snow White lived behind seven hills, and Mother Hulda (Frau Holle) lived in a strange underworld deeper than the bottom of the well. In the "Seven Ravens" a little girl walked to where sun and stars rise at the end of the world, and in the Norwegian folktale the destination lay "east of the sun and west of the moon."

This distant world of folktales, however, was the shelter of humanity where everyone would feel at home. In folktales it was not the primitive or cruel element that dominated but rather the naive worldview of the simple man living a simple style of life. Beauty and goodness were one and the same thing, simply because goodness was beautiful to the simple man, as much as evil to him appeared ugly. The white bride and the black bride were symbolic of good and evil. Wilhelm Grimm had used the attribute of *schön* (beautiful) in connection with that of *lieblich* (lovely, graceful): *"schön und lieblich."* *Lieblich* in that sense did not imply commercial beauty but was used synonymously with kind, friendly, and graceful, qualities that had a healing effect on the wounded soul. Sometimes the Grimms also used to say, *"Sie war lieblich von Angesicht."* By *Angesicht* they did not mean the regularity of her features but a kind and spirited facial expression standing for a kind and benevolent soul. *Angesicht* was a somewhat archaic expression, yet Wilhelm preferred its poetic ring to the flat expression of *"Sie hatte ein schönes Gesicht (She had pretty features).* [115]

Peuckert believed that the folktale affirmed, embraced, and enhanced primarily not the creatures of evil but the pure and innocent human being. If "sins" happened, they were not conscious acts of evil. In that sense, both Rapunzel and the Goose Girl were persecuted because of their innocence not because of their "sins." In loving the Prince, Rapunzel was innocent because she embraced him inexperienced, unknowingly, and without even thinking that he might help her to escape from the tower. The miller's daughter in "Rumpelstiltskin" was equally innocent, as she had driven into a situation over which she had no control. Wicked was undoubtedly the fisherman's wife in "The Fisherman and His Wife," as she was greedy and ambitious, but because she ended up where she had begun, in her old hovel or *Pißpott* (literally, chamber-pot), evil did not win out at the end.

If good triumphed over evil, it meant that the order and justice of the world had been restored. Peuckert insisted on calling it "order and justice" and not "ethics or morality," for folktale protagonists did not always act ethically. Occasionally, they broke a promise or an oath, they cheated, or they stole. The morality of the folktale was characterized by what he called a *"naive Sittlichkeit"* ("naive ethics").[116]

In regard to the naive concept of ethics, he leaned on André Jolles's work *Einfache Formen (Simple Forms)*. Jolles had in part supported the ritual conception of folktales but he also contradicted it, as he primarily considered folktales as primitive forms of art guided by a primitive concept of justice, a naive moralistic demand to set things "right." In his view, it was neither reason nor logic but magic that brought about such a justice in folktales. Magic—along with an element of fairness—reversed bad fortune and resolved all conflicts that had arisen from such natural disadvantages as being the youngest one, the most stupid one, poor, ill, abused, or just unhappy. Jolles claimed that folktales were far remote from reality or had *Wirklichkeitsferne*, which also meant that they were distant from time and place. Guided by good fortune, the protagonists acted with an inner certainty and ultimately overcame all obstacles. Whereas reality was cruel and unjust, folktales, in their distanced view from reality, were full of magic and fairness.[117]

Neither Jolles nor Peuckert identified folktale ethics with everyday morality. In fact, they thought it was unrealistic as well as antididactic in the sense that it did not reflect how the world was or should be but rather how it might be. As such, it expressed wishful thinking rather than realistic situations or strict moralistic demands.

To this interpretation of primitive justice, or "naive ethics," Peuckert added Lüthi's theories to show that many folktales had a meaning beyond the simple satisfaction granted by fairness and wish fulfillment.[118] This meaning, however, was not to be found in a "lesson," for children certainly did not listen to folktales in order to study ethics. If folktales kept them spellbound by marvelous adventures, difficult tasks, and dazzling possibilities, it was because they involved their own imagination in the dangers, obstacles, failures, and successes faced by their protagonists. Folktales spoke to the child in a vivid picture language and actions symbolic of human endeavors, regardless of whether the child understood their deeper meanings or not.

Sometimes the Grimms' folktales merely followed the course of good fortune that lay beyond morality. Even though good luck seemed to favor those who were spiritually pure and good at heart, everyday morality had very little to do with reward and punishment. It was the naive and innocent character, the one that was "good at heart" who would win out at the end, not the one who "did a good deed" according to Sunday school morality.[119]

If the folktales were not designed to teach morals, were they useless because they taught nothing? They did teach something, said Peuckert, but not morality in the strict sense of the word, and never explicitly. Rather, they implicitly taught some lessons about life itself. One of these was the value of innocence and purity. Another one was the value of taking a challenge seriously by fighting for it to the very end. Only by fighting for their goals could heroes and heroines prove themselves—not by living it up. For the sake of a sacred goal it was necessary to sacrifice comfort, and even to risk one's life. Folktale heroes cut their paths through deep forests, climbed through thistle beds and thorny hedges, crossed the vast wilderness, endured hunger and thirst, and struggled with wild bests. Suffering was their lot on the road toward the final destination. In that sense, the folktales taught by example about the nobility of the soul characterized by a spirit of determination, perseverance, integrity, and dedication. One of the finest "lessons" that folktales had to offer was that of love in its purest form, a love for which no sacrifice was too great. Innocence, sacrifice, and purity of love might gain him what André Jolles had called the immortality of the world or, as Peuckert put it, "the eternal values" born of a noble spirit.[120]

In view of such conclusions reached by students and professors together at the Marburg folktale workshop after World War II, one may think it a pity that the representatives of the occupation forces were not invited to listen, for all of the cruelties in the Grimms' folktales appeared to be sublimated by the noble spirit of the immortal soul. Peuckert's summary, at any rate, gave no hint that the conference participants in any way interpreted the tales from a realistic, social-historical, or cultural-anthropological perspective. Instead, they relied on the views of Jolles and Lüthi to answer the specific accusations that had been laid out against the Brothers Grimm. No apology was needed in such a literary and symbolic context, as it raised even the most cruel and gruesome folktale motifs to forces in the universal struggle of good and evil.

In addressing the question of folktale ethics in our time, Hermann Bausinger presented a related view by emphasizing their symbolic value rather than their "realistic" features.[121] In referring to the folktale style, he called attention to its dichotomy, a juxtaposition of two extremes that belonged to its characteristic elements. Like Lüthi (and to some degree also like Wilhelm Grimm), he perceived in folktales a mythical element corresponding to the concept of ethics, in the sense that the powers of light prevailed in their struggle against the powers of darkness. The figurative language and symbolic form of folktales spoke in terms of contrasting black-and-white images. Whereas fables juxtaposed clever and stupid characters, wise ones and foolish ones in a rather rigid way, folktales sometimes reversed the characters' roles and overall were more flexible than fables. On the other hand in comparison with the farce or joke in the Middle Ages, in which evil sometimes triumphed over good, thus bringing about a humorous reversal of expectations, the folktale was less flexible for it clearly defined the roles of good and evil.

Which character traits and attitudes emerged as "good" in the folktale, and which ones emerged as "evil"? Since so much attention had already been given to evil characters in folktales, Bausinger thought it necessary to balance the discussion by focusing on the so-called good characters in the Grimms' *Kinder- und Hausmärchen*. In analyzing the nature of the protagonists' virtues, he found that the good heroes and heroines were usually courageous and enduring. They were humble, patient, diligent, punctual, generous, and well-meaning, they were willing to bring sacrifices and to endure hardships, and, above all, they had pity on others, even on animals, and went out of their way to help those in need. Like Peuckert, Bausinger observed that such virtues were not merely described but that they arose in the context of the characters' *actions*. Neither did they arise only occasionally or as individual traits, he added, but they occurred in patterns and were quite characteristic of the Grimms' folktale characters as a whole.

In comparing the Grimms' original manuscript of folktales with later editions of the *Märchen*, especially the 1825 shorter edition intended for children, Bausinger admitted that some dialogues and elaborations seemed to convey moralistic intentions. Still, he insisted that the Grimms had been far from moralizing. It was a very different matter when the public schools later edited folktales with a decidedly moralistic emphasis.

How uninterested the Grimms themselves had been in conveying a sense of ethics to their readers one might gather from a closer analysis of their folktales. Contrary to popular belief, folktales did not always reward the good characters nor did they punish the evil ones. Neither did folktale characters themselves, whether male or female, act in the interest of ethics. The Valiant Little Taylor, for example (in the folktale by the same title), showed as much trickery and deceit as did the Master Thief. Like others, they deviated from the path of virtue, acted out of self-interest, and got away with it—in fact, even reaped a reward. Bausinger cited half a dozen other examples of the Grimms' tales in which evil reigned supreme.

Following the symbolic interpretation of von Beit and von Franz, Bausinger explained that folktale characters did not pursue the path of virtue but a quest for development and self-realization (*Entfaltung und Selbstverwirklichung*).[122] Contradicting Jolles's conception of the "naive morality" of the folktale hero's quest for justice, he concluded that folktales were not primarily ethical in nature but aesthetic, for their protagonists followed the call for "inner harmony" through self-realization, not the call of virtue.

Jungian critics might have talked in this connection more about the "inner struggle" or even the "inner battle of subconscious forces" than about harmony. In her work *Shadow and Evil in Fairytales*, Marie-Louise von Franz linked a number of folktale motifs suggesting archetypal darkness, such as possession by evil, the power of magic, witches, old kings, tricksters, dwarfs, and wolves with the anima, pointing out their resemblances to dreams. In her interpretation, such "dark forces" were not agents of evil, nor were their counterparts, the "light forces," agents of goodness or virtue. She explained that in comparative mythology, symbols of darkness had generally stood for whatever was nocturnal, unworldly, or earthly, yet also for the powers of the unconscious and the cult of fertility. Symbols of light, on the other hand, had stood for light and the color white, but also for clarity and order — not for goodness in the conventional sense.[123]

Von Franz answered the question of ethics in folktales in terms of the complementary qualities provided by the conscious and unconscious forces, not by the struggle of "good versus evil." Both the conscious and unconscious forces had multiple facets that evaded a clear-cut definition. The complexity of multifaceted meanings might be observed in such a folktale creature as the wolf, for example, whose image had both negative and positive connotations. He was a dark and destructive force in "Little Red Riding Hood" and "The Wolf and the Seven Little Kids," probably on account of his ancestor Fenris Wolf in Norse mythology, who had swallowed the Sun and the Moon prior to the onset of *Ragnarök*, or Doomsday. He was a positive force in relation to Roman mythology, perhaps on account of his role as a companion of Mars, and also in ancient Colombia, where he appeared as a luminous creature representing higher consciousness. If in myths and folktales all creatures contained their own opposites in terms of positive and negative forces, this was so because in the shadow of the unconscious lay hidden the seeds of creation as well as destruction. Even a pitch-black raven in folktales might be equipped with some snow-white feathers.

In similar Jungian terms, Bruno Bettelheim offered some insight into the folktale's language of good and evil, suggesting that they represented the struggle of the conscious and unconscious within each individual. In their polarization of good and evil, the images of folktales were easily grasped by the child. Overall, children were not interested so much in the question of right or wrong as in sympathy and antipathy. If they liked a hero, it was not on account of his goodness but because he appealed to them positively. Should parents protect children from the dark and evil forces in folktales? There was no need for it, suggested Bettelheim, for as far as fears and phobias were concerned, children had them anyhow, regardless of the folktales they read or listened to. Yet in reading about them within the context of folktale actions, they learned how to deal with them successfully.

Without specifically addressing the tales of the Brothers Grimm, Bettelheim made a strong plea for the "uses of enchantment" in fairy tales. In this connection he played down the question of ethics as well as aesthetics in favor of the theory that in fairy tales internal processes had been externalized in images and symbols that aided the child substantially in gaining self-knowledge and maturity.[124]

It might be pleasant to end with Bettelheim's response to the question of folktale ethics, but the reader should be alerted to the fact that it has not been resolved by any means. While some critics of the historical and psychosociological orientation have continued to blame the Grimms for imposing too many "bourgeois virtues" upon the tales, some feminist critics have accused them of having reinforced female stereotypes and horrid images of male domination. Still others have pointed at their portrayal of cruelty,[125] their insensitivity to questions of race, and their lack of interest in morality. Some modern writers have imposed upon the tales their own views of morality by controlling or censoring the tale selections in anthologies or by making essential changes in the texts. The old didactic school is by no means a thing of the past. It has swung back in a full circle to find new targets in the folktale world of the Brothers Grimm. One may only recall here the many changed endings in modern picture-book adaptations of folktales that are meant to conform to an "acceptable" morality or "political correctness" of a particular school of thought.[126]

NOTES

1. Max Müller, "On Metaphor" in *Lectures on the Science of Language*, delivered at the Royal Institute of Great Britain, Feb., Mar., Apr., and May 1863, 2d ed. (New York: Scribner & Company, 1869), pp. 371–75. See also Richard M. Dorson, "The Eclipse of Solar Mythology," in *Myth: A Symposium*, Thomas A. Sebeok, ed. (Bloomington, Ind.: Indiana University Press, 1965), pp. 33–34.

2. Dorson, p. 33.

3. Müller referred here to the "mythopoeic view" and "mythopoeic men" of Sanskrit literature in particular and the ancient Aryan nations in general. Max (Friedrich Maximilian) Müller, *Chips from the German Workshop* 2 (New York: Scribner & Company, 1872), p. 128. also Max Müller, *Selected Essays on Language, Mythology, and Religion* I (London: Scribner & Company, 1881), pp. 586–603.

4. William Cox, *Mythology of the Aryan Nations* 1 (London: Longmans, Green, 1870), p. 21 and 2, pp. 75–76.

5. Dorson, p. 41.

6. Ibid., pp. 42–45.

7. Wilhelm and Jacob Grimm, *Kinder- und Hausmärchen* 3 (Berlin: Reimer, 1922), pp. 277–79. Specifically, Wilhelm compared here tale number 5, 2 in Basile's *Pentamerone* with a strikingly similar tale in Straparola's *Nights*. Similar examples of linguistic "confusion" may be found throughout Jacob Grimm's *Deutsche Mythologie*, where he often tried to prove by means of etymology that folktales were derived from older myths and that occasionally both were derived from customs, laws, and rituals that had been reinforced orally through formulaic expressions in riddles, proverbs, sayings, and folktales.

8. Ibid., 3, Introduction by Wilhelm Grimm.

9. See, for example, Reidar Th. Christiansen, *European Folklore in America* (Oslo: Universitetsforlaget, 1962), and Kurt Ranke, "Betrachtung zum Wesen und zur Funktion des Märchens," *Studium Generale* 2 (1958), pp. 656–68. Von Sydow's observations on proverbs and common folk expressions as rich and vivid images that gave rise to folktales were closely related to those of Wilhelm Grimm in his preface to *Kinder- und Hausmärchen* 2 (Berlin: Reimer, 1919), in which he analyzed the relationship between folktales and the language and games of children. Wolfgang Mieder, "Ever Eager to Incorporate Folk Proverbs; Wilhelm Grimm's Proverbial Additions to the Fairy Tales" in *The Brothers Grimm and Folktale*, James M. McGlathery et al., eds., (Urbana, Ill.: University of Illinois Press, 1988), pp. 112–32.

10. Andrew Lang, "Household Tales; Their Origin, Diffusion, and Relation to the Higher Myths" in *Grimm's Household Tales*, with author's notes I, Margaret Hunt, trans. and ed. (London: George Bells & Sons, 1910), introduction. This work was originally published in 1884.

11. Dorson, pp. 33–34.

12. Lang, Introduction.

13. Ibid.

14. Ibid.

15. Kenneth and Mary Clarke, *Introducing Folklore* (New York: Holt, Rinehart and Winston, 1965), pp. 28–36. This work also defines a great number of other related theories debated the time.

16. Lang, Introduction.

17. Ibid., pp. lvii–lix. This list represents a summary, not an all-inclusive citation. Lang still compared in detail savage tales and European tales. For further examples see lxxi and p. 508n.

18. Wilhelm Grimm, "Introduction," in *Kinder- und Hausmärchen* 3 (Berlin: Reimer, 1922). See also Part 1, Chapter 5 on Wilhelm Grimm's *various* theories regarding the nature and origin of myths and folktales.

19. Bronislaw Malinowski, "Myth in Primitive Psychology" in *Magic, Science, and Religion and other Essays*, Bronislaw Malinowski, ed. (Garden City: Doubleday, 1954), p. 99.

20. Malinowski, pp. 100–101.

21. Paul Saintyves, *Les contes de Perrault et les récits parallèles* (Paris: E. Nourry, 1923).

22. Sir James Frazer, *The New Golden Bough*, Theodore Gaster, ed. (New York: Anchor, 1968), pp. 608–10; 721–25.

23. Ibid. See chapters on "Death and Resurrection;" "Dying and Reviving Gods," pp. 273–439.

24. Lord Raglan, *The Hero* (first published in London, 1936) (New York: Vintage, 1956), and Lord Raglan, "Myth and Ritual" in Sebeok, pp. 122–34.

25. Otto Rank, *The Myth of the Birth of the Hero; and Other Writings*, Philip Freund, ed. (New York: Vintage, Alfred A. Knopf, Inc. and Random House, Inc. 1964). The work was originally published in Vienna in 1914 by the *Journal of Nervous and Mental Disease* and first appeared as a book in 1932.

26. See Chapter 4 of this work on the Grimms' own views of folktale characters.

27. Joseph Campbell, "Folkloristic Commentary" in *The Complete Grimms' Fairy Tales*, Padraic Colum, ed. (New York: Random House, 1972), pp. 851–54. The mentioned study of *Die Zwei Brüder* (*The Two Brothers*) was a pioneering comparative folktale analysis that appeared in *FF Communications* No. 114 (Helsinki: 1934).

28. Pirkko-Liisa Rausman, "Aarne, Antti Amatus" in *Enzyklopädie des Märchens* 1 (Berlin: Walter de Gruyter, 1979), pp. 2–3. Rausman gives special credit to Aarne's various monograph series (that followed the Finnish geographical-historical method) on folktales, riddles, and epic literature, especially the *Kalevala*.

29. Ibid.

30. Campbell, pp. 854–55.

31. Friedrich Ranke, "Märchenforschung. Ein Literaturbericht (1920–1934)," *Deutsche Vierteljahresschrift für Literatur und Geistesgeschichte* 14, 2 (1936), pp. 247–304. See also Vilmos Voigt, "Anordnungs prinzipien" in *Enzyklopädie* 1, pp. 565–76.

32. Stith Thompson, *The Types of Folktale; A Classification and Bibliography* (Helsinki: 1928), *FF Communications* No. 74.

33. Stith Thompson, *Motif Index of Folk Literature* (Helsinki: 1932–1935). *FF Communications* No. 106–09 and 116–17, and *Motif Index of Folk Literature: A Classification of Narrative Elements in Folktales, Ballads, Myths, Fables, Mediaeval Romances, Exempla, Fabliaux, Jest-Books, and Local Legends* 6 vols. (Bloomington: Indiana University Press, 1948).

34. Stith Thompson, *The Folktale* (New York: The Dryden Press, 1946).

35. Johannes Bolte and Georg Polivka, *Anmerkungen zu den Kinder- u. Hausmärchen der Brüder Grimm* 6 vols. (Leipzig: Dieterichsche Verlagsbuchhandlung, 1913–32. Reprint ed. (Hildesheim: Georg Olms Verlag, 1963–72).

36. Ranke, "Märchenforschung," 301–02.

37. Ibid., p. 302.

38. Bolte and Polivka, Vol. 5, Preface.

39. Ranke, "Märchenforschung," p. 302.

40. See *Kinder- und Hausmärchen* 3, Part 2. The table of contents arranged the tales by countries, thus emphasizing visibly the international scope of the study.

41. Lutz Mackensen, ed., *Handwörterbuch des deutschen Märchens*, issued by Johannes Bolte et al. (Berlin: Walter de Gruyter, 1930–35).

42. Between 1979 and 1990 five volumes were published with well documented scholarly articles. The chief editor of all volumes has been Kurt Ranke, but a great number of German and Swiss scholars also edited sections of individual volumes, among them Hermann Bausinger, Lutz Röhrich, Elfriede Moser-Rath, Max Lüthi, Wolfgang Brückner, Rudolf Schenda, and Rainer Wehse.

43. Vladimir Propp, *Morphology of the Folktale* (originally published in 1923) 2d rev. ed., Laurence Scott, trans., with a preface by Louis A. Wagner and a new introduction by Alan Dundes (Austin: University of Texas Press, 1968).

44. Ibid. This pattern specifically fits the Russian folktales but it has only a limited applicability to *Kinder- und Hausmärchen*.

45. Linda Dégh, *Folktales and Society. Storytelling in a Hungarian Peasant Community* (Bloomington: Indiana University Press, 1969), Chapter 1.

46. Ibid. See also Linda Dégh, "What did the Grimm Brothers Give and Take from the Folk?" in James McGlathery et al., eds., pp. 66–91. On the basis of extensive fieldwork research Dégh concluded that traditional storytellers today to some extent do rely on the printed media, sometimes creating new versions on the basis of the Grimms' *Kinder- und Hausmärchen* and other sources. See p. 82.

47. James R. Dow and Hannjost Lixfeld, eds. and trans., *German Volkskunde. A Decade of Theoretical Confrontation, Debate, and Reorientation (1967–1977)* (Bloomington: Indiana University Press, 1986), pp. 14–19 and Rosemary Levy

Zumwalt, *American Folklore Scholarship. A Dialogue of Dissent*, with a foreword by Alan Dundes (Bloomington: Indiana University Press, 1988). See especially Chapter 7 on conflicts in contemporary folklore theory.

48. Elliott Oring, "Sigmund Freud" in *Enzyklopädie des Märchens 5*, pp. 272–75. The citation relates to Freud's *Aus der Geschichte einer Infantilen Neurose* (1910). See also Sigmund Freud, "Märchenstoffe in Träumen," *Internationale Zeitschrift für ärztliche Psychoanalyse* 1 (1913), pp. 142–51 and Sigmund Freud and D. E. Oppenheim, *Dreams in Folklore* (New York, 1958).

49. Freud, "Märchenstoffe." On a related psychological interpretation of Cinderella see also Bruno Bettelheim, *The Uses of Enchantment; The Meaning and Importance of Fairy Tales*, original title: *Kinder brauchen Märchen*, (New York: Random House, Vintage Books, 1977), pp. 266–67.

50. Carl Gustav Jung, "On the Relation of Analytical Psychology to Poetry" in *The Portable Jung*, Joseph Campbell, ed. and F. C. Hall, trans. (New York: Viking Press, 1983), pp. 301–02. This translation is based on the Zurich lecture of 1922 that bore the title: "Über die Beziehungen der Psychologie zum dichterischen Kunstwerk."

51. Ibid.

52. Ibid., p. 262. The applications of psychoanalysis to sociology, anthropology, and history have had a significant bearing on folklore interpretations in the twentieth century. See Fred Weinstein and Gerais M. Platt, *Psychoanalytic Sociology* (Baltimore: The Johns Hopkins University Press, 1973), and Leonard Tennenhouse, ed., *The Practice of Psychoanalytic Criticism* (Detroit: Wayne State University Press, 1976). See also Alan Dundes, "The Psychoanalytic Study of the Grimms' Tales with special reference to 'The Maiden Without Hands' (AT 706)," *The Germanic Review* 62, 2 (Spring 1987), pp. 50–66.

53. Marie Louise von Franz, *An Introduction to the Interpretation of Fairy Tales* (New York: Spring Publications, 1970), Introduction and Chapter 1.

54. Bettelheim, Chapter 1.

55. Ibid., pp. 288–91.

56. Ibid., pp. 289–90.

57. Ibid., p. 289 and p. 314 notes. In his notes, Bettelheim made reference to works by Jung and the Jungian analysts, among them Marie Louise von Franz, Hedwig von Beit, and Erich Neumann. He felt that these writers treated fairy tales much more comprehensively. As did Julius E. Heuscher in *A Psychiatric Study of Fairy Tales* (Springfield, Ill.: Charles Thomas, 1963), Bettelheim tried to maintain an intermediate position between Freud on the one hand and Jung and the Jungians on the other.

58. Bettelheim, pp. 26–27. Bettelheim called the fairy tale "therapeutic," for the thought that the patient would find in it his own solutions. He considered reading fairy tales as "comforting" to children and patients alike, mainly because they supposedly did not at all refer to the external world but reflected the individual's inner conflicts in symbolic form.

59. Hedwig von Beit, *Symbolik des Märchens; Versuch einer Deutung 2* (Bern: Francke Verlag, 1952–56), Introduction. See also Erich Fromm, *The Forgotten Language. An Introduction to the Understanding of Dreams, Fairy Tales, and Myths* (New York: Rinehart, 1951).

60. Ibid., p. xxi.

61. Ibid., p. xxiii. See also Hermann Bausinger, "Aschenputtel: Zum Problem der Märchensymbolik," *Zeitschrift für Volkskunde* 52 (1955), 144–55.

62. Rudolf Steiner, *Märchendichtungen im Lichte der Geistesforschung*. Vortrag 1908 (first published in Basel, 1942) 3d ed. Berne: Dorch, 1969, and Fritz Eymann, *Die Weisheit der Märchen im Spiegel der Geisteswissenschaften Rudolf Steiners* (Bern: Troxler, 1952). Steiner's anthroposophical interpretation of folktales had a considerable influence on the Waldorf Schools, where folktales

were used from the third grade onwards. See also Vilmos Voigt, "Anordnungs-prinzipien" *Enzyklopädie des Märchens* 1, pp. 565–66.

63. Voigt, p.566. Related views based on Steiner's conception of fairy tales appear in Friedel Lenz, *Bildsprache der Märchen* (Stuttgart: Verlag Urachhaus, 1972), pp. 1–18.

64. Max Lüthi, *The Fairy Tale as Art Form and Portrait of Man* (Bloomington: Indiana University Press, 1984). This work was originally published in 1964 under the title of *Volksmärchen als Dichtung*. On the "book fairy tale" (*Buchmärchen*) see pp. 87, 163, 167.

65. Ibid., pp. 154–57.

66. Ibid., pp. 40–75. For a thorough analysis of the so-called "folktale style," see also Max Lüthi, *The European Folktale: Form and Nature* (New York: Institute for the Study of Human Issues, first Midland edition, 1986).

67. Lüthi, *The Fairy Tale as Art Form*, pp. 152–66.

68. Max Lüthi, "Europäische Volksliteratur: Themen, Motive, Zielkräfte" in *Weltliteratur und Volksliteratur*, Albert Schäfer, ed., (Munich: Verlag C. H. Beck, 1972), pp. 55–79.

69. Friedrich Schlegel, "Rede über die Mythologie" in *Friedrich Schlegel 1794–1802. Seine prosaischen Jugendschriften* 2, Jacob Minor, ed. (Vienna, 1882), pp. 357–63. ("Die Mythologie ist ein solches Kunstwerk der Natur. In ihrem Gewebe ist das Höchste wirklich gebildet; alles ist Beziehung und Verwandlung, angebildet und umgebildet, und dieses Anbilden und Umbilden eben ihr eigentümliches Verfahren, ihr inneres Leben, ihre Methode, wenn ich so sagen darf") See also Ernst Behler, "Introduction" in *Kritische Friedrich-Schlegel Ausgabe*, Ernst Behler, ed. (Munich: Schöningh, 1966). Friedrich W. J. Schelling's *Philosophie der Mythologie* was first published in 1858. On Schelling's romantic worldview consult Burton Feldman and Robert D. Richardson, eds. *The Rise of Modern Mythology 1680–1860* (Bloomington: Indiana University Press, 1972); pp. 315–28.

70. Marie Louise von Franz, *Problems of the Feminine in Fairytales* (Dallas: Spring Publications, 1988), pp. 18–30.

71. Ibid. See also "Lecture IV."

72. Ruth Bottigheimer, *Grimms' Bad Girls and Bold Boys; The Moral and Social Vision of the Tales* (New Haven: Yale University Press, 1987), pp. 71–81.

73. Ibid., pp. 101–12.

74. Ibid., "Patterns of Speech," Appendix B, pp. 177–92.

75. Ibid., Preface, pp. xi–xii.

76. See Chapter 4 on Grimms' own perception of folktale characters.

77. Wilhelm Grimm, "Über die Märchen" in *Kinder- und Hausmärchen* 2d ed., 1 (Berlin: Reimer, 1819), Introduction. See also in Vol. 3 the notes to the individual tales.

78. Maria Tatar, *The Hard Facts of the Grimms' Fairy Tales* (Princeton, N.J.: Princeton University Press, 1987), pp. 87–88, 114–16, 151. Tatar referred here to Bettelheim's concept of the dual mother, which, however, according to Bettelheim's own notes, originated with Hedwig von Beit.

79. Ibid., p. 190, xix, 234.

80. Ibid., p. 105. Nevertheless, Tatar did recognize the women's lot of spinning and hard work in previous centuries—also in fairy tales.

81. See Chapter 4 of this work regarding the Grimms' own views on the subject. The Grimms recognized certain parallels to the German folktale character of *Dummling* (or "*der tumbe klare*") in Grimmelshausen's Simplizius Simplizissimus, Wolfram von Eschenbach's epic character of Parzival, the English Perceval, the French Rennevart, and numerous folktale characters of other countries, especially Russia, suggesting that the influence may have been mutual. They emphasized, however, that Dummling's purity and wisdom set him off from the mere *Dummkopf* (stupid fool) of the medieval jests. See also Max Lüthi, "Dummling, Dümmling" in *Enzyklopädie des Märchens* 3, pp. 937–46.

82. Sigrid Früh und Rainer Wehse, eds., *Die Frau im Märchen*, series issued by the Europäische Märchengesellschaft Rheine (Kassel: Röth, 1985), pp. 6–22. Also Mario Jacoby, Verena Kast, and Ingrid Riedel, *Das Böse im Märchen*, Series: *Psychologisch gesehen*, Hildegund Fisehle-Carl, ed., number 33 (Fellbach: Verlag Adolf Bonz, 1978).

83. Heinz Rölleke, "New Results of Research on Grimms' Fairy Tales," in James M. McGlathery et al., eds., pp. 101–02. In this essay Rölleke humbly stated some of his reservations regarding our knowledge of how much the Grimms may have added to the tales, yet with confidence he judged that overall they had been loyal to the spirit of tradition.

84. Ibid., pp. 6–12.

85. Ibid., pp. 103–04.

86. August Nitschke, *Soziale Ordnungen im Spiegel der Märchen* (Stuttgart: Frommann, 1959).

87. Lutz Röhrich, *Märchen und Wirklichkeit. Eine volkskundliche Untersuchung* (Wiesbaden: Franz Steiner, 1956). See also Lutz Röhrich, "Rumpelstilzchen. Vom Methodenpluralismus in der Erzählforschung," *Schweizer Archiv für Volkskunde* 68/69 (1972/73), pp. 567–96.

88. See Ranke, "Märchenforschung," pp. 306–10, and Albert Wesselski, *Versuch einer Theorie des Märchens* (Reichenberg im Breisgau: Sudetendeutscher Verlag: Franz Kraus, 1931).

89. Otto Kahn, "Hat Rumpelstilz wirklich gelebt? Textvergleichende Studie über das Märchen vom Rumpelstilzchen und eine Erklärung mit Hilfe der Rechtsgeschichte," *Rheinisches Jahrbuch für Volkskunde* 17/18 (1966/67), 143–84.

90. Ibid., p. 163.

91. Otto Gmelin, *Böses kommt aus Kinderbüchern. Die verpaßte Möglichkeit kindlicher Bewußtseinsbildung* (Munich: Kindler, 1972).

92. Dieter Richter und Johannes Merkel, *Märchen, Phantasie und soziales Lernen* (Berlin: Basis, 1974). For an extended bibliography pertaining to Bernd Wollenweber's *Märchen-Soziologie* (*Sociological Approach to Folktales*) and Christa Bürger's concept of folktales as a mirror of social repression, see: Gerhard Haas, "Märchen, Sage, Schwank, Legende, Fabel und Volksbuch" in Gerhard Haas, ed., *Kinder- und Jugendbuch. Zur Typologie und Funktion einer literarischen Gattung* 2d ed. (Stuttgart: Philip Reclam junior, 1976), pp. 174–76.

93. Jack Zipes, "Dreams of a Better Bourgeois Life; The Psychosocial Origins of the Grimms' Tales," in McGlathery et al., ed., pp. 213–15.

94. Ibid., p. 281. Zipes claimed that "Cinderella," "Little Red Riding Hood," "Sleeping Beauty," and "Snow White," among other tales, had been especially cultivated to socialize children, not just in Germany but also in other countries around the world.

95. Jack Zipes, *The Brothers Grimm. From Enchanted Forests to the Modern World* (New York: Routledge, Chapman and Hall, Inc., 1988). pp. 19–22, 28–42.

96. Christa Kamenetsky, Thomas Mann's Concept of the *Bürger*," *Journal of the College Language Association* 5, 3 (March 1963), pp. 134–41, and Christa Kamenetsky, "*Dichter* vs. *Literat*: Thomas Mann's Ironic View of the Literary Man," *Journal of the College Language Association* 14, 4 (June 1971), pp. 420–31.

97. Jack Zipes, "The Grimms and the German Obsession with Fairy Tales" in *Fairy Tales and Society: Illusion, Allusion, and Paradigm,* in Ruth B. Bottigheimer, ed. (Philadelphia: The University of Pennsylvania Press, 1986), pp. 272–85.

98. Jack Zipes, *Fairy Tales and the Art of Subversion; The Classical Genre for Children and the Process of Civilization* (New York: Methuen, Inc., 1988), p. 57.

99. Ibid., p. 58.

100. Louis L. Snyder, *Roots of German Nationalism* (Bloomington: Indiana University Press, 1978).

101. Carl Franke, *Die Brüder Grimm. Ihr Leben und Werk* (Leipzig: Weidmannsche Buchhandlung, 1894), and T. Matthias, *Der deutsche Gedanke bei Jacob Grimm* (Leipzig: R. Voigtländer, 1915).

102. Franke, Introduction.

103. Snyder, p. 38.

104. Snyder relied here on a fragmentary quote from Grimm, cited in Hans Kohn, *Prophets and Peoples; Studies in Nineteenth Century Nationalism* (New York: Macmillan Company, 1946), without further investigating the issue. Instead, he might have consulted Jacob's own letter on this behalf in Wilhelm Schoof, ed., *Briefwechsel zwischen Jacob und Wilhelm Grimm aus der Jugendzeit* 2d ed. (Weimar: Hermann Böhlaus Nachf., 1963).

105. Snyder, p. 194n.

106. See Chapter 1 of this work regarding Jacob Grimm's recognition by the French Ministry.

107. Robert M. Berdahl, "New Thoughts on German Nationalism," *American Historical Review* 76, 1 (Feb. 1972), 65–80.

108. See Chapter 1 of this work.

109. Dorson.

110. Snyder, pp. 47–48.

111. Ibid., pp. 49–50.

112. *Kinder- und Hausmärchen* 2d ed., 3 (1922). See chapters on Italian folktales: Straparola and Basile.

113. Snyder, p. 42.

114. Will Erich Peuckert, *Wiedergeburt. Gespräche in Hörsälen und unterwegs* (Frankfurt am Main: Weidmannsche Verlagsanstalt, 1949).

115. Ibid., pp. 122–24.

116. Ibid., p. 132.

117. André Jolles, *Einfache Formen* (Darmstadt: Wissenschaftliche Verlagsanstalt, 1958).

118. Snyder, p. 135.

119. Ibid., pp. 137.

120. Ibid.

121. Hermann Bausinger, "Gut und Böse in *Enzyklopädie des Märchens* 5 (1989), pp. 316–24.

122. Ibid.

123. Marie Louise von Franz, *Shadow and Evil in Fairytales* (Dallas, Tex.: Spring Publications, 1987).

124. Bruno Bettelheim, *The Uses of Enchantment*, Chapter 1.

125. For a historical discussion of the relationship between cruelties in folktales and the medieval concept of justice, consult Lutz Röhrich, "Grausamkeit" *Enzyklopädie des Märchens* 5, pp. 99–101. In this connection he made reference to an article, published in 1910, that took Grimms' folktales at face value, namely as evidence of criminal aspects of society. E. Wulffen, "Das Kriminelle im deutschen Volksmärchen," *Archiv für Kriminalanthropologie und Kriminalistik* 38 (1910), pp. 340–70.

126. For objections to folktales from an interracial and humanistic perspective, see Robert Moore, "From Rags to Riches: Stereotypes and Anti-Humanism in Fairy Tales," *Interracial Books for Children Bulletin* 7 (1975), pp. 1–3. For arguments against folktales based on a feminist point of view, see Maria L. Lieberman, "'Some Day My Prince Will Come'; Female Acculturation Through the Fairy Tale," *College English* 34 (December 1972), pp. 383–95.

11. DIFFERENT VERSIONS OF THE
KINDER- UND HAUSMÄRCHEN

[Children's Book Editions and Translations]

INCE ITS FIRST PUBLIcation in 1812, the Grimms' *Kinder- und Hausmärchen* has appeared in many languages and has delighted children around the world. Next to the Bible, the work has achieved the largest numbers of reprints and translations. Presently, the Library of Congress lists close to five hundred titles related to various children's-book editions of the Grimms' folktales, and annually dozens of new editions appear in the *Children's Catalog*. Even though English and American children may be less familiar with the complete edition of the tales than German children, they are equally fond of the tales they do know and hardly realize that they originated in another country.

Among the books containing folktales of the Brothers Grimm that are in circulation among children are at least three different types. The first of these consists of a mixed "fairy tale" variety, including both folktales and literary fairy tales or fantasies. The second type consists of anthologies with an international emphasis, and the third type is exclusively dedicated to the tales of the Brothers Grimm.

In the first type with the mixed "fairy tale" approach, some of the Grimms' folktales appear side by side with selected stories of such authors as Hans Christian Andersen, Madame d'Aulnoy, or George MacDonald. Andrew Lang used such a mixed-genres approach in his *Blue Fairy Book*, and it is evident in *The Provensen Book of Fairy Tales*[1] and many others. As children generally do not worry too much about a classification of tales but are primarily interested in reading some good stories, there seems to be nothing wrong with an anthology that brings together under one cover all of their favorite "fairy tales," from "Snow White" to "The Ugly Duckling." On the other hand, it might be advisable to separate in an anthology traditional folktales from literary fairy tales so as not to confuse children about the tales' respective origins. A clearer distinction of these two genres would also be more conducive to teaching children about individual folk cultures, either separately or by means of cross-cultural comparisons. Children might learn to recognize in traditional folktales some variants belonging to different countries, and they would learn to appreciate in literary fairy tales the individual creative merits of a given author. If all stories are treated alike as "fairy tales," the concept of folk culture will be rendered insignificant.

Some advantages also arise from a separation of traditional folktales and fantasies on the library bookshelves and in card catalogs. All too often, we still find a colorful variety of books that are grouped together simply because they seem to fit under the conglomerate term of "fairy tale." Whereas the more recent scholarly debate regarding the authenticity of the Grimms' folktales may not contribute much to motivate skeptics to observe the distinction between folktale and fantasy, some modern curricular developments may. Especially teachers in the areas of social, multicultural, and ethnic studies have made substantial use of the folktale in an effort to explore the cultural folk heritage of various nations.

Early in this century, Charlotte Bühler stated that the best years for children to read and enjoy folktales would be between the ages of five and seven. She coined the term "folktale age" ("*Märchenalter*"), contending that folktales appealed mainly to younger children because of their swiftly moving story plot, vivid imagery, definite conclusions, and sense of justice.[2] Until the early seventies, psychologists and educators largely supported this view, suggesting that folktales be read in the early elementary grades. Both in Germany and in the United States, this theory considerably influenced the reading curriculum in the public schools. More recently, however, the emphasis has shifted to include folktales also for older children of the junior high and even senior high school age. The reason for this shift lies in the discovery of anthropologists and ethnographers that folktales are an excellent medium for teaching multicultural values to older students, urging teachers to make ample use of them in the social and ethnic studies curriculum. Children's literature anthologies used by prospective teachers in children's literature classes at the college level clearly reflect this trend by including a wide range of folktales from many lands, of which a great number appeal to an older age group.[3] Folktales have thus become again *Kinder- und Hausmärchen* in the sense that the Grimms originally understood the title: tales for young and old in the entire household.

The second type of book, the anthology with an international orientation, corresponds to the increasingly international orientation of our literature and social studies curriculum. In this category of publications, selected tales of the Brothers Grimm either are grouped together with other German tales under the category of "Germany," or appear side by side with tales from other countries, such as France, Italy, or China, under headings that are arranged thematically. The Brothers Grimm would have applauded such an international orientation on several accounts. Their vast correspondence with foreign scholars clearly indicated that they themselves tried to promote collections of folktales in various countries. They also spent much love and energy on translating tales and reviewing folktales from other lands. And finally, Wilhelm Grimm's extensive folktale analysis of tales from more than thirty countries gave evidence that it was quite in their spirit to promote an interest in countries and cultures other than their own.

In Germany, it was initially the Grimms' own international folktale analysis of 1822 that stimulated a considerable interest in folktales of other lands,[4] a trend that culminated in the world folktale publications of Heinrich Wolgast. In England, Andrew Lang promoted a similar interest by twelve volumes of *The Colour Fairy Books* (1889–1910). The British interest in international collections increased even more after the English translation of the Norwegian folktales collected by Asbjörnsen and Moe.

Of the many international folktale publications issued in the twentieth century, two deserve special mention. Beginning with 1965, Friedrich von der Leyen published an international folktale collection in more than eighty volumes under the title of *Die Märchen der Weltliteratur*[5] (*Folktales of World Literature*). Other editors of this series included Felix Karlinger and Kurt Schier. In the United States, Richard Dorson published in those years an outstanding series under the title of *Folktales of the World*.[6] He added prefaces and notes to the tale collection of various countries, in each case classifying the tales according to the folktale-type system of Aarne-Thompson. The tales of the Brothers Grimm appear together with other German folktales in one volume within the series. Such an approach not only emphasizes the national uniqueness of certain collections but it also makes the reader aware of international variants and cross-cultural comparisons.

Among the works that are exclusively dedicated to the Grimms' folktales are complete editions, smaller editions of selected tales, and single folktale editions in picture-book format. This category of book again shows a great variety of tale versions, all of which are supposedly by the Brothers Grimm. Among them are, for examples, some stories that are only loosely related to the Grimms' tales yet that a given author has altered for one reason or another. Some tales may have a didactic slant, others may show softened endings, and still others may be satires or fantasy adaptations that include major plot and character alterations.[7] Besides, there are many editions that reflect great loyalty to the spirit of the original tales. Yet even among the relatively loyal editions a great variety of choices exists. This is partially so because each editor usually makes somewhat different selections from the 211 tales of the Grimms, and partially because in their selection process they seldom rely on the same editions of the *Kinder- und Hausmärchen*. Since the Grimms in many cases used different tale variants (which they themselves collected, received by mail, or obtained through other sources) and also changed the tales stylistically, none of the seven editions published during their lifetime were identical.[8]

We must still consider another reason why there are so many variations among the English-language versions available to children, namely the nature of the translation. Translators differ both in regard to their philosophy of translation and their choice of vocabulary, syntax, and style. Edgar Taylor believed in a free rendering of the original and did not worry too much about rearranging a few plots and characters in the process. Neither did he feel obliged to confine himself to the Grimms' tales only but also included other German tales under the same title of *German Popular Stories*.[9] The first American translations did not differ much from Taylor's, as his edition served as a model. In fact, when the first American edition of the work was published in 1828, it was merely taken over from Taylor without a new translation. Evidence of the copying process also lies in the odd subtitle that the American edition added to the work. Due to a misreading of the Gothic characters in Taylor's work, it said that the book was based on the Grimms' "*Rinder und Hans Marchen*," which literally means "Cattle and Jack Tales." Someone more familiar with the German language should have caught this error at once. A variety of translations set in during the 1850s and 1860s, among them those by Matilda Davis in 1855, Edward H. Wehnert in 1861, and Mrs. H. H. B. Pauli in 1868.[10] Margaret Hunt's translation of 1884 for a long time was considered the best English translation, also in the United States, mainly because hers was more complete but also more accurate than earlier ones. This translation especially pleased folklorists, educators, and philologists, as it included a translation of the Grimms' notes, even if not all of them. To those who did not know German fluently enough or had limited access to the German complete edition of 1857, Hunt's work was a godsend. Even Padraic Colum still acknowledged having consulted Margaret Hunt's edition before bringing out his own *The Complete Grimm's Fairy Tales* in 1944.[11]

A still greater variety of translations has occurred in more recent decades with the efforts of Ralph Manheim, Brian Alderson, Maria Tatar, David Luke, and Jack Zipes, to mention just a few, who all consciously tried to go one step beyond accuracy, namely to capture the oral tone of Wilhelm Grimm's folktale style. Aldersen used the English colloquial style, rendering some of the Grimm's dialectical tales in a regional English dialect, and Zipes used the American colloquial style.[12] David Luke presented several Low German originals in a Scots translation and two in a Dublin idiom, hoping to preserve in this way the natural speech patterns of the Grimms' folktale style. To aid readers and storytellers in the Scots translation, he prepared a glossary, so as to get them closer to the original flavor of the tales.[13] At first, these tales may appear as strange in print as do *Tales of Uncle Remus* to the uninitiated reader, but if read aloud, they have a vivid and humorous appeal. Their homey touch may also appeal to older children.

The warning that Jacob Grimm gave to storytellers regarding an all-too-accurate yet "dry and pedantic" rendering of the tales applies to translators as well.[14] It appears that both in England and the United States most storytellers and translators are well aware of that danger and consequently have rather moved away from pedantry toward a freer translation. Taking liberties in translation is a different matter, and most are aware of that danger as well. A good translator tries to strike a balance between loyalty to tradition and the art of improvisation.[15] While respecting the spirit and flavor of the original, he tries to preserve the natural flow of language. Such an attempt at translation has added new vigor also to modern children's-book editions of the Grimms' tales, even though in a few cases translators have turned the tales into their own fantasies.

In a way, we may consider Wilhelm Grimm the first translator of the *Märchen*—and a good one at that—for he successfully translated tales from more than thirty dialects into High German. If he had had a choice, he once wrote, he would have rendered them all in the original dialect, so as to preserve the vivid expressions of natural speech. He did so in the case of Runge's tale of "The Fisherman and His Wife" and a few others that are still acclaimed as some of his best stories.

Variety in Grimm editions also has its roots in the different illustrations that have been added to the tales.[16] Some of the greatest book illustrators have added to our choice. Next to such well-known German illustrators as Emil Ludwig Grimm, Ludwig Richter, Moritz von Schwindt, and Else Wenz-Viëtor, some of the best-known English and American illustrators have contributed to the variety and success of the tales in their unique ways. Among these were George Cruikshank, Arthur Rackham, Walter Crane, Edmund Dulac, Josef Scharl, Wanda Gag, Ingri and Edgar D'Aulaire, Fritz Eichenberg, Kurt Wiese, Nonny Hogrogrian, and Maurice Sendak. Wanda Gag's *Snow White and the Seven Dwarfs* was cited as a Caldecott Honor Book in 1938, and Maurice Sendak's *The Juniper Tree* has become a classic in its own right.[17]

[Folktales from the Grimm Archives]

Among the anthologies of folktales available today are also some that are based on previously untranslated tales or unpublished stories collected by the Brothers Grimm. The first category is of special interest to American readers unfamiliar with the less well-known tales from the complete edition of the Brothers Grimm. The second category is a bit more problematic, as it includes archival materials that the Grimms did not wish to publish for certain reasons, such as tales that they re-corded themselves and then rejected or others that they received from friends or acquaintances, either directly or by mail.

Wilhelm Hansen's edition of *Grimms' Other Tales*, translated by Ruth Michaelis-Jena and Arthur Ratcliff, belongs to both categories. It in-cludes previously published tales that Edgar Taylor ignored in his first English translation of the 1812 edition of the *Kinder- und Hausmär-chen* and published tales that the Grimms omitted from the second edition of 1819. Yet, it also contains some tales from the Grimms' archives that they themselves and others had recorded but were never printed before.

Some of the Grimm's annotations to these tales that are listed in the appendix of the work give clues to the reasons of why they were not printed. Jacob Grimm's comment on "The Old Witch," for example, tells that it was taken down before October 1810 from "a modern and badly told story." What Hansen did not explain to the reader is that the word "modern," as the Grimms used it, referred to fantasy elements or "invented stories" that had nothing to do with the genuine folk tradi-tion. "Badly told story,"[18] in Grimms' terminology, did not refer to the grammar of the tale (which they would have corrected, as they did in other cases), but to a mannerism that they thought to be un=charac-teristic of colloquial speech patterns. In summary, then, Jacob's anno-tations reveal that he considered the story "made up," and for that reason he did not think it worthy of inclusion in the *Kinder- und Hausmär-chen*. The reader might have wished for an explanation as to why Hansen considered the tale worthy of printing.

Hansen also included in his anthology fragmentary tale pieces that the Grimms had discarded. One may wonder why he would do so in spite of the fact that the Grimms had clearly rejected them for publica-tion. As translators, Ruth Michaelis-Jena and Arthur Ratcliff did give an explanation in their introduction to the work, namely that in modern times a recording of folktales "without veneer"[19] had gained in interest. They claimed that tales that the Grimms had discarded provided folklorists with a better insight into their nature than the edited tales, simply because they were relatively not "written-up." Such an undertaking is admirable in view of modern folklore research methods. Ironically, however, it is evident that the Grimms had discarded some of them exactly because they were "written-up," namely based on too much personal fantasy rather than on the folk tradition. It must be observed that the title *Grimms' Other Tales* consequently is somewhat misleading, as one may assume that these were folktales that the Grimms collected and approved for publication on the same basis as those that made it into the various editions of the *Kinder- und Hausmärchen*.

Heinz Rölleke proceeded in a similar way by utilizing unpublished archival material of the Brothers Grimm, including tale contributions from some acquaintances and friends that the Grimms had annotated in the margins. Yet in both his goal and his method he differed widely from Hansen. He clearly stated that instead of wishing to add another anthology of less well-known folktales to the *Kinder- und Hausmärchen*, he aimed at establishing the different sources and informants used by the Grimms, as well as the criteria by which they had judged the various folktale contributions they received. He undertook this project in cooperation with his graduate students of German in Wuppertal. Taking his clues from the Grimms' annotations, he tried to define carefully and in scholarly terms the Grimms' principles of tale selections.[20]

Among the stories included were some variants that the Grimms had considered redundant because they had already been printed in the *Kinder- und Hausmärchen*. These provided a basis of comparison with the published versions, in a similar way as the *Oelenberg* manuscript had served other scholars before. Among others, there were also some tales in the archival materials that the Grimms did not plan to publish under any circumstances, because they considered them too fragmentary, too insignificant, or too sketchy to be restored.

The accuracy with which Rölleke and his students proceeded in examining these texts makes readers conscious of the fact that the Grimms were far from publishing oral tales indiscriminately. The Grimms' marginal notes appear in full, and the reader receives firsthand insight into a pattern of notes that, with astonishing consistency, point to the very criteria that the Grimms had stated in their prefaces to the *Kinder- und Hausmärchen*.

In a longer essay, "Texts That Almost Became Grimms' Tales,"[21] Rölleke analyzed two late medieval texts and three literary fairy tales by Ernst Moritz Arndt and Karoline Stahl, which the Grimms planned to include in the second edition of the *Kinder- und Hausmärchen* yet then dropped from their publishing plans. In that case, too, he elaborately cited from the Grimm's notes and correspondence to establish the reasons for their rejection of the tales. He concluded that even though by 1820 Wilhelm Grimm had already begun to rely heavily on written folktales submitted to him rather than depending merely on oral contributions, he continued to scrutinize all submitted tales for authenticity before deciding whether or not to include them in the folktale collection. Rölleke's findings thus far have confirmed the view that the Grimms were looking for genuine folktales and certainly were not "faking it," as Dundes and Ellis suggested.

[Ironic and Satirical Versions]

Neither ironic nor satirical versions of folktales were first discovered in the twentieth century. Prior to the Grimms' publication of the *Kinder- und Hausmärchen* Ludwig Tieck used irony as well as satire in his dramatic piece "Puss in Boots" ("Der gestiefelte Kater").[22] He brought onto the stage not just the actors but also the playwright, the play direc- tor, the stagehands, the audience, and even the critics, thus dazzling the real audience by reflections and romantic rereflections as if they were in a hall of mirrors. By creating an illusion and simultaneously destroying the illusion, he actually allowed the play to discuss itself. In this way Tieck, the playwright, was not only the creator of the play but also the observer, manager, and critic of his own creation.[23]

Like other fantasy writers of German Romanticism, Tieck turned the folktale into an art form—a fantasy that took special pleasure in mirroring itself. Friedrich Schlegel coined the term "poetry of poetry" for such an art that was capable of portraying itself, thus legitimizing the poet's freedom to rise above his creation while destroying its illu- sions. By employing multiple dimensions simultaneously, some writers of the Romantic "fairy tale" removed the folktale from its single-stranded narrative and traditional naivete.[24] By placing it into a new literary con- text, they transformed it into an artistic means of reflections about literature, drama, art theory, and literary criticism. The concept of loyalty to tradition, as the Grimms demanded, would have interfered with the free flow of their creativity.

The ironic and satirical fairy tales of German Romanticism appealed to a more sophisticated audience of adults yet neither to simple folk nor to children. Drawing upon the inexhaustible possibilities of the individual imagination, their writers rejoiced in a certain agility of the mind that turned thought processes into creative play. Being no longer satisfied with searching for the spirit of naivete in nature, peasants, or the souls of children, they followed Fichte's intellectual demand that art rise above oneself. Whereas some of the motifs and images of these fantasies came astonishingly close to those of traditional folktales, the poets imposed upon them a highly subjective flavor that was alien to the *Volksmär- chen*. Following a freedom of creativity, they transgressed the limits set by reason and tradition, changed folktale plots and characters, and replaced the naive faith of the folktale world by their own subjective views. By casting doubt upon the fulfillment of man's dream for unity and the infinite, some tales turned dark and gloomy. Tieck's "fairy tales," like those of Novalis (Friedrich von Hardenberg) and E. T. A. Hoffmann, touched upon the "night side" of German Romanticism, which evoked the mood of dark dreams and nightmares bordering on the shadowy world of the unconscious.[25]

A grotesque portrayal of folktale themes and characters appeared in the late nineteenth century in the humorous works of Wilhelm Busch.[26] In the 1860s he began to look at the folktale from a satirical point of view, utilizing the shock effect of reversing some traditional expectations. He, too, used the device of creating an illusion and destroying an illusion, but his grotesque exaggeration (by means of verse and cartoonlike illustrations) altogether ridiculed Romantic dreams and longing and never ended on a gloomy note. Frequent targets of Busch's satire were domestic virtues and hypocrisies of villagers and small-town citizens, but among others also an all-too-Romantic perception of the folktale world. What happened when a young shepherdess kissed her prince? He instantly turned into a green, scaled, ice-cold, and repulsive frog. What happened to naughty little Tom Thumb just after he managed to escape the huge fangs of a nasty spider? He fell from the tree into the high grass below and joined the grasshoppers in a drink of honey wine, getting so tipsy that he could hardly keep himself upright. Who would ever have thought of drunk Tom Thumb? The satire showed that life does not always teach us a good lesson or that the best lesson is one that you can swallow with pleasure! And what happened to Hansel and Gretel upon returning home from their excursion to the witch's house? With a long rod in her hands, their mother was waiting for them behind the entrance door, ready to give them a good whipping![27] In this case, Busch satirized those starry-eyed folktale lovers who forgot what life was really like.

Busch also used fables to satirize the didactic theme that was so prevalent in his time. In "A Tale Told to Children in 1860," he related how one day a big cat swallowed with one gulp two baby mice and their mother. Inside the cat's stomach, the mother scolded her babies: "You should have watched out, kids!" she said. "It's too late now!" the baby mice replied.[28] Evidently, Busch wished to hold up a mirror to mothers who never get tired of preaching to their young. We may be reminded here of the duchess in Lewis Carroll's *Alice's Adventures in Wonderland*, who always ends her conversation by stating: "And the moral of that is . . . ."

In following his own satirical style, Busch freely changed the plots of traditional folktales, adding realistic features, gross incidents, and scenes from everyday village life. While his touch of local color brought his readers closer to the mores and customs of the village folk, his irony undermined their make-believe and enchantment. In a style that sometimes resembled that of slapstick comedy, he destroyed the Romantic folktale illusion by the shock effect of topsy-turvy adventures based on stark reality and a sense of exaggeration. By making jests of tales that were no jests and by letting illusions clash with stark reality, he turned the sublime into the ridiculous and made his readers laugh. In Busch's tales, serenade singers inevitably end up in a bush of prickly thorns, just as romantic lovers end up in a ditch or get caught in a hail storm.

The styles of Tieck and Busch belong to very different worlds. Tieck delighted the sophisticated audience with varying perspectives and a versatility of mind, yet Busch appealed to a popular audience enjoying the jovial caricature of the disillusioned Romantic dreamer. Tieck's literary fairy tales or *Kuntsmärchen* still belonged to the Romantic movement while Busch's witty verse stories belonged to the awakening realistic movement of the late nineteenth century.

The sarcastic tone of "reworked" folktale versions has become more dominant in the twentieth century, perhaps because the skeptics have raised their voices. A good example of a modern ironic approach to folktales may be observed in Tomi Ungerer's "Little Red Riding Hood."[29] By creating an illusion and destroying an illusion, Ungerer engages the reader, like Tieck, in a play with infinite possibilities. The tale's shock effect arises from the reversal of the reader's expectations regarding the end of the story. Rather than dwelling upon the sad consequences of Little Red Riding Hood's disobedience, his tale encourages her defiance and nonconformity. Little Red Riding Hood (whose headdress makes her look like a stop sign, as Ungerer put it) ends up happily ever after by joining the ever-so-elegant wolf in a castle that is lavishly equipped with a swimming pool. Being a shrewd and materialistic young lady, who carefully calculates her advantages, she finally decides to marry the wolf and move to his castle. The grotesque quality of Ungerer's writing especially emerges in his portrayal of the grandmother who in the end turns into a shrinking rat locked up in a cage.

As a tale of the grotesque, Ungerer's story has mainly entertainment value. Perhaps he aimed at a satire on the cautionary theme of traditional folktales, but the target of his satire does not emerge as clearly as does his desire to entertain.

Satirists seem to enjoy using the folktale as a foil because it provides familiar characters and settings. By changing the well-known plot structure and reversing the characters' roles and actions, they try to get across to the reader a certain point in the hope of improving a given situation in real life. As an art form and in children's literature, a satirical approach to folktales has its legitimate place. Its success ultimately depends on the author's capacity to let his story rise above the level of a common joke or trivial message. At best, it sharpens the intellect and appeals to the critical faculty in older children or adults. There is no harm in letting children enjoy this genre—as long as they do not confuse the satirical tale with the original folktale.

In recent years we have come to know many jokes or simplistic cartoons that take a single shot at folktale characters, just for the fun of the shock effect.[30] Such journalistic approaches to the folktale are different from satirical versions based on entire folktale plots and involving a more sustained creative effort on the part of the author. The line between a mere joke and an art form is not always easy to draw. Readers must decide on their own whether some of the poems that Wolfgang Mieder anthologized in *Disenchantments*,[31] for example, are truly humorous and creative and to what degree they resemble mere jokes or cartoons. Throughout the book, the poets use folktale characters mainly as a springboard for their own imagination. Some of the poems allude to cruelties and sexual abuses in such a pointed way that they are perhaps more shocking than anything one may encounter in the entire collection of the Grimms' *Kinder- und Hausmärchen*. Others try to get across an author's personal philosophy of life and, as such, are to be understood just as poems, not as a satire on the Grimms' fairy tales. This applies in particular to Anne Sexton's lesbian slant in "Rapunzel" but also to Susan Mitchell's cynical tale "From the Journal of a Frog Prince." In Mitchell's poem the prince has already been married to the princess and obviously not too happily, for he is now longing to regain his former state of enchantment in the mud and slime of the pond. He wonders if he should drag his young wife down to the river and show her "the green flame" of his own self by the stream. Feeling alienated amidst a corrupt world of kings, princesses, and castles, he is horrified at the idea of having been transformed into a human being. To stay with his wife means for him to give up his natural state of innocence forever. Whereas the Grimms' frog seemed to count his blessings when he was transformed into a human being, Mitchell's prince altogether doubts if happiness can be obtained among human beings.[32]

In the same volume, Hyacinthe Hill went a step further by showing the frog in the companionship of other rebels who defy mankind: "We are the frogs who will not turn to princes."[33] In preferring their "bug-eyed brides" to human brides, they insist on the right to be themselves. The poem takes the frog's point of view and also suggests a rebellion of the lower class against the haughty nobility. When he throws back the ball at the princess in defiance, with no claims attached, he asserts his self-pride and dignity along with his freedom from human bondage.

Roald Dahl's poems depict a grotesque situation in a similar way as those of Wilhelm Busch by creating a clash between a Romantic illusion and some stark realistic elements, sometimes brought about by a reversal of common expectations. In his poem "Little Red Riding Hood and the Wolf," we meet neither a sweet and kind nor disobedient little girl but a liberated young lady practicing the art of self-defense. When the wolf appears on the scene, she simply "whips a pistol from her knickers . . . bang, bang, bang, and shoots him quite dead."[34] Far from being a victim of seduction of one sort or another, she resourcefully emerges as an agent of her own fate. The target of Dahl's satire may be the stereotypical role of women as victims in folktales or else the traditional cautionary character of the folktale itself. The recast ending of the tale suggests that modern girls are independent enough to handle their own affairs without their mother's advice. Not only does she kill the wolf and enjoy it too, but she is also calculating enough to profit from the adventure by enriching her wardrobe by an elegant wolf-fur coat. By warning his readers of Little Red Riding Hood, Dahl reverses the old moral and makes them realize that times have changed indeed.

Recently, even some comparative studies of folktale variants have turned satirical in tone. This applies, among others, to Alan Dundes's *Little Red Riding Hood: A Casebook.* By moving beyond the familiar variants of Perrault and Grimm to variants of the tale from such countries as China, Japan, and Korea, Dundes said that he hoped to lead readers beyond an "unnecessarily and arbitrarily limiting scope of investigation" based only on what he considered "two standard literary versions of the tale."[35] The last phrase gives away his skeptical attitude regarding the authenticity of the *Kinder- und Hausmärchen.* In his preface Dundes logically stated that no single interpretation could possibly do justice to folktale variants of different countries—a view that might best be supported by Aarne-Thompson's comparative motif studies—yet in his own essay within the anthology Dundes justified an endless variety of interpretations of the tale on the assumption that the Grimms themselves had been "at least one full step removed from pure oral tradition."[36] He charged them outright with the folklorists' "cardinal sin" of having combined variants and creating composite texts consisting of different versions of the same tale type.

The consistency of his argument escapes the reader, for one may wonder why he did include the Grimm version at all if he did not consider it an authentic oral tale type. If indeed he was convinced that the Grimms' tales were "fakelore" rather than folklore, why would he use them as folktale "variants" in an international context? Neither a subtitle nor the preface made it clear that he would concern himself with more than folktales—and nothing less than folktales should have been used within the context of Aarne's definition of "variants."

A similar inconsistency may also be noted in some other anthologies combining essays with a study of folktale "variants." Jack Zipes, for example, also followed the notion that the Grimms did not publish genuine folktales but rather imposed upon the collected tales their personal and social values and frustrations. In *The Trials and Tribulations of Little Red Riding Hood,*[37] he contended that the literary fairy tales had been employed since the seventeenth century to reinforce the Western civilizing process and social norm. While avoiding a clear-cut distinction between folktale and literary fairy tale, he discussed both the *Volksmärchen* (folktale) and the *Kunstmärchen* interchangeably, thus placing Tieck's "The Life and Death of Little Red Riding Hood: A Tragedy" on the same level as the Grimms' version of "Little Red Cap."

Zipes followed in this design his own theory that every tale collection bears the personal stamp of its collector and the social environment in which he happens to live. From that point of view, he obviously felt justified to ignore the distinction between folktale and fantasy, or even folktale and satire. In doing so, he undoubtedly gained more freedom for himself to interpret the various tales within a sociocultural context. Whether he did justice to the Grimms' *Kinder- und Hausmärchen* in this context is a matter of interpretation.

A growing skepticism regarding the authenticity of the Grimms' tales has even stimulated the writing of satires and parodies on the great variety of critical approaches to the *Kinder- und Hausmärchen*. In *Die Wahrheit über Hänsel und Gretel* (*The Truth About Hansel and Gretel*),[38] Hans Traxler took as his target the pseudo-scientific approaches of anthropologists and historians who have desperately tried to find some scraps of "reality" in folktales, even in cases where magic and make-believe seemed to predominate. Assuming the role of a newspaper reporter investigating an archaeological digging, he described in meticulous detail the excavations of the remains of the witch's gingerbread house in a wooded area in Hesse, using maps and simulated photographs to support his "documentation." By exaggerating the anthropological and historical approach, he made them appear ridiculous.

Iring Fetscher, too, based his satirical approach on the premise that the Grimms themselves had not taken their folktale collections too seriously and that, consequently, it didn't really matter what critical approach one might employ in relation to the tales, as they might well be interchangeable. By satirizing the various interpretations of the folktales under the title of "Methods of Confusion" ("Verwirrmethoden"),[39] he hardly left a simple approach untouched, be it linguistic, philological, anthropological, psychological, or historical. Following Basil Bernstein's definition of folktales as "verbal messages with a maximum of verbal redundancy," he tried to match what he considered the arbitrary critical method by his own arbitrariness. As the ultimate joke, he introduced his readers to the do-it-yourself-method-of-interpretation by inviting them to top all of the others by means of their own creativity, suggesting that they create a "variant" to their liking. Without troubling himself to provide evidence, Fetscher tried to convince his readers that the Grimms themselves had invented most of the tales and that they deserved to be called *Kunstmärchen* rather than *Volksmärchen*.

In his musical "Into the Woods," Stephen Sondheim represented a collage of revisionist folktale plots, thus following a similar skepticism regarding the authenticity of the Grimms' tales. Turning his skepticism into a free creative approach to the tales, Sondheim permitted none of the characters to live happily ever after in the setting of the evergreen forest. Rather, he let them age and die, survive, or learn to cope. It didn't matter in this case if Sondheim used the Grimms' or Perrault's version as an inspiration for his story, for he reshaped it into a witty musical intended for grown-ups. The audience is not meant to feel pity for Cinderella if she loses her prince, for having been raised to be "charming and playful," the prince is not to be taken seriously anyway. Where there is no sincerity and no naivete, one cannot ask for true compassion. The reversal of expectations causes laughter rather than tears also in the case of Rapunzel, who finally turns mad and is squashed under a giant's foot—a fate that children might have wished on the old witch instead. The grotesqueness of Sondheim's "fairy tale" is especially evident when the witch, upon losing her magic powers, turns into a charming fairy with a sex appeal. How could one be angry with Sondheim for "spoiling" the folktales with his humor? His witty verse and musical score have to be judged on their own creative merits, not by their "loyalty" to tradition.[40]

Satirical writers do not worry too much about the issue of loyalty to tradition—and why should they? The art of exaggeration and distortion have always belonged to their craft. It has not been their business to respect tradition but to challenge it. One simply has to judge the stories for what they are, on the basis of their own creativity, be it within the context of fantasy writing or a musical score. It is mandatory, however, that readers themselves should not confuse folktales with fantasies or satires.

It seems that the more critics have come to buy the idea of the Grimms' folktales as "fakelore" rather than genuine folklore, the more they have felt encouraged to treat them like literary fairy tales. The modern trend to anthologize folktale versions under the same cover with fantasy pieces and satires shows that editors, too, have been affected by this skepticism. While satirical writers have always followed their personal impulse, with no obligation to tradition or convention, critics have customarily worked under certain limitations to set logic, evidence, or at least an author's frame of reference. Is it really true that there are no limits to interpretations, as Dundes said, and that every critic may, at will, create his own "variant" of a folktale? Granted, the dividing line between a folktale and a literary fairy tale is a legitimate subject of debate, but it may be helpful to keep in mind that the Grimms themselves were very conscious of this distinction and that their notes and commentaries do support it.

NOTES

1. Andrew Lang, *The Blue Fairy Book* (1889; reprint, New York: Dover Publications, 1974); Alice and Martin Provensen, eds., *The Provensen Book of Fairy Tales* (New York: Random House, 1971).

2. Charlotte Bühler and Josephine Bilz, *Das Märchen und die Phantasie des Kindes* (Munich: J. A. Barth, 1961).

3. See, for example, Donna Norton, ed., *Through the Eyes of a Child. An Introduction to Children's Literature*, 3d ed. (New York: Macmillan Company, 1991), p. 274. In introducing the unit on folktales, Norton emphasized the importance of teaching children about cultural diffusion and traditional folk values through a comparative study of international folktales. Various children's literature anthologies for college-level students, such as Judith Saltman, ed., *The Riverside Anthology of Children's Literature*, 4th ed. (Riverside, N.Y.: Houghton Mifflin Company, 1987), also emphasize a rich collection of international folktales, usually listed under the names of individual countries.

4. *Die Kinder- und Hausmärchen*, 2d ed., Vol. 3 (1922).

5. Friedrich von der Leyen, *Die Märchen der Weltliteratur*, series (Jena: Eugen Diederichs Verlag, 1965–).

6. Richard M. Dorson, *Folktales of the World*, series (Chicago: University of Chicago Press, 1965).

7. Among these are also a number of cartoons, caricatures, and jokes.

8. See The Editing Process in Chapter 7 of this work.

9. Jacob and Wilhelm Grimm, *German Popular Stories* (London: Murray, 1823).

10. Wayland D. Hand, "Die Märchen der Brüder Grimm in den Vereinigten Staaten" in *Brüder-Grimm Gedenken* 1, Ludwig Denecke, ed. (Marburg: Elwert Verlag, 1963), pp. 540–43.

11. Wilhelm and Jacob Grimm. *Grimm's Popular Tales* trans. Margaret Hunt, intr. by Andrew Lang (London: 1884). A modern version based on this translation but adapted for younger readers is Frances Jenkins Olcott, ed., *The Complete Grimm's Fairy Tales* (New York: Follett, 1968), Intr. Frances Clarke Sayers. See also Jacob and Wilhelm Grimm, *The Complete Grimm's Fairy Tales* rev. ed. by James Stern, intr. by Padraic Colum, with a folkloristic commentary by Joseph Campbell (New York: Pantheon, 1944).

12. Jacob and Wilhelm Grimm, *Grimms' Tales for Young and Old: The Complete Stories* (Garden City, N.Y.: Doubleday, 1977), trans. Ralph Manheim; Jacob and Wilhelm Grimm, *The Brothers Grimm Popular Folktales* (New York: Doubleday, 1978); Jacob and Wilhelm Grimm, *The Brothers Grimm Popular Folktales* (New York: Doubleday, 1978), trans. Brian Alderson; *Jacob and Wilhelm Grimm: Selected Tales* (New York: Farrar, Straus and Giroux, 1973), trans. David Luke; and Jacob and Wilhelm Grimm, *The Complete Fairy Tales of the Brothers Grimm* (New York: Bantam Books, 1987). Also see Maria Tatar's translations of the Grimms' prefaces to *Kinder- und Hausmärchen*, Vol. 1 (1812) and Vol. 2 (1815) of the first edition and Vol. 1 (1819) of the second edition in *The Hard Facts of the Grimms' Fairy Tales* (Princeton, N.J.: Princeton University Press, 1987).

13. Luke, trans., Preface.

14. Jacob Grimm, "Über das Pedantische in der deutschen Sprache" (Vorgelesen in der öffentlichen Sitzung der Akademie der Wissenschaften, 2. Oktober, 1847). Jacob Grimm, *Kleinere Schriften*, Vol. 1 (Berlin: Ferdinand Dümmler, 1882), pp. 327–74.

15. As an example of "bookish language" he cited the colloquial and dialectical use of strong verbs (past tense) such as *buk* instead of *backte* (baked) and *wob* (wore) instead of *webte* (weaved). Storytelling still preserved these older forms and added a lively touch to the tales. See also Chapter 5 in this work on The Art and Age of Storytelling.

16. See Betsy Hearne, "Booking the Brothers Grimm: Art, Adaptations, and Economics," in James M. McGlathery et al., eds., *The Brothers Grimm and Folktale* (Urbana: University of Illinois Press, 1988), pp. 220–32.

17. Wilhelm Hansen, Ruth Michaelis-Jena, and Arthur Ratcliff, eds. *Grimms' Other Tales; A New Selection* (Edinburgh: Canongate, 1984).

18. Ibid., Appendix.

19. Ibid., Introduction.

20. Heinz Rölleke, ed., *Märchen aus dem Nachlaß der Brüder Grimm* 3rd rev. ed. (Bonn: Bouvier, 1983).

21. Heinz Rölleke, "Texte die beinahe Grimms Märchen geworden wären," *Zeitschrift für Deutsche Philologie* 102, 4 (1983), pp. 481–500.

22. Ludwig Tieck (pseudonym: Peter Leberecht). *Der gesticefelte Kater*, Ed. Helmut Kreuzer (Stuttgart: Reclam, 1964). The play was originally published in 1797.

23. The literary fairy tales or *Kunstmärchen* of German Romanticism received detailed attention in Richard Benz, *Märchendichtung der Romantiker* (Jena: Diederichs, 1926), and in Marianne Thalmann, *The Romantic Fairy Tale: Seeds of Surrealism* (Ann Arbor, Mi.: University of Michigan Press, 1970; original title: *Das Märchen und die Moderne*, Stuttgart: Reclam, 1961). Some modern critics proclaim the view that there is no single "folktale style," just as there is no single style for literary fairy tales. See Clemens Heselhaus, "Die romantische Gruppe in Deutschland" in *Die europäische Romantik*, Ernst Behler, ed., (Frankfurt am Main: Athenäum, 1972), pp. 135–45.

24. On romantic irony and romantic satire, consult Oscar Walzel, *German Romanticism* (New York: Frederick Ungar Publishing Company, 1965), pp. 34–76, 185–223.

25. Ibid., p. 73. Walzel referred to Friedrich Schlegel's warning that an ironic style such as Tieck's that mimicked the style of an Italian comedian, at the hands of a less-gifted writer might easily be degraded into a new type of didacticism bombarding the reader with programmed messages.

26. Ibid., pp. 202–03.

27. Wilhelm Busch is best known in children's literature for his grotesque portrayal of Max and Moritz, two village pranksters. Wilhelm Busch, *Und die Moral von der Geschicht'* (Gütersloh: Mohn & Company, 1959), intr. Theodor Heuss. See "Hänsel und Gretel," pp. 501–02; "Die zwei Schwestern" ("The Two Sisters," a satirical version of the "Frog Prince") pp. 770–78; and "Hänschen Däumeling" ("Thumbling"), p. 786–94. See also Wilhelm Busch, *Humoristischer Hausschatz mit 1500 Bildern*, 2 vols. (Munich: Verlag von Fr. Bassermann, 1949). Busch was also one of the most famous contributors to the nineteenth-century *Bilderbogen* (a large-size picture-book poster in a portfolio format). Michael Schwarze, ed., *Eine lustige Gesellschaft. 100 Münchener Bilderbogen in einem Band* (Zurich: Edition Olms, 1978).

28. "Was die Amme den Kindern anno 1860 erzählt" in Busch, *Und die Moral*, pp. 106–07.

29. Tomi Ungerer, *Storybook* (New York: Franklin Watts Inc., 1974). Considering the diversity of critical approaches to "Little Red Riding Hood" that range from the wolf as a symbol of male domination to Red Riding Hood as a symbol of budding female sexuality or bourgeois social norms, it is possible that Ungerer used these as a target for his satire.

30. Wolfgang Mieder, "Grim Variations: From Fairy Tales to Modern Anti-Fairy Tales," *The Germanic Review* 62 2 (Spring 1987), pp. 90–103. Mieder uses the term "*Anti-Märchen*" (Anti-Fairy Tales), which was coined by André Jolles in *Einfache Formen* (Halle: Niemeyer, 1930).

31. Wolfgang Mieder, ed., *Disenchantments. An Anthology of Modern Fairy Tale Poetry* (Hanover, N.H.: University Press of New England for the University of Vermont, 1985). See also by the same author *Grimms Märchen—Moderne Prosa, Gedichte, Karikaturen*. Series: Arbeitstexte für den Unterricht. (Stuttgart: Reclam, 1979), and *Mädchen, Pfeif auf den Prinzen. Märchengedichte von Günter Grass bis Sarah Kirsch* (Cologne: Diederichs, 1983).

32. Susan Mitchell, "From the Journals of a Frog Prince," in Mieder, ed., *Disenchantments*, pp. 38–40.

33. Hyacinthe Hill, "Rebels from Fairy Tales," Ibid., p. 27.

34. Roald Dahl, "Little Red Riding Hood and the Wolf," Ibid., pp. 113–14. For various versions of the Grimms' fairy tales rewritten from a feminist perspective, as well as related essays on the topic, see Jack Zipes, ed., *Don't Bet on the Prince; Contemporary Feminist Fairy Tales in North America and England* (New York: Methuen, Inc., 1986).

35. Alan Dundes, ed., *Little Red Riding Hood: A Casebook* (Madison, Wis.: University of Wisconsin Press, 1989). Preface. For related comparative studies, see also Marianne Rumpf, *Rotkäppchen. Eine vergleichende Untersuchung* (diss., University of Göttingen, 1951), and Hermann Bausinger, "Möglichkeiten des Märchens der Gegenwart," in *Märchen, Mythos, Dichtung. Festschrift zum 90. Geburtstag Friedrich von der Leyens*, Hugo Kuhn and Kurt Schier eds. (Munich: C. H. Beck, 1963); Alan Dundes, ed. *Cinderella: A Folklore Casebook* (New York: Garland Publishing Company, 1982).

36. Dundes, ed., p. 195.

37. Jack Zipes, *The Trials and Tribulations of Little Red Riding Hood; Versions of the Tale in Sociocultural Context.* (South Hadley, Ma.: Bergin & Garvey Publ., Inc., 1983).

38. Hans Traxler, *Die Wahrheit über Hänsel und Gretel. Die Dokumentation des Märchens der Brüder Grimm. Eine glaubwürdige Parodie* (Munich: Heyne, 1967).

39. Iring Fetscher, *Wer hat Dornröschen wachgeküßt? Das Märchenverwirrbuch* (Frankfurt am Main, Fischer Verlag, 1974), p. 17.

40. John Beaufort, "'Into the Woods': A Fairy Tale for Adults; Sondheim's Music Charms while Plots Take New Twists," *The Christian Science Monitor* (Nov. 6, 1987), p. 26.

12. CONCLUSION

[Dispelling the Myths]

HE DIVERSE AND OFTEN contradictory approaches that critics of the *Kinder- und Hausmärchen* have taken to the subject might induce readers to become skeptical about the validity of any critical perspective on folktales and the Brothers Grimm. In this case, however, the controversy itself is proof that the tales are still with us and alive, as an enjoyment for children and a puzzle for adults. Yet could we go so far as to say that the truth lies in the eye of the beholder? What this work has emphasized throughout is that the Grimms themselves did not view folktales as mere "stories for the nursery" but within a broader framework of Romantic thought and multidisciplinary scholarly studies. It is this context that deserves greater attention if we wish to do justice both to the Grimms themselves and to their folktale collection. For all too long many critics have relied on judgments formed by their own particular discipline while frequently imposing their personal value systems upon the tales. This is even true for some modern folklorists who expect to find in the collection what belongs to a present-day approach.

This work has attempted to dispel some myths regarding the Grimms, their claims, their informants, their sources, their methods, and the folktales themselves. Taking as a vantage point Herder's influence on

Romantic thought and the Grimms' own theories pertaining to *Natur-poesie*, it has shown that their folktale collection formed a logical extension of their other scholarly endeavors. This is particularly true for their international orientation regarding folktale variants and its intimate connection with their studies of language, law, and medieval literature.

Without consulting the Grimms' multidisciplinary approaches to the topic within the framework of German Romanticism, it would be difficult to find out what they were looking for in *Naturpoesie*. Still to this day, some persons do consider folktales on the same plane as "nursery tales," failing to grasp their relationship to myths and epics. Grimms' own notes and essays have given insight into such interconnections as they perceived them.

While Grimms' scholarship is impressive in many respects, some readers may have wondered why it also included such seemingly simple things as the language and games of children, as well as nonsense verse, proverbial expressions, and superstitions. The answer is that in childhood games and folktales alike the Grimms perceived the language of *Naturpoesie* that was archaic yet still alive in modern colloquial speech. By analyzing Grimms' concept of *Naturpoesie* in relation to Jacob's language theory and Wilhelm's conception of medieval literature, this work has added another perspective to the various issues mentioned that applies to Wilhelm Grimm's studies of the language and games of children.

Both Jacob Grimm's theory of language dynamics and Wilhelm's theory of universal folktale origins prepared the ground for comparative studies of variants in the living folk tradition in Germany and abroad. Their linkage to storytelling has revealed that both theories encouraged loyalty to the "core" of tradition yet also a spontaneous recital involving variations in folktales from one storyteller to the next. Such individual differences, in Grimms' views, accounted for many "unexplainable" variants of folktales around the world. Consequently, they did not see the ideal storyteller as one who slavishly repeated folktales word-by-word without modifications. Even though they admired in Frau Viehmännin a fabulous memory regarding certain phrases and passages, they also praised her freedom of expression which they considered a prerequisite for keeping alive the oral tradition.

Such insights have implications for an understanding of Grimms' approaches to editing the tales. In their demand of loyalty to the spirit of tradition, they did make an allowance for individual modifications and the use of variants, while rejecting a "clinging" to individual words. Such an editing concept, however, should not be confused with an arbitrary embellishment or a subjective rewriting of the tales based on an editor's personal fantasies or social frustrations. In reality, it corresponded to the Grimms' work in restoring old manuscripts that were close to the oral tradition, requiring a keen sense of traditional speech patterns.

Both Jacob and Wilhelm Grimm believed that editing folktales required a firm grasp of traditional tales' substance or "core," along with certain skills acquired by an intimate knowledge of *Naturpoesie*. The Grimms possessed such a knowledge through their acquaintance with various older languages, dialects, and colloquial speech patterns in epics and folk narratives but also through their familiarity with the laws, customs, and ethics that governed the themes and characters in folktales at home and abroad. Such an understanding gave them the necessary clues to make selections among the many tale contributions which they received. Both their published notes to the tales and their unpublished notes on behalf of the tales which they rejected have given evidence of their principled approach to the initial selection process. Secondly, their literary and linguistic knowledge was especially helpful to them in the editing process itself, aiding them in some instances to supply some missing links or tale portions, just as it had been helpful in regard to the restoration of medieval manuscripts. If at times Wilhelm Grimm took more liberties in editing the tales than he and Jacob together were willing to grant to other collectors, he did so not because he was hypocritical or dishonest but because he trusted his unique qualifications for such an editing job. This work has shown that some differences did indeed exist in conceptions of both brothers toward editing the tales but that these were less pronounced than they are thought to be, as they both believed in the need for certain limited modifications before committing the tales to print. While such editing does not measure up to the high standards of accuracy required by modern folklore research, it was consistent with the Grimm's own Romantic theories regarding loyalty to the core of tradition. They applied the same principles to their use of printed sources, which they considered as published variants, or an extension of the oral folk tradition, not as a substitute for it. The very nature of the sources mentioned by the Grimms has shown their close link with traditional characters, themes, and colloquial speech patterns prevalent in oral tales.

Did the Grimms intend their folktale collection for children or for grown-ups? Did they censor the collected tales, so as to make them more "suitable for children," or did they ignore children as potential readers? Already in the second edition of the *Kinder- und Hausmärchen* Wilhelm did make certain changes in the language of the tales, specifically for children, by weeding out some offensive expressions. Children also played a significant role in the initial recording of the tales, served as informants to the collection, and as an inspiration to the tale selection in the *Kleine Ausgabe* (*Small Edition*) of 1825. On the other hand, both Wilhelm and Jacob were uncompromising as they refused to give in to didactic voices urging them to make changes in traditional folktale characters, plots, and themes, for they firmly believed that folktales should not be tailored to teach certain lessons or morals. This does not mean, however, that they disregarded children as a reading audience. Rather, it implied that they refused to alter the substance of the tales while "talking down" to children. The Grimms' extensive notes to the tales place the collection in a category of folk literature for all ages and scholars as well.

Are *Kinder- und Hausmärchen* still to be viewed as genuine folklore? Such critics as Felix Karlinger, Max Lüthi, Heinz Rölleke, and Maria Tatar have taken a safe middle position on the subject while placing Grimms' tales between traditional folktales and literary fairy tales. Depending on how much weight they have attached to the Grimms' perceived editorial changes of the oral tales, they have leaned more to one side or the other. Of these critics, possibly Rölleke has been the most serious defendant of Grimms' fine perception of what was genuine in the traditional folktale. While not denying some of the changes which they imposed on the original tales, he gave them much credit for having come close to the oral tradition.

This work has added a new perspective to the issue by showing that neither Jacob nor Wilhelm believed in the existence of a static *Urmärchen* or primeval tale to which storytellers or editors were bound by a pedantic word-by-word recital. To the degree that the Grimms required spontaneity as a prerequisite for keeping the tales alive in the oral tradition while insisting only on loyalty to the substance or "core" of the tales (rather than to individual words), the issue of changes in the wording of folktales has been rendered irrelevant. The Grimms expected changes, as they expected variants to occur, as a natural process of language dynamics and language development, but never as an arbitrary process based on personal fantasies. For that reason, too, they thought that their folktale collection was unique and should be distinguished from the literary fairy tale or *Kunstmärchen*.

The international and comparative perspective of Grimms' folklore activities, a much neglected topic in Grimm research, holds the key to their sustained correspondence with scholars and collectors in other lands, their translations, folktale theories, and comparative notes. The chapters on didacticism, nationalism, and the Third Reich have explored various reasons of why the Germans themselves at one time or another preferred to ignore Grimms' international scholarship by editing their essays and prefaces in a highly selective and distorted way. There is no doubt that the Grimms promoted an intensive study of the German folk heritage, yet they did not do so at the expense of other cultures and traditions. Sharing Herder's ideas on the folk soul of ancient nations, they perceived no contradiction in searching for national folklore while simultaneously pursuing an active interest in international folklore as well. In that sense, too, they embraced the spirit of early German Romanticism in which national and universal ideas still flourished side by side.

Those critics who have preferred to see Grimms as nationalist scholars have usually ignored their translation of Croker's *Fairy Legends*,

Wilhelm's pioneering essay on folklore of the British Isles, and Jacob's translations of Old French epics, Spanish romances, Stepanovic's Serbian grammar, the French and Flemish *Reynard the Fox*, and the Old Slavic epic of *The Song of Igor*, along with his prefaces and reviews pertaining to Serbian, Cossack, and other national fairy tale collections. They have also been conspicuously silent on behalf of the third volume of the second edition of the *Kinder- und Hausmärchen* that not only contains Grimms' notes on German folktales but also Wilhelm's extensive analysis of Basile's *Pentamerone* and other comparative studies of folktale collections around the world.

The question of whether or not Grimms' folktales are quite as old as they themselves thought they were must be answered with caution, for contrary to popular belief the Grimms did not cling exclusively to the idea that all folktales evolved from myths or from Norse mythology. The exaggerated notion of the Grimms' exclusive German, "Nordic," orientation has been traced back to Edgar Taylor's misunderstanding in his first English translation of the work. Taylor was also responsible for the myths that the Grimms had printed all tales exactly as they had originally recorded them, and solely from the German peasant folk. The idea of a chauvinistic German and "Nordic" orientation is also evident in the writings of some overzealous German nationalists among the interpreters of Grimm around the turn of the century, and even more so in the Nazis' distorted folkish and racial folktale interpretations in the Third Reich. In reality, Grimms' concept of folktale origins was partially rooted in the Indo-European language theory (in contrast to the Nazis' exclusive Nordic "Aryan descent" theory), and partially in the belief of a spontaneous creation of the same tales in remote and different cultures—a theory that leaned more toward anthropological theories. Sometimes the Grimms were eclectic in their theoretical approaches but not ethnocentric.

The satirical treatments of Grimms' folktales have merit of their own in literary terms, to the extent that they are viewed as an art, not as critical interpretations of the folktales themselves. The chapter on irony and satire has suggested that modern skepticism and a lack of background knowledge regarding the conception and basis of Grimms' research have promoted the satirical approach to the tales.

The ethics of folktales have been viewed from various angles, as they are still the subject of an on-going issue. Against the background of so many moralistic, didactic, pragmatic, and political treatments of Grimms' *Kinder- und Hausmärchen*, possibly the literary and psychological views offer the most enlightened perspectives, as these tend to be free from a didactic bias that should belong to a by-gone age.

BIBLIOGRAPHY

PRIMARY SOURCES: WORKS BY WILHELM AND JACOB GRIMM

• *Kinder- und Hausmärchen*

Kinder- und Hausmärchen. Vol. 1 Berlin: Reimer, 1812; Vol. 2, 1815. The subsequent editions were issued during the lifetime of the Brothers Grimm: 2d enl. ed., 3 vols. Vols. 1 and 2, 1819; Vol. 3, 1822. Vol. 3 contained in its first part the *Anmerkungen* to the tales (notes), and in its second part Wilhelm Grimm's comparative study of folktales around the world, including a separate preface on folktale theories and additional comparative annotations.

Kleine Ausgabe (Small Edition), published in a single volume. Berlin: Reimer, 1825. Ill. by Ludwig Grimm.

3d enl. ed., 2 vols. Göttingen: Verlag der Dieterichschen Buchhandlung, 1837.

4th enl. ed., (Grosse Ausgabe (Large Edition). Göttingen: Verlag der Dieterichschen Buchhandlung, 1840. Additional introductory essay contained Grimms' book reviews of international folktale editions that had appeared in the wake of the *Kinder- und Hausmärchen* since 1812.

5th ed., 2 vols. Göttingen: Verlag der Dieterichschen Buchhandlung, 1843.

6th enl. and improved ed. *Grosse Ausgabe* (Large Edition), 2 vols. Göttingen: Verlag der Dieterichschen Buchhandlung, 1850.

7th ed., *Grosse Ausgabe* (Large Edition). Göttingen: Verlag der Dieterichschen Buchhandlung. Vol. 3 of 1856 contains revised notes of 1822, with an abridged comparative historical part and new bibliographical entries pertaining to folktale publications around the world. Vols. 2 and 3, containing the "complete" folktale collection, were published in 1957.

• Modern German Editions of the *Kinder- und Hausmärchen* (Selective Listing)

Brüder Grimm: Kinder- und Hausmärchen. Ausgabe letzter Hand. 3 vols. Ed. Heinz Rölleke. Stuttgart: Reclam, 1980. This edition is based on Grimms' *Grosse Ausgabe* of 1857. Vol. 3 is a reprint of the 1856 edition of Grimms' notes.

Kinder- und Hausmärchen der Brüder Grimm. Vollständige Ausgabe in der Urfassung. Ed. Friedrich Panzer. Foreword by Friedrich Panzer. Wiesbaden: Emil Vollmer Verlag, 1975. The text is based on the first edition of the tales (2 vols. 1812–1815) and includes Grimms' notes to the tales that were originally included in these two volumes.)

Die schönsten Märchen der Gebrüder Grimm. Series: *Märchen der Weltliteratur,* Vol. 4. Hamburg: Verlag Olde Hansen, 1978.

Grimms Kinder- und Hausmärchen. 2 vols. Ed. Heinz Rölleke. Cologne: Diederichs Verlag, 1982.

Grimms Märchen. Introd. by Inge Weber-Kellermann. Frankfurt am Main: Insel Verlag, 1984.

Die Märchen der Brüder Grimm. Vollständige Ausgabe. Introd. Kurt Wasselowsky. Augsburg: Wilhelm Goldmann Verlag, 1984. (The text is based on the Grimms' 1857 edition, yet replaces some archaic expressions by modern colloquial speech.)

Kinder- und Hausmärchen. Munich: Deutscher Taschenbuch Verlag, 1985.

Es war einmal. Zurich: Racher, 1920. Series: Manesse Bibliothek der Weltliteratur. Repr. ed. Stuttgart: Manesse, 1947.

ENGLISH TRANSLATIONS OF THE *KINDER- UND HAUSMÄRCHEN* (SELECTIVE LISTING)

German Popular Stories. 2 vols. Trans. Edgar Taylor. London: Murray, 1823–1826. Ill. George Cruikshank. The 2d. ed. followed in 1829.

German Popular Stories and Fairy Tales as Told by Gammer Grethel. 3 rev. ed. Trans. Edgar Taylor. London: Bell & Sons, 1878.

The Fairy Ring: A New Collection of Popular Tales. Trans. John Edward Taylor. Ill. Richard Doyle. London: Murray, 1846.

German Popular Stories and Fairy Tales as Told by Gammer Grethel. 3rd rev. ed. Trans. Edgar Taylor. London: George Bell & Sons, 1878.

Grimm's Household Tales with the Author's Notes 2 vols. Trans. Margaret Hunt. Intr. Andrew Lang. Pref. John Ruskin. London: George Bell & Sons, Ltd., 1878.

Household Stories from the Collection of the Brothers Grimm. Trans. Lucy Crane. Ill. Walter Crane. Macmillan & Company, 1886.

Folktales of Germany. Trans. Lotte Baumann. Foreword by Richard Dorson. Chicago: University of Chicago Press, 1966.

The Juniper Tree and Other Tales from Grimm. Trans. Lore Segal, with four tales trans. by Randall Jarrell. Selected by Lore Segal and Maurice Sendak. Ill. Maurice Sendak. New York: Farrar Straus and Giroux, 1973.

The Complete Grimm's Fairy Tales. Reprint of 1944 ed. Trans. Margaret Hunt. Rev. James Stern. Intr. Padraic Colum, with a folkloristic commentary by Joseph Campbell. Ill. Josef Scharl. New York: Pantheon, 1975.

Grimms' Tales for Young and Old: The Complete Stories. Trans. Ralph Manheim. Garden City, N.Y.: Doubleday, 1977.

The Brothers Grimm: Popular Folktales. Trans. and Introd. Brian Alderson. Ill. Michael Foreman. New York: Doubleday, 1978.

Jacob and Wilhelm Grimm: Selected Tales. Trans. and Intr. David Luke. New York: Penguin, 1983.

The Complete Fairy Tales of the Brothers Grimm. Trans. Jack Zipes. New York: Bantam, 1987.

OTHER WORKS PUBLISHED JOINTLY BY THE BROTHERS GRIMM

Deutsche Sagen (German Legends). 2 vols. Berlin: Verlag der Realbuchhandlung, 1816–1818. Reprint ed. in the series: *International Folklore*, eds. Richard M. Dorson, Issachar Ben Ami, and Vilmos Voigt. New York: Arno Press, 1977. *The German Legends of the Brothers Grimm.* 2 vols. Trans. and ed. Donald Ward. Philadelphia: Institute for the Study of Human Issues, 1981.

Altdeutsche Wälder (Old German Forests). A journal edited by the Brothers Grimm, to which they also contributed essays and reviews. Kassel and Frankfurt: 1813–1816.

Der Arme Heinrich. (Poor Henry). A poem by Hartmann von der Aue, ed. by the Brothers Grimm. Berlin: Verlag der Realbuchhandlung, 1815.

Lieder der alten Edda (Songs of the Elder Edda). Trans. based on the manuscript, ed., and interpreted by the Brothers Grimm. Berlin: Verlag der Realbuch-handlung, 1815.

Die beiden ältesten deutschen Gedichte aus dem 8. Jahrhundert: Das Lied von Hildebrand und Hadubrand und Das Weißenbrunner Gebet. (The Two Oldest German Poems of the Eighth Century: The Song of Hildebrand and Hadubrand and the Prayer of Weißenbrunn). Eds. Kassel: Thurneisen, 1822.

Irische Elfenmärchen. Trans. by Jacob and Wilhelm Grimm. (Based on the first volume of Thomas Crofton Croker's, *Fairy Legends and Traditions of the South of Ireland.* London: Murray, 1825). Leipzig: Friedrich Fleischer, 1826. This translation included Wilhelm Grimm's introductory essay "Über die Elfen" (About the Fairies).

Deutsches Wörterbuch (German Dictionary). The first three volumes were published by the Grimms alone. Leipzig: Weidmann'sche Buchhandlung, 1852 (Vol. 1) and Leipzig: S. Hirzel, 1854–62 (Vols. 2 and 3). Vol. 4, which was partially based on the Grimms' contributions, was continued by Karl Weigand and Rudolf Hildebrand. With the help of distinguished German linguists, the final volume of this etymological dictionary was completed a century later. 16 vols. Leipzig: Hirzel, 1854–1960/71.

Volkslieder (Folk Songs), 3 vols. Grimms' collection of folk songs deposited at the University Library of Göttingen. Eds. Charlotte Oberfeld et al., Marburg: N.G. Elwert Verlag, 1985–1988.

SEPARATE PUBLICATIONS BY JACOB GRIMM (SELECTIVE LISTING)

Über den altdeutschen Meistergesang (About the Old German Master Singers). Göttingen: Heinrich Dieterichs, 1811.

Irminstrasse und Irminsäule (Irmin Street and Irmin Column). Vienna: Carl Gerold, 1815.

Circular wegen Aufsammlung von Volkspoesie (Round-Letter on Behalf of Collecting Folk Poetry). Vienna: 1815. (Printed in Vienna, yet distributed and mailed by Jacob Grimm.)

Deutsche Grammatik (German Grammar). 4 vols. Göttingen: Dieterichs, 1819–1837.

Wuk Stephanowitsch, Kleine serbische Grammatik (Vuk Stepanovic, Small Serbian Grammar). Berlin: Dieterichs, 1828.

Deutsche Rechtsalterthümer (German Legal Antiquities). Göttingen: Dieterichs, 1828.

"Vorwort" (Preface) in Anton Dietrich, ed. *Russische Volksmärchen in den Urschriften gesammelt und ins Deutsche übersetzt (Russian Folktales collected in the original and translated into German)*. Leipzig: Weidmann'sche Buchhandlung, 1831.

Reinhart Fuchs (Reynard the Fox) Berlin: Reimer, 1834.

Deutsche Mythologie (German Mythology, also trans. as *Teutonic Mythology)*. 3 vols. Göttingen: Dieterichsche Buchhandlung, 1835–1837. Jacob Grimm. *Teutonic Mythology*. 4 vols. Trans. from the 4th ed. with notes and appendix in a separate volume. New York: Dover, 1966.

Über meine Entlassung (About My Dismissal). Basel: Schweighauser, 1838.

Lateinische Gedichte des X. und XI. Jahrhunderts (Latin Poems of the 10th and 11th Century) Göttingen: Dieterichsche Buchhandlung, 1838.

Weistümer (Works of Wisdom). 7 vols. Göttingen: Dieterichsche Buchhandlung, 1840–1878.

Andreas und Elena (Gedicht) (Andrew and Helen—A Poem). Kassel: Theodor Fischer, 1840.

Über das Pedantische in der deutschen Sprache (About the Pedantic Element in the German Language). Berlin: Druckerei der Königlichen Akademie der Wissenschaften, 1847.

Geschichte der deutschen Sprache (History of the German Language). 2 vols. Leipzig: Weidmannsche Buchhandlung, 1848.

Das Wort des Besitzes (The Word "Property"). Berlin: Druckerei der Königlichen Akademie der Wissenschaften, 1850.

Rede auf Wilhelm Grimm und Rede über das Alter (Oration on Wilhelm Grimm and Lecture about Old Age). Ed. Hermann Grimm. Berlin: Druckerei der Königlichen Akademie der Wissenschaften, 1863.

Kleinere Schriften von Jacob Grimm (Smaller Publications of Jacob Grimm). 8 vols. These volumes include speeches, essays, reviews, prefaces, and personal notes and references). Vols. 1–5 ed. Karl Müllenhoff. Berlin: Ferdinand Dümmlers Verlagsbuchhandlung, 1864–1871. Vols. 6–7 ed. Eduard Ippel. Berlin: Ferdinand Dümmlers Verlagsbuchhandlung, 1882–1884. Vol. 8 ed. Eduard Ippel. Gütersloh: Bertelsmann, 1890. Reprint ed. Hildesheim: Georg Olms Verlagsbuchhandlung, 1965.

Jacob Grimm. *Selbstbiographie. Ausgewählte Schriften, Reden und Abhandlungen*. Munich: Deutscher Taschenbuch Verlag, 1984.

SEPARATE PUBLICATIONS BY WILHELM GRIMM (SELECTIVE LISTING)

Altdänische Heldenlieder, Balladen und Märchen (Old Danish Heroic Songs, Ballads, and Folktales). Trans. and Preface by Wilhelm Grimm. Heidelberg: Mohr und Zimmer, 1811.

Drei altschottische Lieder im Original und Übersetzung (Three Old Scottish Songs in the Original and in Translation). Heidelberg: Mohr und Zimmer, 1813.

Über deutsche Runen (About German Runes). Göttingen: In der Dieterichschen Buchhandlung, 1821.

"Über die Elfen" (About the Fairies) Wilhelm's comparative essay on English, Irish, Scottish, and Welsh fairylore, attached as an introduction to *Irische Elfenmärchen*. Trans. by Jacob and Wilhelm Grimm of Thomas Crofton Croker's *Fairy Legends and Traditions of the South of Ireland*. Leipzig: Fleischer, 1826.

"Fairy Legends" (review article). *Göttingische Gelehrte Anzeigen* (Ja. 12, 1826). Reprinted in *Kleinere Schriften von Wilhelm Grimm*. Vol. 2. Berlin: Dümmler, 1881.

Zur Literatur der Runen. Nebst Mittheilung runischer Alphabete und gotischer Fragmente aus Handschriften (On the Literature Regarding Runes, including Communications regarding Runic Alphabets and Gothic Fragments, based on Manuscripts). Vienna: Carl Gerold, 1828.

Grave Ruodolf (Count Rudolf). Göttingen: In der Dieterichschen Verlagsbuchhandlung, 1828.

Die deutsche Heldensage (The German Heroic Legend). Göttingen: In der Dieterichschen Verlagsbuchhandlung, 1829.

De Hildebrando antiquissimi carminis teutonici fragmentum (The Song of Hildebrand: A Teutonic Fragment). Göttingen: (Verf.) (Author), 1830. Facsimile edition Kassel: Studienwerkstätten der Gesamthochschule, 1984.

Vridanks Bescheidenheit (The Modesty of Freidank). Göttingen: Verlag der Dieterichschen Buchhandlung, 1834.

Ruolandes Liet (The Song of Roland). Göttingen: Dieterichsche Buchhandlung, 1838.

Sämtliche Werke von Ludwig Achim von Arnim. 22 vols. Berlin: Veit, 1839–1850. Ed. and Introd. by Wilhelm Grimm. These works include novels, short stories, poems, and dramas.

Kleinere Schriften von Wilhelm Grimm (Smaller Publications of Wilhelm Grimm). These include speeches, essays, reviews, prefaces, and personal notes and references. 4 vols. Ed. Gustav Hinrichs. Vol. 1, Berlin: Ferdinand Dümmlers Verlagsbuchhandlung. 1881. Vols. 2–4, Gütersloh: Bertelsmann, 1887.

Kolleg zum Nibelungenlied. Series: *Schriften der Brüder Grimm Gesellschaft*, Kassel, Nr. 10. (*Lectures on the Nibelungenlied*. Series: *Publications of the Brothers Grimm Society*, Kassel, No. 10). Transcribed by one of Wilhelm's students at the University of Göttingen. Ed. Else Ebel. Marburg: N.G. Elwert Verlag, 1985.

Irische Land- und Seemärchen. Wilhelm's translation of Thomas Crofton Croker's collected tales, published posthumously. Series: *Schriften der Brüder Grimm*

Gesellschaft, Kassel, Nr. 14. (*Irish Land-and Sea Fairy Tales*. Series: *Publications of the Brothers Grimm Society*, Kassel, No. 14). Ed. and published by Werner Moritz, Charlotte Oberfeld, and Siegrid Heyer. Marburg: Elwert Verlag, 1986.

Published Documents, Manuscripts, and Correspondence

Andersen, Hans Christian. *Das Märchen meines Lebens. Briefe und Tagebücher*. Trans. from the Danish with an afterword by Erling Nielsen. Munich: Winkler Verlag, 1967.

Arbeitsgemeinschaft für deutsche Volkskunde. Berlin: Zentralverlag der N.S.D.A.P., 1938. (Papers and documents related to a workshop on folklore, sponsored by the National Socialist Party).

Brill, Edward V.K. "The Correspondence between the Brothers Grimm and Sir Walter Scott." In *Brüder Grimm Gedenken*. Vol. 1. Ed. Ludwig Denecke. Marburg: N. G. Elwert Verlag, 1963.

Catalogue of the Public Library, Bay City. Bay City, Mi.: Public Library, 1878.

Daffis, Hans. *Inventar der Grimm-Schränke der Preussischen Staatsbibliothek*. Series: *Mitteilungen der Preussischen Staatsbibliothek*, Vol. 5. Leipzig: Hiersemann, 1923.

Gerstner, Hermann, ed. *Brüder Grimm in Selbstzeugnissen und Bilddokumenten*. Monograph No. 20 by Rohwohlt. Reinbek: Rowohlt, 1973.

Gregory, John M. *School Funds and School Laws of Michigan; with Notes, Forms, to which are added Elements of School Architecture, with Lists of Text Books and Library Books*. Lansing, Mi.: Office of the School Superintendent, 1859.

Grierson, H. J. G., David Cook, and W. M. Parker, eds. *The Letters of Sir Walter Scott 1811–1814*. Centenary edition. London: 1933.

Grimm, Hermann, and Gustav Hinrichs, eds. *Briefwechsel zwischen Jacob und Wilhelm Grimm aus der Jugendzeit*. 2d enl. and rev. edition, ed. by Wilhelm Schoof. Weimar: Böhlaus, Nachf., 1963.

Gürtler, Hans, and Albert Leitzman, eds. *Briefe der Brüder Grimm*. Jena: Verlag der Fromannschen Buchhandlung, Walter Biedermann, 1923.

Harder, Hans-Berndt, and Ekkehard Kaufmann, eds. *200 Jahre Brüder Grimm. Die Brüder Grimm in ihrer amtlichen und politischen Tätigkeit*. 2 parts. Series: *Ausstellungskataloge*, Vol. 3. Kassel: Verlag Weber & Weidemeyer, 1985–1986.

Hartwig, Otto. "Zur ersten englischen Übersetzung der Kinder- und Hausmärchen der Brüder Grimm." *Zentralblatt für Bibliothekswesen* 15 (1898): 1–23. (The article contains reprints of letters by Jacob Grimm, Edward Taylor, and Georg Benecke.)

Hennig, Dieter, ed. *Katalog der Ausstellung im Palais Bellevue, Brüder Grimm Museum*. Kassel: Bärenreiter Verlag, 1973. Hennig, Dieter and Bernhard Lauer, eds. *200 Jahre Brüder Grimm: Dokumente ihres Lebens und Wirkens*. Series: *Ausstellungskataloge*, Vol. 1. Kassel: Verlag Weber & Weidemeyer, 1985.

Hennig, John. "The Brothers Grimm and T. C. Croker." *Modern Language Review* 41 (1946): 44–54.

Koszinowski, Ingrid, and Vera Leuschner, eds. *Ludwig Emil Grimm 1790–1863. Maler, Zeicher, Radierer*. Series: *Katalog der Ausstellung*, Vol. 2. Kassel: Verlag Weber & Weidemeyer, 1985.

Lefftz, Joseph, ed. *Märchen der Brüder Grimm: Urfassung in der Orginalhandschrift der Abtei Oelenberg im Elsaß*. Series: *Wissenschaftliche Reihe der Lothring. Wissenschaftl. Gesellschaft: Reihe C*. Vol. 1. Strasbourg: Wissenschaftliche Gesellschaft zu Straßburg, 1927.

Leitzmann, A., ed. *Briefwechsel der Brüder Grimm mit Karl Lachmann*. Jena: Diederichs, 1927.

Michaelis-Jena, Ruth and Arthur Ratcliff, eds. *Grimm's Other Tales*. A New Selection (based on manuscripts in Grimm's archives). Wood engravings by Gwenda Morgan. New York: A.S. Barnes & Co., 1956.

Ottendorff-Simrock, Walther, ed. *Die Grimms und die Simrocks in Briefen*. Bonn: Ferdinand Dümmlers Verlag, 1966.

Pfeiffer, Franz and Karl Bartsch ed. *Briefwechsel mit unveröffentlichen Briefen der Gebrüder Grimm*. Ed. Hans Joachim Koppitz. Cologne: Greven, 1969.

Rölleke, Heinz. *Die älteste Märchensammlung der Brüder Grimm: Synopse einer handschriftlichen Deutung*. Monograph. Geneva: Fondation, Martin Bodmer, 1975.

———, ed. *Märchen aus dem Nachlaß der Brüder Grimm*. 2d ed. Series: *Schriftenreihe Literaturwissenschaft*. Wuppertal: Gesamthochschule, 1979.

Reichsministerium des Innern (Reich Ministry of the Interior), eds. *Die Reichsschulkonferenz 1920. Ihre Vorgeschichte und Vorbereitung und ihre Verhandlungen. Amtlicher Bericht*. Leipzig: Dürr'sche Buchhandlung, 1921.

Reifenscheid, Alexander. *Freundesbriefe von Wilhelm and Jacob Grimm; Mit Anmerkungen*. Heilbronn: Henninger, 1878.

Rißmann, Jutta. "Eine bisher unbekannte handschriftliche Fassung; "Sechse kommen durch die Welt." In *Brüder Grimm Gedenken*. Vol. 3. Marburg: N. G. Elwert Verlag, 1981.

Schmidt, Ernest, ed. *Briefwechsel der Gebrüder Grimm mit nordischen Gelehrten*. Berlin: Dümmlers Verlagsbuchhandlung, 1885.

Schnack, Ingeborg, ed. *Die Selbstbiographien von Jacob und Wilhelm Grimm*. Kassel: Brüder Grimm Gesellschaft, 1956.

Schoof, Wilhelm, ed. *Briefwechsel zwischen Jacob und Wilhelm Grimm aus der Jugendzeit*. 2d ed. (originally edited by Hermann Grimm and Gustav Hinrichs). Weimar: Hermann Böhlaus Nachf., 1963.

———, ed. *Die Grimms und die Simrocks in Briefen: 1830–1864*. Bonn, Munich: Dümmler, 1966.

Schoof, Wilhelm, and Ingeborg Schnack eds. *Briefe der Brüder Grimm an Savigny. Aus dem Savignischen Nachlaß*. Berlin: Erich Schmidt Verlag, 1953.

Schoof, Wilhelm, and Jörn Göres, eds. *Unbekannte Briefe der Brüder Grimm. Unter Ausnutzung des Grimmschen Nachlasses*. Bonn: Athenäum, 1960.

Schulte-Kemminghausen, Karl. *Westfälische Märchen und Sagen aus dem Nachlaß der Brüder Grimm*. 2d ed. Münster: Beiträge des Droste-Kreises, 1957.

Schulz, Franz, ed. *Die Märchen der Brüder Grimm in der Urform. Nach der (Ölenberger) Handschrift herausgegeben*. Offenbach am Main: Gebrüder Klingspor and the Frankfurter Bibliophilen Gesellschaft, 1924.

Scott, Sir Walter. *The Journal of Sir Walter Scott*. Ed. E. K. Andersen. Oxford: Clarendon, 1972.

———. *The Letters of Sir Walter Scott*. Edited by Herbert John C. Grierson, David Cook, W. M. Parker, et al. London: Constable, 1932–1937.

———. *The Journal of Sir Walter Scott*. Text rev. from a photostat in the National Library of Scotland. Westport, Connecticut: Greenwood Press, 1978.

OTHER WORKS CONSULTED

"A–Zypressenzweig." *Der Spiegel* 15, 12 (1961): 65–74.

Aarne, Antti Amatus. *Leitfaden der vergleichenden Märchenforschung*. Series: *FF Communications* No. 13, 1913. Helsinki: Academia scientiarum fennica, 1913. Reprint 1950.

———. *The Types of Folktale: A Classification and Bibliography*. 2d rev. ed. Trans. and enl. Stith Thompson. Helsinki: Academia Scientiarum Fennica, 1981.

_____. *Verzeichnis der Märchentypen.* Series: *FF Communications* No. 3, 1928. Reprint. Helsinki: Academia Scientiarum Fennica, 1950.

Andersen, Hans Christian. *The True Story of My Life.* Trans. from the German by Mary Howitt. London: Longman, Brown, 1847.

Antonsen, Elmer H. "Rasmus Rask and Jakob Grimm. Their Relationship in the Investigation of Germanic Vocalism." *Scandinavian Studies* 34 (1962): 183–94.

Aries. Philippe. *Centuries of Childhood.* New York: Knopf, 1862.

Arnim, L. Achim von, and Clemens Brentano, eds. *Des Knaben Wunderhorn: Alte deutsche Lieder* (originally published 1806–1808). Reprint: Munich: Winkler Verlag, 1974. Postscript, Willi A. Koch.

Asbjörnsen, Peter Christian and Jörgen Moe. *Popular Tales from the Norse.* Trans. Sir George Webbe Dasent. New York: D. Appleton, 1859.

Auden, W.H. "In Praise of the Brothers Grimm." *New York Times Book Review* 12 Nov. 1944: 1.

Aulnoy, Marie Catherine Comtesse d'. *The Fairy Tales of Madame d'Aulnoy.* Newly trans. into English with an introduction by Anne Thackeray Ritschie. London: Lawrence & Bullen, 1892. See also: *The Tales of the Fairies in Three Parts, Compleat.* Extracted from the 2d ed. in English of *The Diverting Works of the Countess d'Anois* (originally published in 1715). Reprint New York: Garland Publishing Inc., 1977. Pref. Michael Patrick Hearn.

Avery, Gillian. "Fairy Tales with a Purpose." In *Nineteenth Century Children: Heroes and Heroines in English Children's Stories 1780–1900.* Ed. Gillian Avery. London: Hodder and Stoughton, Limited, 1965.

Azzolina, David S. *Tale-Type and Motif Indexes; An Annotated Bibliography.* New York: Garland, 1987.

Bachofen, J. J. *Myth, Religion and Mother Right.* Trans. Ralph Manheim. Princeton: Princeton University Press, 1967.

"Bad Literature." *Isabella County Enterprise.* Mt. Pleasant, Mi. (May 21, 1879), Youth Column: 3.

Bamberger, Richard. *Jugendlektüre.* Vienna: Verlag für Jugend und Volk, 1965.

Basile, Giambattista. *The Pentamerone or the Story of Stories; Time for the Little Ones,* trans. and ed. by John Edward Taylor. London: David Boyne and J. Cundall, 1847.

Bastian, Ulrike. *Die Kinder- und Hausmärchen in der literaturpädagogischen Betrachtung.* Frankfurt: M. Haag und Herchen, 1986.

Baumgärtner, Alfred Clemens. "Ach Du bist's, alter Wasserpatscher!" Zur aktuellen Rezeption Grimmscher Märchen" in Baumgärtner, Alfred C. und Kurt E. Maier, eds. *Mythen, Märchen, und moderne Zeit.* Series: *Beiträge zur Kinder- und Jugendliteratur.* Volkach: Akademie der Kinder- und Jugendliteratur, 1986.

Baumgärtner, Alfred C., and Kurt C. Maier, eds. *Mythen, Märchen und moderne Zeit.* Series: *Beiträge zur Kinder- und Jugendliteratur.* Volkach: Akademie der Kinder- und Jugendliteratur, 1986.

Bausinger, Hermann. "Aschenputtel: Zum Problem der Märchensymbolik." *Zeitschrift für Volkskunde* 52 (1955): 144–55.

_____. "Archäische Züge im Märchen. *Enzyklopädie der Märchen.* I. Ed. Ludwig Denecke. Marburg: N. G. Elwert Verlag, 1963.

_____. "Möglichkeiten des Märchens der Gegenwart." In *Märchen, Mythos, Dichtung. Festschrift zum 90. Geburtstag Friedrich von der Leyens.* Eds. Hugo Kuhn und Kurt Schier. Munich: C. H. Beck, 1963.

_____. *Märchen, Phantasie und Wirklichkeit.* Frankfurt: Dipa Verlag, 1976.

_____. "Gut und Böse." In *Enzyklopädie des Märchens.* Vol. 5. Ed. Kurt Ranke et al. Berlin: Walter De Gruyter, 1989: 316–24.

Beane, W.C. and Wm. Doty. *Myths, Rites, and Symbols.* New York: Harper & Row Inc., 1976.

Bechstein, Ludwig. *Märchenbuch.* Leipzig: Verlag Georg Wigand, 1845.

Beer, Gundula. "Charles Perrault und die Brüder Grimm." Typescript. Munich: International Youth Library, 1968.

Beaufort, John. "'Into the Woods': A Fairy Tale for Adults; Sondheim's Music Charms while Plots Take New Twists." *The Christian Science Monitor* (Nov. 6, 1987): 26.

Behler, Ernst. "Nachwort." *Deutsches Museum. Die Geschichte einer Zeitschrift.* Ed. Ernst Behler. Darmstadt: Wissenschaftliche Buchgesellschaft, 1975.

————. "Kritische Gedanken zum Begriff der europäischen Romantik." In *Die europäische Romantik.* Ed. Ernst Behler et al. Frankfurt am Main: Athenäum Verlag, 1972.

————, ed. *Kritische Friedrich-Schlegel Ausgabe.* Intr. by Ernst Behler. Munich: Schöningh, 1966.

Beit, Hedwig von. *Symbolik des Märchens: Versuch einer Deutung.* 3 vols. Berlin: Francke Verlag, 1952–1956. Title of Vol. 2: *Gegensatz und Erneuerung im Märchen.*

Ben Amos, Dan, ed. *Folklore Genres.* Austin: University of Texas Press, 1976.

Benz, Richard. *Die deutsche Romantik. Geschichte einer geistlichen Bewegung.* Stuttgart: Klett, 1956.

————. *Märchendichtung der Romantiker.* Jena: Diederichs, 1926.

————. "Johann Gottfried Herder." In *Die Grossen Deutschen: Eine Biographie.* Eds. Hermann Hempel, Theodor Heuss, Bruno Reiffenberg, et al. Berlin: Deutsche Buch-Gemeinschaft, 1965.

Berdahl, Robert M. "New Thoughts on German Nationalism." *American Historical Review* 76, 1 (Feb. 1972): 65–80.

Berendsohn, Walter A. *Grundformen volkstümlicher Erzählkunst in den Kinder- und Hausmärchen der Brüder Grimm: Ein stilkünstlicher Versuch.* Hamburg: W. Gente, 1921.

Berlin, Isaiah. *Herder and Vico. Two Studies in the History of Ideas.* New York: Vintage, 1976.

Bettelheim, Bruno. *The Uses of Enchantment. The Meaning and Importance of Fairy Tales* (original title: *Kinder brauchen Märchen*). New York: Random House, Vintage Books, 1977.

Bietak, Wilhelm, ed. *Romantische Wissenschaft.* Series: *Deutsche Literatur, Reihe Romantik*, Vol. 13. Ed. Paul Kluckhortn. Darmstadt: Wissenschaftliche Buchgesellschaft, 1966.

Bingham, Jane, ed. *Writers for Children: Critical Studies of Major Authors Since the Seventeenth Century.* New York: Charles Scribner's Sons, 1987.

Birkhäuser-Oeri, Sibylle. *Die Mutter im Märchen: Deutung der Problematik des Mütterlichen und des Mutterkomplexes am Beispiel bekannter Märchen.* Series ed. Marie Louise von Franz. Stuttgart: Verlag Adolf Bonz, 1976. Biskin, D., and K. Hoskissen. "An Experimental Test of the Effects of Structural Discussion of Moral Dilemmas Found in Children's Literature." *The Elementary School Journal* 77 (May 1977): 407–16.

Bolte, Johannes, and Georg Polivka. *Anmerkungen zu den Kinder- und Hausmärchen der Brüder Grimm.* 6 vols. (Leipzig: Dieterichsche Verlagsbuchhandlung, 1913–1932); 2d unrev. ed. Hildesheim: Georg Olms Verlag, 1963–1972.

Bottigheimer, Ruth. *Grimms' Bad Girls and Bold Boys.* New Haven: Yale University Press, 1987.

————. "Tale Spinners: Submerged Voices in Grimms' Fairy Tales." *New German Critique* 27 (1982): 142–50.

————. ed. *Fairy Tales and Society: Illusion, Allusion, and Paradigm.* Philadelphia, Pa.: University of Pennsylvania Press, 1986.

Bracher, Helmut, ed. *Und wenn sie nicht gestorben sind . . . : Perspektiven auf das Märchen.* Frankfurt: Suhrkamp, 1980.

Bracher, Helmut, and Volkmar Sander, eds. *German Fairy Tales: Jacob and W. Grimm* and Others. Foreword by Bruno Bettelheim. Freiburg I. Breisgau: Kurt Schmidt Verlag, 1973.

Briggs, Katherine M. *The Anatomy of Puck. An Examination of Fairy Belief among Shakespeare's Contemporaries and Successors.* London: Routledge and Kegan Paul, 1959.

_____. *A Dictionary of Fairies.* London: Lane, 1976.

_____. *Englische Volksmärchen.* Aus dem Englischen übersetzt von Uta Schier. Düsseldorf: Diederichs, 1970.

_____. *The Fairies in Tradition and Literature.* London: Routledge and Kegan Paul, 1967.

_____. *The Vanishing People. A Study of Traditional Fairy Beliefs.* London: Batsford, 1978.

Briggs, Katherine, and Ludwig Denecke. "Edgar und John Edward Taylor, die ersten englischen Übersetzer der Kinder- und Hausmärchen." In *Brüder Grimm Gedenken.* Vol. 2. Ed. Ludwig Denecke. Marburg: N. G. Elwert Verlag, 1975.

Brooke, Henry. *A New Collection of Fairy Tales; Containing many Useful Lessons, Moral Sentiments, Surprising Incidents, and Amusing Adventures* 2 vols. London: Holborn C. Hitch in Pater Noster Row. Printed for R. Dodsley in Pall Mall, W. Bowyer in Whitechapel, S. Fryer and G. Woodfall at Charing-Cross, 1750.

Brüder-Grimm Symposium zur Historischen Wortforschung. Berlin: Walter De Gruyter Verlag, 1986.

Brunvand, Jan Harold. *The Study of American Folklore.* New York: W. W. Norton, 1968.

Bühler, Charlotte and Josephine Bilz. *Das Märchen und die Phantasie des Kindes.* Munich: J. A. Barth, 1961.

Busch, Wilhelm. *Und die Moral von der Geschicht'.* Gütersloh: Mohn & Companie, 1959.

_____. *Humoristischer Hausschatz mit 1500 Bildern* 2 vols. Munich: Verlag von Fr. Bassermann, 1949.

Büsching, Johann Gustav. *Volks-Sagen, Märchen und Legenden.* Leipzig: Carl Heinrich Reclam, 1812.

Camman, Alfred. "Eine deutsche Märchenerzählerin aus der Ukraine." *Jahrbuch für deutsche Volkskunde* 18 (1975): 88–177.

_____. "Neues aus Bezestowo: Ein Nachtrag zu meinem Aufsatz 'Eine deutsche Märchenerzählerin aus der Ukraine.'" *Jahrbuch für deutsche Volkskunde* 19 (1975): 79–82.

Campbell, Joseph. *The Hero with a Thousand Faces.* Böllinger Series 17. New York: Pantheon, 1949.

_____. *The Power of Myth.* Ed. Bill Moyers. New York: Doubleday, 1988.

_____. "Folkloristic Commentary." In *The Complete Grimm's Fairy Tales.* Ed. Padraic Colum. New York: Random House, 1972: 851–59.

Carpenter, Humphrey, and Mari Prichard, eds. *The Oxford Companion to Children's Literature.* New York: Oxford University Press, 1985.

Chambers, Robert. *Popular Rhymes, Fireside Stories, and Amusements of Scotland.* Enl. ed. Edinburgh: William Robert Chambers, 1872.

Christiansen, Reidar Th. *European Folklore in America.* Oslo: Universitetsforlaget, 1962.

Clarke, Kenneth and Mary. *Introducing Folklore.* New York: Holt, Rinehart and Winston, 1965.

Cole, Sir Henry (pseudonym: Felix Summerly), ed. "Little Red Riding Hood," "Beauty and the Beast," and "Jack and the Beanstalk" in *Traditional Fairy Tales.* Series: *The Home Treasury of Books, Toys, etc. purposed to cultivate the Affection, Fancy, Imagination, and Taste of Children.* London: Joseph Cundall, 1845. Reprinted in *The Classics of Children's Literature* Vol. 1. Ed. Justin Schiller. New York: Garland, 1978. Introduction by Margaret Crawford Maloney.

Commager, Henry Steele. *The American Mind. An Interpretation of American Thought and Character Since the 1880s*. New Haven: Yale University Press, 1950.

Comstock, Sarah. "The Story Corner." *St. Nicholas* 41, 4 (Feb. 1914): 308–13.

Cook, Elizabeth. *The Ordinary and the Fabulous: An Introduction to Myth, Legends, and Fairy Tales for Teachers and Storytellers*. Cambridge: Cambridge University Press, 1969.

Coss, August. "Wurzeln der Romantik bei Herder." *Modern Language Quarterly* 2 (1941): 611–18.

Cox, George William. *Mythology of the Aryan Nations*. 2 vols. London: Longmans, Green, 1876.

Cox, M. and E. Roalfe. *Cinderella: Three Hundred and Forty-Five Variants of Cinderella, Catskin and Cap O'Rusher*. London: Folklore Society, 1893.

Crane, T. F. "The External History of the *Kinder- und Hausmärchen* of the Brothers Grimm." *Modern Philology* 19 (1917): 557–611.

Creuzer, Friedrich. *Symbolik und Mythologie der alten Völker*. 4 vols. Leipzig: Leske, 1814–1821.

Croker, T. P. F. Dillon. "Obituary" (for Thomas Crofton Croker, his father) *Gentleman's Magazine* 42 (Oct. 1854): 397–401.

Croker, Thomas Crofton. *Fairy Legends and Traditions of the South of Ireland*. 2 vols. London: Murray, 1925–1928. (Vol. 1 trans. Wilhelm Grimm. *Irische Elfenmärchen*. Leipzig: Fleischer, 1826. Vol. 2 is dedicated to "Dr. Wilhelm Grimm." The 2d ed. of 1832 contains a letter by Sir Walter Scott, dated April 27, 1825.)

––––––. *The Keens of the South of Ireland*. London: Printed for the Percy Society, 1844.

––––––. *The Popular Songs of Ireland*. Collected and edited with an introduction and notes. London: Henry Colburn, 1839.

Cruikshank, George. "Cinderella." In *The Fairy Library*. Ed. George Cruikshank. London: Bell and Daldy, 1870.

Danhardt, R. "Grimm-Editionen im Kinderbuchverlag Berlin." In *Die Brüder Grimm: Erbe und Rezeption; Stockholmer Symposium 1984*. Series: *Stockholmer Germanische Forschungen*, No. 32. d. Astrid Stedje. Stockholm, Almqvist & Wiksell International, 1985.

Darton, Harvey. *Children's Books in England*. 3d ed. Ed. Brian Alderson. Cambridge: Cambridge University Press, 1982.

David, Alfred, and Mary Elisabeth David. "A Literary Approach to the Brothers Grimm." *Journal of the Folklore Institute* I, 5 (1964): 172–88.

De Boor, Helmut. "Rezension vom *Briefwechsel der Brüder Jacob und Wilhelm Grimm und Karl Lachmann*." *Zeitschrift für Philologie* 55 (1930): 400–404.

Degen, Rolf. "New Light on Origins of Grimm's Fairy Tales." *The German Tribune* (26 Aug. 1984): 8–9.

Dégh, Linda. *Folktales and Society; Storytelling in a Hungarian Peasant Community*. Trans. by Emily M. Schonberger. Bloomington: Indiana University Press, 1969.

––––––. "Grimms' 'Household Tales' and Its Place in the Household: The Social Relevance of a Controversial Classic" *Western Folklore* 38 (1979): 83–103.

––––––. "What did the Grimm Brothers Give and Take from the Folk." In *The Brothers Grimm and Folktale*. Ed. James M. McGlathery, et al. Urbana: University of Illinois Press, 1988.

Delarue, Paul. *Borzoi Book of French Folk Tales*. Commentary by Paul Delarue. New York: Knopf, 1956.

Demers, Patricia, and Gorden Moyles, eds. *From Instruction to Delight. An Anthology of Children's Literature to 1850*. Toronto: Oxford University Press, 1982.

Denecke, Ludwig, ed. *Brüder-Grimm Gedenken*. 6 vols. Marburg: Elwert Verlag, 1963–1990.

––––––, ed. *Jacob Grimm's Circular-Brief: An die gesammten Freunde altdeutscher Poesie und Dichtung (Vienna: 1815)*. Facsimile edition. Kassel: Brüder Grimm Museum, 1968. Afterword by Kurt Ranke.

_____, ed. *Jacob Grimm und sein Bruder Wilhelm*. Stuttgart: Metzler, 1971.

_____. "Bibliographie der Briefe von und an Jacob und Wilhelm Grimm." *Aurora* (1983): 169–227.

Denecke, Ludwig, and Ina M. Greverius. "Brüder Grimm Gedenken." *Hessische Blätter für Volkskunde* 54 (1963): 64–65

Denecke, Ludwig, and Irmgard Teitge. *Die Bibliothek der Brüder Grimm: Annotiertes Verzeichnis des festgestellten Bestandes*. Ed. Friedhilde Krause. Weimar: Hermann Böhlaus Verlag, 1969.

Deutsche Bibliothek and Goethe Institut, eds. *Aus 150 Jahren norwegischdeutschen Geistesaustausches: Zwei Vorträge*. Oslo: Deutsche Bibliothek, 1965.

Dickens, Charles. "Frauds on the Fairies." *Household Word* 184 (Oct. 1859). Reprint in Nicholas Tucker, ed. *Suitable for Children? Controversies in Children's Literature*. Berkeley: University of California Press, 1976.

Dietrich, Anton. *Russische Volksmärchen in den Urschriften gesammelt und ins Deutsche übersetzt*. Introduction by Jacob Grimm. Leipzig: Weidmann'sche Buchhandlung, 1831. I.

Diewerge, Heinz. *Jacob Grimm und das Fremdwort*. Series: Arbeitsgemeinschaft zur Germanischen Philologie, No. 34. Leipzig: Arbeitsgemeinschaft zur Germanischen Philologie, 1935.

Dilkey, Marion C. and Heinrich Schneider. "John Mitchell Kemble and the Brothers Grimm." *Journal of English and Germanic Philology* 11 (1941): 461–79.

Dobers, Ernet, and Kurt Higelke, eds. *Rassenpolitische Unterrichtsgestaltung der Volksschulfächer*. Leipzig: Klinckhardt, 1940.

Doderer, Klaus. *Über Märchen und Kinder von heute*. Weinheim: Beltz, 1983.

_____. "Das bedrückende Milieu der Kinderfiguren in den Grimmschen Märchen. In *Klassische Kinder- und Jugendbücher*. Series: *Kinder- und Jugendliteratur*. 3d ed. Ed. Klaus Doderer. Weinheim: Beltz Verlag, 1975.

Dorson, Richard. *The British Folklorists. A History*. Chicago: University of Chicago Press, 1968.

_____. *Folklore*. Bloomington: Indiana University Press, 1972.

_____. "The Eclipse of Solar Mythology." *Journal of American Folklore* 68 (1955): 393–416. Reprint in *Myth: A Symposium*. Ed. Thomas A. Sebeok. Bloomington: Indiana University Press, 1965.

_____, ed. *Folktales of the World*. Series. Chicago: University of Chicago Press, 1965–.

Dow, James R., and Hannsjost Lixfeld, eds. and trans. *German Volkskunde: A Decade of Theoretical Confrontation, Debate and Reorientation (1967–1977)*. Bloomington: Indiana University Press, 1986.

Dundes, Alan, ed. *Cinderella: A Folklore Casebook*. New York: Garland, 1982.

_____, ed. *Little Red Riding Hood: A Casebook*. Madison, Wis.: University of Wisconsin Press, 1989.

_____, ed. *The Study of Folklore*. Englewood Cliffs: Prentice-Hall, 1965.

_____. "The Psychoanalytic Study of the Grimms' Tales with Special Reference to 'The Maiden without Hands' (AT 706)." *Germanic Review* 62, 2 (Spring 1987): 50–66.

Edgeworth, Maria. *The Parent's Assistant*. London: Stockdale, of Piccadilly, 1796.

Edwards, Carol, ed. "The Fairy Tale Snow White." *Making Connections Across the Curriculum: Readings for Analysis*. Eds. Patricia Chittenden and Malcolm Kiniry. New York: St. Martin's Press, 1986.

Ellis, John. *One Fairy Story Too Many: The Brothers Grimm and Their Tales*. Chicago: University of Chicago Press, 1983.

Emmonds, Christian et al., eds. *Literatur für Kinder und Jugendliche in der DDR*. Von einem Autoren-Kollektiv unter Leitung von Christian Emmonds. Berlin: Kinderbuchverlag, 1979.

Enzyklopädie des Märchens. Handwörterbuch zur historischen und vergleichenden Märchenforschung. 6 vols. Eds. Kurt Ranke et al. Berlin: Walter de Gruyter, 1975–90. (Other volumes are in preparation).

Eyman, Fritz. *Die Weisheit der Märchen im Spiegel der Geisteswissenschaften Rudolf Steiners.* Berne: Troxler, 1952.

"Fairy Legends and Traditions of the South of Ireland" (review). *Quarterly Review* (June/Oct. 1815): 197–210.

"Fairy Tales, or the Lilliputian Cabinet containing Twenty-Four Choice Pieces of Fancy and Fiction, collected by Benjamin Tabart." *The Quarterly Review* 8 21 (1819): 91–114.

Federspiel, Christa. *Vom Volksmärchen zum Kindermärchen.* Vienna: Notring, 1968.

Feldman, Burton, and Robert D. Richardson, eds. *The Rise of Modern Mythology: 1680–1860.* Bloomington: Indiana University Press, 1972.

Fergurson, Anna. *The Young Lady.* Lowell, Mass.: N. L. Dayton, 1848.

Fetscher, Iring. *Wer hat Dornröschen wachgeküsst? Das Märchenverwirrbuch.* Frankfurt am Main: Fischer Verlag, 1974.

Fine, Elizabeth. *The Folklore Text: From Performance to Print.* Bloomington: Indiana University Press, 1984.

Fischer, John L. "The Sociopsychological Analysis of Folktale." *Current Anthropology* 4 (1963): 235–93.

Fowkes, Robert A. "The Linguistic Modernity of Jacob Grimm." *Linguistics* 8 (1964): 56–61.

Frank, Manfred. "Das Motiv des 'kalten Herzens' in der romantisch— symbolischen Dichtung." *Euphorion* 71 (1977): 383–405.

Franke, Carl. *Die Brüder Grimm. Ihr Leben und Werk.* Leipzig: Weidmannsche Buchhandlung, 1894.

Franz, Marie Louise von. *An Introduction to the Interpretation of Fairy Tales.* New York: Spring Publications, 1970.

_____. *Problems of the Feminine in Fairytales.* Dallas, Tex.: Spring Publications, 1988.

_____. *Shadow and Evil in Fairytales.* Dallas, Tex.: Spring Publications, 1987.

_____. "Zur Methode der Jungschen Märchendeutung." In *Traumgesicht und Zauberspuk: Märchenforschung, Märchenkunde, Märchendiskussion.* Ed. Frederik Hermann. Frankfurt am Main: Fischer, 1982.

Frazer, Sir James. *The Golden Bough.* 12 vols. London: Collier-Macmillan, Ltd., 1890.

_____. *The New Golden Bough.* ed. Theodor H. Gaster. New York: American Library, 1959.

Freud, Sigmund. *Gesammelte Werke.* London: Imago, 1941.

_____. "Märchenstoffe in Träumen." *Internationale Zeitschrift für ärztliche Psychoanalyse* 1 (1913): 142–51.

Freud, Sigmund, and D. E. Oppenheim. *Dreams in Folklore.* New York: International University Press, 1958.

Friderici, Robert. "Wer entdeckte die Märchenfrau?" *Hessische Blätter für Volkskunde* 60 (1969): 166–67.

Fromm, Erich. *The Forgotten Language. An Introduction to the Understanding of Dreams, Fairy Tales, and Myths.* New York: Rinehart, 1951.

Fronemann, Wilhelm. *Das Erbe Wolgasts.* Langensalza: Beltz Verlag, 1927.

Früh, Sigrid, and Rainer Wehse, eds. *Die Frau im Märchen*, Series issued by the Europäische Märchengesellschaft Rheine. Kassel: Röth, 1985.

Führer, Maria. *Nordgermanische Götterüberlieferung und deutsches Volkstum. 80 Märchen der Gebrüder Grimm vom Mythus her beleuchtet.* Munich: Neuer Filser Verlag, 1938.

_____. "Nordgermanische Götterüberlieferung und deutsche Volksmärchen." *Jugendschriften-*Warte 44, 7 (July 1939): 94–114.

Ganz, Peter. *Jacob Grimm's Conception of German Studies*. An inaugural lecture delivered before the University of Oxford on 18 May, 1973. Oxford: At the Clarendon, 1973.

Gardner, Howard. "Brief on Behalf of Fairy Tales." *Phaedrus: An International Journal of Children's Literature Research* 5, 2 (1978): 14–23.

Geiger, Rudolf. *Mit Märchensöhnen unterwegs. Prüfung und Bewährung in 12 Märchen der Brüder Grimm.* Stuttgart: Urachhaus, 1968.

Gerstl, Quirin. *Die Brüder Grimm als Erzieher.* Munich: Ehrenwirth, 1964.

Gerstner, Hermann. *Die Brüder Grimm im Reich der Poesie und Sprache.* Murnau: L. Uhland, 1962.

———. *Die Brüder Grimm. Biographie mit 48 Bildern.* Gerabonn, Crailsheim: Hohenloher Verlag, 1971.

Gieser, Dietmar. *Mit den Brüdern Grimm durch Hessen.* Series: Die Hessen-Bibliothek. Kassel: Thieles und Schwarz, 1983.

Ginschel, Gunhild. "Der Märchenstil Jacob Grimms." *Deutsches Jahrbuch für Volkskunde* 9 (1963): 131–68.

Gödden, Walter. "Wilhelm Grimms Freundschaft mit Jenny von Droste-Hülshoff. Eine biographische Reminiscenz anhand neuen Quellenmaterials." In *Brüder Grimm Gedenken.* Vol. 6. Ed. Ludwig Denecke. Marburg: N. G. Elwert Verlag, 1986.

Gmelin, Otto. *Böses kommt aus Kinderbüchern. Die verpaßte Möglichkeit kindlicher Bewußtseinsbildung.* Munich: Kindler, 1972.

Görres, Johann Joseph, ed. *Die teutschen Volksbücher* (sic.). Heidelberg: Mohr und Zimmer, 1807.

Graebsch, Irene (Dyrenfurth). *Geschichte des deutschen Jugendbuches.* Leipzig: A. Harrassowitz, 1942.

Greverius, Ina Maria. "Wege zu Wilhelm Grimms 'Altdänischen Heldenliedern.' " In *Brüder Grimm Gedenken.* Vol. I. Ed. Ludwig Denecke. Marburg: Elwert Verlag, 1963.

Grimm, Albert Ludwig. *Kindermärchen.* Heidelberg: Mohr und Zimmer, 1809.

———. *Lina's Mährchenbuch. Eine Weihnachtsgabe* (sic.). 2 vols. Ill. with copper engravings. (Weinheim, 1809.) 2d ed. Frankfurt am Main: Gebrüder Wilmans, 1816.

Grimm, Ferdinand (Pseudonym: Lothar). *Volkssagen und Mährchen der Deutschen und Ausländer* (sic.). Leipzig: 1820.

Grimm, Hermann. "Wilhelm Grimm" and "Ralph Waldo Emerson." In *Literatur* (original title: *Fünfzehn Essays.* Ed. Hermann Grimm. Gütersloh: Mohn Verlag, 1882). Trans. Sarah Adams. Boston: Cupples, Upham & Company, 1886.

Gummel, Hans. "John Kemble." *Nachrichten aus Niedersachsens Urgeschichte* 20 (1951): 3–54.

Haacke, Ulrich. "Germanisch-deutsche Weltanschauung in Märchen und Mythen im Deutschunterricht." *Zeitschrift für deutsche Bildung* 12, 12 (Dec. 1926): 608–12.

Haas, Gerhard, ed. "Märchen, Sage, Schwank, Legende, Fabel, Volksbuch." *Kinder- und Jugendbuch. Zur Typologie und Funktion einer literarischen Gattung.* 2d ed. Stuttgart: Philip Reclam junior, 1976.

Haase, Donald. "John Ellis: 'One Fairy Tale Too Many' and Jack Zipes, 'Fairy Tales and the Art of Subversion.'" *Monatschefte* 79 (1987): 114–17.

Hagen Rolf. "Perraults Märchen und die Brüder Grimm." *Zeitschrift für deutsche Philologie* 74 (1955): 392–410.

Halliwell, James Orchard. *Descriptive Notices of Popular English Histories.* London: Printed for the Percy Society, 1848.

Hamann, Heinrich. *Die literarischen Vorlagen der Kinder- und Hausmärchen.* Series: *Palaestra. Untersuchungen und Texte aus der deutschen und englischen Philologie.* Berlin: Mayer & Müller, 1906.

Hand, Wayland D. "Die Märchen der Brüder Grimm in den Vereinigten Staaten." In *Brüder Grimm Gedenken*. Vol. 1. Marburg: N. G. Elwert Verlag, 1963.

―――. "Status of European and American Legend Study." *Current Anthropology* 6 (1965): 439–46.

Handwörterbuch des deutschen Märchens. Ed. Lutz Mackensen. Issued by Johannes Bolte et al. Berlin: de Gruyter, 1930–1940.

Handwörterbücher zur deutschen Volkskunde. Bolte, Johannes et al., eds. Berlin: Walter de Gruyter, 1930–1935.

Hanks, Carol and D. T. Hanks Jr. "Perrault's 'Little Red Riding Hood': Victim of the Revisers." *Children's Literature* 7 (1978): 69–77.

Harig, Ludwig. "Als wollt's die ganze Welt satt machen: Leibgericht der Deutschen: Die Märchen der Brüder Grimm." *Die Zeit*. (11 Ja. 1985): 116–17.

Harris, Joel Chandler. *Uncle Remus: His Songs and His Sayings*. Ill. F.S. Church and J.H. Moser. New York: D. Appleton, 1880.

Harrold, Charles Frederick. *Carlyle and German Thought 1819–1834*. New Haven: Yale University Press, 1934.

Hartland, Edwin Sidney. *The Science of Fairy Tales. An Enquiry into Fairy Mythology*. London: Walter Scott, 1890. Reprint Detroit: Singing Tree Press, 1968.

Hasubek, Peter. *Das Deutsche Lesebuch in der Zeit des Nationalsozialismus Ein Beitrag zur Literaturpädagogik zwischen 1933 und 1945*. Hannover: Hermann Schrödel Verlag, K.G., 1972.

Hazlitt, W. Carew. *Fairy Tales, Legends, and Romance; Illustrating Shakespeare and Other Early English Writers*. London: Frank and William Kerskajem, 1875.

Heisig, James. "Bruno Bettelheim and Fairy Tales." *Children's Literature* 6 (1977): 107–12.

Hennig, John. "The Brothers Grimm and T. C. Croker." *Modern Language Review* 41 (1946), 44–54.

Heselhaus, Clemens. "Die romantische Gruppe in Deutschland." In *Die europäische Romantik*. Ed. Ernst Behler. Frankfurt am Main: Athenäum Verlag, 1972.

Herder, Johann Gottfried. *Sämmtliche Werke*. 33 vols. Ed. Bernhard Suphan, et al. Berlin: Weidmannsche Buchhandlung, 1877–1913.

―――. *Volkslieder. Stimme der Völker in Liedern*. 2 vols. Leipzig: Weygandsche Buchhandlung, 1778–1779.

Hetman, Frederik, ed. *Traumgesicht und Zauberspur. Märchenforschung, Märchenkunde, Märchendiskussion*. Frankfurt am Main: Fischer Taschenbuch Verlag, 1982.

Heuscher, Julius E. *A Psychiatric Study of Fairy Tales*. Springfield, Il.: Charles Thomas, 1963.

Hiemesch, Karl-Heinrich. *Der Gesinnungsunterricht*. Leipzig: Dürr, 1925.

Hildebrandt, Irma. *Es waren ihrer fünf: Die Brüder Grimm und ihre Familie*. Cologne: Diederichs Verlag: 1984.

Höck, Wilhelm. "Märchen—nicht für Kinder." *Der junge Buchhandel* 17, 3 (1964): 25–28.

Horn, Katalin. *Der aktive und passive Märchenheld*. Basel: Schweizerische Gesellschaft für Volkskunde, 1983.

―――. "Helfer." In *Enzyklopädie des Märchens*, Vol. 5. Eds. Kurt Ranke et al. Berlin: Walter de Gruyter, 1987.

Hürlimann, Bettina. *Three Centuries of Children's Books in Europe*. (Original title: *Europäische Kinderbücher in drei Jahrhunderten*). Trans. and ed. Brian W. Alderson. Cleveland: World Publishing Co., 1968.

Jacek, Gertrude. *Madame de Staël and the Spread of German Literature*. New York: Oxford University Press, 1915.

Jackson, W. T. H. *The Hero and the King*. New York: Columbia University Press, 1982.

Jacoby, Mario, Verena Kast, and Ingrid Riedel. *Das Böse im Märchen*. Series: *Psychologisch gesehen*, vol. 33. Ed. Hildegund Fisehle-Carl. Fellbach: Verlag Adolf Bonz, 1981.

Jacobs, Joseph. *English Fairy Tales*. Ill. John D. Batten. London: Nutl, 1890.

Jalkotzy, Alois. *Märchen und Gegenwart*. 2nd ed. Vienna: Jungbrunnen Verlag, 1952.

Janosch (pseud.). *Janosch erzählt Grimms Märchen*. Weinheim: Beltz Verlag, 1972.

Janning, Jürgen, Heino Gehrts, Herbert Ossowski et al., eds. *Gott im Märchen*. Kassel: Erich Röth Verlag, 1982.

Jolles, Andre. *Einfache Formen*. Darmstadt: Wissenschaftliche Verlagsanstalt, 1958.

Jones, Ernest. "Psycho-Analysis and Folklore." In *The Study of Folklore*. Ed. Alan Dundes. Englewood Cliffs: Prentice-Hall, 1965.

Jung, Carl Gustav. *Symbolik des Geistes. Studien über psychische Phänomenologie*. Zurich: Rascher Verlag, 1948.

_____. *Archetyp und das kollektive Unbewußte*. Olten (Freiburg im Breisgau): Walter Verlag, 1976.

_____. *Über das Phenomen des Geistes in der Kunst und Wissenschaft*. Olten (Freiburg im Breisgau): Walter Verlag, 1971.

_____. *The Portable Jung*. Ed. Joseph Campbell. Trans. F. C. Hall. New York: Viking Press, 1983.

_____. "On the Relation of Analytical Psychology to Poetry." In *The Portable Jung*. Ed. Joseph Campbell. Trans. F. C. Hall. New York: Viking Press, 1983.

Jürgens, A., ed., *157 Alte und Neue Lieder mit Bildern und Singweisen*. Repr. ed., Mainz: Wilhelm Goldmann Verlag and B. Schott's Söhne, 1981.

The Juvenile Review or Moral and Critical Observations on Children's Books intended as a Guide to Parents and Teachers in Their Choice of Books of Instruction and Amusement. (London: Printed for N. Hailes, Juvenile Library, London Museum, Piccadilly, 1817.) Reprint edition sponsored by The Friends of the Osborne and Lillian H. Smith Collections, Toronto Public Library. Afterword Marjorie Moon. Cumulative index Dana Tenny. Toronto: Plow and Watters, 1982.

Kahn, Otto. "Rumpelstilz hat wirklich gelebt. Textvergleichende Studie über das Märchen vom Rumpelstilzchen und eine Erklärung mit Hilfe der Rechtsgeschichte." *Rheinisches Jahrbuch für Volkskunde* 17/18 (1966/67): 143–84.

Kaltwasser, Karl. *Lebendiges Erbe. Rede zur feierlichen Eröffnung der Brüder Grimm Gesellschaft in Kassel*. Kassel: Bärenreiter Verlag, 1942.

Kamenetsky, Christa. *Children's Literature in Hitler's Germany: The Cultural Policy of National Socialism*. Athens, Ohio: Ohio University Press, 1984. 2d ed. 1986.

_____. "Thomas Mann's Concept of the 'Bürger.'" *Journal of the College Language Association* 5, 3 (March 1963): 134–41.

_____. "In Quest of Virtue; Popular Trends Reflected in Children's Literature in Nineteenth Century Michigan." *Keystone Folklore Quarterly* (Summer 1965): 63–85.

_____. "Political Distortion of Philosophical Concepts: A Case History—Nazism and the Romantic Movement." *Metaphilosophy* 3, 3 (July 1972): 198–218.

_____. "Herder und der Mythos des Nordens." *Revue de littérature comparée* (Paris) 47 (Ja.–Mar. 1973): 23–41.

_____. "Herder and the Romantic Folklore Revival." *Journal of Popular Culture* (1973): 54–68.

_____. "The Brothers Grimm: Folktale Style and Romantic Theories." *Elementary English* 2 (Mar. 1974): 379–83.

_____. "*Dichter* vs. *Literat*: Thomas Mann's Ironic View of the Literary Man." *Journal of the College Language Association* 14, 4 (June 1971): 420–31.

_____. "Folktale and Ideology in the Third Reich." *Journal of American Folklore* 90 (1977): 168–78.

_____. "Jacob and Wilhelm Grimm (1785–1863 and 1786–1859)." *Writers for Children: Critical Studies of Major Authors Since the Seventeenth Century*. Ed. Jane Bingham. New York: Charles Scribner's Sons, 1987.

_____. "Folklore as a Political Tool in Nazi Germany." *Journal of American Folklore* 85, 337 (July/Sept. 1972): 221–38.

_____. "The Irish Fairy Legends and the Brothers Grimm." In *Proceedings of the Ninth Annual Children's Literature Convention in Gainesville, Florida, 1981*. Ann Arbor, Mi.: Malloy Lith. and the Children's Literature Association, 1983): 77–87.

Karlinger, Felix. *Grundzüge einer Geschichte des Märchens*. Darmstadt: Wissen-schaftliche Buchgesellschaft, 1983.

_____. *Wege der Märchenforschung*. Darmstad: Wissenschaftliche Buchgesell-schaft, 1973.

Karutz, Richard. *Die Mär in Mythen und Märchen*. Stuttgart: Klett Verlag, 1962.

Keightley, Thomas. *The Fairy Mythology*. Reprint edition. Detroit: Gale Research Company, 1975 (originally published in 2 vols., London: Murray, 1828).

Kerenyi, Carl. *The Gods of the Greeks*. New York: Thames and Hudson, 1951.

Kiefer, Emily. *Albert Wesselski and Recent Folktale Theories*. Bloomington: In-diana University Press, 1947.

Kingsley, Charles. *The Heroes; or Greek Fairy Tales for My Children* (originally published in 1856). 2d ed. New York: E. P. Dutton, 1885. Preface by Charles Kingsley.

Klagges, Dietrich. "Die Märchenstunde als Vorstufe des Geschichtsunterrichts." *Jugendschriften-Warte* (July/Aug. 1940): 49–51.

Klose, Werner. *Lebensformen deutscher Jugend. Vom Wandervogel zur Popgenera-tion*. Munich: Günter Olzog Verlag, 1970.

Klotz, Volker. "Weltordnung im Märchen." *Neue Rundschau* 81 (1970): 78.

Kochs, Theodor, "Nationale Idee und nationalistisches Denken im Grimmschen Wörterbuch." In *Nationalismus in Germanistik und Dichtung*. Eds. Benno von Wiese and Rudolf Heuss. Dokumentation des Germanistentages in München v. 17 bis 22. Oktober 1966. Berlin: E. Schmidt, 1967.

Kohler, Rudolf. *Aufsätze über Märchen und Volkslieder*. Berlin: Weidmann'sche Buchhandlung, 1894.

Kohn, Hans. *Prelude to Nation-States*. The French-German Experience 1781–1815. Princeton: Princeton University Press, 1964.

_____. *Prophets and Peoples; Studies in Nineteenth Century Nationalism*. New York: Macmillan Company, 1946.

Köster, Hermann Leopold. *Geschichte der deutschen Jugendliteratur*. Reprint of 4th ed., 1927. Berlin: Verlag Dokumentation, 1972.

Krause, Joachim, Norbert Oellers, and Konrad Polheim, eds. *Sammeln und Sichten: Festschrift für Oscar Fainbach zum 80. Geburtstag*. Bonn: Bouvier, 1982.

Krippendorf, Klaus. *Content Analysis: An Introduction to Its Methodology*. Beverly Hills: Sage Publications, 1980.

Krohn, Rüdiger. "Brothers Grimm Overcame Small-Town Provincialism." *The German Tribune* 20 (185): 11–12.

Kuhn, Hugo, and Kurt Schier, eds. *Märchen, Mythos, Dichtung. Festschrift zum 90. Geburtstag Friedrich von der Leyens*. Munich: C. H. Beck, 1963.

Kunze, Horst, ed. *Schatzbehalter alter Kinderbücher. Vom Besten aus der älteren deutschen Kinderliteratur*. Hanau, Main: Verlag Werner Dausien, 1965.

Lacqueur, Walter Z. *Young Germany: A History of the German Youth Movement*. New York: Basic Books, 1962.

Laiblin, Wilhelm, ed. *Märchenforschung und Tiefenpsychologie*. Darmstadt: Wissenschaftliche Buchgesellschaft, 1969.

Lang, Andrew. *The Blue Fairy Book* (originally published in 1889). Reprint New York: Dover Publications, 1974.

_____. *The Fairy Books* (series) 12 vols. London: Longmans, Green, 1889–1911.

_____. *The Andrew Lang Fairy Tale Book.* Afterword: Michael Patrick Hearn. New York: Signet, New American Library, 1981.

_____. "Household Tales; Their Origin, Diffusion, and Relation to the Higher Myths." In *Grimm's Household Tales*, with the author's notes. Trans. and ed. Margaret Hunt. London: George Bell & Sons, 1878.

Langer, Heinz. *Grimmige Märchen.* Pref. and selections by Lothar Borowsky. Munich: Heinrich Hugendubel Verlag, 1984.

Lemmer, Manfred. *Die Brüder Grimm.* Leipzig: Bibliographisches Institut, 1967.

Lenz, Friedel. *Bildsprache der Märchen.* Stuttgart: Verlag Urachhaus, 1971.

Levin, Isidor, "Das russische Grimmbild." In *Brüder Grimm Gedenken.* Vol. I. Ed. Ludwig Denecke. Marburg: N. G. Elwert Verlag, 1963.

Leyen, Friedrich von der. *Das Märchen.* 4th ed. Heidelberg: Mohr und Zimmer, 1958.

_____. *Das deutsche Märchen und die Brüder Grimm.* Series: Märchen der Weltliteratur, ed. by Friedrich von der Leyen. Düsseldorf: Diederichs Verlag, 1964.

_____. "Traum und Märchen." In *Märchenforschung und Tiefenpsychologie.* Ed. W. Laiblin. Darmstadt: Wissenschaftliche Buchgesellschaft, 1969.

_____, ed. *Märchen der Weltliteratur.* Series. Jena: Eugen Diederichs Verlag, 1965–.

Lieberman, Maria L. " 'Some Day My Prince Will Come'; Female Acculturation Through the Fairy Tale." *College English* 34 (December 1972): 383–95.

Linke, Werner. *Das Stiefmuttermotiv im Märchen der germanischen Völker.* Berlin: Ebering, 1933.

Locke, John. *Diaglogues Concerning Education* (originally published in London, 1745. Reprinted in: John Locke. *The Educational Writings of John Locke.* Ed. James L. Axtell. Cambridge: Harvard University Press, 1970. See also the same essay under the title of *Some Thoughts Concerning Education.* Cambridge: The University Press, 1880.

Lüthi, Max. *Volksmärchen und Volkssage: Zwei Grundformen erzählender Dichtung.* Bern: Francke Verlag, 1961.

_____. *Märchen.* 2nd rev. ed. Series: Realienbücher für Germanisten. Stuttgart: Metzlersche Verlagsbuchhandlung, 1964.

_____. *Once Upon a Time: On the Nature of Fairy Tales.* Bloomington: Indiana University Press, 1970.

_____. *The Fairytale as Art Form and Portrait of Man.* Trans. Jan Erickson. Bloomington: Indiana University Press, 1984.

_____. *The European Folktale: Form and Nature.* (Original title: *Das europäische Volksmärchen: Form und Wesen*). Trans. John D. Niles. New York: For the Institute for the Study of Human Issues, first Midland edition, 1986.

McClellan, Edwin. "The Educational Ideas of Philip Tappan." *Michigan History* (Mar. 1954): 69–78.

McDowell, Edwin. "Once Upon a Time: Sister for Cinderella." *Detroit Free Press* 29 Sept. 1983: Sec. 18A.

_____. "A Fairy Tale by Grimm Comes to Light." *New York Times* 16 Sept. 1983: 1.

McGillis, Roderick. "Criticism in the Woods: Fairy Tales as Poetry." *Children's Literature Quarterly* 7 (1982): 2–8.

McGlathery, James M. et al., eds. *The Brothers Grimm and Folktale.* Urbana: The University of Illinois Press, 1988.

Malinowski, Bronislaw. "Myth in Primitive Psychology." In *Magic, Science, and Religion and other Essays.* Garden City: Doubleday, 1954.

Mallet, Carl-Heinz. *Fairy Tales and Children. The Psychology of Children Revealed through Four of Grimm's Fairy Tales.* New York: Schocken Books, 1980.

Manheim, Ralph. *Grimm's Tales for Young and Old.* New York: Doubleday, 1977.

Marquardt, Ulrike. "Neu aufgefundene Bildnisse Grimmscher Märchenträgerinnen." In *Brüder Grimm Gedenken*. Ed. Ludwig Denecke. Vol. 4. Marburg: Elwert Verlag, 1984.

Matthias, T. *Der deutsche Gedanke bei Jacob Grimm. In Grimms eigenen Worten dargestellt*. Leipzig: R. Voigtländer, 1915.

Mavrogenes, Nancy A. and Joan S. Cumming. "What Ever Happened to Little Red Riding Hood? A Study of a Nursery Tale." *The Horn Book Magazine* 4 (June 1979): 344–49.

Mayo, Robert S. *Herder and the Beginnings of Comparative Literature*. Series: University of North Carolina Studies in Comparative Literature. Ed. Werner P. Friedrich. Vol. 48. Chapel Hill: University of North Carolina Press, 1969.

Michaelis-Jena, Ruth. *The Brothers Grimm*. New York: Praeger, 1970. Michaelis-Jena, Ruth, and Ludwig Denecke. "Edgar and John Edward Taylor, die ersten englischen Übersetzer der Kinder- und Hausmärchen." In *Brüder Grimm Gedenken*. Vol. 2. Ed. Ludwig Denecke. Marburg: N. G. Elwert Verlag, 1968.

Mieder, Wolfgang, ed. *Disenchantments: An Anthology of Modern Fairy Tale Poetry*. Hanover, N.H.: University of New England for the University of Vermont, 1985.

_____. *Grimms Märchen: Moderne Prosa, Gedichte, Karikaturen*. Series: Arbeitstexte für den Unterricht. Stuttgart: Reclam, 1987.

_____. *Mädchen, Pfeif auf den Prinzen. Märchengedichte von Günter Grass bis Sarah Kirsch*. Cologne: Diederichs, 1983.

_____. *Tradition and Innovation in Folk Literature*. Hanover, N.H.: Pub. for the University of Vermont by the University of New England, 1987.

_____. "Grim Variations: From Fairy Tales to Modern Anti-Fairy Tales." *The Germanic Review* 62, 2 (Spring 1987): 90–103.

Minor, Jacob, ed. *Friedrich Schlegel 1794–1802. Seine prosaischen Jugendschriften*. 2 vols. Vienna: Konegen, 1906.

Mönckeberg, Vilma. . . . *dann leben sie noch heute*. Münster, Westphalen: Aschendorf, 1962.

_____. *Das Märchen und unsere Welt: Erfahrungen und Einsichten*. Düsseldorf: Eugen Diederichs Verlag, 1972.

Moore, Robert. "From Rags to Riches: Stereotypes and Anti-Humanism in Fairy Tales." *Interracial Books for Children Bulletin* 7 (1975): 1–3.

Moser, Dietz-Rüdiger. "Altersbestimmung des Märchens." *Enzyklopädie des Märchen*. vol. 1. Eds. Kurt Ranke et al. Berlin: Walter de Gruyter, 1975: 417–19.

_____. "Keine Unendliche Geschichte: Die Grimm'schen Märchen—eine Treppe in die Vergangenheit?" *Journal für Geschichte* 3, 1984: 18–23.

Moser, Hugo. "Volks- und Kunstdichtung in der Auffassung der Romantiker." *Rheinisches Jahrbuch für Volkskunde* 4 (1953): 69–78.

Mosse, Georg. *The Crisis of German Ideology. Intellectual Origins of the Third Reich*. New York: Grosset and Dunlap, 1964.

Müller, Elisabeth. *Das Bild der Frau im Märchen. Analyse und erzieherische Betrachtung*. Munich: Profil, 1986.

Müller, Friedrich Maximilian. *Chips from a German Workshop*. New York: Scribner and Company, 1869.

_____. *Comparative Mythology*. 2d ed. London: G. Routledge, 1909. Reprinted New York: Arno Press, 1977.

_____. *Contributions to the Science of Mythology*. New York: Longmans, Green and Company, 1897.

_____. *Lectures on the Science of Language*. Delivered at the Royal Institution of Great Britain. London: Scribner, Armstrong and Company, 1861. Reprinted New York: Arno Press, 1978.

_____. *Selected Essays on Language, Mythology, and Religion*. London: Scribner and Company, 1881.

Musäus, Johann Carl August. *Volksmärchen.* 5 vols. Gotha: Carl Wilhelm Ettinger, 1782–1787. The 2d ed. was titled: *Die Deutschen Volksmärchen.* Halle: Von Wiel & Co., 1789–1805.

Naubert, Christiane Benedicte Eugenie. *Neue Volksmährchen der Deutschen. (sic)* 5 vols. Leipzig: Weygandsche Buchhandlung, 1789–1793.

"The National Fairy Mythology of England." *Frazer's Magazine* (July 1834): 51–62.

Newbery, John. *Mother Goose's Melody; Sonnets for the Cradle; Instruction with Delight.* London: John Newbery, about 1765.

Nissen, Walter. *Die Brüder Grimm und ihre Märchen.* Göttingen: Vanderhoeck & Ruprecht, 1984.

_____. *Das Mädchen ohne Hände.* Series: *New York University Studies in Germanic Languages and Literature.* Ed. Robert A. Powers and Volkmar Sander. St. Louis: Washington University Press, 1963.

_____. *Das Mädchen ohne Hände. Märchen Nr. 31 aus der Grimmschen Sammlung.* Olten (Freiburg im Breisgau): Walter Verlag, 1981.

Nitschke, August. *Soziale Ordnungen im Spiegel der Märchen.* Stuttgart: Frommann, 1959.

Nodelmann, P. "What Makes a Fairy Tale Good? The Queer Kindness of the Golden Bird." *Children's Literature in Education* 8 (1977): 101–08.

Norton, Donna, ed. *Through the Eyes of a Child. An Introducton to Children's Literature.* 3d ed. New York: Macmillan Company, 1991.

Oberfeld, Charlotte. "Der Tod als Freund und 'Der arme Junge im Grab' (KHM 185): Ludwig Auerbacher und die Brüder Grimm." In *Brüder Grimm Gedenken.* Vol. 5. Ed. Ludwig Denecke. Marburg: N. G. Elwert Verlag, 1985.

Opie, Iona and Peter. *The Classic Fairy Tales.* New York: Oxford University Press, 1974.

O'Sullivan, Sean. *Folktales of Ireland.* Chicago: University of Chicago Press, 1965.

Paede, Paul. *Krankheit, Heilung und Entwicklung im Spiegel der Märchen.* Frankfurt am Main: Vittorio Klostermann, 1986.

Panzer, Friedrich. "Märchen." In *Deutsche Volkskunde,* insbesondere zum Gebrauch der Volksschullehrer, im Auftrage des Verbandes deutscher Vereine für Volkskunde. Ed. John Meier. Berlin: Walter de Gruyter, 1926.

Parker, Richard Green. *Fairy Fairstar's Cabinet of Gems.* Series: *New and Original Toy Books.* London: A. Park, 1854.

Peppard, Murray B. *Paths Through the Forest.* New York: Holt, Rinehart and Winston, 1971.

Perrault, Charles. *Contes de ma mère l'oye. Histoires du temps passé avec des moralités.* Paris: Claude Barbin, 1697.

Petersen, Julius. *Die Wesensbestimmung der deutschen Romantik.* Leipzig: Dürr, 1926.

Petzold, Leander. *Volksmärchen und Materialien.* Stuttgart: Klett, 1982.

Peukert, Herbert. "Jacob Grimm und die Slawen." Vortrag zur Grimm-Ehrung der Philosophischen Fakultät der Friedrich-Schiller-Universität, Jena. *Zeitschrift der Friedrich-Schiller Universität Jena* 13 (1964), 211–20.

Peuckert, Will Erich. *Wiedergeburt. Gespräche in Hörsälen und unterwegs.* Frankfurt am Main: Weidmannsche Verlagsanstalt, 1949.

_____. "Wilhelm und Jacob Grimm." In *Die Grossen Deutschen.* Vol. 3. Eds. Hermann Hempel, Theodor Heuss, and Benno Reifenberg. Darmstadt: Deutsche Buch-Gemeinschaft, 1966.

Piaget, Jean. *A Child's Conception of the World.* London: Routledge & Kegan Paul, 1919.

Pickard, P. M. *I Could a Tale Unfold: Violence, Horror, and Sensationalism in Stories for Children.* London: Tavistock, 1961.

Pickering, Jr., Samuel F. *John Locke and Children's Books in Eighteenth Century England.* Knoxville: University of Tennessee Press, 1981.

Praesant, Wilhelm. *Märchenhaus des deutschen Volkes: Aus der Kinderzeit der Brüder Grimm.* Kassel: Brüder Grimm Gesellschaft, 1957.

_____. *Ludwig Emil Grimm: Ein deutsches Bilderbuch.* Kassel: Bärenreiter Verlag, 1940.

_____. "Im Hintergrund Steinau: Kleine Beiträge zur Familiengeschichte der Brüder Grimm." In *Brüder Grimm Gedenken.* Vol. 1. Ed. Ludwig Denecke. Marburg: N. G. Elwert Verlag, 1963.

Prestel, Josef. *Handbuch der Jugendliteratur. Geschichte der deutschen Jugendschriften.* Freiburg, Brsg.: Herder Verlag, 1933.

_____. "Märchen als Schaubild." *Deutsches Bildungswesen. Erziehungswissenschaftliche Monatsschrift des N.S.L.B. (German Education.)* Scientific Journal of Education, monthly, published by the National Socialist Teachers Association. (July 1933): 101–07.

_____. "Sendung des Märchens." *Jugendschriften-Warte* 43, 7/8 (1940): 137–42.

Propp, Vladimir. *Morphology of the Folktale.* 2d ed. Trans. Laurence Scott (originally published in 1923). Rev. and ed. with a pref. by Louis A. Wagner. New intr. by Alan Dundes. Scott. Austin, Tex.: University of Texas Press, 1968.

Provensen, Alice and Martin, eds. *The Provensen Book of Fairy Tales.* New York: Random House, 1971.

Quinn, Gerstl. *Die Brüder Grimm als Erzieher. Pädagogische Analyse des Märchens.* Series: *Unterricht, Erziehung, Wissenschaft und Praxis.* Vol. 4. Munich: Ehrenwirth Verlag, 1964.

Raglan, F. R. S. Lord. *The Hero* (first published in London, 1936). New York: Vintage, 1956.

Rank, Otto. *The Myth of the Birth of the Hero; and Other Writings* (originally published in Vienna in 1914 in the *Journal of Nervous and Mental Diseases,* and as a book in 1932). Trans. Charles Francis Atkinson. Reprint ed. Philip Freund. New York: Vintage, Alfred A. Knopf, Inc. and Random House, Inc., 1964.

Ranke, Friedrich. "Märchenforschung. Ein Literaturbericht (1920–1934)." *Deutsche Vierteljahresschrift für Literatur und Geistesgeschichte* 14, 2 (1936): 277–304.

Ranke, Kurt. "Die zwei Brüder: Eine Studie zur vergleichenden Märchenforschung." *FF Communications* No. 114. Helsinki: Academia scientiarum fennica, 1934.

_____. "Der Einfluss der Grimmschen Kinder- und Hausmärchen auf das volkstümliche deutsche Erzählgut." Stockholm: *Papers of the International Congress of European and Western Ethnology,* 1955: 126–33.

"Betrachtung zum Wesen und zur Funktion des Märchen." *Studium Generale* 11 (1958): 656–68.

_____. "Charaktereigenschaften und -proben." In *Enzyklopädie des Märchens.* Vol. 2. Eds. Kurt Ranke et al. Berlin: Walter de Gruyter, 1980: 1240–48.

_____, ed. *Folktales of Germany.* Foreword by Richard Dorson. Series: *Folktales around the World.* Chicago: Chicago University Press, 1966.

Rauch, Karl. *Deutsche Märchen vor den Brüdern Grimm.* Series: *Märchen europäischer Völker.* Vol. 4. Hamburg: Verlag Olde Hansen, 1975.

Rausman, Pirkko-Liisa. "Aarne, Antti, Amatus," in *Enzyklopädie des Märchens.* Vol. 1. Ed. Kurt Ranke. Berlin: Walter de Gruyter, 1979.

"On Reading; Editorial." *Sergent's School Monthly* (Jan. 1858): 3.

"On Reading." *Fourth Reader. National Series of Selections for Reading.* New York: A. S. Barnes & Company, 1856.

Richter, Dieter, and Johannes Merkel. *Märchen, Phantasie und soziales Lernen.* Berlin: Basis, 1974.

Richter, Ludwig and A. E. Marschner, eds. *Alte und Neue Volks-Lieder.* Leipzig: Verlag Georg Wigand, 1847.

Ritz, Hans. *Die Geschichte vom Rotkäppchen: Ursprünge, Analysen und Parodien eines Märchens.* Emstal: Muri Verlag, 1981.

Röhrich, Lutz. *Märchen und Wirklichkeit: Eine volkskundliche Untersuchung.* Wiesbaden: Franz Steiner, 1956.

_____. "Mensch und Tier im Märchen." *Schweizer Archiv für Volkskunde* 49 (1953): 163–93.

_____. "Die Grausamkeit im deutschen Märchen." *Rheinisches Jahrbuch für Volkskunde* 6 (1955): 176–224.

_____. "Rumpelstilzchen: Vom Methodenpluralismus in der Erzählforschung. *Schweizer Archive für Volkskunde* 68/69 (1972/73): 567–96.

_____. *Märchenerzählforschung heute.* Freiburg im Breisgau: Herder Verlag, 1976.

_____. "Grausamkeit." In *Enzyklopädie des Märchen.* Vol. 5. Ed. Ludwig Denecke et al. Berlin: Walter De Gruyter, 1989.

Rölleke, Heinz. *Die Märchen der Brüder Grimm: Eine Einführung.* Series: *Artemis Einführungen.* Vol. 18. Munich: Artemis Verlag, 1987.

_____. "Allerleirauh. Eine bisher unbekannte Fassung von Grimm." *Fabula* 13 (1974): 87–94.

_____. "Drei Bildnisse der Märchenvermittlerin Marie Hassenpflug." In *Brüder Grimm Gedenken.* Vol. 3, Ed. Ludwig Denecke. Marburg: Elwert Verlag, 1981.

_____. " 'Wie ein Lämmerschwänzchen.' Zur Herkunft einer Resensart in Grimms Märchen" *Wirkendes Wort* (March/April 1983): 152–63.

_____. "Schneeweißchen und Rosenrot. Rätsel um ein Grimmsches Märchen" *Wirkendes Wort* (March/April 1983): 481–500.

_____. "Discovery of Lost Grimm Fairy Tale Not the Sensation It Is Claimed To Be." *The German Tribune* 27 (No. 1983): 11. Reprint from *Frankfurter Allgemeine Zeitung für Deutschland* 17 Oct., 1983.

_____, ed. *'Wo das Wünschen noch geholfen hat.' Gesammelte Aufsätze zu den 'Kinder- und Hausmärchen' der Brüder Grimm.* Bonn: Bouvier Verlag, Herbert Grundmann, 1985.

Roberts, Warren E. *The Tale of the Kind and the Unkind Girls: Aa–Th 480 and Related Tales.* Berlin: de Gruyter, 1958.

Rosenkötter, Rose. "Kindheitskonflikte und Reifungserleben im Märchen." In *Literaturpsychologische Studien und Analysen.* Ed. Walter Schönau. Amsterdam: Rodopi, 1983.

Rötzer, Hans Gerd. *Märchen.* Bamberg: C. C. Buchners Verlag, 1988.

Rousseau, Jean Jacques. *Emile.* Trans. B. Foxley. London: J. M. Dent & Sons, 1911.

Rumpf, Marianne. *Rotkäppchen. Eine vergleichende Untersuchung.* Diss. University of Göttingen, 1951.

Rüttgers, Severin. *Literarische Erziehung. Versuch über die Jugendschriftenfrage auf soziologischer Grundlage.* Berlin: Beltz, 1931.

Sahr, Michael. *Zur Wirkung von Märchen: Kinderliteratur und Rezeption.* Battmannsweiler: Wilhelm Schneider, 1980.

Sale, Roger. *Fairy Tales and After. From Snow White to E. B. White.* Cambridge: Harvard University Press, 1978.

Saltman, Judith, ed. *The Riverside Anthology of Children's Literature.* 4th ed. Riverside, N.Y.: Houghton Mifflin Company, 1987.

Schade, Ernst. "Märchen als Literatur für Kinder: Rezeptionstheorien für und wider Märchen." (Typescript of a lecture). Kassel: Brüder Grimm Museum, n.d.

Schäfer, Albert, ed. *Weltliteratur und Volksliteratur.* Munich: Verlag C. H. Beck, 1972.

Schenda, Rudolf. *Volk ohne Buch. Sozialgeschichte populärer Lesestoffe.* Series: *Wissenschaftliche Reihe.* Stuttgart: Deutscher Taschenbuchverlag, 1977.

Schenk, H. G. *The Mind of the European Romantics: An Essay in Cultural History.* London: Constable, 1966.

Scherer, Wilhelm. "Jacob und Wilhelm Grimm." In *Allgemeine Deutsche Biographie,* Vol. 9. Leipzig: Weidmann'sche Buchhandlung, 1879.

Scherf, Walter. *Lexikon der Zaubermärchen.* Stuttgart: Alfred Kröner, 1982.

Schiller, Friedrich von. *Über naive und sentimentalische Dichtung.* Stuttgart: Reclam, 1966.

Schlegel, Friedrich. "Rede über die Mythologie." In *Friedrich Schlegel 1794–1802. Seine prosaischen Jugendschriften*. Ed. Jacob Minor. Vol. 1.

Schmidt, Ferdinand, ed., *Das Märchenbuch für Kinder.* Leipzig: Otto Wigand, 1850.

Schmidt, Kurt. *Die Entwicklung der Grimmschen Kinder- und Hausmärchen seit der Urhandschrift; nebst einem kritischen Texte der in die Drucke übergegangenen Stücke.* Series: *Hermaea. Ausgewählte Arbeiten aus dem Deutschen Seminar zu Halle.* Eds. Philip Strauch et al. Halle: Niemeyer, 1932.

Schoof, Wilhelm. *Die Entstehungsgeschichte der Grimmschen Märchen.* Hamburg: Hauswedell, 1959.

_____. *Die Brüder Grimm in Berlin.* Berlin: Haude & Spener, 1964.

_____. "Neue Beiträge zur Entstehungsgeschichte der Grimmschen Märchen." *Zeitschrift für Volkskunde* 52 (1955): 112–43.

_____. "150 Jahre Kinder- und Hausmärchen. *Wirkendes Wort* 12 (1962): 331–35.

_____. "Englische und französische Beziehungen der Brüder Grimm." *Wirkendes Wort* 14 (1966): 394–407.

_____. "Die Grimmschen Märchen. Zur Erinnerung an die 150-jährige Wiederkehr ihres Erscheinens." *Börsenblatt für den deutschen Buchhandel* (Frankfurter Ausgabe) 100, 18 (Dec. 1962): 2207–10.

Schopenhauer, Adele, *Haus-, Wald- und Feldmärchen.* Ed. Karl Wolfgang Becker. Berlin: Buchverlag Der Morgen, 1987.

Schuler, Theo. "Jacob Grimm und Savigny: Studien über Gemeinsamkeit und Abstand." *Zeitschrift der Savigny-Stiftung für Rechtsgeschichte* 80 (Weimar, 1963): 197–305.

_____. "Westfälische Märchen und Sagen der Brüder Grimm: Aus dem Nachlaß der Brüder Grimm. Beiträge des Droste-Kreises." In *Brüder Grimm Gedenken.* Vol. 2. Ed. Ludwig Denecke. Marburg: N. G. Elwert Verlag, 1975.

Schulte-Kemminghausen, Karl, and Ludwig Denecke. *Die Brüder Grimm in den Bildern ihrer Zeit.* Kassel: Röth, 1963.

Schwarze, Michael, ed. *Eine lustige Gesellschaft. 100 Münchener Bilderbogen in einem Band.* Zurich: Edition Olms, 1978.

Schwietering, Julius. "Volksmärchen und Volksglaube." Lecture at the Deutsche Volkskunde-Tagung, Heidelberg, Sept. 18, 1934. *Dichtung und Volkstum* 36, 1 (1938): 68–78.

Scott, Sir Walter. *Poetical Works of Sir Walter Scott.* London: Cadell & Whitacker, 1833. Printed in Edinburgh: Ballantyne & Co.

_____. *Letters on Demonology and Witchcraft.* With a new intr. and notes by Raymond Lamont Brown. Republished from the 1884 edition. Wakefield: Yorkshire, 1968.

"Sir Walter Scott and Mr. Crofton Croker." *Gentlemen's Magazine* (Oct. 1854): 453–56.

Sebeok, Thomas A. *Myth: A Symposium.* Bloomington: Indiana University Press, 1965.

Seitz, Gabriele. *Die Brüder Grimm: Leben—Werk—Zeit.* Munich: Winkler Verlag, 1984.

Sexton, Anne. *Transformations.* Boston: Houghton Mifflin, 1977.

Siecke, Ernst. *Über die Bedeutung der Grimmschen Märchen für unser Volksthum.* Rede gehalten in der Ortsgruppe Berlin des Alldeutschen Verbandes am 15. März, 1895. Series: *Sammlung wissenschaftlicher Vorträge* no. 11. Hamburg: Königliche Hofverlagshandlung, 1896.

Siegmund, Wolfdietrich. *Antiker Mythos in unseren Märchen.* Kassel: Eugen Röth, 1984.

Simrock, Karl. *Das deutsche Kinderbuch. Altherkömmliche Reime, Lieder, Erzählungen, Übungen, Rätsel und Scherze für Kinder.* Gesammelt von Karl Simrock. Frankfurt am Main: Brönner, 1848.

Smith, David Nichol, ed. *Eighteenth Century Essays on Shakespeare.* New York: Russell and Russell, 1962.

Smith, W. L. *Education in Michigan*. Lansing, Mi.: Office of the Superintendent, 1881.

Snyder, Louis L. *Roots of German Nationalism*. Bloomington: Indiana University Press, 1976.

_____. "Nationalistic Aspects of the Grimm Brothers' Fairy Tales." *Journal of Social Psychology* 23 (1959): 219–21.

Spender, C. "Grimm's Fairy Tales." *Contemporary Review* 102 (1912): 673–79.

Spies, Otto. *Orientalische Stoffe in den Kinder- und Hausmärchen der Brüder Grimm*. Series: *Beiträge zur Sprach- und Kulturgeschichte des Orients*. Walldorf, Hessen: Verlag für Orientkunde, 1952.

Spiess, Karl von. *Deutsche Volkskunde als Erschließerin deutscher Kultur*. Berlin: Stubenrauch, 1934.

_____. "Was ist ein Volksmärchen?" *Jugendschriften-Warte* 43, 6 (June, 1938), 37–39. The essay is continued in no. 7 (July, 1938), 34–48.

Spörk, Ingrid. *Studien zu ausgewählten Märchen der Brüder Grimm: Frauenproblematik — Rollentheorie — Psychoanalyse — Überlieferung — Rezeption*. Series: *Hochschulschriften für Literaturwissenschaft* no. 66. 2d ed. Maisenheim, Königstein: Verlag Anton Hein, 1986.

Stedje, Astrid, ed. *Die Brüder Grimm: Erbe und Rezeption*. Stockholmer Symposium 1984. Series: *Stockholmer Germanische Forschungen* no. 32. Stockholm, Almqvist & Wiksell International, 1985.

Steig, Reinhold. *Clemens Brentano und die Brüder Grimm*. Stuttgart: Cotta, 1914.

_____. *Achim von Arnim und Jacob und Wilhelm Grimm*. Stuttgart: Cotta Verlag, 1940.

_____. "Wilhelm Grimm und Herder." *Vierteljahresschrift für Literatur* 3 (1890): 573–78.

_____. "Zur Entstehungsgeschichte der Märchen und Sagen." *Archiv für das Studium der neueren Sprachen*. 107 (1901): 378–87.

Steiner, Rudolf. *The Interpretation of Fairy Tales*. New York: Anthroposophic Press, 1929.

_____. *Märchendichtungen im Lichte der Geistesforschung*. Vortrag 1908. (Basel: 1942) 3d ed. Berne: Dornach, 1969.

Stellmacher, Wolfgang. *Herders Shakespear-Bild*. Berlin: Rütten & Loening, 1978.

Stern, Leo. *Der geistige und politische Standort von Jacob Grimm in der deutschen Geschichte*. Berlin: Akademie-Verlag, 1963.

Stockley, Violet A. *German Literature as Known in England, 1750–1830*. London: Routledge and Sons, 1929.

Stokoe, Frank W. *German Influence on the English Romantic Period, 1788–1818*. Cambridge: Cambridge University Press, 1926.

Stone, Kay. "I Won't Tell These Stories to My Kids." *Canadian Ethnic Studies* 7, 2 (1975): 33–41.

Straparola, Giovanni Francesco. *The Nights of Straparola*. 2 vols. First trans. W. G. Waters. Ill. E. R. Hughes. London: Lawrence & Bullen, 1894.

Strutynski, Udo. "The Survival of Indo-European Mythology in Germanic Legendry: Toward an Interdisciplinary Nexus." *Journal of American Folklore* 97 (1984): 42–56.

Summerly, Felix (see: Cole, Sir Henry)

Sydow, Carl W. von. "Anthropologische Märchentheorie." In *Handwörterbuch des Märchens*. Vol. 1. Ed. Lutz Mackensen et al. Berlin: Walter de Gruyter, 1930–1940: 79–81.

_____. "Ethnologische Märchentheorie." In *Handwörterbuch des Märchens*. Vol. 1: 630–34.

Tabart, Benjamin. *Fairy Tales of the Lilliputian Cabinet; Containing twenty-four Choice Pieces of Fancy and Fiction*. London: Tabart & Company, 1818.

Tatar, Mary. *The Hard Facts of the Grimms' Fairy Tales*. Princeton: Princeton University Press, 1987.

Taylor, Peter, and Hermann Rebel. "Hessian Peasant Women: Their Families and the Draft: A Social Historical Interpretation of Fairy Tales from the Grimm Collection." *Journal of Family History* 6 (1981): 349–56.

Tennenhouse, Leonard ed. *The Practice of Psychoanalytic Criticism*. Detroit: Wayne State University Press, 1976.

Tetzner, Lisa. *Aus der Welt der Märchen*. Münster: Aschendorf, 1965.

Textor, Georg. "Die Ahnen der Märchenfrau. *Heimatbrief* 9 (1965): 4–15.

Thalmann, Marianne. *The Romantic Fairy Tale: Seeds of Surrealism*. Ann Arbor: University of Michigan Press, 1970. (Original title: *Das Märchen und die Moderne*. Stuttgart: Reclam, 1961).

Thomas, Joyce. *Inside the Wolf's Belly. Aspects of the Fairy Tale*. Sheffield: Sheffield Academic Press, 1989.

Thompson, Stith. *The Folktale*. New York: The Dryden Press, 1946.

_____. *Motif-Index of Folk Literature. Classification of Narrative Elements in Folktales, Ballads, Myths, Fables, Mediaeval Romances, Exempla, Fabliaux, Jest-Books, and Local Legends*. 6 vols. Bloomington: Indiana University Press, 1955.

_____. *The Types of Folktale; A Classification and Bibliography*. Helsinki: 1928. F. F. *Communications* No. 74.

Tieck, Ludwig (pseudonym: Peter Leberecht). *Der gestiefelte Kater*. Ed. Helmut Kreuzer. Stuttgart: Reclam, 1964. (Original publ. date: 1797).

_____. *Ritter Blaubart: Ein Ammenmärchen (in vier Akten)*. Leipzig: Karl August Nicolai, 1797.

_____. *Werke* 4 vols. Ed. Marianne Thalmann. Munich: Winkler Verlag, 1964.

Tismar, Jens. *Kunstmärchen*. Series: Sammlung Metzler, Realien und Literatur, Vol. 155. Stuttgart, Metzler, 1977.

Töppe, Frank. *Das Geheimnis des Brunnens. Versuch einer Mythologie des Märchens*. Düsseldorf: Gisela Töppe Verlagsgesellschaft, 1988.

Townsend, John Rowe. *Written for Children. An Outline of English Language Children's Literature*. 2d. ed. Boston: The Horn Book and Lippincott Company, 1975.

Träger, Claus. "Johann Gottfried Herder as a Theorist of Literature." In *Proceedings of the 8th Congress of the International Comparative Literature Association*. Eds. Bela Kopeczi and Vjda György. Stuttgart: Bieber, 1980.

Traxler, Hans. *Die Wahrheit über Hänsel und Gretel. Die Dokumentation des Märchens der Brüder Grimm. Eine glaubwürdige Parodie*. Munich: Heyne, 1967.

Tucker, Nicholas, ed. *Suitable for Children? Controversies in Children's Literature*. Berkeley: University of California Press, 1976.

Ungerer, Tomi. *Storybook*. New York: Franklin Watts, 1974.

Velten, H. V. "The Influence of Charles Perrault's '*Contes de ma mére l'oye*' on German Folklore. *Germanic Review* 5 (1930): 4–18.

Very, Lydia. *Red Riding Hood*. Boston: L. Prang & Company, 1863.

"The Vice of Reading." *Littell's Living Age* 8 No. 2582 (Oct. 3, 1874).

Voigt, Vilmos. "Anordnungsprinzipien," in *Enzyklopädie des Märchens*. Vol. 1, Ed. Kurt Ranke. Berlin: Walter de Gruyter, 1979.

Vogt, Friedrich. *Dornröschen—Thalia*. Series: *Germanistische Abhandlungen*. Breslau: Hirt, 1876.

Vordtriede, Werner. "Jacob Grimm zum 100. Todestag (20. IX. 1963)." *Merkur* 17, 3 (1963), 910–13.

Wales, Ruth Johnstone. "Hometown Festival West German Style: Tiny Schwabendorf Celebrates Its 300th Anniversary as a Refuge for French Huguenots." *Christian Science Monitor* Aug. 11, 1987: 21–22.

Walzel, Oscar. *German Romanticism*. New York: Frederick Ungar Publishing Company, 1965.

_____. "Jenaer und Heidelberger Romantik über Natur- und Kunstpoesie." *Deutsche Vierteljahresschrift für Literatur- und Geistesgeschichte* 13, 4 (1935): 226–59.

Ward, Donald, ed. *The German Legends of the Brothers Grimm.* 2 vols. Intr. by Donald Ward. Philadelphia: Institute for the Study of Human Issues, 1978.

_____. "New Misconceptions about Old Folktales: The Brothers Grimm." In *The Brothers Grimm and Folktale.* Ed. James M. McGlathery et al. Urbana: The University of Illinois Press, 1988.

Weber, Eugen. "Fairies and Hard Facts: The Reality of Folktales." *Journal of the History of Ideas* 42 (1981): 93–113.

Wegehaupt, Heinz. *Hundert Illustrationen aus zwei Jahrhunderten zu Märchen der Brüder Grimm.* Hanau: Verlag Dausien, 1985.

Wegehaupt, Heinz, and Renate Rupert. *150 Jahre Kinder- und Hausmärchen der Brüder Grimm.* East Berlin: Kinderbuchverlag, 1972.

Weinrebe, Helga. *Märchen—Bilder—Wirkungen. Zur Wirkungs- und Rezeptionsgeschichte von illustrierten Märchen der Brüder Grimm nach 1945.* New York: Peter Lang, 1987.

Weinstein, Fred, and G. M. Platt. *Psychoanalytic Sociology.* Baltimore: The Johns Hopkins University Press, 1973.

Weishaupt, Jürgen. *Die Märchenbrüder Jacob und Wilhelm Grimm: Ihr Leben und Wirken.* Kassel: Thiele & Schwarz, 1985.

Wellek, René. *Confrontations; Studies in the Intellectual and Literary Relations between Germany, England, and the United States in the Nineteenth Century.* Princeton: Princeton University Press, 1965.

_____. "The Name and Nature of Comparative Literature." In *Comparatists at Work. Studies in Comparative Literature.* Eds. Stephen Nichols et al. Waltham, Mass.: Blaisdell Publishing Company, 1968.

Wesselski, Albert. *Deutsche Märchen vor Grimm.* Brünn: Verlag Rudolf M. Rohrer, 1938.

_____. *Versuch einer Theorie des Märchens.* Series: *Prager Deutsche Studien.* Reichenberg im Breisgau: Verlag Franz Kraus, 1931.

Wiese, Benno, and Rudolf Heuss, eds. *Nationalismus in Germanistik und Dichtung.* Dokumentation des Germanistentages in München v. 17. bis 22. Oktober 1966. Berlin: Erich Schmidt Verlag, 1967.

Wittgenstein, Ottokar Graf zu. *Märchen, Träume, Schicksale, Autoritäts-Partnerschafts- und Sexualprobleme im Spiegel zeitloser Bildersprache.* Munich: Kindler, 1973.

Wolf, Hanna, ed. *Mudder, Mudder, de Melk kokt över! Kinderspiele und Geschichten aus der Raabestraße im alten Geestemünde.* Bremerhaven-Langen: Hanna Wolf and Druckhaus Lehe-Nord, 1985.

Wolgast, Heinrich. *Das Elend in unserer Jugendliteratur; Beiträge zur künstlerischen Erziehung unserer Jugend.* Reprint ed. Hamburg: Selbstverlag, 1950). "Der Wörterbuchmacher Jacob Grimm als Literaturkritiker." Editorial. *Die Zeit* (Ja. 11, 1985): 16.

Wulffen, E. "Das Kriminelle im deutschen Volksmärchen." *Archiv für Kriminalanthropologie und Kriminalistik* 38 (191): 340–70.

Wyss, Ulrich. *Die wilde Philologie: Jacob Grimm und der Historismus.* Munich: Beck'sche Verlagsbuchhandlung, 1979.

Yearsley, Macleod. *The Folklore of Fairy-Tales.* London: Watts & Co., 1924.

Yonge, Charlotte. *The History of Sir Thomas Thumb.* Incl. notes and poetry about the fairies. Ill. Jane Blackburn. Edinburgh: Thomas Constable & Co., 1855.

Ziegler, Matthes. *Die Frau im Märchen.* Leipzig: Köhler and Amelang, 1937.

_____. *Volkskunde auf rassischer Grundlage. Voraussetzungen und Aufgaben.* Series: *Deutsche Volkskunde für Schulungs- und Erziehungsarbeit der N.S.D.A.P.* Munich: Hoheneichen Verlag, 1939.

Ziller, Tuiscon. "Die Bremer Stadtmusikanten; Ethisch-psychologische Zergliederung." In *Ethisches Lesebuch.* Leipzig, Dürr: 1897.

Zipes, Jack. *Breaking the Magic Spell: Radical Theories of Folk and Fairy Tales.* New York: Methuen, Inc., 1984.

_____. *Fairy Tales and the Art of Subversion; The Classical Genre for Children and the Process of Civilization.* New York: Heinemann, 1983.

_____. *The Trials and Tribulations of Little Red Riding Hood. Versions of the Tale in Sociocultural Context.* South Hadley, Me.: Bergin and Garvey Publishers, Inc. 1983.

_____. *The Brothers Grimm. From Enchanted Forests to the Modern World.* New York: Routledge, Chapman and Hall, Inc., 1988.

_____. "The Grimms and the German Obsession with Fairy Tales." In Ruth Bottigheimer, ed. *Fairy Tales and Society: Illusion, Allusion, and Paradigm.* Philadelphia, Pa.: University of Pennsylvania Press, 1986.

_____. "Der Prinz wird nicht kommen. Feministische Märchen und Kulturkritik in den U.S.A. und in England." In *Die Frau im Märchen.* Ed. Sigrid Früh and Rainer Wehse. Series issued by the Europäische Märchengesellschaft. Kassel: Röth, 1985.

_____. "A Second Gaze at Little Red Riding Hood's Trials and Tribulations." *The Lion and the Unicorn* 7–8 (1985): 78–107.

_____. "The Enchanted Forest of the Brothers Grimm: New Modes of Approaching the Grimms' Fairy Tales." *Germanic Review* 62, 2 (Spring 1987): 66–75.

_____, ed. *Don't Bet on the Prince; Contemporary Fairy Tales in North America and England.* New York: Methuen, Inc., 1986.

Zuckmayer, Carl. *Die Brüder Grimm. Ein deutscher Beitrag zur Humanität.* Frankfurt: Suhrkamp, 1948.

Zumwalt, Rosemary Levy. *American Folklore Scholarship: A Dialogue of Dissent.* Bloomington: Indiana University Press, 1988.

INDEX

A Note about the Author

Christa Kamenetsky studied at the universities of Freiburg, Munich, Central Michigan, and Washington and is the author of *Children's Literature in Hitler's Germany* (Ohio University Press). She is professor of English at Central Michigan University where she teaches children's literature and comparative literature.